BUSINESS COMMUNICATION FUNDAMENTALS

Bobbye D. Sorrels
The University of Oregon

Charles E. Merrill Publishing Company
A Bell & Howell Company
Columbus Toronto London Sydney

Published by
Charles E. Merrill Publishing Company
A Bell & Howell Company
Columbus, Ohio 43216

This book was set in Optima.
Production Coordination: Cherlyn B. Paul
Text Design: Cynthia Brunk
Cover Design Coordination: Tony Faiola
Cover photograph courtesy of Shaklee Corporation.

Library of Congress Catalog Card Number: 83-061495
International Standard Book Number: 0-675-20096-2
Printed in the United States of America

1 2 3 4 5 6 7 8 9 10—88 87 86 85 84

To my mother, Amorita Sorrels,
and the memory of my daddy, Cecil D. Sorrels

PREFACE

Business Communication Fundamentals recognizes the need for competent communicators in the business world. Because people who work in business spend 90 percent of their time in some form of communication, business success depends on clear communication.

Because writing requires particular attention, over half of this book deals with developing and refining written messages. It first treats the general principles of writing and then applies the principles to neutral, good-news, bad-news, and persuasive messages as they appear in letters, memoranda, reports, forms, questionnaires, employment forms, policy statements, and other written messages. It describes the "just-write" technique of writing first and editing later, as well as other approaches to writing. An extensive appendix reviews grammar, spelling, word usage, and other mechanics important to the use of language.

Oral communication represents 75 percent of all business communication. Therefore, this book includes substantive coverage of task-centered conversations, dialogues, group discussion, role-playing, platform speaking, and listening. The chapters on listening and oral messages detail the processes, providing illustrations and practice.

Beyond written and oral communication, this book covers nonverbal communication, which carries 65 to 93 percent of the message in face-to-face exchanges. In business transactions students need to learn how to "read" underlying nonverbal messages. For example, if a supervisor expresses pleasure with a worker's job, but avoids eye contact, grimaces, and stamps out a cigarette, the worker might have cause for concern. Thus, salespeople, customer service representatives, and other workers and managers alike need to understand the importance of the nonverbal message. Such understanding will help them solve problems, overcome objections, sell a company's product, and accomplish the innumerable other objectives associated with business activity.

The organization of the book emphasizes the importance of the receiving acts—reading, listening, and observing nonverbal messages. By strengthening receiving skills, students will learn how to gain and retain more information and to understand how to send clear messages that receivers will understand correctly.

The coverage of reading represents one unique feature of this book. Because information bombards decision makers faster than they can process it, improving speed and comprehension in reading can help business executives reach better decisions. The self-contained treatment of reading provided in the book frees instructors from the necessity to devote extensive blocks of class time to cover the material. Nineteen marked passages for timed reading and nineteen self-tests with solutions help students improve their own reading abilities without the extensive involvement of instructors.

The text highlights six basic guidelines for communication throughout. The guidelines focus on purposes, participants, channels, interference, sending and receiving messages, feedback, and evaluation of communication. The best communicators apply these guidelines to every transaction.

The final section of the book covers written, oral, and nonverbal communication in conjunction with gaining employment and developing a career. Topics include the résumé, the letter of application, follow-up messages, interviews, dress and appearance, career planning, and a review of the importance of communciation to careers.

To assist students in developing better communication skills, the book provides numerous self-teaching elements in addition to the self-timing and self-testing of reading passages. Over 400 exercises and comprehensive illustrations appear throughout the book. Each chapter includes both oral and written exercises, a test over the chapter, and a vocabulary list.

By presenting business communication in all of its forms—sending and receiving written, verbal, and nonverbal messages—I write this book with the goal of developing proficient, all-around business communicators.

ACKNOWLEDGMENTS

Many people helped make this book possible. My daughter Lynne Persing (graduate student, The University of Oregon) made invaluable contributions. Not only did she make creative suggestions, but she developed the first draft of Appendix B, some of the examples and cases, and many of the exercises and their solutions. My appreciation also goes to Jan Tuepker, Martha Perry, and Jan Clayton for their typing; to Colene Maxwell for her help in editing some illustrations; to my family, my friends, and my colleagues at Central State University (Oklahoma) and The University of Oregon for their interest and support; to Cindy Manning and Beth Clayton for their clerical aid; and to the editors at Merrill for their suggestions.

I am also indebted to the following reviewers: Prof. Carol Baxter, University of North Carolina at Charlotte; Prof. Jean Johnston, University of Akron; Prof. Philip H. Kelly, Gannan University; Prof. Lila Prigge, University of North Dakota; Prof. Marcia K. Shallcross, Palomar College; and Prof. Anne Sostrom, Capital University.

CONTENTS

BUSINESS COMMUNICATION FUNDAMENTALS

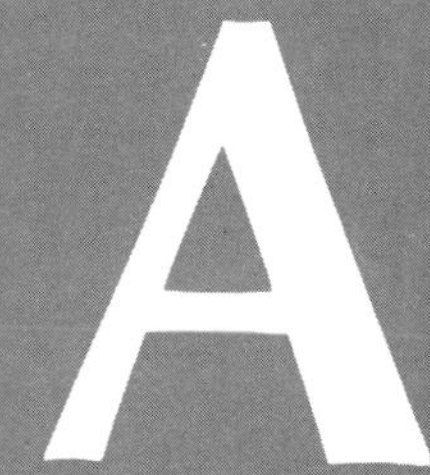

UNDERSTANDING AND APPLYING THEORY AND GUIDELINES

STUDENT'S OBJECTIVES:

1 To understand the importance of improving communication skills

2 To understand the human communication process

1

THE PROCESS OF COMMUNICATION

3 To apply a model of communication

4 To learn a definition of business communication

Have you ever thought, "I know what I want to say, but I just can't find the right way to say it"? After a conversation, have you ever thought, "I heard what she said, but I'm not sure what she meant"? If so, you have experienced the kinds of frustration all of us experience as we try to communicate. Yet communication provides the key to success in business—indeed, to success in life itself. Anything you can do to advance your development as a communicator will prepare you for the challenge of competing and succeeding in the business world.

Business communication takes many forms, including telephone conversations, meetings, letters, written reports, memos, computer printouts, electronic mall, and videotapes. This chapter defines business communication as a special case of the overall human communication process and presents a model of this process. Chapter 2 provides practical application of the definition and model.

DEFINITIONS

In a business transaction each participant gives something of value and expects value in return. This chapter extends the concept of transaction to business communication; the word *transacting* represents the exchange of meanings that takes place in effective business communication.

To develop a working definition of business communication, we start with a definition of business:

> Business is the activity conducted by organizations of paid people working together to produce and market goods and services for profit.

Next, we add a definition of human communication:

> Human communication is the process of transacting meanings through written, oral, and nonverbal messages.

Finally, if we merge the definitions of business and human communication, we may define business communication in the following way:

> Business communication is the process of transacting meanings through written, oral, and nonverbal messages internal and external to organizations of paid people working together to produce and market goods and services for profit.

Most of the examples in this book present common business situations. However, because business communication represents a special case of human communication, skills developed while studying the examples will apply to all arenas of life.

HUMAN COMMUNICATION

The preceding definition provides a convenient basis for understanding human communication. This section highlights each key word in the definition, thus emphasizing the importance of each part of the communication process. It also illustrates that these elements interlock to define the communication process as a dynamic, rapidly changing whole.

Process

The word *process* in the definition means that communication involves much more than the one-way function of sending (Figure 1–1a) or sending and receiving (Figure 1–1b). Instead it involves a two-way loop created by a return or response (feedback) from the receiver to the sender (Figure 1–1c). Even a loop, however, suggests that the feedback returns to a beginning point and simply repeats itself.

As suggested by communication theorist Frank E. X. Dance, a more realistic view of communication emphasizes a dynamic process by visualizing sending and receiving as a dynamic spiral[1] (Figure 1–1d). The spiral builds as the sender and receiver both grow from the continual process. Feedback from one to the other increases the growth rate, and the spiral continues.

Observe that the spiral in Figure 1–1d does not take a graceful form. Instead it shows the awkwardness that accurately portrays the communication process: senders and receivers rarely have the same abilities, start at the same

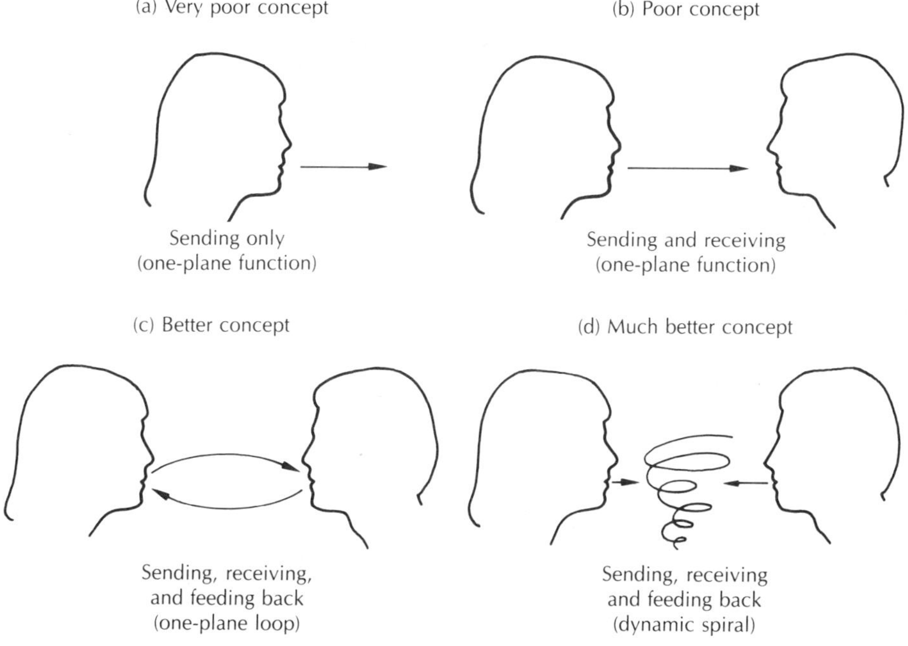

FIGURE 1–1 Concepts of the communication process.

level, or grow at the same rate. Interference occurs. Meanings assigned to symbols differ. Other factors distort the spiral.

As an example of how a dynamic spiral works, think about a simple exchange of business letters. You send a letter to Mary Jones, an employee at another company. Her receipt of your letter completes the first tier of a spiral. She learns something from reading your letter, then writes a second letter and sends it to you. Your receipt completes the second tier. Then, when you learn from her letter and write a third letter, you initiate a third tier. The spiraling process continues as long as the two of you continue the exchange. For oral exchanges, the spiral grows even more rapidly.

The concept of a dynamic spiral applies at every level of communication. Writers differ on classification schemes for the levels at which communication takes place. However, the five levels used here cover the various schemes quite well: (1) intrapersonal, (2) interpersonal, (3) mediated, (4) person-to-group, and (5) mass.

Intrapersonal Communication

When you think, you use intrapersonal communication. You initiate, receive, and process messages within yourself as you play both sending and receiving roles. Human growth depends on this internal communication. Through it you know yourself and develop your self-concept, self-determination, and self-motivation. Intrapersonal communication also provides the vehicle for dealing with the environment.

For example, each morning you decide how to dress appropriately for the expected weather, decide which route will get you to your destination quickest, and decide how much you need to eat for breakfast. This kind of internal communication forms the foundation for the other four levels of communication.

Interpersonal Communication

Interpersonal communication occurs when two (or a few) people talk face to face. Conversations, dialogues, and small-group discussions are interpersonal exchanges. Each person also operates intrapersonally during the exchange. Thus, an exchange with just two people involves at least three communication elements—the unique thinking done by each person and the overriding process created by the interpersonal exchange.

For example, imagine that you and a client have just ended a meeting in your office and now want to set another appointment. You are thinking, "I want to meet as soon as possible, but I have meetings all day today and tomorrow morning." Your client is thinking, "I'm really pressed for time and have a flight to catch tomorrow afternoon at two o'clock." After some discussion, you agree to meet for lunch tomorrow at the airport coffee shop.

Mediated Communication

This level of communication occurs when two (or a few) people use some intermediate means for carrying their messages. They do not communicate face to face and thus do not have direct feedback. Mediated communication often uses a mechanical or electrical device to transmit or receive messages. Examples include the telephone, closed-circuit television, mobile radio, radar, teletype, and the communication satellite. Mediated communication also occurs through letters, reports, forms, and interoffice memoranda.

Person-to-Group Communication

The person-to-group level involves one speaker and an audience. The speaker usually faces the audience, and the audience usually contains people with similar interests. A small, private person-to-group situation often has some of the characteristics of interpersonal communication. However, for large public groups, the person-to-group level lacks the benefits provided by interpersonal exchanges.

The traditional speaker-and-audience setting may include microphones, projectors, and tape players. They usually supplement the speech, rather than interfere with it. However, if a microphone or other equipment functions improperly, interference can occur.

Mass Communication

Mass communication includes messages sent to large, public, dissimilar, anonymous, distant audiences using some intermediate instrument of transfer. The instruments include electronic (for example, radio, television, tape, film) and print (for example, newspaper, magazine, book, pamphlet, brochure, direct-mail campaign). The restricted opportunity for feedback is the most serious barrier to effective mass communication.

Transacting

The word *transacting* forms the second important concept in the communication definition. In support of the concept, Don Fabun, a well-known researcher in communication, writes:

> It is sometimes useful to think of human communication as "transactions." In the sense we mean here, a transaction involves the interaction of the observer and what . . . [the observer] observes. This can take place between ourselves and the world-outside-our-skin. Or it can take place between two or more human beings.[2]

The phrase "world-outside-our-skin," as Fabun defines it, thus covers both intrapersonal and interpersonal levels of communication. For example, communication occurs on an intrapersonal level when you consider the colors at sunset or the rhythmic sounds of a passing train. A transaction takes place between you and your environment. On an interpersonal level, transactions require both active senders and receivers. Such transactions require the fullest possible use of feedback to enable observers to learn more about themselves and the others in the exchange.

Meanings

Just what do people transact or share as they communicate? Ultimately, they share meanings. In his book, *Communications: The Transfer of Meaning,*

Fabun supports meaning as the focus of transaction, concluding that "it is the transfer of meaning that is the goal of interhuman communication."[3] Rudolph F. Verderber also emphasizes meaning as the essence of communication: "By definition, then, communication is the process of stimulating meanings."[4]

Meanings exist within and between people and develop through one's social interaction in the world. Because each human's world differs from every other, each person's set of meanings differs from every other. These differences create the greatest single barrier to effective communication. As a classic example, communication often breaks down between management and labor because each group operates from a different set of concepts—a different view of the world of work. Even the word *management* has a different meaning for managers than it does for laborers.

Because humans cannot transfer meanings directly from one mind to another, they must use *symbols*—both the verbal (written and spoken words) and nonverbal (nonwords)—to represent and share those meanings.

Since meanings for symbols vary from person to person, good communicators develop the art of using symbols. They evaluate, find, and create symbols, whether written words, spoken words, or nonwords. As senders, they thus improve their chances of choosing symbols that will call out the desired meanings within receivers; as receivers, they improve their chances of accurately interpreting senders' symbols.

Written, Oral, and Nonverbal Messages

The last part of the definition of communication specifies three categories of messages: (1) written verbal, (2) spoken verbal, and (3) nonverbal. Notice the use of the word *verbal* to mean *consisting of words,* rather than to mean *oral.* This definition of verbal clarifies that both written verbal *and* oral verbal messages use words as symbols, and that nonverbal messages use symbols *other* than words.

The final word, *messages,* also carries important meaning for the definition of human communication. It does so for two reasons: (1) Symbols form messages, and thus only *represent* meanings. (2) Messages develop in the minds of both senders and receivers as *internal* messages, but move between them in different forms—*external* messages. Letters, notes, speeches, and a clenched fist all form external messages; however, they only *represent* the true messages—the internal ones.

A MODEL OF THE COMMUNICATION PROCESS

Figure 1-2 illustrates a graphic model of the communication process, picturing the first stage for communication between two people.

The model includes two human units—the sender and the receiver—and two units external to the human—the external message and the channel. It includes one unit both internal and external to the human—interference. Refer to Figure 1-2 as you review the units.

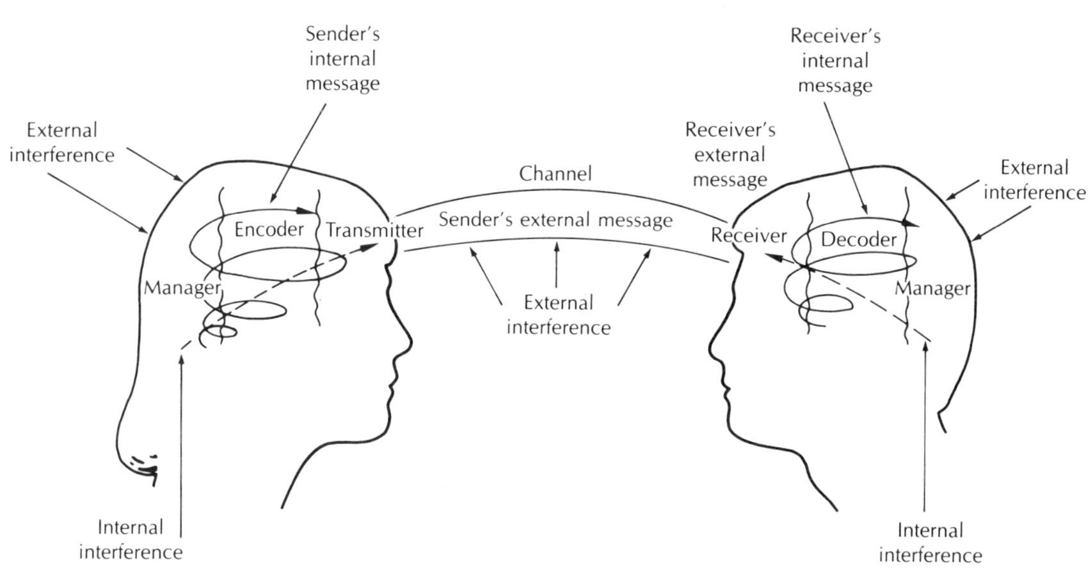

FIGURE 1–2 The first stage of the two-person communication model.

Sender

The sender initiates the communication spiral through the *interaction* of (1) source and manager, (2) encoder, and (3) transmitter. The first two function in the mind, but the transmitter requires both mental and physical activity.

The *source and manager* serves as the fountainhead for sending. It stores and supplies such elements as knowledge, values and beliefs, socialization, emotions, acculturation, attitudes, symbols, and communication methods. It selects meanings and turns them into internal messages. It also plans, organizes, activates, motivates, and controls the entire sending process.

The *encoder* works with the source and manager to convert the internal message into the external message. To do so, the encoder assigns external symbols to the meanings that make up the internal message.

The *transmitter* works with the encoder to thrust the external message into the selected channel. For example, the voice sends both verbal and nonverbal messages. The fingers manipulate pens, pencils, typewriters, musical instruments, paint brushes, styluses, and other such instruments. The body appears, touches, moves, creates sounds, and even emits odors. As an example of the sending process, suppose you must review a financial report before it goes out for printing. As you do so, you find an error in the addition of a column of figures. The following mental interactions take place: Your source says, "Oh, no!" Your manager says, "I must make the correction now!" Your encoder says "Cross out the wrong total and write in the correct figure." Your hand, the transmitter, reaches for a red pencil. You have just become a sender.

Channel and External Messages

As the physical forms in which messages occur, channels fall into three broad categories: written verbal, oral verbal, and nonverbal.

Written verbal channels include notes, memoranda, letters, telegrams, reports, newspapers, magazines, books, and other similar forms. Oral verbal channels include telephones, televisions, radios, platform speeches, interviews, conferences, conversations, and other such media. Virtually all sensory avenues—touches, sights, sounds, aromas, and flavors—carry nonverbal messages. They supplement or take the place of written verbal and oral verbal messages.

The channel carries the *sender's external message* through time and space to the receiver. When it reaches the receiver, it becomes the *receiver's external message*. These two messages may differ because interference often changes the sender's external message on the way to the receiver. Thus, the receiver may receive a different message than the sender put into the channel.

Receiver

The receiver's external message activates sophisticated mental activities. For example, listening involves much more than hearing. The receiver must *decode* the external message and convert the symbols of the received message into the internal message. The decoder works with the destination and manager to do so.

After developing the internal message, the *destination and manager* interprets and assigns meanings to it. Then the destination and manager organizes, evaluates, and stores those meanings as they relate to such elements as the knowledge, values and beliefs, socialization, emotions, acculturation, attitudes, symbols, and communication methods already stored there. Of course, the destination and manager also activates, motivates, and controls the entire receiving process.

Interference

Interference with the communication process arises in conjunction with two basic elements: (1) the human mind and (2) the channeled message. Interference associated with the mind creates by far the more serious threat.

Human Mind

Interference within the mind comes from both internal and external sources. It affects both sender and receiver and can occur at any stage of communication. Examples of internal interference with mental processes include the following:

- The storage of incorrect information leads to inaccurate messages.
- The sender's value system conflicts with the receiver's value system.
- The sender and receiver have weaknesses or differences in the ability to function as sources, destinations, managers, encoders, decoders, transmitters, and receivers.
- Symbols hold different meanings for sender and receiver (for example,

a sender may refer to a "slab," but a receiver does not understand "slab" to mean "highway").

- The mind strays (for example, thoughts about a party can play havoc with study for an exam).
- Emotions such as sadness, anger, and even joy override the transmitted topic.

Examples of external sources of interference with mental processing include (1) a cold office, (2) a jackhammer outside the window, (3) another person's movements or talk, (4) a loud stereo, (5) poor lighting, (6) the aroma of a baking pie, and (7) thirst or hunger.

External Message

The external elements that affect the message overlap with those that affect comprehension. For example, a jackhammer interferes with understanding for a reader, but it interferes with the external message for a listener. Other examples of interference in oral and nonverbal transactions include distractive whispers, a howling microphone, static on a radio, crackling on a telephone line, and a pillar between the speaker and a member of the audience. Examples of interference with written messages include the loss of time between transmission and receipt of messages, postal delays, and letters damaged by postal equipment.

Feedback

Although not shown in Figure 1-2, feedback, of course, forms the next stage of the transaction. Once meanings lodge in the destination of the receiver, the receiver becomes the sender and initiates feedback. Then the process simply recycles as described for the original sender. The addition of feedback creates a second stage to the spiraling model. Of course, the communication spiral can grow indefinitely—just as long as sender and receiver choose to create feedback to the other.

This communication model attempts only to break a dynamic process into parts for analysis; no model can capture the intricacies of the communication process or the speed at which it takes place. Thus, as you study the basic components of the process, try to think of them as stop-action frames from a complex motion picture.

BUSINESS COMMUNICATION

The definition, model, and principles of human communication apply directly to business communication. Remember the definition given at the beginning of this chapter:

> Business communication is the process of transacting meanings through written, oral, and nonverbal messages internal and external to organizations of paid people working together to produce and market goods and services for profit.

This combined definition reinforces the concept that people define business—people communicating within themselves and with one another. Because the individual human being is the basic unit for business, business communication always includes the intrapersonal level. As communication moves to the interpersonal, mediated, person-to-group, and mass levels, human transactions still remain at the core of the process.

SUMMARY

Human communication—the process of transacting meanings through written, oral, and nonverbal messages—provides the key to success in business and in life. As a process, communication takes a dynamic, spiraling form between senders and receivers at five levels of communication: intrapersonal (within oneself), interpersonal (two-way, face-to-face), mediated (two-way, not face-to-face), person-to-group (one-way, face-to-face), and mass (one-way, not face-to-face). Transacting, or sharing meaning, requires that active senders and receivers learn about each other and use feedback. Meanings exist within people, not within the verbal and nonverbal symbols used to transact them. Symbols form messages, and messages take written, oral, and nonverbal forms.

A model of the communication process features the sender, receiver, external message, channel, and interference. The sender engages the source and manager and the encoder to develop the internal message and external message. The transmitter thrusts the external message into the channel. The message moves through time and space to the receiver. The receiving apparatus picks up the message. The decoder and destination and manager convert the internal message into meanings. Then the receiver become a sender, initiates feedback, and the spiral continues to grow.

Business communication applies the human communication process to the internal and external activities of organizations of paid people working together to produce and market goods and services for profit.

EXERCISES

1. You are a business communication consultant. Write a short note to your new client explaining the importance of good communication. Include in your letter a definition of human communication.
2. Three students are needed to complete this exercise. Each student reads a part (Ms. Jones, the manager; Mr. Higgins, the secretary; and Ms. Phillips, the job applicant). After you have read "A Play," discuss the questions listed at its end.

A PLAY

(Ms. Jones and Mr. Higgins are speaking on the intercom.)

Ms. Jones: Has Ms. Phillips arrived yet?

Mr. Higgins: No, she's ten minutes overdue. Would you like me to call her?

Ms. Jones: Let's wait another five minutes.

(Ms. Phillips enters Mr. Higgins's office.)

Mr. Higgins: May I help you?

Ms. Phillips: Yes. I'm Sara Phillips. I have an interview with Ms. Jones. I'm sorry I'm late.

Mr. Higgins: No problem. Ms. Jones's office is to my right. Knock and walk in.

Ms. Phillips: Thank you.

(Ms. Phillips knocks, then immediately walks into Ms. Jones's office.)

Ms. Jones: You startled me. Are you Sara Phillips?

Ms. Phillips: Yes. I'm sorry I'm a bit late. My car . . . .

(Ms. Jones interrupts.)

Ms. Jones: No need to explain. Have a seat.

END

a. Explain how "A Play" illustrates the spiraling communication process.
b. Were the people operating at a mediated level? If not, at what level or levels were they operating? Explain.
c. Did Ms. Phillips's late arrival affect the situation? Does her late arrival constitute a form of communication? Explain.
d. Is it possible that Mr. Higgins wanted Ms. Phillips to pause after she knocked on Ms. Jones's door, but that Ms. Phillips thought he wanted her to knock and walk in immediately? Can words and phrases hold different meanings for different people? Explain.

3. Meet with your group to discuss the five levels of communication (intrapersonal, interpersonal, mediated, person-to-group, and mass). Work together to develop three examples of communication at each level. Also discuss some of the problems that could exist in communicating at each level. Have one member of the group present the examples and conclusions to the class.

4. Determine which level of communication each of these situations represents. Remember that some situations do not fall into just one of the five categories.
a. You shield your face from the sun.
b. You speak to the League of Women Voters.
c. You ponder your future.
d. You talk to your professor.
e. You write to your colleague in New York.
f. You listen to a television program.
g. You publish a newspaper.
h. You read a section of a book to a class.
i. You ask a friend to tell your manager that you will be late for work; your friend does as you ask.
j. You write a letter that will be duplicated and sent to 200 people.
k. You solve a present-value problem.

5. You work for the John Melton Corporation. You have been asked to conduct an in-house training program on human communication. You have been told that the program should run two hours a day for five days. Your boss wants a one- or two-page outline of the program tomorrow morning. Write the outline.

6. You teach a business communication course in a local high school. You are familiar with the definition of human communication set forth in this book. Rewrite the definition so that it can be understood easily by your fifteen-year-old students. Also develop at least one example that clearly illustrates each part of the definition.
7. *[Your professor will time this exercise.]* Write a few paragraphs on the importance of understanding the human communication process. Include several of the relevant aspects of communication theory.
8. List several channels you could use to make it known that you are running for mayor. Note the types of interference that could distort your message. What channel(s) would best serve your purposes?
9. Two students are needed to complete this exercise. One student should communicate the following to the other student without the use of the voice or paper.

   I am not feeling well. As soon as this class is over, I am going to go to see the doctor.

   Was the message too complex to be transmitted nonverbally? Discuss.
10. You own the Rugs for You Carpet Warehouse. You want to prepare a flyer announcing your first annual shag carpet sale. You will distribute the flyer to people in a working-class neighborhood. What should you consider before composing the flyer? What sorts of symbols could be misinterpreted? After you have explored the potential problems, prepare the flyer. Do you think your flyer will communicate what you intend it to communicate? Why?
11. Form groups to discuss the model of the communication process. Use the model to analyze this situation:

    Sara Mason decides that she needs to contact her client, John Dorn, because he seems to want daily progress reports. She uses her telephone to call John. After Sara says "Hello," static interrupts their conversation. John then says: "Bad connection, isn't it?"

    Answer these questions for both the sender (Sara Mason) and receiver (John Dorn):
    a. What parts did the source/manager and destination/manager play?
    b. What was the involvement of the encoder? the decoder?
    c. What functions did the transmitter and receiver play?
    d. What types of interference occurred in the communication sequence?
    e. What, if anything, constituted feedback?
    Have one member present your group's analysis to the members of another group.
12. Read the section on dictation in Chapter 14 (pages 402–403). Then write a rough draft of a memorandum to your colleagues at the Norris Systems Management Corporation explaining the possible applications of the model of the communication process. Meet with your group. You and every other group member then dictate the memorandum to some other group member. Evaluate each other's dictating style.
13. You are a loan officer for a bank. You notice that the letter your superiors and colleagues send customers are full of typographical and grammatical errors,

strange jargon, and arithmetic errors. The letters are written on hot orange stationery. Write a memorandum to your superiors and colleagues explaining that these practices constitute interference and should be avoided. Remember that the memorandum should not offend your superiors or co-workers.

14. Outline the definition of business communication. Meet with your group. You and every other group member dictate a complete version of the definition from your outline into an imaginary dictating machine. Evaluate each other's performance by answering these questions:
   a. Was the dictator prepared?
   b. Did the dictator speak clearly?
   c. Did the dictator speak at an appropriate speed?
   d. Was the dictator able to dictate a coherent message from the outline?
   e. Did the dictator hesitate or correct herself or himself repeatedly?
   f. Did the dictator use correct grammar and idiom?
   g. Did the dictator provide enough instructions to allow a typist to transcribe with relative ease?

15. Consult your dictionary and thesaurus to create meanings for these words. Use the words when you think, write, and speak so that you feel comfortable using them.

a. Acculturation	**g.** Fundamental	**m.** Introspection
b. Compel	**h.** Hypothetical	**n.** Mediated
c. Composite	**i.** Imagery	**o.** Obliterate
d. Contemporary	**j.** Impel	**p.** Socialization
e. Dynamic	**k.** Inherent	**q.** Successive
f. Extraneous	**l.** Integral	**r.** Unique

16. Complete and score this comprehension test over Chapter 1.

SELF-TEST 1
Chapter 1

A. Recall (10 points each). For each multiple-choice question, select the most accurate answer.

   1. Intrapersonal communication:
      a. Takes place between or among two or a few people
      b. Takes place between a complex organization and many people
      c. Takes place within oneself
      d. Is primarily nonverbal
      e. Takes place between two people who know one another relatively well

   2. Mediated communication:
      a. Takes place between two people speaking face to face
      b. Involves some intermediate means for carrying the messages
      c. Excludes the use of letters, reports, or memoranda
      d. Is communication through television and newspapers
      e. Takes place within oneself

   3. Human communication may be defined as:
      a. The two-way exchange of ideas between people
      b. Sending messages and receiving feedback

c. A spiraling process
d. The perfect exchange of information
e. A one-way process

4. All human communication:
   a. Involves a simple process
   b. Involves the transaction of meanings through symbolic action
   c. Is verbal
   d. Involves inanimate objects
   e. Is static
5. Which of these is not a part of the first stage of the two-person communication model?
   a. Debugger/translator
   b. Source/manager
   c. Encoder
   d. Decoder
   e. Transmitter
6. The channel is best defined as:
   a. Air waves
   b. Sound waves
   c. The form in which the message occurs
   d. A letter or television broadcast
   e. A messenger service
7. When the receiver's external message reaches the receiving person, what element is activated first?
   a. Destination/manager
   b. Decoder
   c. Receiver
   d. Transmitter
   e. Debugger/translator
8. Business is defined in this chapter as:
   a. A name given to an organization of paid people working together to produce and market goods or services for profit
   b. A name given to an organization of paid people or volunteers who produce goods and/or services for profit or charity
   c. A name given to an organization of people who provide services and manufacture products
   d. A name given to any group of people who work together
   e. A name given to any organization that provides goods and services for a 10 percent profit

B. Inference (10 points each). Indicate whether these statements are true or false.
   1. The model of the communication process set forth in this book is an attempt to look at and understand some rather arbitrarily labeled parts of the communication process.
   2. The sending act is the most important part of the communication process.

SOLUTION

A. Recall (10 points each)

1. c	5. a
2. b	6. c
3. c	7. c
4. b	8. a

B. Inference (10 points each)

1. True
2. False

ENDNOTES

1. Frank E. X. Dance, "Toward a Theory of Communication," in *Human Communication Theory: Original Essays* (New York: Holt, Rinehart and Winston, Inc., 1967), 296.
2. Don Fabun, *Communications: The Transfer of Meaning* (New York: Glencoe Publishing Co., Inc., 1968), 32. Copyright 1968 by Kaiser Aluminum & Chemical Corporation. Reprinted by permission.
3. Fabun, 26.
4. Rudolph F. Verderber, *Communicate!* (Belmont, Calif.: Wadsworth Publishing Company, Inc., 1975), 4.

STUDENT'S OBJECTIVES:

1 To convert an understanding of communication theory into an understanding of communication practice

2 To learn to apply six guidelines for effective communication:

- Define purposes, participants, and environment
- Identify the channel
- Control interference
- Select, encode, decode, transmit, and receive messages
- Use feedback
- Evaluate

2

GUIDELINES FOR EFFECTIVE COMMUNICATION

3 To build a foundation for the applications in the remainder of the book: reading, listening, receiving nonverbal messages, writing, preparing presentations, speaking, and seeking employment

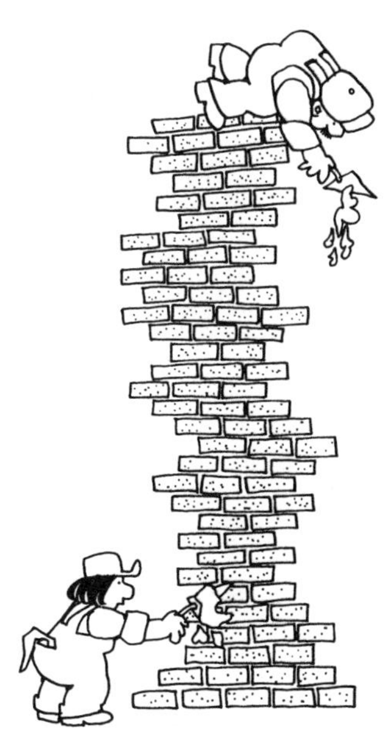

Six guidelines for effective communication bring theory into practical ap-plication. If you apply the following guidelines when you send and receive messages, your communication will improve noticeably.

1. Define purposes, participants, and environment
2. Identify the channel
3. Control interference
4. Select, encode, decode, transmit, and receive messages
5. Use feedback
6. Evaluate

Because most of *Business Communication Fundamentals* deals with Guideline 4 (encoding, decoding, transmitting, and receiving messages), this chapter develops the other five guidelines.

GUIDELINE 1: DEFINE PURPOSES, PARTICIPANTS, AND ENVIRONMENT

This guideline requires careful definition of three important factors: (1) the purposes of both sender and receiver, (2) the participants, and (3) the environment.

Purposes

Business has purpose—with profit as the general goal. Business firms set, review, and revise goals at every level of activity. These purposes take many forms. Some examples that illustrate the variety include the following:

- The receipt of an order for party hats and napkins represents a short-term objective. Increased sales of party hats represents an intermediate objective. Profitability represents a long-term objective.
- Subconscious, secondary objectives to obtain the boss's approval and retain the job accompany a conscious, primary objective to complete an excellent report by the time the boss needs it.
- The writer (sender) of a notice about a job opening has the objective of receiving applications from qualified people. However, the reader (receiver) has the objective of learning about jobs by reading notices.

Whether sending or receiving, dealing with the short term or the long term, or setting primary or secondary objectives, consider not only your own purposes, but also those of the other participant. When purposes coincide, the transaction runs smoother than when they differ. When purposes differ, try to adjust to address some of the other's purposes.

Purposes for Sending

As a purposive sender, you will consider the receiver and the desired action. What do I want the receiver to do? What do I want her to believe? What do I want him to say? How do I want her to behave? What do I want him to become? Without defining your purpose, your messages may miss their targets. You may unwisely emphasize the process of sending (writing, speaking, drawing, etc.) instead of desired outcomes.

Some examples of purposes that suggest action by the receiver include:

- To return the card
- To buy the clock
- To send the list
- To sign the agreement
- To return the report
- To laugh

Purposes for Receiving

To become an active receiver, identify your specific purposes for receiving messages. What action will result from the reception? How will the action help you satisfy your needs and wants? Examples of such purposes for receiving messages include:

- To choose best product
- To pass test
- To laugh
- To please boss
- To keep job
- To learn to operate machine

Ethics and Purpose

With purposes and profits come responsibilities for ethical behavior. As rules of moral conduct, ethics govern the decisions that business people make as they try to reach their goals. Ethics not only reflect your personal morality but also help you to recognize the morality of those with whom you interact.

Participants

Effective communication requires careful definition of yourself and the other participants in the transaction. Self-definition depends on both intrapersonal and interpersonal levels. In addition, definitions of self and others depend on understanding a broad base of psychological, social, cultural, and physical factors. Analysis of key factors will help to define participants in the context of any given transaction.

1. Name
2. Address
3. Age
4. Sex
5. Marital and family status
6. Education and intelligence
7. Occupation
8. Income and spending
9. Reference groups
10. Interests
11. Nationality, race, and ethnicity
12. Physical characteristics
13. Dress and appearance
14. Religion

Avoid stereotyping people; human beings vary widely. For example, even though people in a certain age bracket have some similarities, they all do not fit the same mold. Each person has a unique blend of interests and abilities. As a sender, try to send messages to fit that person's world. As a receiver, try to interpret messages in light of the sender's world.

To understand the other's world, develop and practice *empathy*. Use your imagination to project yourself into the feelings and ideas of others. Participate in those feelings and ideas. As you walk a mile in the other's moccasins, you can both encode and decode messages as if transacting with yourself. Nothing can do more to improve communication than developing empathy.

Environment

Factors other than the purpose and the participants require analysis to improve communication. These environmental factors include the topic, circumstances, time, and physical conditions under which the communication occurs.

This example shows how the *topic* has an impact on transaction: If a company (the sender) grants credit (the topic), you (the receiver) likely will have a positive view of the company. On the other hand, if denied credit, you may have a negative view of the sender. Knowing the receiver's interest level and the relevance of the topic can also help to understand the environment in which the transaction takes place.

Circumstance also significantly affects a transaction. Some of the circumstantial factors include channel, formality, number of participants, interference, status of everyone involved, political situation, extent of participation, distance of participants, aural qualities, and visual qualities.

The *time* dimension can affect communication in important ways. Examples of the facets of time requiring consideration include: time of day, position in a business cycle (prosperity, recession, depression, recovery), length of the transaction, timing relative to other events, punctuality of the participants, and customs of the participants.

The *physical* surroundings of a transaction also affect its success. Some of the factors include location, space, distance, furnishings, crowding, seating arrangements, aesthetics, temperature, weather, and climate.

GUIDELINE 2: IDENTIFY THE CHANNEL

The second guideline requires understanding communication channels. Senders should choose the best channel for the particular communication. Receivers should assess the implications of the choice made by the sender, as well as the strengths and limitations of the channel itself.

Channel Effectiveness

Make channel effectiveness the first consideration when defining channels. A hierarchy of channel types from best to worst would include the following:

- interpersonal
- mediated (such as telephone and two-way radio)
- person-to-group
- mass and some mediated (such as letter and report)

Because of the importance of human interaction, you should strive to use the best channel possible. Even when circumstances dictate a relatively poor channel, you should try to improve the transaction by adding some of the features of the more effective channels.

Potential for Feedback

Avoid the tendency to think that businesses have only the letter and the telephone available to them. For example, try to arrange for personal meetings with clients or suppliers, recognizing that such direct communication provides the best potential for feedback. Even when forced to use a poor channel, establish some mechanism for feedback. For example, with a sales letter, include a stamped envelope for a response. Similarly, include a coupon in a newspaper advertisement.

Custom

If tradition calls for written invitations to a reception, avoid using the telephone. On the other hand, do not blindly follow custom. For instance, suppose that your firm has always contacted suppliers by telephone. A personal visit by someone from your firm might improve relations.

Impact

Marshall McLuhan felt so strongly about the impact of channels that he proposed that the medium (the channel) *is* the message. His theory suggests that the channel absorbs the message. The channel becomes the message, and the impact upon the receiver comes from the channel. Therefore, messages packaged in highly effective channels may cause the receivers to assign them different meanings than those packaged in less effective channels.

Difficulty

Another criterion for channel definition stems from the complexity of the material contained in the message. Certain channels simply do not have the capacity to carry difficult messages. For example, a two-way interpersonal channel alone cannot carry the extensive data needed for an annual report to stockholders.

Do not overload a channel, but do not waste the capacity of a channel either. The error of underloading a channel becomes particularly serious. For example, why write a letter when a telephone call or personal visit could handle the subject matter—and provide a more successful transaction?

Storage and Retrieval

When a communicator must retain many messages for future reference, human minds alone will not suffice. Minds continually reinterpret, bury, and lose material. Minds disagree with one another. Minds become inaccessible. Minds die. Thus, written communication provides the best potential for storage and retrieval.

The computer provides an essential part of the communication system. It uses symbols and it even interacts with humans and other computers. In addition, computers provide an extensive capacity for storage and retrieval.

Number of Receivers

The number of receivers also influences the choice of channel. By definition, if more than a few people constitute the intended receiving group, the transaction cannot take place through the interpersonal and mediated levels.

Time

Time emerges as a factor in choice of channel, particularly when the transaction requires speed. In addition, time itself can form an element of a channel. For example, a night letter represents a different channel than does a telegram—simply because of the time of day for the transmission of each. The night letter simply does not carry as much psychological weight as a telegram.

Distance

The distance between sender and receiver also has an impact on channel usage. If five hundred miles separate sender and receiver, one cannot casually walk over to see the other for interpersonal transaction. However, distance alone should not dictate the choice. Make channel selection decisions on the basis of an analysis of all relevant factors, particularly the cost/return and subject matter.

Cost/Return

An important criterion for selecting channels involves analysis of costs and return on investment. To illustrate, people tend to think that letters cost much less than telephone calls. In reality, including all labor, material, service, postal, and overhead expenses for both, the letter often costs more. A five-minute call from Oklahoma City to New York during business hours costs about $3 (including the wages of the participants and the overhead). Depending on the wages of the people involved, estimates of the cost to produce and mail a single letter range from $2 to $7, with an average of about $5. Thus, for the illustration, a telephone transaction at $3 costs less than even the minimum for a two-letter transaction at $4.

Such a comparison becomes particularly appropriate for companies with access to a Wide Area Telephone Service (WATS) line. For one fixed fee, employees may make as many long-distance telephone calls as they wish. As the number of calls increases, the average cost for a call decreases. In addition, toll-free numbers allow people to make free long-distance calls to a firm.

Similar cost comparisons can be made for other channels. The long-distance travel of humans for communication at the interpersonal level often proves most expensive. Yet, as one conclusion from their research related to cost-benefit considerations, Holland, Stead, and Leibrock write:

> Managers should be careful not to preclude the use of richer forms of information transfer. . . . Unfortunately, many organizations tend to *reduce* information budgets (restraining long-distance calls, trips, etc.) during periods of uncertainty since such periods may coincide with increased economic constraints. . . .[1]

GUIDELINE 3: CONTROL INTERFERENCE

Interference involves senders and receivers, emanates from humans and nonhumans, and occurs at all stages of the communication process. This section explains some of the concepts of general semantics, discusses relationships between perceptions and meanings, and suggests some specific devices for overcoming a major source of human interference—the use of symbols.

General Semantics

General semantics, a branch of linguistics, deals with the relations between *symbols* and *meanings*. The basic semantic obstacle exists because of the one-word, one-meaning misconception. However, meanings actually vary from one person to another. As soon as words begin to take on relatively common meanings, their meanings seem to shift, or usage adds new words with similar meanings.

Symbols in the form of words make communication possible, but they also act as major obstacles. For example, the word *run* has about ninety meanings listed in the dictionary. The word *blue* can mean a color or a mood. The term *labor union* holds one set of meanings for its members and another for management.

Symbols carry both rational and emotional parts of meanings. Thus, a safe symbol for some people might draw out negative meanings from others. Remember that meanings exist within the minds of people, not within the symbols themselves. Symbols (words and nonwords) merely *represent* meanings.

Perceptions and Meanings

Perception provides the means for converting sensations (received through the five senses) into internal meanings. The senses themselves serve as *filters*—potential barriers to communication.

The major filters, however, exist within the mind, because the mind assigns meanings to what the senses receive.

In his basic textbook, David K. Berlo suggests four types of meanings: denotative, structural, contextual, and connotative.[2]

Denotative Meanings

Denotative meanings exist as widely accepted, uniform meanings for physical objects. Even though denotation can lead to a basic level of shared meanings, the frequent lack of physical objects creates a serious limitation. Illustrations and pictures can, however, substitute for physical objects.

For example, use of the simple word *shoe* without pointing to the actual shoe (or a picture of it), does not create a denotative meaning. The word *shoe* could refer to one of a variety of human shoes—men's, women's, canvas, leather, hiking, jogging, tennis, etc. It could also refer to a horseshoe, a brake shoe, or the shoe of a tire.

Structural Meanings

Structural meanings depend on grammar, syntax, and the sequencing of symbols into sentences. For example, consider this sentence: "Several chairpersons selected committee members on the basis of friendship instead of qualifications." A significant revision of meaning would occur by interchanging the phrases "several chairpersons" and "committee members." A dramatic revision of meaning would occur by converting the final segment to read ". . . on the basis of qualifications rather than friendship." This sentence provides another example: "That machine operator said the supervisor is a thief." As punctuated, the meaning differs substantially from: "That machine operator," said the supervisor, "is a thief."

Contextual Meanings

To illustrate contextual meaning, read a paragraph containing some contrived denotative "words" for which you need to supply meanings. As you read the paragraph, analyze how you substitute familiar words for the artificial ones.

> A large number of *outalucks* have the *druc*. Some of them have had to go to the Infirmary. Because many of the *outalucks'* professors have the *druc* too—coughing and sneezing all over the place—the professors will let the *outalucks* make up their final *sockos*. At least three professors are already so *gloop* that graduate *bools* will administer their *sockos*. Most of the professors will also accept term *duples* late.

Connotative Meanings

As private and vaguely sensed meanings, connotative meanings represent dynamic abstractions of a person's social experience. For example, the words *liberal* and *conservative* are symbols for abstract meanings. The meanings exist as a result of a person's previous encounters with the words and the socially based concepts associated with them.

Any given symbol can have a combined effect—denotative, structural, contextual, and connotative. As an example, suppose that at 12:30 P.M. a colleague states to you: "My boss is out to lunch." The word *boss* has structural meaning as a noun serving as the subject of the sentence. It denotes in the sense that it refers to someone higher on the organizational chart than your colleague. The limited contextual meaning would suggest that the person labeled "boss" has gone to a restaurant to eat the noon meal (also a denotative meaning).

Suppose your colleague made the same statement at 6:00 P.M. with this inflection: "My boss is 'out to lunch.'" The meanings differ significantly. Without the benefit of preceding or subsequent sentences, contextual meanings remain incomplete. Connotative meanings about the word *boss* could differ between you and your colleague, depending on your respective "boss" experiences and perceptions.

When selecting or observing symbols, think of their wide ranges of potential meanings. The more abstract a symbol, the greater the likelihood that its meaning will differ among people. Thus, use denotative and low-abstraction connotative symbols when possible, and use high-abstraction connotative symbols carefully.

Overcoming Barriers

This summary of the major barriers created by the use of symbols—and means for overcoming them—highlights ten rules developed by Schneider, Donaghy, and Newman from the literature of general semantics.[3] Detailed discussion of their research is beyond the scope of this book, but you may consult their text for additional information.

Rule 1: Go to the reality

Barriers often arise when communicators function from a *map* rather than the *territory*. For example, an executive might deal with employees based on memories of his own treatment (the map), rather than the real situation that exists now (the territory).

To deal with narrow and internal symbols, move into the broad and external world of reality. Observe the territory, not just recollections and impressions that constitute your internal maps.

Rule 2: Determine denotative, connotative, and contextual meanings

A major type of interference occurs when communicators confuse denotative and connotative meanings and respond to meanings within themselves as if they were responding to the physical things.

To overcome such problems, look beyond the denotative meanings to the possible connotative meanings that symbols may carry for the other participants. Choose and interpret your words in light of both sets of meanings. Ask questions, restate the messages, and observe the context of the messages.

Rule 3: Distinguish between facts and generalizations

Risks occur when a communicator treats a generalization as a fact. To overcome the confusion between facts and generalization, habitually ask yourself: "Is this statement I've just made (or heard) limited to facts or does it generalize beyond facts?"

Rule 4: Attach "etc." to all messages

A major obstacle to sharing meanings lies in the assumption (usually false) that a message contains everything known about the subject. Arrogance, prejudice, closed-mindedness, and intolerance could result. No one can ever know everything about a subject. Suspect yourself any time you feel too certain about a topic; such a moment proves quite dangerous. Search for more on the very topic you think you have conquered. Attach a mental "etc." to all messages sent and received.

Rule 5: Date information

Miscommunication often occurs simply because people draw conclusions from the past and treat them as correct for the present and the future. Recognize change and always date information. When viewing any person, place, or thing, do not assume time stands still.

Rule 6: Index information

When communicators do not differentiate between similarities and differences within groups, they increase the chances for the form of semantic interference known as stereotyping.

The great danger in stereotypes lies in the unconscious labeling process. Many people create and accept caricatures about whole classes of people and things without challenge or differentiation. Correcting the interference requires a conscious effort to index the similarities and differences in available information.

Rule 7: Look for the middle ground

People often create interference by taking extreme positions. They act as if all situations exist at two poles, with no middle ground. Some situations do exist as clear dichotomies (for example, taxpayers either mail their federal tax returns by April 15 or they do not). Most communication transactions, however, explore a range of alternatives about the subject at hand. If participants ignore such ranges and act as if only two contradictory classes exist, interference occurs. Thus, you can reduce such interference if you look for the middle ground.

Rule 8: Use "to be" correctly

Misuse of the "to be" verbs can lead to serious interference. Avoid restrictive statements that project stereotyped attributes and imply an absolute equation between the elements joined with a "to be" verb. Avoid projecting arrogant, final-word images of permanent truth. Insert qualifiers such as the words *likely, probably, may, seems,* and *in my opinion*. Acknowledge that very little in life deserves the finality of *is*.

Rule 9: Question affective symbols used in place of informative ones

The use of affective (emotional) symbols instead of informative ones introduces another category of semantic barriers. For example, name-calling arouses negative feelings—particularly when directed at the receiver.

Try to avoid the misuse of affective symbols by thinking of the paired nature of words—their denotative and connotative functions. Use *euphemisms* (positive substitutes) for words that may create negative meanings (*dysphemisms*). As an example, if a person calls someone else a "wild-eyed radical," do not accept that label without analysis. The replacement of dysphemisms by euphemisms often results in the self-fulfilling prophecy of success instead of failure.

Rule 10: Think before reacting

Many obstacles to effective communication arise simply because people react without thinking. The basic correction for *all* types of miscommunication calls for thinking before responding. Therefore, take the time to use the appropriate devices for overcoming interference that this section has provided.

GUIDELINE 4: SELECT, ENCODE, TRANSMIT, AND RECEIVE MESSAGES

As stated at the beginning of this chapter, Guideline 4 forms the subject for most of the remaining chapters in this book; therefore, this chapter does not cover it.

GUIDELINE 5: USE FEEDBACK

The word *feedback* originally referred to technical systems, particularly computer systems. Systems feed back errors or deviations to the control center so that it can correct them. As a closed-loop system, communication has output that produces an effect on the input, just as for technical systems. Feedback provides control by reinserting the results of previous performances into the communication process.

Feedback takes many forms: a question calling for more information or for clarification, the answer to a question, a paraphrase of the sender's message, a puzzled expression, a nod of acceptance, silence, applause, a completed questionnaire, a progress report, passing the salt as requested.

The continual nature of feedback in face-to-face encounters enables the participants to evaluate and revise messages during transactions. Even with less effective channels, however, feedback provides useful information. For example, in an exchange of business letters, each letter gives the receiver the opportunity to make necessary adjustments before writing again.

Not only does feedback benefit individual transactions, but it also adds to the cumulative growth of the user. Therefore, analyze and evaluate all feedback; you can benefit even from the mistakes.

Many problems arise from an insufficient flow of good organizational feedback, particularly because organizations often restrict communication to formal, upward-flow channels. A mere declaration of an open-door policy at the upper-management level usually does not overcome the restriction.

The formal communication system too often prohibits employees from freely generating and receiving upward, downward, and lateral feedback. In those organizations, informal systems, notably the grapevine, flourish.

Positive feedback serves as an effective communication technique because it does not attack the person. It uses constructive, objective, and specific action in a direct, supportive way. Positive feedback softens criticism—or bad news of any kind—by wedging it between sincere expressions of good news.

Pretend that as a trainer for an office-machine operation, you demonstrate the pattern and then have each employee move through it. Trainee Joe does not do well, and you supply feedback to help him. Contrast the impact of these two types of feedback:

- "There's no way you're ever going to learn this operation. Here, let me demonstrate one more time." (*negative*)
- "Hey, you're doing OK. Let me stand here behind you and take your arm through the pattern a few times. It'll get easier." (*positive*)

Both messages acknowledge the improper motion of the trainee. However, Trainee Joe would probably react better to the positive feedback of the second example.

Stimulating Feedback

Senders should plan how to stimulate feedback even as they formulate messages. Each level of communication requires feedback stimulation. The following suggestions will help you at each level.

Interpersonal Level

- Ask questions that check perception through feedback: "Which one of my suggestions do you like best?" "What do you think?" "What do you like or dislike about my solution?" "Have you ever had a similar experience?"
- As a group leader, stop the discussion when two consecutive statements conflict. Then ask one person to restate her or his comment so that it shows understanding of the other person's statement.
- Do not dominate a conversation. Use nonverbal cues to invite feedback at comfortable intervals. Display a sincere interest in listening to the other person.
- In training discussions, announce any end-of-meeting tests at the beginning so that people will organize feedback during the session.

- Develop and exhibit a nondefensive attitude. Establish receptiveness to both good and bad news. Mentally meet people on their own levels. Use nonverbal invitations for the other to respond. Avoid formality. Establish warmth and openness.
- Learn about the other person so you can picture what feedback you might receive in addition to feedback you want. Create a climate that acknowledges the value system, attitudes, and customs of the other person. At least avoid an atmosphere that flies in the face of strong feelings the other person holds.
- Tap into the grapevine to learn about morale, attitudes toward policies, solutions to problems, reactions to decisions, and feelings of the employees.
- Develop upward, interpersonal flows of information from workers to management. Establish a regular pattern of management-employee meetings and a genuine open-door policy. Interview all departing employees. Establish grievance procedures that include face-to-face conversations at each step.
- Provide appropriate physical arrangements, such as a central lounge and snack area. Move people who need to gather feedback close to each other with open doorways between associated offices.

Mediated Level

- When talking by telephone, use tone, volume, pitch, inflection, speed, pauses, and other such elements to invite feedback. Questions such as "I'm wondering if I'm making myself clear?" and "Would you repeat that?" also solicit immediate feedback.
- Include a postage-paid, addressed envelope or card to promote returns to promotional or survey letters. Send a check-off or short-answer form. Use self-carboned, tear-off reply forms. They allow both you and the receiver to keep copies of the messages.
- Conduct attitude surveys in organizations by questionnaires, a suggestion box, or a special telephone recorder number. Ask for news items and suggestions in the company newsletter, and give prizes for the best responses. Have supervisors prepare detailed records on employee tardiness, absenteeism, productivity, exceptional performance, and innovative ideas.

Person-to-Group Level

- Weave an incident common to the group into the speech.
- During the speech, interject some questions directly to well-liked people for simple one- or two-word answers. A humorous question works particularly well.
- Ask a question that calls for a show of hands by the members of the audience. Raise your hand as you call for them to do so.

- Include some statements that call for laughter, groans, applause, or other nonverbal participation.
- About halfway through a long speech, have people stand for a minute.
- In a small group, have each person introduce herself or himself at the beginning of the meeting.
- If possible, follow the speech by a question-and-answer session.

Mass Level

- Use surveys, readership studies, polls, and television-viewing rating systems.
- Use coded "cents-off" coupons, refund offers, contests, giveaway drawings, postage-paid return envelopes and cards, and phone-in radio and television shows.
- Ask product-testing panels to complete and mail questionnaires or diaries about the products they test.

Sending Feedback

As a receiver, try to determine what senders want as feedback. For situations in which you want to give uninvited feedback to senders, consider asking them first. For example, if you think a colleague should improve her use of the telephone, ask, "Would you like me to share some hints that I have learned about telephone techniques?"

Feed back quickly; immediate feedback contributes much more than delayed feedback. Use as many channels as needed. Use the best possible channels, and use both verbal and nonverbal expressions. Even if the original message took a negative form, respond positively. Describe, interpret, and clarify. Feed back in a mature, accepting fashion; avoid defensiveness. Make feedback appropriate, straightforward, specific, and factual. Assess actions, not personalities.

If you cannot decide what a sender wants, try to ask questions or rephrase the received message as a check of your perception. If the answers clarify the situation, formulate the desired type of feedback.

Use particular sensitivity when generating unsolicited feedback about the other's behavior or personality. Make it constructive. Make it relate to something the other person can change.

GUIDELINE 6: EVALUATE

Evaluation of transactions measures attainment of goals and shows which communication procedures work best. The ability to evaluate communication also contributes to your personal growth and self-confidence.

Evaluate not only at the end of a transaction, but continually during it. Continual evaluation allows for adjustment even during ongoing transactions. Whether mental, oral, or written, ongoing or terminal, brief or extensive, informal or formal, individual or organizational, communication evaluation should raise questions such as the following:

- To what extent does (did) the transaction meet the objectives of the sender? the receiver?
- Does (did) the channel serve the transaction well?
- What strengths and weaknesses does (did) the sender exhibit? the receiver?
- Does (did) the transaction provide sufficient feedback?
- How does (did) interference affect the transaction?
- What action could improve this transaction or subsequent transactions?

Formal communication audits can extend evaluation to the total organization. Communication consultants usually conduct the audits and make the diagnoses. Audits allow managers to improve many facets of organizational life: job enrichment, job satisfaction, feedback systems, counseling, interpersonal relationships, human development programs, motivation, participation, retention, commitment, and perceptions and attainment of organizational goals.

Evaluating helps establish a healthy communication climate—one free of adversary relationships.

With the completion of this review of the guidelines for effective communication, we will move to applied communication. Part B covers receiving, beginning with reading in Chapter 3.

SUMMARY

Six guidelines for effective communication help convert theory into application: (1) Define purposes, participants, and environment. (2) Identify the channel. (3) Control interference. (4) Select, encode, decode, transmit, and receive messages. (5) Use feedback. (6) Evaluate.

Whether sending or receiving, define the purposes of both you and the other participants. State purposes for sending as actions desired by the receiver. Tie them to the receiver's needs, wants, and motivation. State purposes for receiving to identify the action you want to take as a result of receiving the message. Ethics must govern purposive activities.

Defining yourself and the others in a transaction depends a great deal on understanding psychological, sociological, cultural, and physical factors. Try to analyze these factors in each transaction, but avoid stereotyping on the basis of such information. Instead use it to bring about empathy and adaptation.

The environment contributes a great deal to a transaction. Identify, adapt to, and control such things as the topic, circumstance, time, and location.

Choose and receive from the various communication channels in light of their effectiveness, availability, potential for feedback, custom, impact, difficulty of message, storage and retrieval, number of receivers, time, distance, and cost/return. For channel effectiveness, apply this hierarchy in order from best to worst.

Control interference from both human and nonhuman sources. For the major source, the human, understand the principles of general semantics (meanings are in people, not in words) and perceptions and meanings (denotative, structural, contextual, and connotative). To overcome human barriers to communication:

- Go the reality
- Determine denotative, connotative, and contextual meanings
- Distinguish between facts and generalizations
- Attach "etc." to all messages
- Date information
- Index information
- Look for the middle ground
- Use "to be" correctly
- Question affective symbols used in place of informative ones
- Think before reacting

Encode, decode, transmit, and receive in light of the purposes, participants, environment, channel, and interference.

Stimulate, use, and create feedback to the fullest. For example, at the interpersonal level, ask perception-checking questions such as: "Which one of my suggestions do you like best?" "Do I understand correctly that you want me to . . . ?"

Evaluating transactions—at the end and at every stage along the way—measures attainment of goals and improves communication procedures. Use feedback as a major source of information for evaluation. Communication audits serve to evaluate an entire organization's communication effectiveness.

EXERCISES

1. You must present a paper in your marketing class. The paper is worth half of your grade. Though you would like an "A" in the course, you need only a "C" to get your degree. What are your purposes? What are the professor's purposes? Explain.
2. You bought a miniature electric train. After you operated it for an hour, it ceased to work. You are angry. You put the train in its box and walk to the store where you bought it. You fear that the store will not take it back because it was a sale item. You wish to be firm and communicate that you want your money back or you want a train that works. You also want to relate that the salesperson who sold you the train misled you about its capabilities. In brief, clear terms, what are your objectives? What will your first statement be?
3. What does the word "cool" mean to you? What might it mean to a rock star? a ghetto inhabitant? a scientist? a socialite? a grave digger? a chef?

4. You are the supervisor of a group of salespeople who sell a line of children's books directly to grocery stores. You aren't satisfied with the performance of your salespeople and suspect that they do little or no planning before they meet with their potential customers. Write a memorandum that clearly explains the importance of defining purposes, the participants, and the environment. Include some practical suggestions on how to gather, analyze, and use the information.
5. You want a face-to-face meeting with your accountant to discuss his failure to keep your tax records in order. He insists that you put your complaints in writing and mail them to him. What do you do? Assume he avoids meeting with you. Write a letter that clearly states your complaints and demands. Will your letter be as effective as a face-to-face conversation might have been? Why?
6. Choose the specific channel or channels that you feel would be most appropriate for these communication situations. Explain your choices.
   a. Your manager sends a memorandum asking you what amount you would like your raise to be.
   b. You need to get in touch with your London office to relay some very important, detailed financial information.
   c. You need to let your 150 employees know that a major company reorganization will begin next week.
   d. You need to decide whether or not to apply for a promotion.
   e. You are the chief marketer for a large oil company. You know that your company's public image is deteriorating rapidly because consumers are upset over the fact that your company is making unusually high profits. You wish to improve that image by letting the consuming public know that you are using those profits to develop solar energy systems.
   f. You are dissatisfied with the man with whom you share an office. He talks all of the time and smokes several packs of cigarettes a day. You are allergic to cigarette smoke. You know that Ms. Andrews, your supervisor, is the person who makes office assignments.
7. Describe the communication channel which would be most effective for each of these situations.
   a. You need to communicate with a customer whom you know to be illiterate.
   b. You need to convey important information to 72 centrally located employees immediately.
   c. You need to communicate with a customer who reacts negatively to sexist language. Your personal style still includes such sexist terms as the "-man" words and "he," "his," and "him" as "neutral" references, though you are trying to eliminate them. You could choose a written channel so that you could edit to remove the offending language. However, you prefer a richer channel. What could you do?
   d. You have to lay off an employee.
   e. You receive a telephone call from a supplier. The supplier spends ten minutes reciting stock numbers, quantities of back-ordered items, prices, terms, and other such numerical data, evidently expecting you to capture all of it. The supplier makes no mention of supplementing the call with a written document. What might you do to change the channel choice?
   f. You want to contact a client in an office in Atlanta. It is 4:30 on a Friday afternoon in Chicago.
8. Meet with your group. Discuss the following situations. All you know about each of these potential clients is what you read here. As a life insurance salesperson, how would you approach each person? Why?

a. Elaine "Lou-Lou" Werner, the owner of a garden supply store, dresses in rather loud colors. She likes big cars, and works long hours. She dislikes long meetings.
b. Willard Fasteau just retired from his job. He had worked as a welder for 40 years. He lives alone, wears dressy clothes, has never been married, and flies an American flag in front of his small house. You heard that he is nice once you get to know him.
c. Sharon Torres is a teller at a bank. She is married and has four children. She is a member of the League of Women Voters, and she dresses very conservatively. A "No Peddlers" sign is nailed to the door of her house.
d. Mike Frank is a graduate student in sociology at the local university. He shares an old house with three other students. You have seen him playing softball with neighborhood children. He is a chain smoker, and he usually wears jeans and Hawaiian shirts.

Have one of your group members present one of your answers to the class.

9. You quite likely will work with a number of "others" who will not share your view of the world. Most of these people will be tolerant of you, but some of your co-workers will be preachers—they will try to convert you to their way of thinking. Because you do not want to fight with these people, you must think of ways to keep the peace and yet get your work done. List some tactful techniques that you might use.

10. What can you do to overcome the problems associated with the channels used in these situations?
    a. You just completed a short report you wrote for your Washington, D.C., office. You cannot mail the report because it is due in Washington today; thus, you must transmit its contents by phone.
    b. Though you believe that complex financial information should be transmitted in written form, your boss wants you to make an oral presentation of this year's sales figures to your company's managers at the annual sales meeting. Your boss does not want you to use visual aids or written handouts.
    c. Because the company for which you want to work cannot afford to fly you to North Dakota for an interview, you must conduct the entire interview process by mail and telephone.

11. Meet with your group. Discuss how you would handle each of these communication problems.
    a. Bill dominates the conversation at almost every staff meeting. When asked to allow someone else to speak, Bill usually says: "I'll be through in a minute." He is rarely through in a minute.
    b. Sally, your department's computer expert, is very shy. When you ask her important computer-related questions, she doesn't give you much information. She expresses herself beautifully on paper, but sometimes you need your questions answered immediately.
    c. Clark, your boss, usually interrupts you when you speak. You often have something very important to say.

12. Do you believe that the profit motive significantly distinguishes business organizations from not-for-profit organizations? Why? If you believe that the profit motive does make a substantial difference, what effect does it have on communication in business organizations?

13. You have worked at the Fancy Company for two years. You have yet to receive a raise, though your performance ratings have always been high. You make an

appointment with Mr. Biggs, the company president, to discuss a raise. What are your purposes? What do you think Mr. Biggs's purposes will be? How can an understanding of Mr. Biggs's purposes beforehand help you prepare your case?

14. You are a debt collector for the Anne Johnson and Daughters Department Store. You must call three people today to give them notice that they have a week to make their overdue payments. If they do not make the payments within a week, your company will have to take legal action. You are a good communicator and are aware of the importance of the environment of the other. You know the following about the debtors:
    a. John is a carpenter who always makes late payments. He hates to talk on the telephone.
    b. Elizabeth was just fired from her job. You do not know why. You do know that she is the sole support of her two children and that she is in dire financial straits.
    c. Bob is a Wall Street executive who has never been behind on a payment before. The last time you called (when the bill was 60 days overdue) he referred you to his accountant, who said that she would put the payment in the mail the next day.

    How would you handle each call?

15. Knowing who and what you are is important in order to communicate effectively. Write a short paper assessing your strengths, weaknesses, and personal values. Here are some questions you might answer in writing the assessment. (You may add to or subtract from the lists for each of the questions.)
    a. How would you rank these in order of importance to you? (You may add to or subtract from the list.)

        - ☐ Love
        - ☐ Achievement
        - ☐ Affiliation/Friendship
        - ☐ Wealth
        - ☐ Hobbies
        - ☐ Religion
        - ☐ Recognition
        - ☐ Family
        - ☐ Recreation
        - ☐ Health
        - ☐ Power
        - ☐ Career

    b. What do you believe concerning these issues or subjects?

        - ☐ Separation of church and state
        - ☐ The death penalty
        - ☐ Human rights
        - ☐ Regulation by the government
        - ☐ Conservation
        - ☐ Nuclear power
        - ☐ Civil rights
        - ☐ Women's movement
        - ☐ Management styles (authoritarian or nonauthoritarian)
        - ☐ Gun control
        - ☐ Labor unions
        - ☐ Living together before marriage
        - ☐ Euthanasia
        - ☐ Abortion
        - ☐ Corporate responsibility
        - ☐ Mass transportation

c. Which of these are your strengths? weaknesses?

- □ Are you intelligent?
- □ Are you skilled?
- □ Are you kind?
- □ Are you hard-working?
- □ Do you like your personality?
- □ Are you graceful?
- □ Do you speak well?
- □ Do you write well?
- □ Do you listen well?
- □ Are you sentive to other people's feelings?
- □ Are you usually happy?
- □ Do you get along well with others?
- □ Do you eat the right foods?
- □ Do you exercise regularly?
- □ Are you tolerant?

16. For the following situation, identify the actual interference, identify the feedback and explain how you would use it, and describe how you would evaluate at each stage.

Mary Harris, a good friend of yours, wrote you a letter asking you to think about opening a financial management firm with her in New York City. You call her and ask her if you would be equal partners in the firm. She says that you would have to contribute $50,000 to the firm if you want partner status. You ask when she needs the money. "Soon," she says. "When exactly?" you ask. "In a month or two," she replies. She then says she needs to go to a meeting, so she will talk to you later.

17. You have been asked to give a short, serious talk at the beginning of your company's Thanksgiving banquet. All religions as well as agnosticism and atheism are represented in your company. Write the short talk.

18. Two of your friends argue a great deal. Both take strong, extreme stands on opposite sides of almost every issue. Neither will admit that any other stand exists, though you know better. List at least one other position that could be taken on each of your friends' issues.

a. John believes that unions are the answer to all of labor's problems. Susan believes that unions cannot solve any of labor's problems.

b. John believes that all workers would be very productive if managers would get out of their way. Susan believes that managers must closely supervise workers because workers will not work on their own.

c. John believes that people should be hired only on the basis of their experience. Susan believes that people should be hired only on the basis of their education.

d. John believes that the office coffee-making chores should be shared by clerical, professional, and managerial personnel alike. Susan believes that the secretaries should always make the coffee.

e. John believes that people cannot exercise any control over communication interference. Susan believes that people can overcome all communication interference.

19. Describe the differences among the denotative, structural, contextual, and connotative meanings of the word "servant."

20. John, your best friend, tells you that your office mate is a "crazy alcoholic." Though you do not know her well, she seems to be kind and competent. But the statement that John made about her sticks in your mind. Is it possible that John is wrong? Could John intend the words "crazy alcoholic" to be a compliment? If the description is somehow true, does her "alcoholism" affect her work or her relationship with you? What should you do?

21. The top manager of the company for which you work has heard that you are taking a business communication course. He sends you a note asking you to write a one- or two-page essay on interference and how to overcome it. He asks you to give the essay to your immediate supervisor who will in turn give it to him. What is important to consider before you write the essay? Can you identify potential sources of interference in carrying out this task? Write the essay. Would you have worded it differently had your colleague asked for it? Your teacher? Your mother?
22. You will meet separately with each of your ten employees to discuss their work over the last six-month period. What types of internal and external interference could be a part of each meeting? How will the interference affect the quality of each meeting?
23. Some people believe that even the absence of outside noise and activity can constitute interference. Do you agree? Why?
24. Your friend believes that people agree on the meanings of most words because the dictionary defines them. You realize that your friend is somewhat misguided. You know that even if every person in the world had access to and used the same dictionary, each person would interpret the dictionary's descriptions differently. Explain the saying "meanings are in people, not in things" to your friend.
25. Your friend always calls adult women "girls." Every time he uses the word "girls," you think of female children. In fact, one time he told you that your girl was welcome at the manager's banquet, so you brought your eight-year-old daughter. She was the only child at the banquet. Your friend had meant for you to bring your secretary, a forty-year-old woman. How would you tactfully clear up the confusion surrounding the word "girl"?
26. Develop your own evaluation form for use in appraising your communication transactions. Include questions that are of particular interest to you.
27. Use your dictionary and thesaurus to develop meanings for these words. Use the words when you think, write, and speak so that you will feel comfortable using them.
    a. Affective
    b. Cognitive
    c. Compatible
    d. Context
    e. Criterion, criteria
    f. Differentiation
    g. Diminish
    h. Dysphemism
    i. Enigma
    j. Euphemism
    k. Hierarchy
    l. Hypothesis
28. Take and score Self-Test 2 over Chapter 2.

SELF-TEST 2
Chapter 2

A. Recall (6 points each). For each multiple-choice question, select the most accurate answer.
   1. Which of these statements is *not* true?
      a. Business communication is purposive communication—with profit as the ultimate goal.
      b. Purposes can be immediate or ultimate, conscious or subconscious.
      c. The specific goal of purposive communication is to bring about some desired action or interaction.

   - d. Communication purposes are independent of the environment for which they are defined.
   - e. The source/destination and evaluator functions as the generator of purposes.

2. When you consider human factors, consider:
   - a. Educational background
   - b. Ability to hear, see, and speak
   - c. State of mind
   - d. Rank in the company
   - e. a–d
3. In order to control external interference:
   - a. Learn what constitutes good form and composition.
   - b. Learn to evaluate what has been transmitted or received by you.
   - c. Learn to select appropriate people and equipment to accomplish what you want accomplished.
   - d. Listen carefully and ask for clarification.
   - e. a–d
4. Which of these does *not* describe positive feedback?
   - a. Does not attack a person
   - b. Deals with specific acts in a direct and supportive way
   - c. Can occur even when the message does not bring good news
   - d. Always occurs when the response is yes
   - e. Respects human dignity
5. Connotative meanings are defined as:
   - a. Meanings on which most people agree
   - b. Meanings that are personal, private, and not shared
   - c. Meanings that the dictionary lists for words
   - d. Meanings shared by people of similar cultures
   - e. Meanings that cannot be expressed or understood by anyone
6. A communication audit:
   - a. Is similar to an accounting audit
   - b. Represents a contemporary evaluative process for organizations
   - c. Often involves outside consultants
   - d. Involves measuring the effectiveness of critical communication flows
   - e. a–d
7. You will more than likely act ethically if you
   - a. Always pursue a course of action that allows your company to make the greatest profits
   - b. Remain loyal to your superiors at all times
   - c. Pursue the course of action that is good for people and your company
   - d. Always do your work exactly as you are told
   - e. Never question the decisions of others
8. What is the major potential barrier to any communication exchange in which you participate?
   - a. You
   - b. Noise
   - c. Your health
   - d. Cultural differences
   - e. Purposes
9. Which one of these is *not* a semantic barrier?

   a. Treating the map as if it is the territory
   b. Operating at the poles—the extremes
   c. Treating symbols as having only denotative meanings
   d. Attaching "etc." to everything you send or receive
   e. Using affective dysphemisms
10. Which one of these statements is true?
   a. Letters are usually less expensive than telephone calls.
   b. Custom has nothing to do with channel choice.
   c. Sometimes a firm is wise to invest in transportation in order to bring people into face-to-face transactions.
   d. The potential for feedback is an unimportant factor in choosing channels.
   e. The company newsletter cannot be used to stimulate feedback.

B. Inference (10 points each). Indicate whether these statements are true or false.

1. The good communicator needs to strike a reasonable balance between quantitative and qualitative evaluation of communication effectiveness.
2. Interference is anything that somehow alters intended messages or makes them less than correct in the first place.
3. An easily determinable, morally sound course of action exists for every business situation.
4. You cannot assess purposes, the participants, and the environment if you do not know beforehand that the communication event will occur.

SOLUTION

A. Recall (6 points each)

1. d
2. e
3. e
4. d
5. b
6. e
7. c
8. a
9. d
10. c

B. Inference (10 points each)

1. True
2. True
3. False
4. False

ENDNOTES

1. Winford E. Holland, Bette Ann Stead, and Robert C. Leibrock, "Information Channel/Source as a Correlate of Technical Uncertainty in a Research and Development Organization," *IEEE Transactions on Engineering Management* EM-23 (November 1976): 166–67.
2. David K. Berlo, *The Process of Communication: An Introduction to Theory and Practice* (New York: Holt, Rinehart and Winston, 1960), 190.
3. Arnold E. Schneider, William C. Donaghy, and Pamela Jane Newman, *Organizational Communication* (New York: McGraw-Hill Book Company, 1975), 19. Schneider, Donaghy, and Newman list as sources: Samuel J. Bois, *Explorations in Awareness* (New York: Harper & Brothers, 1957); Stuart Chase, *The Power of Words* (New York: Harcourt, Brace and Co., 1954); Wendell Johnson, *Your Most Enchanted Listener* (New York: Harper & Brothers, 1956); S. I. Hayakawa, *Language in Thought and Action,* 2d ed. (New York: Harcourt, Brace & World, Inc., 1964); Kenneth S. Keyes, *How to Develop Your Thinking Ability* (New York: McGraw-Hill Book Company, 1950); Irving Lee, *Language Habits in Human Affairs* (New York: Harper & Brothers, 1941); and Harry L. Weinberg, *Levels of Knowing and Existence* (New York: Harper & Row, Publishers, Inc., 1959).

B

RECEIVING

STUDENT'S OBJECTIVES:

1 To become a more proficient reader

2 To learn the importance of reading speed, comprehension, and efficiency

3 To learn to calculate reading speed (words per minute), comprehension rate (score on a test), and reading efficiency score (words per minute times comprehension test score)

3

READING

4 To learn to choose from four reading types: careful reading, rapid reading, skimming, and scanning

5 To adopt practices to increase reading efficiency, including active reading and use of knowledge about the reading process

6 To increase retention of information gained from reading

GUIDELINES FOR EFFECTIVE READING

- ☐ *Define purposes, participants, and environment for reading and writing*
- ☐ *Identify reading channel*
- ☐ *Control interference with reading and writing*
- ☐ *Select, read, and decode message*
- ☐ *Use feedback to and from writer*
- ☐ *Evaluate at each stage and at end of transaction*

Most people spend about 16 percent of their waking hours reading. Busi-nesspeople often spend an even higher percentage because their work requires it. Thus, the more quickly the businessperson reads and comprehends, the more efficiently the business runs.

Obviously, you already read. Perhaps you read well, or perhaps you do not read as well as you would like. You may have already taken some specialized work in reading improvement. If not, you may want to do so now. If you want to read better, your institution probably has a reading center to aid you.

Whatever your level of ability and experience, a review of reading fundamentals will help sharpen your skills. This review covers four major categories: (1) speed, comprehension, and efficiency; (2) types of reading; (3) increasing reading efficiency; and (4) increasing retention.

SPEED, COMPREHENSION, AND EFFICENCY

Self-timing and self-testing can improve your reading. Therefore, you should locate a stopwatch, a standard watch with a second hand, or a digital watch that displays seconds.

To check your reading efficiency, first record how many seconds you take to read the passage on page 46–47. Read it carefully for content, but read it as quickly as you can.

John N. Mangieri and R. Scott Baldwin deal with comprehension, speed, and types of reading in the following excerpt. Time yourself on the material between the clock faces.

Rate of comprehension rather than rate per se should be your primary objective in any reading task. In general, the more complex and expansive the requirements of comprehension, the slower your rate of reading will need to be in order for you to properly absorb information. There are four basic types of reading: careful reading, rapid reading, skimming, and scanning.

Careful reading is the slowest kind of reading, ranging from 50 to 350 words per minute, again depending upon the intricacy of the material.

Careful reading is normally employed to . . . [conquer] detail, analyze content, or solve problems. You generally use this style of reading when you are . . . going to be tested on the material read.

Rapid reading can proceed at rates ranging from 300 to 600 words per minute. It is employed when the conceptual burden in the material is light, or when the retention of large amounts of specific information is not especially critical.

Skimming is a subcategory of reading which allows the reader to greatly increase reading rate by sacrificing exposure to detail. The purposes of skimming are to absorb main ideas, to grasp the general nature of the content, or to review previously read material. With practice, people can learn to skim efficiently at rates as high as 1500 words per minute.

Scanning is the fastest kind of reading. It is also the most restrictive in terms of the actual amount of information processed. The purposes of scanning are finite and highly specific. At speeds approaching 3000 words per minute, a reader can search for names, dates, numbers, textbook subheadings, or the answers to specific questions. It should be noted that a person proficient in scanning will see little or nothing other than the information which he [or she] is seeking.[1]

(294 words)

Just record your time now; you will calculate your speed and efficiency rating after taking a comprehension test—Self-Test 3. Self-Test 3 and its solutions, as well as the other self-tests and their solutions in this chapter, will depart from the established format of appearing at the end of the chapter. In Chapter 3 only, for the convenience of the reader, they will be found in the body of the text. Self-Test 3 has two parts: immediate recall (what you remember just after reading) and immediate inference (what you infer just after reading). When taking the self-test, do not look back on the passage you just read. Now take Self-Test 3.

SELF-TEST 3
Excerpt about Types of Reading (Careful Reading)

A. Recall (20 points each). For each multiple-choice question, select the most accurate answer.

1. The primary objective in any reading task:
   - **a.** Is speed
   - **b.** Depends on the type of reading
   - **c.** Is comprehension
   - **d.** Can be summarized as the rate of reading
   - **e.** Is a good rate of comprehension
2. The four basic types of reading are called:
   - **a.** Careful reading, rapid reading, skimming, and scanning
   - **b.** Reading for pleasure, for main ideas, for specific information, and for total recall
   - **c.** Slow, moderately fast, fast, and speed reading
   - **d.** Reading for absorption, comprehension, central themes, and review
   - **e.** Problem-solving, analysis, retention, and searching

3. The fastest kind of reading involves:
   a. A great deal of processed information
   b. Speeds approaching 3,000 words a minute
   c. Grasping the general nature of the content
   d. Reading material for broad and unspecified purposes
   e. Seeing everything in the passage, but using rapid eye movement
4. The slowest kind of reading involves:
   a. Speeds ranging from 200–400 words a minute
   b. A light conceptual burden
   c. The need for retention of small amounts of specific information
   d. Conquering detail, analysis, or problem-solving
   e. Searching for specific details, while blocking out all other information in the passage

B. Inference (20 points). For the multiple-choice question, select the most accurate answer.

1. The excerpt indicates that:
   a. Mangieri and Baldwin consider only the slowest kind of reading to be appropriate for business situations.
   b. The insertion of an ellipsis or bracketed words cannot slow the reading speed.
   c. Mangieri and Baldwin's views are too old to be considered valid.
   d. The fastest reading rate allows for virtually no information processing.
   e. Mangieri and Baldwin do not favor any one of the four types of reading over the others.

SOLUTION

A. Recall (20 points each)
1. e **3.** b
2. a **4.** d

B. Inference (20 points)
1. e

Check and score your performance on the self-test. Because the points total 100, your score forms a percentage.

Now that you have recorded your *reading time* and *comprehension test score* (c.t.s.), next determine how fast and how efficiently you read. To find your *reading rate,* in words per minute, multiply the total number of words read by 60 (because your reading time is in seconds). Then divide the product by your reading time, in seconds:

$$\text{words per minute (w.p.m.)} = \frac{\text{(total number of words read)} \times 60}{\text{(reading time in seconds)}}$$

For example, if someone read the excerpt in 86 seconds, the person read at 205 w.p.m.:

$$\text{w.p.m.} = \frac{294 \times 60}{86} = \frac{17{,}640}{86} = 205$$

As the passage you just read conveys, speed alone does not give enough information. Comprehension must enter into any proper assessment of reading ability. You can use the concept suggested by Lee A. Jacobus of calculating a reading efficiency score (r.e.s.).[2] To find the r.e.s., multiply the w.p.m. figure by the c.t.s. score:

$$\text{r.e.s.} = \text{w.p.m.} \times \text{c.t.s.}$$

For the preceding example (205 w.p.m.), if that person scored 70 percent on the comprehension test, the calculation yields a reading efficiency score of 144:

$$\text{r.e.s.} = 205 \times .70 = 144$$

In contrast, suppose that another person read at a rate of 300 w.p.m., but scored only 40 percent on comprehension. That person's r.e.s. drops to 120. If still another person had a reading rate of only 150 w.p.m., but scored 100 percent, the reading efficiency score stays at 150. (Note that the units of r.e.s. are words per minute.)

Did you read the excerpt at a rate of 50–350 w.p.m., the appropriate range for careful reading? Did your r.e.s. still fall in the 50–350 range?

Reading tests appear throughout the remainder of this book—several more times in this chapter and at least once in each subsequent chapter. You will have the opportunity to time and test yourself over a passage marked by two clock faces. The end of each chapter contains the self-tests and answers to the self-tests for that chapter. The passages differ in length and difficulty.

If you decide to use the passages and tests, try varying your reading speed among the four types of reading. However, you will want to choose careful reading more often than the other three types.

If you want to time and test yourself over an entire chapter, a full-chapter test appears at the end of each chapter. You may estimate the number of words in a chapter by multiplying the number of pages by the average number of words on a page.

Before continuing with the analysis of reading as a topic, turn to Appendix A and examine the forms for recording performance on timed readings. The forms include separate sections for the four types of reading. They provide places for the date, the self-test number or material read, the number of words, the number of seconds, the w.p.m., the c.t.s., and the r.e.s. In addition, graphs for each of the four types provide an opportunity to plot your progress in both reading speed and efficiency.

If you keep a record of reading improvement throughout the term, view the long sweep of the charts. Avoid accepting isolated changes as absolute signs of general changes. The level of difficulty, length of passage, kind of test questions, and other factors will affect individual entries.

TYPES OF READING

The Mangieri and Baldwin excerpt you read describes the following classification of types of reading:

- *Careful reading* (complex reading)—50–350 w.p.m.
- *Rapid reading* (simple reading)—300–600 w.p.m.
- *Skimming* (main-idea reading)—up to 1,500 w.p.m.
- *Scanning* (search-for-preset-information reading)—up to 3,000 w.p.m.

Careful Reading

Use the *careful reading* type when reading for learning-level comprehension and long-term retention of both general information and details. Also use it when analyzing, solving problems, proofreading, and checking for accuracy.

Rapid Reading

For light or pleasure reading, take in "chunks" of material—even as you cover virtually all of it. Get the essence of the content and continue reading. Do not try to remember every detail.

Time yourself as you use the rapid-reading style to read these paragraphs:

There are many differences in each person's ability to see. One person may have difficulty seeing objects that are close, while another may find it difficult seeing objects that are some distance away. If you must hold ordinary written material either very close to your eyes or at arm's length in order to read it, if the material you are reading seems blurred, or if your eyes tire easily or hurt, then you should consult an eye doctor. You may need to wear glasses, perhaps only for reading. If you already wear glasses, you may need to have them changed.

Whether or not you wear glasses, you should practice good eye hygiene. Here are a few suggestions:

1. Rest your eyes every half hour or so by looking into the distance or by closing your eyes for a few minutes.
2. Exercise your eyes from time to time, particularly after doing close work. One good eye exercise is to rotate the eyes slowly, without moving your head. Move your eyes far to the right; then to the left; then up; and finally, down. These exercises will help to strengthen your eye muscles.
3. Avoid reading in bright sunlight or while riding in a car, train, or other vehicle.
4. Have eye injuries or sties attended to at once by a doctor. . . .

Poor lighting contributes to eye tiredness and loss of clear vision. Of course, nonglaring daylight provides the best light for reading, and light-colored walls and furnishings permit the best use of daylight. Indirect lighting, rather than semidirect or direct lighting, is the best artificial lighting. Therefore, make certain that there are no glaring light bulbs visible to the eyes or any other glaring or shiny spots anywhere near where you are reading.

For the best reading conditions, sit comfortably in a well-ventilated (not overheated) room that is free from distracting sights and sounds. Above all, do not attempt to do serious reading with the radio, television, or stereo on.[3]

(331 words)

After recording your reading time, take Self-Test 4. Then score the test, find your reading speed and reading efficiency scores, and record them in Appendix A.

SELF-TEST 4
Excerpt about Eyes and Reading Conditions (Rapid Reading)

A. Recall (20 points each). For each multiple-choice question, select the most accurate answer.

1. You should rest your eyes:
   a. About every 15 minutes
   b. About every 30 minutes
   c. About every 45 minutes
   d. By staring for a few minutes
   e. By rubbing them
2. Good eye hygiene may be practiced by:
   a. Reading in bright sunlight
   b. Reading in a car, train, or other vehicle
   c. Reading ordinary material held at arm's length
   d. Reading ordinary material held one or two inches from your eyes
   e. Giving eyes a rest occasionally by closing them for a few minutes or looking into the distance
3. Good conditions for reading can be provided by:
   a. Light-colored walls and furnishings because they permit the best use of daylight
   b. Direct lighting
   c. Very bright light bulbs
   d. Semidirect lighting
   e. Shiny spots near where you are reading
4. Which one of these is good for your eyes?
   a. Taking care of eye injuries or sties without seeing a doctor
   b. Going without prescribed glasses at times to strengthen eye muscles
   c. Exercising your eyes by blinking rapidly 15 times
   d. Rotating the eyes slowly, without moving your head
   e. Consulting an eye doctor only when you reach the point that you can no longer see the words

B. Inference (20 points). For the multiple-choice question, select the most accurate answer.

1. Concerning the eyes and conditions for reading:
   a. Eyes can be hurt by too much light, just as they can be hurt by too little.
   b. An 85° room is perfect for reading.
   c. A room cannot be too cold for reading.
   d. Reading is perfectly all right in an airplane.
   e. Far-sightedness is more serious a problem than is near-sightedness.

SOLUTION

A. Recall (20 points each)

1. b
2. e
3. a
4. d

B. Inference (20 points)

1. a

A high-school textbook written at a relatively low level of difficulty yielded the paragraphs about eye care. Therefore, you probably established a reading efficiency score (r.e.s.) in the 300–600 w.p.m. range.

Skimming

Though the eyes touch all of the material, skimming involves extremely rapid reading. You move past details in order to gain perspective on the whole or the central thesis.

You probably often skim newspapers and magazines. In addition, skimming also serves well in textbook reading, particularly as a preview or a postview technique. It allows you to establish or reconstruct the whole before or after dwelling on the parts during the careful-reading process.

To establish your skimming speed, comprehension, and reading efficiency levels on a preview basis, skim the section titled "The Importance of Listening," pages 70–71. Try to skim it in 15 seconds or less. It contains 368 words, and you want to reach for the 1,500 w.p.m. upper limit. Then take Self-Test 5, check it, do the calculations, and record the data on the skimming table and graphs.

SELF-TEST 5
Excerpt about the Importance of Listening (Skimming)

A. Recall (33 points each). For each multiple-choice question, select the most accurate answer.

1. A person spends about what percentage of her or his waking time listening?
   - **a.** 5 percent
   - **b.** 95 percent
   - **c.** 85 percent
   - **d.** 45 percent
   - **e.** 15 percent
2. The ability to listen:
   - **a.** Represents a major element of human relations
   - **b.** Is not important
   - **c.** Is important only to people in management
   - **d.** Is a natural ability only certain people possess
   - **e.** Does not play a role in gaining knowledge

B. Inference (34 points). Indicate whether the following statement is true or false:

1. Listening can be practiced.

SOLUTION

A. Recall (30 points each)

1. d
2. a

B. Inference (40 points)

1. True

When you later reach the point for carefully reading the section you just skimmed, you may well read more quickly than you would have otherwise.

Scanning

Unlike skimming, scanning does not require that you read every word. Instead start with a preset mental list of the kinds of facts you want from the material. Then move through it at speeds of up to 3,000 w.p.m., and block out everything other than the facts desired.

You have scanned many times. For example, you have searched for specific data in an encyclopedia. You have skipped through a textbook looking only for certain words or sections. You have scanned a newspaper article to find a dollar amount, a Consumer Price Index, or a date. You have scanned a telephone directory page looking for a name.

To practice scanning, turn to page 88 and time yourself on the introduction to Chapter 5. Search for just two things: (1) the percent of social meaning Birdwhistell suggests nonverbal communication contributes in a two-party exchange and (2) the name of the author who suggests that nonverbal communication contributes 93 percent of the message. When you have located them, do two things: Jot down the time it took and mark the last word that you read. Then return to this section and take and score Self-Test 6 before calculating your reading rate.

SELF-TEST 6
Excerpt about Nonverbal Communication (Scanning)

A. Recall (33 points each). Fill in the blank for each fact asked for.
   1. Birdwhistell's proportion: ____________________
   2. Name of the author suggesting 93 percent: ____________________

B. Inference (34 points). For the multiple-choice question, select the most accurate answer.
   1. Nonverbal communication:
      a Contributes as much to written as to oral exchanges
      b. Has little impact on transactions
      c. Never occurs independent of verbal communication
      d. Has a significant impact on virtually all interchanges

SOLUTION

A. Recall (33 points each)
   1. 65 percent
   2. Albert Mehrabian

B. Inference (34 points)
   1. d

To estimate the number of words scanned, first count two or three lines to determine the typical number of words per line (about 12 in this book). Then multiply that figure by the number of lines scanned. Once you know the number of words, you may proceed with the calculating and recording.

You will, of course, give a careful reading to the introduction of Chapter 5 as you move into that material. At this point, though, consider some suggestions that can help increase reading efficiency.

INCREASING READING EFFICIENCY

Improvement of one aspect of reading skills—either speed or comprehension—obviously improves overall efficiency. Two major suggestions can help in that improvement: (1) Become an active reader. (2) Apply knowledge of the reading process.

Become an Active Reader

All too often readers take on passive or resistant postures—unable or unwilling to participate assertively in the communication process. In effect, these postures reflect an inner attitude that says, "I am under control of the writer; I have no active role in this communication transaction."

Indeed, however, you do have a great deal of control. By applying the proper techniques, you can become an active reader. These techniques include:

- Select proper reading type(s)
- Set time schedules
- Control personal and environmental factors
- Improve vocabulary
- Practice

Select Proper Reading Type(s)

Reading carefully, when skimming would suffice, wastes time. On the other hand, reading carefully without scanning first may also waste time and reduce comprehension. Thus, always choose the correct reading type(s) to accomplish the task.

For example, if the reading requires comprehension and retention of relatively difficult material, preview it before beginning the careful reading. The preview should include scanning, skimming, or rapid reading. For example, in previewing a textbook, scan for headings, lists of rules or objectives, or similar key points. After scanning, perhaps read through the material rapidly to pick up whatever information you can before moving into the careful reading.

Just as you preview material to improve comprehension, review it following a careful reading. Again, use any or all of the other types of reading to accomplish the review, for reinforcement of learning occurs with each one.

Somewhat surprisingly, the best comprehension does not necessarily coexist with the slowest speed. Instead the optimal comprehension usually occurs when speed approaches the maximum for the selected range of reading. Therefore, always read as quickly as you can for the chosen reading type.

Set Time Schedules

Use time schedules to aid reading efficiency. However, set them realistically. If you set too little time for a task, you may not taste success, but only become frustrated and dissatisfied. On the other hand, if you set too much time, you may take all of the time allotted whether you need it or not, thus wasting some time. Have you not dawdled over something simply because you had the time to do so?

You cannot, of course, become a computer—spitting out work at previously established rates down to the fraction of a second. However, because time has value—whether used for work or pleasure—you no doubt can improve your ability to spend it wisely.

Control Personal and Environmental Factors

Your own personal characteristics and your environment make up the reading setting. Speed, comprehension, and retention suffer without good physical, psychological, and external conditions.

Your physical condition contributes a great deal to your ability to read. Obviously, the eyes are the major physical element. Therefore, have them tested periodically and care for them as reviewed earlier.

Psychological state also has an important impact upon the ability to read well. When beginning to read, first try to separate yourself physically from any persons or places that distress you emotionally. Then concentrate on the task at hand by overcoming your own psychological obstacles. Keep your mind from wandering to topics other than your reading. Ignore everything else. Improve your ability to remain seated for long periods of time.

Control external conditions as much as you can. For best reading, try to establish these conditions:

- Comfortable and pleasant surroundings
- Good seating at a desk or table
- Proper lighting
- Appropriate temperature and ventilation
- Quietness
- Reading aids (pencil, paper, dictionary, thesaurus)

Improve Vocabulary

Reading includes seeing words, transferring them to the brain, and giving meaning to them. The meaning-giving stage draws on both experience and creativity.

To expand your ability to supply meanings for words, read a great variety of publications. With some reasonable priorities, read everything you can find. Read as rapidly as you can at the reading level you have chosen.

All kinds of communication can improve your ability to use symbols. Every time you send or receive written, oral, or nonverbal messages, you have an opportunity for such improvement. The secret lies in an eagerness to understand and use new words and other symbols.

Use word lists, glossaries, dictionaries, and thesauruses as aids to learning. When encountering a word list, first supply those meanings you already hold. Then check a dictionary for expanded definitions. Look up the words in a thesaurus to determine synonyms and antonyms for as many as you can. Then write several sentences for each, carefully thinking about the meanings they have for you. Deliberately use the words in conversations or writings.

Make your own vocabulary lists. As you encounter words for which you cannot recall satisfactory meanings, jot them down. However—and herein lies the advantage of this approach—copy the entire sentence (or at least the phrase), rather than just the word. Once you have a list of several sentences or phrases, proceed to the reference books.

Practice

Though implicit in other hints for becoming an active reader, the final one calls for practice. Nothing can possibly do more to help improve reading than reading can. Of course, the value of repetition and practice depends on the *quality* of the time spent practicing. Reinforcement of bad habits rather than good ones can prove counterproductive.

Apply Knowledge of the Reading Process

Reading involves extremely complex visual and mental processes. First, your eyes make a point fixation. For left-to-right reading, the fixation focuses just to the left of the symbols to be read. The fixation encompasses a number of words for a duration of about one-fourth second. After each fixation your eyes jump forward to another fixation. The jump lasts only about one tenth as long as the fixation itself.

The actual transfer of information from the eyes to the brain occurs during the point fixations. However, the stages unfold so rapidly that the eyes seem to move continuously from left to right. Only the sweeping return from the end of one line to the fixation at the beginning of the next seems to interrupt the movement. In truth, the only continuous motion exists within the return itself.

In addition to fixations, forward jumps, and sweeping returns, the eyes also engage in regressions. Regressions involve movements in which the eyes move rapidly back from one point to a fixation to the left of it. As natural, reinforcing acts, regressions can actually improve reading performance—unless overdone.

The mental part of reading proves more complicated than the visual part. As your eyes accomplish their work, your mind simultaneously accomplishes its task. It processes visual perceptions already received, receives new ones, and controls the entire operation—including the difficult choices of fixation points. Researchers still do not understand how the mind does what it does.

The wider the span of words in point fixations, the shorter the durations of fixations, jumps, and returns. The fewer the number of unnecessary regressions, the faster the speed and comprehension.

From this brief review of the reading process come several techniques for improving reading:

- Keep eyes moving
- Read in logical blocks of words
- Read just enough to capture thought
- Hold speaking apparatus still and quiet
- Underline and take notes sparingly

Keep Eyes Moving

Even though the reading motion does not represent a continuous, smooth flow, keep your eyes ever moving. The general suggestion to keep your eyes moving applies to all four types of reading. However, scanning involves such wide fixation spans that it creates a gross downward motion seemingly devoid of left-to-right movement.

Avoid unnecessary regressions and breaks in eye movement. For example, if your mind does not hold any meaning for a given word, you may tend to regress a few times or even stop to locate the word in a dictionary before proceeding. However, before doing so, try to keep moving through the passage. Frequently the context supplies sufficient clues to permit you to infer a meaning good enough to allow you to continue without a break.

If you still have to use a dictionary, mark the point at which you stopped reading. After using the dictionary, return to the passage with an undiminished eye-movement momentum.

Slowing to a pace that reduces the need for regressions and extensive rereading forms another way to keep eyes moving in careful reading. Even though reading slower, you may have a net gain in speed because of the elimination of some rereading.

Read in Logical Blocks of Words

To illustrate the importance of reading logical blocks of words, time yourself separately on each of the two following passages. Read carefully for comprehension, take the tests, and calculate reading efficiency scores. You need not record these scores.

SEGMENT 1: Order some things. Get towels, pencils, small nails, memo pads, bolts, paper clips, and grass cutters. Also call the office manager, bus driver, chief accountant, florist, receptionist, and hairdresser to remind them of the meetings next Tuesday and Friday.

(39 words)

Do the following self-test now.

SELF-TEST
Segment 1

A. Recall (50 points each). For each multiple-choice question, select the most accurate answer.
   1. Which one of these is *not* listed for the order?
      a. Grass cutters
      b. Towels
      c. Bolts
      d. Small nails
      e. Ballpoint pens
   2. Which one of these is *not* mentioned in the segment?
      a. A meeting on Friday
      b. Bus driver
      c. Bookkeeper
      d. Receptionist
      e. Office manager

SOLUTION

A. Recall (50 points each)
   1. e
   2. c

SEGMENT 2: As you complete assignments, make checkmarks beside appropriate instructions. Also count number of requests for new supply catalogue, and report number in memo to shipping room. Write thank-you note for gift. Invite usual participants to my meeting next Wednesday.

(39 words)

Do the following self-test now.

SELF-TEST
Segment 2

A. Recall (50 points each). For each multiple-choice question, select the most accurate answer.
   1. Which one of these is *not* part of the segment?
      a. Report number of requests to shipping room.
      b. Count requests.
      c. Complete assignments.
      d. Place checkmarks beside appropriate instructions.
      e. Write to payroll department.
   2. Which one of these is *not* part of the segment?
      a. Write a thank-you note.
      b. Invite people to meeting.
      c. A supply catalogue

d. Write a letter.
e. Meeting next Wednesday

SOLUTION

A. Recall (50 points each)
1. e
2. d

First, compare your reading rates for the two segments. You probably read Segment 2 more quickly than Segment 1, even though each has 39 words and includes instructions. For one thing, Segment 1 includes a series of relatively unrelated words divided by commas. With Segment 2 you had greater opportunity to read logical phrases. If you took advantage of the expanded context, you swept up several words in one eye fixation. Segment 1 required you to read much of it a word at a time.

Now compare the scores on the comprehension tests. Again, you probably scored better on the second than on the first. Though both segments contain many facts to recall, those in Segment 2 form natural units of information.

Finally, contrast your reading efficiency scores. If you read Segment 2 by taking in related blocks of words rather than by reading one word at a time, this final score no doubt reflects the superiority of that approach by being higher than that for Segment 1.

One final illustration should serve to emphasize the importance of reading thought units rather than words. Notice your arrested progress as you read this sentence word for word as marked:

> The • efficient • reader • moves • smoothly • from • the • beginning • of • one • word • or • phrase • to • another— • reading • just • enough • to • capture • the • thought.

Now observe the efficiency with which you read the same sentence in logical blocks as marked.

> The efficient reader moves smoothly • from the beginning of one word or phrase • to another— • reading just enough • to capture the thought.

Read Just Enough to Capture Thought

Consider another rule for increasing speed: read just enough of a word or phrase to capture the thought. To illustrate, maintain a smooth eye movement as you read this sentence:

> Busi____ communi____ is noth____ more__ th__ th__ applica____ of t__ univers__ princi____ __ hum__ com_____.

As you read, you usually skip past "a," "an," "the," and other such short, relatively unimportant, and transitional words. Make an overt effort to perform the same sort of rapid eye movement as you slide past endings on longer words—or even several words in a phrase. As you practice this approach, your gains in speed will reflect a real growth on your part.

Read another skeleton sentence. Again, keep moving.

> To be __ bet____ communi____, adop__ as ma__ prov__ tech____ as you c__, as soon __ you ____.

Reading such vacated words and phrases may seem like playing a game. The game leads to skipping letters, syllables, and words even when someone has not removed them for you. Make a concerted effort to read normal material in the same way.

Read this final sentence while maintaining the resolve that you will read only enough of the word and phrase beginnings to create meanings in your mind:

> As a communication receiving act, reading represents one of the most complex and dynamic mental and physical processes in which you will ever participate.

Did you cut off some words and phrases after picking up just a few letters?

Do you ever feel that you are "cheating" if you do not read every word, every syllable, every letter? If so, reject that attitude. You only read improperly when you do not take advantage of your mind's awesome ability to fill in the logical gaps left as you bound forward through reading passages.

Hold Speaking Apparatus Still and Quiet

To increase your reading speed, do not make vocal sounds or movements while reading. Such acts slow you toward oral reading speed—a speed much slower than silent reading.

As an example, time yourself as you read the next narrative paragraph aloud. (You may be in a place where you cannot read aloud. If so, simulate the process by moving your throat muscles, tongue, and even your lips as if speaking aloud.) Read for your comprehension and for the comprehension of others who may or may not actually be present. Begin reading aloud now.

As you read these words aloud, observe how you can still read thought units, but how much slower you move. Observe also that you cannot read just the beginnings of words and phrases; you must cover everything. Think how, if you can read aloud well, you probably do not engage in regressions as much as you do in silent reading. In contrast, though, notice how you sometimes must regress to correct the pronunciation of a word or to place proper emphasis on a phrase. In summary, oral reading is much slower than silent reading.

(94 words)

Calculate your reading speed for the preceding paragraph and compare it with your other careful-reading speed(s). Because of its simple content, this passage requires no comprehension test or reading efficiency score. Even with the simplicity of the material, you probably read more slowly than in the segments read silently.

Underline and Take Notes Sparingly

A serious interruption of eye movement occurs when you stop to underline or make notes. The loss in comprehension often outweighs any potential gain from the underlining. Therefore, unless you have absolute control over your pencil, avoid using it.

If you need a pencil only to make a dash or dot in the margin of an occasional passage to which you may need to return, then keep one in your hand. Excessive marking interferes with the momentum of the reading process. It may also become a crutch for avoiding genuine mental activity.

Even if you make an outline or compile notes after the actual reading, keep them brief. Many people tend to write too much. Copying from one page to another will not magically cause learning.

Instead of that laborious, time-killing exercise, engage the mind fully in the task of comprehending directly from the pages of the book. Make only skeleton summary notes—and then only if they actually do improve your recall.

INCREASING RETENTION

To this point, this chapter has featured efficiency focused on the goals of immediate understanding and recall. However, mid-range and long-range recollection of material also plays an important role in communication.

Some say that everything perceived remains in the brain, subject to recall, no matter how much time elapses between storage and recall. That theory, of course, represents the ultimate in retention. However, if all learning remains stored forever, much of it lies deeply recessed—so deep that most people cannot recover it without the aid of psychiatry or hypnosis.

The major concern here, however, lies far from such extreme measures. It rests with improving the practical ability to retain information for recall even after long periods of time. Though overlapping somewhat, these five steps facilitate such retention:

- Use memory aids
- Set priorities
- Think
- Reinforce
- Develop resolve

Use Memory Aids

Mechanical approaches to retention include developing acronyms, abbreviations, merged words and letters, or special designations for key points. For example, one plan for remembering the requirements for granting financial credit uses the three C's (character, capital, capacity).

If used wisely, memory aids form effective devices for improving retention. However, if the aids require time-consuming activities, learning probably can take place in the same period of time without them.

Set Priorities

Another approach to retention calls for setting priorities. Information seems to fall into layers as you read. Hence, the closer to the surface information lies, the easier the recall becomes.

To expand your ability to recall, then, choose carefully the items to place in predominant positions in your mind. For example, unless telephoning has your highest priority, why memorize dozens of phone numbers? Instead use your primary data bank for *important* data. Although you have the capacity to remember telephone numbers *and* the important material, why clutter the top strata of your mind with trivia you can store outside of your mind?

Think

Sheer thinking contributes to retention. To remember things, think about them. Think not only about their level of significance, but how they relate to other knowledge, about how they can contribute, and about their importance to future intake of material.

Though many learning theories attempt to explain thinking, it still remains largely a mystery. Therefore, experiment with your own thinking process to learn which methods work best for you.

Reinforce

Obviously, the one-time-over capture of material forms the most efficient way to learn for retention and recall. However, such capture proves impossible for most people. Therefore, repetition becomes necessary.

Variations in the avenues of reception usually improve the quality of repetition. For instance, you may learn educational material through the performance of several acts: reading a textbook passage several times, reading other publications on the same subject, listening to a lecture, participating in a discussion, and viewing a film.

Another way to reinforce reading material requires summarizing it aloud—even if only for yourself. Better yet, talk with someone about it. If you make brief notes or underline, review them periodically. Such acts call the information to the mind's surface and fix it firmly for retention.

You also may reinforce by integrating new material into other material. Interweave it; do not consider it an end unto itself. Relate it to other topics and other communication situations. Think of it as part of a larger whole and, thus, review it as you combine it with other information.

Of course, each added reinforcement takes time that could be used for another topic; therefore, avoid unnecessary review. Try to reach goals in as few repetitions as possible, but use reinforcement as long as it contributes to learning and retention.

Develop Resolve

A final set of procedures for retention involves the *resolve*—the commitment—to retain knowledge. Some of your memories exist so indelibly that you cannot shake them even if you wish you could. However, many other memories exist because you overtly decided to keep them existing. Recollections involving things learned during formal education often fall into the latter class. Therefore, unless you have only such pleasant or awful experiences that you cannot help but remember them, you need to develop a disciplined resolve for retention.

Chapter 4 moves from the receiving act of reading to another receiving act—listening. As you read the next chapter, notice both the similarities and differences between reading and listening.

SUMMARY

Good business communicators read well. To improve your reading, consider working with a reading center and using the suggestions in this chapter to improve your speed, comprehension, and efficiency.

This chapter reviews four kinds of reading and associated speeds (words per minute): (1) careful reading (complex reading)—50–350 w.p.m.; (2) rapid reading (simple reading)—300–600 w.p.m.; (3) skimming (main-idea reading)—up to 1,500 w.p.m.; (4) scanning (search-for-preset-information reading)—up to 3,000 w.p.m. To calculate reading speed, w.p.m., multiply the number of words read by 60; then divide that result by the number of seconds required to read the passage.

To check comprehension (understanding) on a reading passage, test yourself over the information contained in it. This book contains self-tests over selected passages; clock faces mark the test passages. The tests establish comprehension test scores (c.t.s.).

Neither reading speed (w.p.m.) nor comprehension (c.t.s.) alone determines reading efficiency. However, the composite of the two does. Therefore, to calculate a reading efficiency score (r.e.s.), multiply w.p.m. by c.t.s.

To increase reading efficiency, become an active reader and apply knowledge of the reading process. The active reader selects the proper reading type(s), sets time schedules, controls personal and environmental factors, improves vocabulary, and practices. The reading process involves fixations, forward jumps, sweeping returns from the end of one line to the beginning of the next, and regressions (rapid backward movements). Based on this definition of the reading process, some additional suggestions for improving reading include: Keep eyes moving. Read in logical blocks of words. Read just enough to capture thought. Hold speaking apparatus still and quiet. Underline and take notes sparingly.

In addition to speed and comprehension, long-term retention of reading material contributes to communication effectiveness. To improve retention, use memory aids, set priorities for what you want to remember, think as you read, reinforce through channels other than reading, and develop the resolve to remember.

EXERCISES

1. Time yourself as you read a recent *Wall Street Journal* article from an inside page (to avoid having to locate a "continued" portion of the article). Read for main ideas. Upon completion, and without looking back, write down the main ideas. Estimate the number of words in the article by determining the average number of words per line and multiplying that average by the number of lines. Calculate your speed. Ideally, it will approach 1,500 w.p.m. You can test yourself for comprehension by reviewing the article for main ideas and determining what proportion of them you wrote down correctly. You can then calculate your r.e.s.
2. Write a short pencil or typewritten draft of a memorandum to go to all of the employees in your office. Make up a company name. In the memorandum name and briefly explain the meaning of the six guidelines for communication as they apply to reading. (An example of a memorandum appears in Figure 10–2.)
3. Read several paragraphs in one of your textbooks. Consult a dictionary on the words you do not know. After you have read the definitions of the words in question, write sentences using the words. Make a determined effort to use the words appropriately in conversations.
4. Proofread an assignment you have prepared. Time yourself and figure your w.p.m. score. Proofread the assignment again, record your time, and figure your w.p.m. score. Did you miss any errors the first time through? If so, note the types of errors you overlooked. Did you find a pattern to what you overlooked? Practice catching the kinds of errors you missed.
5. Read the letter in Figure 7–10 for comprehension, and time yourself. Then take and score Self-Test 7.

SELF-TEST 7
Import Car-Talog Sales, Inc., Letter (Careful Reading)

A. Recall (30 points each). For each multiple-choice question, select the most accurate answer.

1. Eleanor Parkins' order:
    a. Will be shipped on time
    b. Will be shipped late
    c. Cannot be shipped
    d. Is in the mail, except for one item
    e. Was lost
2. Which of the following does the writer offer Ms. Parkins?
    a. A refund
    b. A substitute for the items not in stock
    c. A discount on substitute items
    d. An apology
    e. A free gift

B. Inference (40 points). Indicate whether the following statement is true or false.

1. The primary purpose of Y.R. Self's letter to Eleanor Parkins is to thank her for her order.

SOLUTION

A. Recall (30 points each)
1. d
2. b

B. Inference (40 points)
1. False

6. On your own, write a one-page paper on the importance of improving your reading skills. Then form groups of four or five students. You and every other group member read your papers to the group. You may then want to evaluate each paper and select one from each group to be read before the whole class. This exercise will allow you to review this chapter, practice writing, practice speaking, and practice listening, the subject of the next chapter.
7. You are the training and development director for a major corporation. A new employee tells you that though he is doing well with most of his work in the engineering department, he sometimes has trouble reading what he considers to be difficult material. What advice would you give him?
8. Assume that your professor will give you an examination in one week over the first chapter of this textbook. Your professor suggested that you concentrate on the major concepts set forth in the chapter. The fifty-minute examination will consist of seven essay questions, and you must answer six of the seven. You realize that though you have read the chapter, you can recall very little of its content. You decide that you must read it again. This time you want to retain the important information you read so that you can do well on the examination. You know that to improve retention you may (1) use memory aids, (2) set priorities, (3) think, (4) reinforce, and (5) develop resolve. Now write a one- or two-page plan that answers these questions.
   - **a.** What, if any, memory aids will I use? Why do I believe that they will prove helpful to me?
   - **b.** To what subjects within the chapter should I assign priority status? Why do I believe these subjects are the ones on which I should concentrate my efforts?
   - **c.** How can I assure that I will actively think about what I am reading?
   - **d.** What, specifically, can I do to reinforce the information that I wish to retain?
   - **e.** Most important, what steps can I take to develop my resolve to complete the established study process and to remember what I read?
9. *[Your professor will time this exercise.]* You must study for an examination that will be given next week. You want to find or prepare a good reading environment. Write a paragraph explaining what reading environment you will seek and why you will seek it.
10. Concentration is often difficult to accomplish. Make a list of internal and external devices that have helped you concentrate in the past. Make another list of new devices that might help you concentrate now and in the future. For example, you might always have taken a walk just before you studied, and you might plan to start keeping a glass of water at your study place.
11. You meet a fourth-grader who says that she does not like to read. She says that she finds it "boring and hard." What suggestions would you make that would help her find reading more interesting? What advice would you give that would help her find reading less difficult? Remember, she is both very young and quite dismayed.
12. Consult your dictionary and thesaurus to create meanings for the following list of words. Use these words when you think, write, and speak so that you feel comfortable using them.

a. Assessment
b. Efficacy
c. Explicit
d. Helix
e. Implicit
f. Interpersonal
g. Intrapersonal
h. Kaleidoscope
i. Myriad
j. Persevere
k. Pertinent
l. Procrastinate
m. Regress
n. Reverie
o. Semantics
p. Subconscious
q. Subsequent
r. Thesaurus

13. Take and score Self-Test 8 over Chapter 3.

SELF-TEST 8
Chapter 3

A. Recall (16 points each). For each multiple-choice question, select the most accurate answer.

1. The meanings of words:
   a. Are inherent
   b. Are assigned by people
   c. Do not change
   d. Do not differ among people
   e. Relate to their pronunciation
2. Which of the following statements does *not* accurately characterize careful reading?
   a. Careful reading involves reading for learning-level comprehension and long-term retention.
   b. Proofreading is one type of careful reading.
   c. Careful reading should be undertaken at 200–1,500 w.p.m.
   d. Mangieri and Baldwin put the range of speeds for careful reading at 50–350 w.p.m.
   e. Careful reading is used in problem solving.
3. Which of the following is *not* set forth in this book as a major reading classification?
   a. Careful reading
   b. Skimming
   c. Scanning
   d. Fixing
   e. Rapid reading
4. Which of the following does *not* contribute to efficient reading?
   a. Reading in indirect artificial light or non-glaring daylight
   b. Using a pen or marker to underline many words and phrases
   c. Practicing reading and recording w.p.m. and r.e.s. scores
   d. Reading in a quiet place where distractions are kept to a minimum
   e. Developing the resolve to read without allowing your mind to stray
5. Which of the following does *not* contribute to increasing reading speed and comprehension?
   a. Selecting the proper reading type
   b. Taking copious notes as you read
   c. Reading as quickly as you can for the reading type chosen
   d. Concentrating
   e. Being an active reader
   f. Reading in logical blocks of words
   g. Improving your ability to manipulate symbols and meanings

h. Underlining and taking notes sparingly
i. Previewing careful-reading material
j. Reviewing careful-reading material
k. Practicing

B. Inference (20 points). For the multiple-choice question, select the most accurate answer.

1. The guidelines for reading:
   a. Can be used only when the communicator has fully developed her or his communication arts and skills
   b. Are guidelines written specifically for use in business situations
   c. Define, in detail, every aspect of the communication process
   d. Are known to all managers
   e. Are guidelines that can be expanded to apply to all forms of human communication

SOLUTION

A. Recall (16 points each)

1. b
2. c
3. d
4. b
5. b

B. Inference (20 points)

1. e

ENDNOTES

1. John N. Mangieri and R. Scott Baldwin, *Effective Reading Techniques: Business and Personal Applications* (New York: Harper & Row, Publishers, Inc., Canfield Press, 1978), 66–67.
2. Lee A. Jacobus, *Improving College Reading,* 3d ed. (New York: Harcourt Brace Jovanovich, Inc., 1978), 334.
3. Marie M. Stewart, Frank W. Lanham, Kenneth Zimmer, Lyn Clark, and Bette Ann Stead, *Business English and Communication,* 5th ed. (New York: Gregg Division/McGraw-Hill Book Company, © 1978), 30. Reprinted by permission.

STUDENT'S OBJECTIVES:

1 To understand the importance of listening and the proportions of time spent in listening (45 percent) and in the other communication acts

2 To increase listening efficiency by becoming an active listener and by applying knowledge of the listening process

3 To become an active listener by selecting the proper listening mode, previewing and reviewing, controlling personal and environmental factors, improving vocabulary, and practicing

4 LISTENING

4 To apply knowledge of the listening process by keeping the process flowing, listening for logical blocks of words, taking notes sparingly, and providing and using feedback

5 To increase retention from listening by using memory aids, setting priorities, thinking, reinforcing, and resolving to remember

GUIDELINES FOR EFFECTIVE LISTENING

- ☐ *Define purposes, participants, and environment for listening and speaking*
- ☐ *Identify listening channel*
- ☐ *Control interference with listening and speaking*
- ☐ *Select, listen to, and decode message*
- ☐ *Use feedback to and from speaker*
- ☐ *Evaluate at each stage and at end of transaction*

Most people spend about 45 percent of their interhuman communication time listening/hearing. The term *listening/hearing* appears in the preceding sentence because people do not always listen; too often they just hear. All listening involves hearing, but not all hearing involves listening. Listening represents an active, thinking communication act, whereas hearing represents a passive, physical one.

Listening plays such an important role in communication that its neglect in education shocks the thinking person. Schools stress reading and writing and usually have some formal training in speaking. However, they rarely offer even one learning unit on listening. This chapter helps to fill that void.

THE IMPORTANCE OF LISTENING

To emphasize the importance of listening, examine the table on page 71. It shows the apportionment of a typical person's time among communication acts. Virtually all writers keep the relative sizes of the proportions shown in the table about the same. They all say that people generally take part in more communication with other people than in communication within themselves, in more oral than written communication, in more reading than writing, and in more listening than speaking.

Listening allows people to gain knowledge, to take in the ideas and opinions of others, to receive instructions, to increase banks of communication symbols, and to improve the ability to use symbols. Listening also reinforces other received messages, gives pleasure, and lets people use their minds in satisfying ways. To a greater extent than reading, listening plays a major part in human relations—the social interactions that define a great deal of life itself.

Think of the different kinds of listening you do: You listen as you converse informally—in person, by telephone, or by two-way radio. You listen as you participate in a dialogue. You listen to speakers and lecturers in formal situations. You listen when someone screams "Fire!" You listen to the cooing of a baby or to a symphony orchestra.

Think also of the importance of listening to business. Many of the kinds of listening cited in the preceding paragraphs apply. In addition, picture the extent to which a manager depends on listening to carry out her or his duties.

Estimated Proportions of Typical Person's Time Spent in Various Communication Acts.

Typical Person	Percent Spent
Communication within oneself	30
Communication with other humans	70
Total communication	100
Communication time with other humans	
Speaking	30
Listening	45
Total in oral transactions	75
Writing	9
Reading	16
Total in written transactions	25
Total communication with other humans	100

Listening helps the manager know the all-important details about things and people, maintain motivation and morale, and make wise decisions.

Listening proves just as important for any other business position. Picture for example the work of a salesperson, a secretary, a computer programmer, an accountant, a stockbroker, a loan officer, a personnel interviewer, an in-service-training instructor, and a collection officer.

(368 words—including table)

INCREASING LISTENING EFFICIENCY

Suggestions for increasing listening power bear a striking resemblance to those given in Chapter 3 for reading improvement. As *receiving* acts, both quite naturally have common criteria for accomplishment. Helpful techniques for listening improvement fall into two categories: (1) active listening and (2) knowledge of the listening process.

Become an Active Listener

Active listening, as opposed to passive listening, results from following the six communication guidelines and the other hints given in this chapter. The concept of active listening adds a critical dimension to the listening process. It recognizes that the listener alone has the power to listen, and thus to affect dramatically the quality of the communication.

If you view yourself as helpless, you do not provide the impetus necessary for communication to flourish. If you listen actively, the speaker also may become more active, and as a result, the communication has a better chance to attain its goals.

Empathy, the ability to understand another person's feelings, contributes to listening, but it does not substitute for active listening. Active listening includes feedback—an open, frank response to the speaker.

As an example, suppose that you have listened intently, politely, and courteously for twenty minutes to a co-worker's grievance against a supervisor. You may understand his position; however, you will not become an active listener until you translate that empathy into feedback. You might state exactly what you think he should do. You could help him analyze the situation so that he arrives at his own decision. You might simply state your concern for the difficult situation. You may say nothing at all, but provide feedback with supportive body language.

Whatever the decision, however, you made it overtly. You did not just sit with folded hands and a wandering mind, or at most a polite, distant attitude that said, "I feel sorry for you." You entered the arena. You played an active role.

The active listening approach described in the preceding example also involves critical listening. As you share responsibility for the exchange, you develop a critique. The critique deals not only with the content of the message, the speaker, and yourself, but with the communication process itself.

For example, you may decide through active, critical listening that a speaker at a formal affair may be sincere, but has the facts wrong. You may decide that she makes grammatical errors and has distracting mannerisms. You may decide that you have an innate prejudice against her "type." However, as an effective listener, you can still benefit from the experience.

Analyze how the speaker could have improved the development of her topic. Make notes about the facts you think are wrong so that you can check them for accuracy. Consider how you could improve communication with this audience. Objectively determine whether your rejection of the speaker's poor grammar could be a form of snobbishness. Challenge your own dismissal of her words by considering that you might have rejected them because of your prejudgment about her "type."

Whether you employ empathy, critique, self-interest, or some other technique, never act as a receiving spectator at your own communication events. The toss of the coin simply placed you as the first receiver—but a receiver just as responsible as the sender for making the exchange into an exciting game.

Techniques for moving from passive to active listening include:

- Select proper listening mode
- Preview and review
- Control personal and environmental factors
- Improve vocabulary
- Practice

Select Proper Listening Mode

Always try to anticipate or at least make a rapid decision about the kind of listening you will do. Such a decision usually improves the transaction. Choose from these types:

- *Careful listening:* Comprehension and retention not only of the general idea of *heavy* material, but the details as well.
- *Attentive listening:* Comprehension and retention not only of the general idea of *light* material, but the details as well.
- *Skimming:* Comprehension and retention of only the general idea.
- *Scanning:* Location and retention of only preset and specific kinds of information.

These four types of listening naturally parallel the four types of reading discussed in Chapter 3. However, they differ in the concept of speed. The reader controls the speed, whereas the listener rarely can. A listener can sometimes convey, verbally or nonverbally, the desire for the speaker to change the speed, but the speaker does not always comply.

Speed does add a dimension to listening, although it differs from the concept of reading speed. People talk socially at about 125 w.p.m. and at about 100 w.p.m. before an audience. However, they think at about 400 w.p.m. Therefore, a great disparity exists—a disparity that creates problems in the ability to concentrate while listening. As a listener, your mind may wander because of such a difference in the capacities for sending and receiving. Speed, then, remains a consideration for listening effectiveness.

Preview and Review

Preparation gives listening the best possible chance of success. If you know ahead of time that you will do some listening, particularly careful listening, preview the situation. Simulate as clearly as possible the upcoming event in your mind. Review any titles, outlines, or agenda provided. Anticipate everything you can about who will say what, preview questions you might ask, and determine just what points you want to cover.

Some skeleton notes prepared ahead of time can contribute significantly to your mental organization during a transaction. You might even leave blanks to fill in during the conversation. Arrange related written material in logical order for ready reference during the session.

Prepare yourself to concentrate, and to assert control over tendencies to be mentally lazy or intolerant of the speaker. Determine that you will comprehend and retain what you have heard.

Previewing requires the direct application of the communication guidelines discussed in Chapter 2: defining the purposes, participants, environment, channel, and possible interference. Previewing indirectly considers the remaining guidelines: how you will decode, stimulate feedback, and evaluate.

Following a listening encounter, review the content and quality of the transaction. Evaluate to determine whether you accomplished your purposes and whether you performed well in all other aspects of the communication process. Reliving the experience briefly will help fix material in your mind, and it will improve your performance the next time you participate in a listening experience.

Control Personal and Environmental Factors

As a good listener, try to understand and control three important elements of the setting: (1) your own physical condition, (2) the psychological makeups of both you and the speaker, and (3) the external physical setting in which you function.

Personal physical conditions Physical condition plays an important role in the listening process. The ears, of course, dominate. Thus, even if you do not seem to have any problems, have your ears tested. Most campuses provide a free or inexpensive hearing clinic. If you find that you have some hearing loss, pursue the problem with a specialist.

Avoid loud noises—particularly repeated earsplitting noises endured over long periods of time. The loudness of factories, radios, stereos, and many live-music performances may cause serious damage to your hearing abilities.

Psychological conditions Try to know your own psychological background and present psychological state, as well as those of the speaker. An empathetic and knowledgeable view of human psychology provides the beginning of the solution for many communication problems.

Use positive thinking. Avoid excusing inattention by labeling the topic uninteresting. Do not allow yourself to become defensive or to stop listening simply because a speaker does not suit your tastes in looks, dress, grooming, accent, values, beliefs, or attitudes. Separate content from the distracting features of the person delivering it.

Do not become so emotional about some of the speaker's words that you make a judgment before hearing the speaker out. Avoid interrupting the speaker. Do not think so much about what you will say next that you miss the speaker's message. On the other hand, do not pretend to pay attention when, indeed, you allow your mind to wander.

Establish and maintain concentration throughout the transaction. As introduced earlier, the time dimension has quite an impact on listening because humans think faster than they can speak. For that reason, a potentially dangerous mental gap exists between the processes—a gap that can play havoc with your concentration. Therefore, the effort required to concentrate becomes more important for listeners than for readers. Readers can go back to the point of the lost concentration. Listeners generally cannot.

These critical (analytical) tactics strengthen concentration and learning:

- Search for deep meanings in the content of the speaker's message
- Anticipate the speaker's next words
- Find points that support or refute the speaker's points
- Summarize points already made by the speaker
- Evaluate not only the content of the message, but the reliability of the speaker and the information as well

When using these tactics, do not let them do more than fill the gap between listening and thinking speeds. Otherwise, they become obstacles to comprehension and retention rather than contributors. Use willpower and the magnificent ability of the brain to perform both acts: listening to the speaker at the same time that you use the suggested tactics.

(341 words)

Take and score Self-Test 9 over the excerpt about psychological conditions on pages 81–82.

External conditions For optimal listening, control the elements of sound and sight in your surroundings. Sit or stand comfortably but alertly. Locate yourself so that you can see and hear well. Adjust the temperature appropriately and try to have good ventilation. If you have a choice, make the surroundings reasonably attractive and tidy. However, avoid preoccupation with such factors.

Ward off any foreseeable interference. Avoid sitting by people who whisper to you during oral presentations. Stay away from potential outside noises such as those emanating from a foyer or hall. Because visual cues aid listening, try to sit where you can see the speaker well.

Improve Vocabulary

The listening process centers upon the ability to decode—to create meanings for messages composed of words and other symbols selected by someone else. Therefore, just as for reading, develop a broad-ranging internal library of symbols and meanings. Also improve your ability to create meanings for new symbols.

Whereas reading focuses on words, listening focuses on both words and nonwords. The color, texture, and quality of paper in a reading situation simply do not have the impact of the color, texture, and quality of a voice. Therefore, to become an improved listener, expand your command of all types of symbols.

Recall the suggestions in Chapter 3 for improving vocabulary in conjunction with reading (pages 55–56). With minimal revisions, these techniques apply just as well to listening. Therefore, no repetition of them appears here.

Practice

As for any mode of communication, take advantage of every opportunity you have to apply the principles for good listening. Because you spend so much of your interhuman communication time listening, you have many chances for their application.

Practice the techniques of listening during the discussions and lectures in classes. Practice them during meetings of organizations. Practice them during conversations and dialogues. Practice them during speeches and radio and television shows. With such concerted practice, your personal and academic growth will surely benefit.

Apply Knowledge of the Listening Process

The listening process encompasses three broad stages: (1) selecting, (2) receiving, and (3) changing symbols into meanings.

Because you listen to much less than you hear, selecting the listening message begins the process. That selection involves a deliberate mental act. For example, think of how you function in a room crowded with conversational groups. You hear all the sounds around you, but selectively listen to only the few people in your group. Have you ever so successfully shut out everything else that someone had to call your name several times before you shifted the focus of your attention? The intensity of concentration often makes the shift difficult; many times only a shocking or startling event can redirect attention.

Once you select the sound to which you will listen, receiving begins. The complicated hearing mechanism picks up the chosen sound waves and transfers them to the brain. Even as the transfer takes place, the mind begins the next step.

The most complicated part of listening requires your mind to take the internal message symbols, interpret them, and convert the messages into meanings for you. As described earlier, only you can create meanings correct for you. Neither the written nor the spoken word has any inherent meaning.

These techniques apply this knowledge of the listening process:

- Keep the process flowing
- Listen for logical blocks of words
- Take notes sparingly
- Provide and use feedback

Keep the Process Flowing

Even more than for reading, keep the listening process flowing smoothly and rapidly. Without a continual, but controlled flow, the transaction may simply roll by without you.

Always stay alert to the need to turn attention from one communication transaction to another. Make selections of messages carefully and in line with your objectives. You simply cannot listen to everything that surrounds you. Once you have selected a message, engage your hearing mechanism and your mind fully in the listening process. Avoid the mental laziness that often slows or stops the flow of receiving and decoding messages.

Listen for Logical Blocks of Words

Because the words usually just keep coming, gulp them in as logical blocks of words, not as one word after another. Listen for the main ideas in broad, sweeping strokes.

In the *careful* listening mode, add the details logically to the outline created by identifying key blocks. Concentrating on the blocks allows the details both to build the blocks and then to fall naturally into the categories created by them.

Take Notes Sparingly

Again echoing a tactic for efficient reading, take only a few notes during a listening encounter. Used wisely, skeleton notes of major points and key details can reinforce comprehension and retention. However, trying to capture everything usually becomes a distraction. It often detracts from the concentration necessary for good listening.

Similarly, although tape-recording a presentation makes relistening possible for clarification or reinforcement, it cannot become a substitute for listening. Therefore, use recording instruments only for particularly weighty presentations and careful-listening situations. Even then, use recordings only to supplement active listening. Of course, always obtain the speaker's permission to record.

Provide and Use Feedback

When possible, provide verbal and nonverbal feedback to the speaker. Show genuine attention. You can express support or disagreement by using nonverbal messages during a monologue and with words at appropriate points in a two-way exchange. Ask for clarification of points you do not understand. Suggest that the speaker slow down, or speed up, or repeat.

When a speaker does provide feedback in response to a request, listen and observe just as carefully as you did to the original message. Continue to reengage feedback processes until completion of the transaction.

INCREASING RETENTION

Comprehension and retention have the same importance in listening as in reading. However, because you usually cannot relisten as you can reread, the danger of misunderstanding and forgetting becomes greater for listening. The typical person can remember only about half of what he or she just heard, and can recall only one fourth of it a short time later. With slight changes, the tactics for reading retention work just as well for listening. Memory aids, priorities, thinking, reinforcement, and resolve can once again prove useful.

Use Memory Aids

If the speaker presents an acronym, saying, gimmick, or clever outline, definitely use it to help you remember. You probably will not have time to create your own memory aids during any ongoing listening activity. You might do so later from tapes or notes, as an aid to reinforcement. As you listen to the speaker, make mental lists. Also create mental images from the words you hear.

When introduced to people, try to think of some word association for the name, occupation, home town, address, interests, or other distinguishing characteristics about the person. For example, in a conversation, remember a new name by associating it with the name of someone you know. Picture the spelling of the name. Say the name aloud several times during the conversation. It not only adds a personal touch, but also helps to fix the name in your mind. Repeat some of the facts that you want to recall and tie them to something familiar. You might say, "Oh, you live in New Lenox. I have a cousin who lives there."

Following such a conversation you may want to capture the facts in writing. Writing not only provides immediate reinforcement for learning, but also forms the basis for additional reinforcement through later reading.

You should try to remember the information without looking at your notes. Use notes only as security in case of forgetfulness, and not as a substitute for retention.

A related device for dialogue calls for questioning the speaker or restating in your own words the ideas and concepts spoken by another. Not only does such a device help you remember, it often serves to clarify the intent of the speaker. Consider this summary of a communication transaction that actually occurred in a committee meeting. One member said, "I am absolutely opposed to listing the policy items in a priority order." A second member then said, "No matter what we do, the final implementation depends on the quality and good faith of the people who implement the policy." A supporter of the priority listing then said to the second speaker, "Do you mean, then, that you do not favor a priority listing?" The second speaker replied, "No, as a matter of fact, I like the concept of a priority listing."

You, too, have likely rephrased something a speaker said, just to find that you had not understood at all. However, you probably also have accepted countless other statements as you thought you heard them, when actually you misunderstood.

Rephrase and question anything that has left even an inkling of confusion in your mind. Not only will you have more vivid recall of the transaction, but you may alter its course entirely.

Immediately after listening to a speaker with whom you cannot interact, find someone with whom you can discuss the content. Just saying something aloud can do as much to help remember it as any other procedure. If you cannot say it aloud, say it to yourself. Picture yourself telling someone what you just heard. You probably have experienced the frustration of forgetting a joke if you did not retell it to someone immediately after hearing it.

Set Priorities

As with information gained through reading, you cannot possibly keep everything you hear at the tip of your fingers. Therefore, establish priorities for recollection. Then store everything according to the ranking. This process may prove slightly more difficult for listening than for reading, but its adoption nonetheless improves the retention significantly. Your mind can accomplish the feat. It can simultaneously carry an outline of major points, select details for storage, assign value weights according to the relative importance of those details, and store them in keeping with that valuation.

Think

As mentioned in Chapter 3, thinking contributes to remembering. As you listen, activate your mind, and then continue to think about what was said. Think *about* the messages gained through listening. Think about how they apply to your life, to solving your problems, to meeting your goals.

Think of how you will retain the information even as you listen to it. Overtly put it into storage and assign mental triggers to it so that you can recall it upon demand. Use association with the familiar to accomplish the feat.

Reinforce

Retention improves as you repeatedly allow into your mind the material judged to be important. Taping and replaying the material provides a useful repetition of the entire listening sequence. In addition, for important material, make a typewritten transcript of the tape. Reinforcement improves through the use of different channels for repeated reception.

If you take notes, review them as soon as possible after completion of the communication. As with the tape recording, you may want to convert hand-written notes into typewritten form for easier reading.

Develop Resolve

All mental activity rests on motivation. Unless you genuinely want to store information for ready recall, you probably will not. Only the most startling occurrences stay with you without determination on your part. Therefore, your willpower, your resolve, and your commitment can do more to improve comprehension and recall than all of the mechanical aids you can devise.

From the topic of listening, we will now turn to the third category of symbols—the nonverbal. Chapter 5 develops the concepts of nonverbal communication, with emphasis on interpreting received wordless messages.

SUMMARY

Most people spend about 45 percent of their interhuman communication time listening, 30 percent speaking, 16 percent reading, and 9 percent writing. Thus, listening occupies more time than any other act, yet probably receives the least attention in instructional settings.

To increase listening efficiency, become an active listener and apply knowledge of the listening process.

Techniques for active listening include: (1) Select the proper listening mode. (2) Preview and review. (3) Control personal and environmental factors. (4) Improve vocabulary. (5) Practice.

The listening modes include careful listening (comprehension and retention not only of the general idea of heavy material, but the details as well), attentive listening (comprehension and retention not only of the general idea of light material, but the details as well), skimming (comprehension and retention of only the general idea), and scanning (location and retention of only preset and specific kinds of information). In selecting the proper listening mode, recognize that people talk socially at about 125 w.p.m. and at about 100 w.p.m. before an audience, but think at about 400 w.p.m.

Some critical (analytical) tactics help to close the gap between speaking and thinking speeds and thus improve concentration and the control of personal and environmental factors. Such tactics include: (1) Search for deep meanings in the content of the speaker's message. (2) Anticipate the speaker's next words. (3) Find points that support or refute the speaker's points. (4) Summarize points already made by the speaker. (5) Evaluate not only the content of the message, but the reliability of the speaker and the information as well.

The listening process encompasses three broad stages: selecting, receiving, and changing symbols into meanings. Some additional techniques for recognizing this process include: (1) Keep the process flowing. (2) Listen for logical blocks of words. (3) Take notes sparingly. (4) Provide and use feedback.

To increase retention of information gained through listening, use memory aids, set priorities, think (concentrate) all the time, reinforce by using repetition and by using additional channels for receiving, and resolve to remember what you hear.

EXERCISES

1. Your professor or another student will read a selection from another chapter in this book or play a recording. Apply the techniques you have just reviewed as you listen and take brief notes. Then complete the comprehension test that the professor will administer.
2. Attend a session of another class or ask a colleague to tape a discussion or lecture in one in which you are not a student. Prepare for listening as well as you can, and then listen to that unfamiliar presentation—taking brief notes as you do. Without relistening, write a one-page summary of your findings.
3. Apply effective listening techniques to one entire session of the class in which you use this book. Write a one-page summary of the session.
4. Apply effective listening techniques to a meeting of another class in which you are a student. Write a one-page summary of the meeting.
5. Your professor will divide the class into small groups and give each member of the group a short biographical sketch of a hypothetical person. Each then tries to become that person by studying the sketch for a few minutes. Then, each person fully introduces herself or himself as the hypothetical character. After all have spoken, each will tell or write down as much as possible about each of the others. Evaluate how well each person listened to and recalled what each hypothetical character said.
6. Have another student who has some knowledge in a particular business field pretend he or she is your manager at a firm in that field. Ask your "manager" to tell you about the way business is conducted at the firm. Listen and participate, making use of the six guidelines for effective listening. Write a summary of how you answered or employed each of the six guidelines. How could the interchange have been improved?
7. Keep a log on one whole day's communicating time. How does the time you spent listening compare to the time you spent speaking, reading, writing, hearing, and in other forms of communication?
8. Using the techniques for effective listening, prepare for and attend a speech. Write a summary of the speech. Also summarize how you made use of the listening techniques.
9. Watch and listen to instructional programs on an educational network. Practice

listening and make a record of what you believe your listening strengths and weaknesses are.

10. You are a member of a local civic organization and must present a light, even humorous, five-minute talk on self-improvement at the next meeting. You choose the topic of listening. Write a one- or two-page presentation. (Your professor may ask some of the class members to present the statements orally.)
11. You are a department manager at the Huge Corporation. You hold weekly meetings with your 32-member staff. At the beginning of each meeting, you give a brief talk on the department's successes and problems and on current issues. After each talk, though, your staff members inevitably ask you questions that you already had answered in your beginning-of-the-meeting speech. You know that you are a good speaker; so you conclude that many of your staff members just do not listen to you or to each other. You now decide to prepare a two- or three-page speech for next week's meeting. The subject of the speech will be the importance of listening and techniques for good listening. Prepare the speech. Remember, your staff doesn't listen, so you will need to include attention-getting devices in your speech.
12. Many people have trouble remembering other people's names. They probably did not listen to the names when the people were first introduced to them. Meet with a group with which you have met before. Without talking, you and each other group member try to recall and write down the names of the other group members. Check your work. Did some of you forget each other's names? Now discuss ways in which you can learn to listen to and then remember people's names.
13. Consult your dictionary and thesaurus to create meanings for these words. Use the words when you think, write, and speak so that you will feel comfortable using them.

    a. Anticipate
    b. Approximate
    c. Clarify
    d. Continuum
    e. Critique
    f. Decode
    g. Manipulate
    h. Mode
    i. Nonverbal
    j. Participative
    k. Random
    l. Verbal

14. Take and score Self-Test 10 over Chapter 4.

SELF-TEST 9
Excerpt about Psychological Conditions

A. Recall (14 points each). For each multiple-choice question, select the most accurate answer.
   1. Which of the following does *not* represent a good psychological condition for listening?
      a. Separating content from distracting features of the speaker
      b. Avoiding emotionality so as to hear the speaker out
      c. Avoiding defensiveness
      d. Pretending to pay attention so that you can think of what you will say next
      e. Using empathy
   2. Concentration is important to listening because:
      a. You think faster than you speak and may lose your concentration on subjects.

   - **b.** You may miss important points of a speech because of lack of concentration.
   - **c.** You speak faster than you think and may lose your train of thought.
   - **d.** Both a and b
   - **e.** Both b and c

3. Critical listening does *not* involve which of the following?
   - **a.** Evaluating the content for reliability
   - **b.** Determining the degree of accuracy of the information being transmitted
   - **c.** Skimming the material and retaining only the general ideas
   - **d.** Determining the quality and soundness of the speaker's ideas
   - **e.** Determining the reliability of the speaker
4. Concentration may be improved by:
   - **a.** Willpower
   - **b.** Overcoming barriers
   - **c.** Proper application of listening guidelines
   - **d.** a–c
   - **e.** b and c only
5. Which of the following is a true statement regarding effective listening?
   - **a.** Critical listening cannot improve comprehension.
   - **b.** Concentration is less critical for listening than for reading.
   - **c.** Making a rapid decision about the kind of listening you will do may improve listening ability.
   - **d.** Determining a listening mode will not allow you to participate more effectively in the communication process.
   - **e.** Not a–d
6. Which of the following is *not* a concentrative tactic?
   - **a.** Anticipating what the speaker will say next
   - **b.** Reviewing previous points made by the speaker
   - **c.** Focusing on the message—looking for deeper meanings
   - **d.** Being preoccupied with your own views on the subject
   - **e.** Focusing attention upon the subject at hand

B. Inference (16 points). For the multiple-choice question, select the most accurate answer.

1. The act of listening:
   - **a.** Is merely a function of hearing a person speak
   - **b.** Is a function of such ongoing processes as concentrating and thinking
   - **c.** Requires the use of few or no acquired skills
   - **d.** Is merely an attitude about what one hears
   - **e.** Can easily be maintained with little or no concentration of the part of the listener

SOLUTION

A. Recall (14 points each)

1. b **3.** c **5.** c
2. d **4.** d **6.** d

B. Inference (16 points)

1. b

SELF-TEST 10
Chapter 4

A. Recall (14 points each). For each multiple-choice question, select the most accurate answer.

1. Listening:
   a. Is the same as hearing
   b. Does not involve hearing
   c. Is a passive, physical function
   d. Always involves hearing, though hearing does not always involve listening
   e. Is not a communication act
2. The interhuman communication time spent in listening and receiving related nonverbal messages is:
   a. 1 percent
   b. 45 percent
   c. 16 percent
   d. 90 percent
   e. 30 percent
3. The first broad stage of the listening process is selection. In this context, selection refers to:
   a. Choosing the appropriate channel
   b. Choosing the listening type
   c. Choosing that to which you will listen and tuning out the rest
   d. Choosing the location for the interchange
   e. Not a–d
4. While listening to a live speech:
   a. Take as many notes as possible.
   b. Try to anticipate what the speaker will say next.
   c. Think about different subjects in order to keep your mind active.
   d. Look up the words you do not understand.
   e. a–d
5. Which of the following is *not* a guideline for effective listening?
   a. Define purposes, participants, and environment.
   b. Identify listening channel.
   c. Control interference.
   d. Select, hear, and decode speaker's messages in light of purposes, participants, environment, channel, and interference.
   e. Select, hear, and revise speaker's messages in light of personal biases.
   f. Use feedback to and from speaker.
   g. Evaluate at each stage of interchange.
6. Which of the following is *not* a technique for listening effectively?
   a. Practice.
   b. Preview.
   c. Review.
   d. Select proper listening mode.
   e. Concentrate and think.

f. Be a passive listener.
g. Improve symbol/meaning manipulation.
h. Take notes sparingly.
i. Control physical and psychological setting.
j. Listen for retention.

B. Inference (16 points). Select the most accurate answer.

1. Listening:
    a. Requires no real preparation
    b. Can take place only when the speaker is physically present
    c. Is an art and skill that takes considerable effort to develop
    d. Should be practiced by only those people who do not speak very often
    e. Is productive only when both the speaker and listener are in agreement

SOLUTION

A. Recall (14 points each)

1. d	**3.** c	**5.** e
2. b	**4.** b	**6.** f

B. Inference (16 points)

1. c

STUDENT'S OBJECTIVES:

1 To learn the importance of nonverbal (wordless) messages

2 To understand and apply the concepts of immediacy (tendency to approach the things we like and avoid the things we dislike), power (tendency to equate size, dominance, strength, and high status with power), and responsiveness (adaptive actions such as anger, joy, and surprise in response to the environment)

5

RECEIVING NONVERBAL MESSAGES

3 To understand and apply the meanings carried by nine nonverbal elements: (1) face, (2) voice, (3) movement, (4) touch, (5) appearance, (6) space, (7) time, (8) silence, and (9) environment

GUIDELINES FOR EFFECTIVE RECEIVING OF NONVERBAL MESSAGES

- ☐ *Define purposes, participants, and environment for receiving and sending nonverbal messages*
- ☐ *Identify nonverbal channel*
- ☐ *Control interference with receiving and sending nonverbal messages*
- ☐ *Select, observe, and decode nonverbal message*
- ☐ *Use feedback to and from sender*
- ☐ *Evaluate at each stage and at end of transaction*

"Actions speak louder than words." "A picture is worth a thousand words." "What people do is more important than what they say." "First impressions [virtually always nonverbal ones] are lasting impressions." These sayings illustrate the common understanding of the importance of nonverbal communication—communication without words.

Some evidence of the impact of nonverbal communication lies in the findings of Birdwhistell, an acknowledged authority in the field. As Mark L. Knapp reports, Birdwhistell estimates that the typical person spends only about 10 or 11 minutes each day in speaking words, with an average spoken sentence of about 2.5 seconds. He also suggests that in a two-party conversation, the nonverbal elements carry 65 percent of the social meaning, leaving only 35 percent to the verbal level.[1]

Other estimates place as much as 80 percent[2] or even 93 percent[3] of the message load on the nonverbal. Whatever proportion holds true for a given situation, the nonverbal elements contribute substantially to oral exchanges.

For written messages, the verbal elements may carry a greater proportion of the meaning than do the nonverbal elements. However, the proportion carried by the nonverbal elements still remains significant.

(184 words)

Nonverbal messages can repeat, contradict, complement, accent, or regulate verbal communication. When verbal and nonverbal messages conflict, many people tend to believe the nonverbal instead of the verbal. People often assume, usually subconsciously, that humans have more difficulty manipulating nonverbal messages than they do the verbal ones. Thus, people often place greater trust in the nonverbal elements than the verbal elements.

The nonverbal category can stand alone as a primitive communication type. For example, all of these things communicate without words:

Paintings/photographs
The roar of the wind
A finger pointed upward
Dance
A handshake
The aroma of baking bread
Tears
A bugler playing taps
A poignant silence
The wag of a dog's tail

Nonverbal messages deal primarily with emotions and attitudes. Nonverbal symbols lack the sophistication needed to carry complex messages.

Some theorists do not even treat the tools of nonverbal communication as symbols. In this book, however, the word *symbols* refers to both words and nonwords used in the communication process.

Nonverbal receiving includes reception of wordless messages through all five senses. At the same time, nonverbal receiving includes more than seeing, hearing, touching, smelling, and tasting, for it draws on at least as much perceptual ability and mental processing as do reading and listening.

The lack of dictionaries, thesauruses, and grammars cataloging nonverbal symbols erects a major barrier to learning. Thus, a nonverbal communicator does not have equal access to the kinds of aids available for verbal communication. General inattention to nonverbal communication in formal education presents another obstacle. The largest barrier, however, lies in the subtleties of nonverbal messages and the delicate and personal nature of interpreting them. Thus, the key to using nonverbal communication rests with the cultivation of keen awareness and sensitivity to nonverbal messages. A review of some of the findings in the field of nonverbal communication will help you in that cultivation.

IMMEDIACY, POWER, AND RESPONSIVENESS

Researchers and writers suggest many different classifications of nonverbal communication. Albert Mehrabian asserts that nonverbal behavior and related communication occur in only three primary dimensions: (1) immediacy, (2) power, and (3) responsiveness.[4]

Immediacy

The concept of *immediacy* springs from the tendency to approach the things we like and avoid the things we dislike. For nonverbal communication, then, the like-dislike metaphor deals with both physical and perceptual distances. Mehrabian writes, "Approach and immediacy indicate preference, positive evaluation, and liking, whereas avoidance and nonimmediacy indicate lack of preference, dislike, and, in extreme cases, fear."[5]

Positive, physical immediacy between people includes such acts as sitting or standing close to one another, maintaining a face-to-face posture, and touching or leaning toward the other. A lack of immediacy occurs when opposite behaviors occur. Figure 5–1 illustrates some of the behaviors associated with immediacy.

Power

The second metaphor relates to size, dominance, strength, and high status. For example, a person who strides or struts exhibits more power than one who takes small steps or shuffles. One who slouches or bows shows much less power than one who stands fully erect. The relaxed person who occupies a

FIGURE 5–1 Illustrations of three classes of nonverbal behavior: immediacy, power, and responsiveness.

great deal of physical space shows more status than one who is tense and occupies minimal space.

Through the size and conspicuousness of such things as cars, houses, furniture, jewelry, and clothing, people reveal much about their relative status—or at least their views of what constitutes status. Similarly, the more the relaxation, the greater the power. Leaning back in a chair and crossing legs demonstrates more power than sitting forward on the chair with arms close to the body and legs straight with knees pressed together. The examples in Figure 5–1 show how power and powerlessness manifest themselves through nonverbal messages.

Responsiveness

As shown in Figure 5–1, responsiveness, probably the most basic way to communicate emotion, involves adaptive actions ranging from the comatose to the frenzied. Response to the environment appears through anger, joy, surprise, fear, boldness, happiness, sadness, anxiety, quietude, petulance, pity, or benevolence. Such responses prove particularly valuable for human communication transactions.

SOURCES OF NONVERBAL MESSAGES

The nonverbal classification including immediacy, power, and responsiveness applies to all elements of nonverbal activity. Therefore, subsequent sections of this chapter tie the three concepts to another common classification scheme. The second scheme includes nine categories that recognize the human and environmental sources of nonverbal messages: (1) face, (2) voice, (3) movement, (4) touch, (5) appearance, (6) space, (7) time, (8) silence, and (9) environment.

Face

Theorists suggest that the face reveals more about emotional state and personality than any other human part. For example, Mehrabian[6] suggests this formula for communicating any feeling:

$$\text{Total feeling} = \begin{cases} 7\% \text{ verbal feeling} \\ 38\% \text{ vocal feeling} \\ 55\% \text{ facial feeling} \end{cases}$$

Notice how this formula leads to the earlier reported suggestion that humans receive about 93 percent of feeling from nonverbal components, with only 7 percent from the words uttered by the person.

Facial Expressions

The face can make hundreds of emotional expressions with different blends of available facial movements. However, researchers have consistently identified only six primary ones: surprise, fear, anger, disgust, happiness, and sadness.

Each person has unique expressions for even the six—and many more for the combinations that come from them. Therefore, interpreting facial expressions often proves difficult. People's ability to mask emotions adds to the difficulty. They can pretend interest or attention while their minds race on to other subjects. They can hide behind expressions that belie the truth.

The face also helps to regulate conversations. Flashing the eyebrows, pursing the mouth, and winking often regulate by inviting or starting communication transactions. These and other facial expressions also help to control conversational turn-taking and conclusion.

Applying Mehrabian's classification, we can see that the face contributes to expressions all along the scale between the poles of liking/disliking, dominance/submission, pleasantness/unpleasantness, intensity/control, and action/passivity.

Paul Ekman and Wallace V. Friesen identify eight facial styles exhibited consistently by many people:

- The Withholder—Inhibited, with little facial movement
- The Revealer—Uninhibited, with a great deal of facial movement
- The Unwitting Expressor—Limited number of expressions thought to be masked, but not
- The Blanked Expressor—Blank face instead of the emotion the person thinks is there
- The Substitute Expressor—Emotion shown but different than expressor thinks
- The Frozen-Affect Expressor—Permanent display of a given emotion (e.g., always looks sad because sadness forms a permanent feature of facial configuration)
- The Ever-Ready Expressor—Display of the same initial emotion (e.g., happiness) no matter what the stimulus
- The Flooded-Affect Expressor—Overriding state (e.g., anger) colors all other emotions.[7]

Smiling Smiling contributes greatly to facial expressions. Though it centers on the mouth, it also affects other facial expressions. Elizabeth McGough describes three major types of smiles. In the first, the *simple* smile, the lips barely touch, and no teeth show. This private smile shows happiness, and usually occurs when a person is alone. The upper teeth show in the *upper* smile, used when greeting another person. It involves some eye contact. Both upper and lower teeth show in the third type of smile, the *broad* smile. The broad smile usually occurs when a person laughs; it involves little eye-to-eye contact.[8] (See Figure 5–2 for illustrations.)

Smiles do not always indicate happiness, though, and often mask true feelings. McGough writes: "Most of us have seen the oblong, or polite, smile. This smile has no depth to it, although upper and lower teeth show. We may

FIGURE 5–2 Types of smiles.

recall disliking the person who flashed this toothy grin at us. This smile conveys condescension."[9] Figure 5-2d illustrates the polite smile.

McGough also identifies a smile that shows that a person feels inferior—the *lip-in smile*. The lip-in smile parallels the upper smile, but the lower lip draws over the teeth.[10] Figure 5-2e shows a sketch of the lip-in smile.

Eyes Eye appearance and gaze contribute a great deal to nonverbal communication. They do so on their own or as they contribute to facial expressions.

Many factors associated with the eyes, eyebrows, and accompanying facial elements enter into nonverbal communication. Shape, color, eye size, pupil size, position, blinking, wrinkles, and eye movements contribute to the overall expressions that emanate from the eye region. For example, heavy eyebrows unbroken across the nose communicate something quite different than do two thin and distinct eyebrows. Many attribute different qualities to people with blue eyes than to those with dark eyes. People often associate large, wide eyes with frankness or naivete and small or narrow eyes with untrustworthiness.

Mehrabian's immediacy metaphor fits the concept of eye gaze well. Research shows that, generally, people's eyes approach what they like and avoid what they do not like. For example, eye contact between a speaker and audience increases the audience's assessment of the speaker as a credible source.

People generally maintain more eye gaze and mutual eye gaze with those whose approval they want, those to whom they bring good news, and those whom they like. They also do so with people toward whom they feel positive, in whom they have an interest, and whom they know and trust.

Averted eyes show anger, hurt feelings, and a hesitancy to reveal the inner self. They show a reticence in one who bears bad news and the avoidance of a competitor, a stranger, or someone who offends. They also reveal negativism and the need to increase psychological distance, as in an elevator, waiting room, or other small space.

Eye gaze relates to power also. If a person of status initiates eye contact, the subordinate must maintain it. However, if the subordinate initiates it, the dominant person need not maintain it. The person of higher status may look away or even gaze into the distance. Dominance generally places the person of highest status at the head of the table. Such placement puts this powerful individual in a position of flexibility and control over eye contact, yet leaves her or him free to look elsewhere when a subordinate initiates it. Side-by-side seating does not satisfy the person of highest status because of the difficulty of controlling eye contact.

When subordinates keep their eyes on the dominant individual, their behavior sometimes seems to run counter to the approach/avoidance theory, for they sometimes approach someone whom they dislike. Power, and responsiveness to it, take precedence over liking in such a situation. A similar exception occurs when a person dislikes another, but fears that person's power. In these circumstances, the eyes remain riveted on the feared one. The subordinate honors the nonverbal "rule" by maintaining eye contact with the person of power. By following the "rule," the subordinate may curry favor and prevent an action feared from that person. In addition, eye gaze allows the subordinate to pick up clues about how to behave to avoid the wrath of the feared one.

Voice

Because the voice carries verbal messages, its function as the bearer of nonverbal messages often receives less attention than it should. However, paralanguage—the vocal cues that accompany spoken words—contributes significantly to the richness of communication.

G. L. Trager suggests that paralanguage includes four major categories: (1) vocal qualifiers, (2) vocal segregates, (3) vocal differentiators, and (4) vocal qualities.[11]

Vocal Qualifiers

Variations in pitch, rate, and volume of the voice create vocal qualifiers. A high pitch may indicate nervousness, anxiety, tension, fear, surprise, dynamism, anger, joy, cheerfulness, or impatience. A low pitch may show affection, sadness, boredom, pleasantness, intimacy, or empathy.

The rate of speech also seems to change with emotions or personality types. A slow rate often accompanies intimacy, affection, boredom, or sadness. A rapid or clipping rate of speed seems to go with anger, cheerfulness, impatience, joy, animation, stress, or extroversion.

Vocal volume tends to vary with emotional and personality characteristics in the same direction as pitch and rate. Loudness seems to occur with anger, cheerfulness, joy, strength, fearlessness, activity, and high status. Softness appears with affection, boredom, sadness, intimacy, empathy, fear, passivity, weakness, and low status.

Low pitch, slow rate, and softness tend to appear together, just as high pitch, fast rate, and loudness do.

Vocal Segregates

Sounds, unnatural silences, and meaningless words used only to fill gaps between meaningful words act as vocal segregates. Examples include "uh," "ah," "uh-huh," "um," "er," and even "I mean," "ya know," "man," "OK," and "well." Such fillers often indicate stress and create a negative impact on the receiver.

To reduce the number of vocal segregates in your speech, listen to tapes of yourself, become aware of segregates even as you speak, and practice mental control instead of the audible segregates or unnatural silence. To cope with the segregates of others, apply the listening principles that call for concentration on content, not style.

Vocal Differentiators

Specialized sounds made with the voice create nonverbal symbols called vocal differentiators. Most differentiators lead to negative meaning within receivers. For example, think of your reaction when you hear these differentiators:

Yawning	Snoring	Sharp exhaling/inhaling
Laughing	Yelling	Spitting
Crying	Clearing throat	Hissing
Belching	Whining	Moaning
Giggling	Coughing	Groaning
Whispering	Hiccoughing	Slurping
Sniffing	Sighing	Gurgling

Because a good communicator avoids using vocal differentiators, use awareness, concentration, and practice to remove them from your communication. When hearing the vocal differentiators of other people, try to ignore them and to evaluate them on the basis of other factors.

Vocal Qualities

The summary tone or quality of a voice arises from many factors, including pitch, volume, rate, resonance, rhythm, inflection, and enunciation. Although temporary changes in pitch, volume, and rate act as vocal qualifiers, they also contribute to the general quality of the voice.

Resonance (timbre) relates to the amplitude of the vibrations—the resounding nature of the voice. It ranges from the fully amplified tones associated with sadness, boredom, and affection, to the thin or blaring tones associated with joy, impatience, cheerfulness, and anger.

Rhythm arises from the regularity or irregularity of the vocal pattern. Regularity often expresses confidence, sincerity, satisfaction, fear, activity, surprise, joy, cheerfulness, or affection. Irregularity may express anger or sadness.

Inflection involves the rising and falling pitch of the voice. Monotones seem to express boredom. Steady or slightly upward inflection often shows affection, impatience, or satisfaction. Upward inflection usually indicates cheerfulness or joy. Irregular inflection may show anger. Downward inflection may reveal sadness.

Enunciation describes the distinctness with which one pronounces or articulates words. A slurred sound often accompanies sadness and affection, and, to some extent, boredom and satisfaction. At the other extreme, a clipping style frequently belongs to anger and impatience.

Other blending factors contribute to the quality of voice expression—and to the value judgments made about it. Recall reactions to such voice characteristics as throatiness, thinness, quaking, breathiness, stridency, flatness, dialects, accents, and tenseness. Think also of the dramatic messages conveyed by poignant pauses and extended periods of silence in a church, synagogue, funeral home, courtroom, or government chamber.

Consider how combinations of verbal and nonverbal symbols can create inconsistent messages. Positive words can combine with negative tones of voice, and negative words with positive tones to create double-edged messages. Sarcasm often results. When it does, the ultimate decision about meaning usually tips in the direction of the nonverbal vocal qualities rather than the words. For example, think about how the tone and emphasis of delivery make the difference in how you react to phrases such as these: "You're really weird." "I hate you." "You're so cute." "That was so clever." "You certainly handled that well."

Recall how Mehrabian's research suggests that receivers gain 38 percent of the total feeling of a message from vocal cues. The proportion falls second only to the 55 percent conveyed by facial expression.

Movement

Nonverbal communication arising from human movement (motile or kinesic behavior) forms five categories: (1) emblems, (2) illustrators, (3) regulators, (4) adaptors, and (5) postures and gestures. The first four derive from the work of Ekman and Friesen, who also included affect displays (facial expressions) in their classification.[12]

Emblems

Many body movements act as symbols with relatively fixed verbal translations. They often replace verbal messages entirely. Such symbols become emblems. H. G. Johnson, Ekman, and Friesen recorded about seventy emblems.[13] This list includes some examples:

- Patting the stomach—"I'm full of food"
- Patting the adjacent seat—"Sit beside me"
- Shaking fist—"I'm angry"
- Cupping hand behind ear—"I can't hear you"
- Circling the first finger parallel with the side of the head—"That person's crazy"
- Moving one index finger across the other or making a clicking sound with the tongue—"For shame"
- Forming the first and second fingers in the shape of a *V*—"Peace" or "Victory"
- Shrugging shoulders and raising palms of hands upward—"I don't know"
- Tapping finger against skull—"I'm thinking"
- Rolling eyes—"I'm exasperated"

Illustrators

When people move and gesture as they speak, they use illustrators. Illustrators synchronize with and complement words. For example, picture a man telling you about the size of a fish he caught. Can you imagine the description using only words?

Consider other kinesic illustrators. Suppose you make the vehement statement, "I will *not* allow this to happen." Would you slap a fist into the palm of the other hand or make a sharp downward motion of one hand as you say the word *not*? Do you automatically wave an arm as you call "Taxi"? When you talk about an object in your presence, do you point or gesture toward it as you say words such as "Take this desk." Do you usually nod your head as you answer "Yes" to a question?

Regulators

When body motions serve to add instructions or controls to oral transactions, those motions act as regulators. Examples of such nonverbal symbols include:

Mutual gazes	Grooming actions	Embraces
Waves	Smiles	Shoulder slaps
Head movements	Forward leanings	Handshakes
Head nods	Posture changes	Shifts in eye contact

Conversational turn-taking involves such acts as raising and lowering eyebrows, leaning forward and backward, and moving hands. Initiating and breaking away from conversations involve a great deal of nonverbal regulation. For example, have you ever consciously or subconsciously looked at your watch in an attempt to shorten a conversation with someone? Similarly, have you ever slapped your hands on the arms of your chair or on your thighs while rising to indicate the termination of an exchange?

Adaptors

Examples of adaptors include picking or holding things, scratching, pinching, rubbing, covering eyes, self-grooming gestures, and manipulation of objects. They can reveal something of the emotional state of the individual exhibiting them.

Adaptors develop as responses to learning situations, many of them in childhood. They tend to associate with negative emotions and seem to occur for some instrumental purpose: controlling emotions, getting along with others, or satisfying needs. They often appear as adaptive means for coping with discomfort created by negative feelings about oneself, other people, or the environment.

Postures and Gestures

Various postures and gestures serve as emblems, illustrators, regulators, and adaptors. However, they also combine to serve as collective expressions of attitudes. Mehrabian provides an excellent summary of the clusters of postures and gestures that relate to his three categories of nonverbal communication. Portraying immediacy, for example, postures that lean toward or open to another tend to show liking or warmth. Those that slouch, lean away, or close off from another tend to reveal disliking and coldness.

In terms of power, Nancy M. Henley suggests that different clusters of postures associate with a person of power and status in communication than with one of lesser status. The clusters of the powerful person include relaxation, informality, close proximity, touching, staring and ignoring, showing emotion, and a nonsmiling expression.[14] In contrast, Henley concludes that the subordinate assumes postures that include tension, circumspection, distance, nontouching, averting eyes while watching furtively, hiding emotion, and smiling.[15] Henley also concludes that the postures and gestures between men and women often virtually parallel those for status nonequals, with men in the position of power.[16]

Fitting with the concept of responsiveness—of adaptation—people straightforwardly exhibit many expressions. Such expressions include cheerfulness, affection, pleasantness, joy, fear, anger, nervousness, caution, worry, and defensiveness. They also attempt to hide emotions. Knapp[17] suggests that clues to deception include:

- Shifty eyes
- Passing hands over mouth
- Uncertain hand-shrug emblems
- Tearing at fingernails
- Looking at ceiling
- Drawn-out smile
- Scissoring legs
- Averted eyes
- Fewer illustrators
- Less nodding
- Tense leg positions
- High-pitched voice
- More speech errors
- Frequent leg-position shifts
- Hands holding onto knees
- Hand pressed into cheek

Though research into cues of deception yields incomplete results, one finding shows consistency: "Obviously, failure to perform nonverbal acts which ordinarily accompany verbal acts is a sign something is wrong."[18]

Touch

Ashley Montagu and Floyd Matson suggest that as Americans leave childhood, their ability to communicate through the largest human organ—the skin—deteriorates significantly.[19] Though this culture sublimates the power of the tactile sense, touch still can carry a great deal of a message. Touching can show tenderness, affection, encouragement, and the full range of emotions.

The infant begins its communicative life largely through the sense of touch. During feeding, suckling, nuzzling, hugging, kissing, cradling, changing, powdering, cuddling, and stroking, human exchange begins to unfold. The denial of extensive touching can have serious negative impact upon the infant's development, possibly even leading to brain damage.

For children and adults the amount of accepted touching varies with many factors such as sex, age, culture, environment, the state of a relationship, intimacy, power and status, and immediacy. The greater freedom of the male to touch the female illustrates differences in power and dominance.

Negative attitudes toward touching in this culture arise from diverse sources. They include the Puritan ethic and attitudes about sex, the emotionalism associating same-sex touching with homosexuality and lesbianism, and the ritualism of handshakes and backslaps.

Touching actions serve as regulators (guiding, attention-getting, accenting) that convey and elicit both positive and negative feelings. Touching conveys the total range from highly impersonal to highly personal meanings. If a person touches a portion of another person's body considered unavailable at a given stage of a relationship, a negative reaction likely will result. However, even a nonintimate's pat on the back with a compliment acts as a positive stroke.

Controlled research conducted by Jeffrey D. Fisher, Marvin Rytting, and Richard Heslin yielded this discussion of the results:

> . . . a casual touch of a very short duration in a Professional/Functional situation [library clerks checking out books to university students] had positive consequences for the recipient. . . . subjects in touch conditions evidenced more positive responses than subjects in no touch conditions. Further, . . . [the analysis] suggests that while the response to the touch condition was uniformly positive for females, it was more ambivalent for males. . . . It is suggested that females, who have had more experience as recipients of touch from significant others, may be more comfortable than males when receiving momentary interpersonal touches from strangers.[20]

The movement toward sensitivity training, body awareness, encounter groups, and the psychiatric use of touch indicates the rekindling of an interest in understanding touching.

Appearance

Your appearance both reflects and creates your own self-image—as well as the image that others have of you. Three categories can organize a review of the nonverbal communication inherent in appearance: (1) the person, (2) clothing, and (3) accessories.

The Person

Many human characteristics contribute to one's general appearance. Height and weight carry meaning in people's minds. Body hair also serves as a point of judgment about a person. Though the debate has settled somewhat, the length of the hair on the male head has led to major contention. Fights, banishments, and even killings have occurred because of parents' demands that sons have their hair cut.

Hair color—particularly for women—also creates (usually erroneous) nonverbal messages. For example, some think red hair goes with a fiery temper; blonde, with stupidity; and brunette, with seductiveness.

Moustaches, beards, and sideburns make nonverbal statements to some. Moreover, most people consider hair on the male's chest and even on legs and arms to be manly. However, most people consider facial and body hair for the female to be unattractive.

Skin color leads to racial stereotypes. In addition, many light-skinned people struggle to obtain deep suntans because they think of pale skin as unhealthy and unattractive. A person's appearance also depends on age, culture, occupation, and sex. General standards exist for how a person should look on the basis of these factors.

Grooming and cleanliness also communicate. A common phrase during the height of the debate raging over the length of male hair was, "I don't care how long he lets it grow if he'll just keep it combed and clean." Although the statement did not always reflect true feelings, it did indicate a reliance upon cleanliness and grooming as symbols of a person's values.

Another category of nonverbal personal characteristics deals with general attractiveness. The premium placed on beauty in this culture has worked in a particularly detrimental fashion toward females. Research has shown, moreover, that unattractive children receive significantly less positive attention from parents and teachers than do their attractive counterparts. This lack of attention often results in poorer self-images for the less attractive children.

Handicaps also communicate nonverbally in a negative way to many people. Unfortunately, people often underestimate those who have some abnormality or deformity in face or form—whether from birth, accident, or disease. This false perception of "difference" often drives a wedge, preventing real communication between them and other participants.

The general carriage and demeanor of a person communicate something of that person's importance. Contrast your evaluation of a person who walks firmly with chin held high and one who shuffles with a dejected look. Picture someone you know who has a charismatic aura. Do such qualities emanate more from the nonverbal realm than from the verbal one?

Clothing

A brief recitation of some words and phrases should illustrate the powerful communicative role that clothing plays. Make mental associations as these types of garb call types of people to mind:

Black leather	White socks	Jeans
Miniskirts	Evening gowns	Fur coats
Polyester knit pantsuits	Cashmere sweaters	Imprinted T-shirts
Leisure suits	Tailored suits	Bow ties
Sheer fabrics	Frills	Plunging necklines
Corduroy	Boots	Tight-fitting clothing
Hats	Stockings	Sandals

Choices of clothing speak quite loudly about one's personality, status, power, attitudes, values, behavior, occupation, and confidence. Clothing for the business executive has assumed such importance that several best-selling books have as their sole purpose the description of the kinds of clothing that establish an image of power.

Accessories

Articles other than garments contribute to appearance and dress. Recall the imagery you associate with these examples of such accessories:

Tatoos	Leather briefcases	Emblems	Buttons
Eyeglasses	Earrings	False eyelashes	Cosmetics
False fingernails	Sunglasses	Gold inlays	Scarves
Billfolds	Rings	Canes	Tinted hair
			Bow ties

Space

Like animals do, humans stake out and maintain territories and attempt to control bubbles of space around themselves. This inclination proves so strong that encroachment on another's space can lead to serious miscommunication.

The use of space and territory (proxemics) varies from culture to culture. However, cultures do have many common features. For example, ownership of land and other real property provides evidence of territorial concerns in most cultures. Disputes over boundaries between nations tragically form the basis for devastating breakdowns in communication—wars.

Question yourself about some aspects of space and territory. Have you ever:

- Held a book or newspaper in front of your face, looked out a window, feigned sleep, or stared into space on public transportation or in a crowded waiting room?
- Looked straight ahead or at the floor indicator or averted your eyes so as not to meet those of someone else in an elevator?
- Identified a chair, an area on a library table, or a desk as yours—and felt perturbed if someone else occupied it?
- Received a scolding for sitting in your father's chair?
- Sat between two people on a sofa or in the seat of a car and talked straight ahead rather than consciously acknowledging them as occupying some of your space?
- Felt uncomfortable or threatened by someone sitting down beside you when the room had other empty, isolated seats available?
- Sat next to someone in a situation such as that described in the last example and observed the person squirm or even move to a new location?

As you read the questions, you probably thought, "My feelings in these situations depend on other factors as well." Indeed, the reaction to territorial invasion does vary with the circumstances. Knapp suggests:

> Although we often think people vigorously defend their territory, the type of defense is highly dependent on who the intruder is, why the intrusion is taking place, what type of territory is being encroached upon, what type of encroachment is used, . . . how long the encroachment takes, and where it occurs.[21]

Massing of Humans

Massing of humans has an impact on communication, though not always negative. Many people regularly seek out and enjoy settings that include large numbers of other people; witness the popularity of dining out. However, crowding may create an emotional state brought on by the undesirable presence of too many "trespassers."

Distances

Another refinement calls for distinctions among the types of distances over which people communicate. Edward T. Hall's writings suggest four types: public distance, formal distance, informal distance, and intimate distance.[22]

- *Public distance* marks off speeches or lectures to an audience where the closest person sits or stands about ten or more feet away.

- *Formal distance* calls for about four to eight feet between participants in such activities as job interviews.
- A distance of about three feet—about an arm's length away—identifies *informal distance* for such exchanges as casual conversations.
- People reserve *intimate distance* (about eighteen inches or less) strictly for those invited into it. Encroachment upon it by nonintimates often leads to significant reactions.

Respect for space

People tend to honor the space of others. They avoid violating it and become quite uncomfortable when they must do so. You probably have apologized many times to people whose territory you have entered accidentally or against your will.

Time

The passage of time divides human life into centuries, decades, years, weeks, days, hours, minutes, and seconds. Time has dimensions in lightness and darkness, the seasons, hormonal and other biological cycles, and the life cycle itself. Thus, time plays both indirect and direct roles in communication.

The time clocks within people affect how they communicate both verbally and nonverbally to others. For example, some managers set staff meetings in the morning because people interact better in the mornings than in the afternoons. As additional examples of the impact of time upon communication, think about how arriving late for an interview creates a negative impression, how a person making a long-distance call must take account of time zones, how people become disgruntled when a business meeting lasts too long, and how the length of coffee breaks provides a universal bone of contention between employers and employees.

Evidence of the time-bound nature of Americans becomes apparent through these vignettes:

- Workers punch time clocks.
- Passengers become upset because of a late bus (plane, train).
- Transportation schedules include departure and arrival times stated as precisely as 9:02 A.M.
- People place clocks in virtually every room and office in which they live and work.
- A worker tells everyone who will listen about cutting three minutes off the trip to the job that morning.
- Time-management seminars abound.
- One of the major analytical approaches to business and economic conditions involves time series.
- Production experts conduct time-and-motion studies.
- People feel complimented or honored when others "take the time" to do something for them.
- A supervisor reminds an operator, "Time is money."

- People complain about jet lag, changes from the day shift to the evening shift, and the adjustment to daylight saving time.
- A member of an audience says, "I really liked that speaker's timing."

Preoccupation with time leads to stereotypes about the proper durations of time for given activities. Generally, managers require employees to work five eight-hour days a week, beginning and ending at the same times each day. Many of them resist the four-day week and the concept of flexible working hours. Students become upset if a professor keeps them two or three minutes past the end of the class or keeps them the full period on the first day of class.

People expect movies of no longer than two hours—including commercials when shown on television. They expect television shows of 30 minutes or an hour long. Although plays may have some flexibility, the two-hour limit, including expected intermissions, prevails. A sermon or a speech should take 20 to 30 minutes. Even when a lunch break takes only 30 minutes, people call it a lunch hour. Similarly, academic people still call a 50-minute examination an hour exam.

Another type of concern about time relates to what people consider the proper time of day to do certain things. For example, people who have dinner at 8 P.M. consider those who eat the main meal of the day near midday and call it "dinner" uncouth. They also misunderstand those who eat the third meal of the day at 4:30 or 5:00 P.M. instead of later.

Treatment of time introduces another important nonverbal element. An applicant late for an interview probably loses any chance for the job. Coming late to a party, however, does not constitute impropriety. In fact, people often treat those who arrive exactly on time or, perish the thought, early, as social novices.

The higher the status, the later one can arrive for a scheduled beginning time. For example, doctors expect patients to arrive on time for appointments, but doctors may come late. Professors may walk into classrooms late, but they expect students to arrive on time. To use time as an effective communication tool, first understand its impact on people, then act in concert with that understanding.

(638 words)

Take and score Self-Test 11 over the excerpt about time on pages 113–14.

Silence

Silence is an important vehicle for nonverbal communication. Its impact crosses all levels of human activity.

External silence improves the quality of communication within oneself. For most people, thinking proceeds more efficiently without the interference of outside noises.

Silence also contributes to the ultimate self-communication: dreaming. Some psychologists suggest that we need sleep at least as much for the therapy provided through dreams as for the physical rest it provides. Thus, as an important element of sleeping and dreaming, silence again has an impact on internal communication.

People also use silence in transactions between or among themselves. They often provide periodic silences of many minutes to improve the thinking power of people involved in group activities. They include silences of a few seconds' duration even during conversations. Not only do such silences allow people to think, but they help to pace the conversation, provide cues for turn-taking, and generally control the conversation. Of course, unnatural silences can act as vocal segregates and thus lead to interference.

To use silence as a tool of power, many speakers have learned to use the intimidating pause—a pause of 7 to 10 seconds. They maintain control of the exchanges through other nonverbal means and through status, while those of lesser power squirm in discomfort.

Communicators also use silence for dramatic effect—to gain or maintain attention, to persuade, or to entertain—often by introducing silence when the receivers expect something else. At other times people effectively use silence when it does match expectations. For example, no thinking communicator would interrupt the silence mandated for a period of meditation at a banquet or for portions of religious observations.

Because silence makes such an important contribution to nonverbal communication, learn to use and interpret it. As with other forms of nonverbal communication, the key to its use and interpretation lies in awareness and sensitivity.

Environment

The nonverbal environment substantially affects communication. The environment includes other people, things, and nature.

People

This book deals primarily with communication between or among specifically identified participants. However, other people also indirectly affect communication transactions. The section on space, earlier in this chapter, deals with one of them—the effect of massing.

When people communicate as active or passive outsiders, their presence often has a negative effect. Recall making a telephone call while other people could see or hear you. As long as you felt that the others did not enter into the process, they probably had little impact. However, as soon as you noticed them listening or reacting to your words, your conversation probably took a different form. You no doubt can recreate similar occurrences involving conversations in an office, a waiting room, an airplane, a train, or a bus.

The presence of other people can have a positive impact on a communication transaction. For example, for angry participants, the presence of others may lead them to control themselves. The interjection of a third party can also create silences that allow participants to collect their thoughts. It can also allow them to end a conversation that they already wanted to terminate.

Things

Have you ever entered a home or office and hesitated to touch anything? Have you entered other homes and offices and felt engulfed with warmth and invitation? As an example in the business world, picture two kinds of banks. Traditional banks take the form of cold, austere, echoing, uncarpeted, pillared, marbled bastions of clinical finance. Contemporary banks take the form of warm, woodtoned, carpeted, inviting, human places for dealing with money matters. The *layouts and structural features* of rooms, buildings, and even cities affect communication. Building design can allow people to encounter or avoid one another. Offset office or apartment doors on either side of a hall lead to less communication than occurs when doors face each other. Offices or apartments near elevators or stairway landings lead to more interchange than do those removed from them.

Locations, sizes, and designs of offices relate to power and status. Generally, the higher the status of an individual, the higher the office in a multistoried building. The office frequently has a great deal of floor space and requires visitors to overcome great distances and barriers to reach it. It probably has an outside wall with windows. The executive with the most power usually occupies the corner room with the most windows. It may have a private elevator to an exit by a private parking space.

The nonverbal symbols of power tend to cut people off from colleagues with whom they need to communicate. Therefore, wise executives reserve their bastions of privacy for the kinds of creativity that require it. However, they move out into the outer offices, hallways, and workplaces for as much of the day as they can. Otherwise, executives may find that the trappings of status destroy the interactions that allowed that status to develop in the first place.

Fences, walls, dividers can erect barriers to communication. Though sometimes desirable, the separation also can prove detrimental. In many ways the people who work in large, central, open areas have the advantage. Thrown into regular contact with one another, they learn a great deal about business and about human relations.

Furniture illustrates the importance of things in the communication environment. For example, picture a classroom with hard, straight-backed, colorless, arm-desk chairs arranged in rows facing the teacher. Then picture a room with colorful molded chairs in a circle or semicircle. Usually, more exchange takes place in the second setting than in the first.

Furniture in a home or office also often affects conversation. The types and arrangements of chairs, sofas, tables, and other furniture may facilitate, interfere with, or at least alter conversational patterns.

A desk often serves as a barrier between communication participants or as a symbol of power. Thus, the desk becomes an important nonverbal element.

Other *furnishings* affecting people and thus their communication include draperies, blinds, fabrics, decorations, plants, floor coverings, and wall coverings. Such furnishings help create a range of settings from invigorating to debilitating.

Lighting also has an impact on communication. Bright lights stimulate activity. Dim lights contribute to intimacy between intimates, but may create some discomfort between nonintimates.

The *temperature, humidity, and ventilation* of a room can have a significant impact upon the communication that transpires there. Recall communication events in your life affected positively or negatively by these factors.

As suggested, *colors* do seem to affect people's communicative efforts. Hues with a possible positive or stimulating influence include yellow, yellow-green, green, blue, violet, purple, red, and orange. Colors with the potential for a negative effect include black, brown, and white.

To establish the impact of *sounds,* recall a time when you changed environments and had difficulty adjusting to the new set of stimuli. The classic example occurs when a city dweller goes to the country or the country dweller goes to the city. Either person finds the unfamiliar mix of noises (or lack of them) so disconcerting that he or she becomes edgy and cannot even sleep well. Undesirable noises may interfere with activity. Many communities, offices, factories, and even homes have taken action to overcome noise pollution.

Research has shown that the type and volume of *music* people hear communicates nonverbally with them. Plato urged only martial types of music to keep people in the tight, militaristic, functional mode. In 1979 Khomeni outlawed music on radios and televisions in Iran because he believed that it destroyed the desired religious attitude and had a "numbing" effect on the mind. Elsewhere, though, music plays in homes, cars, offices, factories, supermarkets, mental institutions, bus stations, and even dairy barns and chicken houses. Great performance halls spend enormous amounts of money just to assure good acoustics.

The type of music and its intensity relate to the site, the people, the time of day, and the type of activity desired. Soothing, quiet music plays in mental institutions. Office workers may begin the day hearing soft music, but find it slowly intensified for the times when people tend to tire—particularly just after lunch and near quitting time. Supermarket shoppers often hear fast, upbeat music to keep them moving and buying.

Any pervasive *odor* can play a part in the creation of an environment. For example, think how odors from these sources might affect your behavior.

Cooking and foods	Flowers
Human bodies	Musty closets
Pets	Garbage
Shaving lotions	Chemicals
Perfumes	Gasoline

Another example of the importance of odors to human interaction exists in the controversial topic of smoking. Though all of the controversy does not center on the smell alone, a great deal of it does. The battle between smokers and nonsmokers often creates a severely destructive wedge between communication participants—all from a nonverbal factor.

Nonverbal surroundings include things that *touch* as well as those that affect the other senses. Such things include the textures of the throw pillows, upholstery fabrics, woods, and metals used in construction of chairs, sofas, and other furniture.

Even through their shoes people experience a different nonverbal sense from a carpeted floor and a tile, concrete, or wooden floor. Assess the impact of floor material by considering the person who stands and walks on concrete all day, compared to one who does so on carpet. The tired and aching feet that result from the concrete have a significant impact on the person who must cope with them. The cushioned seat and the hard metal or wooden seat can make a difference in the behavior of persons sitting on the two types.

Nature

Natural elements create an atmosphere that affects humans. For example, if you work ten miles from home and a blizzard occurs, your well-being is affected—no matter how nearly perfect your immediate environment. Thus, the *weather* influences personality. Heat, cold, barometric pressure, humidity, wind, ice, rain, snow, sunshine, and cloudiness all affect moods and performance. Gray, overcast, rainy days put some people into a state of depression.

In a clearly related way, the *climate* of a region contributes to the undercurrent of general human activity. People in the temperate climates tend toward alertness, activity, and achievement more than those people in the tropical ones. Cold and low humidity serve as stimuli; heat and high humidity serve as depressants.

Variety in the elements of weather and climate also adds a stimulating dimension to human interchange, a dimension missing in areas in which the weather rarely changes. However, too much variety can prove unsettling.

Different combinations of weather and climate have varying effects on human behavior. A 25-mile-an-hour wind has a quite different meaning for someone sailing on a beautiful lake on a warm spring day than for someone standing on a drab street corner in a cold rain waiting for a bus.

The seasons of the year can also have a dramatic effect. You doubtless can recall emotional lows associated with the starkness of winter and emotional highs associated with the burst of spring. Consider one more piece of evidence of the importance of temperature: the relationship between summer heat and certain kinds of mass human unrest. Events such as the destructive urban riots of the 1960s relate to complex factors including the state of politics, the level of the economy, racial discrimination, and ghetto conditions. The factors existed all year, yet the riots erupted in the heat of summer.

Some research has related *solar and lunar activities* to mood changes or "swings." A great deal of skepticism greets those who claim the relationships; however, research suggests that behavior becomes predictably more agitated with a full moon and that accidents relate to the cycles of both the sun and moon.

This review of nonverbal communication completes the coverage of the three receiving acts. Part C (Chapters 6–14) moves to the three sending acts: writing, sending oral messages, and preparing tables, illustrations, and other supplemental presentations (basically nonverbal). Chapter 6 begins with some general principles for writing.

SUMMARY

Nonverbal (wordless) communication carries from 65 percent to 93 percent of the message load in social communication transactions. Obstacles to using nonverbal messages to the fullest include the lack of dictionaries of nonverbal symbols, the inattention to them within formal education, their subtleties, and the delicate and personal nature of interpreting them.

One classification for types of nonverbal communication includes immediacy, power, and responsiveness. The concept of immediacy springs from the tendency to approach the things we like and avoid the things we dislike. Power relates to size, dominance, strength, and high status. For example, a person who strides or struts exhibits more power than one who takes small steps or shuffles. Responsiveness involves adaptive actions such as anger, joy, surprise, and fear. These actions occur in response to the environment, including other humans.

Another scheme for classifying nonverbal communication includes these categories: (1) face, (2) voice, (3) movement, (4) touch, (5) appearance, (6) space, (7) time, (8) silence, and (9) environment.

Theorists suggest that the face reveals more about emotional state and personality than any other human part, carrying about 55 percent of any feeling. Facial expressions include many blends, perhaps identified by eight facial styles: the Withholder, the Revealer, the Unwitting Expressor, the Substitute Expressor, the Frozen-Affect Expressor, the Ever-Ready Expressor, and the Flooded-Affect Expressor. Smiling contributes to facial expression. The three major types of smiles include the simple (private) smile (no teeth showing), the upper smile (upper teeth showing in greeting), and the broad smile (both lower and upper teeth showing while laughing). Two other smiles—the polite smile (condescending smile) and the "lip-in" smile (a smile of inferiority)—do not convey happiness. The eyes contribute through their physical characteristics (color, size, etc.) as well as through their use (eye gaze, eye contact, etc.).

Vocal qualifiers, segregates, differentiators, and qualities serve as cues to accompany spoken words. Vocal qualifiers stem from variations in pitch, rate, and volume of the voice. Vocal segregates include sounds, unnatural silences, and meaningless words ("uh," "er," "ya know," "I mean," "well," etc.). Vocal differentiators represent specialized sounds such as yawning, laughing, crying, giggling, and slurping. Vocal qualities arise from the summary tone created by pitch, volume, rate, resonance, rhythm, inflection, and enunciation.

Messages through movement arise from emblems (symbols that carry relatively fixed verbal translations, such as shaking a fist), illustrators (movements and gestures that synchronize with and complement words), regulators (motions that add instructions or controls to oral transactions), adaptors (responses to learning situations such as picking, scratching, and rubbing), and postures and gestures showing immediacy, power, and responsiveness.

Touch can introduce the full range of human emotions—from a tender caress to the clenched fist making contact with another's jaw. Thus, it contributes positively, negatively, and in every intermediate state, including simple regulation of conversations.

The nonverbal elements associated with appearance fall into three categories: the person, clothing, and accessories. Characteristics of the person include height, weight, body hair, hair color, skin color, grooming, cleanliness, attractiveness, handicaps, and general carriage—all creating meanings within the observer. Also creating meanings, choices in clothing speak loudly about one's personality, status, power, attitudes, values, behavior, occupation, and confidence. Accessories, articles other than clothing (e.g., eyeglasses, jewelry, canes), also communicate.

The use of space and territory includes such categories as massing of humans, distances, and respect for the space of others. The massing of humans can lead to positive or negative input. Proper distances define public space, formal space, informal space, and intimate space. Good communicators respect the space of others.

Time adds dimensions to communication both indirectly and directly. Through the division of life into units (lightness, darkness, seasons, years, weeks, days, hours, and life cycles), time shapes all communication. If affects communication directly in such ways as the lengths of workdays, expectations about the lengths of speeches, lunch breaks, and TV shows, and the concepts about arriving "on time."

The use of silence has an impact on communication in many ways: External silence helps intrapersonal processing, including dreaming. Natural silences within conversations allow for improved thinking and turn-taking. Unnatural silences can lead to interference. The deliberate use of silence can intimidate or create a dramatic effect.

Environmental factors contributing to nonverbal messages include people, things, and nature. The presence of outsiders can change the course of a given transaction significantly. Such things as buildings, locations, walls, furniture, lighting, temperature, humidity, colors, and sounds have an impact. Contributing natural elements include climate, weather, and even solar and lunar activities.

EXERCISES

1. Describe what type of person each of the following is. What is the person's mood? Is he or she "saying" something? What?

JOHN

ELIZABETH

RODNEY

NORA

2. Read the following sentence aloud several times to express alternately happiness, anger, fear, discomfort, boredom, and condescension.

The general carriage and demeanor of a person report something of the status and power of that person.

What was your tone of voice and facial expression for each mood?

3. Watch for and record the nonverbal actions of a professor in one of your other classes. Pay particular attention to facial expressions, body movements and gestures, and appearance as described in this chapter. Does the professor's nonverbal behavior support or contradict her or his verbal actions? Explain. (Do not identify the professor in your record.)
4. In your opinion, what forms of dress and types of grooming habits make a person look strong and serious? Weak and frivolous? You may want to discuss this in a four- or five-person group.
5. Height, race, sex, physical handicaps, and a great deal of a person's physical appearance cannot be changed. Make a list of at least five ways you can overcome any prejudices you have against people who are tall or short, of another race, of the other sex, physically handicapped, or not particularly good-looking.
6. What is communicated by each of these nonverbal states?

   a. A business executive with dirty hair
   b. Loud music in a medical doctor's office
   c. A professor with her arms folded across her stomach
   d. A colleague with perspiration on his brow
   e. An open book on an unoccupied desk
   f. An overflowing trash can in an otherwise clean office
   g. A sigh
   h. A soft, comfortable visitor's chair outside the manager's office
   i. A crowded, noisy, hot room
   j. High-heeled shoes and a short, sheer dress
   k. An unbuttoned shirt and tight slacks
   l. Strong cologne or after-shave
   m. Dyed hair
   n. A person who smells of onions
   o. A person whose face is within inches of your face
   p. A person who interrupts your sentences

7. Meet in groups. Choose one person to read the paragraph provided. The speaker should try to support nonverbally the intent of the paragraph (a welcoming speech). Evaluate her or his performance. What nonverbal acts supported or contradicted the speaker's message?

   Welcome to the Snelton Automobile Plant. As you tour the main assembly line, feel free to ask questions or make comments. We are particularly interested in your criticisms. Thanks for coming. We have looked forward to your visit for weeks. Enjoy!

8. What nonverbal aspects of your person or your behavior do you wish to change? How can you go about changing them? Will the changes allow you to communicate more honestly and effectively?
9. Videotape or at least audiotape yourself. Listen to, view, and evaluate the nonverbal messages you send. Invite others to participate.
10. What nonverbal states and behaviors do you find distracting or downright maddening? For instance, some people do not like to have others yawn in their faces. Why do you find each of the states and behaviors distracting? What do they communicate to you? Do you sometimes exhibit these states and behaviors?

11. Meet with your group. You and each other group member give a short talk on what you would wear to a job interview with a conservative accounting firm. Center your evaluation of each group member's performance around these questions:
    a. Did the speaker use vocal segregates during her or his speech? If so, what were they?
    b. What did the speaker's vocal qualifiers communicate?
    c. What, if any, vocal differentiators did the speaker use?
    d. What was the general quality of the speaker's voice (pitch, volume, rate, resonance, rhythm, inflection, and enunciation)?
12. Six potential clients will be visiting your data processing firm in August. You have been chosen to give a sales presentation to the visitors. Your manager wants the presentation to last about an hour, with a thirty-minute discussion period to follow the presentation. You also are in charge of all of the arrangements for the meeting. What can you do before and during the meeting to overcome these nonverbal communication problems?
    a. Your office building is not air-conditioned. All of your offices are very hot in August, particularly in the afternoon.
    b. One of your company's conference rooms holds 200 people. The other conference room holds fifteen people, but is next to a noisy print shop.
    c. You want to wear a conservative suit, but you fear that you will get very hot in it.
    d. When you speak in front of a group of people, you wave your arms a great deal and frown frequently, both out of nervousness.
    e. All of your potential clients are much older than you.
    f. You fear that an hour-long presentation could bore the audience.
13. You are one of 20 management analysts in the program management department of the Aztec Corporation. You have noticed that several of your colleagues are sending sloppy letters and reports to your clients. The letters and reports are written in pencil or pen on notebook or scrap paper, are stuffed in dirty or wrinkled envelopes, and are mailed late. Your department's manager does not understand the problem, but said that he would not mind if you would write a memorandum addressing the nonverbal message problem. Write a memorandum that covers the most important aspects of making choices of stationery, envelope, printing, format, and time. Try to convince your colleagues that inappropriate nonverbal accompaniments detract from the written message. Remember that your boss and your colleagues do not recognize that a problem exists.
14. You are the manager of the Finance Department of a major corporation. You know that your employees regard you as closed-minded, pretentious, and frightening. Every time you talk to one of your employees, he or she seems very nervous and eager to end the conversation. You realize that you cannot be an effective manager if most of your employees fear you, so you decide that you can begin to change your image by changing the furniture in your office.

    Your office seems cold and forbidding, and you want to give your employees a chance to relax when they visit you.

    Draw a plan for changing your office. Use the space provided or a separate piece of paper. Assume that you have plenty of money to buy new furnishings. Explain the reasoning behind the changes that you make.

    After you have drawn up a plan, list several other nonverbal changes that you could make that might contribute to your new image. For example, you could plan to use a mirror to practice making kind and open facial expressions.

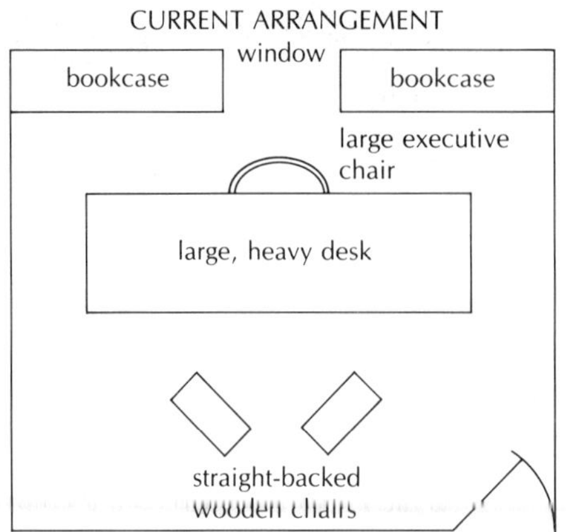

15. Study the following illustrated scene. Write a brief statement in response to each of these questions:

a. What is the relative status of each character?
b. What is the emotional state of the person seated behind the desk?
c. What is the emotional state of the person standing in front of the desk?
d. What nonverbal components in the scene led to the impressions stated in a–c?

You may want to meet with your group to discuss your written statements, the feelings associated with both roles, and how to overcome the nonverbal problems evident in the scene.

16. Hints for good time management include:
   a. Use a good reminder system.
   b. Increase reading and writing skills.
   c. Make routine decisions the first time you encounter the problems requiring them.
   d. Make monthly, weekly, and daily plans; put them in written form.
   e. Use the most efficient channel for each communication transaction.

f. Announce meetings in advance.
g. Cut the time spent on social conversation.
h. Deliberately neglect low-priority problems; they may solve themselves.
i. Have someone else take telephone calls, open mail, etc., and arrange the messages in order of importance for you.

Think of two or three additional hints. Write a one- or two-page memorandum to your employees about time management. (Supply any information you need.) In the memorandum include expanded and illustrated versions for at least five of the hints listed here or suggested by you.

17. Use your dictionary and thesaurus to create meanings for these words. Use the words when you think, write, and speak so that you feel comfortable using them.
    a. Acuity
    b. Bastion
    c. Cliché
    d. Condescend
    e. Contradict
    f. Dominant
    g. Metaphor
    h. Novice
    i. Poignant
    j. Punctual
    k. Ramification
    l. Status
    m. Stereotype
    n. Triad
18. Take and score Self-Test 12 over Chapter 5.

SELF-TEST 11
Excerpt about Time

A. (33 points each). For each multiple-choice question, select the most accurate answer.

1. Which one of these statements is true?
   a. Time plays only an indirect role in communication.
   b. Stereotypes about durations of time associated with given activities support the concept of flexible working hours.
   c. Americans generally consider being early for a party a faux pas.
   d. A person's status has nothing to do with how he or she may use time.
   e. People usually become restless when a committee meeting exceeds ten minutes.
2. Which one of these statements is *not* true?
   a. Time-management seminars reinforce the importance of time as a nonverbal communication factor.
   b. The precision of a plane schedule is evidence of the time-bound nature of Americans.
   c. Both professors and students have expectations about the timing of classes.
   d. Attitudes about "wasting" time have no impact on communication.
   e. To be late for an appointment with a president probably is more serious than to be late for an appointment with a supervisor.

B. Inference (34 points). For the multiple-choice question, select the most accurate answer.

1. Which one of these statements is *not* true?
   a. Seasonal changes have an effect on nonverbal communication.
   b. The concept of "timing" can be just as important for a speaker as for a comedian.
   c. Age is actually a function of time, and thus overlaps with other factors in communication.

d. Einstein's theory of relativity held the key that unlocked the secrets of nonverbal communication.
e. Attitudes about the coffee break have a nonverbal impact on transactions.

SOLUTION

A. Recall (33 points each)
1. c
2. d

B. Inference (34 points)
1. d

SELF-TEST 12
Chapter 5

A. Recall (20 points each). For each multiple-choice question, select the most accurate answer.

1. Which of the following is a true statement?
   a. According to authoritative estimates, nonverbal elements may carry 65, 80, or even 93 percent of the social meaning in interpersonal exchanges.
   b. The power metaphor is that humans approach the things they like and avoid the things they dislike.
   c. Responsiveness (adaptation) generally relates to size.
   d. The Withholder is inhibited, but uses a great deal of facial movement.
   e. Subordinates do not keep their eyes on dominant people.
2. Humidity can affect communication performance. Which of the following also affect(s) communication?
   a. Layout and location of a room
   b. Presence of other people
   c. Lighting
   d. Color of walls
   e. a–d
3. Physical appearance and dress:
   a. Do not affect communication events
   b. Have nothing to do with nonverbal communication
   c. Completely define the person
   d. Can communicate a great deal about people
   e. Not a–d
4. Which one of these statements is *not* true?
   a. The vocal segregates ("uh," "er," etc.) can interfere with communication.
   b. Emblems are nonverbal symbols that have relatively fixed interpretations.
   c. The deliberate use of silence can intimidate or create a dramatic effect.
   d. People generally enjoy invading the territories of others.
   e. Human masses do not always have a negative impact on communication.

B. Inference (20 points). For the multiple-choice question, select the most accurate answer.

1. Nonverbal communication:
   a. Cannot exist without verbal communication
   b. Is virtually beyond the communicator's control
   c. Does not lend itself to research
   d. Lacks some sophistication, but contributes significantly to transactions—especially oral ones
   e. Has received deserved attention from academicians

SOLUTION

A. Recall (20 points each)
1. a **3.** d
2. e **4.** d

B. Inference (20 points)
1. d

ENDNOTES

1. Mark L. Knapp, *Nonverbal Communication in Human Interaction,* 2d ed. (New York: Holt, Rinehart, and Winston, 1978), 30. Reprinted by permission.
2. Charles U. Larson, *Communication: Everyday Encounters* (Belmont, Calif.: Wadsworth Publishing Co., Inc., 1976), 50.
3. Albert Mehrabian, *Silent Messages* (Belmont, Calif.: Wadsworth Publishing Co., Inc., 1971), 43–44.
4. Mehrabian, *Silent Messages,* 113, 115, 116.
5. Mehrabian, *Silent Messages,* 114.
6. Mehrabian, *Silent Messages,* 44.
7. Paul Ekman and Wallace V. Friesen, *Unmasking the Face* (Englewood Cliffs, N.J.: Prentice-Hall, 1975).
8. Elizabeth McGough, *Your Silent Language* (New York: William Morrow and Co., 1974), 30–31.
9. McGough, *Silent Language,* 31–32.
10. McGough, *Silent Language,* 32.
11. G. L. Trager, "Paralanguage: A First Approximation," *Studies in Linguistics* 13 (1958): 1–12.
12. Paul Ekman and Wallace V. Friesen, "The Rhetoric of Nonverbal Behavior: Categories, Origins, Usage, and Coding," *Semiotica* 1 (1969): 63–70, 82–92.
13. H. G. Johnson, Paul Ekman, and Wallace V. Friesen, "Communicative Body Movements: American Emblems," *Semiotica* 15 (1975): 346–50.
14. Nancy M. Henley, *Body Politics: Power, Sex, and Nonverbal Communication* (Englewood Cliffs, N.J.: Prentice-Hall, 1977), 124–50. Reprinted by permission.
15. Henley, *Body Politics.*
16. Henley, *Body Politics.*
17. Knapp, *Nonverbal Communication,* 229–32.
18. Knapp, *Nonverbal Communication,* 231.
19. Ashley Montague and Floyd Matson, *The Human Connection* (New York: McGraw-Hill, 1979).
20. Jeffrey D. Fisher, Marvin Rytting, and Richard Heslin, "Hands Touching Hands: Affective and Evaluative Effects on Interpersonal Touch," *Sociometry* 39 (December 1976): 419.
21. Knapp, *Nonverbal Communication,* 141.
22. Edward T. Hall, *The Silent Language* (New York: Doubleday & Co., Inc., 1959), 163–64. Reprinted by permission.

C

SENDING

STUDENT'S OBJECTIVES:

1 To apply guidelines for effective communication to sending, with emphasis on principles of writing

2 To choose, apply, and practice an appropriate drafting process

6

WRITING

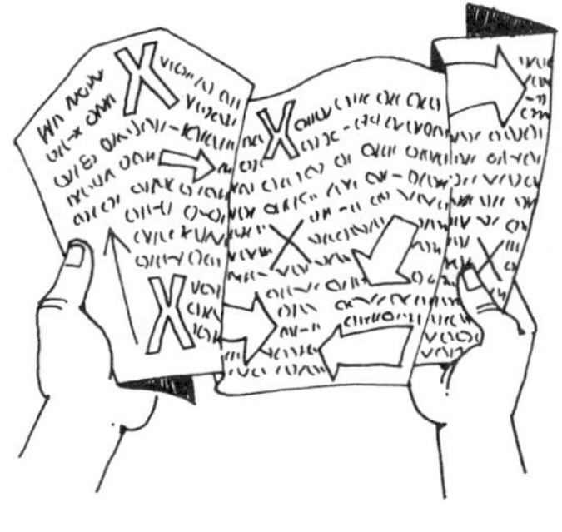

3 To apply different developmental patterns, outlines, and parts for messages

4 To revise messages for correctness, conciseness, clearness, colorfulness, considerateness, and coherence

5 To use personal and external transmitting instruments well, with emphasis on modern equipment, services, and word-processing systems

GUIDELINES FOR EFFECTIVE WRITING

- ☐ *Define purposes, participants, and environment for writing and reading*
- ☐ *Identify writing channel*
- ☐ *Control interference with writing and reading*
- ☐ *Select, write, and transmit message*
- ☐ *Use feedback from and to reader*
- ☐ *Evaluate at each stage and at end of transaction*

This chapter shifts from *receiving* activities to *sending* activities, beginning with basic principles of writing. Chapters 7–13 provide applications of these principles to letters, memoranda, reports, and other written messages. This chapter emphasizes Guideline 4 of the six communication guidelines discussed in Chapter 2. However, good selecting, encoding, and transmitting depend on careful application of the other guidelines as well. Use the guidelines in Chapter 2 to define purposes, participants, environment, and channel, to control interference, to stimulate and use feedback, and to evaluate the whole writing process.

Because written communication channels do not involve face-to-face interaction and feedback, you should choose more direct channels whenever possible. Particularly avoid blind acceptance of a written channel simply because "it's always done that way." Written messages do provide permanent and accurate records of complex, technical, and legal information. They also prevent the emotional interference that can occur in oral transactions, add formality, meet strict traditional requirements, or complete distant or time-consuming communication not possible through oral channels. When using written messages, supplement them with oral interactions whenever you can.

The application of Guideline 4 calls for the selection of a message. However, that selection begins at the instant of awareness of the need for a message and continues to grow through the application of Guidelines 1, 2, 3, and 4. Of course, the selection of a message eventually takes place in the sender's mind. Because the mind may not contain all of the necessary information, Chapter 12 describes how to collect such information through written, oral, and nonverbal processes.

The remainder of this chapter deals with encoding (writing) and transmitting. First, it covers writing in two parts: drafting and revising.

DRAFTING

The sender may choose from several approaches to convert messages in the sender's mind to written drafts of external messages. All of the effective approaches involve both writing and organizing.

Approaches to Writing and Organizing

Many writers recommend organizing first and writing second, others recommend writing first and organizing second, and some recommend a combined approach.

The writers who recommend *organizing first and writing second* claim that they save time and effort by:

- Including all important elements and eliminating unnecessary ones
- Placing parts in logical order according to a developmental plan and outline—even before collecting information
- Putting elements where they belong
- Spending time on important parts, not unimportant ones
- Including the proper amount of information

At the same time, writers who recommend *writing first and organizing second*—the *just-write method*—claim that this method saves time and effort. To apply the just-write method, begin by just writing. Forget developmental patterns, outlines, spelling, logic, grammar, transitions, punctuation, factual accuracy, format, courtesy, and anything else that will slow progress. Just spill the thoughts as quickly as they come. Unload them before they escape.

One problem with the just-write method is that people think at a speed of 400 w.p.m., but they can write longhand at only 25 w.p.m. Therefore, if you use this approach, try to overcome some of that gap by: (1) using shorthand or a typewriter, (2) abbreviating words, (3) writing single key words or sentence fragments, (4) crossing through words rather than erasing them, (5) keeping a pad and pencil handy for random outpourings, and (6) using a tape recorder.

If you fear or dislike writing, the just-write method may help overcome those feelings. You may no longer sit and stare at a blank sheet of paper, or write one or two words and then crumple the paper and throw it in the wastebasket. You cannot avoid the process by sharpening pencils, collecting more data, or deciding to put off the writing until tomorrow.

Even when your thoughts simply will not focus on the subject, begin writing anyway. Write anything—any words, phrases, or off-the-topic thoughts you may have. Miraculously, the words quickly turn to those needed for your topic. With the just-write method, you complete the entire draft before organizing. Organizing becomes part of the revising stage.

Perhaps the best method results from *combining* the two polar approaches just described:

- Use the just-write technique to spill key words on paper.
- Quickly organize the key words into a rough preliminary outline for a chosen developmental pattern. Still do not worry about correctness of form.
- Use the just-write technique to unload thoughts about each part of the outline. Add other parts or reorganize as desired.
- Quickly revise the outline if necessary. Leave it rough.
- Use the just-write technique to write the entire draft of the message.
- Complete the organization during the revising stage.

Organizing

Whether accomplished before or after writing, organizing involves two major elements: developmental patterns and outlines.

Developmental Patterns

The *pattern of development* chosen for the parts (for example, chapters of a book) has an impact on its evolution. This chapter covers seven developmental patterns: (1) indirect, (2) direct, (3) chronological, (4) spatial, (5) analytical, (6) comparative, and (7) ranked.

The *indirect* pattern moves from factual bits to a general conclusion or principle built from them. The indirect pattern proves particularly useful for delivering bad-news messages because it softens the blow. For example, a letter refusing a request for credit might cite such factors as poor credit record and insufficient income before making the refusal.

The *direct* pattern moves from the conclusion (or principle) to the factual bits that support it. The direct plan works well for messages that include routine or pleasant information. For instance, a message of invitation usually begins with the invitation. Then it supplies the details.

If a message features the *order* of events, then it uses the *chronological* pattern. Examples include the step-by-step sequence of the occurrence of events for an automobile-accident insurance claim and instructions for assembling a tricycle.

Some messages logically fit a *spatial* pattern. For example, a report about a firm's international operations often unfolds through geographical areas. Other spatial patterns cover the topic from top to bottom, from bottom to top, from left to right, from right to left, from inside to outside, from outside to inside, from near to far, or from far to near.

The word *analyze* means to separate the whole into its constituent elements for careful scrutiny. Therefore, an *analytical* pattern proves logical for many kinds of messages. For instance, a résumé usually contains descriptive parts such as education, experience, personal data, and references.

The organization of a message often involves a *comparative* pattern. To illustrate, a report could compare qualities of decentralized and centralized management.

The components of a message may fall in the *ranked* pattern—either ascending or descending. The ascending style overlaps the indirect pattern, and the descending style overlaps the direct. For example, an arrangement of budget requests in order of importance takes the ranked pattern.

Outlines

As a skeleton display of the parts of the message, an outline can include topics or short sentences.

The topic outline includes phrases or sentence fragments that identify the subjects of the parts. The sentence outline includes complete sentences. Such sentences may eventually serve as topic sentences for paragraphs of the message itself.

For simple writing—most letters, memoranda, notes, and forms—the topic outline serves well. However, for more involved messages, try writing the topic outline first and then converting it into a sentence outline.

To develop message outlines, you must make two decisions: (1) Establish the parts of the message. (2) Select a format for the outline.

Parts First, establish an appropriate number of major *parts* for your message. The appropriate number depends on the nature of the subject matter and other factors, including the length of the message. A six-hundred-page book, for example, may properly include twenty major parts (chapters). On the other hand, a five-page report probably should not contain twenty major parts.

To determine the appropriate major parts, carry in mind the basic concepts of a three-part message: beginning, middle, and ending. However, establish major parts of relatively equal importance as they relate logically to the subject, not as they relate to the three-part plan. As an obvious example, do not label the major parts as "Opening," "Body," and "Ending." Such an outline would communicate nothing about the subject matter and it would lump the bulk of the subject matter into one section—the body.

To divide the message into logical major parts of relatively equal importance, first look at the subject as a whole. For instance, if you write a letter to request a major credit card and a high line of credit, you would not name your political party as a major factor. Political party membership does not logically belong to the subject. Even factors that meet the test of logic may not meet the test of equivalency. For the credit-request letter outline, you might place your credit-payment record as a major part, but would not include your checking-account balance of $132.50 at that same level. If you deal with your checking account at all, you would place it within a major part dealing with assets.

Make the major parts cover the entire topic. For example, a comparison of the forms of business organization in the United States that use partnerships and corporations as the only two major parts would not cover the subject. The writer must add sole proprietorships to complete the coverage.

Also establish parts distinct from one another—parts that do not overlap. For example, if training and development constitute two of the major parts in a study of the personnel function, the two categories have many common elements. Thus, they overlap and cause difficulty for classifying subparts. To eliminate the overlap, make training and development a single topic.

The sheer volume of words necessary for each major part also affects decisions. If the number of words differs too much among the parts, try to adjust the outline to make the parts more nearly equal in size. Suppose little information exists about three contributors to management thought—the topic under consideration. Lumping discussion of them into one category called "Other Contributors" might make the section more nearly equal to parts in the message.

Make the word patterns parallel in the headings for the parts. Choices include:

- All complete sentences
- All verbs and verb phrases

- All nouns and noun phrases
- All adjectives
- All questions
- All declarative statements

Consider the following examples of incorrect and correct parallel word patterns.

INCORRECT	CORRECT
The Manager Plans	Planning
Organize	Organizing
Directing	Directing
Controlling Function	Controlling
Collecting Data	Collection
Organization of Data	Organization
Analyze Data	Analysis
Interpreting	Interpretation

After determining the major parts (at least two) of your message, place them in the order dictated by the selected developmental pattern. Next establish the first level of subparts. Then continue subdividing as necessary. Use essentially the same principles for subdivisions as used for major divisions:

- Establish an appropriate number of subdivisions. At this level, include at least two and no more than ten subdivisions for each category, with the best number probably three to six.
- Establish logical subdivision topics of relatively equal importance.
- Make the subdivisions cover the topic with each subdivision distinct from the others.
- Make the word patterns parallel within each level. However, the patterns may vary among levels. For example, the major parts may use noun phrases, one group of subparts may use adjectives, and another group may use complete sentences.
- Place the subjects in logical order according to the developmental pattern.

Formats The classical format for outlines identifies the major parts of the message as capital roman numerals with periods aligned. More contemporary arrangements identify major parts with arabic numbers. (See Figure 6–1.)

The more contemporary styles do not require the indentation that the traditional format does. However, many writers still use the traditional design.

For your own drafting purposes, choose any of the styles shown—or one of your own design. If others will see the outline, you should use a correct, formal style.

Writing As one good way to bring structure to a message, develop the body first, the opening second, and the ending third. This suggestion applies particularly well to long messages.

```
I.
    A.
        1.
            a.
                (1)
                    (a)
                    (b)
                (2)
            b.
        2.
    B.
II.
    A.
    B.
    C.

1.0
    1.1
        1.11
            1.111
                1.1111
                    1.11111
                    1.11112
                1.1112
            1.112
        1.12
    1.2
2.0
    2.1
    2.2
    2.3

1
    1a
        1a1
            1a1a
                1a1a1
                    1a1a1a
                    1a1a1b
                1a1a2
            1a1b
        1a2
    1b
2
    2a
    2b
    2c
```

FIGURE 6-1 Outline formats.

The *body* of a message may include one paragraph or hundreds of paragraphs. Whatever its length, it contains the substance—the meat—of the message.

The *opening* part of a message occupies less space than the body. However, it plays an important role. It often gains the reader's attention, establishes the background, makes a transition, and introduces the material to follow.

The *ending* section of a message also occupies less space than the body. Like the opening, it serves important purposes. It often summarizes the message, spotlights the conclusion, provides a light touch, adds courtesy, and calls for acceptance and action.

To organize a part, first establish all of the topic sentences for it. Then review them for logic and content. However, do not revise them for structural detail at this point. Instead, move to the paragraphs.

A *paragraph* contains one or more sentences—a topic sentence and any other sentences necessary to develop the topic introduced in it. The beginning of a paragraph makes a transition from the preceding material as it gains the reader's attention and even flashes a forecast of the topic. The topic sentence usually follows the opening words or sentence. Whether it falls at the beginning, the middle, or the end, the *topic sentence* acts as the focal point of the paragraph. It communicates the fundamental message. The body develops the topic and subtopics. An ending word, phrase, or sentence completes the paragraph with a result, a conclusion, a summary, or even an emphatic reinforcement of the topic of the paragraph.

A paragraph probably should contain no more than ten sentences. If a paragraph needs more than ten sentences to develop the topic, subdivide the topic and treat each of the subdivisions in a separate paragraph.

(321 words)

Take and score Self-Test 13 over writing the draft on page 147.

REVISING

People do not ever write well; they only *rewrite* well. Therefore, first develop a draft, and then revise the draft to bring it to final form. To revise a draft, review it for these C's of good messages: (1) correctness, (2) conciseness, (3) clearness, (4) colorfulness, (5) considerateness, and (6) coherence.

Correctness

To create a correct message, make it complete and accurate, and make it mechanically sound. These features form the foundation on which the other characteristics can build.

Completeness and Accuracy

A *complete* message contains everything necessary to create the desired meaning within the receiver. For example, the purpose of a message would fall to defeat through the omission of such information as the date, time, or place of an event, the address to which to send an ordered or requested item, or the exact name, description, color, size, or catalog number of an ordered item.

An *accurate* message has all the facts and details right. Inaccuracies may destroy a message. For example, think of what may—or may not—happen as a result of errors in dates, times, places, addresses, descriptions, colors, sizes, statistical data, and other similar bits of information. Collect and review information carefully; then check and proofread drafts and final copy to assure that the information stays correct. Invoice numbers, stock numbers, dollar amounts, totals, and other numbers create particular problems.

Mechanics

Proper revision of messages requires correction of the mechanics—the rules for language and structure. Many readers react so negatively to errors in mechanics that they do not even think about the content.

Grammar controls the structure and forms of words and guides their arrangement and relationships in phrases and sentences. Thus, grammatical rules deal with such topics as subject-verb agreement, noun-pronoun agreement, and subjective and objective cases of pronouns.

The marks of *puncutation* serve to identify, separate, clarify, interrupt, emphasize, and terminate series of words. Without them a page of words would form an unintelligible blur. They help to provide the rhythm for the written word supplied by pauses and vocal qualities for the spoken word.

Probably second only to grammatical errors, errors in *spelling* cause untold anguish for the educated reader. Thus, the good communicator never misspells a word, paying particular attention to the correct spelling of proper names.

The concern for proper *usage of words* relates both to spelling and grammar. Certain kinds of words lead to common problems. Examples include *accept/except, personal/personnel, affect/effect, counsel/council.*

These examples of misplaced modifiers illustrate the need to understand the *structure of sentences:*

- The woman sitting at the desk with the gray hair supervises this section.
- Rotting in the vegetable bin, he threw the potatoes away.
- The chefs discussed how to make a salad with their assistants.

Whether you write a letter, a memorandum, a formal report, or some other message, you should use the appropriate *format.* For example, letters usually have single spacing, whereas many reports have double spacing. Letters often include salutations; memoranda usually do not.

Appendix B covers many elements important to mechanics. It reviews grammar, punctuation, spelling and pronunciation, usage of words, structure of sentences, use of numbers, possessives, syllabication, capitalization, abbreviations, contractions, footnotes, and bibliographic entries. Appendix D reviews the formats and components of letters. In addition, Chapters 7–9 include many examples of letters. Chapter 10 illustrates correct formats for memos, notes, forms, and some other written channels. Chapters 11 and 12 cover proper styles for written reports.

Conciseness

Good messages take a concise form. A concise message says what it needs to say in a brief way.

As one way to write concisely, use short words in short sentences in short paragraphs. Arrange paragraphs so that the topic sentence appears first or just after any transitional words used. Follow the topic sentence with just enough words to develop the idea.

Brevity, however, can interfere with the other features of good messages. Therefore, the careful communicator does not sacrifice the other features of good messages to attain it. Such features include consideration, correctness, and clearness.

An example of how brevity can defeat clarity occurs when one always chooses a shorter word over a longer word. Long words do not necessarily muddy a passage; neither do short words necessarily clarify it. To illustrate, the following lists contrast some words that have similar meanings. The words in the first column contain one or two syllables. Most of the words in the second column contain three or more syllables—long words according to the readability formulas described in a subsequent section. Decide which word in each pair you would choose for the average reader.

abash	embarrass	ken	knowledge
abet	encourage	obtund	paralyze
bane	nuisance	scion	descendant
cede	surrender	surfeit	sufficiency
cogent	persuasive	tyro	beginner

For conciseness, then, examine the message to eliminate or replace words without breaking structural rules or introducing choppiness. Particularly, remove redundant words. In the following example, observe how the second sentence in each pair uses fewer words to convey the same meaning as the first:

- The delayed shipment seriously obstructed, blocked, and impeded our progress on the project.
- The delayed shipment seriously impeded progress on the project.
- Each of the persons made a significant, substantial, important contribution from her or his own functional specialty.
- Each person contributed substantially from a functional specialty.

Clearness

The English language has about one million words, but people actually use and understand only a small portion of them. Estimates suggest that many people live their entire lives using no more than one or two thousand words. Therefore, to make a message clear, try to choose words that the reader will understand in the way you intend them. Some ways to assure clarity call for using synonyms for obscure words, selecting concrete words over abstract words whenever possible, and defining terms.

Synonyms

For an obscure or unnecessarily long word, try to find a familiar, short word that has about the same meaning—a synonym. A dictionary or a thesaurus can help in locating synonyms. Although many words do have synonyms, many others do not. If the reader likely will not understand the best word, at least in the context in which it appears, recast the sentence, use a series of words, or define the word right then and there.

When using new words, take care to join words in customary patterns—to satisfy idiomatic requirements. For example, though *rife* means abundant, the sentence "The report has a rife number of errors" does not use proper idiom. "The report is rife with errors" does. Correct idiom requires the insertion of *with* after *rife*. Check dictionaries and books on grammar for examples of proper idiom.

Concreteness

Concrete (denotative) words refer to things perceived by the five senses. Thus, they not only help make a message clear, but they also hold the reader's interest better than abstract words do. Words like *desk, tape recorder,* and *paper clip* make direct, concrete references to physical objects. Words like *obscure, politics, indecent,* and *dependence* do not, and therefore may create problems of interpretation. Even words like *gravity, highly, soon, fair, good, excellent, superior, slowly, far,* and *near* can create problems. Therefore, use concrete (even quantitative) words whenever possible. As an example of concreteness, you could replace the hazy phrase "as soon as possible" with a concrete phrase, such as "Please ship the materials to arrive no later than May 12."

In contrast, the deliberate avoidance of concreteness can hide information. For example, disappointment over an attendance of only sixty-five at a dinner for the Citizen of the Year could lead to a news release including these words: "A large number of people attended to pay their respects to Archer."

Because abstract words form an important part of advanced human communication, you cannot always avoid them. However, for clarity, explain them with concrete illustrations. For instance, as a supervisor completing an evaluation form for a new employee, you might write: "She does not seem to be adjusting to her job." Because *adjusting* is abstract, you could expand with these sentences:

> She has averaged three or four serious posting errors a week. Even though two others joined the firm at the same time she did, she consistently produces the smallest number of daily postings in her section. Most significantly, however, all but one of the other clerks have complained at least twice each that she is

rude and uncooperative. I have also found her to act that way. Once when I was trying to help her with a complicated posting, she said, "Get off my back, you jerk."

Avoidance of *this* and *these* as nouns also adds concreteness to messages. Contrast the "pointing" effect created by using *this* as an adjective instead of a noun:

This means that	This action means that . . . .

Definition of Terms

To assure understanding, define any terms that have special meaning for the message. For example, suppose that a message refers to "small farms." Without a definition of "small farms," the message remains incomplete. This example from a questionnaire illustrates how problems might arise from using undefined terms:

What is the size of the company you work for?

_______ Large

_______ Medium

_______ Small

As another example, this question on a credit-application form needs some definition of terms:

List your assets:

List your liabilities:

Colorfulness

Colorfulness adds an important dimension to messages. It holds attention, creates interest, and motivates readers to the acceptance or action desired by the writer. These pairs illustrate the contrast between drab and colorful wording:

bad	wicked	receive	pocket
exaggeration	caricature	tease	vex
hate	loathe	tempt	cajole
informer	turncoat	thin	bony
investigate	snoop	worry	fret

To use color creatively, review it in association with verbs, expletives, freshness, and appropriateness.

Verbs

The preceding list of examples contains several verbs. The following examples also illustrate the importance of verbs to colorfulness by showing how a change in the verb and accompanying sentence structure adds vibrancy to the expression:

1.	The children ate their supper.	The children devoured their supper.
2.	Her skills developed rapidly	Her skills ripened rapidly.
3.	The crowd passes by.	The crowd streams past.
4.	She felt for the keys in her purse.	She groped for the keys in her purse.
5.	Planning is a significant part of the managerial process.	Planning contributes significantly to the managerial process.
6.	It is said by managers that	Managers report that . . . .
7.	There are far too many members on the committee.	The committee has far too many members.

Examples 1, 2, and 3 illustrate the brightness supplied by the use of a metaphor. As a figure of speech, the *metaphor* uses a word or phrase denoting one kind of object or idea as a substitute for a word or phrase in a different context. Such use suggests likeness between the objects or ideas. Thus, to replace *developed* with *ripened* in Example 2 creates a metaphor that projects more excitement than the original form.

Examples 5, 6, and 7 in the list illustrate the dullness of the "to be" verbs:

am	shall be	has been	shall have been
is	will be	have been	could have been
are	may be	had been	should have been
was	etc.		etc.

Because the "to be" verbs perform indispensable grammatical functions, most messages contain some of them. However, when the "to be" verbs predominate, they destroy the vitality of a message. Thus, let sparkling verbs, not nouns and adjectives, carry the action.

Use of the active voice instead of the passive voice helps create color. In the active voice, the subject creates the action. In the passive voice, the subject receives the action. Thus, active voice provides more vigor and animation than passive voice. It also often removes the colorless "to be" verbs from the construction. Observe the difference in the liveliness and directness of these paired expressions:

PASSIVE	ACTIVE
The file cabinet was inspected by Elizabeth.	Elizabeth inspected the file cabinet.
Many decisions must be made by me.	I must make many decisions.

Deliberate use of the passive voice may improve the tone of a negative message, however. Contrast these two sentences:

Complete your report by Friday.

Your report should be completed by Friday.

Though no dramatic difference exists between the two sentences, the second one does not contain the demanding tone of the first. The writer probably will complete the report by Friday in both cases. However, the second statement may make her or him feel better about doing it.

Active-voice sentences often use the first-person pronouns (*I, we, my, our,* etc.) in the *personal* style of writing. In contrast, the passive voice often appears in association with the *impersonal* style (writing without first- and second-person pronouns). Although the impersonal style creates a less dynamic tone than the personal style, some formal messages still require the impersonal style.

Expletives

Examples 6 and 7 of the first list in the section on verbs show the weakness of the use of *it* and *there* as expletives. When words serve only as place-holders, they waste space, muddy meaning, and dull the prose. Not only do expletives use the lifeless "to be" verbs, they also show a haziness of reference. The words, "It is said," hedge on the answer to the question, "Who said?" These examples illustrate how the style improves just by eliminating the expletives:

It has been written that	Jones wrote that . . . .
There are many examples of	Examples abound to explain . . . .
There is no significant difference between	No significant difference exists between . . . .
It is clear that	Clearly
It is too bad that	Unfortunately
It is a foregone conclusion that	Obviously

Expletives prove useful when subordinating negative information, however. Contrast the tones of these two sentences:

You should have said . . . .

It is better to say . . . .

Even in this circumstance—as indeed in most others—the writer may still avoid the expletive by adopting a third choice: "I think you might have said . . . ." The introduction of "I think" into this sentence also illustrates the importance of "owning" one's behavior. Most people accept suggestions better from someone who establishes them as opinions than from someone who treats them as some pronouncement of permanent truth.

Freshness

Form your messages with fresh words. Worn-out, trite, jargon-ridden phrasing usually creates boredom or even arouses negative feelings within receivers. A conversational, personal writing style can make your message warm and fresh. Use contractions and a natural flow of words. However, avoid slipping into the overly casual, "cute," and ungrammatical constructions often used in conversation. Written messages just cannot carry the informality that conversations can.

To keep messages fresh, avoid clichés. The fresh, usually briefer words shown in the right column of the following list replace the clichés in the left column:

along the lines of	like
as a case in point	as an example
as of this date	now
due to	because
effectuate	effect
finalize (prioritize, routinize, positionize, etc.)	finish (replace contrived "ize" words with others)
first and foremost, try to	try to . . . .
for the purposes of	for
for the reason that (on the grounds that)	because
impact on	affect
in accordance with	by
in case of	if
in terms of	in
in the nature of	like
last, but not least	last
on the basis of	by
. . . said as follows:	. . . said:
satisfaction reaction (and other double nouns)	satisfaction (remove one of the nouns or rephrase)
To make a long story short, Mary said	Mary said . . . .
with reference to	about

Appropriateness

When choosing words for color, keep an eye to the appropriate level of formality. These groups of words illustrate the range of formality available for some expressions:

gut feeling	hunch	premonition
all set	ready	prepared
chow down	eat	dine
bellyache		complain
	won't	will not
big shot		celebrity
place	home	abode

The choice of words depends on such factors as the receiver's preferences, the occasion, and the communication channel. An invitation to a formal ball would not call the affair a *bash*. In contrast, an invitation to a few friends to a home would not refer to a *festivity*.

Considerateness

Review messages to show *considerateness* for the receiver. Check for (1) courtesy, (2) positive style, (3) "you" attitude, and (4) nondiscriminatory words and other symbols.

Courtesy

Common courtesy strengthens messages. These examples show the simple kinds of words that help greatly to convert blunt messages into courteous ones:

Best wishes	Ladies and Gentlemen
Dear Ms.	May I
I look forward to	Please
If you can	Thank you
If you like	You are invited

Positive Style

Courtesy alone cannot overcome a negative style. Therefore, the whole message should reflect a positive style, as these pairings of negative and positive expressions illustrate:

You obviously did not follow the instructions.	The instructions suggest that you . . . .
You should have known that the warranty does not provide for	Although the warranty does provide for . . . it does not include . . . .
We are sorry, but we no longer carry the sweater you ordered in tan.	Although we no longer have the sweater you orered in tan, we can give it to you in the attractive beige shown in the enclosed brochure.
Because you sent the wrong . . . we cannot	As soon as you send . . . we shall be able to . . . .

"You" Attitude

The "you" attitude concentrates on the other person. With genuine empathy—focus on the reader's needs and point of view—the "you" attitude will pervade the entire message. These examples show how words can introduce the "you" attitude:

Would you like to . . . .

Thank you for the . . . .

I liked working with you on the project.

You may want . . . .

You now have credit at . . . .

Some teachers and receivers suggest that the first-person pronouns (*I, we, my,* etc.) detract from the "you" attitude. Others suggest that the first-person pronouns contribute to a vital writing style without defeating the "you" attitude. The scales seem to tip *toward* the use of first-person pronouns.

To avoid offending receivers who do not like the first-person pronouns, avoid *overusing* them. Particularly avoid beginning every sentence or paragraph with *I* or *we*. In most cases you can keep the active voice and personal style without overuse of the first-person pronouns.

Of course, the impersonal writing style required for some formal channels prohibits the use of either first- or second-person pronouns. When using the impersonal style, then, incorporate the "you" attitude through dynamic writing and substantive content. Make your interest in the reader shine through in spite of the impersonal style.

Nondiscriminatory Symbols

Consideration of the reader calls for the use of nondiscriminatory symbols, symbols that do not stereotype individuals on the basis of some characteristic common to or imputed to a class of humans. Such characteristics include race, ethnicity, age, sex, handicap, and religion.

The most pervasive discrimination in communication attaches to the characteristic of sex. The language proves unfair to both sexes, but particularly unfair to females. Therefore, to avoid sexist messages, remove all references that treat the male as the norm and that cast people into sex-based roles.

Because of the extensiveness of sexism in the language, Appendix C includes guidelines for nonsexist communication. However, a few examples appear here, along with some for the other kinds of discrimination. Observe how the revised expressions remove discriminatory references without hurting the idiom at all:

Each manager should be sure that his	All managers should be sure that their . . . .
Suppose an executive told his secretary that she should	Suppose an executive told a secretary to . . . .
In all the history of mankind	In all the history of humankind . . . .
The firemen, policemen, and garbagemen	The firefighters, police officers, and garbage collectors . . . .
As drunk as an Indian	Drunk
Welfare recipients do not support this legislation, because it would take away their gravy train.	Some welfare recipients do not support this legislation, because they say it would remove some deserving people from the rolls.
I tried to Jew the salesman down on the price.	I haggled with the salesperson over the price.

Did you hear the joke about the Polack who	Did you hear the joke about the man/woman/person who . . . .
Neither black nor white	Neither bad nor good
Old fogy	Fogy
Golden years	Older years
Plain Jane	Ordinary in appearance
At the meeting she came across like a cross-eyed fool.	At the meeting she came across as a frenzied person.
Holy Rollers	Emotional worshipers

Nondiscriminatory symbols support human dignity, and they avoid the legal implications of discriminatory language. People have begun to file and win suits on the basis of discrimination in messages such as job descriptions and job titles.

Coherence

The final stage of revision requires a review of the entire message to assure coherence. Coherence occurs when the parts fit together in an orderly way to form a unified whole. To assure coherence, check for (1) transition, (2) awkward construction, (3) pace, (4) consistency, and (5) readability.

Transition

Transitional devices connect the parts—whether phrases, sentences, paragraphs, or sections. The following suggestions contribute to transition:

1. Prepare the reader for what will follow. Example: *"Although you may know that . . . "*
2. Use transitional words such as:

accordingly	finally	on the other hand
afterwards	for example	otherwise
again	furthermore	rather
also	however	similarly
and	in addition	still
as a result	in contrast	subsequently
at the same time	in spite of	then
besides	like	therefore
but	likewise	thus
conversely	moreover	to illustrate
despite	nevertheless	unlike
even so	next	yet

3. Use a pronoun to refer to a word or phrase in the preceding sentence. Example: "Avoid the 'to be' verbs. Compared to many other verbs, *they* have no spirit."
4. Use the same word or phrase to introduce successive sentences. Example:

"*Select words* carefully. *Select words* that make the message correct, concise, clear, colorful, considerate, and coherent."

5. Use numerical sequences of items. Example: "Use three steps to accomplish the task. *First, . . . Second, . . . Third, . . .* "
6. Use the same word in successive sentences. Example: "Avoid *using* 'this,' and 'these' as nouns. *Using* them introduces a weak, indefinite writing style. Also avoid *using* nouns as adjectives, as in 'this type person.' Nouns do not modify other nouns."
7. Use the first and last sentences of paragraphs to carry the meaning forward. Example: ". . . *Transitional devices* contribute a great deal to coherence.

   One such transitional device requires the writer to. . . . "

Awkwardness

To assure unity and coherence, restructure awkward sentences. All of the rules for good writing apply to such restructuring. This example of revision shows some ways to remove awkwardness:

> Though 15 people from our department (accounting) attended the workshop, 12 of them, including Jerry Bale, had no background for the topic of the workshop ("Advanced Sampling Techniques for the Auditor") offered by the CPA Association of Des Moines last week.

> Last week 15 people from our accounting department attended the workshop on Advanced Sampling Techniques for the Auditor. The CPA Association of Des Moines conducted it. Of the 15 who attended, Jerry Bale and 11 others did not have the background for it.

Pace

Appropriate *pace* also contributes to the coherence of a message. Good pace uses emphasis, subordination, and variety.

Emphasis of ideas can occur through several devices:

1. Place an important idea in context with other important ideas.
2. Position the key idea at the beginning or the end of the structural unit—sentence, paragraph, section, or longer unit.
3. Choose the developmental pattern on the basis of desired emphasis.
4. Repeat key ideas.
5. Place the vital idea in an independent clause, with the subordinate clauses and phrases supporting it.
6. Use transitional words and phrases that feature the most important idea.
7. Use attention-getting words.
8. Choose words that present the idea in the most vivid and active forms.
9. Preview and summarize key ideas.
10. Use, but do not overuse, mechanical devices: underlines, exclamation points, spacing, frames built with lines or space, indented formats, blocked formats, all capitals, dashes, different styles of type, different colors, special arrangements of letters, and variations in headings.

To *subordinate* ideas, simply reverse the suggestions for emphasizing ideas. For instance, place a negative idea in the body of a message—not at the beginning or ending.

To give a message a pleasant pace, use a *variety* of sentence structures. Mix the four basic sentence types to do so.

Standard sentences place the subject first and the verb second. They may also include modifiers, direct objects, indirect objects, and complements:

- Lynne sang well.
- The purchasing manager ordered the materials.
- Harold is a blonde.

The *parallel sentence* emphasizes coordinate parts. The featured words, phrases, and clauses often appear in a series:

- To communicate well is to live well.
- Courtesy, positiveness, empathy—these qualities contribute significantly to good tone.

Like the parallel sentence, the *balanced sentence* spotlights coordinate elements. However, the balanced sentence contrasts the coordinate ideas. The appropriate conjunction becomes *but* instead of *and*:

- People should use nondiscriminatory language—not because they fear lawsuits, but because they respect human dignity.
- The true test of the manager lies not in the ability to issue orders, but in the ability to order issues.

The *periodic sentence* uses a series of words, phrases, or clauses to build to a climax:

- To understand others, to understand the interaction between you and others, understand yourself.
- Through thinking, through face-to-face transactions, through mediated transactions, through person-to-group transactions, one becomes a whole communicator.

Consistency

Consistency contributes to coherence in messages. Thus, establish consistency in such factors as writing style, format, use of numbers and abbreviations, and parallel structure. In the following examples, observe the improvement evident in the second message of each pair:

He likes swimming, to jog, and tennis.	He likes to swim, to jog, and to play tennis.

The men's group and the ladies' group met for a planning session.	The men's group and the women's group met for a planning session.

Readability

All of the preceding suggestions point toward readable copy. However, a special concept—readability—deals with calculations of message density.

Since the early 1920s researchers have developed more than fifty readability formulas. The Flesch Reading Ease score and the Gunning Fog index represent two of the most-used formulas. Both formulas yield results expressed at *grade level* of reading difficulty. For application of the Flesch formula, see *The Art of Readable Writing*[1] and "A New Readability Yardstick."[2]

Calculation of the Gunning Fog Index follows these steps paraphrased from *The Technique of Clear Writing:*

1. Randomly choose several samples of about one hundred words each. Count the number of words. Count the number of sentences. Find the average sentence length by dividing the number of words by the number of sentences.
2. Count the number of hard words (words of three or more syllables). Do not count proper names. Do not count words formed by combining short, easy words (for example, bookkeeping, grandmother). Do not count verb forms that become three syllables because of the addition of "-ed" or "-es." Divide the number of hard words by the total number of words and multiply by 100. This number is the percent of hard words in the passage.
3. To obtain the Fog Index, add the average sentence length and the percent of hard words. Multiply the result by 0.4.[3]

Apply the Gunning Fog Index to this passage about the use of readability formulas:

> Formulas are for *rating,* not for *writing.* Since the variables in the formula were selected only as indices of difficulty . . . changing them does not necessarily cause the difficulty of the writing to change accordingly. What you frequently get when you make such changes is an artificially altered readability score, one that is not reflected in increased comprehension by the reader. The changes needed in rewriting are more subtle and complex than a formula can suggest. . . .
>
> Once your material has been rewritten (without regard to the formula), *then* apply the formula again. If the material now appears to be appropriate, fine. If not, rewrite again and apply the formula again.
>
> If this business of checking readability, rewriting, checking again, then rewriting again, seems time-consuming or difficult—it is, at first. After some experience, however, you usually get a feel for the appropriate level for a given body of readers, and the process gets much faster and easier. Readers are likely to be turned off by writing that seems unnecessarily difficult. Your extra time will not only save *time* for them, perhaps even thousands of hours; it will also encourage them to read more of what you have written. And that is what readable writing is all about.[4]

For such a brief passage, base your readability calculation on all of it. Counting and calculating yield these data:

Number of words	= 206	Number of hard words	= 35
Number of sentences	= 13	Percent of hard words	= 17
Average sentence length	= 16	Gunning Fog Index	= 13

Thus, the Gunning Fog Index suggests that the material falls at the 13th-grade (college) level.

Robert Gunning places a "danger line" for reading difficulty between the 12th and 13th grades. He labels the 10th grade and lower as the "easy-reading range." Thus, he leaves the 11th and 12th grades in a range of moderate difficulty.[5]

To analyze the difficulty of reading material from another viewpoint, consider Michel Lipman and Russell Joyner's summary of appropriate proportions of adults who can read at the various grade levels:[6]

School Grade Level	Approximate Percent of Adults Who Can Read at This Level
5th	93%
6th	90%
7th	88%
8–9th	76%
9th	52%
College	24%
College graduates	6%

As a warning about application of the summary, Lipman and Joyner write: "Like all charts, this is an approximation. It is intended as a guide to readability rather than . . . [estimates] yielding scientific accuracy."[7]

Occasionally check the readability level of your own writing. If it falls much above the ninth or tenth grade, you may want to examine your style.

TRANSMITTING

Transmitting follows selecting, drafting, and revising a message. For written messages, the transmitting stage includes putting the revised draft into final form, selecting the proper stationery and format, making necessary copies, and delivering them to the receivers. This section reviews the mechanics of letter formats and some of the modern equipment, services, and systems now in use.

Stationery and Format for Business Letters

To write letters, apply the guidelines for effective communication and the principles for good writing. For the mechanics associated with writing letters, use an appropriate format and establish the proper components of the letter, as detailed in Appendix D.

The basic formats of letters include (1) block, (2) modified block with blocked paragraphs, (3) modified block with indented paragraphs, and (4) simplified. The continuation page also has a defined format.

A letter can include as many as 15 parts: (1) stationery and letterhead/return address, (2) date line, (3) special designations, (4) inside address, (5) attention line, (6) salutation, (7) subject line, (8) body, (9) complimentary close, (10) company name, (11) signature block, (12) reference initials, (13) enclosure notation, (14) copy notation, and (15) postscript. The simplified format does not include a salutation and complimentary close; however, it does include a subject line as a fixed part.

Addresses on envelopes should parallel the inside addresses. Do not include the attention line and the special designations in the same position, however. Observe postal regulations when addressing envelopes. Also use correct methods for folding letters for insertion into envelopes. You should become thoroughly familiar with the mechanics of letter transmitting given in Appendix D, and use that reference material frequently.

Equipment, Services, and Systems for Transmitting

Dictation Equipment

Dictation equipment provides for dictation of messages into a recorder for conversion into printed form. Desk-top portable dictation machines use microphones attached to the recorders. Centralized systems use standard telephones connected to a central recorder.

The two basic centralized systems use private wire systems and private branch exchange (PBX). The private systems do not connect with telephone company equipment. The PBX systems do.

Standard and Electric Typewriters

Certainly the typewriter contributes significantly to the encoding and transmitting process. Modern typewriters allow the typist to type faster than ever before. Additional features include rapid correction of errors and the quick change of styles of type.

Automatic Typewriters

By attaching a recorder to the Selectric typewriter, IBM introduced the era of the automatic typewriter. The attachment makes possible the storage, correction, revision, recall, and reproduction of information at rapid rates. Now various makes and models allow operators to insert selected cards containing prerecorded information to produce custom-ordered, errorless messages at speeds of about four hundred words a minute.

Duplicating Equipment

Several kinds of machines for producing copies of messages (reprography) substantially reduce the work of the communicator.

Photocopying equipment contributes significantly to the communication process. For one copy or hundreds, copiers do the work formerly left to carbon paper, spirit duplicators, mimeograph machines, offset press, and printers. Some copiers make copies at the rate of about eighty a minute.

The offset press and printers still serve important duplicating functions. Modern phototypesetting processes have reduced considerably the time necessary to produce good copy. Printing proves particularly good for mass messages because it reduces the demand for space by about forty percent, thus bringing significant savings in paper and distribution costs.

Mail and Messenger Services

The United States Postal Service provides the largest mail service in the country. Details of some of its services appear in Appendix D. Private concerns also provide personal message-delivery service. The United Parcel Service (UPS) specializes in delivering packages. Courier services such as Purolator and Federal Express make one-day deliveries between cities served by major airports.

Electronic Mail Service

Through the use of private lines, telephone lines, Western Union (TWX, Telex, and Mailgrams), laser beams, facsimile equipment, computer-to-computer hookups, and typewriter-to-typewriter hookups, communicators now transmit messages electronically. The encoder inserts a message at one end of the connection, and it appears in readable form at the other.

Electronic mail service requires special equipment. However, because of the speed of transmission, more and more businesses take advantage of it.

Word Processing

Word processing is a relatively new integrated approach to the transmitting act. *Dartnell's Glossary of Word Processing Terms* defines word processing as "the automatic production of typed documents or the automation of secretarial work."[8] Helen M. McCabe and Estelle L. Popham suggest that the "systems approach deals with office procedures, personnel, and equipment as an organized whole, rather than with each part separately."[9]

Someone encodes the unit messages. However, once internal to the word processing equipment, someone may retrieve and even combine them to produce individually typewritten messages at rapid speed.

For a single letter, the dictator usually outlines the letter and dictates it in final form into the recorder—a much more rapid process than handwriting. The word processor uses the appropriate transcribing equipment to listen to the recording and type the final copy.

The transcription process usually involves a rough draft on the automatic typewriter or printer, which stores the draft message even as the processor types it. The processor then proofreads the draft and corrects errors on the stored draft. Then he or she sets the equipment to type the corrected message automatically.

The potential contribution of the word processing concept staggers the mind. McCabe and Popham write:

> Most experts agree that automated office systems are not far off and that word processing is the most likely means for bringing them about. Case studies indicate that a start is already being made to combine word processing and data processing. These efforts—together with new advances in telecommunications and records management—may produce the long-awaited total management information system. . . .[10]

To follow this chapter on basic principles of writing, Chapters 7 and 8 move to the specific types of messages transmitted by letters. Appendix D covers the different formats and components of letters.

SUMMARY

In a shift from receiving activities to sending activities, this chapter covers principles of writing. To write well, apply the guidelines for effective communication (Chapter 2), draft the message, revise the message, and use transmitting instruments efficiently.

Drafting requires two primary activities: writing and organizing. Some people prefer organizing first, then writing; others prefer the *just-write* technique of writing first, then organizing. Perhaps the best method uses a combination: (1) Use the just-write technique to spill key words on paper. (2) Organize the key words into a rough preliminary outline for a chosen developmental pattern. (3) Use the just-write technique to unload thoughts about each part of the outline. (4) Revise the outline if necessary. (5) Use the just-write technique to write the entire draft. (6) Complete the organization during the revising stage.

Developmental patterns for organization include: (1) indirect, (2) direct, (3) chronological, (4) spatial, (5) analytical, (6) comparative, and (7) ranked. Writers of business messages tend to use the indirect and direct patterns more than they do the others.

Outlines may include topics or short sentences. To establish the parts of an outline, divide the whole message into major parts of about equal importance. Then partition each part into subdivisions of about equal importance. Maintain parallel structure for the headings that identify parts. Select a format for an outline from the classical or more contemporary styles. Include at least two headings at each level chosen.

To write a draft, write the body first, the opening second, the ending third. Use topic sentences and paragraphs to form a coherent message.

To revise a draft, review it for (1) correctness, (2) conciseness, (3) clearness, (4) colorfulness, (5) considerateness, and (6) coherence.

For correctness, attend to completeness and accuracy, and to mechanics. For completeness, include everything necessary to create the desired meaning within the receiver. For accuracy, get all the facts and details right. For proper mechanics, take care of grammar, punctuation, spelling, usage of words, structure of sentences, format, and other such factors (reviewed in Appendixes B and D).

A concise message says what it needs to say in a brief way. Basically, use short words in short sentences in short paragraphs. Do not emphasize conciseness to the exclusion of the other qualities, however.

A clear message results from the application of all of the suggestions for good writing. However, some specific aids include the use of familiar words, concrete words, and definitions of terms.

Colorfulness holds attention, creates interest, and motivates receivers to the action desired by the writer. To introduce color, use vibrant and active verbs, avoid the use of "it" and "there" as expletives, use fresh words instead of worn-out words, and keep the words appropriate to the level of formality of the message.

For considerateness, review messages for (1) courtesy, (2) positive style, (3) "you" attitude, and (4) nondiscriminatory symbols. All of these elements emphasize empathy—putting oneself into the ideas and feelings of the other. Appendix C includes some guidelines for nonsexist communication.

Coherence exists when the parts of a message fit together in an orderly way to form a unified whole. To assure coherence, include good transitions, avoid awkward constructions, set a good pace, establish consistency, and make the message readable. One special concept of readability involves the calculation of a readability index, often reported as a grade level. The chapter illustrates the application of one such formula, the Gunning Fog Index.

Basic letter formats include (1) block, (2) modified block with blocked paragraphs, (3) modified block with indented paragraphs, and (4) simplified. A letter can have as many as 15 parts. Appendix D offers a detailed explanation of the proper methods for putting your written message into the form of a business letter.

Both personal and external transmitting instruments contribute to sending a message. Transmitting includes putting the revised draft into final form, selecting the proper stationery and format, making necessary copies, and delivering them to the receivers. External instruments and services include dictation equipment, typewriters, duplicating equipment, mail and messenger services, and electronic mail service. As a contemporary system, word processing involves the automatic production of typed documents through the automation of secretarial work. It integrates office procedures, personnel, and equipment into an organized whole.

EXERCISES

1. You are the personnel manager for a corporation based in Kansas City. Your new hiring procedures have been approved by all of the appropriate people. You must now commit the procedures to paper and distribute them to all of the people involved in the hiring process. Answer these questions:
   a. What are your purposes for printing and distributing the procedures? What are the readers' purposes for reading? Who are you in this situation? Who are the readers? What is the environment?
   b. What writing channel is appropriate for these procedures?
   c. What are the types of potential and actual interference involved in this communication situation? How will you control the interference?
   d. How will you print and distribute the procedures in light of the purposes, the participants, the environment, the channel, and the interference?
   e. How will you use feedback from and to the readers of your procedures?
   f. How will you evaluate at each stage of the communication process?

   You need not write the actual procedures.
2. Meet with your group. Determine and discuss the special problems associated with written messages. What can you as good communicators do to overcome some of the problems? Have a member of your group read your group's conclusions and suggestions to the rest of the class.
3. [*Your professor will time this exercise.*] You are the Director of Employee Communications at an automobile assembly plant. You are asked to write a memorandum that will be distributed to 300 of your employees. In the memorandum you must let the employees know that:
   a. They will be laid off for six weeks.
   b. They are free to look for other jobs.
   c. The automobile industry is currently depressed, hence the decision to lay off employees.
   d. These particular employees are being laid off because they are the most recently hired.
   e. All questions and comments concerning the layoff should be directed to the employee communications office; no other department will accept questions or comments.
   f. The employees' last paychecks will be mailed to them; they are not to come to the plant to get them.

   Write the memorandum. Remember to try to soften the impact of the bad news. You may wish to discuss the difficulty of this task with your group after you have completed the memorandum. One question you might discuss: Would another channel have been more appropriate in this communication situation? Why?
4. Visit the showroom of an office-machines dealer who specializes in word-processing equipment. Learn the characteristics and capacities of four or five different types of equipment. Write a one- or two-page summary of your findings.
5. Write a one- or two-paragraph body of a letter or memorandum for each of these situations.
   a. Jessie Jones is six weeks late on his house payment. He has never been late before. Your company owns the house.
   b. Your company is forced to charge more than was originally agreed upon for the office furniture it is building for Wiggins, Higgins, and Smart, a law firm.
   c. The daughter of one of your company's welders has just received a scholar-

ship to study at the Harvard Business School. You know that the welder, Sara Smith, is quite proud of her daughter. Write one paragraph for a letter to Sara Smith and a different paragraph for her daughter, Elizabeth Smith.

   d. You are ordering six boxes of parchment bond (item 606) and two book cabinets (item 409B) from the Fairlington Office Supply Co. You want the paper in white and the cabinets in oak. You want the paper to be sent within two weeks or not at all. You are in no hurry for the book cabinets.

   e. You wish to set up an interview with Robert James, the accounting manager at the firm for which you would like to work. You earned a B.B.A. in accounting, were an honor graduate, plan to take your C.P.A. examinations next month, and worked as an accounting intern for two summers. You would be willing to relocate if necessary.

   f. You are interested in purchasing the services of the Oklahoma Consulting Group (OCG). You want the OCG to do a communication audit at your firm. You want to know if the OCG has experience in communication auditing, how much an audit will cost, and when the audit could be conducted.

   g. You ordered a copy of *Even Timid People Can Manage a Big Business* from the R. I. Poff Publishing Co. You placed your order six months ago and the check you sent with the order was cashed five months ago. You want your book as soon as possible. If you cannot have the book, you want your money back.

6. You have noticed that your employees' written messages are difficult to read and often do not contain the appropriate information. Several of your employees stated that they are aware of the problem, but really do not know how to approach their writing projects. You assured them that you would give them some assistance in the form of a paper that describes the four steps of writing (selecting, drafting, revising, and transmitting). You promised that your paper would contain practical advice on accomplishing each of the steps. Write the three- or four-page paper.

7. Write one or two paragraphs that illustrate each of the seven developmental plans: (1) indirect, (2) direct, (3) chronological, (4) spatial, (5) analytical, (6) comparative, and (7) ranked.

8. You must write James Sea a letter denying his request for an interview with your company's Transportation Department. Sea wants to work in the department, but no openings exist. He has indicated that he is also interested in a position in the Office Services Department, where you do have an opening. Although he is overqualified for that, you do want to let him know about it. Develop a topic outline for the letter to James Sea.

9. Develop a sentence outline from the topic outline you prepared in Question 8.

10. Using the sentence outline you developed for Question 9, write the letter to James Sea.

11. You have just been asked to write a memorandum that deals with the relative merits of brainstorming. You know that one of the best ways to begin the writing process is to immediately write down every remotely relevant thought that you have on the subject about which you must write. Now take a piece of paper and write down everything that comes into your mind about the subject of brainstorming. You need not put the material into memorandum form.

12. Write end-of-message time-and-place paragraphs for these situations:

   a. You want a job applicant to send you his résumé by September 6. You need the résumé by then because your boss will leave for a two-month vacation on September 7, and she makes all the hiring decisions.

   b. You want an overdue payment to be sent to you by December 1. The overdue amount is $39.43.
   c. You need to know by October 1 whether the receiver will be able to speak at the October 15 conference in Muncie, Indiana.
   d. You want the receiver to meet you at the Carel, Montana, office on either March 6 or March 13. You need to know by March 1 which date is acceptable.
   e. You want 40 reams of 20-pound bond to be sent to you by January 30. If the paper will not reach you by then, you do not want it at all.

13. Find a two- or three-page piece of your own writing, perhaps the paper you wrote for Question 6. Use the Gunning Fog Index to determine the readability index for your work.
14. Use your dictionary and thesaurus to create meanings for these words. Use the words when you think, write, and speak so that you feel comfortable using them.
   a. Albeit
   b. Chronological
   c. Diligent
   d. Discourse
   e. Inevitable
   f. Integrity
   g. Mediate
   h. Realistic
   i. Systematic
   j. Tendency
15. Take and score Self-Test 14 over Chapter 6.

SELF-TEST 13
Excerpt about Writing the Draft

A. Recall (33 points each). For each multiple-choice question, select the most accurate answer.

1. Unless the message is relatively short, which part should you write first?
   a. Opening
   b. Body
   c. Ending
   d. Address
   e. Summary
2. What is the practical upper limit for the number of sentences in a paragraph?
   a. Fifteen
   b. Ten
   c. Five
   d. No limit exists
   e. Six or seven

B. Inference (34 points). Indicate whether this statement is true or false.

1. Once you have written the body of a message, the opening and ending are easier to write.

SOLUTION

A. Recall (33 points each)
1. b   2. b

B. Inference (34 points)
1. True

SELF-TEST 14
Chapter 6

A. Recall (25 points each). For each multiple-choice question, select the most accurate answer.

1. Analytical development is most clearly found in:
   - **a.** A message that unfolds through space rather than time
   - **b.** Comparative messages
   - **c.** Sequential patterns in a message
   - **d.** Chronological ordering of a message
   - **e.** Messages that first describe the wholes and then the parts that make up the wholes
2. An important purpose of the opening of a message is to:
   - **a.** Gain the receiver's attention
   - **b.** Present the major argument
   - **c.** Summarize the message
   - **d.** Establish who the writer is
   - **e.** Describe the main points of the message
3. Which set of words does not represent the correct parallel structure?
   - **a.** Plan, organize, direct, and control
   - **b.** Collecting, analyzing, and interpretation
   - **c.** Explaining, describing, and understanding
   - **d.** Who, what, when, and where
   - **e.** Select, organize, draft, revise, and transmit

B. Inference (25 points). Indicate whether this statement is true or false.

1. The concept of readability is not pertinent to oral messages.

SOLUTION

A. Recall (25 points each)

1. e
2. a
3. b

B. Inference (25 points)

1. False

ENDNOTES

1. Rudolf Flesch, *The Art of Readable Writing,* 25th anniv. ed. (New York: Harper & Row Publishers, Inc., 1974), 247–50.
2. Rudolf Flesch, "A New Readability Yardstick," *Journal of Applied Psychology* 32 (June 1948): 255.
3. Robert Gunning, *The Technique of Clear Writing,* rev. ed. (New York: McGraw-Hill Book Company, 1968), 38. The Gunning Fog Index (SM) is the property of Gunning-Mueller Clear Writing Institute and is used with permission.
4. George R. Klare, *A Manual for Readable Writing* (Glen Burnie, Md.: REM Company, 1975), 48.
5. Gunning, *Technique of Clear Writing,* 40.
6. Michel Lipman and Russell Joyner, *How to Write Clearly* (San Francisco: International Society for General Semantics, 1979), 8.

7. Lipman and Joyner, *How to Write Clearly,* 8.
8. *Dartnell's Glossary of Word Processing Terms* (Chicago: The Dartnell Corporation, 1975), 47.
9. Helen M. McCabe and Estelle L. Popham, *Word Processing: A Systems Approach to the Office* (New York: Harcourt Brace Jovanonich, Inc., 1977), 1–2.
10. McCabe and Popham, *Word Processing,* 1–2.

STUDENT'S OBJECTIVES:

1 To apply the guidelines for effective communication and the principles of writing to neutral and good-news messages

2 To learn to write neutral direct-response solicitors such as orders, inquiries, and requests

3 To learn to write neutral indirect-response solicitors such as announcements, notices, general invitations, and messages of transmittal

7

WRITING NEUTRAL AND GOOD-NEWS MESSAGES

4 To learn to write neutral letters of response such as acknowledgments, approvals, information and explanation, and instructions and directions

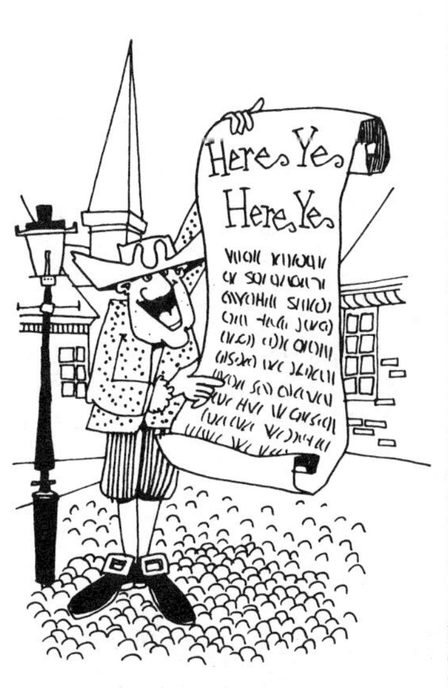

5 To learn to write good-news messages such as favorable responses to substantive requests and personal messages to announce an award or honor

Letters fall into three broad categories: (1) neutral and good-news messages, (2) bad-news messages, and (3) persuasive messages. This chapter covers the first type. Chapters 8 and 9 deal with the other two.

WRITING NEUTRAL MESSAGES

Neutral letters form a major portion of the day-to-day communication transactions of business. As the word *neutral* suggests, such letters carry messages that fall somewhere between good news and bad news. Thus, elements of both good and bad news often spill over into them.

The routineness of neutral letters makes them relatively easy to develop. The style usually requires these features:

- Direct or descending-rank pattern of development
- Straightforwardness
- Courtesy
- Conciseness
- Correctness
- Completeness
- Clearness
- Closing that calls for action (dated when appropriate)
- Provision of channel for feedback

Neutral messages take three forms: (1) direct-response solicitors, (2) indirect-response solicitors, and (3) responses.

Direct-Response Solicitors

Direct-response solicitors overtly ask receivers to supply something or do something in direct response to the messages. To gain the desired response, provide complete, specific information about what you want. Apply this basic principle to these three kinds of direct-response solicitors: (1) orders, (2) inquiries, and (3) requests.

Orders

The letter, telephone, order blank, requisition form, and purchase-order form all provide communication channels for ordering. When ordering goods or services, supply all appropriate information: catalog numbers (if available), names and descriptions of items (including colors, sizes, qualities, and model numbers, if necessary), quantities, unit prices, price extensions (total item prices), and weights. In addition, include shipping instructions, descriptions of how you are paying or will pay, names and addresses of receivers, and desired dates of delivery.

Figure 7-1 illustrates a letter ordering material goods. Observe that the

MODULAR MANUFACTURING

707 S. W. Avenue
Mulga, AL 35118
(700) 221-2111

January 21, 198X

Resa Suppliers
6092 Super Street
Picacho, AZ 85241

ORDER FOR $2,736.33 WORTH OF EQUIPMENT

Please ship these items as listed in your January sales brochure:

Qty.	Name of Item	Cat. No.	Lbs.	Price	Total Price
1	Drill press with ½-HP motor	7-1139A	235	$ 489.48	$ 489.48
2	¾-HP drill	6-2222C	9	74.92	149.84
2	½-HP automatic scroll saw	9-4123A	9	84.39	168.78
1	Metal-turning lathe and cabinet	7-2491A	500	2,148.60	2,148.60
			753		$2,956.70
	Less 10% Preferred Customer discount				295.67
					$2,661.03
	Plus Shipping Charges @ $.10 a lb.				75.30
					$2,736.33

Please ship the equipment, freight prepaid, to arrive no later than February 28. Please bill us at the established 2/20, n/60 terms.

Y. R. Self

Y. R. Self
Shop Supervisor

YRS:jt

FIGURE 7-1 Order for merchandise.

letter meets the principles for writing this response-soliciting message: directness, courtesy, conciseness, correctness, completeness and detail, clearness, a closing that calls for dated action, and clear provision of a channel for feedback. Notice that the use of columns contributes to efficient application of these principles.

Inquiries

As indicated by its name, the inquiry simply seeks information by asking questions. To develop successful inquiries, again make sure that the receiver knows exactly what you want and how you want to receive it.

Business inquiries deal with products, services, employment, credit, operations and procedures, and other topics.

Employment A potential employer often writes to a former employer to inquire about a job applicant's qualities, attitudes, and performance. The name of the former employer may or may not appear as a reference on the applicant's data sheet. A potential employer also often writes to character references listed by an applicant.

In either a preprinted form or a letter, the potential employer can ask specific questions about a prospective employee. To illustrate, which of these queries would better elicit an informative response:

> What kind of employee was Ms. Milam when she was with your firm?
>
> Would you please briefly evaluate Ms. Milam's abilities as an employee with your firm by rating these factors from 10 (high) to 1 (low): (1) job performance, (2) written and oral communication arts and skills, (3) dependability, (4) cooperativeness, and (5) absenteeism?

Most respondents prefer the second type, because answering specific questions proves easier than having to write general statements or trying to guess what kind of information the inquirer wants.

Confidentiality becomes an important consideration when inquiring about people. Court rulings and legislation have opened many personnel files. Therefore, no one can ever promise absolute confidentiality. However, if writers assure receivers that they act as professionals and will keep all information confidential, they reduce the likelihood of legal action significantly. Because of even the slight chance of legal action, however, many respondents to inquiries about people avoid making any negative statements. Therefore, as a potential employer, question the validity and value of any such responses that you receive.

Figure 7-2 provides an example of a letter of inquiry about a former employee. Examine it for all of the qualities of good routine direct-response solicitors. Particularly observe that the letter courteously asks specific questions in concise form. It includes suggestions for quantitative criteria upon which to base a part of the evaluation. It also assures confidentiality.

Credit Many letters involve simple inquiries about the payment records and credit ratings of applicants for credit with a company. Credit investigators use

ALLTHEANGLES, INC.
21918 44 Street, N.W.
Dover, DE 19901

April 19, 198X

Elsburg Corporation
3221 Daniel Avenue
Nixon, NJ 08818

Attention: Mr. Watergate

Ladies and Gentlemen:

Katherine Jones-Bush has applied to us for a position as a computer programmer. She has listed you as a former employer. Acting in your professional capacity, would you please answer a few confidential questions about Ms. Jones-Bush's tenure with you:

1. How long did she work for you as a computer programmer?
2. Relative to all computer programmers who have worked for you, in which of these classes would you place her performance? Upper 5%, upper 10%, upper 25%, upper 50%, lower 50%, lower 25%, lower 10%, lower 5%.
3. Under what circumstances did she leave your employ?
4. How did she get along with her co-workers?
5. How did she get along with her supervisors and managers?
6. How was her attendance?
7. Would you hire her again as a computer programmer? Why?

We shall appreciate your responses to these questions—and any other information that might help us in our decision.

Sincerely yours,

Y. R. Self

Y. R. Self
Director of Personnel

jt

FIGURE 7–2 Inquiry about an applicant for employment.

forms and telephone queries as much as they use letters. The same kinds of precautions about confidentiality apply to credit transactions as apply to employment transactions.

As an illustration of a routine credit inquiry, suppose that you work in the credit department of a large retail store and receive a completed application blank from Myron Dalton. You then call or write agencies such as his bank, the credit references he listed on the application, the appropriate credit bureau, and, if he owns a business, such reporting organizations as Dun & Bradstreet. Figure 7-3 illustrates one such message. The letter contains direct, brief questions in a courteous package. It provides blanks within the letter itself so that the respondent can answer easily. It also refers to confidentiality.

Operations and procedures Case Study 1 illustrates the evolution of an inquiry about organizational operations and procedures. As you read the case study, notice how it applies the six guidelines developed in Chapter 2.

Case Study 1: Inquiry Letter

You want to open a motorcycle dealership in Bend, Oregon. You know that dealerships already exist there for David Harleyson, Zukisu, Yemehee, and Cudati motorcycles. Therefore, you decide that the dealerships for Sakikawa and Dohaka form the best business possibilities. You set out to gain the information that will help you know whether you want or have the capacity to acquire the dealerships. In addition, you want to know how to apply for the dealership. You apply the guidelines and make these decisions:

1. Purposes, participants, and environment
   a. My objectives
      (1) Long term: To acquire the one or more dealerships that will lead to maximum profit
      (2) Intermediate term: To analyze information about the Sakikawa and Dohaka dealerships to determine which dealership or combination would yield the most profit
      (3) Short term: To receive from the two distributors the information necessary to begin the analysis
   b. Distributors' objectives
      (1) Long term: To grant significant numbers of dealerships to high sales achievers
      (2) Intermediate term: To analyze the data provided by applicants for a dealership to find whether they appear to be potential high sales achievers
      (3) Short term: To provide the necessary information to potential applicants
   c. Receivers
      (1) Sakikawa Motorcycles
      1818 Kihei
      Honolulu, HI 96802
      (2) Dohaka Distributors
      P.O. Box 222, South Branch
      Long Beach, CA 90803
   d. Environment not a major factor
2. Channel
   a. Dismiss interpersonal at this stage because of expense and uncertainty
   b. Dismiss telephone because too much information needed
   c. Choose letter because it will provide a consistent basis for obtaining information from two different distributors

ANGELO'S DEPARTMENT STORES, INC.

Omaha Branch/1700 East Drive/Omaha, NE 68102/(504) 777-7777

December 19, 198X

Credit Manager
Pratt & Pratt Sales
9823 West Boulevard
Lincoln, NE 68503

Dear Credit Manager:

CREDIT RECORD OF MYRON DALTON

Myron Dalton, 17 West Circle, Omaha 68104, is an applicant for a credit line of $1,000 with Angelo's. He has listed your firm as a credit reference, stating that he has had an account with you for the past eight years.

Please help in the evaluation of Mr. Dalton's application by responding to some questions. Space is provided after each so that you may answer directly on this letter if you like.

1. Has Mr. Dalton had credit with you for the stated eight years? If not, for how long?
2. Have you placed a credit limit on the Dalton account? If so, how much?
3. How many purchases has he charged to his account in the years he has been with you?
4. What is the largest amount he has ever owed you?
5. How many times has he been late with a payment? If he has been late, what is the average number of days he has been late?
6. How much does he owe you now?
7. If he owes you now, is any of the amount past due? If any is past due, how much? For how long?
8. If you were Angelo's, would you grant credit to Mr. Dalton? If so, for a $1,000 line?

Your answers will be kept confidential. We hope that we may have the opportunity to help you in a similar way sometime.

Yours sincerely,

Y. R. Self

Y. R. Self
Credit and Collections

YRS:mjj

FIGURE 7-3 Inquiry about credit.

3. Interference
   a. Interference possible with incomplete list of information needed
   b. No serious external interference
4. Writing
   a. Select list of information needed from each distributor
      (1) Capital requirements for me?

      ....

      (10) How to apply for dealership?
   b. Draft
      (1) Use just-write method
      (2) Organize
         (a) Select indirect pattern
         (b) Outline
   c. Revise
   d. Transmit
      (1) Choose simplified style
      (2) Typewrite same message for each of two distributors, with only distributor name changed (Figure 7–4)
      (3) Mail first class
5. Plan for feedback
   a. Use feedback responses from two distributors to complete analysis set out in objectives
   b. Feedback to distributors if more information or clarification is needed
   c. Send completed application to distributors if decision warrants
6. Evaluate
   a. My objectives met
      (1) Short term: When complete replies to inquiries received
      (2) Intermediate term: When analysis of information yields the most profitable dealership combination
      (3) Long term: When profitable dealership(s) acquired
   b. Distributors' objectives met
      (1) Short term: When replies to inquiries completed
      (2) Intermediate term: When analysis of applications completed
      (3) Long term: When dealerships granted to high sales achievers

Figure 7–4 illustrates the first letter resulting from Case Study 1. It shows application of the six communication guidelines, the general writing principles covered in Chapter 6, and the specific principles covered in this chapter. Particularly observe how the development of specific questions should lead to desired responses. Even if the distributor sends preprinted brochures or flyers, they will more likely answer the questions than if the distributor had no guidance on what to send. The letter does use the indirect developmental style, whereas most letters of inquiry use the direct style. However, the introductory information borders on a persuasive technique to interest the distributor in you as a potential dealer.

Requests

Simple requests closely parallel inquiries and orders. However, the writer asks for more than information—often for free goods or services, for routine monetary transactions, for corrections of errors, or for attendance at an event.

2323 Sisters Lane
Bend, Oregon 97701
January 7, 198X

Dohaka Distributors
P.O. Box 222, South Branch
Long Beach, CA 90803

INQUIRY ABOUT DEALERSHIP

At age 14 I rode my first motorcycle. Fifteen years later I am still an enthusiast. For 11 of the past 12 years I have been fortunate enough to combine my enthusiasm for the sport with my jobs. I have worked for three different motorcycle dealers during that time–with the work involving just about everything associated with motorcycles. I have held jobs in mechanics, sales, parts, shop supervision, and office management—all quite successfully.

A year ago I moved to Bend and presently work as a salesperson for an automobile agency. However, I want to return to motorcycles. With my savings, the backing of a relative, and the establishment of a good line of credit with a local bank, I will be able to set up my own motorcycle sales and service shop here in Bend within the next year. Therefore, I am now looking into the possibilities for dealerships.

Bend does not have a Dohaka dealer. I like the Dohaka and am beginning my analysis of the potential for a Dohaka dealership now. To help me make the analysis, would you please answer these questions:

1. How much capital do you suggest I need in order to become a Dohaka dealer?
2. If I become a Dohaka dealer, do you grant me an exclusive Dohaka dealership for a given area? If so, how do you define the area?
3. If I carry the Dohaka, may I also carry other makes of motorcycles?
4. Do you provide service schools for Dohaka mechanics? If so, where are they located? What are the costs to the dealer?
5. Would you help me make a market analysis of the Bend area?
6. Do you provide customer mailings and showroom displays? local radio and television spots and newspaper ads? readership analysis for magazines and newspapers carrying your ads?
7. How do you handle the costs of warranty service?
8. What Dohaka models are now available? Will you have any new models coming out in the next six months?
9. What is Dohaka's share of the motorcycle market in the United States? Could you send me a copy of the latest annual report of Dohaka, Inc.?
10. How do I apply for a Dohaka dealership?

Please supply this information by February 1. I am making my analysis now and must make dealership decisions by April.

Y. R. Self

Y. R. Self

FIGURE 7–4 Inquiry about operations and procedures.

If a request moves beyond the simple and routine, it can become a persuasive message. For example, if you invite someone from the local telephone office to make a speech or media presentation about the company, you need not use persuasion. Such personnel want to take their messages to the public. However, if you ask a busy and popular person to speak at the monthly meeting of your organization, you might have to use some of the persuasive techniques described in Chapter 9.

1771 Alfalfa Trail
Independence, MO 64001
(010) 010-0101

February 9, 198X

Ms. Catherine Dors
Communication Specialist
Elko Whosesalers, Inc.
Two Allendale Drive
Independence, MO 64004

Dear Ms. Dors:

Brada Allen and Sol Degiusti told me how much they enjoyed working with all of you at Elko. They are particularly pleased that you feel that both the in-service sessions and the communication audit were productive contributions to the progress of Elko.

As agreed when the consultation began, the basic fee for the services of the team is $200 an hour. For the 15 hours spent with you, then, the basic fee is $3,000. The cost of the special supplies and materials is $389.43 (itemized on the attached sheet). Therefore, the total due Central Communication Consultants is $3,389.43.

Thank you for the opportunity to work with you. If you decide you would like the additional sessions you mentioned, we shall be glad to talk with you about them.

Sincerely,

Y. R. Self

Y. R. Self, Director
Corporate Relations

YRS:stu

Encl.

FIGURE 7-5 Request for consultation fee.

To write good requests, again apply the principles. Focus on the development of a detailed description of what you want the receiver to do. Figure 7–5 provides an illustration of the principles. It requests a routine payment for a service even as it introduces some "soft sell." It features the indirect developmental style and a personal, easy-going approach to a request.

Figure 7–6 illustrates the principles applied to a request for correction of an error in filling an order. Because the receiver clearly made the error, the writer properly used the direct developmental style and a straightforward, but tactful, request for correction by a given date. Such a request should defuse any defensiveness that might arise in the receiver because of making the mistake.

In one type of request, the sender *expects* the receiver to attend some event. Such messages often include this kind of sentence: "If you cannot attend, please notify my secretary." Such requests come close to forming directives.

With the inclusion of "R.S.V.P." or "Please reply," a message indicates at least two desired modes of response—assurance of attendance and actual physical presence at the event. When including the "R.S.V.P." or "Please reply" line, provide within the message a phone number or an address for reply. In addition, indicate the desired date of reply. If asking for responses by mail, writers often include forms and postpaid, addressed envelopes.

Indirect-Response Solicitors

Unlike direct-response solicitors, *indirect-response solicitors* do not overtly seek distinct and immediate responses. For example, when a company sends out 500 copies of a letter announcing that it has just received a prestigious award for public service, it does not *expect* an immediate, tangible response (though it may receive some messages of congratulation). Instead it expects to build goodwill and gain business from the receiver sometime in the future.

Examples of indirect-response solicitors include announcements, notices, invitations, and messages of transmittal. All of them require care in assuring completeness, detail, and clarity.

Announcements

Figure 7–7 illustrates the application of the writing principles to an announcement. Notice how the focus of the message—the new address—appears three times.

Behind all announcements lies the desire that the receiver take some action. However, direct observation of the desired action and evaluation of the message become difficult. For example, even if a number of people come to a new store or attend a lecture, the sender rarely knows exactly who came because of the announcement.

Notices

Many government and private contracts and programs require notices for certain events. For example, corporations, electric cooperatives, and credit

SELLSALOT CORP.
20202 Fielding Avenue
Warren, Ohio 44401

October 19, 198X

Louisiana Instruments, Inc.
999 Cajun Avenue
Vieux Carre, LA 70112

Ladies and Gentlemen

Please send me the adaptor and the SA Statistical Analysis module for the LI-62. Please send them both to arrive by October 28, because I am undertaking an important analytical project then and need to be able to use my new LI-62 in conjunction with it.

Your shipment (your Invoice No. 74099 and our Purchase Order No. 20205) arrived today, but did not include the adaptor. It did include two modules, but one (enclosed) is the RE Real Estate instead of the SA Statistical Analysis as ordered.

I like the LI-62 very much and look forward to receiving the adaptor and SA module so that it becomes fully useful for my work.

Sincerely yours

SELLSALOT CORP.

Y. R. Self

Y. R. Self
Market Research Specialist

YRS:er

Enclosure: RE Module

FIGURE 7–6 Request for correction of error in filling order.

unions must notify their stockholders and members of impending annual meetings and elections. Managers send notices to employees to tell them of changes in company policy. Another kind of notice applies when a mass error necessitates mass correction. For example, if a catalog mailed to 1,500 customers last week includes an incorrect price list or mailing address for orders, 1,500 notices must go to those same customers.

I. R. ESS TAX SERVICES
12 Honor Heights/Swanlake, ID 83281/(707) 707-0707

January 3, 198X

Mr. Bill Chronister
Ms. Jane Delgado
1314 Dodge Blvd., Apt. 302
Swanlake, ID 83281

Dear Mr. Chronister and Ms. Delgado:

The offices of I. R. Ess Tax Services have been moved to 12 Honor Heights—next door to Singleton's Sporting Goods in the new Honor Heights Mall in southeast Swanlake.

We have been pleased to prepare your tax returns for you in the past and look forward to preparing them again this year.

Yours sincerely,

Y. R. Self

Y. R. Self
Tax Consultant

lol

Tax time is here. Remember, the new address of I. R. Ess Tax Services is 12 Honor Heights.

FIGURE 7–7 Announcement of new location.

Figure 7–8 shows a notice to employees about a revision of their retirement program. The form letter goes to each employee's home address. It illustrates how the writer briefly and directly conveys information, though expecting direct responses only from those who have questions about how the provisions apply to them or about their accounts.

Invitations

Many invitations qualify as indirect-response solicitors. They may differ from the requests for attendance described earlier for any of these reasons: (1) They go to a large mailing list chosen without a great deal of selectivity. (2) A large proportion of the receivers do not attend the event. (3) The writer cannot expect to observe individual responses to the message—only general ones.

Waystein Pianos
22 IVORY AVENUE
EIGHTY EIGHT, KY 42130
(333) 333-3333

June 18, 198X

Dear Employee:

NOTICE OF MODIFICATION IN RETIREMENT PLAN FOR WAYSTEIN EMPLOYEES; EMPLOYER I.D. NO. 22-2222222; PLAN I.D. NO. 002

Upon approval by the Board of Directors, and subject to approval by the Internal Revenue Service, effective July 1, 198X, the Waystein Pianos Retirement Plan will be changed in this way: Waystein Pianos will credit to retirement accounts the prior service of all regular full-time employees who have had breaks in service, provided they meet either of these conditions:

1. Fulfillment of vesting requirements (8 years of continuous employment and attainment of age 30) before the break in service

2. Length of the break in service does not equal or exceed the length of continuous employment before the break

If you have had a break in service with Waystein, check the enclosed statement to determine how the change affects you. If the statement is not enclosed or if you believe it contains an error, contact Larry Tooner in our Eighty Eight office. If you should like to call, his extension number is 333.

Respectfully,

WAYSTEIN PIANOS

Y. R. Self

Y. R. Self, Chairperson
Retirement Plan Administration
Committee

yy

Encl. for affected employees:
Statement of effect of change

FIGURE 7–8 Notice of change in retirement plan.

Indirect-response invitations ask people to attend the same kinds of events that direct-response invitations do. However, these contrasting situations illustrate the difference.

Direct-response solicitor: Invitations with R.S.V.P. notations go to 30 carefully selected people asking them to the opening of law offices and to the reception associated with it.

Indirect-response solicitor: In addition to an ad in the newspaper, invitations without R.S.V.P. notations go to a mailing list of 5,000 people asking them to the grand opening of a new northside Floor-Mart discount store. The invitation offers free soft drinks and popcorn to those who attend.

Transmittals

A transmittal serves primarily to accompany something sent to the receiver. Transmittals often accompany such things as catalogs, product samples, schedules of events, convention programs, telephone directories, questionnaires, special publications, manuscripts of books, or reports. Because a transmittal letter (cover letter, covering letter) accompanies something else of more importance than the letter itself, it qualifies as a routine type. However, it may include tinges of persuasion.

Transmittals often lead only to indirect responses. For example, the transmittal of a catalog may eventually lead to an order of some kind, but tying the order to the transmittal itself may prove difficult.

When writing a letter of transmittal, avoid using worn-out opening phrases. Particularly avoid such phrases as "Enclosed please find," "Enclosed herewith," and "Attached you will find." Even avoid "Enclosed is" and "Attached is" when you can. Acceptable phrases include:

"As suggested by Lee Engle, I am sending you this copy of. . . ."

"Please accept this copy of . . . with our compliments."

"Take a look at the . . . included in this envelope."

"We are pleased to send you this trial-size bar of Sunup Soap."

"Because of the importance of knowing your views about current topics, I am asking you to complete this questionnaire."

An example of a transmittal letter appears in Figure 7-9. It accompanies the annual report of a company. Thus, it includes only a simple, but complete, message of description and conveyance.

Responses

Letters of response should provide feedback messages appropriate to the initiating communication. For instance, if a representative of Dohaka Distributors replies to the letter asking for information about a Dohaka dealership (Figure 7-4), he or she should answer all the questions in a straightforward and precise manner.

This type of routine letter forms a good channel for responses to both direct- and indirect-response solicitors. Such responses take the forms of acknowledgments, approvals, information and explanation, and instructions and directions.

Acknowledgments

Sometimes a letter confirms the receipt of something or reports that some action will occur. These circumstances lead to messages of acknowledgment—

synergy pharmaceuticals, inc.

2098 Aspurn Drive
Mineral Springs, Arkansas 71851
(602) 026-2060

August 2, 198X

Dr. James Lo
Suite 900
Pastour Complex
Radium, CO 80472

Dear Dr. Lo:

You will want to examine this copy of the 198X annual report of Synergy Pharmaceuticals, Inc.

As a stockholder of Synergy, you will particularly enjoy reading page 16. It presents a summary of the major indicators of a corporation's financial position—all of which show marked stability and growth for Synergy.

If you have comments or questions about the report, please contact us.

Respectfully yours,

Y. R. Self

Y. R. Self, Director
Owner Relations

ss

Enc.: 198X Annual Report

FIGURE 7–9 Unsolicited transmittal of annual report.

messages that serve in much the same way as written receipts for payments of money.

An acknowledgment always provides an excellent avenue for feedback during the time lapse between communication actions. You might recall the uncertainty associated with sending a watch or a calculator to a factory for repair and hearing nothing for two months. You might also recall the feeling when you can relieve someone else's frustration just by sending a simple acknowledgment. Then act from that base of empathy.

Acknowledgments usually confirm receipt of such direct-response solicitors as orders, inquiries, requests, and messages in oral communication channels. Acknowledgment of *orders* for both goods and services occurs for many situations. Such situations include the first order from a potentially good customer, an unusually large order from a regular customer, the receipt of goods or services, or hotel and transportation reservations.

Figure 7–10 illustrates a letter acknowledging an order. It also reports the necessity of delaying part of the order and offering a substitute, a circumstance that borders on bad news. Observe how the letter uses a direct, though

Tiaf · Yoytota · Wolksvagen · Leop · Nodah · Snudat · Pacri

IMPORT CAR-TALOG SALES, INC.

1802 South Grand Prix
Durants Neck, NC 27930

Telephone: 333-333-3334
Toll Free: 800-333-3333

Replacement Parts · Accessories · Supplies · Custom Parts

September 3, 198X

Ms. Eleanor Parkins
4298 15 Street
Seabrook, NH 03874

Dear Ms. Parkins

Thank you for your order for parts and accessories for your 1980 Tiaf Sedan. As you can see by the enclosed invoice, today we shipped six of the seven items you ordered. You should receive them in six to ten days.

We are temporarily out of the 86 TF 20622CR Star Mag Wheel at $78.90. Our supplier promises that we will have a shipment by September 22. Therefore, we could send the four you ordered to arrive no later than the first week in October.

As another alternative, we can ship immediately four 89 TF 21622CR Super Star Mag Wheels at $80.90. The Super Star is identical to the Star except that it has a triple-chrome-plated center cap instead of a single-plated one.

Just call our toll free number (800-333-3333) and tell me your decision. If I should be out when you call, Dee Stone will take your message.

Sincerely yours

Y. R. Self

Y. R. Self, Supervisor
Shipping Department

rr

Enclosure: Invoice

FIGURE 7–10 Acknowledgment of order with statement of necessity to delay or substitute for part of order.

(206 words)

courteous, style for both the basic acknowledgment and the delivery of the news about the delay and the substitution. Notice also how the writer offers clear alternatives and makes response easy.

Occasionally, *inquiries* have such importance that receivers acknowledge them immediately, rather than waiting until making full responses. As an illustration, suppose that as the president of a corporation you receive a personal letter from the governor asking for your opinions on several current topics. Even if you plan to respond within the week, you should promptly acknowledge the governor's message and say when you will respond.

A related circumstance arises when a letter of inquiry comes into the office of a receiver away for an extended period. If the receiver empowers someone to check the mail during such a period, he or she should send an acknowledgment explaining to the inquirer the necessity for delaying the response.

Acknowledgments of *requests* parallel closely those of orders for goods and services. However, orders involve money, and requests usually do not. These examples clarify the need for such acknowledgments:

1. A request comes from a high school teacher for 50 copies of the company's brochure *Careers in Insurance*. The receiver acknowledges the request, sends 10 copies, and promises the other 40 within two weeks.
2. A letter asks the receiver to lead a local library discussion group for four weeks in September. She writes that she cannot because she will be out of town during two of the scheduled meetings. She adds that she could, however, lead the October or November discussions.
3. A receiver writes to the Chamber of Commerce to express thanks and to accept its invitation to the annual dinner.
4. A personnel director writes to acknowledge receipt of a letter of application.
5. A chairperson of a company committee writes each member to acknowledge excellent performance.

A written message often confirms a telephone conversation, an agreement, something said by a speaker, or a message through other *oral communication channels*.

Figure 7-11 illustrates a letter acknowledging an oral agreement to lend some films. The letter has an appropriate conversational style but shows firmness and clarity in reinforcing the agreement.

Approvals

Although the word *approval* carries a good-news tone, many approval messages become quite routine. They involve such acts as:

- Issuing a credit card to someone who had no doubt about receiving it
- Approving the repair of merchandise under warranty
- Correcting a mistake in filling an order
- Replacing a faulty piece of new merchandise
- Agreeing to speak to a club

SILVERAY ELECTRONICS
1800 Spacecraft Landing
Airway Heights, WA 99001
(200) 000-0000

July 31, 198X

Mr. Chris Jenks, Director
Human Resource Development
Galaxie Manufacturing
One North Aether Way
Airway Heights, WA 99001

Dear Chris

Thanks for the lunch and the pleasant and productive conversation. I always enjoy these chances to combine "shop talk" with some moments of relaxation.

Thanks also for offering to lend me your two films on human relations. As we decided, I will be in your office at 3:15 p.m. on Friday, August 7, to pick them up. I will show them to Silveray employees during the week of August 10 and return them to you at 8:30 a.m. on Monday, August 17.

Let's meet for lunch again soon. Perhaps we can schedule a good time for both of us when I see you next Friday.

Cordially

Y. R. Self

Y. R. Self
Training Specialist

FIGURE 7-11 Acknowledgment of transaction in oral communication channel.

Use courtesy when approving requests—even those that call attention to some error by you or that involve a questionable claim. For example, consider how you would feel if a company sent you a negative, blaming message like this one:

Dear Ms. Ellis:

Your toaster was received. We just cannot believe that the malfunction could be our fault. However, we are repairing it *this time.* In the future, remember that your warranties with A. Pliance, Inc. do not cover any misuse by you.

Sincerely,

Next, think about how the same message improves slightly because of the removal of some of the blaming and negative overtones in the following form:

> Dear Ms. Ellis:
>
> We received your toaster yesterday and examined it immediately. Although we have some question about the cause of the malfunction, we will repair it because it is still under warranty.
>
> Sincerely,

Finally, think about how the change to a positive, gracious, nonblaming approach improves the message significantly:

> Dear Ms. Ellis:
>
> Thank you for the chance to put your fine A. Pliance toaster back into good working order. You should receive it in like-new shape by August 10.
>
> Sincerely,

Figure 7-12 shows an example of a simple letter of approval. It uses empathy to establish a positive approach to an approval of a request. Such an approach should cause the customer to do more business with the company.

Information and Explanation

In letters of information and explanation, clear-cut facts, data, news, and interpretations form the bulk of the messages. For example, the letter of recommendation for Katherine Jones-Bush, the job applicant (Figure 7-2), will explain and inform. Some other examples of responses providing information or explanation include:

- The messages describing Myron Dalton's credit record with Pratt & Pratt Sales (Figure 7-3)
- A message to a university student explaining your ideas about the importance of communication in business
- A message giving information about attic-insulation service

Make messages of information and explanation complete, concise, correct, and courteous. Use the direct developmental pattern.

Instructions and Directions

The message giving instructions or directions often logically follows a chronological development. It also depends on concrete words and illustrations for clear expression. Of course, it calls for the completeness, correctness, conciseness, and courtesy necessary for other neutral messages.

Examples of messages containing instructions or directions include:

- A step-by-step description of how to assemble or dismantle anything from a toy train to a giant refinery engine motorsaplenty, inc.

February 9, 198X

Mr. Michael Storie
789 Fourth Street, West
Volborg, MT 59351

Dear Mr. Storie:

You are right. The motor you returned to us overheats badly. We shipped a carefully tested replacement today, and you should receive it by Monday of next week.

Because you had the bother and expense of returning a brand-new piece of equipment, I am enclosing a check for $15. It should at least cover your freight cost.

Please check with us again the next time you need quality equipment. I can assure you that the experience will be better next time.

Sincerely yours,

Y. R. Self

Y. R. Self
Customer Relations

att

25 Deece Avenue
Electric Mills, MS 39329

FIGURE 7–12 Approval of a claim.

- A travel route
- The procedure for using a computer terminal
- A computer program for the solution of a specified problem
- The communication channels an employee should use in order to talk directly with the president
- The required sequences for ordering materials both within and outside the firm

WRITING GOOD-NEWS MESSAGES

Neutral and good-news letters differ only slightly. For example, consider how these messages slip ever so slightly from the neutral to the good-news category:

- An announcement congratulates the receiver for an unusual honor.
- A message approves the adjustment of a claim for an adjustment not under warranty and not really expected.
- A notice informs recipients that they have passed the C.P.A. or bar examination.

arroyo industries, inc.
19 Isla Verde
Descalabrado, PR 00757
(888) 888-8888

December 9, 198X

Ms. Nikita Waukomis, Director
South Dakota Foundation for
the Native American Arts
2098 East Cheyenne Trail
Brandon, SD 57005

Dear Ms. Waukomis:

Please consider the enclosed check for $10,000 the contribution of Arroyo Industries, Inc., to the fine work of the South Dakota Foundation for the Native American Arts.

Each year the Arroyo Board of Directors carefully chooses the five considered most deserving from the requests for contributions received that year. Each of the five then receives a check for $10,000.

Arroyo Industries, Inc., wishes you continued success as you preserve and perpetuate the rich contributions made by Native American artists.

Sincerely yours,

Y. R. Self

Y. R. Self, Chair
Board of Directors

ll

Enclosure

FIGURE 7–13 Good-news response to request for contribution.

- An announcement informs employees of a substantial Christmas bonus this year.
- A message gives unexpected approval to a request for a loan.

The direct and descending-rank developmental patterns prove most appropriate for the good-news letter. Put the good news first. Report dramatically, but not falsely. Give additional information as needed, and conclude. The pleasantness of the news itself removes the burden of a difficult encoding process.

(135 words)

Take and score Self-Test 15 over writing good-news messages on pages 177–178.

Two brief sample messages illustrate the minor features that distinguish a good-news letter from a neutral letter. Figure 7–13 shows a favorable response to a request for a contribution. It also serves as a transmittal, but not a routine one.

In the letter presented in Figure 7–14, Ronald Clemons receives credit although his record would not be viewed by every credit manager as warranting it. Because Clemons did not think that he would be approved, he obviously will view the message as good news.

From this discussion of neutral and good-news messages, we now turn to probably the most difficult of all writing—bad-news messages. Chapter 8 not only describes the difficulties, but suggests solutions for overcoming them.

SUMMARY

Letters fall into three broad categories: (1) neutral and good-news messages, (2) bad-news messages, and (3) persuasive messages. This chapter covers the first category.

Neutral messages emphasize the direct or descending-rank pattern of development, straightforwardness, courtesy, conciseness, correctness, completeness, clearness, action-eliciting closing, and provision of channel for feedback. Direct-response solicitors, indirect-response solicitors, and responses form three major types of neutral messages.

Direct-response solicitors directly ask receivers to supply something or do something. Such solicitors include orders, inquiries, and requests. For all three types, provide complete, specific information about what you want the receiver to do.

Orders deal with both goods and services. Inquiries ask for information about such topics as products, services, employment, credit, and operations and procedures. Confidentiality forms an important consideration for employment and credit messages. Neutral requests ask for such things as free goods or services, routine monetary transactions, correction of errors, and attendance at an event.

PASSPORTACARD CREDIT CENTER
One Foundation Circle/Charleston, WV 25301
(918) 918-9189

March 19, 198X

Mr. Ronald Clemons
22 West Hardship Road
Prosperity, WV 25909

Dear Mr. Clemons:

In the belief that the strength of your credit record this past year offsets your record for the two years preceding it, we approve your request for a full $300 line of credit with PASSPORTACARD.

Your temporary card and an explanatory brochure are enclosed. Your laminated card should arrive within two weeks. Note that as standard procedure your card will expire one year from now, but is renewable as a virtual formality if your record warrants it.

Use your PASSPORTACARD well. It can be your passport to financial strength.

Sincerely,

Y. R. Self

Y. R. Self, Manager
New Customer Service

iou

Encs.: Temporary card
Brochure

FIGURE 7–14 Good-news approval of request for credit.

Indirect-response solicitors do not overtly seek distinct and immediate responses. Examples of such messages include announcements, notices, general invitations, and messages of transmittal. All of them require care in assuring completeness, detail, and clarity.

Letters of response should provide feedback messages appropriate to the initiating communication. Such responses take the forms of acknowledgments, approvals, information and explanation, and instructions and directions. Make responses straightforward, precise, and courteous.

Good-news messages differ only slightly from neutral messages. They ordinarily use the direct or descending-rank developmental style. They put the good news first, give additional information as needed, and conclude. Examples of types of good-news messages include favorable responses to substantive requests and personal messages to announce an award or honor.

Neutral and good-news messages often overlap with one another and sometimes overlap with persuasive and bad-news messages. The classification does not matter so much as does the application of the principles appropriate to the message's emphasis.

EXERCISES

1. You are interested in hiring Don Santiago, a consultant, to conduct several writing workshops for your firm. You want to know what he charges for his services and how he conducts his workshops before you decide whether or not to hire him. Write the letter, supplying whatever additional information you need.
2. You need to buy some accounting reference books for your office. You want two hardbound copies of *International Accounting,* one soft-bound copy of the fifth edition of *Managerial Accounting Practices in Europe* (without appendixes), four copies (either soft- or hard-bound) of the *Financial Accounting Reference Manual,* and, if it costs less than $75, one copy of *Depreciation Methods for Natural Resources* (soft-bound). You also want the microfiche edition of *Who's Who in Accounting*. Write the letter, supplying whatever additional information you need.
3. The mayor of your city, Christine Falk, is running for reelection. You would like her to participate in your business club's candidates' forum. Because she is campaigning, you know that she would be glad to participate in the forum. Write the letter, supplying whatever additional information you need.
4. You wish to hire the John Westfall Janitorial Service to clean your office building Wednesday and Sunday evenings. You know that Westfall charges $50 per janitor per six-hour work period. This figure includes all supplies and supervisors' salaries. You feel that you need five janitors on a regular basis, and one additional janitor the second Sunday of each month for special cleaning jobs. You want to hire the service for a six-month trial period. If you like the janitors' work, you will hire the service on a year-to-year contract. Write the letter, supplying whatever additional information you need.
5. Meet with your group. Discuss the messages from Don Spelling and Susan Telephone on the following page; determine what, if anything, is wrong with them. Add information and correct them if necessary.
6. Every year you write a letter to your employees (to be sent to their homes) asking them to donate canned goods to your company's Drive for Needy Families. You want only nonperishable canned goods, canned meats in particular. As usual, you want the employees to put the food in the special bins located by the soft-drink machines on each floor. The drive will run from September 6 through October 1. Write the letter. (You may make up the necessary names, addresses, and so forth.)
7. [*Your professor will time this exercise.*] You hired a temporary secretary through Humanpower Temporaries, Inc. You were told that the cost would be $180 for five days. You paid in advance. The secretary, Tom, did not show up for the last of the five days of work. Write a letter requesting a refund for the day Tom (you do not know his last name) did not work.

IDLE COMPANY
60 Able Avenue
Orville 66660

Prestige Business Card Co.
Mrs. Ann Elizabeth Fry
1616 Filbert Way
Silo, Wisconsin

My dear Miss Fry,

We heard you sell cards. We would like to buy some. We want sets of cards for three of our employees. Here are there names: John Ray, Deborah Leitz, and Mr. W.C. Lord. How much do they cost? I don't want to pay over $30. Could you send paper too?

Thanks so much

Don Spelling

BANK OF THE FIR TREES
1111116 Fir Tree Plaza
Jennifer, Idaho 16160
Monday, August 19

Dear Sirs;

I really appreicate your help. I've heard really nice things about all of you.

A lady by the name of Augusta Aardvark applied for a teller position at my bank. She said she used to work for you.

Would you please tell me everything you know about her?

Susan Telephone
Bank President

P.S. Your a big help!

8. Use your imagination to write an invitation soliciting an individual response. Meet with your group. You and every other group member read your letters aloud. Choose one of the letters and have its author read it to the rest of the class.
9. Sonya Rich orders 400 of your company's best table lamps. This is her first order. You know that Rich owns large hotels in at least 16 major cities. You cannot ship the lamps until the middle of next month. Write the letter of response, supplying whatever additional information you need.
10. Harry Field ordered 60 staplers and 10 pen and pencil sets from your company. You are out of the pen and pencil sets, but do have them on order. You expect them to arrive in two months. Write the letter of response, supplying whatever additional information you need.
11. You are the director of corporate relations for a major grocery store chain. A newspaper reporter, Nancy Von Hoff, writes you a letter asking you a number of questions, most of which deal with your company's rather unconventional pricing practices. You will be out of town on business for a week, but will answer Von

Hoff's questions when you return. You decide that you should at least acknowledge the reporter's inquiry before you leave town. Write the letter, supplying whatever additional information you need.

12. You receive a call from Sam Ching, a broker with a major San Francisco investment firm. Ching says that he may be interested in hiring you, and that he will mail you a company brochure. You decide that you want to write a letter to thank him for his call. You also want to express interest in the job. Write the letter, supplying whatever additional information you need.
13. You just had dinner with an important potential client, Helen Sky. She asked you to send her a copy of your annual report. You discover that you have no reports on hand, but that several hundred copies will be printed by the end of next week. Write the letter, supplying whatever additional information you need.
14. Some communication specialists believe that most neutral letters can be made into good-news letters if written properly. What do you think?
15. *[This is an exercise in dictation.]* You have decided to hire Larry Nagy as a public relations assistant for your firm. His starting pay will be $1,200 a month, and you want him to begin work in your Lafayette office at 8 A.M. on Monday, June 1, 198X. Outline the letter that you will send to Mr. Nagy. Make up the names and addresss, and add information as you wish. Now meet with your group. You and every other group member dictate your letters. Evaluate each person's performance immediately after he or she has spoken.
16. Rewrite each of these neutral or good-news sentences.
    - a. The order will get there in a week or two.
    - b. We've decided to let you have the Ellen F. Bear Scholarship.
    - c. Letterhead stationery is what we want in white or off-white item number 609LS.
    - d. Send the books we ordered immediately.
    - e. Because you want it so much, I'll grant you an interview.
    - f. Your payment is three days overdue. For that reason, we will not allow you to use your charge card anymore.
17. Use your dictionary and thesaurus to create meanings for these words. Use the words when you think, write, and speak so that you feel comfortable using them.
    - a. Allay
    - b. Amenity
    - c. Appraise
    - d. Apprise
    - e. Convey
    - f. Illustrative
    - g. Incur
    - h. Libel
    - i. Neutral
    - j. Ostensibly
    - k. Proxy
    - l. Query
18. Take and score Self-Test 16 over Chapter 7.

SELF-TEST 15
Excerpt About Writing Good-News Messages

A. Recall (33 points each). For each multiple-choice question, select the most accurate answer.
   1. Which of these would *not* be classified as a good-news letter?
      - a. A letter announcing that the Maria Stokes Foundation will again award a scholarship to a promising business student

b. A letter announcing that you have won the Maria Stokes Foundation scholarship
c. A letter inviting the "social elite" to a fund-raising event
d. A letter approving credit for someone who under most circumstances would not receive credit
e. A letter requesting that you join the staff of the First Bank as a vice president, a position few people your age are offered

2. When you write a good-news letter, you should:
   a. Build up the good news
   b. Ask that the receiver call you so that you can give the good news over the telephone, a more personal channel
   c. Put the good news first
   d. Put the good news after the introductory paragraphs
   e. Downplay the good news

B. Inference (34 points). Indicate whether this statement is true or false.
   1. If you are not sure that the letter you are writing should be a good-news letter, try to decide whether your receiver will consider your message good news.

SOLUTION

A. Recall (33 points each)
   1. a
   2. c

B. Inference (34 points)
   1. True

SELF-TEST 16
Chapter 7

A. Recall (25 points each). For each multiple choice question, select the most accurate answer.
   1. Neutral letters:
      a. Carry messages that will have no effect on the receiver
      b. Are really bad-news letters that have been softened
      c. Are letters that you write when you have no definite feelings on an issue
      d. Are rarely written in the business world
      e. Carry messages that fall somewhere between good and bad news
   2. Which of these statements is *not* true?
      a. Direct-response solicitors are letters that involve someone overtly asking another to supply or do something in direct response to the message.
      b. When you write a letter to order services, you should be just as specific and detailed as you are when you order goods.
      c. When you include the "R.S.V.P." or "Please reply" line in an invitation, be sure to provide within the message itself a phone number or an address to which the reader can reply.
      d. When writing an inquiry letter regarding a prospective employee, ask only general questions such as: "Was Ms. Nassed a good employee?"

   e. In contrast to an order letter, the request letter often asks for goods and services free of charge.

3. In which of these situations would an indirect-response solicitor *not* be appropriate?
   a. You wish to invite your 3,500 stockholders to the annual stockholders' meeting.
   b. You wish to announce that your bank has opened a new branch.
   c. You wish to invite several potential clients to a presentation you are giving just for them.
   d. You wish to send a letter with the brochure you will send to the people on your mailing list.
   e. You wish to write a letter that corrects a mistake in your company's widely distributed catalog.

B. Inference (25 points). Indicate whether this statement is true or false.

1. You should write a letter of acknowledgment only when you have been specifically asked to do so.

SOLUTION

A. Recall (25 points each)
1. e
2. d
3. c

B. Inference (25 points)
1. False

STUDENT'S OBJECTIVES:

1 To learn to develop messages that carry bad news by using an indirect, ascending-rank, or chronological developmental pattern, a positive writing style, a buffer opening, a positive sandwich, carefully chosen words, and the "you" attitude—all of which reflect empathy

2 To learn to develop refusal messages that deny credit, refuse requests or claims, refuse to fill an order, or deny a general request or inquiry

8

WRITING BAD-NEWS MESSAGES

3 To learn how to write a message setting out a claim or calling for an adjustment

4 To learn to write unfavorable recommendations for applicants for jobs

5 To learn to initiate messages that convey bad news (for example, informing customers that they can no longer use their credit cards)

Bad-news messages require more finesse than do neutral and good-news messages. Consider a bad-news situation to exist when:

- Content of the message may lead to an irreparable loss of the goodwill of the recipient
- The news probably will disturb the recipient
- The message cannot become neutral by adding a substantive good-news alternative to the bad news
- The news clearly runs counter to the interests of the recipient
- The situation warrants the investment of time and money necessary to develop a bad-news message

PRINCIPLES FOR WRITING ABOUT BAD NEWS

To develop bad-news messages, you need to apply the guidelines and principles developed in earlier chapters. This chapter begins with a discussion of these suggestions:

- Select the indirect, ascending-rank, or chronological pattern of development
- Adopt a positive writing style
- Use a buffer opening
- Create a positive sandwich
- Choose words carefully
- Establish the "you" attitude

Developmental Patterns

Avoid the harshness of the direct and descending-rank plans. Because they would begin with the bad news and then supply the details, they would introduce a psychologically defeating overtone. Instead choose an indirect, ascending-rank, or chronological developmental pattern for the body of the message, because these three plans begin with details and build to the bad news.

As an example of the indirect, even chronological, pattern, a message could begin with:

> Thank you for your letter of June 12 in which you described the claim resulting from cigarette-burn damage to your carpet. On the day it arrived, we began the investigation. First, we checked . . . . Next, we . . . .

The message would then lead naturally to the denial of the claim:

> Although none of these avenues yielded a way to grant this claim, your future claims will always receive the same thorough examination.

A sentence or two would follow this denial to pad the ending of even the indirect method. The section on positive sandwiches includes examples of such endings.

Positive Style

A positive writing style can overcome a great deal of the negativeness of a bad-news message. Positiveness arises from empathy and reaches expression through actions and words that convey that empathy.

If you must write an unfavorable reply (bad news) to a message initiated by another, try to reply just as promptly as you would to deliver good news. Sometimes, such promptness can communicate as much as the words do. It expresses an understanding attitude toward the receiver's needs.

No matter how right your position, maintain self-control and courtesy. Avoid demeaning or blaming the other. Avoid abruptness, condescension, and harshness.

Convey a sense of rationality and avoid worn-out, falsely apologetic phrases such as:

We humbly regret that . . . .

Please forgive the necessity to . . . .

We beg your forgiveness for . . . .

We are so sorry that . . . .

We offer our humblest apologies for having to . . . .

This suggestion does not mean that messages should never include words such as *sorry, regret,* and *apologize*. However, it does mean that the words belong within sincere apologies for situations actually requiring the correction of errors. Such situations do not lead to bad-news messages. In fact, apologies and corrections of errors usually represent good or neutral news.

Develop strategies that will overcome the negative aspects. Try to live up to the classical image of the optimist: write about a half-full glass rather than a half-empty one whenever possible. Emphasize what you can and will do, not what you cannot and will not do. However, try to do so without contrivance.

As examples, the half-full glass might involve substituting merchandise at a discount, or sending another speaker in your place. It could offer a compromise on a claim for which the receiver expects outright denial. It may suggest an alternative supplier.

Explain the bad news itself briefly and clearly. Subordinate it to the positive sections. Always keep in mind the dual nature of your goal—to solve the specific problem *and* to keep the goodwill of the receiver. Appeal to a sense of fairness while attempting to accomplish both parts of the goal.

Buffer Opening

You can improve on the indirect developmental pattern by opening a bad-news message with a buffer. Deliver a sincere compliment, agree with the other about something, or comment on a warm, positive, or perhaps just neutral topic. In all cases, though, relate the buffer to the message in the body of the letter.

Avoid flashy attention-getting devices and false apologies. Instead, use the buffer to establish a controlled approach to the topic. Contrast these openings:

We are sorry, but we cannot	Thank you for writing about . . . .
You should know that we cannot	Your concern about . . . is commendable.
We cannot understand why you would think	We appreciate your interest in . . . .
Your request for is totally out of line.	Your request for . . . caused me to do some thinking.

Positive Sandwich

You might also add a buffer to the end of a message to create a positive sandwich. Wedge the substance of a bad-news message between two positive buffers. Doing so will reduce the intensity of the transaction. The positive sandwich adds two stages to the basic sequence of the indirect pattern. It becomes:

1. Buffer
2. Details
3. Bad news (including any positive option offered)
4. Buffer

Use a pleasant closing buffer for a bad-news message. Avoid apologetic clichés here, too. Make the closing statement either relate to the situation or avoid it entirely. In either case, concentrate on goodwill at this point in the message. Examples of closing buffers include:

> Do not ever hesitate to send in your claims. We shall do everything possible to grant them.
>
> Thanks again for your interest in establishing a credit line with us. As suggested, we look forward to reviewing your request again in February.
>
> Have a wonderful holiday season.
>
> Best wishes for the continued expansion of your business.

Choice of Words

For bad-news situations, you must choose each word carefully. Wise choices can make the difference between a successful and an unsuccessful transaction. Chapter 6 includes suggestions for choosing words to create a positive tone. However, another approach relates to sentence structure itself. For the delivery of the actual bad news, frequently use the complex sentence. A complex sentence has an independent and a dependent clause. Place the bad news in the dependent clause to subordinate it:

> Although no opening presently exists in a position that matches your fine qualifications, I have placed your application in a top-priority position.
>
> Although it does not include the $2,500 credit line you requested, your credit card with a $1,500 credit line is enclosed.
>
> Even though I cannot speak to your group this month, I can speak in September or October.

Contrast the positive tone of the preceding indirect statements with the negative tone of these direct ones:

> Our policies do not allow us to . . . .
>
> To grant your request would be against company policy.
>
> If we adjusted your unwarranted claim, we would have to do the same thing for others.
>
> I personally would like to make the adjustment, but I am just one small cog in a giant wheel.
>
> We received your request; however, we will not be able to grant it.

Notice particularly the negative effect of using *but* and *however.* Such words signal the bad news.

"You" Attitude

The concept of the "you" attitude pervades the preceding paragraphs because empathy represents the cardinal principle of all communication. The "you"-centered approach springs from understanding the needs and wants of the receiver. As that understanding grows, the ability to "get outside" oneself contributes significantly to defusing bad-news messages. Although a genuine "you" attitude usually shines through a message, carefully chosen words also show it. Thus, use considerate words, avoid overusing *I* and *we,* and do use the stated or implied *you.*

TYPES OF BAD-NEWS MESSAGES

The types of bad-news messages include: (1) refusals, (2) claims and adjustments, (3) unfavorable recommendations, and (4) unsolicited news of a negative nature.

Refusals

Chapter 7 suggests how to say *Yes* or not say *No* relatively easily. However, saying *No* requires creativity. This chapter covers four broad types of refusal messages: (1) credit, loan, and insurance; (2) claim and adjustment; (3) order; and (4) general request and inquiry.

Credit, Loan, and Insurance

A firm cannot always grant credit, a loan, or insurance to someone who applies for it. When refusing, try to understand the receiver's disappointment, and write accordingly. Avoid using form rejections. If the volume of work requires forms, it is a good idea to develop several versions. Then you can use the refusal form that best fits the particular case.

In either an individually written or a form rejection, try to give the real reason for the rejection. At least avoid a blanket statement that leaves the receiver without a basis for correcting the situation. Figure 8-1 provides an illustration of a letter rejecting a request for credit. Observe the positive

CHARGERRIFIC, INC.
619 East Valley Street
Wilson, Connecticut 33219

November 9, 198X Telex No. 17-4444

Mr. Samuel Wayne
849 Oakbrook, Apartment 16C
Wilson, Connecticut 06095

Dear Mr. Wayne:

Thank you for taking the time to look into the services offered here at Chargerrific. In addition to issuing charge cards, Chargerrific offers an array of merchandise at discount prices to both its charge customers and its cash customers.

While we cannot give you a charge card at this time because you do not meet our requirement of a $10,000 annual salary, we are adding your name to our mailing list. Now you will receive our discount merchandise catalogues. You will also receive a $5 gift certificate with your first Chargerrific catalogue.

Welcome to Chargerrific as a new customer. Should you wish to reapply for a Chargerrific Card in the future, we will gladly consider your application.

Yours sincerely,

Ellen Fernandez

Ellen Fernandez
Credit Manager

aa

FIGURE 8-1 Rejection of request for credit.

FIRST VALLEY BANK
One Hildegard Plaza
Hildegard, New Jersey 22374
(555) 343-3192

December 15, 198X

Ms. Lee Fong
5006 Knox Road
Hildegard, New Jersey 22374

Dear Ms. Fong:

Thank you for visiting First Valley Bank last Thursday.

After careful analysis of your financial status, we find that you qualify for VIProfessional Checking, a checking account for on-the-go business and professional persons. VIProfessional Checking offers free checks, no service charge, and $100 overdraft protection. Mr. Don Klein, our VIProfessional assistant, will be glad to help you open your account.

Although we cannot grant you the $3,000 loan you requested because you have not lived in Hildegard for two years, we will be happy to consider your loan request when you have fulfilled the residence requirement.

Please come in soon to open your VIProfessional checking account.

Sincerely,

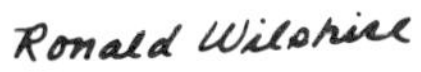

Ronald Wilshire

Ronald Wilshire
Loan Officer

bb

FIGURE 8-2 Refusal of request for loan.

sandwich and the use of the complex sentence in the second paragraph. Figure 8-2 shows a refusal to lend money to an applicant. It grants part of the request, subordinates the bad news, identifies the specific reasons for the denial, and puts buffers at the beginning and the end.

Figure 8-3 illustrates a form rejection of an application for insurance. Even as a form, though, it retains an empathetic tone, a positive sandwich, and a careful choice of words.

Carson Insurance Company
P.O. BOX 52 TAYLOR, MISSISSIPPI 59993

December 1, 198X

Dear Applicant:

Thank you for contacting Carson Insurance Company for help with your insurance needs. Carson offers a number of low-cost health insurance plans to people who have no history of major illness.

Because of your medical history, we are referring you to our subsidiary, Golden Times Insurance. Golden Times insures people with a history of major illness. Golden Times charges only slightly higher rates than Carson and offers the same excellent service. A Golden Times brochure and application blank are enclosed.

We appreciate your contacting us, and we know that the people at Golden Times Insurance look forward to hearing from you.

Sincerely,

Ann Faulkner

Ann Faulkner
Insurance Assistant

AF:cc

Enclosures

FIGURE 8–3 Rejection of request for insurance.

Claim and Adjustment

Sometimes writers use letters to deny requests for claims and adjustments. They may deny requests outright, or they may offer alternatives that bring the messages back into the not-such-bad-news realm.

A letter could carry the news to a claimant that a warranty has expired. It may also report that without proof of date of purchase or warranty registration, the company cannot repair or replace an item.

A written message could notify a claimant that he or she did not meet the terms of an agreement or warranty. One of the most difficult situations involves the decision that someone misused or damaged a product, thus negating the provisions of a warranty.

Written messages sometimes shift the responsibility of a problem to a third party. Some of the possible parties include the shipper, the retailer, the wholesaler, or the producer. A letter might report that the firm cannot match a request exactly, but will assume some responsibility or offer some mutually satisfactory solution. It may offer to repair an out-of-warranty item at cost (or even less). It may offer a replacement for an irreparably damaged item at producer's or wholesaler's cost.

For responses to requests for claims and adjustments, keep the treatment as unbiased as possible. Create a response specific to the circumstances. Do not bury the bad news so well that the receiver thinks that the company will do something that it will not do. Search for a way to offer some good news that will overshadow the bad—even to the extent of offering an alternative not legally or ethically required.

For example, facilitate transfers of claims to others. One way to do so calls for making the transfer yourself rather than telling the reader to do so. As an illustration, contrast these two treatments of the same request:

The matter is out of our hands. You will have to write to	Although we cannot correct the situation here, I have sent a copy of your letter to . . . . I asked for a quick and fair consideration of your request, as you can see in the enclosed copy of my letter.

Notice how the contrast between the two messages again makes the point that *less* does not always mean *better.* Avoid the curtness that can result from a summary dismissal of a problem.

To maintain specificity and clarity, avoid the form message for nonroutine claims and adjustments. When receivers read words that obviously do not apply to their cases, they often become frustrated and angry. With frustration and anger comes the loss of any hope for retaining goodwill.

Certainly cost effectiveness sometimes dictates that a company cannot offer any relief to the requestor—even if it may lose a customer. However, the investment of some time and thoughtfulness can significantly reduce that risk. Try to deal directly with the situation instead of throwing it into a generic class with dozens of others. Use the facts of the specific case to appeal to logic, reason, and fair play. As a result, even the most frustrated of claimants may eventually say, "I don't like the results, but I can see why the company had to make this decision."

A classic tale summarizes the improper consideration of a claimant: A dissatisfied customer writes to a large company to make a complaint. She receives a nonspecific, but courteous response. Still attached to the response, a hand-written note tells a word processor to "use paragraphs A, D, and K to answer this grouch."

To deal with complainers, even those who make unfair attacks, charges, and claims, put yourself in the other's shoes, and adapt your thinking accordingly. No list of "cookbook" methods or "recipes" can do nearly as much as empathy can to aid in developing bad-news messages.

ASKO BUSINESS MACHINES, INC.
446 East Broadway
Lawrence, Massachusetts 64198
(555) 212-9419

April 21, 198X

Mr. Albert VanDunn
Cranston Dormitory, Box 16
Minville University
Minville, Massachusetts 64190

Dear Mr. VanDunn.

Thank you for purchasing your Business Manager II typewriter at Asko Business Machines and for your letter of April 16. We take particular pleasure in serving students.

Asko provides a 90-day warranty on all of the office machines it sells. Berryhill Corporation, the manufacturer of your Business Manager II, provides a five-year limited warranty on its typewriters. Because you purchased your typewriter from us over a year ago, you can take it to any Berryhill Repair Center for service. The enclosed list of Berryhill Repair Centers includes one center in nearby Baileyville.

The new Heavy-Duty Speedtype typewriter makes a perfect machine for students who must do a great deal of typing work. We can offer you the Heavy-Duty Speedtype at a 15 percent student discount.

Come in soon for a complete demonstration at our Lawrence store. No appointment is necessary.

Sincerely,

John Dade

John Dade
Manager

dd

Enclosure

FIGURE 8–4 Refusal of claim.

Figure 8–4 contains an example of the refusal of a claim. Notice the sensitive approach, the positivism, the nonblaming attitude, and the subordination of the bad news.

(651 words)

Take and score Self-Test 17 over claim and adjustment on pages 205–206.

Order

Many bad-news messages have to do with orders. Some messages refuse requests for credit. Others report an out-of-stock item. Still others report increases in prices, call for more information before completing the order, or indicate a delay. If handled well, several of these situations can fall more into the routine than the bad-news category.

Refusing to fill an order because the person does not qualify for a *credit* sale calls for great care. You want to make the sale, receive subsequent orders, and receive payment. Therefore, try to offer the potential customer some compromise. At least suggest the means by which he or she may qualify for credit. Such means might include the number or volume of prepaid orders that would lead to credit-customer status.

If, for an ordered *item not in stock,* the firm can offer a slightly higher-priced item for the same price, the receiver might well accept the potential bad news as good news. In such situations the seller invests a little money rather than run the risk of losing a satisfied customer. For example, suppose someone uses an outdated price list or catalog and sends too little money. Simple courtesy and frankness can reduce the bad news about an increase in price. For an inconsequential amount of money, simply go ahead and ship the order, include a message about the increase as part of a transmittal, and ask for a remittance for the amount owed. For a substantial amount of money, give the customer the chance to withdraw the order before shipping it. Similarly, for any *additional information* required before shipping an order, write a prompt, nonblaming, but straightforward message asking for it. In effect, then, the message shifts into the routine classification, rather than the negative one.

For a *delayed* shipment or the *offer of a substitute,* the firm cannot always supply a higher-priced substitute for the same price as the original item. Sometimes it does not even have a satisfactory substitute and simply must delay the shipment. Of course, the longer the proposed delay, the more distressing it becomes to the person placing the order. Again picture the receiver and weigh which would be the greater loss for your company—the customer or some outright investment of funds. You may even contact another supplier to fill the order for your customer and then contact the customer to explain.

Figure 8–5 illustrates a bad-news message associated with an order. Observe the positive approach. Also observe how the writer took the time to help the customer solve her problem. All too often a writer would just curtly tell the customer "We don't stock dust screens" and no more. Read the letter from the viewpoint of the person who placed the order. Do you think you would feel fairly treated? Would you remain a customer?

General Request and Inquiry

As described in Chapter 7, requests and inquiries relate to many topics other than credit, loans, claims, adjustments, and orders. Therefore, refusals often occur in response to other topics.

Declining an *invitation* to attend an event often amounts to bad news for the person making the invitation. Encode the message as carefully as any bad-news message. Give the reasons sensitively, but as honestly as diplomacy

INTERNATIONAL
TELEVISION
CORPORATION

43 Oak Road, Mason, New York 32907

June 14, 198X

Ms. Irene Lawson
ZEX Property Management, Inc.
1515 Arbor Boulevard
Rilling, Arkansas 96411

Dear Ms. Lawson:

Thank you for your order for 100 dust screens for your ITC Color XI units. We are pleased to know that the television sets have served you well, so well that you wish to keep them in your motels for several more years. Our ITC Color XI sets are built to last a lifetime.

Because of the pressures of inflation, the International Television Corporation no longer produces most of its television accessories, including the dust screens you ordered. Of course, ITC still manufactures a complete line of quality television repair parts, all of which will be available to you at a discount for the life of your ITC television sets. Our new parts catalogue is enclosed.

We feel sure that a number of custom plastics shops would be glad to fill your large order for dust screens. We called one shop in your area, Katz Plastics in Flame, Arkansas. The shop's owner, Joanne Katz, stated that she could produce 100 dust screens in about four weeks. She was unable to give us a price at the time, but assured us that her prices are competitive.

You probably want to deal directly with Katz Platics or another shop. However, we will assist in any way we can.

Sincerely,

Mary Santino

Mary Santino
Service Representative

ms/ee

Enclosures

FIGURE 8-5 Rejection of order because of inability to fill.

allows. You should develop a turndown for a *speaking engagement* just as conscientiously as a denial of credit to a requester. In essence, such a message rejects a request from each member of the potential audience. Adopt a sensitive, but forthright style. Try to suggest an alternative date in addition to the name of another speaker for the event. Express sincere appreciation for the respect accorded by the request.

When refusing to give or lend *materials* requested by someone, consider the impact on the requester. Give the reasons, and try to offer an alternative. Likewise, when denying a requested *service,* courteously explain why. Try to offer another reasonable avenue through which the requester may obtain the service. For example, suppose your firm owns a film that someone would like to borrow to show to an organization. If you cannot lend it, you might suggest that the requester rent it at low cost from a university media center that you know owns a print of the film.

Sometimes a firm receives an *inquiry* that it cannot handle. Whether the inquiry comes from someone of little or great importance, answer promptly and state clearly the reasons for not being able to answer the questions. If possible, suggest another channel through which the inquirer may obtain the desired answers. Figure 8–6 provides an example of a refusal of a request. Observe how Rosen obviously thought about how Faxlin would feel and wrote the message accordingly. Notice also how he offered an alternative course of action.

Claims and Adjustments

Many claims and adjustments deal with routine transactions. On the other hand, messages sometimes relate to claims or adjustments involving large amounts of money, someone's rights, or a delicate personal situation.

Analyze how the news may affect the receiver. Establish purposes in terms of the action desired from the receiver. Of course, not only does such a claim or adjustment carry bad news to the receiver, but it often requires the use of some persuasive processes. Therefore, when reading Chapter 9 on persuasive messages, think of how rational and emotional appeals apply to claims and adjustments. Review Figure 8–7 on pages 196–197 to observe how Miller maintained a delicate balance between communicating bad news and trying to persuade the receiver to take the desired action. She used the positive sandwich, but included some tastefully stated direct statements.

Unfavorable Recommendations

Most recommendation writers tend to describe only the positive qualities of job applicants. However, they sometimes feel ethically bound to describe some negative ones. In such cases, the bad news points toward the applicant rather than toward the receiver of the letter itself. However, even the receiver often may find such news disagreeable because of disappointment about a seemingly good candidate.

The applicant may at one time or another see a letter of recommendation, even if the requester assures confidentiality of the exchange. Therefore, recall the discussion in Chapter 7 on confidentiality. For your own protection and

BARSTOW AND KEEDY MANUFACTURING, INC.
391 Henderson Avenue
Ivell, Wisconsin 39421
(555) 624-2462

March 1, 198X

Mr. Jerome Faxlin
Korsika Chamber of Commerce
P.O. Box 899
Korsika, Wisconsin 39426

Dear Mr. Faxlin:

The Industry Speaks to Korsika workshop series you are planning sounds most interesting. Your idea to include both managers and workers on each panel is brilliant! Workers' views of industry conditions are so often overlooked.

Every year I make a number of trips to our office in Atlanta, Georgia, and I am scheduled to attend two very important meetings there during the week of your workshops. Luckily, Elizabeth McPhree, Barstow and Keedy's top marketing specialist, is free to serve as a panelist on Monday, June 6, or Tuesday, June 7. As you may know, she is a well-known speaker. She also is the co-author of Beyond Selling: Marketing Strategies for Executives, a textbook used in many graduate schools of management. Ms. McPhree shares my enthusiasm about your fine program.

I am honored that you asked me to participate in your workshop series, because I am confident that the series will be a smashing success. Please let us know if you would like Ms. McPhree to serve as a panelist. We would be glad to answer any of your questions.

Again, thank you for giving me the opportunity to be a part of the Industry Speaks to Korsika workshop series. I hope that I can participate in one of your future programs.

Sincerely,

Marvin Rosen

Marvin Rosen
Marketing Manager

ff

FIGURE 8–6 Refusal of request to participate in workshop.

that of the applicant, then, make sure you have a solid foundation for negative comments before writing them.

Just as for any bad-news message, surround the negative elements with good elements. Assure the reader that you made the judgments from the context of your observance; do not leave the impression that the weaknesses you describe exist for the person in every context and for all time.

Figure 8–8 illustrates an unfavorable recommendation. Because so many writers say only glowing things about a job applicant, would you decide that this applicant is indeed poor? Did Warrick maintain a proper balance between objectivity and subjectivity? Between directness and tact?

Unsolicited News of a Negative Nature

Now and again you will have to *initiate* a bad-news message. For example, you may have to:

- Write policyholders to notify them of an increase in premiums or a decrease in coverage
- Write to other types of customers to inform them of rate or price increases or decreases in service
- Remove a customer from the approved credit list
- Notify employees that you will have to lower wages or cut benefits
- Notify employees of a layoff
- Tell your clients that a company in which they invested is defunct

Even though they do not refuse a direct request, such messages require the same empathy and psychology associated with unfavorable responses to requests. In fact, an unsolicited message that contains bad news may devastate the receiver more than a solicited message containing bad news may. After all, a requester knows that a message will come and that it may contain bad news. The recipient of the bad news in an unsolicited message often has no warning. To write the unsolicited message carrying bad news, then, apply the guidelines and principles particularly carefully. Protect the receiver as much as you can, but do not hedge about the truth. Consider the message in Figure 8–9 as an illustration of the unsolicited message of bad news. Project yourself into the mind of the receiver, and evaluate the success of the letter in accomplishing its obvious objective.

The next chapter covers persuasive messages. It emphasizes persuasive requests, collection messages, and sales messages.

R C J SECURITY ALARM, INC.
6298 Perman Street
Jenray, Alabama 38974
(555) 629-9268

June 3, 198X

Ms. Beatrice Albert
Gravely Security Suppliers, Inc.
Route 2, Box 84R
Dorlin, Minnesota 22215

Dear Ms. Albert:

Thank you for responding so promptly to our last order for 40 Deluxe Protection II alarm systems. All of the units arrived last week, and we have already installed several of them in area businesses and homes.

Last year we ordered nine Economy Protection I alarm systems from you. We installed one in our own home and the rest in homes in our neighborhood. Recently, burglars robbed three of our neighbors, all of whom have Economy Protection I systems. Unfortunately, not one of the systems functioned during the burglaries. We checked our own system and found that it does not function either.

Because we are extremely concerned, we spent many hours inspecting the Economy Protection I alarm systems, but we were unable to locate the problem. However, because we installed over a thousand other alarm systems in the last five years and we received no reports of malfunctions, we must conclude that our installation method is not the problem. Thus, we fear that the Economy Protection I alarm systems them selves are at fault.

Because we and our neighbors are eager to protect our homes, please send nine Deluxe Protection I systems as soon as possible to replace the faulty Economy Protection I systems. We will then install the replacement systems at no charge to our

FIGURE 8–7 Claim request letter.

Ms. Beatrice Albert 2 June 3, 198X

somewhat distressed customers. Of course, we know that you will provide the new alarm systems at no cost to us, and we would be glad to send back the faulty systems if you will cover the postage charges. We realize that you would like to have a chance to inspect one of the faulty systems so that you can avoid problems with the Economy Protection I systems you produce in the future.

Again, we have had no trouble with the other alarm systems you have sent to us. We expect to be your customer for years to come because you provide us with such excellent service.

Sincerely,

Lucinda Miller

Lucinda Miller
Co-Owner

gg

FIGURE 8–7 (Continued).

LOGAN NILO SAVINGS & LOAN
One Streil Plaza
Harbor Pond, Maine 62419

July 21, 198X

Mr. Jackson Riley
C & R Savings and Loan
946 Stewart Road
Perry, Missouri 41986

Dear Mr. Riley:

It is a pleasure to help you evaluate Mr. Dan Smith's suitability for a position at C & R Savings and Loan. I both trained and supervised Mr. Smith during the time that he worked at Logan Nilo.

Mr. Smith worked as an assistant loan officer at Logan Nilo for three years. We hired him immediately after he was graduated from Harbor Pond Community College with a two-year degree in accounting. He was very eager to learn about the savings and loan business, and several customers told me that he was one of our most courteous employees. Mr. Smith did a fine job of working with his customers.

Mr. Smith missed 32 days of work in 1977, 41 days in 1978, and 36 days in 1979. Most of his absences were because of illness, and each absence lasted one or two days. On ten occasions Mr. Smith failed to call us to say that he would be unable to come to work.

Mr. Smith also made frequent errors in processing loan applications. Though he seemed to try to avoid mistakes, little of his work was free of errors. In fact, I began reviewing all of Mr. Smith's work in order to correct his errors. He was quite willing to discuss his mistakes so that he could learn to overcome them.

Because of the attendance and the work problems I just mentioned, we asked Mr. Smith to leave Logan Nilo on November 16, 1979. We were somewhat reluctant to ask him to leave because he had developed rapport with his customers. He was also eager to learn, loyal to me and his co-workers, and honest. Mr. Smith had a wonderful sense of humor, and was a very positive influence on office morale. I do believe that he has the ability to become a good loan officer if he can cultivate good health and learn to concentrate on his work.

I trust the confidential information will be of some help to you. Please call or write me if you have any other questions.

Sincerely,

Ellen Warrick

Ellen Warrick
Loan Manager

EW:hh

FIGURE 8–8 Unfavorable recommendation.

CARLETON ELECTRIC COMPANY
P.O. Box 145, Carleton, Indiana 14987

August 1, 198X

Dear Customer:

During the past two years, the Carleton Electric Company has experienced rapidly increasing labor and equipment costs. We at Carleton tried to make a number of internal changes so that you, our valued customer, would not have to shoulder the burden.

As you know, we were successful: Your rates did not increase for two full years. While you were paying more and more for other products and services, you did not pay one penny more for electricity supplied by the Carleton Electric Company.

After conducting a thorough review of our operations, we find that we can no longer absorb all of our still-increasing costs. We have, however, found a way to hold the required rate increase to only 5.5 percent. And 5.5 percent is much less than the 15 percent annual inflation rate. The typical consumer will pay only $2 a month more for service.

The new rates will take effect on August 1, and you can count on no additional rate increases for at least one year after that. We have again succeeded in shouldering a great deal of the inflation burden ourselves.

Please call or write if you have any questions or comments concerning the rate change. Your views are very important to us.

You can continue to rely on us to fight inflation for you.

Sincerely,

Emory L. Thaxer

Emory L. Thaxer
Customer Relations Manager

rr

FIGURE 8–9 Unsolicited letter containing bad news.

SUMMARY

Take great care in writing messages that carry bad news. Use the indirect, ascending-rank, or chronological developmental pattern, a positive writing style, a buffer opening, a positive sandwich, carefully chosen words, and the "you" attitude. All these approaches subordinate the bad news and make empathy the overriding determinant of the structure and content of the message.

Refusal messages deny credit, refuse requests for claims and adjustments, refuse to fill an order, or deny a general request or inquiry. If possible, offer an alternative to soften the blow of the refusal. Make the message clear, but keep it buffered and positive.

When developing a message setting out a major claim and calling for an adjustment, treat it as bad news for the receiver. Maintain a sensitive balance between communicating the bad news and trying to persuade the receiver to take the desired action.

Unfavorable recommendations for job applicants carry bad news for both the applicant and the receiver. To develop such messages, establish a sure foundation for any negative comments, consider the issues of confidentiality, and use statements of fact rather than vague references to unsatisfactory performance. Also try to include the strengths of the person. Few people possess only weaknesses.

You may have to initiate bad-news messages at times. Such *unsolicited* messages might inform customers that they can no longer use their credit cards, or they could notify employees of a cut in their wages and benefits. Again try to offset bad news with a positive alternative or some good news.

DEAD-END JOBS

Yesterday 85 of FJC Computer Corporation's 420 secretaries met with David Levine, FJC's human resources vice president. The secretaries had asked for a meeting with Levine to discuss promotion opportunities in the firm.

At the meeting, many secretaries expressed great concern about having no way to move into professional positions. Although many of them have earned or are working on college degrees, the firm offers professional positions only to graduates of the firm's own year-long computer training program. The program is full-time, and trainees receive half of their eventual starting pay. But unlike most of the young men and women in the training program, the secretaries support families and cannot afford to take a cut in pay to attend the computer school; thus, they are effectively locked into their clerical positions if they wish to remain at FJC.

Levine understands the secretaries' dilemma and worries that those with college degrees may go to competitors' firms to secure professional positions. Levine knows that FJC would lose a number of loyal and exceedingly competent people if such an exodus occurred.

Levine explores ways to allow interested secretaries and other nonexempt employees the opportunity to move into professional positions and thinks of these alternatives:

- Design a special night training program
- Let nonexempt employees participate in the existing training program at no cut in pay
- Design a part-time day program and give employees time off from work
- Design a self-paced, independent study program

Levine knows each alternative has its advantages and disadvantages. He must evaluate each alternative in light of these factors:

- The firm has a limited training budget
- The integrity of the training program must not be compromised
- Many of the firm's nonexempt employees have family commitments in the evening
- The professionals for whom the nonexempt employees work would be reluctant to give them time off during the day
- Some nonexempt employees might not find acceptable a training program that takes more than a year to complete
- Some trainees might never lose the stigma of having been a nonexempt employee
- Some professional employees might feel threatened by the nonexempt employees' attempts to move up in the firm

(This case is fictional.)

EXERCISES

1. This is an unsatisfactory bad-news letter. Correct it and explain the reasoning behind your changes. Concentrate on the content, not the format of the letter.

FIRST BIG BANK
1432 East Creswell Avenue
Leona, Oregon 16154

August 1, 198X

Mr. I. I. Warren
1069 Elm Street
Wixler, Oregon 16165

Dear Mr. Warren:

We cannot give you the $2,000 loan you requested because you have a less-than-satisfactory credit record. We also do not like to give loans to elementary school teachers because they do not make a good salary and they are unemployed in the summer.

We will allow you to keep your checking account at our bank, though.

Sincerely,

F. I. Mouth

F. I. Mouth
Loan Officer

2. This is an unsatisfactory bad-news letter. Correct it and explain the reasoning behind your changes. Concentrate on the content, not the format of the letter.

EXCELO COMPANY
17 MOX ROAD
WINSOME, NEVADA 66663

March 18, 198X

Ramona Sleeve
Arbo Furniture, Inc.
115 North Booth Street
Wales, Vermont 88883

Dear Ms. Sleeve:

The six file cabinets we ordered from you are unsatisfactory. They arrived all dented and scratched, and none of the drawers works correctly. We have used them for only one year.

Pick them up immediately and send a refund.

Sincerely,

T. O. O. Late

T. O. O. Late
Facilities Manager

3. This is an unsatisfactory bad-news letter. Correct it and explain the reasoning behind your changes. Concentrate on the content, not the format of the letter.

DAVIS AND LEVENSON CONSULTING GROUP
99 East Oak Lane
Edmonds, Arkansas 33364
(555) 666–1390

April 1, 198X

Ms. Elizabeth Geil
Geil Systems Management, Inc.
130 Allen Avenue
Edmonds, Arkansas 33364

Dear Ms. Geil:

I am pleased to respond to your request for an evaluation of Frank Smith's performance at Davis and Levenson. Unfortunately, Smith was one of our worst employees. He was late sometimes and I heard that he did not work very hard. It was said that he had a bad attitude. He may have some troubles at home. I just cannot bring myself to recommend him for a job.

I hope that I have been of assistance.

Sincerely,

N.V. Nice

N. V. Nice
Personnel Director

4. This is an unsatisfactory bad-news letter. Correct it and explain the reasoning behind your changes. Concentrate on the content, not the format of the letter.

GRAHAM CABLE TELEVISION, INC.
1149 North Road
Charlestown, California 41963
(555) 439–6629

November 9, 198X

Dear Cable Customer:

We are raising your monthly residential cable fee by $10.50. You now should pay Graham Cable Television, Inc., $22.50 every month. We are forced to raise the residential rate because we are losing money on all of you residential customers. You ask us to make too many service calls.

Make your payments on time, please.

Sincerely,

N.O. Tact

N. O. Tact
Payments Clerk

5. Meet with your group. Discuss and correct these poorly worded sentences that were written for bad-news messages. Have one of your group members read the improved sentences to the rest of the class.
    a. You always make your payments late, so we are lowering your credit limit to $100.
    b. Your request came much too late for us to do anything about it.
    c. You are a bad insurance risk; thus, we must refuse your request for the Golden Sixties coverage.
    d. Your salespeople lied to me.
    e. We won't fill your order until you make a big payment.
    f. However, you can apply for a loan when you start making a good salary.
    g. She was not a decent employee.
    h. Please forgive us for what we had to do, and we hope you will use cash to buy things from us from now on.
    i. Now don't be too mad at us.
    j. We have bad news for you.
    k. Now don't get upset, but you are in grave danger of losing your house.
    l. Why do you always make late payments?
6. You did not choose to hire the receiver of your letter for the production manager position for which he interviewed. Write a letter informing him of your decision. Supply any needed information.
7. You cannot fill the receiver's order because she has not paid for her last order. You also want her to pay what she owes. Write the letter, supplying any needed information.
8. You must refuse an advertisement because it does not meet your magazine's standards. You feel that the advertisement is both sexist and racist. Write the letter, supplying any needed information.
9. You will not grant a requested interview because you do not approve of the general policies and content of the publication the interviewer represents. Write the letter, supplying any needed information.
10. Write a letter in response to T.O.O. Late's message in Number 2. Supply additional information as needed.
11. P. R. Risk has written to you to ask for credit at your clothing store. You investigate and learn that P. R. Risk:
    - Is new in town
    - Has no credit record elsewhere
    - Has a job that pays $10,000 a year
    - Rents an apartment
    - Has debts of $2,000
    - Is a single parent of one two-year-old child
    - Has a high-school education
    - Is 23 years of age

    On the basis of the information, you decide you cannot extend the credit. Write the letter of refusal. Give some reasons, and offer some suggestion about how Risk might become eligible.
12. You must tell your 250 employees that economic conditions are forcing you to close your plant for an indefinite period beginning October 1 (one month from now). You have begun to make some contacts that may allow you to start production again the first of the year, but nothing is firm at this point. You do plan to bring in an employment-counseling team the last week of this month. The team will be available to help the employees conduct job searches. Write a general letter to the employees, supplying additional information as needed.

13. Respond to the order letter in Figure 7-1 with the news that you will not be able to ship the metal-turning lathe and cabinet until March 15. The only lathe you can ship to arrive by February 28 lists at $500 more. However, it has added features enough to warrant the added expense. Your supervisor says that you can cut 10 percent off that $500—in addition to giving the person the Preferred Customer discount.
14. Use your dictionary and thesaurus to create meanings for these words. Use the words when you think, write, and speak so that you feel comfortable using them.
    - a. Buffer
    - b. Commendable
    - c. Contrivance
    - d. Empathy
    - e. Duality
    - f. Finesse
    - g. Gracious
    - h. Hackneyed
    - i. Insincere
    - j. Irreparable
    - k. Pervade
    - l. Rapport
    - m. Subservient
    - n. Tact
15. Take and score Self-Test 18 over Chapter 8.

SELF-TEST 17
Excerpt about Claim and Adjustment

A. Recall (33 points each). For each multiple-choice question, select the most accurate answer.

1. Which of these is *not* a good way to soften a letter that denies the writer's request for a claim or adjustment?
    - a. Offer an alternative.
    - b. If possible, shift the responsibility to a third party (only if it is the third party's responsibility).
    - c. Offer a compromise.
    - d. Try to prove that the writer was completely at fault.
    - e. Offer to send a replacement.
2. Which of these statements concerning denying claim and adjustment requests is *not* correct?
    - a. Do not bury the bad news so well that you mislead the receiver into thinking that you will do something that you do not plan to do.
    - b. Try to be honest so that the receiver does not feel that he is or she is being given the "runaround."
    - c. Try to use a form letter for nonroutine claims and adjustments.
    - d. Try to retain the receiver's goodwill.
    - e. Avoid being curt.

B. Inference (34 points). For the multiple-choice question, select the most accurate answer.

1. Which of the following does not constitute a courteous denial of a claim or request for adjustment?
    - a. Although we cannot repair your watch, we have enclosed a list of excellent discount repair services.
    - b. We know that doing without your radio has been an inconvenience, but because your warranty has run out, we cannot repair or replace it. Because you are a valued customer, we will send you an extremely helpful "do-it-yourself" repair kit.
    - c. We find no record of your April 12 payment. Because it is possible that we have overlooked it, please send a copy of your cancelled check to us in the enclosed postpaid envelope.

d. Because your insurance does not cover dental work, we cannot send you a check at this time. For only an additional $6.50 a month, however, we can cover *all* of your dental bills.
e. All of our products are covered by a 90-day warranty. You have owned your toaster for over a year and should know that we are no longer responsible for any problems. You must bear the repair expense.

SOLUTION

A. Recall (33 points each)
1. d 2. c

B. Inference (34 points)
1. e

SELF-TEST 18
Chapter 8

A. Recall (25 points each). For each multiple-choice question, select the most accurate answer.
1. The best developmental patterns for bad-news messages are:
   a. Indirect, ascending-rank, and chronological
   b. Direct, indirect, and spatial
   c. Chronological, analytical, and direct
   d. Indirect, chronological, and descending-rank
   e. Direct, indirect, and analytical
2. When you write an unfavorable recommendation, try to:
   a. Be vague about the employee's drawbacks.
   b. List as many of the employees' weaknesses as possible.
   c. Be specific about the employee's weaknesses and try also to bring out her or his strengths.
   d. Convince the receiver not to hire the employee.
   e. Make the employee look better than he or she is so that you can get rid of her or him.
3. Which of these is *not* appropriate for bad-news messages?
   a. Sentences containing both an independent and a dependent clause (complex sentence)
   b. A blanket form that covers the rejection of all claims
   c. Buffer opening
   d. Positive sandwich
   e. Empathy

B. Inference (25 points). For the multiple-choice question, select the most accurate answer.
1. Which of these statements is true?
   a. Bad-news messages employ significantly different techniques and principles than neutral and good-news letters.
   b. A person who has sent an article to a factory for repair assumes that no news is good news.
   c. When someone makes unfair demands, your responsibility for making a positive response remains the same as for less-demanding people.

d. Frankness has no place in bad-news messages.
e. The best way to establish a "you" attitude is to use the word "you" several times during the message.

SOLUTION

A. Recall (25 points each)
1. a
2. c
3. b

B. Inference (25 points)
1. c

STUDENT'S OBJECTIVES:

1 To learn to develop persuasive messages—messages that attempt to get people to take some action beyond the routine, including the action of accepting some idea or belief

2 To apply the principles of writing persuasive messages by using the indirect, chronological, and direct plans of development and the AICA pattern (attention, interest, conviction, action)

9

WRITING PERSUASIVE MESSAGES

4 To practice developing collection messages through the routine, persuasive, and demand stages

3 To practice developing persuasive requests

5 To practice developing sales messages, including messages in the continual series, the wear-out series, and the campaign series

Every message involves persuasion. Whatever their other objectives, senders usually at least want to persuade receivers to respect their personal abilities and qualities.

GENERAL CONCEPTS OF PERSUASION

Writers develop persuasive messages to get people to take some action beyond the routine. The desired action might require the receiver to expend large amounts of energy, time, or money for potentially great rewards. It could involve only slight expenditures, but ask the reader to act or accept without apparent benefits. It may even require the receiver to expend energy, time, or money that may lead to risks or painful results.

Action

Persuasive messages try to get people to do many different kinds of things; for example:

Purchase goods or services	Do some kind of favor
Adopt a plan	Donate to a foundation
Pay a bill	Hire or promote
Appear before a group	Change their minds
Attend some function	Fund a research project

Although this book uses the traditional word *persuasive,* the actual spotlight falls upon the desired action, not upon the persuasion itself.

Benefits to the Receiver

The successful persuasive message clearly identifies benefits to the receiver. These benefits must have strength enough to overcome inertia or outright resistance. Thus, defining purposes and understanding the receiver constitute the focus of persuasive activity.

Persuasion involves using knowledge about a receiver in order to achieve goals. Therefore, the topic of ethics again enters into the discussion. Some people equate persuasion with manipulation, and thus with unethical activity. They do so particularly when the activity leads to profit.

Ethics

Everyone in every walk of life uses persuasive techniques. For example, children try to convince others to do what they want. So do politicians, elected government officials, and attorneys. So do teachers, researchers, ministers, newspaper editors, writers, and representatives of not-for-profit organizations. Each of these groups includes some unethical people. However, the use of certain techniques by unethical people does not make the techniques themselves unethical. Ethics reside in people's motives, not in the processes they employ.

Do raise questions about business and persuasion, though. Do you think that advertising creates demand? If you do, do you think the creation of "artificial" demand involves unethical practices? Do you think the use of subliminal suggestion in selling represents an ethical activity?

Do you favor government action restraining advertising? Should the government prohibit or restrict advertisements for sales of "junk" foods? refined sugar? saccharin? tobacco? alcoholic beverages and other drugs? personal products? pornographic literature? adult book stores? X-rated movies? massage parlors? legal services? medical and dental services? eyeglasses? Does government action itself represent unethical interference with business and the professional and private lives of people?

As you raise such questions about the Madison Avenue approach to persuasion, ask the same questions about the use of persuasion in other arenas:

- Should charismatic speakers be allowed to persuade people to accept certain beliefs?
- Should not-for-profit organizations ask people to contribute to their causes?
- Should activist groups demonstrate for or against such things as war, nuclear power, and ecology?
- Should investigative reporters write persuasive pieces—particularly if they do not reveal their sources?
- Should laws prohibit the activities of organizations that espouse beliefs counter to those that prevail in a nation? (Should the Nazi Party, the Communist Party, and the Ku Klux Klan use persuasion to bring members into their folds?)
- Should consumer advocates persuade legislators to enact protective laws?

These questions provide deliberate reminders about the hopelessness of trying to restrict the use of persuasive techniques to the "right" groups or "proper" topics. The definitions of *right* and *proper* vary from person to person and from group to group. No amount of legislation will change that fact.

For business communication, then, consider the ethical ramifications as you create persuasive messages. Decide whether the end justifies the means, whether you will retain self-respect, and how receivers and the larger community will view your persuasive methods. Also use rational, critical approaches as you receive persuasive messages.

PRINCIPLES OF PERSUASION

To develop principles for persuasive messages, recall the communication guidelines in Chapter 2 and the writing suggestions in Chapter 6. The concern with purposes, participants, environment, channel, interference, messages, feedback, and evaluation apply directly to persuasion. Many of the examples in previous chapters involve persuasion to a significant extent. At this point, though, we will review three of the components: purposes, receivers, and messages.

Purposes

For any situation involving persuasive techniques, establish the objectives precisely. In addition, carefully establish the bases for evaluating success in attaining them. Also try to understand the receiver's purposes as completely as possible.

Receivers

To understand receivers, look into human wants, needs, and motivations. Understanding why people behave as they do improves chances of matching appeals to motives. People usually choose to do what will help them attain *their* goals, not yours.

For example, a debtor may not *want* to pay a past-due bill, but a straight-forward statement of the creditor's plans for legal action may make its own appeal. Even a debtor who does not want to pay probably wants even less to engage in illegal acts or receive social disapproval.

As an aid to selecting appropriate persuasive approaches, study the full range of wants, needs, and motivations. They begin with basic needs for food, shelter, and clothing, advance to needs for security, love, and belonging, and go all the way up to needs for self-fulfillment and self-determination.

Values, beliefs, attitudes, and life styles change through time. Appeals that worked 30, 20, or even 10 years ago will not necessarily work today. The review of types of persuasive messages in subsequent sections helps to match appeals to human factors.

Messages

At the writing stage of developing a persuasive message, you must select, draft, revise, and transmit messages carefully. Select messages and appeals to match the receiver's motives identified during the preliminary stages. Draft messages using whatever method works best for you. Revise and transmit messages to meet the standards established for the chosen channels.

Developmental Plans

Persuasive messages lend themselves to indirect, ascending-rank, chronological, direct, and descending-rank plans for development. If a persuasive message also includes some bad news, choose the indirect, ascending-rank, or chronological pattern. Many letters of collection fall into this category. Sales messages and job applications, however, fall quite naturally into the direct and descending-rank patterns.

Parts of Messages

The basic communication outline recognizes that every message has at least three major parts—a beginning, a middle, and an end. For persuasive messages, however, the plan usually involves four parts. These parts take the form of the AICA formula:

1. Attention
2. Interest
3. Conviction
4. Action

Attention The opening of any message should gain the receiver's attention and introduce the topic. However, persuasive messages—particularly sales messages—demand attention-getting openings. Unless the opening captures the reader's attention, he or she may never read past it to the body and the stimulus to action. Even for required reading, attention-getting devices greatly increase interest and concentration.

To gain attention, include some detail that relates to the reader's life or whets the reader's appetite for more information. If you can sweep readers into messages by appealing to human wants and needs, you have a good chance of holding them throughout the messages.

Attention-getting devices include:

1. *Use attractive nonverbal symbols:* paper, color, letterhead, format, layout, graphs, pictures, drawings, size and kind of type, a dash of handwriting, clean type, even margins, short messages.
2. *Open with a natural, conversational lead-in:* "Yes, I agree that . . . ." "You're so right—we should . . . ." "Hi, Dick; how's it going?" "Hello, I'm Y.R. Self. As a representative of Spittinimage Portraits, Inc., I enjoy telling . . . ."
3. *Tie the message to a current topic:* "Gasoline prices affect us all."
4. *Use a striking subject line:* "Money Market Certificates: Exciting Alternatives to Traditional Savings Accounts"
5. *Raise a question:* "Have you ever wished you could have your own personalized stationery"?
6. *Insert the receiver's name:* "Take a look at the enclosed brochure, Ms. Tate; you will like what you see."
7. *Set a scene:* "Transport yourself to a quiet beach . . . the sound of waves as they caress the shore . . . the stirring of a cool breeze through the palms . . ."
8. *Use action words:* "Strike a blow for financial security." "Reach out . . . ." "Control your own . . . ." "Take the plunge."
9. *Make a dramatic or unexpected statement:* "You may be one of the millions who have high blood pressure and do not know it."
10. *Spotlight a single, dramatic key word:* "Energy," "Growth," "Security," "Hunger," "Crime," "Profit."
11. *Use common courtesies:* "Thanks! I appreciate your thoughtfulness." "Please, for the sake of our children, read on."
12. *Enclose something in quotation marks:* "'That's the best cake I've ever eaten.' So said Alma Goren of Rooneyville, West Virginia." "'To err is human'—and are we ever human."

Avoid artificiality—too much of the trite, too much hype, too many buzz words. On the other hand, rise above the drab and the colorless. Choose attention-catching techniques to fit the circumstances of the transaction. For example, when writing to persuade the receiver to speak at a formal occasion, do not begin with a flamboyant attention-getting sentence. However, when writing to persuade someone to buy a product or service, do.

Likewise, when writing a first-stage collection letter, use the opening position for a buffer rather than for anything very striking. Yet, when writing a final-stage collection letter, use a startling opening message to gain the reader's attention.

Interest The second stage of the evolving message attempts to assure that the reader perceives and becomes *interested* in the subject. Although the attention phase introduces the subject, it rarely develops full perception or interest. The attention phase should hold readers long enough to move them into the words designed to clarify the topic.

Interest spins directly out of attention. To illustrate, these examples add interest-building words to some of the examples in the preceding section.

> Complete the first conversational lead-in in the second item: "Yes, I agree that we need to set the date for our conference now." The reader slips quickly from attention into interest.
>
> Add a second sentence to the third item: "Gasoline prices affect us all. But if you change to a Vechette, you'll average close to 40 miles a gallon." The reader would immediately switch from thoughts about gasoline prices in general to a consideration of a Vechette as a gasoline-saving automobile.
>
> Even the example in the seventh item could add words establishing clearer topics: "Hawaii awaits you." "Visit the golden shores of Miami Beach." "How about following the annual conference of the Financial Analysis Association with a weekend at Malibu?"
>
> Add this sentence to the ninth item: "For only $19.95 you can keep a regular check on this serious health problem by owning a Disys brand aneroid blood pressure monitor and stethoscope."

Conviction The stage of *conviction* spirals the reader beyond mere attention and interest into personal understanding and conviction about the whole subject. The development of interest may take only one or two sentences. However, full development of conviction usually requires several sentences, if not paragraphs or sections. Treat the attention-getting stage as the introduction, the conviction-building stage as the body, and the interest-gaining stage as the bridge between the two. Many writers develop the body before developing the other parts.

Action The final stage of a persuasive message calls for *action,* including the mental action of acceptance. The action-getting paragraph(s) (usually just one) clearly define the desired actions (who, what, when, where, how and why). These examples of closings illustrate calls for action:

Please ship the materials to arrive by June 9.

If you cannot attend the meeting on the 30th, please let me know by the 25th.

Would you please send your reply by August 22. I need the information for a project due the end of the month.

Make your payment by October 19 if you want to avoid legal action.

Order now. This special offer expires on April 1.

As suggested, writers sometimes establish goals calling for indirect action or acceptance. Therefore, the final section of a message may not always call for concrete action. For example, trying to persuade thousands of employees to appreciate the company likely would not yield concrete results.

Whichever the case—call to external action or call to internal action—let receivers know what feedback you want, and communicate in a way that motivates them to give that feedback. Thus, make the action-eliciting portion of the message:

- Tie the action to your own and the reader's purposes
- End the message with the clearest possible call to action
- Motivate the reader to complete the desired action
- Make the action as easy as possible by including stamped envelopes, giving telephone numbers and addresses, and offering to do something in return

TYPES OF PERSUASIVE MESSAGES

Obviously, the principles for effective persuasion overlap with those for other types of messages. Many persuasive-request messages fit the neutral classification. Messages of collection include both persuasion and bad news. Even good-news messages sometimes involve some persuasion. Although this chapter features letters, persuasive messages also may appear in memoranda, forms, reports, oral presentations, and other formats.

Four broad classes define the scope of persuasive messages: (1) requests, (2) collections, (3) sales, and (4) employment. Chapters 15 and 16 cover employment; this chapter covers requests, collections, and sales.

Requests

Persuasive requests move beyond the routine. They try to overcome apathy or resistance in the receiver. These examples of desired actions illustrate persuasive requests:

Contribute to a charity
Collect complex information
Lend money
Grant an interview
Grant a personal leave
Complete a questionnaire
Authorize research
Grant a promotion or raise

- Give permission to use private facilities for a meeting
- Approve a transfer to another department
- Rezone property from residential to business
- Grant special privileges
- Endorse a political candidate
- Give permission to buy a special piece of equipment
- Agree to take an organizational office

For persuasive requests you should choose either the indirect or direct developmental pattern and combine it with the AICA design to develop the message. If you select the indirect pattern, open with a mild attention-getting reference to the topic. Then use the interest-gaining stage as the transition from the introduction to conviction. In the body (conviction stage), develop the reasoning fully. Finish with a clear, positive statement of the desired action and a courteous closing statement.

For the direct pattern, deliberately start with the request. Then follow it with the arguments in support of the request at the conviction-building stage. Throughout the process, whether indirect or direct, name or imply the potential rewards of the desired action to the receiver. Appeal to the basic needs and wants of the receiver.

Carefully identify anything that may interfere with your request, and try to prevent its occurrence. The greatest source of interference lies within the minds of you and the receiver. Therefore, cast yourself into the receiver's role and try to anticipate any negative reactions to what you propose. Then write to eliminate or subordinate all points that might lead to objections. Also emphasize points that will likely lead to feelings positive enough to overshadow any negative ones. As an overriding thread through your thinking—and throughout the message itself—anticipate that the receiver will grant the request. Such an attitude often creates a self-fulfilling prophecy of success.

Figure 9–1 illustrates a letter written persuasively. Does the development use the indirect or direct pattern? Do you think the pattern "works" for this persuasive request? Do you think the message would overcome apathy or resistance in the receiver? As the receiver, would you respond as the writer wants? Another persuasive request appears in Figure 9–2. Analyze it as suggested for Figure 9–1.

Collections

Messages designed to collect past-due accounts run the gamut from the routine to the demanding or threatening. Persuasive messages fall at an intermediate stage between the two extremes. Although this chapter concentrates on the application of communication principles to persuasion, it also covers the routine and demanding stages of the collecting sequence.

Importance of Collection

Companies collect money to make a profit or just to survive. In addition to the serious losses sustained when a debtor never pays, a firm loses money when payments arrive late. Of course, the later they arrive, the greater the loss, because:

- The reduction of cash flow often necessitates borrowing at high interest rates
- The collecting procedures themselves require heavy expenditures for the personnel and materials necessary to complete them
- Repossessions of durable goods cost a great deal
- Improper collecting procedures often cause greater losses than sustained with good collection procedures
- Debtors often reduce the number of purchases or even cease to be customers, particularly if the firm uses poor precedures for collection
- Offended debtors often turn other customers or potential customers against a firm

The key to managing delinquent accounts, therefore, lies in recognizing two goals: collecting as soon as possible and retaining the goodwill of the customer. Good procedures, then, depend heavily on good communication.

Communication for Collection

As for any form of persuasion, knowledge about the receiver forms the basis of the collection process. Why do debtors not pay their bills? With correct answers to this question, the chance of developing successful messages improves. From the debtor's point of view, these represent some of the possible answers:

- Am careless or forgetful
- Do not have enough money this month, but will have enough next month
- Have been out of town
- Am ill
- Have moved and mail has not been forwarded correctly
- Creditor made error in billing
- Dissatisfied with product or service and want an adjustment
- Other members of family incurred charges without my knowledge
- Lost my job after incurring the debt
- Owe too many creditors; may get counseling and/or take bankruptcy
- Am just unwilling to pay

Using the appropriate reasons for nonpayment, you should encode the collection message(s) to try to meet the receiver's specific wants and needs. During the middle, nonroutine, stage, offer a positive way out of the dilemma—partial payments, counseling, etc. Combine written messages with telephone messages. Even during the later stages of collection, avoid threats of force. Suggest the possibility of legal action only when intending to use it. Treat collection messages as combinations of bad news and persuasion.

You should use the positive sandwich and indirect formats through the intermediate stage of persuasion. During the initial and ending stages, however, use a more direct approach. At the early stage, even use some originality—perhaps some humor—in conjunction with the direct attention-getting

FULL LIFE, INC.
a nonprofit corporation

32 Lee Road
Marion, Iowa 22659
(555) 621-1213

October 11, 198X

Dear Marion Businessperson:

Over 2,000 people will turn 65 in the Marion, Iowa, area this year. They will join the 62,000 Marion residents who are already members of the 65-and-older generation. They, like Marion's other older people, will likely find that they have more free time, less money, and more medical problems than they had in their younger years.

Marion has one activity center for older persons. It holds only 50 people. Marion has no housing for low-income older people. Nor does our city operate a medical clinic for older people who need medical care at a low cost. In fact, Marion, Iowa, has all but ignored its older people.

We at Full Life, Inc., want to end the neglect of our older friends. And we most definitely need your help.

Full Life, Inc., a nonprofit corporation devoted to helping Marion's older citizens, is asking you and other Marion businesspersons to make donations of $25, $50, $100, or whatever amount you can afford to support Full Life's first major project—the building of the much-needed Full Life Center in the downtown area. The $2 million center will hold 500 people, and it will house a swimming pool, a cafeteria, a small gymnasium, and a number of meeting and game rooms. If enough money is donated, a medical clinic will also be a part of the Center. The Center will provide a number of the services so lacking in our city.

Over 100 Full Life volunteers have already collected $200,000 of our $2 million goal. These volunteers donate both their time and their money to this good cause. They want to give some-

FIGURE 9–1 Request for contribution.

opening. During the final stage, however, put directness in the form of a sharp demand for immediate payment. At whatever stage, include the amount owned in every message; tie the amount to specific due dates. Also include the account number in every message.

For mass collections, where the volume of communication precludes custom-made messages, you can use form messages—often transmitted as a

Marion Businessperson 2 October 11, 198X

thing to the 64,000 Marion residents who are their parents, neighbors, and friends. Again, we need your help too so that we can reach our $2 million goal by January 31.

The enclosed brochure explains the Full Life Center project. Also enclosed are a donation card and postpaid envelope for your contribution. Note that if you donate $100 or more, you will be named a Friend of the Center, and your name will appear on the Friends of the Center plaque that will mark the Center's entrance. Remember that your donation is tax-deductible.

We are all growing older. Your donation will not only help your older neighbor, but it will be an investment for your future as well.

Please return the enclosed donation card and your contribution by November 15, 198X. Feel free to call me at 621-1213 if you havo any questions.

Sincerely,

Jane Woshki

Jane Woshki
Chairperson, Center Fund Drive

hh

Enclosures

FIGURE 9–1 (Continued).

timed series. When well done, even form messages reflect an understanding of people. Develop several series to fit differing circumstances surrounding the need to collect. With or without automatic equipment, leave places to insert amount due, due date, and account numbers on each message. When a firm uses form messages—even if typewritten individually in a word-processing center—management often engages professional writers to develop them.

Big Ninth Accounting Service

Airport Road and Ayers—Madison, WI 53701 · (006) 060-6060

September 1, 198X

Mr. John Childs, C.P.A.
Partner, Debit Accounting Co.
19 North Solstice Avenue
Milwaukee, WI 53207

Dear Mr. Childs:

Will you please be the speaker for the October 19 meeting of the Madison C.P.A. Association? When I was the guest of Esther Murray at the meeting of your Association last March, I had the good fortune to hear you speak. Right then I vowed to try to bring that same good fortune to the other Madison Association members.

The dinner meeting begins at 7:30 p.m. in the Crystal Room of the Wilburton Hotel. Preceding it is a hospitality hour starting at 6:30 p.m. in the adjoining Applewood Room.

Your presentation would begin at about 8:00 and end at about 8:30, with another 10 minutes for questions if you like. A business meeting follows the speaker. Therefore, though you would be welcome to stay, you could leave immediately after your presentation in order to return to Milwaukee by a reasonable hour.

Please speak on any subject that you choose. Your presentation "There's No Accounting for Inflation" would be excellent.

The Association will, of course, provide your dinner and hospitality-hour refreshments. In addition, Esther will be pleased to drive you over from Madison, or the Association will provide $35 to cover your expenses if you prefer to provide your own transportation.

I hope you will accept this invitation, and also look forward to learning the subject of your speech. If you decide you would like Esther to drive you, let me know, and I will ask her to contact you to make the arrangements. Could you let me know by September 20 whether you will be able to come?

Sincerely yours,

Y. R. Self

Y. R. Self, C.P.A.
198X Programs
Madison C.P.A. Association

st

FIGURE 9–2 Request for speaker.

A review of the concept of a series will help you understand the principles and psychology involved.

Collection Series

As already implied, a series of collection messages goes through three major stages: routine, persuasive, and demanding.

Routine stage The first stage includes routine contacts with the debtor. The first message often just duplicates the original bill with words like *Reminder* stamped across it. The sample letter shown in Figure 9-3 illustrates the use of the direct pattern, an attention-getting opening, and an easy-going, nondemanding tone.

A second message in this early stage may simply repeat the statement, but with a clearer reminder. The reminder may use words like "Third Notice: Please Pay Promptly," "Second Reminder," or even a humorous "Did you

HILLEY GIFTS, INC.
4213 Avery Street · Mill, Ohio 62198

August 15, 198X

Mr. David Bonrell
130 West Sixth Street, Apt. 3
Allen, Wyoming 86619

R E M I N D E R

Dear Mr. Bonrell:

JUST A REMINDER—that all Hilley Gifts, Inc., payments are due within 30 days of the date that you receive your bill. We have not yet received your July 15 payment for $60.

Please take the time to send us a check for $60 in the enclosed postpaid envelope. Then you will have the satisfaction of knowing that your account is paid through July.

You are one of our most valued customers.

Sincerely,

Donna Raren

Donna Raren
Credit Manager

jj

Enclosure

Account No. 55151

FIGURE 9-3 First routine-stage collection message.

Forget?" The humorous approach might accompany a sketch of a person scratching her or his head, or a finger with a string tied around it. Figure 9–4 illustrates a reminder. Observe how the message remains nondemanding, but does become bolder in its reminder.

If one or two simple reminders fail, and the customer has usually paid on time, perhaps you should send a message of inquiry about why the customer has not paid. Stress the need for payment, but give the customer a chance to explain. Continue to give the receiver the benefit of the doubt. Figure 9–5 is an example of a letter of inquiry still in the first (routine) collection stage. Notice that it borders on insistence even as it leaves the door open for the customer to explain or pay as a routine transaction.

HILLEY GIFTS, INC.
4213 Avery Street · Mill, Ohio 62198

September 15, 198X

Mr. David Bonrell
130 West Sixth Street, Apt. 3
Allen, Wyoming 86619

SECOND NOTICE

Dear Mr. Bonrell:

WE ALL FORGET TO DO THINGS SOMETIMES!

HAVE YOU FORGOTTEN TO SEND US
YOUR LAST TWO PAYMENTS?

Perhaps both your July 15 and August 15 Hilley Gifts payments have just slipped your mind.

Please send the $120 in overdue payments to us promptly in the postpaid envelope enclosed for your convenience.

Don't forget to send your payment today!

Sincerely,

Donna Raren

Donna Raren
Credit Manager

jj

Enclosure

Account No. 55151

FIGURE 9–4 Second routine-stage collection message.

HILLEY GIFTS, INC.
4213 Avery Street · Mill, Ohio 62198

September 30, 198X

Mr. David Bonrell
130 West Sixth Street, Apt. 3
Allen, Wyoming 86619

CAN WE HELP?

Dear Mr. Bonrell:

We are puzzled. You usually make your payments promptly, yet you are two payments behind now. In fact, you will be three payments behind if we do not receive a check from you in 15 days. We are concerned because you are one of our best customers.

Perhaps you have merely forgotten. Or you have been out of town. Or you are just having a little trouble paying your bills right now. But whatever the reason, we need to know so that we can help.

Please send us your check for $120 to cover your overdue July 15 and August 15 payments. The enclosed postpaid envelope is for your convenience. Or, if something prevents you from making a prompt payment, let us know by writing us today.

We expect to hear from you before October 10, 198X.

Sincerely,

Donna Raren

Donna Raren
Credit Manager

jj

Enclosure

Account No. 55151

FIGURE 9-5 Third routine-stage collection message.

Persuasive stage If reminders and inquiries fail to gain a response, move into the second stage. The persuasive stage changes the emphasis from the rather routine into the persuasive. Along with the shift to persuasion comes a shift in developmental patterns. Though routine messages usually take the direct pattern, persuasive collection messages often take the indirect pattern.

The interest-getting and conviction-building segments of the persuasive message require careful development of the facts. Pay particular attention to the potential benefits of payment for the receiver. Basically appeal to the receiver's sense of fair play, pride, and social approval.

Build the pressure on the receiver at a steady pace through two or three well-timed messages. However, maintain a positive, correctly buffered approach. Leave receivers with alternatives that allow them to recover from the transaction with dignity. However, end each persuasive message with a call to action—a call for payment.

Figures 9-6, 9-7, and 9-8 serve as examples of the intermediate, persuasive stage of a collection series. They illustrate the progressively heavier stress on the need for action. They also continue to include the amount due, the due

HILLEY GIFTS, INC.
4213 Avery Street · Mill, Ohio 62198

October 10, 198X

Mr. David Bonrell
130 West Sixth Street, Apt. 3
Allen, Wyoming 86619

Dear Mr. Bonrell:

You are proud of your good credit rating, aren't you? It allows you to enjoy all manner of goods and services. We want you to continue to enjoy the privileges that a good credit rating affords you.

Because you do want to protect your excellent credit rating, we at Hilley Gifts are confident that you will promptly pay the $180 you owe us. We have sent you several reminders and are very concerned that you have not made your last three payments—July 15, August 15, and September 15.

Protect your good credit rating by mailing your payment today!

Sincerely,

Donna Raren

Donna Raren
Credit Manager

jj

Account No. 55151

FIGURE 9-6 First persuasive-stage collection message.

HILLEY GIFTS, INC.
4213 Avery Street · Mill, Ohio 62198

October 20, 198X

Mr. David Bonrell
130 West Sixth Street, Apt. 3
Allen, Wyoming 86619

Dear Mr. Bonrell:

A string of overdue bills can do great damage to a good credit rating. Most people who have worked hard to earn their good credit ratings do not want to do anything to hurt them.

We doubt that you want to endanger your credit rating, Mr. Bonrell. Unless we receive the $180 you owe us for your last three payments, however, we will be forced to begin a review of your account. The review process does involve a critical reevaluation of your credit standing.

Send $180 for your July, August, and September payments today so that we do not have to begin the review. Remember that your credit rating is one of your most valuable assets.

Sincerely,

Donna Raren

Donna Raren
Credit Manager

jj Account No. 55151

FIGURE 9–7 Second persuasive-stage collection message.

date, and the account number. However, they no longer include postpaid envelopes.

Demanding stage If the persuasive stage fails, shift to the final stage: demand. Use a direct style. Set a date by which you must receive payment, or, occasionally, a response that includes a partial payment and a clear, believable plan for completing payment. Stand ready to go through with any stated actions. Figures 9–9 and 9–10 illustrate these features of the demanding stage of a series of collection messages.

If the debtor does not meet the final demand, turn the debt over to the legal department. Then notify the debtor courteously, but directly, of the action. Figure 9–11 shows such a post-collection message.

HILLEY GIFTS, INC.
4213 Avery Street · Mill, Ohio 62198

November 1, 198X

Mr. David Bonrell
130 West Sixth Street, Apt. 3
Allen, Wyoming 86619

Dear Mr. Bonrell:

When we are forced to review one of our customer's charge accounts, we must also review that customer's credit standing. We will be forced to begin a review of your account at Hilley Gifts, Inc., if we do not receive the $240 you owe us by November 15. You are now four months behind on your payments, and you have given us no reason for the delay.

Five reminders have been mailed to you concerning the four payments that will be overdue on November 15:

July 15—	$ 60
August 15—	$ 60
September 15—	$ 60
October 15—	$ 60
TOTAL	$240

You can avoid a review of your account by sending a check for $240 now!

Sincerely,

Donna Raren

Donna Raren
Credit Manager

jj Account No. 55151

FIGURE 9–8 Third persuasive-stage collection message.

Whether using individually developed messages or form messages, think of the collection process as including routine, persuasive, and demanding stages. Also observe careful timing and sequencing of messages. Transmitting the various messages should create an unfolding, increasingly persuasive sequence. Even with a chain of collection messages, however, try to maintain some flexibility, thus meeting the unique characteristics of each situation. In certain circumstances, you might skip the routine or persuasive stages entirely. In others, you might vary the timing from the typical sequence of messages.

HILLEY GIFTS, INC.
4213 Avery Street · Mill, Ohio 62198

November 15, 198X

Mr. David Bonrell
130 West Sixth Street, Apt. 3
Allen, Wyoming 86619

Dear Mr. Bonrell:

You did not respond to our last request for payment; therefore, we have begun a review of your account. One result is that we will not allow you to make any more charges on your Hilley charge card. And as you know, your credit rating is also in grave danger.

You are seriously behind in your payments—four months, in fact. Unless you send the $240 you owe us or make other arrangements by December 1, we will be forced to take even more drastic collection action.

Time is running out. Send your payment today.

Sincerely,

Donna Raren

Donna Raren
Credit Manager

jj Account No. 55151

FIGURE 9-9 First demanding-stage collection message.

Sales

Business firms often engage professionals to create mass selling messages. A review of some of the principles of mass selling will improve your understanding of both persuasion and communication.

Characteristics of Selling Messages

Selling messages may take many forms, including letters, memoranda, leaflets, flyers, newspaper and magazine advertisements, catalogs, outdoor advertisements, and television and radio commercials. Although the examples in this section take the form of letters, the concepts also apply to the other communication channels.

HILLEY GIFTS, INC.
4213 Avery Street · Mill, Ohio 62198

December 1, 198X

Mr. David Bonrell
130 West Sixth Street, Apt. 3
Allen, Wyoming 86619

FINAL NOTICE

Dear Mr. Bonrell:

We have completed the review of your account. On December 15, you will be five months—$300—behind on your payments, and you have responded to none of our letters. We have no choice but to make this your last chance to send your payment or to call us to discuss other arrangements.

If we have not heard from you by December 15, we will refer your overdue account to our attorneys. Please send your $300 payment now so both of us can avoid the legal collection process.

Sincerely,

Donna Raren

Donna Raren
Credit Manager

jj

Account No. 55151

FIGURE 9–10 Final demanding-stage collection message.

Originality Selling messages allow for more originality and creativity in design and development than do any other types of business messages. The sender may use unlimited imagination in designing them, and may use virtually any developmental pattern. Include or omit salutations in letters. Write formally or informally. Use both rational and emotional appeals. Use dramatic or subtle techniques. Include or offer free gifts. Enclose coins, stick-on stamps, return cards or envelopes marked "Yes" and "No," product samples, and other such objects related to the topic. Include lavish photographs, pictures, charts, sketches, tables, tapes, small records, and even scratch-patches that give off the fragrance found in a soap, cologne, or shaving lotion.

Analysis Learn about the prospective buyer. Learn about the product or service offered to the buyer. Use the procedures described in Chapter 2 to define the prospective buyer. The general items from the list of key factors

HILLEY GIFTS, INC.
4213 Avery Street · Mill, Ohio 62198

December 23, 198X

Mr. David Bonrell
130 West Sixth Street, Apt. 3
Allen, Wyoming 86619

Dear Mr. Bonrell:

We have referred your account to our law firm, Williams, Fong & Micci, P.C., for legal action. The firm will now handle all facets of the collection process concerning your Hilley Gifts, Inc., charge account. An attorney will call you within the next two weeks.

Call Williams, Fong & Micci, P.C., at (555) 614–9987 if you have any questions. The firm's address is 1319 Elm Street, Mill, Ohio 62198.

Sincerely,

Donna Raren

Donna Raren
Credit Manager

jj

Account No. 55151

FIGURE 9–11 Post-collection message.

contribute particularly well to developing messages for distribution to the masses. Motivational research (briefly discussed in Chapter 11) may also help in the definition. To learn about the product or service, meet with the designers and producers.

Appeal Match the product or service to the prospective customer. Then select two or three major features and build an appeal around them. Avoid using so many features that the receiver does not accept any of them. Build the entire appeal around the desired action—the purchase of the goods or services. Make the purchase both attractive and easy. Enclose return envelopes, order blanks, and simple, complete instructions.

Use the AICA pattern to its fullest. Review the attention-getting devices discussed earlier in this chapter. Relate the attention to the basic appeal and unfold the other sections naturally from that initial statement. Spotlight the action properly. Call for the purchase while recalling the basic rational or emotional appeal and the beneft of the purchase to the buyer.

Selling messages have their foundation in a multitude of human needs and wants, both rational and emotional. The Direct Mail Advertising Association suggests that beyond the basic needs for food, shelter, and clothing, people spend money to:

Save money	Conserve possessions
Make money	Avoid criticism
Save time	Provide security
Avoid effort	Live in style
Provide comfort	Have beautiful possessions
Assure cleanliness	Satisfy appetite
Have enjoyment	Emulate others
Gratify curiosity	Show individualism
Bring good health	Protect reputation
Escape physical pain	Take advantage of opportunities
Receive praise	Avoid trouble
Gain popularity	Attract the opposite sex

Variety Most selling messages aim for direct sales. However, other, less-direct objectives also exist; for example:

- To create general demand for a service or product instead of specific sales
- To prepare prospects for a salesperson's call
- To solicit or respond to inquiries
- To announce the results of tests on products and services
- To establish goodwill that may ultimately lead to sales

Types of Selling Messages

The major types of written sales messages include enclosures, personal messages, one-time mass mailings, and sales series.

Enclosures Transmittal messages often include messages that attempt to sell. Such messages may accompany filled orders, coupons, product samples, refunds, and responses to other messages. Figure 9–12 illustrates such an enclosure. Notice its simple, concentrated "pitch" for a product.

Personal messages Selling often becomes part of individually created messages. Inquiries about products and services provide perfect opportunities for selling responses. Similarly, acknowledgments of orders prior to shipping offer a chance to try to persuade the purchaser to buy something else.

One-time mass mailings Firms often prepare a sales message, duplicate it, and distribute it to a mailing list—one time. Figures 9–13 and 9–14 illustrate such letters. Examine each of them carefully. Notice the mixture of traditional

F.R.M. Sutical Corp.
783 Capsule Road
Iron Springs, AZ 86330

Dear Consumer:

Here's the free sample of VIMVIG VITAMINS you asked for.

As you will discover, VIMVIG is a special vitamin compound. VIMVIG consistently leaves you with more energy and without as many colds.

VIMVIG is available in most grocery, drug, and discount stores in bottles of 50, 100, or 200 capsules.

Thank you for responding to our free sample offer. We feel sure you will like VIMVIG so well that you will want to purchase VIMVIG when the sample is gone.

Good health,

Carroll Jeeves

Carroll Jeeves

F.R.M.S.80 D7418–6/5/80

FIGURE 9–12 Selling message as an enclosure.

format and nontraditional placement and repetition of words. Also notice the amount of space devoted to the attention-getting devices and the concerted thrust toward action.

(To the student: Skip over the figures that serve as examples when taking the following timed exercise. Return to them later.)

Series Direct-mail selling often requires sending unsolicited letters in a series. This chapter covers three types of series: (1) the continual (sometimes called *continuous*) series, (2) the wear-out series, and (3) the campaign series.

Through a *continual* series, sellers send pieces at regular intervals for an indefinite length of time. The selling messages often accompany other pieces such as statements, catalogs, price lists, and first- and even second-stage messages of collection. Such enclosures serve to resell existing customers—an important concept in selling.

Because continual-series pieces accompany other messages, they cost less than series mailed independently. Figure 9–15 includes an example of a continual-series enclosure. Notice that the letter uses a brash "hard sell," and

CAREFUL CAR WASH
317 Harrison Way
Lakeview, Arizona 81941

March 25, 198X

(There's an offer in this letter that you can't pass up.)

Dear Neighbor:

Careful Car Wash wants to get acquainted with you, our neighbor. We could think of no better way to get to know you than to offer to clean your car—inside and outside—for a special price!

YOUR CAR WILL RECEIVE

A WASH,

A WAX,

A SHINE, AND

AN INSIDE VACUUM

FOR JUST $2.50—EXACTLY HALF THE REGULAR $5 PRICE.

This special offer is YOURS because we want to get to know YOU. We also want you to know what a fine job Careful Car Wash does on YOUR car. No automatic car wash could compete with the thorough job our people do at Careful. Just come on in and see for yourself!

Bring this letter in between 9 and 7 Monday through Saturday to have your car receive the BEST cleaning, shining, and vacuuming it has ever had—all for just $2.50! Hurry, though, because this extra special offer ends on April 15!

We're looking forward to getting to know you.

Sincerely,

Lisa Johnson

Lisa Johnson
Owner

FIGURE 9–13 Message advertising "get acquainted" offer.

Laurel Boutique

25 North Park Street Vine, New Mexico 33219

August 1, 198X

Dear Preferred Customer:

SALE

SALE

SALE

SALE

SALE

SALE

SALE

Most other stores have sales, and they all seem to be alike. But when we allow only our Preferred Charge Card customers to buy anything in our store at a 25 percent discount, it is an event.

We are holding our very special event for you on Friday, August 17, from 10 to 5. And only you, our Preferred Charge Card customer, can buy elegant dresses, silky scarves, and anything in the boutique for a mere 75 percent of the regular price.

Most sales last for weeks. Our event lasts only one day.

Be there.

Sincerely,

Priscilla Poteau

Priscilla Poteau
Owner

FIGURE 9-14 Message advertising special sale.

puts too much information on the page. Yet also realize that these kinds of messages do, indeed, sell. Why?

With the *wear-out* series, begin with a mailing list of prospective purchasers. Then create and mail a sales message that stands on its own. After a period of time, check the returns from the first mailing. Then mark off the names of those who responded to the first mailing. However, leave the original purchasers' names on the list if you think a second mailing might bring

PARCHMENT-LIKE, PERSONALIZED STATIONERY FOR JUST $4.95?

YOU'VE GOT TO BE KIDDING?

But at Elegant Economy Stationery, we never KID. We just make beautiful, heavy-bond, personalized stationery at a price most everyone can afford. For only $4.95, you can receive 50 personalized letter sheets, 50 plain sheets, and 50 personalized envelopes.

AND AGAIN, WE'RE NOT KIDDING. JUST LOOK:

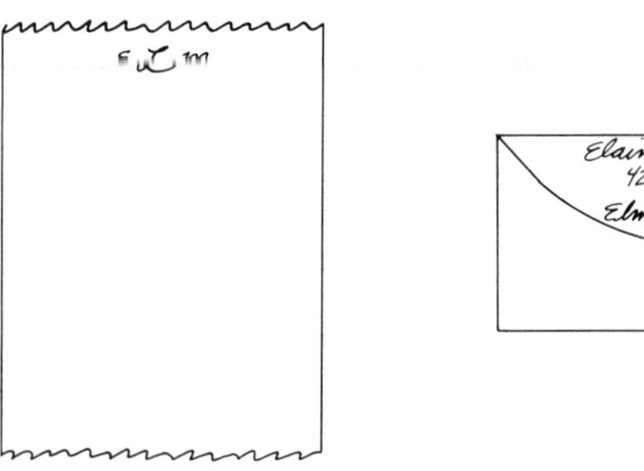

The price is low because our letter sheets and envelopes come in only one size and one color. We also use only one print style, color, and size. The sheets are 8″ x 11″, and both the parchment-like sheets and envelopes come in an elegant Golden White color.

Your initials and name are printed in Night Bark, a deep, bold brown. Your name and full address go on all of your 50 envelopes; and your initials—with your last initial in the middle—go on 50 of your letter sheets.

WHY NOT WRITE YOUR LETTERS ON ELEGANT STATIONERY?
ORDER NOW!

Name and address as you want them to appear on your envelopes
________________ (Name)
________________ (Street)
________________ (City, State, Zip)

Mailing address
________________ (Name)
________________ (Street)
________________ (City, State, Zip)

Please allow six weeks for delivery.

Initials as you want them to appear on your letter paper

____
First Last Middle

Send a $4.95 check or money order to:
Elegant Economy Stationery
P. O. Box 69
Ware, New Jersey 60492

FIGURE 9–15 Continual-series enclosure.

additional sales. Then send a second mailing to the revised list. Develop a new message or use the same message included in the first mailing.

Following the second mailing, revise the list again, and send another mailing. Continue the process until the returns do not warrant continuing the process—until the list "wears out." Figures 9-16 and 9-17 illustrate two letters from a wear-out series. Observe how each message remains self-contained, yet relates to the other messages. Analyze each letter for developmental pattern, the matching of service and appeal, and the unfolding of the AICA formula. Particularly decide whether the messages would lead you to action—and why. Because it involves a series of independent mailings, the wear-out system costs more than the continual system. However, it costs less than the campaign series.

The *campaign* series involves careful development of several coordinated mailings—all of which go in sequence to every person on the mailing list. Because everyone receives every piece, the series itself may build through the AICA plan. All letters contain all four components. However, the first letter may emphasize attention; the second, interest; the third, conviction. Even with such shifting emphasis, each message calls for action—the placement of an order. Because of the high cost of the campaign series, you should restrict its use to sales of the kinds of expensive items that warrant large expenditures. (429 words)

Take and score Self-Test 19 over the sales series on page 246.

Figures 9-18 and 9-19 show the combined effect of a series of letters in a sales campaign. Observe how the messages complement one another. Analyze each letter for application of the principles of persuasion. Suppose as a customer, you had a deck built between March 1 and April 30, only to learn that if you had waited until after May 1 you could have saved $50? What would you do?

The next chapter introduces some formats and types of messages other than the letter. It covers memoranda, forms, cards, telegrams, and other such channels.

Dawson Lucci Dance Company

2319 West Ninth Avenue
El Paso, Kansas 23999
(555) 236-1984

July 1, 198X

Dear Friend:

Larry Blieve of the Kansas Weekly called the Dawson Lucci Dance Company "Brilliant!," and Meredith Morris of the El Paso Courier wrote: "The Dawson Lucci Dance Company shines brighter than any star in the sky."

We want to give you a special, before-the-box-office-opens opportunity to become a subscriber to the full season of the dance company that practically always receives rave reviews, El Paso's own Dawson Lucci Dance Company. The Dawson Lucci Dance Company will give you many evenings of exciting performances if you subscribe.

The company is composed of 25 dancers, all of whom studied under some of the greatest teachers in New York and Europe. And the Dawson Lucci Dance Company does not limit itself to one dance form: It performs ballet, jazz, and modern dance with equal ease.

This year's Dawson Lucci season includes six concerts, all of which will be held at the beautiful El Paso Performing Arts Center. You can see all six concerts for just $25—that's six concerts for the price of five.

Last season all but one of the Dawson Lucci Dance Company's performances were sold out. You can be sure to see all of this season's concerts from your reserved seat if you become a season subscriber now. Just fill out the enclosed subscription card and mail it with your check or money order today. And hurry! Only a limited number of season subscriptions are available.

Don't risk missing even one of the "Brilliant!" Dawson Lucci Dance Company performances.

Sincerely,

Allen Santini

Allen Santini
Manager

AS/ln

Enclosures

FIGURE 9–16 First letter in wear-out series.

Dawson Lucci Dance Company

2319 West Ninth Avenue
El Paso, Kansas 23999
(555) 236-1984

August 17, 198X

Dear Friend:

The Dawson Lucci Dance Company just got back from its summer road tour. The dancers went to New York, Montreal, and London. And everywhere they went, they received high praise.

Mary Frankel of the New York Guard wrote: "No other regional dance company could match last night's performance of the Dawson Lucci troupe." "Absolutely fantastic!" were the words Harold Jarms, a Montreal World critic, used to describe the Dawson Lucci Dance Company. And Maureen O'Dean of the London Week in Review called Dawson Lucci ". . . the best American dance company I have seen in years."

The Dawson Lucci Dance Company's home is also your home: El Paso, Kansas. And you can see all of the company's El Paso performances from your reserved seat if you subscribe now.

The 25 dancers of the Dawson Lucci Dance Company will perform all six of this season's concerts at the elegant El Paso Performing Arts Center. The company will perform jazz, ballet, and modern dance, and each performance is something to remember.

You can see all six concerts for just $25—that's six concerts for the price of five. To become a season subscriber, just fill out the enclosed subscription card and mail it with your check or money order today. We regret that we cannot give you a third chance to subscribe after this second one. Our mailing costs are high and the season subscriptions are going fast. So this is essentially your last chance to subscribe.

The critics in New York, Montreal, and London seemed to agree that a performance of the Dawson Lucci Dance Company should not be missed. If you subscribe now, you won't miss a single one.

Sincerely,

Allen Santini

Allen Santini
Manager

AS/ln

Enclosures

Don't delay! Complete the enclosed subscription card and mail it with your check or money order for $25 TODAY.

FIGURE 9–17 Second and final wear-out series letter.

DECK CARPENTERS, INC.
2211 Sunnyvale Road, Sherman, Washington 42226
(555) 916-6116

March 1, 198X

Dear Home Owner:

In a few weeks beautiful weather will move into the Sherman area for its usual seven-month stay. The sun will shine nearly every day. And you will want to spend more and more of each wonderful day outdoors in the midst of the sun and the grass and the flowers.

Deck Carpenters make your outdoor life more comfortable and more beautiful. We build wood patios and decks that make any yard into a summertime paradise. And why use expensive gasoline to get away from it all when you can escape to your own lovely back yard?

We would be very happy to visit your home to discuss your deck and patio needs and to give you a free estimate. Or, if you want us to begin work now, just give us a call and we'll begin construction on your deck or patio within a week. You can choose one of many designs (we've enclosed our brochure which includes some of our most popular designs) or work with one of our associates to design your own personalized deck or patio.

You can call us at 916–6116. Or drop by our office at 2211 Sunnyvale Road. We'd love to talk to you.

You can have your own deck or patio before summer starts if you call Deck Carpenters today.

Yours sincerely,

Mary Jane Francis

Mary Jane Francis
Owner

MJF/rp

Enclosure: Brochure

FIGURE 9–18 First letter in campaign series.

DECK CARPENTERS, INC.
2211 Sunnyvale Road, Sherman, Washington 42226
(555) 916-6116

May 1, 198X

Dear Friend:

You may think that we at Deck Carpenters would have to charge high prices for our quality work and our quality materials. Actually, our rates are competitive with the rates charged by other patio and deck builders in this area, and we know our wood and construction techniques are superior.

Just to prove our point, we enclosed our price list. And because we want you to know that our prices are more than reasonable, we included the prices of two of our competitors.

REMEMBER: We always use the highest quality materials that are on the market. In addition, we take the time to include the "little extras" that make our decks and patios very strong as well as very beautiful.

Summer is almost upon us. You still have time to enjoy most of the sunny season from your Deck Carpenters deck or patio. If you call now, we can start building your fully guaranteed backyard paradise within ten days. And just to make things a little easier, we've enclosed a $50 gift certificate to apply to any deck or patio we build for you. Hurry, though, because the $50 gift certificate is good only through May 25.

Please call us at 916–6116 for a free home consultation—or come by our office at 2211 Sunnyvale Road.

Make your yard into a paradise. Use your $50 gift certificate on a beautiful, solid, reasonably priced Deck Carpenters patio or deck today!

Sincerely,

Mary Jane Francis

Mary Jane Francis
Owner

MJF/rp

Enclosures: Price list
Gift certificate
Brochure

FIGURE 9–19 Final letter in campaign series.

SUMMARY

Persuasive messages attempt to get people to take some action beyond the routine or to accept some idea or belief. Concentrate on the desired action, not the persuasion itself. Pay particular attention to the purposes, benefits to the receiver, and the content of the message.

Persuasive messages fit into indirect, ranked, chronological, and direct plans of development, but require the indirect plan when messages also contain bad news. The parts of a persuasive message fall into the AICA pattern (attention, interest, conviction, action).

Four broad classes of persuasive messages exist: (1) persuasive requests, (2) collection messages, (3) sales messages, and (4) employment messages (covered in Chapters 15 and 16).

Persuasive requests move beyond the routine. They ask the receiver to do such things as complete a questionnaire, endorse a candidate, or grant a promotion. For such requests, choose either the indirect or direct developmental pattern, coupled with the AICA design.

Collection messages seek to collect past-due accounts in order to make profits. In addition to collecting money, the message sender wants to retain the goodwill of the customer. Try to understand why people do not pay their debts. Tie that understanding to a three-stage series. The first (routine) stage includes one or more *routine* reminders written in the direct style. The intermediate (persuasive) stage includes two or three *persuasive* messages written in the indirect style. The final (demanding) stage involves one or more direct-style *demands* for payment. The final message of the demanding stage usually notifies the debtor that the legal department now has the case.

Selling messages take such forms as letters, memoranda, leaflets, flyers, newspaper and magazine advertisements, and television and radio commercials. Sales messages require originality, perceptive analysis of receiver and product, appeals to human needs and wants, and a clear understanding of purposes. Selling messages using letters, notes, and memoranda include enclosures, personal messages, one-time mass mailings, and sales series. Types of series include the continual, the wear-out, and the campaign. The continual series involves inserts with periodic mailings. The wear-out series uses mailings of self-contained messages to the same mailing list, reduced at each stage by removing the names of those who have made purchases. The campaign series requires several coordinated mailings sent in sequence to every person on the mailing list.

COMPUTERIA

Susan Frans' dreams are about to come true. She has received news that the bank approved her small business loan. She now has the capital to open her personal and business computer outlet, Computeria, in Sagewood, California.

Frans already owns a small stock of computer hardware and software; moreover, she rented a storefront last week in anticipation of the loan's approval. Because Frans carefully laid all the groundwork for her computer store, she can hold the store's grand opening the first week in September. The first week of September brings children back to school, their parents back to work, and other business and professional workers back to their offices after a summer of three-day weekends and vacations. That week is also fall orientation week at California State University—Sagewood.

Frans knows the prime selling season for home and business computers comes in late summer and fall. And her survey of Sagewood residents shows that businesspersons, college students, and parents of schoolchildren have the most interest in actually purchasing computer systems. Because she thinks businesspersons will order the larger computer systems and college students and parents will buy the personal computer systems, she wants to attract these groups to the grand opening of Computeria.

Frans offers business computer systems priced from $4,800 to $106,000. The personal or home computer systems run from $2,100 to $5,200. These prices include the computer, a monitor (display screen), a printer, and the two software packages of the purchaser's choice. Frans wants the majority of her customers to buy the entire computer system; she can offer much more competitive prices when items such as the printers are not sold separately.

Frans thinks she and her sales personnel will be busy demonstrating computers and educating potential buyers during the hectic two-week grand opening. But many businesspersons, college students, and parents will not need the general demonstrations and instructions that the less sophisticated customers require; they are simply waiting for the right system wth the right price tag. Frans believes she can offer both the right system and the right price. But she worries that the grand opening sale will not attract the sophisticated buyers who will not want to brave the mob scenes.

After much thought, she decides a private sale one evening during the grand opening might appeal to the knowledgeable consumer. Frans not only wants these businesspersons, college students, and parents to attend the private sale, she also wants them to come eager to buy a computer system.

(This case is fictional.)

EXERCISES

1. You are the collection manager for the Berry and Flom Department Store. Every month you must close the accounts of thirty or forty people because they have not made payments in the preceding six months. Because you cannot write a personal letter to every customer, you prepare a form letter that will be sent to the customers whose accounts must be closed. In the form letter, you inform them that their accounts are being closed and that a collection agency has been hired to collect the debt. Write the form letter.

2. These are poor persuasive messages. Correct each message and explain the reasoning behind your changes. Concentrate on the content, not the format, of each message.

a.

DIMCO, INC.
Staple Plaza, Suite 900
Winner, Montana 46218
(555) 336–9412

January 29, 198X

Dear Customer:

Now that you have had a chance to use your new Dimco Typewriter, we know that you really want a Dimco Copier.

The Dimco Copier works just as well as the Dimco Typewriter.

We will be expecting your order.

Sincerely,

N. T. Bright

N. T. Bright
Salesperson

b.

FRISCO'S DRY CLEANERS

BRING YOUR DIRTY, SMELLY CLOTHES TO US !!!

COUPON
25 % OFF
COUPON

c.

AMERICAN CHARITIES, INC.
1700 East Park Street, Suite 1200
Monroe, Florida 76660
(555) 343–3157

October 9, 198X

Mr. Milton Vance
84 Macon Street
Palm Springs, Georgia 84611

Dear Mr. Vance:

We know that you are a relatively wealthy man and a proud American. We want your donation so that we can help poor children all over the world.

We are a reputable organization, so send at least $100.

If you do not give, your conscience will hurt you.

Please! Please! Please!

Sincerely,

S. L. Zee

S. L. Zee
President

d.

LAMONT, INC.
602 Vella Street
Thorne, Arizona 99962
(555) 462–9914

February 16, 198X

Ms. Ellen Stake
3960 Benton Road
Thorne, Arizona 99962

Dear Ms. Stake:

Why in the world are you a month late on your Lamont Charge payment? You have never done this to us before!

Please send the payment right now so that we do not have to ask you again.

We value our customers.

Sincerely,

O. V. React

O. V. React
Collection Clerk

e.

QUANTITY PURSES, INC.
P.O. Box 19B
Dover, Idaho 41163

Dear Housewife:

We know that you are having trouble making ends meet. We also know that you like to look good when you leave the house. So, you need our LUXURY PLASTIC PURSE! It's cheap, yet it looks expensive. Just look:

Even you can afford this magnificent purse. It's only $9.95 plus postage and handling.

You do want to look decent when you leave the house, don't you?

Order now!

Sincerely,

I. N. Sulting
Consumer Sales

QUANTITY PURSES, Inc., P. O. Box 19B, Dover, Idaho 41163

I want _____ LUXURY PLASTIC PURSES at $9.95 plus $1.50 for postage and handling. I want my purse in ___ white ___ pink ___ red ___ green. I have enclosed a check for $__________.

Name ______________________ Address ______________________
Allow nine weeks for delivery.

3. Prepare a four-letter wear-out series for a new monthly magazine, *Kever Life*. You publish the magazine and hope to reach prospective subscribers in the Kever, Oregon area. The magazine includes local news; short stories, essays, and poetry

written by local writers; quizzes and crossword puzzles; a special children's section; numerous full-color photographs; a calendar of local cultural events; and book, movie, and theatre reviews. A one-year subscription to *Kever Life* is $10, a two-year subscription is $18, and a three-year subscription is $25. The first 250 subscribers will receive two extra months of *Kever Life* free. The first issue will be mailed in early April. You want subscribers to enclose their checks with their orders and send them to:

KEVER LIFE
Route 6, Box 492
Kever, Oregon 88814

4. [*This is both a timed exercise and a dictation exercise.*] Barry Bones, your best customer, called to complain that one of your salespeople just insulted him. Because of the insult, Mr. Bones told you that his grocery store chain will not carry your company's line of canned vegetables—Tasty Veggies—any longer. You do not want to lose Mr. Bones as a customer. You cannot get in touch with the salesperson in question, so you decide to write Mr. Bones a letter of apology. You also want to try to persuade Mr. Bones not to drop your Tasty Veggies line. You want to get the letter in the mail as soon as possible. Outline the letter. Make up the necessary names and addresses. Now dictate the letter (from your outline) to another student. Then have that student dictate her or his letter to you. You and the other student evaluate both your letters and your dictating skills.
5. Because most of your colleagues at the Extremely Big Corporation do not understand the "you" attitude, write a memorandum persuading them of its importance. Include at least one example of a "you"-attitude persuasive letter.
6. Write sentences that tactfully express each of these messages. The sentences that you write will constitute the main part of persuasive letters. You want:
   a. The receiver of your letter to speak to a group of your employees. The speaker usually charges for her speeches, but you have no money to pay her.
   b. Your boss to promote you to the position of chief economist.
   c. The receiver to grant you an exclusive interview.
   d. The receiver to complete an enclosed questionnaire.
7. Write one reminder, two persuasive, and two demand letters for the collection of $432.80 from Darlene Tenmire. Supply any information you need.
8. Write a letter to convince your boss to let you buy an expensive piece of equipment for your work. Make up the facts or cite information about an actual piece of equipment.
9. You are an accountant employed by the Simmons-Norman Corporation. You are performing an audit of the company's books and discover that the company is giving sizable bribes to foreign diplomats who are helping the company establish offices overseas. You then overhear that your company is planning to try to justify a rate increase by pointing to higher labor costs. You know that the bribery expenses are much higher than the increase in labor costs. What will you do? What should you consider before making a decision? Would your response be different if the amounts of the bribes were so small that the company's customers weren't affected? Write a brief paper answering these questions and trying to persuade the reader to accept the validity of your answers.
10. Write a humorous reminder to be sent to your customers who miss their payments by a few days. Supply whatever information you need.
11. Collect five or more actual sales letters. Analyze each. Identify the developmental plan, the treatment of the AICA pattern, the writing style, and any other relevant

factors. Evaluate the quality of the message. Pay particular attention to the attention-getting and action-seeking sections.

12. Write a simple enclosure sales message to accompany refunds you make when customers send you three boxtops. Supply needed information.
13. Use your dictionary and thesaurus to create meanings for these words. Use the words when you think, write, and speak so that you feel comfortable using them.

a. Compose	**g.** Continuous	**l.** Exploit
b. Comprehension	**h.** Crux	**m.** Motivation
c. Comprise	**i.** Emanate	**n.** Persuasion
d. Concept	**j.** Espouse	**o.** Relevant
e. Constitute	**k.** Ethics	**p.** Subliminal
f. Continual		

14. Take and score Self-Test 20 over Chapter 9.

SELF-TEST 19
Excerpt about Sales Series

A. Recall (25 points each). For each multiple-choice question, select the most accurate answer.

1. The continual series involves:
   - **a.** Solicited messages
   - **b.** Smaller expenditures than the wear-out series
   - **c.** A special, one-time mailing
   - **d.** Mailing lists purchased especially for the series
   - **e.** Inserts for the demand stage of the collection series
2. The campaign series involves:
   - **a.** The careful development of several coordinated mailings—all of which are sent in sequence to every person on the mailing list
   - **b.** Less expense than the wear-out series
   - **c.** Inexpensive products or services
   - **d.** Several independent messages
   - **e.** Messages that include only one of the AICA elements
3. The wear-out series involves:
   - **a.** The most expensive products
   - **b.** At least three independent mailing lists
   - **c.** Letters that cannot stand alone
   - **d.** Never sending a second letter to a person who has made a purchase
   - **e.** Continuing the mailings until the point of diminishing returns

B. Inference (25 points). Indicate whether this statement is true or false.

1. Sales series letters fall at the mediated level of communication.

SOLUTION

A. Recall (25 points each)

1. b
2. a
3. e

B. Inference (25 points)

1. False

SELF-TEST 20
Chapter 9

A. Recall (16 points each). For each multiple-choice question, select the most accurate answer.

1. Which one of these statements is true?
   a. The goal of every persuasive message is an action observable through the five senses.
   b. Persuasive techniques are ethical when used by an evangelist, but unethical when used by business.
   c. Persuasive messages should use only the deductive developmental pattern.
   d. The appeal in a sales message should match the receiver to the product or service.
   e. The larger the number of appeals in a sales letter, the better.
2. Which one of the statements is *not* true?
   a. The attention phase need not relate to the topic at all.
   b. "Please" and "Thank you" are not always considered attention-getting devices.
   c. The interest stage ties the attention stage to the body.
   d. The conviction phase probably should be written first.
   e. Job applications are persuasive messages.
3. Which one of these statements is true?
   a. Persuasive messages fall into the routine category.
   b. The best rule for all collection messages is to assume the worst about the debtor.
   c. Some messages include both persuasion and bad news.
   d. The collection series need not keep repeating the amount owed.
   e. The only objective of collection letters is to collect the money—eventually.
4. Which of these statements concerning sales messages is *not* correct?
   a. Sales messages allow a great deal of originality and creativity in design and development.
   b. You should build your appeal around the qualities of the product or service, the qualities of the prospective buyer, and the desired action.
   c. Avoid overwhelming the prospective buyer with too much information.
   d. The major purpose of sales messages is to let consumers know that a product or service exists.
   e. Be sure that the attention section is related to the basic appeal.
5. Business ethics concern:
   a. Mores, values, and honesty
   b. Specific ways to act in all situations
   c. Hiding misdeeds
   d. Only the people in the public relations department
   e. Learning to emphasize the positive

B. Inference (20 points). Indicate whether this statement is true or false.

1. You need not conduct motivational research if your product or service is not complicated.

SOLUTION

A. Recall (16 points each)

1. d
2. a
3. c
4. d
5. a

B. Inference (20 points)

1. False

STUDENT'S OBJECTIVES:

1 To learn to develop written business messages (other than the letter and the report)

2 To apply the writing principles to the development of memoranda

10

WRITING MEMORANDA, FORMS, AND OTHER MESSAGES

3 To apply the writing principles to the development and use of forms

4 To apply the writing principles to the development of other messages such as telegrams, cards, press releases, agendas, motions, minutes of meetings, statements of policy, and job descriptions and specifications

Memoranda, forms, and other written-message channels represent important avenues for communication. They carry the same kinds of messages as letters and reports, but do have special features and applications.

MEMORANDA

Many messages within business organizations use the format of a memorandum (memo). In fact, because of its close identification with internal business communication, it often has the name *interoffice memorandum.*

Stationery

The firm usually provides stationery with the memo heading desired for the company's internal use. The writer may also supply a memo heading on plain paper or letterhead stationery. Examples of formats appear in Figure 10–1. Stationery for the memorandum often consists of 16-pound paper without any

(a)

February 12, 198X

To: Members of the Committee on Personnel Policies
(Bates, Estes, Farmer, Kyle, Perry)

From: Y. R. Self *YRS*

Subject: Meeting of February 18, 198X

(b)

Interoffice Memo — Cagey, Inc.

TO: Sara Brains — DATE: 12/17/198X
FROM: Y. R. Self *YRS* — FILE NO. 410129

(c)

TO: Doris Eckles — DATE: 3 August 198X
FROM: Y. R. Self *YRS* — SUBJECT: Draft of report

FIGURE 10–1 Formats for memorandum headings.

fabric and is smaller than letter stationery. Common sizes include the half sheet (8½ by 5½ inches) and the quarter sheet (4¼ by 5½ inches).

Memoranda often take the form of self-carboned packs of stationery. Some packs include three sheets and use a format that allows the receiver's response to be placed on the same sheet as the original message. The sender can write the message on the top half of the first sheet, tear off and retain a carbon copy, and send the original and one copy to the receiver. The receiver then writes the response on the bottom half of the original, returns it, and keeps the copy (which now contains both messages).

Format

The memorandum often omits a courtesy title for the addressee. It does not include an inside address, a salutation, a complimentary close, or a standard signature block. Senders usually place their initials or signatures beside the typewritten names placed after "From." The memo omits official titles after names unless receivers do not know those titles.

The memo has single spacing within paragraphs, and double spacing between. It has a double or triple space after the last line of the heading.

Writing

Apply the six guidelines developed in Chapter 2 and the writing principles developed in Chapter 6. Use the direct developmental method. Emphasize correctness, conciseness, and clearness, but, of course, maintain considerateness. Spotlight objectives in the subject line and the first paragraph. Add only enough developmental information to reinforce these objectives. Figure 10–2 illustrates the application of these principles for writing memoranda.

Figure 10–3 shows an example of a handwritten business note. Observe its informal way of conveying information.

FORMS

As suggested in Chapter 7, forms carry many routine business messages. Forms may save a great deal of time and money when compared with letters and memoranda. However, they do not have the warmth of more personal messages.

Creating Forms

When developing forms, carefully apply the principles for writing presented in Chapter 6. Revise the first draft, paying particular attention to the qualities of correctness, conciseness, clearness, considerateness, and coherence. After revising, use the form during a trial period and then revise it again before committing it to permanent use. Here are some specific suggestions for creating good forms:

- Give the form a title.
- Include an empathetic introduction to put the reader at ease, along with complete and clear instructions.

MEMORANDUM AFTERTASTE SODA, INC.

TO: Members of Retirement Dinner Committee
(Baird, Farris, Hale, Jardin, Lacy, Rust)

FROM: Y. R. Self *yrs*

DATE: March 2, 198X

SUBJECT: Meeting of March 9, 198X

The Retirement Dinner Committee will meet at 2 p.m. on Thursday, March 9, in Conference Room B. The purpose for the meeting is to make these decisions:

1. Date
2. Site
3. Menu
4. Program
    a. Speaker
    b. Tributes
    c. Entertainment
    d. Emcee
5. Retirees' names
6. Gifts
7. Establishment of subcommittees
8. Date of next meeting

Please do some preliminary thinking about these topics before next Thursday. We will plan to adjourn at about 5:30.

FIGURE 10–2 Interoffice memorandum, setting date and agenda for meeting.

- Write clear questions and lead-in statements for all items. (Chapter 11 contains suggestions for writing unambiguous questions.)
- Write for the lowest readability level anticipated in the audience.
- Arrange the elements in logical groupings and in logical order.
- Exhaust all elements associated with the topic.
- Leave plenty of space for each answer.
- Leave space for providing additional information not specifically requested, or suggest that the writer may attach additional pages.
- Use a size of type large enough that people can read the form.
- Condense the form as much as possible without crowding or sacrificing other qualities.
- If forms go to people who do not request them, make return easy and

FROM THE DESK OF Y. R. SELF

1-28-8X

George—

Thanks for the invitation to the computer demonstration on Monday. I'll be there.

Y.R.

FIGURE 10–3 Handwritten business note.

desirable by enclosing postpaid return envelopes and providing incentives such as money, products, and gifts.

- When appropriate, assure confidentiality.
- If promising anonymity, do not try to identify the respondent by using some hidden or secret identification on forms or envelopes. Such secret codes represent unethical and perhaps illegal practices.
- If the person completing a form must return it by mail, include the mailing address on both the cover letter and form.
- Regularly revise forms to keep them up to date.

(270 words)

Take and score Self-Test 21 over creating forms on page 279.

Figures 10–4 through 10–9 show examples of forms. Put yourself into the role of one who must complete each form, and examine each to determine whether it meets the suggestions for good forms. Notice how the form in Figure 10–6 allows the sender to add specific information to the message.

Using Forms

Just as the communication guidelines and principles apply to designing forms, they apply to completing them. These suggestions aid proper completion of forms:

- Read instructions carefully and skim the entire form before beginning.
- Follow instructions precisely; use script, printing, or typewriting as specified.
- Before beginning to write, determine whether the information goes above or below the line.

Send me more information about:

- ☐ Life insurance
- ☑ Health insurance
- ☑ Home insurance
  - ☐ Homeowner
  - ☑ Renter
  - ☐ Condominium Owner
  - ☐ Mobile Home Owner/Renter
- ☑ Auto insurance
- ☐ Business insurance
- ☐ Small Employers Group Insurance
- ☐ ROC Motor Club

ROC INSURANCE
One Queen's Drive
Amorita, OK 73719

Name C.L. Korda

Address 14 South Central

City Lynn

State AR Zip 72440

Phone 333-333-3333

I understand that no sales representative will come to my home without my permission. I also understand that I am under no obligation.

2009

FIGURE 10–4 Completed form requesting information.

MESSAGE

For Mr. Roland

Date 2/19/8X Time 9:27 a.m.

M J.T. Manning

From Surety Corp.

Phone No. 444-4444

✓	Telephoned
	Returned your call
	Came to see you
	Will call again
✓	Wants to see you
✓	Wants you to phone

Message Wants to set up an appointment to go over the Surety account with you. She will be in her office today, but not tomorrow.

by it

FIGURE 10–5 Completed form for message.

PURPLE EX
PURPLE ARMOR
of Renfrew

1818 West 7
P.O. Box 4343
Renfrew, PA 17053

Fred R. Quicksilver
P.O. Box 893
Leroy, OH 44251

Date: 5/31/8X
Group Number: ______
Process Number: 79845
Processor: jt

Thank you for your recent request for membership in PURPLE EX/PURPLE ARMOR of Renfrew. We shall be glad to proceed with the processing as soon as we receive the information identified in this listing:

☐ Please take the ______ enclosed form(s) for medical examination to a physician who will give the listed person(s) physical examination(s) and complete the form(s). Please complete the examination(s) and have the physician return the form(s) in the enclosed envelope within three weeks of the date of this letter.

☑ Please sign the 3 enclosed form(s) authorizing the release of medical information. Then send each form to the physician listed on it. Send each form soon so that the physician may return it to arrive in this office within three weeks of the date of this letter. The form itself includes a notation asking the physician to return it within two weeks of receipt.

☑ Please answer the following question(s) directly on this letter and return it in the enclosed envelope within two weeks of the date of this letter.

1. Though you are applying only for yourself, what is your wife's name?
______
2. Does your wife have any group insurance? ______ If so, with what company? ______ what group number? ______

Sincerely yours,

Processing Department

2.33 (7–81)

FIGURE 10-6 Completed form requesting additional medical information.

CATHY COMPANY

Requisition for Purchase 9184

Date 6/1/80 Account No. 39214CT

Requisitioned by Arnold Dietrich

Department Accounting

Required Delivery Date 10/1/80

Name of Vendor Daymar Furniture, Inc.

Address of Vendor 9864 Farrell Avenue

Pixie, Wisconsin 98640

Terms offered by vendor 2/10, n/30

Qty.	Catalog Number	Description	Unit Price	Total Price	Shpg. Wt.
6	84EB	Safety File Cabinet	129.95	779.70	240 lbs.
2	662F	Deluxe Walnut Desk	389.95	779.90	400 lbs.
			Total	1559.60	640 lbs.

Required Signatures:

Arnold Dietrich — *6/1/80*

Requisitioner — Date

Anna Mavis — *6/1/81*

Department Head — Date

FIGURE 10-7 Completed form requisitioning materials to be supplied from outside the organization.

I'll take you up on the FREE SAMPLE!

ACHESAWAY TABLETS
Relief for arthritis, but no stomach upset

Do you presently use a medication for arthritis?

☒ Yes Brand Arthritabol

☐ No

Name Don Miller
(Please print clearly)

Address 3470 East Baynes Street

City Lorma State CA Zip 44492

One sample per family and household. Not available outside U.S. Void where prohibited, taxed, or otherwise regulated. Offer restricted to persons 18 years or older. Offer expires 9/30/8X.

FIGURE 10–8 Completed form requesting a free sample (on mail-in card with address on other side).

TRAVIVI CAMERA REGISTRATION

Please return this form within two weeks of date or purchase.

☐ Mr. ☐ Ms. ☑ Other title: Dr.

Name

Ruth Holden-Sayres

Address

1991 East 107 Street

City State Zip

Dorothy NJ 08317

Serial Number: TR-7543A Date of Purchase: 7/11/8X

Name of Store at Which Puchased: Y.G.&T.

Address of Store: Trails Shopping Center
Dorothy, N.J. 08317

FIGURE 10–9 Completed form registering a product under warranty (on mail-in card with address on other side).

- Put something in each blank, even if just a dash, a zero, "none," or "NA" ("not applicable," "not available").
- If typewriting, set machine so that the bottoms of the letters just clear the lines.
- If the instructions do not specifically permit the addition of extra pages to the form, put all information in the spaces allowed.
- When adding pages, refer to them on the form, and arrange them logically.

Figures 10–4 through 10–9 illustrate some properly completed forms. Review each from the standpoint of the company that prepared the form.

OTHER BUSINESS CHANNELS

Businesses use many written communication channels in addition to letters, reports, memoranda, and forms. The channels range from catalogs to company newsletters, from annual reports to procedural manuals. Too many channels exist for full coverage in this book. Business firms often employ specialists to develop the messages for many of these channels. Therefore, this chapter includes suggestions for only a limited number of additional written business communication channels: cards, telegrams, press releases, agendas, motions, minutes of meetings, statements of policy, and job descriptions and specifications.

Telegrams

Telegraphic services provide relatively speedy, low-cost channels for sending messages. They prove particularly valuable for reaching people on the move or in significantly different time zones. Operators transmit full-rate *telegrams* during the day for immediate delivery. However, they can also transmit lower-rate overnight telegrams with a guarantee to arrive by 2 p.m. the next day.

To send a *mailgram,* the local telegraph office transmits the message directly to one of nearly three hundred post offices in the United States that participate in the service. The post office then delivers the mailgram the following day as part of the regular mail.

Radiograms, cablegrams, and *letter telegrams* (lower-rate night telegrams) provide special versions of telegrams for transmission overseas. Using radios and cables for transmission, these channels provide reasonably rapid service. The sender places the message with a local telegraph office or a toll-free telephone number.

The speed of telegraphic services falls somewhere between that of the telephone and the postal service. Choose the telegram when unable to reach someone by telephone, or when you need a written record of detailed or complex information.

Analyzing the cost of telegraphic services shows that generally, for the same number of words, full-rate telegrams, radiograms, and cablegrams cost more than either telephone calls or first-class letters. However, the costs of mailgrams, overnight telegrams, and letter telegrams compete well with them.

To use telegraphic services, choose one of two procedures: (1) Dictate the message over the telephone to the local telegraph office or toll-free number, or (2) submit the message directly to an employee at a telegraph office counter. Personnel in the receiving telegraph office usually telephone messages to the addresses. The offices rarely use messengers to deliver telegrams anymore.

Whether dictating a message over the telephone or delivering it in person, write it ahead of time. Concentrate on the writing qualities of directness, conciseness, clarity, and completeness. Test and revise the drafts by playing the role of the receiver. Make every word count.

Figure 10–10 shows the abbreviated pattern of a message in a full-rate telegram. Observe the different elements of the form. Notice that the body of the message contains the maximum of ten words, and that the names of both participants, the address, and punctuation marks do not count. Also notice how the writer omitted unnecessary words and did not make the first statement a complete sentence.

Cards

Cards provide good channels for brief, nonconfidential messages not inserted into envelopes. Businesses use them extensively, particularly to provide convenience of feedback from receivers.

The United States Postal Service sells both single and double postpaid postal cards. However, many senders print their own cards and pay the postage in addition to the cost of the printing. The sender may obtain a special presort rate or business-reply rate.

The card saves money over the cost of a letter. Not only does the postage cost about 50 percent less than the letter, but preparation also costs less. The card includes the receiver's name and the sender's return address only once. In addition, a card requires no expenditure of time for folding, inserting into an expensive envelope, and sealing. Of course, to write an effective card, do not try to force too much information onto it. Write concisely, clearly, and correctly. Test placement of the message on the card for attractiveness. Figure 10–11 illustrates a card. Notice how much information it conveys without clutter.

Businesses sometimes use both sides of a card for messages. Thus, neither side contains an address. When receivers return such cards, they use return envelopes provided by the senders.

Figure 10–12 shows such a card. The credit union inserted copies of the card in envelopes containing the quarterly statements of activity in credit-union accounts. Examine the two sides of the card. Do they clearly, correctly, and concisely present their messages?

Press Releases

Business writers sometimes use traditional journalistic channels such as newsletters, news magazines, and press releases. Press releases (news releases) go western union **Telegram**

MSG. NO	NO. WDS. CL. OF SVC.	PD.—COLL.	CASH NO.	ACCOUNTING INFORMATION	DATE	FILING TIME	SENT TIME
				Charge 666-666-6666		A.M. P.M.	A.M. P.M.

Send the following message, subject to the terms on back hereof, which are hereby agreed to.

☐ OVERNIGHT TELEGRAM
UNLESS BOX ABOVE IS CHECKED THIS MESSAGE WILL BE SENT AS A TELEGRAM

CARE OF OR APT. NO.

TO Mr. Harold Diggs

ADDRESS & TELEPHONE NO. Miltonia Hotel, 908 Fors Drive (999) 999-9999

CITY — STATE & ZIP CODE Dialville, TX 75761

Additional information on customer. Call me before contacting her.

Dana

SENDER'S TEL. NO. 666-666-6666 **NAME & ADDRESS** Hale's Sales, 2 Cliff Mall, Oshtemo, MI 49077

OFFICE USE ONLY

EOM (BILL TO) / (ADDRESS) / (CITY - STATE - ZIP) / (CHG. METH.)

(CHG #) / (OPR #) / (HF) / (PC CODE) / (PC AMT.) / (GIFT AMT.) / (TAX) / (AGT. I.D.) / (SG) **X-OFF**

FIGURE 10–10 Completed telegram.

Plan to join us at the next meeting of your ASQC Chapter:

Dinner: 6:30 p.m.	Twill's Cafeteria 18 Pilar Drive (Just go through the line)
Speaker: 7:15 p.m.	J. T. Wyatt, QC Engineer, Eastern Electric "Nonparametric Statistics—Sturdy Techniques"
Business: 8:00 p.m.	Plans for national convention Selection of scholarship recipient Awards to winners of membership drive Welcome to new members Plans for fund-raising drive

FIGURE 10-11 Postcard invitation to a meeting.

As required for your protection, the Sensible Corporation Employees Credit Union is undergoing its annual audit by a Certified Public Accounting firm. One part of the audit involves a direct check with members to determine whether the records reflect correct transactions and balances.

If the transactions and balances on the enclosed statement are correct, PLEASE DO NOT REPLY. If, however, you find an error, please complete the reverse side of this notice and mail it directly to:

HOUSE WATERPRICE & CO.
Certified Public Accountants
Suite 1200
8 Park Drive
Security, MD 21235

DO NOT CONTACT ANY EMPLOYEE OR OFFICER OF THE CREDIT UNION. ONLY CONTACT HOUSE WATERPRICE & CO.

If you find errors in your statement, list them here:

Name As It
Appears on Statement ______________________________

Signature ______________________________ Date ____________

Account Number ______________________________

FIGURE 10-12 Audit verification on a card inserted with credit union's statement of account. (Both front and back are shown.)

to newspapers, magazines, radio, television, and other mass channels for distribution to the public.

A press release includes the desired date of the release, the date of the message, the name of the sender, and the source(s) of information. It sometimes indicates the area of the release—local, statewide, or national. When writing press releases, take particular care to use the direct writing style and to establish the six "W's"—who, what, when, where, how, why. Write concisely, correctly, and clearly. Write colorfully when appropriate. Write the message for the larger public. Do not use the sexist styles sometimes practiced by news writers. (See Chapter 6 and Appendix C.)

Transmit the release to the appropriate media. Depending upon the nature of the news, use the mail, messenger service, telegram, telephone, or other channels for the distribution. Figure 10–13 shows a simple press release. Observe how the writer developed the message so that reporters in the media can use it intact or select segments from it easily.

INCHESAWAY SALONS
1818 Steam Drive/Carrie, KY 41725
(777) 777-7777

April 3, 198X

AREA RELEASE FOR APRIL 5, 198X

INCHESAWAY PLANS NEW SALON

Construction will begin in May on a building for a new Inchesaway Salon at 7 Runway Court. So reported Nora Fields, District Manager for the corporation.

When completed in January, 198X, the building will bring the number of salons in Carrie to four. The others are located at the corner of Boecking and Slye, 14 Treadmill Circle, and in the Fitzgerald Plaza.

The building will cost about $850,000 for 14,000 square feet of space. It will house complete salon facilities as well as a suite of administrative offices on the top floor of the split-level, cedar-sided structure.

Fields said that Angle, Level, and Hammer Architects designed the building. The contractor is Steele Construction Co.

FIGURE 10–13 Press release.

Agendas

Businesspeople attend many meetings. Agendas can contribute a great deal to the smooth functioning of those meetings, particularly when distributed ahead of time. An agenda lists the planned events for the meeting in the order of their occurrence. It also lists the name of the group meeting and the time and place of the meeting. It may include the names of the people responsible for various segments, brief summaries of reports and items of business, and the texts of motions. The writing style depends heavily on directness, clarity, and conciseness.

Figure 10–14 illustrates some of the features of a simple agenda. Notice that it contains parallel listings and follows the traditional formal order. (Figure 10–11 also includes an abbreviated agenda.)

AGENDA
MANAGEMENT SOCIETY
Tuesday, April 17, 198X
Room 222
Mercer Hall
7:30 p.m.

1. Call to order: Cecil D. Ray, President
2. Consideration of minutes for March 13, 198X: Melba Harris, Secretary
3. Treasurer's report: Lynne Quinn, Treasurer
4. President's report: Cecil D. Ray
5. Vice President's report: Amorita Gerald
6. Committee reports
   a. Finance: Erma Irby
   b. Service: Edra Persing
   c. Scholarship: S. J. Grace
   d. Business Day: Edith John
   e. Tour of Eastern Electric: M. C. Earl
   f. Homecoming reception: Irene Carl
7. Unfinished business
8. New business
9. Adjournment

FIGURE 10–14 Agenda for meeting.

Motions

For the actual conduct of meetings most organizations establish some procedural rules through their constitutions, bylaws, and operating codes. Then they usually supplement the specific rules with some standard set such as *Robert's Rules of Order.*

Whatever rules it follows, however, any formal meeting requires motions as part of the operating procedure. Most motions take the oral form. However, participants sometimes write out complex information ahead of time. Directness, conciseness, and clarity again define the writing style. Avoid saying "I make a motion that . . . ." Instead, say, "I move that . . . ." Figure 10–15 illustrates a written motion. Observe the detailed description of the committee proposed in the motion.

Minutes

Minutes of meetings constitute the official record of the formal activities of that organization. Thus, they follow a relatively prescribed form. Minutes should include at least every key element of the meetings: who, what, when, where, how, and why. Some organizations want the minutes to include a rather full statement of the decisions and debate in addition to the skeleton features of the meeting. If necessary, use a tape recorder in addition to taking notes. Make minutes complete and correct. Of course, use the chronological pattern of development.

Figure 10–16 includes the outline and some excerpts from the minutes for the meeting outlined in Figure 10–13. Observe how the outline follows the agenda and places the key points from the agenda as side headings. Other formats use no headings at all, put headings centered above the sections, or make headings part of the paragraphs themselves, as in:

> *Members present* (Arst, Carl, Clemons, Crane, Dearborn, Dormain, Earl, J. Ellis, S. Ellis . . . .)

Statements of Policy

Statements of policy act as broad guides for the personnel of an organization as they act and interact to carry out the functional operations necessary to

MOTION

I move that we form a committee made up of five members, with one member selected by nomination and secret-ballot election in each of the five departments in the division. The committee shall select its own chairperson. The committee shall have the responsibility to develop a plan by which departmental employees may participate significantly in the policy-making of the company. The committee shall complete its work during May so that this body may review the plan at its June meeting.

FIGURE 10–15 Motion in written form.

MINUTES OF THE MANAGEMENT SOCIETY MEETING
April 17, 198X, Room 222, Mercer Hall
Scholar Lee University, Goin, TN

Members Present	Arst, Carl, Clemons, Crane, Dearborn, Dormarn, Earl, J. Ellis, S. Ellis, Frank, Fulcher, Gerald, Grace, Hall, Harris, Henthorn, Hilldegard, Irby, John, Karne, Kitely, Lanier, Lipps, Manning, Mitchell, Moore, Myers, Persing, Quinn, Ray, Watkins
Members Absent	Adair, Bearden, Bundrick, Hair, Olvan, Parker
Call to Order	With a quorum present, President Hall called the regular monthly meeting to order.
Minutes of March 13	The minutes of the meeting of March 13, 198X, were approved as written.
Treasurer's Report	Secretary-Treasurer Lanier distributed a copy of the activity in the Management Society account since the beginning of the year (copy attached). The balance on April 12 was $287.15.
President's Report	President Hall reported on his meeting with the President's Council of the School of Business on April 8 and his participation in the regional Management Society conference in Memphis, March 17–19. He reported that ....
Vice President's Report	Vice President Gerald listed the programs for the remainder of the semester. They are: (1) .... She introduced two new members: Donya Ellis and Vern Lipps.
Committee Reports	Finance. Chairperson Irby listed five fund-raising projects: (1) ... Irby moved that the committee report be accepted and that the projects be considered one at a time in order. Mitchell seconded. The motion carried. Irby moved and Moore seconded that project No. 1 be approved. Discussion followed. The motion failed. Irby moved ....
Unfinished Business	....
New Business	....
Adournment	The meeting was adjourned at 9:15 p.m.

Respectfully submitted

J. R. Lanier
Secretary-Treasurer

FIGURE 10–16 Minutes of meeting.

accomplish established goals. Therefore, a good statement of policy comes only after people with authority engage in extensive research and careful formulation based on clear objectives. Once the appropriate people establish a policy, the actual writing must reflect the intent clearly, completely, and concisely. Couch a policy statement in symbols understood by the readers. Too often written policies appear in jargon inappropriate for the level of the message.

People who implement policies must have some latitude in their interpretation. A policy should not and cannot cover every detail. In addition, the conditions on which policies depend change frequently. Therefore, formulate, examine, and revise statements on a regular basis. Figures 10–17 and 10–18 illustrate simple statements of policy. Cast yourself in the role of an employee reading these statements in an employees' manual. Would you understand these policies for posting jobs and filing grievances? Observe that both statements involve procedures and thus use the chronological pattern of development.

Job Descriptions and Specifications

Job analysis, job descriptions, and job specifications (job requirements) require substantial research and decision-making by skilled people. Thus, at this point we will discuss only formats and proper writing style.

1.72. POLICY ON JOB POSTINGS

Effective April 1, 198X all job openings for Grade 6 and higher will be posted so that employees may bid on them. The jobs will remain posted for ten working days.

To bid for a job, the employee will obtain a form from any office or supervisor, complete it, and return it to the office of the manager of the department in which the opening occurs. The employee must submit the bid no later than 5:00 p.m. on the tenth day of the posting.

When the posting period closes, a management-appointed screening committee will interview all bidders. They will then select the top three and notify them of their selection for a second interview. They will send letters to the remaining bidders explaining why they were not chosen to be in the top three.

The supervisor for the area in which the open job occurs will join the screening committee for the interviews with the top three bidders and for the decision. The supervisor and committee will notify the top bidder that he or she has been selected for the job. They will also send letters to the other two explaining why they were not chosen.

FIGURE 10–17 Statement of policy on job postings.

GRIEVANCE PROCEDURE

The grievance process involves the person filing the grievance, the Grievance Committee, the affected officers, and any other persons affected by the process or the final decision. The grievance procedure takes this sequence:

1. The aggrieved person first exhausts all established channels for solving the problem, following the chain from the immediate superior through the division manager. If the grievance is with a superior in that chain, the person should still discuss the matter in the order dictated.

2. If the exhaustion of the established channels does not satisfy the person, s/he reviews the definition of a grievance (page 17 of this manual) to determine whether the particular case fits it.

3. If the person decides that the case fits the definition, s/he obtains a grievance form from the Personnel office and completes it. S/he attaches any additional pages or materials thought necessary to present the grievance and supporting evidence.

4. The person submits the completed form and accompanying materials to the Chairperson of the Grievance Committee (defined on page 18).

5. The Grievance Committee meets within five days of receipt of the grievance and as many times thereafter as necessary to complete the work. (See page 18 for a description of Committee procedures.)

6. The Committee reaches a decision, writes a report, and sends copies to the aggrieved person, to the vice president for the division in which that person works, and to others if deemed appropriate. (See page 18.)

7. The vice president reviews the report, completes whatever additional investigation s/he needs, and reaches a decision. S/he communicates the decision to the aggrieved person and to any other persons affected by it.

8. If the decision requires some action, the affected persons then participate in that action.

FIGURE 10-18 Statement of grievance procedure contained in employees' manual.

Job Descriptions

As the name suggests, a job description describes the nature of a job—the duties and responsibilities that define it. Above all, make a job description complete, concise, and clear. Appraisals of performance naturally flow from descriptions. Therefore, if written well, the job description helps the worker to know both the responsibilities of the position and the criteria for judging performance.

Figure 10–19 includes a typical design for a job description. It also illustrates application of the suggestions for correct writing style. Analyze both the form and the content to determine whether the job description would help both the supervisor of word processing and the evaluator of the supervisor.

Job Specifications

Job specifications describe the qualifications required of the person who fills a job, including education, experience, arts, and skills that the person should possess. Therefore, the statement on job specifications complements the job description. Job specifications require the same writing style as job descriptions do. The major principles, then, include clearness, conciseness, completeness, and directness. Figure 10–20 illustrates the job specifications for the word-processing supervisory position described in Figure 10–19. Observe how the form forces the writer to consider all the qualities that a job requires of the person performing it.

While this chapter covers some miscellaneous channels for written messages, the next two chapters deal specifically with business reports. Chapter 11 begins by discussing the research process and giving some suggestions for collecting data.

SUMMARY

The memorandum, form, and other written-message channels represent important avenues for business communication. They carry the same kinds of messages as letters and reports, but have special features and applications.

Business writers often use typewritten interoffice mmoranda (memos) for messages within their organizations. Companies usually provide special stationery for memos. A memo does not include an inside address, a salutation, a complimentary close, or a standard signature block. It usually does include a subject line. It uses the direct developmental method and emphasizes conciseness, correctness, and clearness. For messages even less formal than memoranda, business writers send notes, often in handwritten form.

Many routine messages fit into a standard form. When creating forms, maintain the qualities of correctness, conciseness, clearness, considerateness, and coherence. Examples of specific suggestions include: (1) leave plenty of space for each answer; (2) arrange the elements in logical groupings and order; (3) include complete and clear instructions; and (4) give the form a title.

JOB DESCRIPTION*

Job Title Supervisor of Word Processing Salary Grade 10

Job Number B-82 Department Word Processing

Effective Date 12/3/8X

The Supervisor of Word Processing, under the supervision of the Manager of the Word Processing Center, performs supervisory duties including interviewing, selecting, and appraising the performance of personnel; planning, organizing, directing, and controlling the personnel and work of the department; and maintaining standards and confidentiality.

JOB DUTIES

Interviews applicants

Chooses personnel

Appraises performance of personnel

Trains personnel

Creates a positive climate for work

Develops annual budget

Defines work procedures and controls

Schedules and coordinates work flow

Maintains performance standards

Presides at regular staff meetings

Corrects problems arising between users and Center

Establishes and uses a reporting system for work measurement and standards

Protects confidentiality of information processed in the Center

---

*This job description includes enough information to evaluate and differentiate it from other jobs. However, it is not written to be a complete description of the function and every duty and responsibility associated with it.

FIGURE 10–19 Job description.

JOB SPECIFICATIONS

For Job no. B–82, Supervisor of Word Processing

Education

Four-year college degree or completion of two-year or business-college program supplemented by appropriate experience.

Experience

About six years of experience in related fields, with at least two years in word processing. Some supervisory experience. Some secretarial experience.

Special Arts

Ability to train and motivate employees.

Special Skills

Ability to perform word-processing activities and develop budgets.

Responsibility

Extensive responsibility for human interactions, establishing and maintaining standards, and solving problems.

Resourcefulness

Ability to make judgments related to personnel selection and appraisal, solving problems, and creation of a good work environment.

Supervision

As a supervisory position, requires complete range of administrative abilities.

Mental Ability

Medium to high intellectual ability.

Physical Ability

Minimal, except for skills for using word-processing equipment.

Contacts

Ability to maintain productive contacts with management, with users of the Center, and with employees.

General Abilities

Abilities to adapt to the pressures of a demanding and fast-paced activity.

FIGURE 10–20 Job specifications.

When completing forms, read and follow the instructions, determine whether the information goes above or below the line, typewrite the answers if necessary, and arrange information logically.

Other types of business channels include telegrams, cards, press releases, agendas, motions, minutes of meetings, statements of policy, and job descriptions and specifications.

For telegrams, make messages concise and correct. Choose them for speed somewhere between that of the telephone and the postal service.

Use cards for brief, nonconfidential messages. The card saves money over the cost of a letter.

Press releases (news releases) should include the desired date of the release, the date of the message, the name of the sender, the source(s) of information, and the area(s) for the release. Use the direct writing style; establish the who, what, when, where, how, and why. Write concisely, correctly, clearly, and colorfully, if appropriate.

An agenda lists the planned events for a meeting in the order of their occurrence. Use directness, clarity, and conciseness. Put complex motions for a formal meeting in writing for distribution to the participants.

The minutes of meetings constitute an official record and thus follow a prescribed form. Minutes should include at least the who, what, when, where, how, and why of the meeting. Several acceptable formats for minutes exist.

Statements of policy act as broad guides to the personnel of an organization. Thus, couch them in symbols understood by the readers, and make them accurate and complete in every detail.

Because a job description describes the duties and responsibilities that define a job, make it complete, concise, and clear. A statement on job specifications complements the job description by describing the qualifications required of the person who fills the job. Therefore, apply the same principles of clearness, conciseness, completeness, and directness to the writing.

EXERCISES

1. You have decided to change your Program Management Department's rules on working hours. The current rules state that all employees must arrive at work no later than eight o'clock and cannot leave before five o'clock. Employees may take an hour for lunch. You now want to allow your employees to arrive between six o'clock and ten o'clock and leave after they have worked at least eight hours. If they wish, they may do without lunch, eat while working, take a long lunch period, or take one or several breaks, just as long as they work eight hours. You also want your employees to operate on an honor system: they need not check with you every time they take a break, go to the dentist, or decide to come to work earlier or later than usual. You do want them to let their secretaries know where they can be contacted, though, in case of an emergency. Write a memorandum describing your new rules.
2. Meet with your group. You and every other group member read one of these situations to the rest of the group. The group members who are not reading should write short notes appropriate to each situation. Evaluate the notes.

BINKS, BANKS, AND BUNKS, P.C.

John Bacon sighs loudly as he begins his first day of work as office manager of Binks, Banks, and Bunks, P.C., a law firm. Not only has the law firm existed for over ten years without an office manager, but it has virtually no records of its transactions. Therefore, Bacon must start from scratch to give the 20-person law firm some administrative direction.

By talking to several lawyers and secretaries in the firm, Bacon learns about these problems:

1. For billing purposes, the lawyers are required to keep records of how they spend their time. Lawyers use legal pads, napkins, or anything else they can find to jot down the time they spend on each of the dozens of cases they handle for their clients. Sometimes these slips of paper get lost, making it difficult or impossible to bill the client. Furthermore, no guidelines govern how time is to be recorded; thus, some lawyers record actual time spent and others round the figure to the nearest half hour.
2. Every year lawyers and clerical personnel receive raises ranging from 2 to 20 percent of their salaries. Unfortunately, the raise just shows up on each employee's first January paycheck; the recipient does not know whether the amount of the increase should be interpreted as a reward or as a punishment. Apparently, no performance evaluation criteria have been established; consequently, the process of assigning raises is less than scientific or systematic.
3. The firm frequently runs out of critical office supplies. In fact, just last week several secretaries could not complete important typing assignments because they had no typewriter ribbons. It took two days to have the special ribbons shipped in from another state.

Based on his assessment of the firm's immediate needs, Bacon decides he must develop forms:

1. For the lawyers to use in recording the time they spend on each client's case.
2. For the partners to use in appraising each employee's performance and in determining pay raises. The form also might be given to each employee to explain her or his pay increase as well as the strengths and weaknesses of her or his performance.
3. For all employees to order supplies long before the stock is depleted.

(This case is fictional.)

a. The person with whom you share an office, Aaron Silkel, is ill today. You answer his phone, and the caller asks if Aaron is in. When you respond that he is ill, the caller asks you to tell Aaron that the Dixon plan will not be finished for six weeks and that the progress report should reflect the delay. The caller, Jane Bachrach, wants Aaron to contact her as soon as possible.
b. You go to Joan Dann's office to ask her to join you for lunch. She is not at her desk. You leave a note.
c. Matthew Timms asked you to review his integrated logistics support plan. You read it and thought it was quite good. You found only one mistake: he left out an important paragraph on reporting requirements on page 17. You write a note that you will attach to the plan.
d. You would like to discuss a work problem with your boss, Andrea Frame. When you call her, neither she nor her secretary is in. You would like to talk to her today if possible. You write a note that you will place on Frame's desk.
e. You want six of your colleagues to review your marketing plan for Naturally Sweet Bran Cereal. You want each of them to read for major content flaws only. You want the plan to go to Rick first, and then to Catherine, Willie, Margaret, Jason, and Sandra, in that order. You want each reader to write her or his comments in the margins of the plan itself.

3. Design a form for your use in checking the accuracy and completeness of memoranda you write. This is an example of part of such a form:

MEMORANDUM CHECKLIST

TODAY'S DATE ________ DATE MEMORANDUM SHOULD BE TYPED ________

DATE MEMORANDUM SHOULD BE DISTRIBUTED ________________

SUBJECT OF MEMORANDUM ________________________

Use yes, no, or NN for not necessary

Have I checked:		Have I included:	
1. Spelling	____	1. Date	____
2. Grammar	____	2. File number	____
3. Format	____	3. My name	____
4. Accuracy of information	____	4. Receiver's name	____
5. Clarity of message	____	5. Subject	____
6. Completeness of message	____	6. Meeting date	____
7. Conciseness of message	____	7. Meeting time	____
		8. Meeting place	____

4. You have noticed that a great deal of the work in your department is routine; thus, the employees could do it more efficiently through the use of forms. You realize that most of the employees probably know better than you what forms they need, but do not know how to design or use them. Write a memorandum that describes how to develop and use forms.
5. Meet with your group. Develop a simple brochure (fold one sheet of plain paper and use all sides) that includes at least this information (you may add more information if necessary):
   a. Company name, address, and phone number:
      Diet-for-Life Service
      9844 Del Mar Court, Suite 1100
      Samson, Florida 99446
      (555) 555-1213

b. Hours:
   Monday through Friday—10 A.M. to 6 P.M.
   Saturday—10 A.M. to 4 P.M.
   Closed Sunday
c. Products and services offered:
   Diet counseling
   Nutrition counseling
   Exercise counseling
   Physical inventories
   Health check-ups
   Special diet plans and books
   Medical library
   Personalized diet program
d. Personnel:
   Registered nurses
   Dieticians
   Trained diet counselors
   Exercise specialists
e. Motto:
   "You need never worry about losing weight again."
f. Description of program:
   No pills
   No strenuous exercise
   No starving
   Customer can see a counselor daily if he or she chooses
g. Special offers:
   First two counseling sessions are free.
   If a person does not lose at least fifteen pounds in the first three months of the program, he or she will receive a full refund from the Diet-for-Life Service.

After you have finished developing the brochure, have one of your group members (preferably someone who has not spoken in front of the class very often) display and describe your group's brochure to the rest of the class.

6. You are responsible for putting together the program for your department's monthly meeting. Prepare the agenda from the following information:
   a. Robert Lasser wants to give a 15-minute presentation on the proposal he is writing for the Onyx contract.
   b. Jane Lee wants to invite department members to attend the computer simulation workshop she will conduct.
   c. Albert Leung wants to discuss the results of his employee survey.
   d. Rachel Stein, your department's manager, will give a special talk on the company's new management plan. She will also preside over the meeting.
   e. David Sams, Alice Strong, Henry Arlington, Ann Bailey, and Jane Tucson each has a departmental problem he or she wishes to discuss.
   f. All group leaders will give work progress reports.
   g. Arnold Fitzbinder wants to ask department members for their suggestions concerning the company dance.
   h. One coffee break should be scheduled.
   i. Anna Greentree wants to ask department members to join her softball team.
7. *[Your professor will time this exercise.]* What, if anything, is wrong with this brief job description for a classified advertisement or bulletin-board posting? Make corrections and add information if necessary (use your imagination).

JOB DESCRIPTION

SECRETARY II JANUARY 6, 198X

We need one girl to type, file, and answer phones. She should be under 30 years of age. She should have five years of secretarial experience and take good shorthand. She should do good work and type fast to. She should have some college background. She should work long hours and on Saturday. She should be reliable. We want references. She should be ~~xxxxxxx~~ willing to write short letters. She should apply soon.

8. Correct this memorandum:

LEASETRUCK, INC. MEMORANDUM

MEMO TO: Employees
FROM: Don
DATE: January 11, 1981
SUBJECT: Meeting

We will start the meeting at 8 A.M. Please submit your topics ahead of time. Albert will provide the coffee. We need some doughnuts. Joan will give us her dept.'s progress report. Wayne will give his dept.'s problems before that. We'll have this dept. mgrs.' weekly staff meeting in the Lincoln Room. It's on the eighth floor. Lonnie will talk about his experiences at the Leasetruck Sales School in Lamone, Ohio. He was there for two months.

9. You want to order 36 light bulbs (item number 466B) at 50 cents each, 10 ladders (item number 1226C) at $40 each, and 8 pairs of scissors (item number 322S) at $8 each. The sales tax is 10 percent of the total order price. Shipping costs are included in the item price. You are submitting this order for your company, Very Huge Company, 6413 Elm Street, Townville, South Dakota 66116. Your company's telephone number is (555) 232-2323. You'll send a check with your order. Fill out the order form.

ALLYOUWANT SUPPLIES, INC.
ORDER FORM

(Please Print)

COMPANY NAME ______________________________

YOUR NAME ______________________________

COMPANY MAILING ADDRESS ______________________________

CITY ______________ STATE __________ ZIP __________

COMPANY TELEPHONE NUMBER ______________________________

ITEM NUMBER	NAME OF ITEM	PRICE EACH	QUANTITY	TOTAL PRICE
Type of Payment		TOTAL		
CHECK ☐ MONEY ORDER ☐		SALES TAX		
Send to:		TOTAL AMOUNT		

ALLYOUWANT SUPPLIES, INC.
42 Industrial Boulevard
Dooley, South Dakota 66449

10. Obtain two or three simple blank forms (job application, credit application, insurance application, loan application, simple contract, questionnaire, insurance claim, etc.), and make a copy of each. Complete each copy, using hypothetical information if necessary. As you complete each, make a list of its strengths and weaknesses.
   a. For each form write a one-page summary of its strengths, weaknesses, and your overall evaluation of the form.
   b. Redesign the poorest of the blanks and type it in final form.
   c. Submit the one-page summaries, the redesigned form, and the three original blank forms to your professor.

11. Contact a telegraph office to determine rates and word allowances for the various services offered. Write a one-page summary of your findings.

12. Condense the message in Figure 7–13 into ten or fewer words as if for a telegram.

13. Revise the information in Figure 10–2 to fit onto a postal card in an attractive format. Instead of wasting an actual postal card, draw a rectangle the size of a postal card on a piece of paper.

14. Select a controversial business topic and write a two- or three-page position paper presenting your views on it.
15. You just learned that your company has been named the recipient of the prestigious annual Craig Foundation Award of Excellence in Human Relations. Supplying any needed information, write a one-page press release about the award.
16. You are the parliamentarian for a local professional organization. Though the organization does not need or want to observe every detail of parliamentary procedures, it does want to observe the basic ones to maintain order during meetings. Obtain a copy of *Robert's Rules of Order,* and examine it carefully. Write a one- or two-page outline of major points—an outline to which you can refer during meetings.
17. Use your dictionary and thesaurus to create meanings for these words. Use the words when you think, write, and speak so that you feel comfortable using them.

a. Compromise	**e.** Precise	**i.** Sarcasm
b. Discreet	**f.** Prior	**j.** Specification
c. Discrete	**g.** Quasi-	**k.** Trait
d. Generic	**h.** Routine	**l.** Trappings

18. Take and score Self-Test 22 over Chapter 10.

SELF-TEST 21
Excerpt about Creating Forms

A. Recall (33 points each). For each multiple-choice question, select the most accurate answer.

1. Which one of these suggestions does *not* contribute to creating a good form?
   - **a.** Condense the form as much as possible.
   - **b.** Write clear questions.
   - **c.** Word the items at the highest readability level anticipated in the audience.
   - **d.** Give the form a title.
   - **e.** Regularly revise forms to keep them up to date.
2. The good form does *not*:
   - **a.** Need to apply the standard principles for writing
   - **b.** Need an introduction
   - **c.** Have to apply the six guidelines for effective communication
   - **d.** Ever have a postpaid return envelope accompany it
   - **e.** Sacrifice completeness to accomplish conciseness

B. Inference (34 points). Indicate whether this statement is true or false.

1. Because of the simplicity of forms, writers need not use empathy in developing them.

SOLUTION

A. Recall (33 points each)
1. c **2.** e

B. Inference (34 points)
1. False

SELF-TEST 22
Chapter 10

A. Recall (25 points each). For each multiple-choice question, select the most accurate answer.

1. A memorandum usually exhibits the ______________ style of writing.
   - **a.** Direct
   - **b.** Indirect
   - **c.** Journalistic
   - **d.** Chronological
   - **e.** Comparative
2. Develop and use forms for:
   - **a.** Virtually every written business exchange
   - **b.** Routine business messages
   - **c.** Most external correspondence
   - **d.** Most formal written messages
   - **e.** Transmitting quantitative data only
3. Which is *not* true regarding the minutes of a meeting?
   - **a.** Minutes constitute the official record of the formal activities of the meeting participants.
   - **b.** Minutes are the program for a meeting.
   - **c.** Minutes should include every key element of the meeting.
   - **d.** Minutes follow a relatively prescribed form and order.
   - **e.** Accuracy is a cardinal requirement for good minutes.

B. Inference (25 points). Indicate whether this statement is true or false.

1. Regardless of what you write, you should strive to be as concise as possible without allowing accuracy and completeness to suffer.

SOLUTION

A. Recall (25 points each)

1. a **3.** b
2. b

B. Inference (25 points)

1. True

STUDENT'S OBJECTIVES:

1 To learn the importance of business reports

2 To understand the research process and its relationship to business communication

3 To review how to collect data from secondary sources through a review of types of sources, the use of the library, and the use of bibliographic and note cards

11

WRITING REPORTS: The Research Process and Collection of Data

4 To learn to collect primary data through oral channels, direct observation using a form, and questionnaires

5 To learn how to design a questionnaire

6 To review and contrast the strengths and weaknesses of three major survey methods: personal interviews, telephone interviews, and mail questionnaires

For large corporations, reports provide the primary information supply line for decision-making personnel. Managers of small organizations also depend on reports to supplement and reinforce directly collected information. In both large and small organizations, reports also are channels for downward and lateral messages. Top managers may send reports down through the organizational structure. In addition, managers often make reports to one another. Organizations also report to external entities—particularly to stockholders and to federal, state, and local governments. Furthermore, reports often flow inward to organizations from external entities such as consulting and auditing firms.

Reports may use both written and oral communication channels. The written channels provide the capacity for handling objective, permanent, complex, and voluminous information. They also accommodate long-distance transmission, review, deliberation, and distribution to large numbers of people. The oral channels provide the capacity for richness, for rapid turn-taking, for expanded feedback and evaluation, and for adjustment based on that feedback and evaluation.

Reports may simply describe a problem, or they may describe a problem *and* a research procedure for trying to solve it. They may suggest a solution to a problem or provide the information by which another person may solve a problem. Reports may result from introspection or scientific research. Reports may deal with production, marketing, finance, or any other function or operation of the firm. They may relate to any management responsibility—planning, organizing, or controlling. Reports may take the style of a completed, preprinted form, a letter, a memorandum, or a traditional manuscript.

Many people claim that businesses prepare too many written reports. Small-business owners frequently object to the number of reports required by government. Consider the volume of reports produced by your company. Often companies can save thousands of dollars by eliminating reports that contribute virtually nothing to performance. Even with the elimination of the unnecessary ones, businesspeople must still prepare many reports. Evaluation of their work depends on their ability to prepare reports effectively—particularly as they rise in management.

This chapter covers the research and data-collecting processes necessary for obtaining information for reports. Then Chapter 12 covers types of reports and the principles for writing them.

THE RESEARCH PROCESS

Research involves the search for solutions to problems. The problems may exist as puzzling questions or as obstacles in the path of the attainment of some goal. Basic research answers puzzling questions, and applied research overcomes obstacles. Thus, most business research falls in the category of applied research.

People use the word *research* in many different ways. To sort out some of those ways, first understand that research does *not* mean the same as:

- Writing—though writing proves important to the process.
- Publishing—though publishing disseminates information gained from the process.
- Quantitative methods—though quantitative methods may contribute significantly to the process.
- Collecting information—though collecting information is a vital stage of the process.

Thus, many people use the word *research* too narrowly. In conjunction with communication, research has the purpose of solving problems, not writing reports or papers. In addition, not all reports and papers result from research. However, research is a process with communication inseparably woven into it, and communication is a process with research inseparably woven into it.

Do not think of a report as an end unto itself; instead, think of it as a means to an end. It captures the results of research or some stage of the process. It summarizes a process suggesting a solution to a problem. It conveys information or possible solutions to a decision-maker, who then attempts to solve the problem. Because of the interwoven nature of research and communication, the good research writer understands and applies the steps of the research process. An assignment like "Write me a report about . . . ." involves much more than writing. Even a report not resulting from research requires professional application of at least the defining and collecting steps of the research process.

While beginning writers may not employ every research step in every assignment, their growth with a company often depends on developing the ability to do so. Rarely does management separate the assignment of research or major elements of it from the report writing. Even if management does assign the research to one person and the writing to another, the writer must understand the process well enough to write about it.

STEPS OF THE RESEARCH PROCESS

The research process uses science, art, technique, and decision-making applied to four stages and these basic steps:

Stage A

1. Recognize and define problem
2. Review literature
3. State hypothesis(es)
4. Design investigation
5. Write proposal

Stage B

6. Collect data
7. Organize data
8. Analyze data

Stage C

9. Interpret results of analysis
10. Draw conclusions
11. Develop recommendations
12. Write and disseminate final report

Stage D

13. Conduct follow-up

Stage A sets the stage, **Stage B** carries out the action, **Stage C** assesses and reports the findings, and **Stage D** checks on the application of the results of the research.

Science, Art, Technique, and Decision Making

Research involves the *scientific method.* In fact, many researchers define steps 1, 3, 4, 6, 7, 8, 9, and 10 as the steps of the scientific method. It adds objectivity to the process because it demands exact procedures, factual observations, experiments, and analysis.

Art brings human creativity into the research process. It contributes particularly to identifying the factors associated with the problem, the hypothesis(es), the design, the interpretation, and the recommendations. Avoid subjective bias, however. Once creativity has opened doors for the research process, you must become the objective scientist. Do not allow bias to affect the observations or analysis. Reengage art only at the stage of interpretation or revision of definitions or design.

A great deal of the work in the research process involves nothing more than sheer *technique*—technical skills. Calculating an arithmetic mean, writing a computer program, using calipers to take measurements, constructing a grammatically correct sentence—all represent the application of technique. Although technical skills may prove mechanical and even tedious, they play a critical role in the completion of research.

Decision-making overlays all of the scientific, artistic, and technical activities associated with research. For example, the researcher must decide which factors to test and which to reject, which method of collection to employ, which analytical tools to use, and which conclusions to draw.

Stage A

Recognizing and defining problem One of the most demanding stages of the research process requires the recognition and definition of the problem. Techniques for doing so include brainstorming, reading, conversing, and observing. The general problem arises from a broad question or obstacle in need of solution. As an example, a researcher may define a decline in productivity as the general problem for a company. Next the researcher will carve the specific problem from the general problem. To accomplish the carving, the researcher isolates a part of the whole—delimits the problem or establishes the scope of the problem. The boundaries of the isolated problem define it in terms of the appropriate W's—the who, what, when, and where, in particular.

For the general-problem example, then, the researcher might define the specific problem as: Do monthly productivity rates for P. R. Blem, Inc., for 1975–198X relate to monthly turnover rates for the same period?

Reviewing literature The efficient researcher searches the literature as an aid to identifying problems, perfecting the definition of a problem, or finding solutions to a defined problem or similar problems. Examining the literature also gives evidence of the researcher's thoroughness and recognition of the work of others—two cardinal elements of the proper research posture.

Stating hypothesis(es) Application of the scientific method requires the statement of a hypothesis or hypotheses. A hypothesis takes the form of a declarative statement that can be tested through the analysis of collected data. It does not take the form of a question or a problem. On the basis of the analysis, the researcher accepts or rejects the prestated hypothesis.

The researchers, then, might state the hypothesis for the P. R. Blem, Inc., productivity problem as: A significant correlation exists between monthly productivity rates and monthly turnover rates at P. R. Blem, Inc., for the period 1975–198X.

Designing the investigation Research design requires decisions about how to collect, organize, and analyze data appropriate to the defined problem and hypothesis(es). Decisions about collection involve precise definition of factors, location of information, methods of observation, and quantity of observation. They also may involve sampling methods and other topics. Decisions about organization and analysis relate to selection of the methods of analysis. Such decisions require a great deal of knowledge about both quantitative and qualitative approaches to examining information and reaching conclusions about it. The quality of research depends on a good design. Thus, the wise researcher makes all of the design-stage decisions before even beginning to collect the data. Otherwise, the research may take an undesirable course—with wasted time, effort, and money as a result.

Writing the proposal The proposal (prospectus) evolves as a written report that includes at least the statement of the problem, a summary of the literature review, the hypothesis(es), and the design of the investigation. The proposal often serves as the basis for requesting permission, authorization, and/or monetary support for the research. Therefore, make it complete, competent, and precise in every detail.

Stage B

Collecting data With a good design, the collecting stage becomes a formality. It simply completes the procedures already established. Collection may involve obtaining information from secondary sources. It may involve primary data gained from direct observation of actual or simulated events, or from indirect observation through surveys. It may involve any or all of the senses.

Organizing data The design also indicates how to organize data. Proper organization aligns the data to fit the chosen analytical approach. It usually requires collation, tables, and graphs.

Analyzing data Once the researcher collects and organizes the data, the analysis proceeds. Many analytical tools fall into the quantitative realm. Others use words instead of numbers.

Stage C

Interpreting results of analysis Interpretation adds art to the scientific methodology of the analysis. It supplies meaning for the results of the analysis. Basically, interpretation answers the question, "Now, what do the results of that analysis mean to me?"

Drawing conclusions Drawing conclusions focuses the analysis and interpretation into a final decision. The conclusion involves acceptance or rejection of the originally stated hypothesis. It also elaborates on why the data, analysis, and interpretation led to that decision.

Developing recommendations Many reports stop with the conclusions (results, findings, discussion) of the research, leaving the decision about action to others. This style occurs quite frequently in business situations: Staff researchers conduct the research, write reports (making no recommendations), and leave the decision-making to the line managers to whom they submit the reports.

Some managers prefer a different style: They charge researchers with the responsibility of developing recommendations. Such recommendations usually follow the conclusions and become modified action components of the reports. However, research reports usually do not include the overt types of requests found in letters, notes, memoranda, and other forms. Instead they include brief and direct recommendations about the needs for additional research or the courses of action decision makers might take. The recommendations tie clearly to the conclusions from which they sprang and may appear in ranked order.

Writing and disseminating final report Like the proposal, the final report includes the statement of the problem, the review of the literature, the hypothesis(es), and the design of the investigation. However, it also includes the collected data in organized form, a summary of the analysis, the interpretation, the conclusion, and recommendation (if appropriate). It may also include an abstract (a summary placed at the beginning of the report), and other sections as well.

In business situations, research reports usually go to a few key managers—including the one who authorized the research. Thus, distribution remains limited and private. For some situations, however, the researcher distributes copies of research results rather widely—even to the extent of submitting them for publication.

Stage D

Conducting follow-up Depending on the instructions from, and relationships with, the authorizing manager, the researcher may conduct a follow-up. The researcher may take any one or a combination of several courses of action:

- Ask whether the manager needs additional information

- Ask which of several recommendations (if included) the manager will implement
- Try to persuade the manager to take a certain course of action or not to take another
- Offer additional recommendations
- Suggest additional research
- Ask the manager to evaluate the report
- Ask the manager to report on the success of the implementation of the recommendation(s) in the report

Types of Research

Many classifications of research types exist. One common system—based on the nature of the data—includes three classes:

- Historical (searching for the meaning of history)
- Survey (using observation to describe or analyze contemporary data)
- Experimental (controlling the research to observe the effect of identified variables upon the outcome)

Historical and most descriptive survey methods involve qualitative (verbal) analysis. The analytical survey, experimentation, and some descriptive survey methods involve quantitative (numerical) analysis. The sophisticated business communicator improves on the use of both words and numbers as tools for research and reporting.

Two special research methods fit particularly well into this review of research and business communication: motivational research and the communication audit. *Motivational research* deals with human behavior. It has as its goal the determination of why people act as they do. One concept underlies all motivational research: People generally cannot or will not directly reveal their motives. Thus, motivational research depends upon indirect methods.

Because of the indirectness required, motivational research uses some special techniques—particularly for the collecting stage. One such technique requires the use of carefully developed open-end questions. For instance, the researcher may begin a story and have the respondent finish it. She may begin a series of sentences and have the respondent finish them. She may simply list words and have the respondent write or say the first thing that comes to mind. She may show pictures, ink blots, and abstract sketches and ask the respondent to react to them.

The *communication audit* deals with written, oral, and nonverbal communication for organizations and individuals. Communication researchers use the laboratory to study simulations of organizations. They also observe actual organizations at work. Researchers study all levels of communication activities. They analyze channels and communication systems. They study internal communication as it flows upward, downward, laterally, and along the grapevine. They analyze the flow of communication to and from external bodies. They conduct research into communication methods, abilities, policies, philosophies, barriers, and needs. They also concentrate upon the readability of messages. As described in Chapter 6, readability formulas exist for this kind of analysis.

COLLECTION OF DATA

As a crucial part of the research process, the collection of information involves both *primary* (firsthand) data and *secondary* (secondhand) data. Primary data usually prove more difficult and expensive to obtain than secondary data. Therefore, after defining the type of information needed, try to find it in written secondary sources before moving to primary sources.

Secondary data

Two categories define how to use secondary sources efficiently: (1) the types of sources and (2) how to locate and record information.

Types of Sources

Secondary information falls into four broad classes: standard types, reference aids, systems for search and retrieval, and unpublished sources. *Standard types of publications* often include the desired type of information. This list includes such publications for the business writer:

Dictionaries
Encyclopedias
Statistical Abstract of the United States
Monthly Labor Review
World Almanac and Book of Facts
Survey of Current Business
Federal Reserve Bulletin
Statistical Yearbook (United Nations)
Demographic Year Book (United Nations)
Monthly Bulletin of Statistics (United Nations)
Business Week
Forbes
Information Please Almanac and Yearbook
Fortune
Sales Management
Textile World
Journal of Accounting
Journal of Business
Journal of Business Communication
Journal of Management Studies
Journal of Marketing
Journal of Marketing Research
Dissertation Abstracts
Congressional Record

If a standard type of publication does not yield the needed data, turn next to *reference aids*. Reference aids identify sources of information. They include organization by topics, authors, and other appropriate classifications. Here is a list of reference aids for business information:

Business Periodicals Index
New York Times Index
Wall Street Journal Index
Accountants' Index
Sources of Business Information (Edwin T. Coman)
Applied Science and Technology Index
How to Use the Business Library (H. Webster Johnson)
Engineering Index
Business Information—How to Find and Use It (Marian Manley)
Social Sciences Index
Humanities Index
Monthly Catalog of United States Government Publications
Biological and Agricultural Index
Cumulative Book Index
Publishers' Weekly
Index Medicus
Chemical Abstracts
Dissertation Abstracts
Education Index
Readers' Guide to Periodical Literature
Vertical File Index
Bulletin of the Public Affairs Information Service

Systems for search and retrieval include *DATRIX* (Direct Access to Reference Information) and *ERIC* (Educational Research Information Center). Both systems use computers to search for sources of information related to an identified topic. Both yield printouts of sources.

Unpublished sources include the records of businesses and other organizations. Such computer systems as the *IBM Remac* disk memory facilitate the storage and retrieval of unpublished numerical information.

Locating and Recording Information

Locating and recording secondary information requires that you know how to use the library and how to use bibliographic and note cards. To *use the library* efficiently, you need to understand and use the elements that define the library system. Such elements include card catalogs, classification systems, maps for locating library sections, microfilm equipment, interlibrary loans, and consultative services.

If you do not feel comfortable with library work, take advantage of the free printed information and orientation sessions offered by most libraries. In addition, never hesitate to ask questions. Most of all, however, avoid letting

PB
MENDE
C1
2H
Mendenhall, William, and Reinmuth, James E.
Statistics for Management and Economics.
4th ed. Boston: Duxbury Press, PWS
Publishers, Wadsworth, Inc, 1982

Taylor, Ronald A. "Explosion of Hi-Tech Products
for the Home." U.S. News & World Report,
December 27, 1982; January 3, 1983. pp.
65-68.

FIGURE 11-1 Bibliography cards for book and periodical.

any insecurity about using the library keep you from obtaining the information you need to solve a problem. Invest the time necessary to take full advantage of the mass of information available. Once you have found a potential source, narrow your search by skimming and scanning tables of contents, prefaces, headings, indexes, and bibliographies for the kinds of information contained.

Then use skimming, scanning, and rapid reading to check into sections that may prove productive.

To *record* information from secondary sources properly, always use cards, *not* paper. Use one set of cards (often 3 by 5 inches) for bibliographic entries. Use another set of cards (often 5 by 8 inches) for notes. By using a separate card for each bibliographic entry or note, you create two permanent decks that you can arrange and rearrange as needed.

When you locate a usable source, immediately make a complete bibliographic entry on a card. Use a consistent style for all entries. (Appendix B of this book and many style manuals present correct formats for such entries.) Always include the library call numbers for books. You may want to develop a classification scheme and coding system for cards. If so, include such a code on each card.

Figure 11-1 illustrates bibliographic cards for a book and a periodical. Observe the completeness of the entries. For efficient recording of notes from publications, first read carefully to decide exactly what you want to use. Never just start copying everything. Once you have selected a passage, decide whether to paraphrase (restate with the substance intact), to use a summary (a brief extraction of key points), or to cite a direct quotation (the actual words of the writer).

On the card, first record the source, then write a full footnote or enough information to allow you to prepare the footnote from the bibliographic card. Take particular care to record correct page numbers. Also include call numbers when appropriate and any code that you have devised. Then write the excerpt itself, putting only one excerpt to a card. Identify the excerpt as a paraphrase, summary, or direct quotation. Figure 11-2 shows a note card. Observe its conciseness and completeness.

Taylor, "Explosion of Hi-Tech Products...,"
p. 67

"With new products emerging almost daily, the telephone is changing from a simple two-way communications device to an all-around information system"

FIGURE 11-2 Note card.

Primary Data

When secondary sources do not yield the desired data, use primary procedures to obtain them. This coverage of the primary collection process falls into three categories: (1) sampling procedures, (2) methods for collecting data orally, and (3) forms for recording direct observations.

Sampling Procedures

A universe (population) contains every elementary unit (person or thing) possessing the characteristic under observation. Sometimes researchers observe every unit of a population. However, at other times they observe only a selected part of it—a sample.

When possible, select samples by a statistical method. Statistical sampling gives every item in the universe equal probability for selection. The major types of probability samples include the simple random sample, the systematic sample, the stratified sample, and the cluster sample.

Sometimes circumstances prevent the use of statistically valid methods. In such nonprobability processes, select samples as representative of the universe as possible. Use validation techniques to overcome the possible bias in nonprobability samples. Many books on sampling, statistics, and research include details on sampling procedures.

Methods for Collecting Data Orally

When seeking information through oral channels, plan the transaction ahead of time. If permitted, use a recorder for complex or extensive information. Take appropriate notes. Ask perception-checking questions when possible. Listen carefully.

For the oral data-receiving situation, try to obtain supplemental written information if possible. For example, to gain a great deal of numerical data to supplement an interview, you can often just ask for a copy of a report that contains it. Place each bit of information on a separate note card. On the card write the preliminary outline number or topic heading. In addition, write the source of the information. Also prepare a card for the source. Later sort the note cards into stacks appropriate to the outline. Also alphabetize the source cards. Chapter 14 includes information on interviewing and brainstorming. These two types of oral transactions prove particularly useful for collection of data.

Forms for Recording Direct Observations

One basic approach to collecting data involves nonverbal, direct observations through the five senses—particularly through the eyes and ears. Such acts may involve counting, measuring, observing the behavior and characteristics of people and things, listening, tasting, smelling, touching, and performing a myriad of other observational acts. Direct observation also often depends on the ability to use simple or technical instruments and equipment.

Using a form for recording results of direct observation can greatly improve the quality of the data-collection process. Such a form should provide:

- A title and/or some other designation such as a code number
- Any special instructions for completion of the form
- Spaces to record specific identifying information—such elements as the date, time, place, name of organization or person, and any special features associated with the observation
- Space to identify the observer
- Identification of all observations to be made along with sufficient space for recording them
- A design that allows the observer to use check marks, X's, or circles—in short, to use a minimum number of words or numbers
- A logical arrangement of the items
- A design that allows the observer to add comments about unusual situations

Figure 11-3 illustrates a form for recording observations of the characteristics of randomly selected parking lots at preselected times. After designing such a form, conduct some trial runs with the form before putting it into use. Take on the role of a field recorder as you examine the form. Does it meet the requirements of a good form for observation?

CONSTRUCTION OF QUESTIONNAIRES

Observations of primary data often occur in an indirect fashion. They still depend upon the senses—again primarily those of seeing and hearing. However, the observations involve reading or hearing what other human beings write or say about the subject of the research. The collection of data through indirect observation moves the research into the category of the survey. The surveying method uses personal interviews, telephone interviews, and mail questionnaires. All three require the careful development of a plan, a set of instructions, and a set of questions designed to obtain the desired information.

Most of the time the instructions and questions take a written form—even if asked in person or over the telephone. Sometimes the interviewer memorizes the instructions and questions for oral delivery. At other times researchers preplan only the introduction to an oral interview—trusting the remainder of the interview to their ability to adapt to whatever course the interview takes. Suggestions for interviewing appear in Chapter 14 and in Chapter 16. Therefore, this chapter covers only the written instruments associated with surveys.

Principles for Construction of Questionnaires

The design of *survey instruments* calls for a blend of communication and research skills. Thus, discussions of survey design appear in the literature on both research and communication. Researchers often differentiate among the basic survey instruments by using such words and phrases as *interview guide, opinionnaire,* and *questionnaire*. However, for convenience, *questionnaire* appears as the generic term in this book. Principles for the construction of

CHARACTERISTICS OF COMMERCIAL PARKING LOTS AND GARAGES IN PARKWAY, MISSOURI, 198X
Researchers Unlimited Corp.
Box 793, Parkway, MO 64130

Observer: Arrive at 8:15 a.m. Show permit to operator on duty. Begin all occupancy observations exactly on time. Make other observations and take meals and breaks in the periods between occupancy observations. Show permit to new operators or supervisors as they come on duty.

Signature of observer ______________________

Date __/__/8X (Mo. Day) Day of week: M ☐ Tu ☐ W ☐ Th ☐ F ☐ Sa ☐ Su ☐

Type of installation: Lot ☐ Garage ☐

Name and location of garage or lot ______________________

____

____

If garage, number of floors ________

Number of parking spaces ________ Parking spaces marked? Yes ☐ No ☐

Dimensions of parking spaces (in feet and inches)

No. _____ at Length ________ Width ________ Total square feet ________

No. _____ at Length ________ Width ________ Total square feet ________

Width of driving lanes (in feet and inches) ________

Number of parking spaces occupied:

8:30 a.m. ________	6:30 p.m. ________
10:30 a.m. ________	8:30 p.m. ________
12:30 p.m. ________	10:30 p.m. ________
2:30 p.m. ________	12:30 a.m. ________
4:30 p.m. ________	

Charges:

Hourly ________	Weekly ________	Other ________
Daily ________	Monthly ________	

On the graph paper provided on the back of this sheet sketch the shape of the lot or of a typical parking floor of the garage. Show the nearest streets on all four sides, directions of one-way streets, the location of the toll booth, the entrances, the exits, and the dimensions of all sides (in feet and inches). You may turn the paper sideways if you wish, but mark clearly which direction is north.

FIGURE 11-3 Form for recording observations.

questionnaires fall into four broad categories: (1) general design, (2) types of questions, (3) qualities of good questions, and (4) types of construction to avoid.

General Design

These guidelines aid in the development of a questionnaire:

1. Introduce yourself, the topic of the survey, and the purpose of the research. However, do not disclose information that may bias the results. Assure confidentiality or anonymity when appropriate.
2. Include good instructions for completing the questionnaire. Questionnaires for interviews often include two sets of instructions—one to the interviewer and one to the interviewee.
3. Use attention-getting, interest-holding, and persuasive devices in the introductory matter. Offer an incentive such as a material gift or a copy of the final report of the research.
4. Provide for ease of feedback; for mail questionnaires, include postpaid envelopes for return.
5. For mail questionnaires, include dates of return and return addresses in the messages themselves. The receivers may misplace the postpaid envelopes.
6. A separate letter or memorandum may accompany a questionnaire. It may include the introduction, topic, title, purposes, instructions, devices for attention, interest, and persuasion, date for return, and return address. In such a message, repeat at least the topic, title, brief instructions, date of return, and return address on the questionnaire form itself.
7. Include filter and classification questions—questions that screen and identify the respondents according to the analytical factors of the research.
8. Include validating questions—questions that ask for the same information in different ways in order to check whether the respondent is answering truthfully.
9. Arrange the questions in logical order.
   a. Use a logical method of development.
   b. Gain and retain attention and interest within the questionnaire itself.
   c. Place the most important questions where the respondents will most likely answer them. Place them as early as possible, but only after proper order of development to that point.
   d. Arrange questions to take account of the impact one question may have on the next one.
   e. Include filter questions early. For example, for a plan to analyze the responses on a questionnaire only if the respondent owns two or more television sets, include early in the questionnaire a filter question about the number of sets owned.
   f. Include classification questions early. For example, to learn the person's sex, age, and income as the basis for analysis, put those questions early so that you will be sure to get the required answers.
   g. Separate validating questions.

   h. Place difficult questions somewhere in the middle—to avoid too early an encounter and also to avoid the fatigue that may set in near the end.
   i. Put similar types of questions together.
   j. Make smooth transitions from part to part and question to question.
10. Attend to the nonverbal aspects of the design—particularly for questionnaires completed directly by the respondent.
    a. Leave plenty of space for response.
    b. Do not crowd the material on the page.
    c. Use appropriate styles of types and printing.
    d. Attend to grammar, spelling, punctuation, and all other such factors.
    e. Use colors, format, and other features to attract the respondent.
11. Match the language level of the questionnaire to the abilities of the respondents.
12. Make the questions as easy to answer as possible for the information needed.
13. Keep the questionnaire reasonably short, even to the extent of redefining the research.
14. Design the questionnaire for ease of tabulation and organization of the information to be collected.
15. Use parallel construction throughout.
16. Pretest and adjust the questionnaire as many times as necessary to perfect the instrument.

Types of Questions

Basic types of questions include (1) the open and (2) the closed. Both require careful development.

Open questions As the name indicates, the *open* question supplies no choice of answers. The respondent must supply all of the words that make the response to the question. Examples of open questions include:

What are your views about nuclear energy?

Describe the events of the accident.

The positive qualities of the open question include:

- Does not lead the respondent into a fixed set of responses
- Allows the respondent to express true feelings freely
- Causes the respondent to think deeply about the topic
- Gives the respondent a sense of participation and importance
- Often provides a good vehicle as an opening question with which to gain interest—particularly in interviews

The negative qualities of the open question include:

- May not yield the kind of information that lends itself to organization for the desired analysis and interpretation

- May elicit no response because it requires too much thinking and time
- Often lacks clarity and specificity
- Interviewer's biases may enter into the transaction as it progresses

On balance, avoid open questions unless they provide the only method to obtain the unstructured kind of information you need. The negative qualities far outweigh the positive ones.

Closed questions *Closed* questions offer responses from which the respondent chooses. The classes of closed questions include the dichotomous question and the multiple-choice question. The *dichotomous* question offers only two possible responses. Certain kinds of questions lend themselves to this form. However, most questions of any consequence have more than two possible answers. These examples illustrate proper dichotomous questions:

1. Did you vote in the presidential election of 198X?
   - ☐ Yes
   - ☐ No
2. Age:
   - ☐ 29 years or less
   - ☐ 30 years or more

The *multiple-choice* question simply extends the number of possible responses from two to a larger number. The number should represent enough responses to encompass the full range of possible responses in mutually exclusive form. The multiple-choice question often must include a final category that allows the respondent to add a response or responses that do not appear in the preset list. Such a category often uses the words *other (please specify).* For such a question, include sufficient space for the respondent or the interviewer to write the response.

Multiple-choice questions may include discrete responses or responses that fall at discrete points along a continuous scale. The continuous rating system generally uses a semantic-differential or Likert scale. First, consider two questions written in a traditional multiple-choice style with discrete (discontinuous) options for responses. (The questions would appear in two different questionnaires.)

Approximate income in 198X:
- ☐ Under $10,000
- ☐ $10,000 but under $20,000
- ☐ 20,000 but under 30,000
- ☐ 30,000 but under 40,000
- ☐ 40,000 but under 50,000
- ☐ 50,000 but under 60,000
- ☐ 60,000 and over

Did you find your meal:

☐	☐	☐	☐	☐
Superior	Excellent	Good	Fair	Poor

Comments:

Observe that the second question combines an open question with a basic closed question. Such combinations often include the positive features of both types.

Next, consider two examples from a rating-scale design for the closed form of question. Again, the two questions would not necessarily appear in the same questionnaire.

How would you rate your immediate supervisor's understanding of the human needs of those whom s/he supervises?

Has no understanding				Understands moderately well				Understands completely
1	2	3	4	5	6	7	8	9

Compared to other programs in the past, how would you rate this one?

Very poor					Same					Superior
-5	-4	-3	-2	-1	0	1	2	3	4	5

A slight variation on the basic construction of the multiple-choice questionnaire allows the respondent to select more than one answer in the checklist. This example illustrates:

Which of these reasons explains why you have not made a credit-card purchase at Freedom's Department Store in the past year? Check as many as you want, and explain if you wish.

____ **a.** Still shop at Freedom's, but pay cash
____ **b.** Have moved from the area
____ **c.** Prefer to shop elsewhere now
____ **d.** Had a problem with a clerk
____ **e.** Had a problem with delivery service
____ **f.** Road construction a deterrent
____ **g.** Other (please specify)

The responses in the previous examples include sentence fragments. However, responses may also take the form of complete sentences.

The positive qualities of the closed question include:

- Except for the open-end components such as *other (please specify),* the responses provide ease of tabulation, organization, and analysis.
- It provides ease of answering.
- If well written, it has more clarity and specificity than an open question about the same topic.
- The rate of response probably will exceed that for the open question.

The negative qualities of the closed question include:

- It sometimes does not include all possible responses.

- It does not provide much opportunity for freedom of expression.
- It may squelch the thinking process by forcing the respondent to choose from among preset responses. Even with the inclusion of the open-end choice, the respondent often chooses one of the listed ones simply to avoid having to think and write.
- The possible range of responses for certain topics becomes so wide that a few responses cannot contain them.

Qualities of Good Questions

Several of the preceding discussions deal with the qualities of good questions. However, these devices for developing good questions summarize and extend them:

- Make the questions clear and understandable; include only words with accepted meanings.
- Use concrete words.
- Write the questions in the most concise language possible.
- Make the questions precise and accurate.
- Draw the questions specifically to the topic.
- Pose the question in the most positive and ethical terms possible.
- Make the questions follow a natural chronology.
- Assure distinctness among responses on closed forms.
- Include all possible responses on closed forms.
- Use indirect questions for embarrassing or emotional topics.
- Handle personal questions by establishing responses showing ranges for such information as income and age.
- When asking respondents to choose and rank responses in order of importance, do not expect them to handle more than three or four.
- When asking for opinions about the status of something, provide a basis for comparison.
- Create questions that do not cause the respondent to have to think or recall too much. For example, to learn about a brand preference of a consumer, ask only about the most recent purchase—not about all purchases within the last year.
- To learn something that might embarrass a respondent, ask what the respondent believes others think about the subject.
- Relate the questions to actual examples when possible; for example, in personal interviews, let the respondent see, hear, or hold something during the questions.
- In personal interviews use certain kinds of open questions to gain psychological and motivational information from people. Examples of such questions include completion of sentences or stories, associations among words, and reactions to pictures, ink blots, abstract drawings, and objects.
- Construct all responses to a question in parallel form—both structurally and psychologically.
- Ask questions that do not threaten feelings of socially acceptable

behavior. For example, provide a buffer statement such as "Many people have looked at pornographic magazines at one time or another out of curiosity about what they contain" before asking, "Have you ever looked at a pornographic magazine?"

- Include among multiple-choice responses *don't know* and *no opinion* when appropriate.
- Retain a courteous and nonprobing tone.

Types of Construction to Avoid

View the development of questions briefly from the other side of the coin—the kinds of questions not to write. Consider these suggestions for avoiding improper construction:

Leading questions Do not write *leading* questions—questions that lead the respondent into a biased answer. Think of the leading nature of these questions:

> You do like comfort in a car, don't you?
>
> Do you prefer an in-ground swimming pool?
>
> Don't you think your supervisor is usually fair?

Loaded questions As an extension of the leading question, the *loaded* question includes words that would make anyone answering the "wrong" way feel foolish. Such questions introduce a bias that indicates a desire to support a predetermined position. Political questionnaires often include such questions. These questions illustrate loading:

> Do you believe that monopolistic, profit-hungry big business should dictate what you may buy in the marketplace?
>
> Do you believe that gang-ridden unions should continue to seize control of the free enterprise system?
>
> Could you ever be un-American enough to speak in support of some Communist organization?

Biased questions and responses Both the misleading and loaded questions introduce obvious bias and emotion into the transaction. However, the *biases* may also appear as leading or loaded words within the responses to multiple-choice questions. This example illustrates:

> Now that you have read the new statement of policy, what do you think? (You may mark more than one.)
>
> ____ I accept it because it controls those who misuse privileges.
> ____ I accept it because I do my job and thus have nothing to fear from it.
> ____ I accept it because I trust my superiors to do what is best for the employees.
> ____ I accept it because I know of no better place to work than here.
> ____ I don't accept it because it takes away some of the soft touches that I have had in the past.

The example also illustrates the flaw introduced by not including a response of *other* and by using declarative sentences as multiple-choice responses.

Multiple-topic questions Do not ask *multiple-topic* questions. Keep each question on one topic only. For instance, what would answers to these questions mean?

Do you support gun-control legislation, anti-inflation measures, and national health insurance?

☐ Yes ☐ No

Do you like to watch comedy, western, and mystery shows on television?

☐ Yes ☐ No

The multiple-topic question introduces an ambiguity that destroys the value of the responses. Unless the respondent moves back to the multiple elements and writes a "Yes" or a "No" above each one, the data prove useless.

Ambiguous questions Avoid all *ambiguous* questions. Ambiguity defeats clarity and specificity. If receivers misunderstand, their answers cannot provide useful information. Even if respondents do not understand a question, they probably will answer anyway, if for no other reason than to leave the *impression* of understanding. Observe the ambiguity in these questions:

Would you be interested in some expensive videotaping equipment?

☐ Yes ☐ No

What type of communication do you like best?

In analyzing the first question, did you wonder whether the word *interest* means *see, know about the technical aspects of,* or *own or lease*? If you decided that the question referred to ownership, did you then wonder whether "interested in some expensive videotaping equipment" relates to buying it or to receiving it as a prize or a gift? In the same vein, what does the word *expensive* mean?

For the second question—an open question—think of just a few of the wildly different kinds of answers that might result:

Good	Telegram
Concrete	Formal
Interpersonal	Television
Concise	Nonverbal

Hop-and-skip questions Keep to a minimum the kind of question that causes the reader to *hop and skip* around to answer. Sometimes a filter question will make such demands, but at least use no more than one such question in any questionnaire. When using a question that causes the reader to hop forward, write clearly and try not to make the jump too great. Try to arrange sets of responses side by side to avoid skipping. This example shows such an arrangement:

5. If your answer to question No. 4 is "Yes," please answer question Nos. 6–10. If your answer to question No. 4 is "No," please answer question Nos. 11–15. After completing either Nos. 6–10 or Nos. 11–15, please complete Nos. 16–22.

6. How many repairs did you . . . ?
   a.
   b.
   c.

11. What is your view of the . . . ?
    a.
    b.
    c.

Unspecified-meanings questions Avoid questions that involve qualitative words with *unspecified meanings*. Consider the various meanings for the qualifiers in this sentence:

> Do you often spend more money than you should for goods or services you do not really need? ____Yes ____No

How often is "often"? How much money is "more money than you should spend"? What goods and services qualify as "goods and services you do not really need"?

Make such questions quantitative when possible. When circumstances require the qualitative construct, at least convert it into a question of opinion based frankly upon the respondent's own definitions of terms. For example, the preceding question could become:

> Have you ever felt that you spent money for goods or services unnecessary to satisfy what you consider to be your basic needs?

Types of Surveys

This section covers three broad classes of surveys: (1) personal interviews, (2) telephone interviews, and (3) mail questionnaires.

Personal Interview

The personal interview occurs at the interpersonal level. The richness of that level and other strengths make it the strongest of the three types.

Strengths The personal interview has these strengths:

- Because it functions at the interpersonal level, the potential for nonverbal messages, immediate feedback, evaluation, and adjustment exceeds that for either the telephone interview or the mail questionnaire.
- The proportion of response exceeds that for mail questionnaires. Therefore, the chances for a truly representative sample also improve.
- Through the interaction made possible by the face-to-face situation, interviewers can explain instructions and answer questions. Thus, they may generate more complete and accurate answers than the mail questionnaire may.

- The interviewer can show products, charts, and other materials and objects that may help the respondent understand the message.
- The potential for going into detail on an issue exceeds that for the other two types.

Weaknesses The personal interview also has some weaknesses.

- It costs more than the telephone interview or mail questionnaire. However, a distribution of the costs over pieces of information obtained reduces costs substantially.
- Wide geographic distribution of the people in the sample often makes the personal-interview survey difficult to accomplish.
- Research often requires a "snapshot" instead of a "moving picture" of the observed variable. Such "snapshots" become difficult through personal interviews.
- Many people view interviews as invasions of their privacy.
- Many high office-holders simply do not grant personal interviews.
- The potential for the interviewer to act consciously or unconsciously to bias the results exceeds that for the other types.
- Locating, training, and retaining enough good interviewers may prove difficult.
- Some respondents will supply personal information in an anonymous mail questionnaire that they will not supply in a personal interview.
- The time allotment for a personal interview often does not allow the interviewer to gain the kind of information that requires the respondent to search some records or do some deep thinking.
- The interviewer often must make several calls before finding the selected person at home.

Telephone Interview

The telephone interview falls second to the personal interview in strength as a survey data-collection method. Though telephoning operates at the mediated level, it still retains some of the qualities of the interpersonal level.

Strengths The telephone interview has these strengths:

- Because of oral interaction, the potential for nonverbal messages, immediate feedback, evaluation, and adjustment exceeds that for the mail questionnaire.
- The proportion of response exceeds that for the mail questionnaires; therefore, the chances for a representative sample also improve.
- Through the interaction made possible by the speaking-and-listening situation, the interviewer may explain instructions and answer questions, thus possibly gaining more complete and accurate answers than from the mail questionnaire.
- The potential for going into detail on an issue exceeds that for the mail questionnaire.

- The telephone directory provides a good basis for applying the systematic sampling technique.
- The contacts may cover even a wide geographic region in a much shorter time than that required for either the personal interviewer or the mail questionnaire.
- Because of the speed of telephone interviews, virtual "snapshots" in time become possible.
- Costs fall below those for personal interviewing, and approach the low costs of the mail questionnaire.
- Some people view a telephone inquiry as less an invasion of privacy than a personal interview.
- Some high office-holders may grant a telephone interview when they will not grant a personal one.
- Some respondents may supply personal information in a telephone interview that they will not supply in a personal interview.
- If one person selected by a probability process does not answer or does not wish to cooperate, the interviewer may easily and immediately choose a replacement by probability methods.

Weaknesses Compared to the other types of survey, the telephone inquiry also has some weaknesses:

- The listed telephone subscribers in a directory on the date of its publication do not properly represent the actual population.
- Compared to the personal interview, the telephone interview loses many of the advantages associated with the interpersonal level.
- The interviewer cannot supply as many nonverbal cues as possible with the personal interview.
- The telephone interview cannot exceed about seven minutes; therefore, it may not have as much potential for a detailed discussion as the personal interview.
- The telephone interview may cost more than the mail questionnaire.
- Many people view the telephone interview as a more serious invasion of privacy than a mail questionnaire.
- Many high office-holders do not grant telephone interviews.
- The potential for the interviewer to act consciously or unconsciously to bias the results exceeds that for the mail questionnaire.
- Locating, training, and retaining capable interviewers may prove difficult (but not as difficult as for the personal interview).
- Some respondents will supply personal information in an anonymous mail questionnaire that they will not supply in a telephone interview.
- The time allotment for a telephone interview does not allow the interviewer to gain the kind of information that requires the respondent to search some records or do some deep thinking.
- The oral-only construct of the telephone interview allows for only simple questions.
- Busy signals and "no-answers" often plague the interviewer.
- Respondents generally feel freer to cut short a telephone interview than a personal one.

Mail Questionnaire

The mail questionnaire has the fewest strengths and the greatest number of weaknesses. It may fit a universe of homogeneous, interested people. However, its weaknesses far outweigh its strengths.

Strengths The mail questionnaire has these strengths:

- Depending upon the number of follow-ups and the difficulties associated with sampling and with instrument construction, the mail questionnaire usually runs lower in cost than any other survey method.
- For a wide geographic distribution of the people in the sample, the mail questionnaire becomes more efficient than the personal interview.
- Many people do not view the mail questionnaire as great an invasion of privacy as personal and telephone interviews.
- Because of the anonymity provided by the mail questionnaire, many people will answer it when they would not respond to an oral interview.
- Some high office-holders will respond to a mail questionnaire when they will not give interviews.
- The potential for the bias introduced by on-the-spot interviewers does not exist in the mail questionnaire.
- Mail-questionnaire surveys do not require the numbers of qualified and trained people that the interview surveys do.
- The mail questionnaire does not have the time restrictions that personal and telephone interviews do; therefore, the respondent has time to search some records or do some deep thinking.
- The mail questionnaire may allow more depth and detail on an issue than a telephone inquiry—but only if the writer of the questionnaire can develop a written probe even approximating that possible through the oral exchange.
- Compared to the telephone interview, the mail questionnaire offers more opportunity to ask complicated questions.

Weaknesses The mail questionnaire has these weaknesses:

- The approach severely limits the opportunities for nonverbal messages, feedback, evaluation, and adjustment.
- The potential for nonresponse bias exceeds that of the other types; proportion of returns often falls as low as 20 percent.
- For a low response rate and anonymous responses, follow-ups and replacements prove difficult.
- Validation of a low-response sample as representative of the universe proves extremely difficult.
- The mail questionnaire cannot satisfy the demands of the kinds of research that require "snapshots" of the factors under analysis.
- Without the advantages of the oral transaction, the interviewer has no opportunity to explain the instructions or answer any questions; accuracy and completeness may suffer.

- Identification of a probability sample from all people in a universe of mailing addresses can prove quite difficult.
- The mail survey takes a significant amount of time.
- In general, to assure good return, questionnaires cannot require more than about twelve minutes to complete. Therefore, the questionnaire usually must ask for only limited information.
- Generally the nature of the mail questionnaire prohibits any in-depth probes of a subject.
- Many people simply will not bother with complex questionnaires.

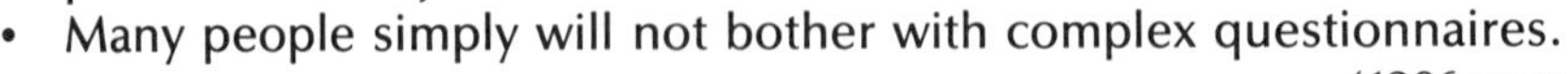

(1306 words)

Take and score Self-Test 23 over the types of surveys on page 314.

The next chapter (Chapter 12) continues the coverage of reports and of writing. It describes the formats and types of reports and the principles for writing them.

SUMMARY

Reports contribute significantly to business communication. This chapter covers the research and data-collecting processes necessary for gaining the information for reports.

Research involves the search for solutions to problems. Most business research falls into the category of applied research, rather than basic research. Because of the interwoven nature of research and communication, the good writer of reports understands and applies the steps of the research process.

The research process uses science, art, technique, and decision-making applied to four stages. **Stage A** includes the first five steps: (1) recognize and define problem, (2) review literature, (3) state hypothesis(es), (4) design investigation, and (5) write the proposal. **Stage B** includes three steps: (6) collect data, (7) organize data, and (8) analyze data. **Stage C** covers steps 9–12: (9) interpret results of analysis, (10) draw conclusions, (11) develop recommendations, and (12) write and disseminate final report. **Stage D** includes one step: (13) conduct follow-up.

One common classification of types of research includes the historical (searching for the meaning of history), survey (using observation to describe or analyze contemporary data), and experimental (controlling the research to observe the effect of identified variables on the outcome). Two special applications of research methods apply well to this review of research and business communication: motivational research and the communication audit.

The collection of information involves primary (firsthand) or secondary (secondhand) data. Try to find data from secondary sources before collecting primary data; secondary data cost less to collect than primary data.

To gather data from secondary sources, you must understand the types of sources: standard publications, reference aids, systems for search and retrieval (such as *DATRIX* and *ERIC*), and unpublished sources. Also use the library efficiently and use bibliographic and note cards for recording information.

When secondary sources do not yield the desired data, use primary procedures. To do so, understand sampling procedures, methods for collecting data orally, forms for recording direct observations, and questionnaires. When possible, select samples by using a probability method. Consult books on sampling, statistics, and research to learn proper procedures.

To collect primary data through oral channels, plan ahead of time, take appropriate notes (or complete a carefully designed interview guide [questionnaire]), ask perception-checking questions when possible, and listen carefully. Use a tape recorder and collect supplemental written information if possible. Apply the suggestions for interviewing found in Chapters 14 and 16.

To collect primary data through direct observation, use a form for recording the results. Such a form includes or provides such elements as a title, instructions, spaces for recording the data, space to identify the observer, and a logical arrangement of the items.

Principles for construction of questionnaires fall into four broad categories: (1) general design, (2) types of questions, (3) qualities of good questions, and (4) types of construction to avoid. Suggestions for general design deal with logic, appearance, and general content. They stress the importance of motivating the respondent to complete a questionnaire. Two basic types of questions define the survey instrument: the open and the closed. The open question supplies no answers from which the respondent may choose. The closed question supplies answers. The closed question appears in dichotomous, multiple-choice, or rating-scale form. The open question allows freer expression. The closed question allows for easier collation and control.

Good questions require qualities that range from simple courtesy to avoiding embarrassment of the respondent. Avoid leading questions, loaded questions, biased questions and responses, multiple-topic questions, ambiguous questions, hop-and-skip questions, and unspecified-meanings questions.

The three major survey methods involve: (1) personal interviews, (2) telephone interviews, and (3) mail questionnaires. All three involve the careful development of a plan, a set of instructions, and a questionnaire designed to obtain the desired information. Each has its strengths and weaknesses. If all other considerations remain equal, however, choose the personal interview.

CROSSLAND UNIVERSITY

As director of external relations at Crossland University in Crossland, Kentucky, Lee Chen wants to have good relations between the merchants in Crossland and the university. Until about two years ago, Crossland's business owners had contributed large sums of money to the university every year. Moreover, these merchants had donated their time for such activities as the Renaissance Faire and some of their products for auctions and other fundraising events. For reasons about which Chen can only speculate, however, the merchants' good will has all but disappeared. Donations of time, money, and goods rarely come from Crossland merchants now; instead, the university must rely on out-of-town and out-of-state contributions, contributions which are typically much harder to get.

Chen also worries about the loss of the Crossland merchants' support because she feels that good town/gown relations are a must at any university. Without good feelings between university and town, the students lose a valuable opportunity to experience life as citizens of the community beyond the university's boundaries. Perhaps the most serious problem resulting from poor relations, however, is the paucity of job opportunities for students.

Because Chen knows she must determine why the deterioration in town/university relations took place before she can attempt to make changes, she decides to go to the very people who have ceased to support the university. Although she knows personal interviews would be far superior to questionnaires, she has an extremely small and overworked

EXERCISES

1. Meet with your group. As a group, try to think of at least five business situations in which you would write a report. Define your purposes for writing the reports, the readers' purposes for reading the reports, the readers, and the environment of the readers. Then discuss the problems inherent in each situation. Have one of your group members present one of the situations and its associated problems to the class.
2. You have been asked by your employer to observe the activities at each of the pizza restaurants in your town. Your employer wants to know:
   - a. The size of each restaurant
   - b. The restaurant's parking arrangements
   - c. The number of tables in the restaurant
   - d. The maximum number of people the restaurant can hold
   - e. The price and size of both the smallest and largest plain cheese pizzas
   - f. The price and size of both the smallest and largest sausage pizzas

staff; therefore, she must use a questionnaire to get the information she needs from the hundreds of merchants in Crossland.

To construct a good questionnaire, Chen knows she should conduct a few preliminary interviews to determine what the problems might be. Then she can design a questionnaire that will stand a reasonable chance of getting at the feelings and frustrations. So she conducts four interviews with seemingly disenchanted merchants and identifies these reasons for their withdrawal of support:

1. Shoplifting has increased markedly, and the merchants think university students are the culprits.
2. The merchants perceive the students as lazy and arrogant. For example, one merchant said he believes that most Crossland University students "haven't put in a good day's work in their entire lives" and "think they are so superior just because they are precious little sorority girls and fraternity boys."
3. The merchants believe the university's administrators hold anti-business views.
4. And the merchants think the university professors are anti-sports. As one businesswoman stated, athletics are "as American as blueberry turnovers." Another shop owner said that sporting events "bring wealthy out-of-town visitors to Crossland most every day."

Now that Chen has some hints about what irks the disaffected merchants, she can design the questionnarie so that residents can readily identify problems and offer possible solutions.

(This case is fictional.)

g. The restaurant's hours
h. The number of customers in the restaurant on the hour every hour on a Friday
i. Whether the restaurant also serves submarine sandwiches

Prepare a form for recording these observations. Include the more basic information (e.g., name of restaurant) as well.

3. You want to interview the 28 third-year computer-science students at a small university in your city, Mapleton, Arkansas. You want them to give you information regarding their career plans. You want to know:
   a. The field into which they plan to go
   b. The beginning salary they expect
   c. Whether they will seek work in Mapleton, outside of Mapleton but in Arkansas, or out of state
   d. Whether they plan to pursue a graduate degree, and if so, in what field
   e. The work title they would like to have in five years, in ten years, and in fifteen years
   f. The salary they would like to have in five years, in ten years, and in fifteen years

Design a survey instrument for your use during each interview. You can use either open or closed questions, whichever you feel would be more appropriate. Explain why you chose the one type of question over the other.

4. These are poorly constructed survey questions. Correct them.
   a. Did you attend former President Ford's lecture yesterday?
      ☐ Yes ☐ I am a Democrat
      ☐ No ☐ Maybe
   b. What is your age?
      ☐ Young ☐ Old
      ☐ Middle ☐ Quite ancient
   c. The employee completes her or his work on time
      ☐ Always ☐ Never
   d. List everything that you like about politics. Be specific.
   e. Do you plan to stop taking advantage of the privileges your company gives you?
   f. How many bags of Pop-Pop Popcorn did you purchase in the last ten years?
   g. Do you advocate the removal of the beautiful trees that God gave us?
   h. Why don't you work hard?
   i. As a basketball player, how do you handle your loss of femininity?
   j. Do you support flexible office hours, better pay, employee lounges, and more vacation days?
      ☐ Yes ☐ No
   k. Would you like better conditions here at Big Corporation?
      ☐ Yes ☐ No
5. [*Your professor will time this exercise.*] You are the manager of the graphics department of a large corporation. You have been asked to keep a record of the attendance of each of your 15 workers for submission to your superior every month. Design an attendance report form. Include spaces for attendance, sick leave, and vacation leave for each worker.
6. Meet with your group. Conduct a complete brainstorming session on any one or several of these topics. Write the findings, appoint a spokesperson, and report the findings to the class.
   a. The advantages and disadvantages of the personal and impersonal writing styles.
   b. The definition and examples of plagiarism.
   c. The relative advantages and disadvantages of formality and informality in reporting style.
7. Meet with your group. Brainstorm to determine the content and design of a mail questionnaire to be sent to selected businesspeople within the college community. The purpose of the questionnaire is to determine the views of businesspeople about the relative importance of business communication and other business courses or specialities to the smooth functioning of business. Before the brainstorming session, you may want to read a section on the topic in Chapter 14 and/or consult some of the sources listed there. After the initial brainstorming session, assign group members to the tasks of drafting (1) a cover letter, (2) the heading and introduction on the questionnaire, and (3) the questions. Meet with the group again to compile the drafts and then develop the second draft. Present the drafts from the groups to the professor and/or class. From them, develop the final questionnaire. Retain it for use with an exercise in Chapter 12.
8. As a marketing research analyst, choose a commonly used household product (e.g., paper towels, detergent, bath soap, shampoo). Develop a telephone inter-

view guide to determine such things as the preferred brand, the last brand purchased, and common and special uses for the product. Also plan to determine such information as the monthly quantity purchased, the number in the family, who in the family makes the purchases, etc. Also develop the introductory statements for the interview. Establish and test the introduction and the guide so that the entire interview takes no more than three minutes. Conduct the interview by telephone with each member of your group or with other acquaintances. Upon completion of the simulation, ask for their evaluation. Revise the guide to reflect the evaluation.

9. Prepare an interview guide to be used to determine the facts and attitudes of people in small business about the numbers and types of reports required by government agencies.
10. Meet with your group. Discuss the steps of the research process. Decide which of the steps might be omitted and still leave the basic research process intact. Select a spokesperson to summarize the discussion to the class.
11. For each of these problems, write at least one hypothesis testable by quantitative methods:
    - **a.** A manager claims that Department F is not operating as efficiently as Department G.
    - **b.** Management is concerned about the level of lost time this year compared with last year.
    - **c.** Customer returns of purchased goods seem to be running unusually high.
    - **d.** Management needs to choose a supplier of production parts from three suppliers who have submitted identical low bids.
    - **e.** A manager thinks that accidents are inversely related to years of experience.
12. For each of these situations, write at least one limitation or assumption:
    - **a.** The researcher is using the telephone directory as the universe for research into levels of income.
    - **b.** To find the public's opinion about a product, the researcher sets up a stand in a shopping mall and asks passers-by to test the product and complete a questionnaire.
    - **c.** To develop an equation for predicting monthly sales for the next two years, the researcher arbitrarily chooses the past two years as a pattern.
    - **d.** A researcher receives a 32 percent return from a mail survey.
    - **e.** One of five field interviewers has a flamboyant style; the others do not.
13. Write a research definition for each of these terms:
    - **a.** Small business
    - **b.** Large manufacturer
    - **c.** Student
    - **d.** Smoker
    - **e.** Manager
    - **f.** Professional worker
14. Use your dictionary and thesaurus to create meanings for these words. Use the words when you think, write, or speak so that you feel comfortable using them.
    - **a.** Charisma
    - **b.** Compendium
    - **c.** Consummation
    - **d.** Dichotomous
    - **e.** Disarm
    - **f.** Disparage
    - **g.** Encompass
    - **h.** Idiom
    - **i.** Inextricabe
    - **j.** Negate
    - **k.** Paraphrase
    - **l.** Probability
    - **m.** Statistics
    - **n.** Valid
    - **o.** Voluminous
    - **p.** Voracious
15. Take and score Self-Test 24 over Chapter 11.

SELF-TEST 23
Excerpt about Types of Surveys

A. Recall (33 points each). For each multiple-choice question, select the most accurate answer.

1. Which of these statements regarding the personal interview is *not* true?
   - **a.** The proportion of response is significantly higher than for mail questionnaires; therefore, the chances for a representative sample also are greater.
   - **b.** Because it functions at the interpersonal level, the potential for nonverbal messages, immediate feedback, evaluation, and adjustment is higher than for either the telephone interview or the mail questionnaire.
   - **c.** Because the interviewer is face to face with the interviewee, the potential for the interviewer to act consciously or unconsciously to bias the results is minimized.
   - **d.** The potential for going into depth and detail on an issue is higher than for either the telephone interview or the mail questionnaire.
   - **e.** The interviewer may show products, charts, and other materials and objects that may help the respondent understand the message.
2. Which of these statements regarding the telephone interview is *not* true?
   - **a.** It is generally better than the mail questionnaire.
   - **b.** The interviewer may explain instructions and answer questions as the interview progresses.
   - **c.** The contacts may be made over a wide geographic region in a much shorter time than that required for either the personal interview or the mail questionnaire.
   - **d.** The costs are significantly lower than those for the personal interview.
   - **e.** The samples taken from the telephone directory are always representative of the population as a whole.

B. Inference (34 points). Indicate whether this statement is true or false.

1. Because the mail questionnaire has so many weaknesses, one would do well not to use it at all.

SOLUTION

A. Recall (33 points each)

1. c **2.** e

B. Inference (34 points)

1. False

SELF-TEST 24
Chapter 11

A. Recall (20 points each). For each multiple-choice question, select the most accurate answer.

1. When you design a survey instrument, do *not*:
   - **a.** Use attention-getting, interest-holding, and persuasive devices in the introductory matter
   - **b.** Include validating questions—questions that ask for the same information in different ways
   - **c.** Arrange the questions in a logical order
   - **d.** Design the instrument for ease of tabulation
   - **e.** Include leading, loaded, biased, ambiguous, or multiple-topic questions
2. Which one of these statements is true?
   - **a.** Research is the same as quantitative analysis.
   - **b.** The purpose of research is to identify problems for a report.
   - **c.** Research methods depend solely on the scientific method.
   - **d.** A hypothesis should be stated in declarative form, not as a question.
   - **e.** Empirical research is inferential research.
3. Which one of these statements is *false?*
   - **a.** Whenever possible, choose a nonprobability sample over a probability one.
   - **b.** Whether conducted in person or by mail or telephone, a survey should involve preplanning and a preprinted form for completion.
   - **c.** The observationnaire is a good instrument upon which to record direct observations.
   - **d.** Filter and classification questions usually appear early in a survey document.
   - **e.** The responses to a multiple-choice question should exhaust the possible answers.

B. Inference (20 points). Indicate whether each statement is true or false.

1. The rating-scale design is particularly adaptable to ranges of qualitative responses to a question.
2. Because it is more precise, quantitative research is more important than qualitative research.

SOLUTION

A. Recall (20 points each)

1. e **3.** a
2. d

B. Inference (20 points each)

1. True
2. False

STUDENT'S OBJECTIVES:

1 To learn how to use the three basic formats for reports: form, letter or memorandum, and manuscript

2 To apply the principles of writing to abbreviated reports—reports that cover only a few of the steps of the research process

12

WRITING REPORTS: Formats, Types, and Principles

3 To apply the principles of writing to comprehensive reports

4 To learn to write a proposal

5 To learn to write a final report of a research project

This chapter completes the discussion of reports started in Chapter 11. It includes reviews of formats and types of business reports and the principles for writing them.

FORMATS FOR REPORTS

Reports usually follow one of three basic formats: (1) form, (2) letter or memorandum, and (3) manuscript.

Form Reports

The form creates an important communication channel for reports. Although it often involves relatively mechanical completion, the form still must capture the desired information in usable terms. Chapter 10 includes reminders for developing and completing forms. Figure 12–1 shows an example of a form report.

Letter and Memorandum Reports

A letter report couples a report with the trappings of a letter (Chapter 7). Likewise, a memorandum report includes paragraphs written under the heading of a memorandum (Chapter 10). However, both types also exhibit some of the characteristics of the traditional manuscript. Some of these characteristics include headings and subheadings, graphs and tables, and multiple pages.

Use the letter report for transactions external to the organization and the memorandum format for internal communications. As an example, outside auditors usually write a report to a firm they have audited in the form of a "management letter"—actually a report in the form of a letter. As another example, internal committees or task forces often write their reports to management in the format of a memorandum. Figures 12–2 and 12–4 illustrate memorandum reports. Figure 12–3 illustrates a letter report.

Manuscript Reports

The traditional manuscript report includes narrative paragraphs with titles, headings, subheadings, footnotes or endnotes, tables, and illustrations. Figures 12–5 and 12–6 use the manuscript format. Examine them as you review the remainder of this section.

The report contains three major parts, with subdivisions under each:

1. Front matter
   - a. Cover
   - b. Title page
   - c. Authorization
   - d. Acceptance
   - e. Transmittal
   - f. List of contents
   - g. List of illustrations
   - h. List of tables
   - i. Preface, foreword, or acknowledgments
   - j. Abstract

2. Body
   a. Introduction
   b. Main body (usually consisting of several clearly defined divisions)
   c. Conclusions and/or recommendations
3. Back matter
   a. Endnotes (if used instead of footnotes)
   b. Appendix(es)
   c. Bibliography

Style manuals describe the components and the complete details for using the manuscript format. However, these suggestions provide some basic information:

- Use 8½- by 11-inch, 20-pound, fabric-content bond paper.
- Use lower-case roman numerals for the front matter and arabic numerals for the body and the back matter. For the first page of a major section that begins a new page, either omit the number (but count it) or center it at the bottom of the page. For subsequent pages, place the number at the upper right margin or centered above the top line. Count the title page, but do not number it.
- Leave one-inch margins on all four sides after binding for most pages. However, for the first page of a major section (the title page, the first page of the report, the first page of a new chapter, the contents, the list of illustrations, etc.) leave a two-inch margin at the top.
- Use double spacing and only one side of the paper. However, to conserve paper, you may use single spacing and both sides of the paper. Such conservation becomes particularly important for situations requiring multiple copies.
- Even with double spacing within the body of a report, you may use single spacing for appendixes. Always use single spacing for footnotes.
- Excerpts from the works of others may call for distinct spacing. Generally, if a direct quotation contains three or fewer lines, place it within quotation marks and merge it into the narrative. However, once it occupies four or more lines, indent, block, and single space it. Eliminate the quotation marks from such blocked direct quotations.
- The placement of titles, headings, and subheadings contributes significantly to the readability of the report. As one basic rule, just as for outlines, include at least two headings at each level introduced.

TYPES OF BUSINESS REPORTS

The types of business reports extend logically from the research process described in Chapter 11. This chapter covers two major categories—abbreviated reports and comprehensive reports. *Comprehensive* reports cover most or all of the steps of the research process. *Abbreviated* reports cover only a few of the steps—very often presenting only a simple problem and the collected, organized information. Although many reports fall into the routine (neutral) category, others use persuasion or bring good or bad news.

To write successful reports, then, apply the six communication guidelines (Chapter 2), the principles of effective writing (Chapters 6, 7, 8, 9, and 10), the appropriate formats (Chapters 7, 10, and 12 and Appendix D), the steps of the research process (Chapter 11), and the suggestions for constructing tables and graphs (Chapter 13).

Abbreviated Reports

Abbreviated reports usually do not include extensive analysis, conclusions, and recommendations. They do not show complete application of the scientific method or the related development of a complex problem statement, hypothesis(es), or methods for solution of the problem. Generally, the abbreviated report:

- Constitutes the most common type of report; often falls in the routine class
- Does not qualify for long retention within the files of the firm
- Numbers no more than ten pages
- Takes the format of a memorandum, letter, or form (usually one to five pages in length) or manuscript (usually six to ten pages in length)
- Deletes or abbreviates some of the developmental passages present in comprehensive reports; for example, does not include an abstract, includes a briefer introduction, includes more enumerated or listed items than the comprehensive report
- Reflects either an informal or formal writing style
- Includes either the personal or impersonal writing style
- Does not necessarily adhere to a rigid developmental plan of organization, but customarily uses the basic direct plan
- Contains simple information and sometimes persuasion
- Includes quantitative data
- Takes the periodic form, hourly, daily, weekly, monthly, quarterly, or annually
- Results from assignment by management

Other names given to the abbreviated report include short report, memorandum report, letter report, form report, informal report, and informational report. Abbreviated reports deal with such topics as operations; management; employee relations; and customer, stockholder, government, and public relations.

(231 words)

Take and score Self-Test 25 over abbreviated reports on page 359.

Figure 12–1 shows an example of an operational marketing report. It shows the completion of a preprinted form. Observe the routine nature of the report. It does not require any advanced writing skills. However, it does call for careful collection of data, correctness, conciseness, and clarity. Section 4, in particular, requires some thinking and decision-making. Does the phrase "doing great" (No. 4c) strike you as appropriate for this kind of report?

Figure 12–2 shows a memorandum report about a personnel activity. Notice that the report takes a neutral approach until the last paragraph. However, even at that point, Armor just offers opinions, not persuasive comments. Also notice the direct, concise, complete writing style that even uses an enumerated listing.

Figure 12–3 illustrates a letter report about operations in the word-processing department. It again illustrates the simplicity of the abbreviated report. What problem did Bethel assign to Lopez? Observe how Lopez obviously used some primary data-collection techniques to gather the information. Also observe the directness and conciseness.

The report of *justification* includes a request for approval of such things as a special purchase, a program, a service, a sale, a bid, or a procedural plan. The abbreviated justification report parallels closely the comprehensive proposal covered in Section 1. However, it differs in the complexity of the request and the overt persuasion sometimes included in a justification report. The abbreviated report may use a more direct, informal, personal, and compact style of presentation.

Case Study 2 illustrates the development of a justification report. It shows application of the communication guidelines and the writing principles appropriate to abbreviated reports.

Case Study 2: Justification Report

As the manager of the Program Management Department, you are quite concerned about the crowded office conditions in your department. You have discussed the problem with your superior (Warren Fein) several times. Now you think that the time has arrived for a firm written message calling for a solution.

1. Purposes, participants, and environment
   a. My objectives
      (1) Long term: To provide a private office for each analyst
      (2) Intermediate term: To gain some relief from the crowding even if each analyst cannot have a separate office
      (3) Short term: To get the commitment of Fein to meet the intermediate- and long-term goals
   b. Fein's objectives
      (1) Long term: To maintain physical conditions conducive to the best performance of all employees
      (2) Intermediate term: To balance the needs for physical space among the departments
      (3) Short term: To receive and analyze information to aid in reaching the intermediate- and long-term goals
   c. Receiver: Warren Fein, Manager, Systems Management Office, a direct, but fair, manager

Form S-3
9/80

LITTLETOWN DEPARTMENT STORE

MONTHLY SALES SUMMARY

Date April 4, 1981 Department Large Appliances (62L)

Name Deborah S. Washington Title Department Manager

Report is for the month of March, 1981

1. List the month's sales (net of sales tax) in each of your department's product areas.

PRODUCT AREA	SALES (NET OF TAX)
Washers	$ 6,298.37
Dryers	2,136.46
Refrigerators	3,998.19
Dishwashers	2,590.13
Trash Compacters	390.90
Stoves/Ovens	4,996.28
TOTAL	$20,410.33

2. List the month's returns (net of sales tax) in each of your department's product areas.

PRODUCT AREA	SALES (NET OF TAX)
Washers	$ 0.00
Dryers	199.50
Refrigerators	0.00
Dishwashers	248.90
Trash Compacters	0.00
Stoves/Ovens	910.30
TOTAL	$1,358.70

FIGURE 12–1 Completed form report for marketing operations.

   d. Environment: A busy, sometimes tense atmosphere; analysts extremely dissatisfied with the office setup
2. Channel: Brief written report reinforced by oral report
3. Interference
   a. Fein receives many such requests; this one may not receive the attention it deserves
   b. Report may not match Fein's communication style
4. Research and writing

3. List the circumstances of each of the returns involving $75 or more.
    a. $199.50 Clean II Dryer—Purchasers did not like the noise that it made.
    b. $248.90 Sparkling I Dishwasher—Did not fit in purchaser's kitchen.
    c. $410.30 Microwave Deluxe III Oven—Did not work at all. Sent back to manufacturer.
    d. $500 Littletown Special Range-Oven—Color did not match the color of purchaser's other appliances.

4. List any sales problems that you believe should be brought to the attention of the store manager.
    a. Have not yet received twelve Clean III Dryers ordered on September 6, 1980. Three customers wanted Clean III Dryers in March if had in stock. Customers would not wait for shipment to come in.
    b. Still do not have replacements for two salespersons who left in February, 1981.
    c. Large Appliances is doing great otherwise.

FIGURE 12–1 (Continued).

a. Define problem and background
b. Interview analysts
c. Propose solutions
d. Draw conclusion
e. Draft
   (1) Outline, using indirect pattern
   (2) Write, using persuasion
   (3) Revise

TO: Jason Jones, Training Director
FROM: Susan Armor, Assistant Training Director
SUBJECT: Speaker for October 10 Writing Workshop Luncheon
DATE: September 6, 1980

As you asked, I talked to several business communication professors at Dane University, Alco State University, and Dane County Community College. Here's what I found:

1. Nora Cambert, Ph.D., of Dane University would be willing to speak to the writing workshop participants at the luncheon. She has spoken at a number of writing workshops and seminars. She is the author of the popular Writing Straight: A Handbook for the Business Writer, and she is both personable and bright. Dr. Cambert would charge $250 to speak at the luncheon, and she needs to know our plans by September 15. Her topic would be: "Writing's Not Difficult if You're Drunk." She stated that the speech would be both informative and humorous.

2. Leonard James, M.A., of Alco State University is free to speak at the luncheon. He has made speeches on two other occasions, and he wrote "Words That Please," an article published in Today's Business Writer magazine. Mr. James, who is rather shy, would charge nothing to speak at the luncheon. He needs to know our plans by September 25, and he does not know on what subject he would speak.

3. Gordon Smith, Ed.D., of Alco State University will be out of town the week of the luncheon.

4. Ann Lee, Ed.D., of Dane County Community College would be glad to speak at the luncheon. She has spoken to over thirty groups, and she is the author of numerous communication articles, including "Writing Wizardry in the Business Office" for the Journal of Technical Communication. Dr. Lee, who was both kind and lucid, would charge $100 to speak at the luncheon. October 1 is the last day that she can accept our offer to speak. "Walking through Writing" would be the title of her speech, and she said that it would be an educational speech.

FIGURE 12–2 Memorandum report in a personnel department.

Jason Jones 2 September 6, 1980

5. Morris Davis, Ed.D., of Dane County Community College would like to speak at the luncheon. He has spoken to a number of local civic and business organizations, and he is the author of two basic business communication textbooks. Dr. Davis was friendly and interesting. He would charge $100 to speak at the luncheon, and he must know our plans by September 28. He does not yet know on what subject he would speak, though he indicated that he tries to make his talks both entertaining and educational.

My impression is that Dr. Cambert would make the most engaging speech. But her $250 fee would put something of a strain on our budget. My second choice is Dr. Davis. His $100 fee would not empty our training bank.

FIGURE 12–2 (Continued).

OFFICE MACHINES UNLIMITED

1818 Indention Boulevard 777 777-7777
Premium, KA 77777

April 8, 198X

Ms. Laura Bethel, Supervisor
Word Processing Center
Acketew Arial Insurance Co.
Premium, KA 77777

Dear Ms. Bethel:

As you requested, I asked each of the 25 typists in the typing pool these questions:

1. What features do you like about the Barrier III Typespeeder?
2. What features do you not like about the Barrier III Typespeeder?
3. If you had to choose between the Barrier III Typespeeder and the Fox-Malcolm Typefaster, which typewriter would you choose?

Each of the 25 typists responded to all three questions. Here are the results of the survey by question number.

1. These are the features the typists liked about the Barrier III Typespeeder:

FEATURE	NUMBER WHO MENTIONED
Rarely breaks down	22
Corrects easily	20
Ribbons easy to change	18
Light enough to move easily	12
Extra keys easy to reach	3
Relatively quiet	1

FIGURE 12–3 Letter report on informal survey for a word processing department.

(4) Transmit
   (a) Use format of memorandum report, modified with elements of manuscript form
   (b) Typewrite, proofread, and deliver

5. Plan for feedback
   a. Impress upon Fein the necessity for positive and quick response
   b. Report orally within one week to stimulate feedback
   c. Use response to develop next stage of persuasion

Ms. Laura Bethel 2 April 8, 198X

2. These are the features the typists did not like about the Barrier III Typespeeder:

FEATURE	NUMBER WHO MENTIONED
Too noisy	16
Paper slips out of place	15
Breaks down too often	3
Correction tape sticks to paper	1

3. These are the typewriter choices that the typists made:

TYPEWRITER	NUMBER WHO CHOSE
Barrier III Typespeeder	19
Fox-Malcolm Typefaster	6

I hope that this information will be of some help. Let me know if you have any questions.

Sincerely,

Arnold Lopez

Arnold Lopez
Manager

jj

FIGURE 12–3 (Continued).

6. Evaluate
   a. My objectives
   b. Fein's objectives

Figure 12–4 contains the justification report in the form of a memorandum. Examine it in light of the development outlined in Case Study 2. Observe the use of three manuscript headings even within the memorandum format. Also observe the conciseness and straightforwardness of the approach. Put yourself in Fein's place and decide how you would react.

TO: Warren Fein, Manager, Systems Management Office

FROM: Y. R. Self, Manager, Program Management Department

SUBJECT: Crowding Problem in Program Management Department

DATE: August 15, 1983

Problem

As you know, the Program Management Department has grown from ten analysts in August, 1979, to thirty analysts in August, 1981. Last year, each of the ten analysts had a private office. Now each analyst must share her or his office with two other analysts, and three analysts are even forced to share their desks.

The offices are extremely crowded, deafeningly noisy, and swelteringly hot. Of the twenty analysts with whom I spoke about this situation, eighteen stated that they would consider looking for other jobs if the crowding problem is not solved before the end of this calendar year.

Alternative Solutions

Three solutions seem practicable by March 31, 1984:

1. If all of the walls were removed in the Program Management Department, the 2,200 square feet of open floor could accommodate thirty analysts' desks and ten secretaries' desks in a sort of "bullpen" setting. The noise level would not be reduced, but the crowding and heat problems would be ameliorated. Though the analysts feel that this is the least appealing solution, they do label it a giant step in the right direction.

FIGURE 12–4 Memorandum report involving a persuasive justification.

Comprehensive Reports

Comprehensive reports result from activities involving all or most of the steps of the research method covered in Chapter 11. Other names given to this type of report include long report, analytical report, formal report, research report, full report, and complete report. Generally, the comprehensive report:

- Appears less often than the abbreviated report; does not fit the routine category

Warren Fein 2 August 15, 1983

2. If the neighboring Engineering Department were moved to another location, its ten offices could be used by the Program Management Department. This alternative would allow ten analysts to have private offices. The remaining ten offices would become two-person offices. The noise level would be reduced significantly, and the crowding and heat problems would be much improved. The analysts consider this a better solution than the "bullpen" alternative.

3. By far the best alternative is to move the Program Mangement Department to the soon-to-be-completed suite of offices on the sixth floor. The Program Management Department could take over the twenty-eight offices in the west wing. Every analyst would have a private office, and the department could provide offices for up to seven new analysts. The analysts believe that this is the best solution.

Conclusion

Of course the third solution would provide the greatest relief to the Program Management Department, but both the first and second solutions would yield some necessary comforts. Regardless of which alternative is chosen, time is of the essence. The help must come quickly so that the analysts in the Program Management Department do not become even more discouraged with the noise, the heat, and the crowding.

FIGURE 12-4 (Continued).

- Qualifies for long retention within the files of the firm
- Numbers six or more pages
- Takes the format of a manuscript
- Includes sections for each of the included research steps
- Reflects a formal writing style
- Uses the impersonal writing style
- Uses relatively fixed indirect, analytical, or comparative developmental plan

- Includes tables, charts, graphs, and other illustrations
- Contains information and/or inherent persuasion (with overt persuasion carried by accompanying letter or memorandum of transmittal)
- Includes quantitative data
- Stands alone rather than taking a periodic form
- Results from assignment by management or occasionally by initiative of the writer

This chapter covers two major types of comprehensive reports: the *proposal* and the *final report.*

Proposal

Through a proposal (prospectus), a researcher identifies a problem and describes the methods for attempting to solve it. The decisions reported in a proposal constitute the biggest step toward accomplishing the desired research. Therefore, even when management does not require a proposal for a project, write one anyway.

Even if left in draft form, the proposal forces careful thinking. The process of committing thoughts to paper aids in the location of flaws and thus can lead to an improved research design. Try to make the proposal so clear and complete that another person could complete the proposed research.

Researchers often seek grants of money from foundations or government agencies. However, whether using grant money, charging a fee to a customer, or using a firm's facilities, the researcher commits resources to the research and becomes accountable for them.

A proposal may cite the need for activities other than research. It might propose a conference or a seminar. It could offer a bid for a contract. It may simply offer to do some work. Written proposals for activities other than research often take on the trappings of other communication channels. Examples include inquiries, requests, and persuasive messages in the forms of letters and memoranda. The examples in this chapter relate to research proposals. However, the business writer may adapt the examples to nonresearch proposals.

In addition to the components of the body, the proposal may include some of the front matter and back matter described earlier in this chapter. For example, a letter or memorandum of transmittal almost always accompanies a proposal. The outline for the body of a proposal parallels that for the research process:

1. Title
2. Introduction
3. Statement of problem
4. Hypothesis(es)
5. Review of related literature
6. Methodology
7. Plans for reporting
8. Schedule of time and work

9. Budget
10. Other sections

Figure 12-5 illustrates a research proposal. Examine it to identify and evaluate its components. Notice that the proposal has the manuscript format. It includes a letter of transmittal, an attachment (a name sometimes used instead of "appendix"), and a bibliography. Observe that although the *title* appears as part of the front matter, it also forms an integral part of the body. It includes the who, what, when, and where, and often the how and why. The body begins with a few sentences of *introduction*. It traces the development of the *problem*. It includes a table illustrating the nature of the problem. The section could also include some excerpts from related research or some graphic figure. (Chapter 13 covers tabular and graphic construction.)

The next section precisely states the *specific*, immediate *problem* attacked by the proposed research. The research problem can take the form of a statement, a question, or even a sentence fragment. The statement of the problem may include more information—the kind of information that answers all of the "W" questions. Alternately, such information may appear in a separate section on the scope of the problem. Some researchers use the word *purpose* to refer to the specific research problem. For these researchers, the problem becomes the obstacle, and the purpose calls for reaching some decisions that will surmount that obstacle.

The proposal specifies the *scope or delimitation*—the boundaries or parameters of the investigation in time and space. Together, the statement of the problem and the statement of the scope or delimitation cover the who, what, when, and where.

Although many researchers use the word *limitations* to mean the same thing as *scope* or *delimitation,* this proposal uses it to identify factors that may restrict the research. Such factors include time, money, research assistance, available data, and difficulties in establishing representative samples. To identify the potential limitations in the latter sense, identify the "gap" between the perfect and practical designs. The "gap" represents the limitations of the research.

Some researchers write about *assumptions* instead of limitations. For example, for the proposal, the first limitation could convert to: "One assumption is that the period of time for the research will yield valid results." Because assumptions and limitations cover the same facets of the research, from slightly different angles, both sections rarely appear in the same proposal.

The proposal includes in declarative form the statements the research will test—the *hypotheses*. The hypotheses take the null form (no difference). However, they can take the positive form (a difference). Avoid the concept of *proving* or *disproving* a hypothesis. The terms indicate too much finality. No research can prove or disprove a hypothesis once and for all.

This proposal (Figure 12-5) summarizes some key pieces of *related literature*. However, it does not try to exhaust such reporting at that point. When reporting from the literature, give full credit to sources of secondary information. When introducing excerpts (summaries, paraphrases, direct quotations),

THE DIFFERENCES BETWEEN TWO COLLECTION SERIES IN

PROPORTIONS AND MEANS OF PAYMENTS RECEIVED

BY RAYLYNNE CO. IN MARCH-MAY, 1983

PROPOSAL

Prepared for

Ms. Cindy Melsa
Credit Manager
Raylynne Co.

Prepared by

Y. R. Self
Research Specialist
Raylynne Co.
January 12, 1983

FIGURE 12–5 Research proposal.

RAYLYNNE CO.

785 Crays Boulevard *Shraft, CO 77777* *888–888–8888*

January 12, 1984

Ms. Cindy Melsa
Credit Manager

Dear Ms. Melsa:

Here is the proposal for the collection-series research we discussed last week. I believe the proposed research could help to answer some of the questions the executive committee raised about the decline in the rate of collections.

The proposed research will require minimal expenditure of time and money—particularly if it helps to solve such a serious problem.

Because the work must begin in February in order to complete the research during the period March-May, I should appreciate having your response by next week. If you would like to discuss the proposal, I shall be glad to meet with you.

Sincerely yours,

Y. R. Self

Y. R. Self
Research Specialist

YRS:aa

Enclosure

FIGURE 12–5 (Continued).

THE DIFFERENCES BETWEEN TWO COLLECTION SERIES IN

PROPORTIONS AND MEANS OF PAYMENTS RECEIVED

BY RAYLYNNE CO. IN MARCH-MAY, 1984

During 1982 and 1983 the rates of collection for delinquent accounts at Raylynne Co. declined significantly. Though inflation and recession undoubtedly explain the major portion of the decline, the age of the collection series may have contributed to rates lower than would have been experienced with a more modern series.

Raylynne Co. created and began to use the presently used Series 17G2 in 1981. Series 17G2 seemed to produce good results that year. However, as shown in this table, 1982 and 1983 do not reflect good collection rates—not even as good as those experienced in 1978 and 1979 with Series 17G1.

ANNUAL RATES OF COLLECTION

RAYLYNN CO., 1978-1983

Year	Percent of Outstanding Dollars Collected After Three Letters	Percent of Outstanding Dollars Collected After All Six Letters
1978	68.5	83.6
1979	68.8	82.3
1980	69.1	83.1
1981	71.7	86.1
1982	64.5	78.2
1983	60.4	72.6

THE PROBLEM

The general problem is the decline in the rate of collections during 1982 and 1983. Thus, the purpose of the proposed research is to find whether a new series of collection letters increases the rate of collections.

FIGURE 12-5 (Continued).

2

Research Problem

The specific problem for the proposed research is to determine whether the collections for a new series—Series 17G3—are significantly greater than the collections for Series 17G2 for the period March through May, 1984.

To establish appropriate controls, employees will randomly divide the outstanding accounts into two groups. Group O will receive Series 17G2, and Group N will receive Series 17G3. The determination will be made for the total collections for all six letters.

Two factors will form the basis for the analysis. They are (1) the proportions of people who make payments any time after the first letter and within two weeks of the sixth letter and (2) the mean sizes of the payments received.

The scope of the delimited research problem, then, is to determine during the period March-May, 1984, whether Group N and Group O differ in:

1. The proportions of payments received and time after mailing the first letter and within two weeks after mailing the sixth letter
2. The mean payments received any time after mailing the first letter and within two weeks after mailing the sixth letter

Limitations

The random division of outstanding accounts into two groups will control such extraneous variables as economic conditions, seasonality, volume of credit, cost of credit, and volume of sales. However, some limitations to the proposed research do exist.

FIGURE 12-5 (Continued).

3

First, a longer period of time might give more valid results. However, the seriousness of the collection-rate problem necessitates taking no more than three months for the initial test of the new series.

Another limitation will arise if the collection staff does not keep accurate records of the added information necessary for the research. For people already pressed to meet their own job requirements, the additional work could add the type of burden that leads to carelessness. The section on personnel training includes suggestions for preventing this limitation.

Hypotheses

So that the statements of hypotheses in this section will not conflict with those necessary for the quantitative analysis, they take the null form:

1. For all six letters, the proportion of payments received from Group N is less than or equal to the proportion received from Group O.
2. For all six letters, the mean payment received from Group N is less than or equal to the mean payment received from Group O.

RELATED RESEARCH

Because of its relationship to circumstances specific to Raylynne Co., the precise topic of the proposed research receives no treatment in the literature. However, two reports were located that do relate to the general subject matter.

Trotter reports on research associated with the instigation of a new collection process (including a new mail collection series) for the Cella Co. in 1977. Though she did not assess the impact of the collection series as an isolated variable, she did suggest:

FIGURE 12–5 (Continued).

The improvement in the rate of collection after the establishment of the new process likely depends a great deal upon the modernized series of five collection letters. Though not tested directly, the new series led the collectors to comment that the new letters brought an obviously improved rate of response.[1]

Similarly, Novick conducted research and concluded: "The 1979 collection series led to a significantly greater average collection than did the 1978 series."[2] However,

Novick's research seems to have one major flaw: He did not hold any sort of control over the other factors that might have related to an increased average. He simply took the mean dollar value of collections for a firm for each of the years and tested to determine whether the means differed significantly. Thus, the increase in 1979 could have been explained by any number of variables other than the collection series.

DEFINITIONS OF TERMS

These definitions may expedite reading this proposal:

Group N—The group receiving the new collection series (17G3)

Group O—The group receiving the old collection series (17G2)

METHODOLOGY

The methodology of the proposed research will involve collection, organization, and analysis of the data.

Collection

These steps will accomplish the collection of the data:

1. Beginning February 2, 1984, design the six letters of series 17G3, and put them into word processing system.
2. On March 2, pull the cards for the accounts to be started on the collection series. Leave the cards in alphabetical order. Number the cards. Use a table of

FIGURE 12-5 (Continued).

random numbers to choose the first card. Assign that card the old collection series, the next card the new series, the next card the old series, etc., until all cards have an assignment. Repeat the process with each new scheduled cycle for collection follow-up.

3. For each cycle, complete the form illustrated as the attachment to this proposal.

Analysis

At the end of the three-month period, the researchers will find proportions of people who have made payments any time after the first letter and within two weeks after the sixth letter for both Group O and Group N. In addition, they will find the mean payments received from each of the two groups. Letters for which the two-week response period has not expired will be eliminated from the analysis. Tables and charts will illustrate the organization.

The first hypothesis will be tested by a one-tailed test for two sample proportions. The test will determine whether the proportion of payments for the new series is less than or equal to the proportion for the old series.

For the test of the second hypothesis, a one-tailed, two-sample-mean test will determine whether the mean payment from Group N the series is less than or equal to the mean payment from Group O for the series.

The two tests will be conducted at the .05 and .01 levels of risk. Each test will lead to a rejection or an acceptance of the associated null hypothesis.

From the decisions will come the conclusions and recommendations. If a test leads to a rejection of the null hypothesis, Series 17G3 will have been successful in improving the rate of collections or the mean size of the payment received.

FIGURE 12-5 (Continued).

6

PLANS FOR REPORTING

At the end of the three-month period, the researcher will prepare a complete report of the research. The report will include a review of the sections included in this proposal as well as a summary of the findings of the collection, organization, and analysis of the data. It will also include the conclusions and recommendations drawn from the analysis.

The reports will be submitted to Credit Manager Cindy Melsa and Collection Supervisor Ken Edah for their desired use and distribution.

SCHEDULE OF TIME AND WORK

The schedule for the work is:

1. Beginning early in February, 1984, Melsa and Edah develop Series 17G3.
2. Late in February, Self, Melsa, and Edah conduct one-hour workshop for collectors.
3. From Monday, March 2, through Friday, March 29, 1984, collectors record data.
4. During the week of June 1, analyze data and prepare report.
5. On June 8, submit report to Melsa and Edah.

PERSONNEL AND TRAINING

Though the research will require no additional personnel, the existing personnel will take on some additional work and will need some brief training and some motivational development.

FIGURE 12-5 (Continued).

To accomplish the training and the motivation, the researcher will schedule and conduct a one-hour session in February for all 26 collectors. They will learn how to divide the delinquents into Group O and Group N and how to complete the forms. Melsa and Edah will also be present to encourage the employees to take the few minutes needed each day to collect the information for it.

A great deal of the responsibility for day-to-day coordination of activities and summarization of the information will fall upon Edah. He will work closely with both the researcher and the collectors.

[1]Jennifer Trotter, "The Collection Process Does Matter," The Collectors' Monthly 22 (February 1978):26.

[2]Walter Novick, "Mean Dollar Collections for the Alabaster Corp. before and after Revision of the Written Collection Series, 1973-1974," Collection Management 95 (Summer 1982):5.

FIGURE 12–5 (Continued).

ATTACHMENT

THE DIFFERENCES BETWEEN TWO COLLECTION SERIES IN
PROPORTIONS AND MEANS OF PAYMENTS RECEIVED
BY RAYLYNNE CO. IN MARCH-MAY, 1984

Date of Mailing ______________, 1984 Letter No. __________

Collector ______________ Group O or N? __________

Surname on Delinquent Account	Account Number	Amount Owed	Date of Payment	Amount of Payment
1.				
2.				
3.				
4.				
5.				
6.				
7.				
8.				
9.				
10.				
11.				
12.				
13.				
14.				
15.				

8

FIGURE 12–5 (Continued).

9

SELECTED BIBLIOGRAPHY

Novick, Walter. "Mean Dollar Collections for the Alabaster Corp. before and after Revision of the Written Collection Series, 1973-1974." Collection Management 95 (Summer 1982): 3-8.

Trotter, Jennifer. "The Collection Process Does Matter." The Collectors' Monthly 22 (February 1978): 23-29.

FIGURE 12–5 (Continued).

use a clear lead so that the reader knows exactly where it begins. Examples include:

In contrast, Jones reports that . . . .

The book *Just-Write Tactics* features a list of . . . .

At the end of an excerpt place some sort of reference to a complete citation of the source. The superior number (superscript) in reference to a footnote or endnote often appears. However, other systems exist.

Footnotes and endnotes follow prescribed formats. Style manuals describe them. In addition, Appendix B includes additional information and illustrations.

Avoid any tendency toward plagiarism in the use of the material of others. Even with summaries, the citation should identify the author as the creator of the ideas.

This proposal contains only two *definitions*. They sometimes appear in a rather lengthy alphabetized list. Such a list may form a section within the body of the proposal or in an appendix or glossary at the end of it. Definitions of only a few expressions may become part of the narrative or footnotes when first introduced. To introduce acronyms for long, cumbersome, well-known, or oft-repeated names, first write the full term. Then follow it immediately with the acronym placed within parentheses. For example, to refer to the Government Accounting Office repeatedly within a report, simply introduce the acronym the first time the reference appears: ". . . Government Accounting Office (GAO) . . . ." Thereafter, simply use "GAO." Avoid overusing acronyms, however; writing sprinkled with them takes on a sloppy, cryptic appearance bothersome to many readers.

The section on *methodology* reports how to *collect* the information, how to *organize* it, and how to *analyze* it. (If you have not had a statistics course you may not fully understand the proposed analysis. However, it just proposes to use some statistical tools to determine whether the results from the old collection series differ from those of the new series.) It even looks ahead to the interpretation, the conclusions, and perhaps the recommendations. Report the size of any required samples. Report how to select the items in the sample. Report the details for making the observations. Design and report any forms (observationnaire, questionnaire, etc.) necessary for the observation. Describe in detail the actual steps of the analysis. Name the exact models or tests projected for quantitative analysis. Name the level of significance, the level of confidence, or any other such predetermined values necessary to the analysis.

The proposal contains a section on *plans for reporting* the results of the research. The section usually includes the names of those to whom the report will go. Sometimes this section contains a complete outline of the proposed final report.

The proposal also contains a schedule of time and work. Time always forms an important consideration for the business researcher. Losing time costs the firm or agency money.

The final section of the proposal covers *personnel and training*. Many proposals also contain sections describing the *budget and qualifications of investigators*.

Final Report

The final report of a research project includes everything that a proposal does. In addition, it includes the results or findings from the research process originally defined in the proposal.

Of all of the business messages, the research report would most likely include all of the front matter, back matter, and body parts listed earlier in this chapter. A research report may even include chapters instead of sections with the customary headings. The final report of the research proposed in Figure 12-5, then, would include the original proposal virtually intact, but written in the past tense. Figure 12-6 includes the additional sections necessary to form the final report.

As a natural topic to follow this discussion of writing business reports, Chapter 13 covers tables, graphs, and other displays that accompany both written and oral messages. Many of the types introduced fit well into business reports.

SUMMARY

Reports usually follow one of three basic formats: form, letter or memorandum, and manuscript. The form report involves relatively mechanical completion. However, it still must capture the desired information in usable terms. Letter reports often travel from inside a firm to outside agencies or from agencies into a firm. The memorandum format moves within the firm—usually upward. The traditional manuscript format often carries comprehensive reports of analytical or research activities. It includes three major parts: front matter, body, and back matter. The three parts contain at least 16 possible subdivisions. Style manuals describe the components and the complete details for using the manuscript.

Business reports fall into two major categories: abbreviated reports and comprehensive reports. Abbreviated reports cover only a few of the steps of the research process. Comprehensive reports cover most or all of the steps. To write both reports successfully, apply the six communication guidelines, the principles of effective writing, the appropriate formats, the steps of the research process, and the suggestions for constructing tables and graphs covered in Chapter 13.

Abbreviated reports usually appear as memoranda, letters, or forms, but occasionally as manuscripts. They usually do not include extensive analysis, conclusions, or recommendations. The justification report provides one example of an abbreviated report. It seeks to persuade someone to take action.

Comprehensive reports usually take the manuscript form. This chapter covers two major types of comprehensive reports: the proposal and the final report.

The proposal identifies a problem and describes methods for solving it. The proposal can include about twenty parts, including the statement of the problem, the hypotheses, the review of the literature, and the design for collecting, organizing, and analyzing the data.

The final report of a research project includes everything that a proposal does. In addition, it includes the results or findings from the research process originally defined in the proposal.

RAYLYNNE CO.

785 Crays Boulevard   Shraft, CO 77777   888–888–8888

January 26, 1984

Mr./Ms. Y. R. Self
Research Specialist

Dear Mr./Ms. Self:

The Executive Committee met last Wednesday to consider your proposal for research into the power of a new collection series to increase the rate of collections. In addition, I met privately with Vice President Allen to discuss it.

As a result of the two meetings, we have decided to proceed with your proposed research as you have designed it.

Mr. Edah and I would like to meet with you this week to begin the development of the new collection series and to make plans for the workshop for the collectors. I will be out of town Wednesday.

Whether we determine that the new series increases the collection rate or not, we need a new series. We also need to know whether we must search for other factors to explain the declining rate. If a change in the series does not make a difference, we might consider an experiment involving telephone collection instead of collection by mail.

Sincerely,

Cindy Melsa

Cindy Melsa
Credit Manager

CM:bb

FIGURE 12–6 Components of final report.

RAYLYNNE CO.

785 Crays Boulevard *Shraft, CO 77777* *888–888–8888*

June 8, 1984

Ms. Cindy Melsa
Credit Manager

Dear Ms. Melsa:

This report summarizes the collection-series research you authorized on January 26. It confirms the findings reported in the preliminary report sent to you on April 17: The new collection series does lead to a significantly improved rate of collection.

As suggested in the recommendations section of the report, we may want to begin exclusive use of the new series, but also conduct research to determine whether a telephone collection process might improve the rate even more. I shall be glad to prepare a proposal for such research if you would like.

Thank you for the opportunity to complete the research—and for all of the aid and support that you provided.

Sincerely,

Y. R. Self

Y. R. Self
Research Specialist

YRS:aa

FIGURE 12–6 (Continued).

CONTENTS

ii

FIGURE 12-6 (Continued).

ILLUSTRATIONS

Figure

iii

FIGURE 12-6 (Continued).

TABLES

iv

FIGURE 12-6 (Continued).

ABSTRACT

During 1982 and 1983 the rates of collection for delinquent accounts at Raylynn Co. declined significantly. This research determined whether a new collection series (17G3) might yield a higher rate of collection and a higher mean collection than Series 17G2.

For the period March-May, 1984, the outstanding accounts were randomly divided into two groups,. Group O received the six letters of Series 17G2, and Group N received the six letters of Series 17G3.

A one-tailed test of the difference between the proportions who made payments in the two groups tested one hypothesis. A one-tailed test of the difference between the mean payments for the two groups tested another hypothesis. The analysis yielded these conclusions:

1. Compared to Series 17G2, Series 17G3 significantly improved the proportion of payments received.
2. No significant difference in mean payments exists between the two groups.

Recommendations flowing from the research include:

1. Change from Series 17G2 to Sries 17G3 for all collections.
2. Test collections after each letter in the two series to determine whether Series 17G3 improves collection when compared to Seris 17G2.
3. Authorize the development of a proposal to conduct research into the possibility of using telephone collections in conjunction with or in addition to mail collections.

RESULTS

The results of the collection and analysis fall naturally into the two major categories of that analysis: proportions of payments and means of payments.

FIGURE 12–6 (Continued).

Proportions of Payments

The numbers of delinquent accounts in Group O and N were 432 and 431 respectively. The number of payments by Group N represents .761 of the total, while the number of payments by Group O represents .616 of the total.

For the one-tailed, normal-distribution test reflected by the z score, the critical points of rejection are 1.64 for the .05 level of risk and 2.33 for the .01 levels of risk. The calculated Z value is 4.598. Compared to the critical points, then, the value of Z calls for a rejection of the null hypothesis at the .01 level of risk. Thus, for the combined data for all six letters, Group N made significantly greater proportions of payments than did Group O.

Means of Payments

As might be expected, the mean size of the payments were not significantly different—subject, of course, to the Type II error. Group O had a mean payment of $101.01, and Group N had a mean payment of $102.44. The Z value is 1.316, thus leading to the acceptance.

CONCLUSIONS AND RECOMMENDATIONS

The conclusions and recommendations flow naturally from the results of the analysis.

Conclusions

The logical conclusions drawn from the research include:

1. Compared to the old collection series, the new collection series significantly improves the proportions of payments received.
2. No significant differences exist in the mean payments for all six letters for Group O and Group N.

FIGURE 12-6 (Continued).

Recommendations

In light of the conclusions and the interpretation of them, these recommendations seem to be in order:

1. Change from Series 17G2 to Series 17G3 for all collections.
2. Test collections after each letter in the two series determine whether series 17G3 improves collections when compared to Series 17G2.
3. Authorize the development of a proposal to conduct research into the possibility of using telephone collections in conjunction with or in addition to mail collections.

FIGURE 12-6 (Continued).

THE TOY BOAT

The BBB Toy Company, Inc., headquartered in Chicago, operates 43 discount toy stores in thirteen states. Each store sells a full line of toys, from the smallest rubber ball to the largest and fanciest train set. Founded in 1935, BBB Toy Company prides itself on its hard-earned reputation of dealing fairly and honestly with its customers. BBB also emphasizes its discount prices on quality items.

The BBB Toy Store in Danish Grove, Indiana, like all BBB toy outlets, holds a month-long toy sale beginning the day after Thanksgiving. During the promotion, the store's employees reduce the price of most toys by at least 25 percent of the discount price. Consequently, almost every toy BBB carries is priced at 30 to 50 percent below the manufacturer's suggested retail price during the holiday sale.

A few special toys receive no reduction in price, however. These toys constitute BBB's Golden Brick Road line, a line of rare, expensive toys that normally cannot be found in most other toy and department stores. Toys in the Golden Brick Road line are never discounted and are so marked by a tag saying *not reduced.*

Two days after Thanksgiving, John B. Miller, a New Yorker visiting his brother in Danish Grove, traveled to the Danish Grove BBB Toy Store to purchase a gift for his adolescent niece. He decided to go to the BBB Toy Store because he had seen BBB's four-page advertisement in the Thanksgiving edition of the *Danish Grove Examiner.* The idea of a storewide reduction in already discount prices appealed to Miller, and he decided on the way to the store that this year he would spend a little extra money on his niece's gift because he thought she was now old enough to take care of a good toy and because the reduced BBB prices would allow him to get his money's worth.

When Miller arrived at the store at noon, over 300 shoppers had made their way through the store since 9 A.M. Many of the shoppers had wanted their purchases gift-wrapped, a service BBB offers free to its customers. Thus, the store's employees had been quite busy all morning.

After looking at a number of toys, Miller decided to buy his niece an elaborate and expensive boat that she could use on the lakes that dotted the Danish Grove area. The boat was three feet long, and it could be run by remote control. Further, the boat was a beautifully constructed limited edition, making it a collector's item.

Miller was slightly reluctant to pay the $599.99 marked on the boat's price tag, but he found comfort in knowing that the amount reflected a 25 percent reduction in the discount price.

Miller had the boat gift-wrapped and took it to his niece.

At the end of that sale day, the Danish Grove store manager noticed that a few of the tags for Golden Brick Road toys were lying on the floor. They apparently had come off during one of the rush periods when aisle room was at a premium.

Miller gave his niece her present that evening. She was ecstatic about the gift, and she, her mother, and Miller immediately tested out the boat on a nearby lake. Its trial run went off without a hitch.

Two weeks later, Miller visited a toy shop near his New York City apartment, because he saw several boats displayed in the store's window. He wanted to see whether the store carried his niece's boat, and if it did, just how much money he had saved by buying it on sale at a discount store. He found his niece's boat, and much to his dismay, its price was $450, $150 less than what he had paid in Danish Grove. In talking with the manager of the New York City toy store, Miller discovered that the manufacturer's suggested retail price for the boat was $600.

In late December, Ellen S. Smith, vice president for customer relations at BBB Toy Company, Inc., in Chicago, received a lengthy letter from Miller. Apparently Miller, an extremely influential consumer advocate, after discovering the retail price of the boat purchased in Danish Grove, had called the manager of the Danish Grove toy store for an explanation and a full refund. Although Miller received an explanation (the special tag must have come off during the rush), he did not receive a refund. The store manager stated that merchandise could not be returned for a refund after it had been used and damaged. (It seems that Miller's other niece, a toddler, had attempted to *board* the boat, crushing its upper deck.)

Smith thinks the manager of the Danish Grove store acted appropriately. Few exceptions are made to this return/refund policy, established at the corporate level, because it keeps customers from suddenly deciding that they do not like the toys they purchased *after* they have used and broken them.

In his letter to Smith, Miller threatened to "show the world that the BBB Toy Stores are not what they claim to be" in the next issue of his *Consumer Warning* newsletter (circulation 550,000) if the BBB Toy Company, Inc., did not take "immediate and appropriate action." Smith checks with her superior and discovers that an exception to the return/refund policy will *not* be made in Miller's case. She is told, instead, to "smooth Miller's ruffled feathers."

(This case is fictional.)

EXERCISES

1. You have noticed that most of your co-workers at the Worthington Corporation do not listen well. You suspect that they have never been taught how to listen. Because you would like to correct this problem, you want to hold three two-day listening workshops for all of the Worthington employees who would like to attend. Write a one- or two-page memorandum proposal for the workshops. The proposal will go to several of your Worthington superiors.
2. Your firm's manager of employee relations asked you to talk to all of the management analysts in your department to find out what they considered to be their major work problems. You did not prepare a questionnaire, but you did ask each of your colleagues to identify work-related problems. You interviewed all of your department's 15 analysts (yourself included). These are the problems that were mentioned, some of the points that the analysts made, and the number of analysts who identified each problem.

PROBLEM	NUMBER OF ANALYSTS WHO MENTIONED PROBLEM
a. Salaries too low ("Our salaries aren't keeping up with inflation.")	13
b. Lack of communication between management and employees ("Managers live in their own little world.")	11
c. Analysts not allowed to make own decisions ("When the managers deign to talk to us, they treat us like children.")	11
d. Vacation days too few ("We need more than two weeks a year away from this place if we are to be effective when we are here.")	10
e. Too few secretaries ("I end up doing my own typing half of the time.")	8
f. Analysts aren't allowed to determine own work hours ("I am old enough to know when I need to come to work or when I can come to work late.")	8
g. Offices too small ("My office mate and I bump into each other every time we move.")	6

PROBLEM	NUMBER OF ANALYSTS WHO MENTIONED PROBLEM
h. Retirement plan not adequate ("Most companies match at least 25 percent of the employee's contribution.")	5

i. Company won't reimburse employees for tuition and books ("I'm spending a fortune for a degree that will be an asset to this company.") 3

j. Company doesn't give enough parties ("My last company gave a party every month.") 1

Write a letter report relating your work and your findings. Include at least one paragraph on conclusions, and use your imagination to add information if you wish. You will give your report to the Employee Relations Manager who asked you to do the work.

3. You are the staff researcher for a large organization. The marketing manager assigns you the responsibility of developing a proposal for research to determine whether the department can use a job-application factor as the predictor of sales performance. You do some thinking and reading and go through all of the preliminary steps. You define yourself, the marketing manager, and the environment within which you operate.
   a. Select one quantitative factor to use as a predictor (from such factors as age, examination score, years of education, and years of experience).
   b. Select the appropriate factor to be predicted (from such factors as average annual sales, average monthly sales, and duration of the sales period under consideration).
   c. Establish the specific problem statement, scope and delimitations, hypothesis(es), and limitations/assumptions.
   d. Develop the design of the investigation.
      (1) Collection
      (2) Organization
      (3) Analysis (using the coefficients of correlation and determination, a test of significance of the coefficient of correlation, and the regression equation)

   Write the draft of these sections of a proposal. Supply additional information as needed.

4. Put each of these into footnote form:
   a. You quoted from Lamar T. Handley's *Managing Your Own Business,* a book that was printed in 1976 by the Wayside Publishing Company of Chapel Hill, North Carolina. Your quotation is from page 16 of the book. This is the first footnote in your paper.
   b. "Business Leaders Wake Up to Crime" is your source. The article was published in the April, 1980, issue of *Big Business,* a magazine. Your quotation was taken from pages 189 and 190 of the magazine. The article's authors are Sara Mason Winecoff and Maren Halvorsell. This is the fifth footnote in your paper.
   c. *The New Jersey Marketer's Guide* is the source for your eighth footnote. The guide was published in New Jersey by the New Jersey Association of Marketing Managers. You quoted from page 92 of the 1980 guide.

5. You interviewed 105 randomly selected clerical workers to learn how they viewed their jobs. You asked each clerical worker ten well-thought-out questions. Your most interesting finding was that 75 of the workers plan to quit their clerical jobs within two years because they find clerical work uninteresting and they do not feel that they are paid well. Of the 75 who plan to quit, 52 want to go to college to earn a four-year degree. Sixty-five of the people who plan to quit said that they would consider staying on at their company if they were given opportunities to train for

entry-level professional positions. Of the 30 workers who do not plan to leave in the next two years, 23 said they plan to stay because they like the people with whom they work. You very much enjoyed working with the clerical personnel. Write an abstract that will introduce your report on the interviews with the clerical workers.

6. Meet with your group. Work as a task force of specialists employed at Meac Co. First, brainstorm to identify the factors that might explain a recent slump in sales for your company, Beef-Jerky Sales, Inc. Complete the brainstorming process by isolating the one or two factors most likely to explain it. Brainstorm again to establish all of the details of a research design for determining whether the factors are related to the slump. Brainstorm and supply all of the information needed to develop a complete research proposal. Divide the work, draft the parts of a proposal, meet to compile and refine the parts, and write the proposal. Use the manuscript form, the impersonal style, and the traditional parts.
7. Choose one of these topics, another suggested by your professor, or one reached through brainstorming with your group or class:
   How business can reduce energy consumption
   The content and features of annual reports
   The content and features of prospectuses
   The field in which you plan to work
   A company for which you might want to work
   The provisions and status of applications of the Equal Employment Opportunity Act
   Organization development as a discipline
   Retirement plans used by business
   The current status of the national economy
   Conflict of interest within business firms
   Japan's productivity and the impact of the Deming approach to statistical analysis on it

   Develop an outline and a plan of attack for the topic. Collect the information from secondary and/or primary sources. Develop a several-page manuscript report of the findings. Include in the report at least three excerpts from secondary sources (one of each of the three types), the footnotes associated with the excerpts, at least one table, and at least one graph. (See Chapter 13 for hints on tabular and graphic construction.) In addition, include headings and subheadings, a bibliography, and all other parts necessary to complete it.
8. Complete at least three personal interviews using the interview guide developed in Exercise No. 9 in Chapter 11. Write a report summarizing the results of the interviews. If made into a class project, select the interviewees by some random process, divide them among the students, and compile the results before each student writes the report.
9. As a communication specialist at P. R. Duce, Inc., write an abbreviated report in memorandum form to persuade D. S. Instred, Marketing Specialist, of the need to apply a readability formula to outgoing messages. Include a description of the chosen formula and apply it to a passage of your choice. Supply any necessary information.
10. For the case described in Exercise No. 7 in Chapter 11, complete the research design, and write a formal proposal for the research.

11. Select a team from the class to choose the best research design from the proposals developed in Exercise No. 10—or to develop a proposal containing the best elements of the others. Divide the work and the expenses (if the institution cannot fund the project) among the class members. Complete the survey and the remainder of the proposed research.
12. Write the final report of the research completed in Exercise No. 11. Put it in the comprehensive, manuscript format for a final research report. Include all necessary parts.
13. Obtain at least three office-equipment catalogs from different firms. Select a type of equipment common to all of them. Put yourself into the role of an employee who wants and needs the type of equipment. Write a justification report in manuscript form comparing the qualities of the various brands and ranking them in order of preference. Include only subtle persuasion for the brand you want. Provide and create whatever information you need.
14. An employee in your department has been unusually irritable and inefficient for the past two weeks. His outbursts have affected the personnel and productivity of the entire department. Write a one-page report on the problem and how you might attack it.
15. *[This exercise is best for students who have some familiarity with statistics.]* As a staff researcher for the Expay Corporation, you have conducted assigned comparison research into the difference between the absentee rates for the East Plant and the West Plant. The assignment resulted from concern that the West Plant's absentee rate exceeded the East Plant's rate—to the detriment of production. Your null hypothesis was that no significant difference exists between the mean absentee rates for the two plants. To conduct the research, you rather arbitrarily chose to use monthly data for the past three years. You found the 36 monthly rates for each of the two plants and then found the mean rate for each. You then used a one-tail test of significance of the difference between two sample means at the .05 level of risk. Results of the quantitative analysis were:

Mean rate for the West Plant = .0647
Mean rate for East Plant = .0524
Standard Error = .0042

$$z = \frac{.0647 - .0524}{.0042} = \frac{.0123}{.0042} = 2.929$$

Tabular value of z at .05 level of risk = 1.645

Because 2.929 is larger than 1.645, the null hypothesis was rejected. Therefore, a significant difference did exist between the two rates—the mean rate for the West Plant was significantly larger than the mean rate for the East Plant.

Supplying additional information as needed, write a comprehensive report to include at least this information:

Letter of transmittal
Introduction and general problem
Statement of specific problem, including scope and delimitations
Limitations/assumptions

Hypothesis
Design
Collection and organization
Analysis
Conclusion
Interpretation
Recommendation

16. Use your dictionary and thesaurus to create meanings for these words. Use the words when you think, write, and speak so that you feel comfortable using them.

a. Ambiguous	e. Design	i. Microcosm
b. Anonymous	f. Disseminate	k. Moot
c. Cryptic	g. Flamboyant	l. Overt
d. Culminate	h. Inference	m. Plagiarism

17. Take and score Self-Test 26 over Chapter 12.

SELF-TEST 25
Excerpt about Abbreviated Reports

A. Recall (33 points each). For each multiple-choice question, select the most accurate answer.
   1. Abbreviated reports usually:
      a. Do not show evidence of complete application of the scientific method
      b. Qualify for long retention within the files
      c. Number at least six pages in length
      d. Rarely fall into the routine class
      e. Never take the manuscript format
   2. Abbreviated reports
      a. Usually flow downward in a firm
      b. Rarely result from assignment from management
      c. Deal with such topics as operations, management, and employee relations
      d. Never appear in the formal writing style
      e. Rarely include quantitative data

B. Inference (34 points). Indicate whether this statement is true or false.
   1. Although abbreviated reports often form a routine type of message, the writer should still apply the principles for developing good messages.

SOLUTION

A. Recall (33 points each)
   1. a 2. c

B. Inference (34 points)
   1. True

SELF-TEST 26
Chapter 12

A. Recall (16 points each). For each multiple-choice question, select the most accurate answer.

1. A typical comprehensive report is *not:*
   a. Usually written in a personal reporting style
   b. From six to many pages long
   c. Usually assigned by management
   d. Written for nonroutine, special-purpose projects
   e. Written in an impersonal, formal reporting style
2. Which one of these statements is true?
   a. Most routine reports appear in the manuscript format.
   b. Every manuscript report should contain a preface, foreword, or acknowledgments.
   c. Each level of headings may include only one heading and accompanying section.
   d. Brainstorming is a form of depth interview; it requires that the group immediately challenge each idea put to the group.
   e. The wise researcher tries to find needed information from secondary sources before engaging in primary investigation.
3. Which one of these statements is true?
   a. Report writers write more long reports than short reports.
   b. The abbreviated report customarily uses the manuscript format.
   c. A justification report may include overt persuasion in addition to the persuasion inherent in the facts and logic of its presentation.
   d. A comprehensive report need not include any analysis.
   e. The abstract is the same as the table of contents.
4. Which one of these statements is true?
   a. Do not write a proposal for a research project unless required.
   b. All comprehensive research reports include recommendations for the action to result from the research.
   c. Operational reports form one of the least common types of reports.
   d. A proposal may cover topics other than research projects.
   e. The review of the literature relates only to the data-collecting stage.

B. Inference (18 points each). Indicate whether each statement is true or false.

1. Because communicators generally use more oral communication than written communication, you need not devote much time to learning how to write reports.
2. In general, comprehensive reports are longer than abbreviated reports.

SOLUTION

A. Recall (16 points each)

1. a　**3.** c
2. d　**4.** d

B. Inference (18 points each)

1. False
2. True

STUDENT'S OBJECTIVES:

1 To apply nonverbal techniques to messages that accompany written and oral presentations

2 To learn to prepare tables

13

PREPARING TABLES, ILLUSTRATIONS, AND OTHER PRESENTATIONS

3 To learn to prepare graphs, charts, pictographs, and maps

4 To learn to prepare and present posters, flip charts, videotapes, movies, audiotapes, slides, films, and photographs

Chapter 5 introduces nonverbal communication by emphasizing body lan-guage. In contrast, this chapter concentrates on the preparation of tables, illustrations, and other such nonverbal messages that accompany written and oral presentations.

NONVERBAL MESSAGES THAT ACCOMPANY WRITTEN MESSAGES

Nonverbal messages that often accompany written messages include photographs, sketches, drawings, maps, blueprints, graphs, and tables. In addition, the stationery, format, envelopes, materials, colors, and quality of the presentation carry nonverbal messages. This section covers tables, graphs, and other illustrations.

Tables

Tables present combinations of numbers and words in a specific format. Tables present information more accurately than graphs because they include precise figures rather than pictorial representations of rounded estimates of the figures.

Table 1. Employment status of the civilian noninstitutional population, January and July 1977

(Thousands of persons 16 years of age and over)

Employment status	1977	
	January	July
Total civilian		
noninstitutional population	155,248	156,547
Civilian labor force	94,704	99,314
Employed	86,856	92,372
At work	82,189	81,111
Full time	59,161	62,767
Part time	23,028	18,343
With a job but not at work	4,667	11,261
On strike	52	138
On vacation	984	8,933
Bad weather	1,248	48
Temporary illness	1,515	1,296
Other	869	846
Unemployed	7,848	6,941
Looking for full-time work	6,211	5,797
Looking for part-time work	1,637	1,144
Not in the labor force	60,544	57,234
Keeping house	34,642	34,740
In school	9,115	1,915
Unable to work	2,617	2,874
Other	14,169	17,706

FIGURE 13–1 Repository table.

Types of Tables

One classification includes two basic types of tables: *repository* and *analytical.*

Repository tables Repository tables simply store descriptive information collected by the people who put it in the tables. Therefore, repository tables usually contain *primary* data.

Governmental agencies often disseminate repository tables to the general public. However, private entities make repository tables available to rather narrowly defined groups. For example, staff members periodically draw from such repositories to perform decision-making analyses. Figure 13–1 shows a repository table. Once transferred from the original source, the information becomes *secondary.* It no longer appears in the exact form created by the original collectors.

Analytical tables An analytical table results from some sort of analysis performed upon the raw or organized data. Such analysis may involve primary or secondary data. The analytical table usually appears in comprehensive reports more often than in abbreviated ones. Quantitative analysis resulting in tables may take a simple or complex form. Figure 13–2 contains an analytical table. It represents the results of a research project involving a moderate level of quantitative analysis.

Parts of a Table

Figure 13–3 shows the parts of a standard table. Not every table contains every part. Unless the report contains only one or two tables, number each table. According to most style manuals, the *table number* appears before the title at the top of the table.

For a short title, center the table *number* in all-capital letters two lines above the title. If the title occupies two or more full-width lines, however, the table number may start at the extreme left position of the table itself, followed by a period and a dash. The next section illustrates such an arrangement. Most style manuals suggest the use of arabic numerals for tables. The order of the tables within the text of the report dictates the numbers for the tables themselves.

Always refer to a table by number within the text before inserting it into the material. Insert the table as soon after that reference as possible. However, put a small table on a single page rather than divide it. If the table occupies more than one page, begin it at the top of the page following the first reference to it. Always fill the space following the reference to a delayed table with narrative. Some simple listings or tabulations do not need numbers or titles. In those cases, simply insert them immediately after the introductory sentences.

Center a reasonably short *title* in all-capital letters in the inverted pyramid style. For a title that occupies two or more complete lines, begin the table number at the extreme left-hand edge of the table, follow it by a period and dash, and begin the title immediately. Complete the line to the right margin, and then begin the second line at the left margin and fill it to the right margin. Continue until the last line; center the last line.

Consumer Price Index
Dallas/Fort Worth, Texas
Standard Metropolitan Statistical Area
(1967=100)
April 1980

GROUP	All Urban Consumers			Urban Wage Earners & Clerical Workers		
	Index	% Change From:		Index	% Change From:	
		4-79	2-80		4-79	2-80
All Items	251.4	19.1	4.0	249.6	18.1	3.6
Food and Beverages	245.6	7.4	1.3	246.4	6.8	1.4
Food	250.4	7.5	1.3	251.3	6.8	1.4
Food at home	238.4	5.1	1.5	241.5	5.5	1.7
Cereals and Bakery Prod.	238.9	12.7	4.8	240.5	13.6	2.7
Meats, Poultry, Fish, Eggs	223.0	-3.9	-0.8	229.2	-2.7	-0.9
Meats, Poultry, & Fish	230.2	-3.5	-1.1	236.4	-2.5	-1.5
Dairy Products	228.5	11.5	2.1	233.9	12.3	1.7
Fruits and Vegetables	222.6	1.5	2.6	222.9	-1.4	4.2
Other foods at home	281.4	10.7	1.6	281.3	12.2	3.2
Food away from home	286.3	12.1	1.1	283.0	9.4	0.8
Alcoholic Beverages	182.1	6.7	-0-	181.4	8.0	0.8
Housing	271.1	25.3	5.7	269.5	24.6	5.6
Shelter	305.8	31.5	7.2	306.8	31.3	7.1
Rent, Residential	186.4	9.6	1.2	186.4	9.6	1.2
Other Rental Costs	258.0	14.9	0.3	255.0	14.5	0.3
Homeownership	358.7	37.7	8.7	363.4	38.4	8.8
Fuel and Other Utilities	227.7	13.4	2.1	228.6	13.8	2.1
Fuels	292.7	18.0	3.0	294.2	18.6	3.0
Fuel Oil, Coal, & Bot. Gas1/	151.4	52.0	2.5	151.4	52.0	2.5
Gas (piped) & Electricity	290.1	16.7	3.1	290.3	16.8	3.0
Household Furnishings & Oper.	204.8	9.5	1.5	200.9	7.4	2.0
Apparel and Upkeep	181.2	5.7	1.6	181.1	8.0	2.4
Apparel Commodities	167.5	4.3	1.6	166.7	6.3	2.1
Men's and Boy's Apparel	180.0	5.4	0.7	181.2	7.9	3.5
Women's and Girl's Apparel	145.5	1.1	4.0	143.0	2.7	3.6
Footwear	196.7	8.8	4.0	197.5	12.4	1.8
Transportation	259.1	25.2	3.5	259.7	24.9	3.2
Private Transportation	260.2	25.0	3.5	260.5	24.8	3.2
Public Transportation	230.0	30.7	1.0	229.5	25.9	0.6
Medical Care	244.2	10.9	3.8	244.3	8.8	3.0
Entertainment	202.8	12.7	5.3	187.1	5.9	0.6
Other Goods and Services	215.1	10.1	0.7	214.4	11.0	0.5
Personal Care	224.6	11.8	1.3	227.4	14.3	1.0
All Items (1963=100)	271.7			269.9		

1/ Based to June 1978=100

The Dallas-Ft. Worth Consumer Price Index covers the counties of Collin, Dallas, Denton, Ellis, Hood, Johnson, Kaufman, Parker, Rockwall, Tarrant, and Wise.

FIGURE 13–2 Analytical table.

For full-width titles, begin only the first word and proper nouns with capital letters. Use lower-case letters elsewhere. This example shows a long title and accompanying table number:

> TABLE 7—Residents of Eugene, Oregon, classified by age, sex, occupation, religious preference, political party, and educational level

Once having selected either the centered or full-width style for the number and title, use that style consistently throughout the report.

Information sometimes appears within a *subtitle* instead of a title. For instance, the example for the long title shown in the preceding section does not include a reference to when the classification was made. The time period could become part of the title itself. However, it could also appear in a subtitle two lines below the last line of the title:

TABLE NUMBER

TITLE

(Subtitle)

(Headnote)

Stub Head	Boxheading	Boxheading	Boxheading	
stub	field	field	field	body of table

SOURCE

*Footnote

FIGURE 13-3 Parts of a table.

Annually for the period 198X-198X

The good title and subtitle should include the W's—at least the who, what, when, and where.

A *headnote* shows such information as the units of measurements within the body of the table. In contrast to the footnote (described subsequently), the headnote refers to every item within the body. These examples illustrate headnotes.

(in percent)

(thousands of dollars)

Place a headnote two lines below the last line of the title or subtitle. As shown, it often appears within parentheses, centered on the line. Use mixed capitals (capitalize the initial word and proper nouns), or use all lower-case letters.

The *body* of a table contains rows (horizontal) and columns (vertical) of numerical information identified by titles.

The *stub* includes the titles for rows of data. Each title forms a stub item. Use the stub items to establish classes that identify the entries fully. The *stubhead* forms the title of the stub. It identifies the information contained in the stub itself. The stubhead forms a special case of the boxheading. *Boxheadings* (column heads, captions) create titles for columns. A *spanner heading* overrides several individual column heads. Make the boxheadings clearly descriptive.

The actual data within the rows and a single column constitute a *field.* Some writers call the collection of fields the body. The field contains the meat of the information. If the table includes totals or subtotals, use them to check the accuracy of the individual entries in a field.

Give credit to the *source* of any secondary information. The source note often appears on the second line below the horizontal rule after the last line of the stub and field. The format of a source note should parallel the style for the footnotes within the text of the message. However, it follows the word *SOURCE,* which itself has a colon after it. It does not include a number.

Footnotes generally begin on the second line below the source note. A footnote refers to a specifically keyed entry within the field of information. A footnote may add information, clarify an entry, explain why an omission occurs, define terms, or transmit other such messages about the individual values. Footnotes may occupy as much space as the body itself. To identify footnotes, use consecutive superior numbers, letters, or special symbols. Use asterisks (*, **, ***, ****) for no more than four footnotes. If most of the footnotes refer to numbers within the fields of data, avoid using superior numbers to identify the references.

These additional suggestions will improve the readability and clarity of a table:

1. Keep footnotes brief and to a minimum.
2. Use rulings correctly.
   a. For only two columns, omit all rules. Even on tables with many columns, omit vertical rules when providing liberal spacing between the columns.
   b. When using rules, include a double rule above the boxheads and a single rule at the bottom of the field. Do not include rules at the sides.
   c. Introduce rules within the table logically. For example, place a rule beneath the entire width of the area defined by a spanner heading, below captions, and below columns of figures which have totals.
   d. Leave space before and after rulings. Omission of such space may create the appearance of an underlined word or number.
   e. Make double rules with the typewriter and single rules by hand. Place the two lines of a double rule close together.
3. Arrange the items in the stub, boxheadings, and fields logically. Arrange them according to size, relationship, emphasis, importance, or interest. Arrange them alphabetically, chronologically, geographically, temporally, or simply according to custom.
4. Check a style manual for other features associated with tabular construction.

Illustrations

Graphs, charts, and other illustrations report the same kinds of data included in tables. However, they do so with lines, bars, circles, stick figures, and maps.

Features

Several features govern the development of illustrations. Careful attention to these features will result in good illustrations.

Within the narrative, introduce a graph by *number* and/or *title*. Then insert it as soon as possible without splitting the graph unnecessarily. Give arabic numbers to illustrations in the order of their introduction. The word *figure* serves well as a label for them. One style calls for referring to the figure in the narrative as "Figure 1," and writing "Fig. 1" for the figure itself.

One design places the figure number and title on the second line beneath the figure itself. Center the number and title or write them in full-width lines. Place the figure number and title on the same line in either case. Capitalize only the first word and proper nouns in either case. Write the multilined title in sentence style the full width of the illustration or with each line centered. These examples show two styles:

Fig. 7. Annual sales of Talent, Inc.

Fig. 9. Relationships among annual sales, advertising expenditures, and number of sales representatives for Sellebrity, Inc., for the period of 198X through 198X.

Use appropriate *scales* to make most charts and graphs approximately square. Do so by establishing the scale on the X-axis first and then calculating an interval for the Y-axis scale that will make the height approximately the same as the width. If one dimension must exceed the other, artists usually make the height the greater of the two.

The graphic grid contains four quadrants identified by the horizontal X-axis and the vertical Y-axis. Because business series tend to involve positive values on both axes, most business graphs fall into the first quadrant of the grid shown in Figure 13–4. Many business and economic graphs include points in time along the X-axis. Therefore, the X-axis scale does not have to begin with zero. Just place the first period of time at the intersection of X and Y. Show zero on the Y-axis for most arithmetic series. However, you may omit the zero for certain business series, such as with index numbers. For a Y series with large numbers, simply begin Y with zero, break the axis, write the smallest value in the scale just above the break, and proceed.

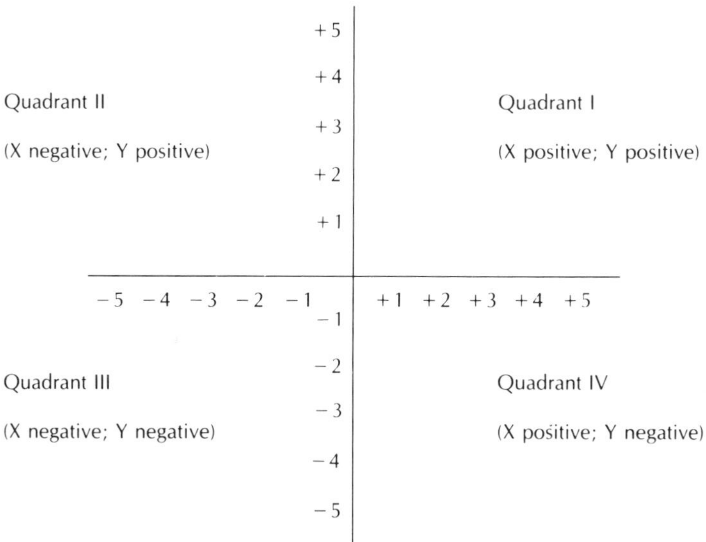

FIGURE 13–4 Grid showing four quadrants.

Check a style manual for information on other matters of style: turning a figure sideways on the page, using several pages for a single figure, and giving credit to the originator of an illustration.

Make graphic presentations clear, concise, complete, accurate, and attractive. Transmit a striking message to engage the reader. Introduce color when appropriate. Employ good artistic and drafting techniques. For example, use a light pencil drawing first, cover it with a pen drawing, and then erase the pencil marking. Also use a straight edge and other such tools to make the illustration crisp.

Include a clear legend to explain the information contained within the figure. Use actual numbers to supplement bars, lines, and areas in pie charts and maps, if you can do so without cluttering the figure.

Types of Illustrations

Choose the type of illustration carefully: (1) To feature the sweep and flow of data, choose the line graph. (2) To feature the differences among the sizes of the classes within a series, use the bar chart. (3) To feature both the total and relative sizes of the parts to the total, use the component line graph, the component bar chart, or the pie chart. (4) To show a series of changing totals, use line graphs or bar charts; do not use a series of area charts. (5) To contrast amounts of difference or change, use an arithmetic scale.

Arithmetic line graphs Arithmetic line graphs form an important type of illustration. This chapter covers four types: simple, multiple, component, and two-directional line graphs. The *simple line graph* contains only one line. That line usually represents the movement of a series of data through time. Figure 13-5 shows a simple line graph constructed on arithmetic graph paper.

A special type of line graph presents the data in a frequency table: the *frequency polygon*. The tabular data in Figure 13-6 form the basis for illustrating the frequency polygon. The "f" in the table stands for *frequency*. The

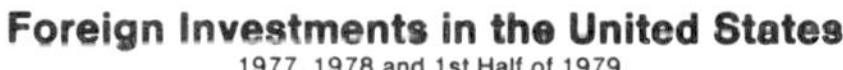

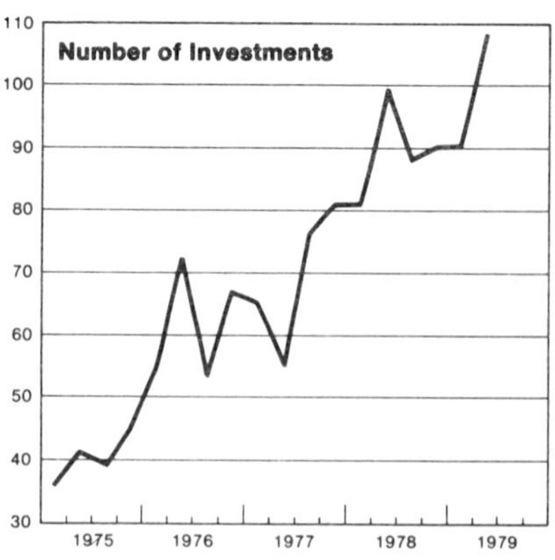

FIGURE 13-5 Simple arithmetic line graph.

HOURLY CHARGES FOR TELEVISION REPAIR
SYLVESTER, OHIO
MAY, 198X

Charges	f
$10 but under $15	2
15 but under 20	15
20 but under 25	25
25 but under 30	60
30 but under 35	12

FIGURE 13–6 Frequency table.

frequency column indicates the number of cases that fall into each class for this distribution. Figure 13–7 shows the corresponding frequency polygon. Observe these features that distinguish the frequency polygon:

1. Only the lower limits go along the X-axis, with the lowest lower limit beginning at least one-half an interval width to the right of the intersection of X and Y.
2. The plots on the Y-axis align with the midpoints of the classes on the X-axis.
3. The polygon closes by showing zero frequency at the midpoints of the classes preceding and following the distribution.

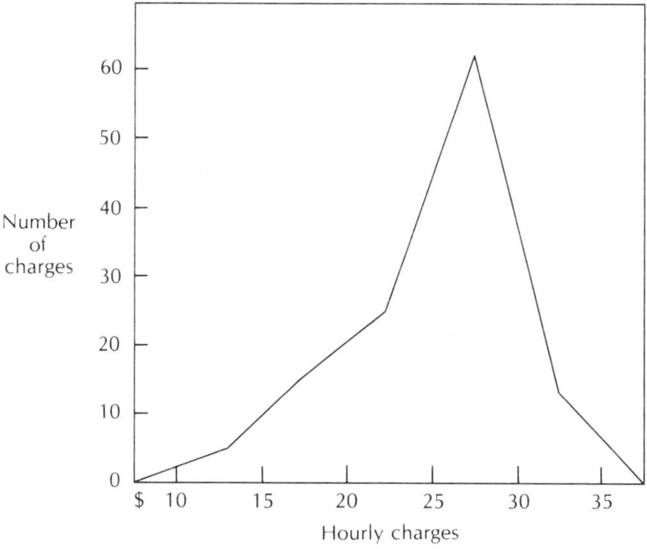

FIGURE 13–7 Frequency polygon for data in Figure 13–6.

The *multiple line graph* simply shows two or more series on the same graph. Figure 13–8 illustrates a multiple line graph with an arithmetic scale on the Y-axis. It also includes a bar chart (described later) and features a break in the Y-axis.

The *component line graph* is useful to show the movement of both a total series and its parts through time. Figure 13–9 provides an example on arithmetic graph paper. Observe how it shows both domestic production and imported oil as they provide the total oil supply.

A *two-directional line graph* illustrates the rise and fall of a series—usually through time. Thus, it adapts well to showing business cycles around a line of normalcy designated as zero. Figure 13–10 shows the visual effect supplied by the two-directional line graph. Notice that it also illustrates a bar chart.

Bar charts Types of bar charts also include simple, multiple, component, and two-directional. The *simple bar chart* involves the placement of a single bar at each point on the axis. Make the bars vertical or horizontal. Arranging the bars in ascending or descending order creates a particularly vivid presentation.

Figure 13–11 illustrates a horizontal bar chart with the bars organized in order of size. Notice that the bars and the spaces between them maintain visually consistent and pleasant perspective in sizes. The bars do not join

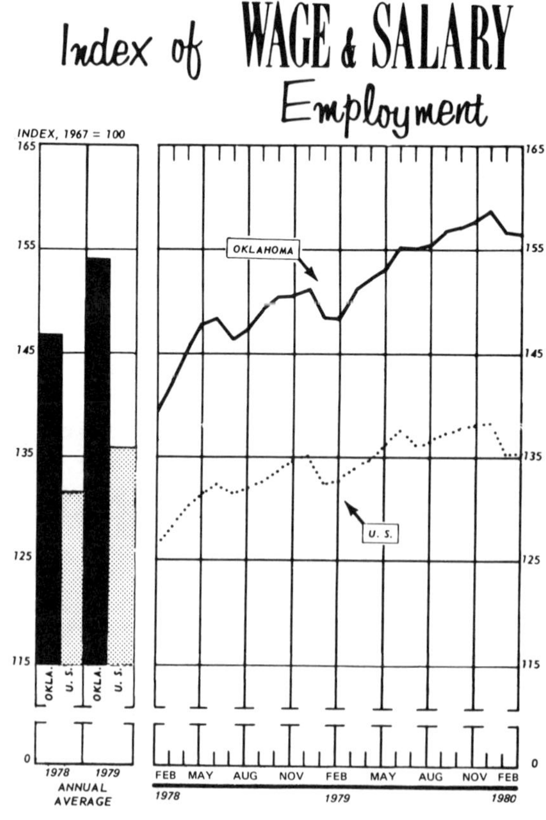

FIGURE 13–8 Multiple line graph.

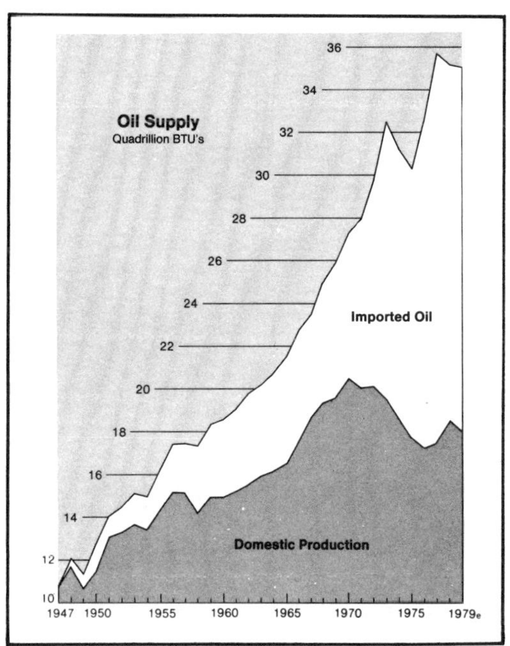

FIGURE 13–9 Component line graph.

because of the qualitative (word) designation for them. Figure 13–12 shows two simple vertical bar charts with time along the X-axis. Because they represent continuous data, the bars could join. Notice the break in the Y-axis.

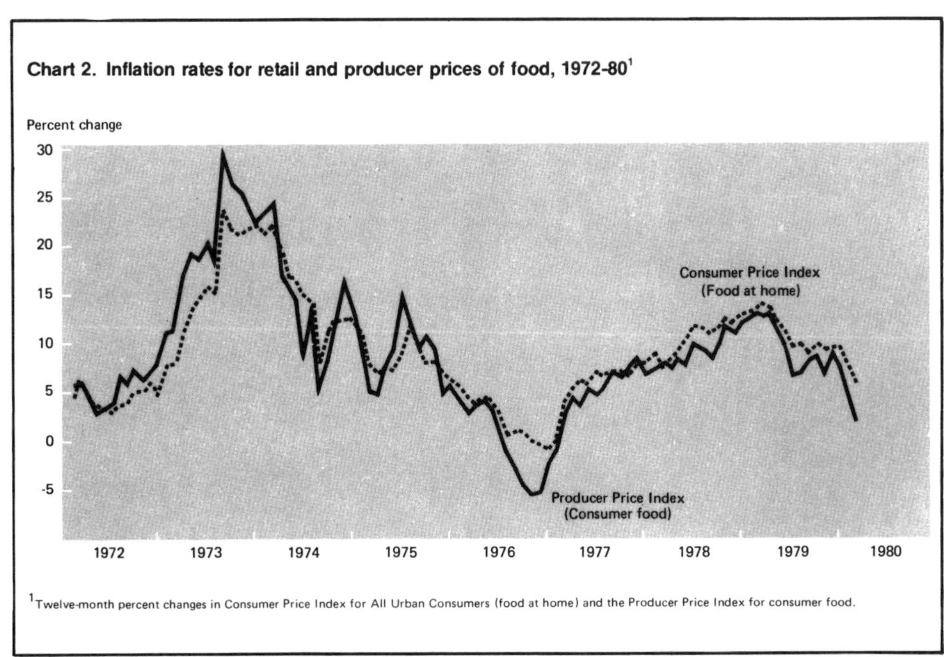

FIGURE 13–10 Two-directional line graph.

Foreign Investments in the United States
1977, 1978 and 1st Half of 1979

States with Most Investments

California 90
New York 88
New Jersey 43
Texas 42
South Carolina 38
Pennsylvania 34
North Carolina 32
Ohio 32
Georgia 31
Virginia 28
Connecticut 26

FIGURE 13-11 Horizontal bar chart.

The *histogram* presents the data in a frequency distribution as a simple bar chart. Figure 13-13 shows a histogram for the data in Figure 13-6.

These suggestions will help to develop a good histogram:

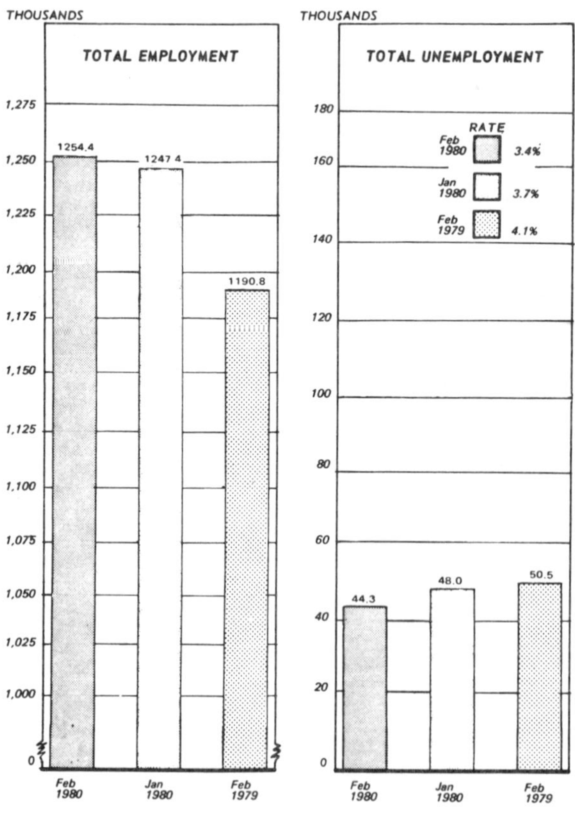

FIGURE 13-12 Vertical bar chart.

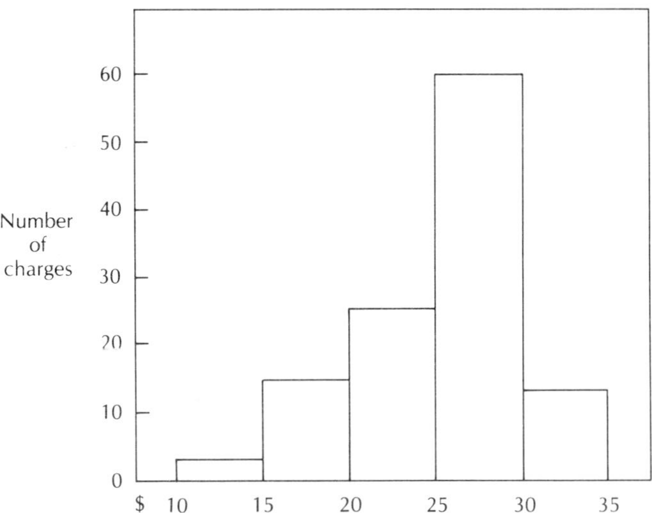

FIGURE 13–13 Histogram for data in Figure 13–6.

- Leave a space the equivalent of at least one-half the horizontal increment at each end of the X-axis.
- For continuous data, show only the lower limits of the frequency-distribution classes. For discrete data, show both the upper and lower limits.
- Do not leave gaps between the bars for continuous data. For discrete data show narrow gaps.
- Make the chart approximately square.

The *multiple bar chart* includes two or more bars at each point on the scale. The chart usually involves vertical bars. Figure 13–14 illustrates the concept. A practical limit exists for the number of bars possible at a single

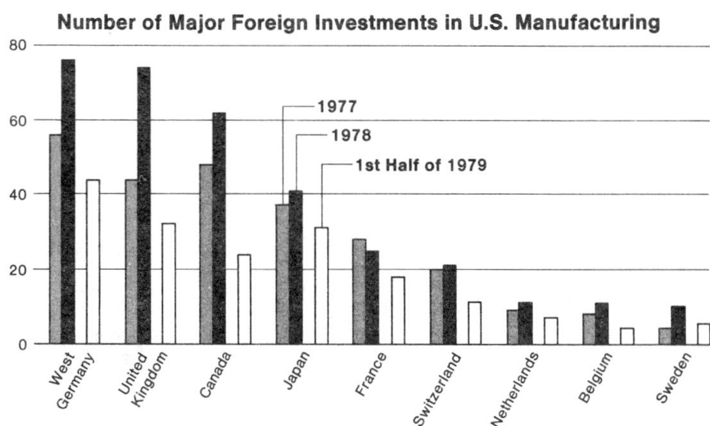

FIGURE 13–14 Multiple bar chart.

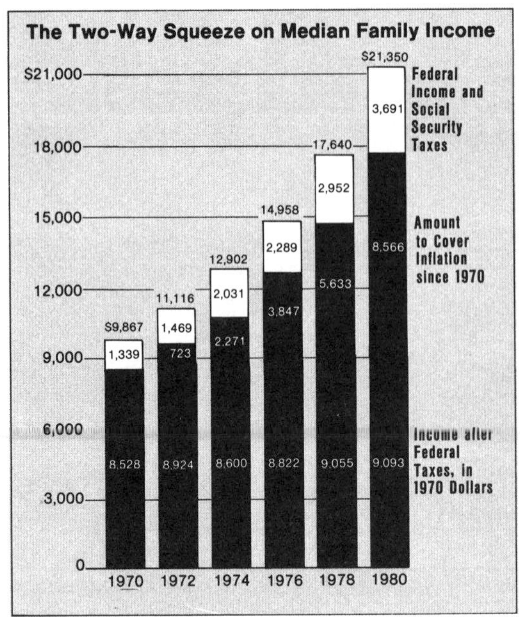

FIGURE 13–15 Component bar chart.

point. Therefore, for more than three or four series, use the multiple line graph.

The *component bar chart* shows wholes and the component parts of wholes. Figure 13–15 illustrates such an approach.

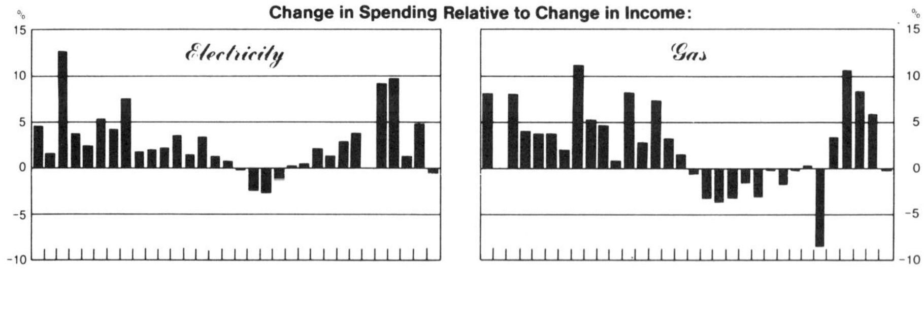

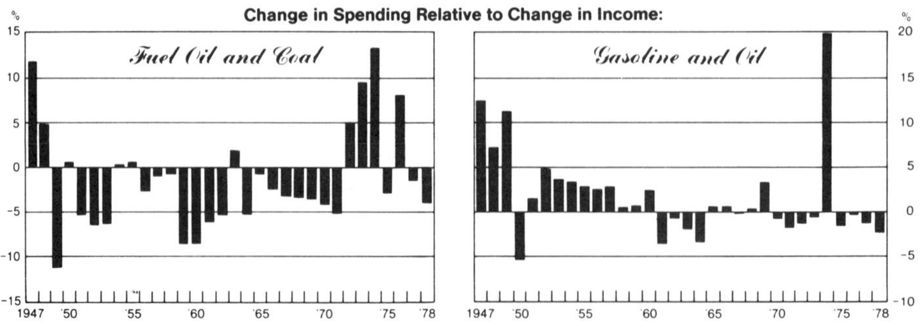

FIGURE 13–16 Two-directional bar chart.

The *two-directional bar chart*—either vertical or horizontal—provides an excellent means for showing percentage changes. Such charts often show the changes in ascending or descending order. Figure 13–16 provides an example.

Pie charts Pie charts show the relative sizes of parts in a whole. However, do not use a series of different-sized circles to try to show different totals. The average viewer cannot grasp changes in areas or volumes well. To construct a pie chart, first determine a percentage distribution for the series. Then arrange the percents in order of size from largest to smallest in clockwise order beginning at the twelve o'clock position. Supply stores usually have paper with a circle divided into 100 equal parts. However, a compass and protractor also will establish the circle and the parts of it. To calculate the degrees to assign to each wedge, multiply the percent represented by that wedge by 360°. Figure 13–17 illustrates four coin-shaped pie charts.

Pictographs Actually a special type of bar chart, the pictograph adds drama to a presentation by using figures to constitute the bars. Keep the figures all the

Global Foreign Investment in Manufacturing
(Number of Investments Announced in 1977, 1978 & First Quarter of 1979)

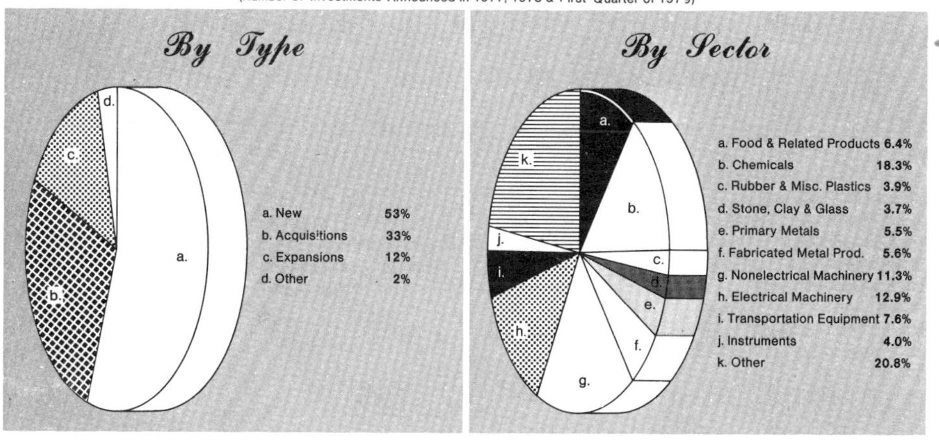

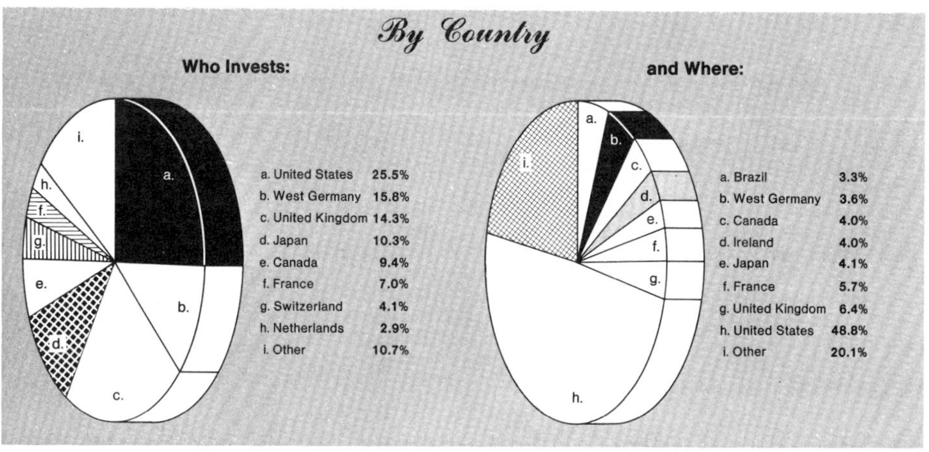

FIGURE 13–17 Pie charts.

same size, but combine them to show a change in only one direction. Figure 13-18 shows a simple pictograph.

Maps A map can present information classified by geographical regions. With the mapping technique, choose the designations of such things as population density carefully. Also be sure to include a clear and complete legend to explain the information. Figure 13-19 shows two informational maps.

NONVERBAL MESSAGES THAT ACCOMPANY ORAL MESSAGES

Virtually all the body language described in Chapter 5 may accompany oral messages. In addition, many of the nonverbal messages that may accompany written messages (for example, charts and graphs) may also accompany oral presentations. This section covers the construction of a few messages for special use in the oral communication channels: (1) transparencies; (2) posters and flip charts; (3) videotapes and movies; (4) audiotapes; and (5) slides, films, and photographs.

Transparencies

Transparencies (sheets of clear plastic material) contain information for projection on a screen behind the speaker. Suggestions for their development and use include:

- Use large type or printing on transparencies.
- Do not try to put too much on a single transparency.

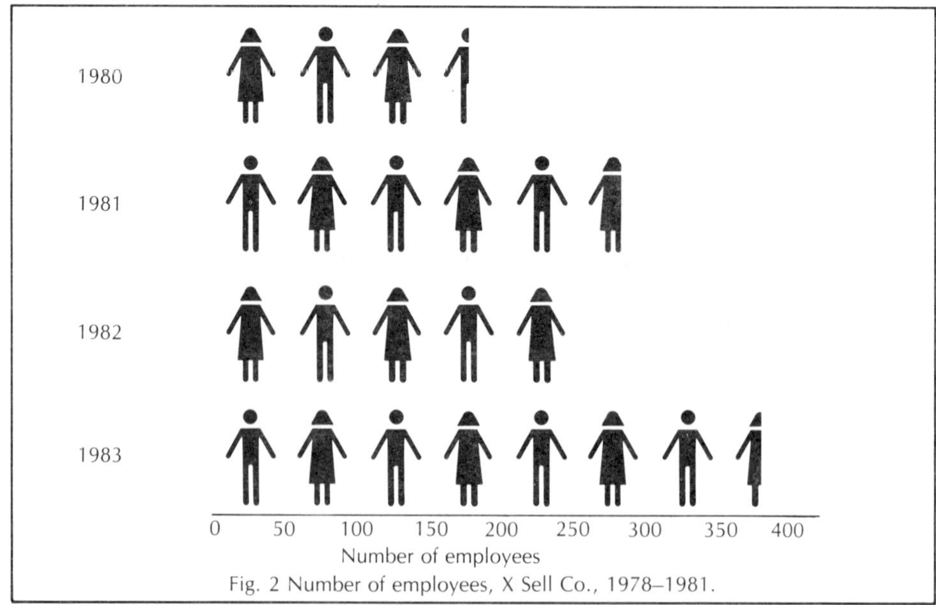

FIGURE 13-18 Pictograph.

Executive Summary

Heading Degree-Days

Heating Degree-Days Accumulated from July 1 through April 27

Departure from last year

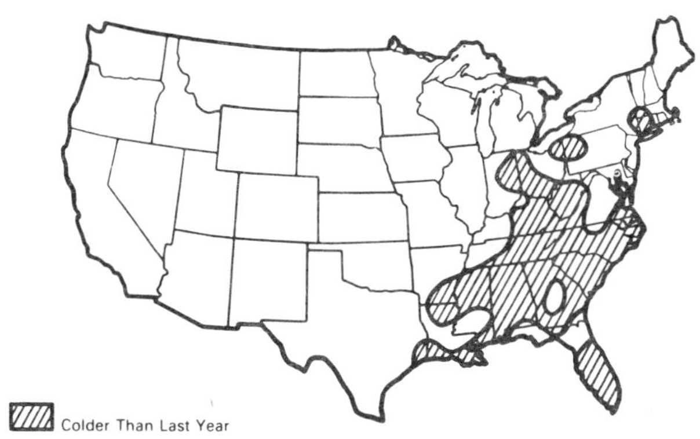

Departure from Normal

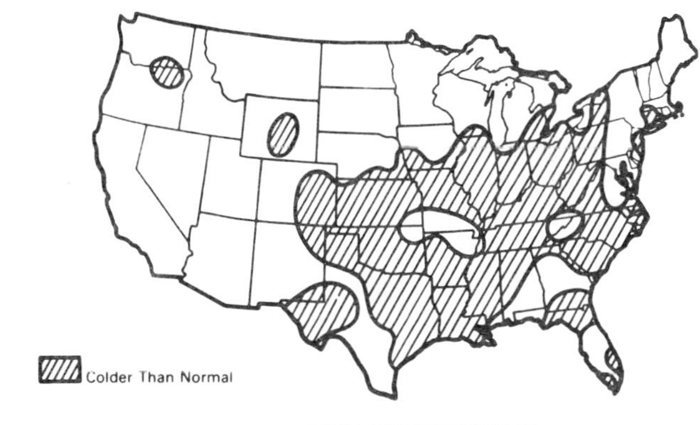

Source: • Department of Commerce – NOAA.

FIGURE 13-19 Maps.

- Use transparencies primarily for well-constructed pictures, sketches, drawings, cartoons, charts, graphs, tables, and other nonverbal messages. Use them also for outlines limited to a few words.
- Bind transparencies if possible.
- Number the transparencies in the order of presentation. Note in the outline of the speech the places for showing the numbered transparencies.
- Do not try to show too many transparencies during a given session.
- Leave a transparency on the overhead projector long enough for the viewers to study it and for the notetakers to outline the major points contained in it.
- Use the transparencies as you practice the presentation. If someone else will change the transparencies for you, practice with that person.

- Whenever possible, practice in the actual room of the presentation.
- On the day of the presentation, set up and test the equipment before beginning the presentation. Place the screen so that the audience can see it.
- Whether you or someone else works the overhead projector, always face the audience. To point to things on the transparencies, use a pointer.
- To write on a transparency during a presentation, operate the overhead projector yourself. However, consider the advantages of preparing overlay transparencies that perform the same function as writing while in the presence of others.
- When the showing requires dimmed lights, have someone control the light switch unobtrusively; still maintain visual contact.

Above all, make the transparency presentation a natural, integrated part of the whole. In fact, if the shuffle of the transparencies overwhelms the oral elements of the presentation, omit them entirely.

Posters and Flip Charts

Suggestions for using posters and flip charts include:

- Make the messages large enough to be observed by everyone in the room.
- Do not crowd the information.
- Use primarily for well-constructed nonverbal messages, not for predominantly verbal ones. Engage a professional artist if necessary.
- Select appropriate paper or card stock for the presentations.
- Organize in the order of display.
- Avoid showing too many in a given session.
- Show each long enough to allow the viewers to study it and take notes from it. Then remove it from view.
- Use posters and charts in practice sessions. Include any other people who might aid in the presentation in at least one such session.
- Whenever possible, practice in the room of the presentation.
- Set up and test the posters and charts just before beginning the presentation. Make sure the audience can see the posters and charts and the information on them.
- Always face the audience without blocking the view of the materials. To point to things, use a pointer.

Just as for transparencies, make posters and flip charts an integral part of the oral presentation. Take care not to use them as crutches for avoiding oral and nonverbal contact with the audience.

You may also use posters and flip charts independently of oral presentations. When placing posters and flip charts on bulletin boards, easels, or walls, do not use too many, place them at eye level, and change them regularly. Such presentations soon make no more direct impact upon the receiver than the draperies.

Videotapes and Movies

Videotape and moving-picture film capture activity for presentation with or independent of a speech. These general suggestions will help in their preparation:

- Use good equipment. Engage a professional photographer if possible. Attend to all of the technical details associated with lighting, distance, focusing, etc.
- Feature the kinds of activities that lend themselves to the visual/aural process.
- Have the people or things being photographed do most of the moving. Move the camera between shots to avoid jerking the camera from one subject to another.
- If you do include a panorama, move the camera steadily and slowly and only on distant subjects. Keep the subject centered.
- Attend to the background. Remove distractions.
- Vary the distances from the camera to the subject when possible. Use some close-ups along with distance shots. Use the zoom-lens technique when available.
- Pay as much attention to the sound as to the picture.
- Make natural presentation a primary goal. When possible, shoot some candid scenes along with the necessary well-rehearsed ones.
- Edit tape or film to remove unnecessary segments and to create a unified whole.
- When using tapes and films produced by others, view and analyze them before showing them to your audience.
- Show videotape or film along with, not instead of, an oral presentation. Discuss the material before, after, and even during its showing (often while stopping the projector and turning up the lights).
- Practice the oral presentation at least once with the media presentation itself—preferably in the room of the presentation.
- Be sure that everyone in the audience can see and hear well.

(514 words)

Take and score Self-Test 27 over posters, flip charts, videotapes, and movies on page 386.

Audiotapes

Audiotapes create fine reinforcement to oral presentations. These hints suggest how to use them.

- Use good equipment and tape. Attend to all of the technical details.
- Choose good voices.
- Feature the kinds of activities that fit the aural mode particularly well. Add music, sound effects, and other such messages.
- Make natural presentations. Capture some candid situations along with the necessary well-rehearsed scenes.
- Introduce variety into the presentation by using many different voices,

different distances, different speeds, and built-in interaction with the audience.

- Edit tape to remove unnecessary segments and to create a unified whole.
- When using tapes produced by others, listen to and analyze them before playing them for an audience.
- Play audiotapes along with, not instead of, oral presentations. Discuss material before, after, and even during its playing.
- Practice the oral presentation at least once with the media presentation itself—preferably in the room of the presentation.
- Make sure that everyone in the audience can hear well.

Slides, Film Strips, and Photographs

Slides, film strips, and photographs make good companions for oral presentations. Suggestions for producing and using them:

- Use good equipment; engage a professional photographer if possible. Attend to all of the technical details associated with the process of photography.
- Spotlight the kinds of activity that belong to the still-shot category. Establish a sense of activity even in still shots.
- Choose subjects carefully.
- Vary the shots in terms of distances, angle, etc.
- Add an audiotape if possible.
- Seek a natural presentation. Shoot some candid scenes along with the necessary well-staged scenes.
- Edit slide, film strip, or photograph presentations in order to remove unnecessary scenes and to create a unified whole.
- Number the slides or photographs in the order of presentation.
- When using slides, film strips, or photographs produced by others, view and analyze them before showing them to your audience.
- Show slides, film strips, or photographs along with, not instead of, an oral presentation. Discuss the material before, after, and even during its showing.
- Practice the oral presentation at least once with the media presentation itself—preferably in the room of the presentation.
- Make sure that everyone in the audience can see well.

This review of tables, graphs, charts, and other channels for nonverbal messages supplements the preceding chapters on writing as well as the next chapter on oral messages. Chapter 14 concentrates upon oral presentations at all four of the communication levels for human transactions.

SUMMARY

This chapter concentrates on the preparation of tables, illustrations, and other nonverbal messages that accompany written and oral presentations.

Tables (rows and columns) present data more accurately than graphs. Repository tables store descriptive information in a form available for general use. They usually contain primary data. Analytical tables result from analysis performed upon raw or organized data. Such analysis may involve primary or secondary data. The traditional table has most of these parts: number, title, subtitle, headnote, stubhead, stub, boxheadings, fields, source note, and footnotes.

Illustrations report the same kinds of data included in tables. However, they do so more pictorially and less accurately. This chapter covers graphs, charts, and other illustrations. Careful attention to features will result in good illustrations. For example, give illustrations numbers and titles, use appropriate scales and legends, apply the rules of the graphic grid when appropriate, and observe other elements of style. Make illustrations clear, concise, complete, accurate, and attractive.

Some of the most-used illustrations include arithmetic line graphs, bar charts, pie charts, pictographs, and maps. Both line graphs and bar charts include four basic types: simple, multiple, component, and two-directional. The frequency polygon and histogram represent special cases of the simple line graph and the simple bar chart. A pictograph uses representational figures to form the bars in a bar chart. Maps present many types of statistical data for geographical regions.

Tables, graphs, charts, maps, and other such illustrations may accompany both written and oral messages. However, some presentations particular to oral messages include transparencies; posters and flip charts; videotapes and movies; audiotapes; and slides, films, and photographs. Prepare and present all of these studio and visual aids carefully to meet the requirements for good communication.

EXERCISES

1. This table could be made to look and read better in another form. A title of some sort would also make it better. Put the table into another form and give it a title.

PRODUCT	GROSS SALES (In Thousands)							
	1974	1975	1976	1977	1978	1979	1980	1981
Hair Dryers	$200	$220	$180	$250	$255	$260	$240	$175
Heating Pads	$185	$190	$195	$190	$190	$185	$180	$180
Can Openers	$105	$110	$110	$115	$120	$125	$120	$100

2. You are writing a report for your boss at Feather Corporation. You have gathered some data that you want to put into table or graph form. Put the data into the form that you think is appropriate. Label the table or graph with a number and a title.
   a. In 1970 the annual turnover rate among upper and middle managers at Feather Corporation was 15 percent. It was 22 percent in 1971, 23 percent in 1972, 28 percent in 1973, 27 percent in 1974, 36 percent in 1975, 41 percent in 1976, 31 percent in 1977, 30 percent in 1978, and 31 percent in 1979.
   b. The turnover rate among line supervisors at Feather Corporation was 18 percent in 1970, 25 percent in 1971, 29 percent in 1972, 28 percent in 1973, 44 percent in 1974, 59 percent in 1975, 57 percent in 1976, 41 percent in 1977, 37 percent in 1978, and 36 percent in 1979.
   c. The turnover rate among staff professionals at Feather Corporation was 22 percent in 1970, 24 percent in 1971, 28 percent in 1972, 28 percent in 1973, 37 percent in 1974, 38 percent in 1975, 61 percent in 1976, 59 percent in 1977, 32 percent in 1978, and 33 percent in 1979.
   d. The turnover rate among clerical personnel at Feather Corporation was 25 percent in 1970, 29 percent in 1971, 27 percent in 1972, 35 percent in 1973, 44 percent in 1974, 45 percent in 1975, 72 percent in 1976, 71 percent in 1977, 64 percent in 1978, and 47 percent in 1979.
3. Write a short (two- or three-minute) statement about the four types of line graphs. Pretend that you will give this lecture at your company's workshop on nonverbal communication. Meet with your group. You and every other group member deliver the statements orally. Answer these questions immediately after each of the statements.
   a. Did the speaker speak at an appropriate pitch, rate, and volume? Why?
   b. Did the speaker use body movements that added to or detracted from her or his speech?
   c. Was the speaker's facial expression appropriate?
   d. In general, what nonverbal messages supported what the speaker said? What nonverbal messages contradicted what the speaker said?
   e. What did the speaker do well? What could be improved?
4. *[This is a dictation exercise.]* Because most of your colleagues at work use transparencies during their speeches, you have been asked to write a one-page memorandum on the use of transparencies. Your colleagues are particularly interested in practical suggestions. Prepare an outline of the memorandum. Now meet with your group. You and every other group member dictate the memorandum from the outline. Discuss these questions after each performance.
   a. Did the speaker dictate clearly?
   b. Did the speaker dictate at an appropriate pitch, rate, and volume?
   c. Was the speaker able to dictate a complete, understandable memorandum from her or his outline?
   d. Did the speaker give the transcriber adequate instructions?
   e. In general, what did the speaker do well? What needs more practice?
5. Given these sales data for CDE Company and three of its eight territories:

	CDE Company	Southeast	South Central	Northwest
1976	$ 995,600	387,100	10,400	135,200
1977	1,033,500	385,400	12,900	134,800
1978	998,700	388,200	13,100	136,100
1979	1,122,100	391,600	20,200	139,200
1980	1,118,500	390,800	24,500	138,900

a. Plot all four series on arithmetic graph paper.
b. Interpret both charts.

6. Given this frequency distribution:

Hourly Wages	No. of Workers
$5.00 but under $5.50	38
5.50 but under 6.00	78
6.00 but under 6.50	114
6.50 but under 7.00	189
7.00 but under 7.50	62
7.50 but under 8.00	7

a. Construct a frequency polygon.
b. Construct a histogram.
c. Interpret and contrast the meanings of the charts.

7. Construct a pie chart from these data:

	Sales ($000)
Department A	38
Department B	182
Department C	12
Department D	59
Department E	203

8. Given this distribution of departmental sales for three years (in thousands of dollars):

	Dept. A	Dept. B	Dept. C	Dept. D	Dept. E
1979	38	182	12	59	203
1980	50	180	22	54	210
1981	47	168	25	62	228

Construct a single graph containing a component bar chart for departmental sales for each of the three years.

9. For the data in Exercise No. 8, construct a component line chart.
10. Meet with your group. Develop, rehearse, and tape-record or videotape a ten-minute presentation on some aspect of tabular and graphic communication. Play each group's production for the class. Evaluate each production.
11. Develop a poster or a series of flip charts to illustrate the concepts associated with the frequency distribution and its associated graphics. Display them for the evaluation of the class.
12. Develop a series of transparencies to illustrate the construction of a semi-logarithmic chart. Prepare a five-minute oral presentation to accompany the transparencies. Make the presentation to the class. Evaluate.
13. Interview a photography professor about some hints for the nonprofessional

photographer. Prepare an interview guide ahead of time. Write a two-page report of the interview.

14. Use your dictionary and thesaurus to create meanings for these words. Use the words when you think, write, and speak so that you feel comfortable using them.

a. Allude	f. Deter	k. Prowess
b. Behest	g. Discern	l. Reticent
c. Codify	h. Inertia	m. Spatial
d. Component	i. Logarithm	n. Temporal
e. Cumulative	j. Nebulous	

15. Take and score Self-Test 28 over Chapter 13.

SELF-TEST 27
Excerpts about Posters, Flip Charts, Videotapes, and Movies

A. Recall (33 points each). For each multiple-choice question, select the most accurate answer.
   1. Posters and flip charts should *not:*
      a. Be organized in the order that you will display them
      b. Contain a great deal of detailed information
      c. Be used primarily for well-constructed nonverbal messages
      d. Contain messages large enough to be viewed and read by everyone in the room
      e. Be used during a practice run of the speech
   2. Which of these message situations least warrants the use of the videotape or moving-picture medium?
      a. Your manager wants to read her annual state-of-the-company speech to your company's 48 centralized employees.
      b. You want to show potential employees the manufacturing operations at your six foreign plants.
      c. You wish to teach all of your company's mechanics how to overhaul your new fleet of delivery trucks. Your company employs over 600 mechanics at a dozen plants across the nation.
      d. This is your company's 25th anniversary. You want to relate your company's most notable accomplishments to your 25,000 employees.
      e. Because your company is concerned about air pollution, you, a communication specialist, have been asked to try to convince your company's employees to ride the bus, join a car-pool, walk, or ride a bicycle to work. You know that most of your employees do not like to read memoranda or listen to speeches.

B. Inference (34 points). Indicate whether this statement is true or false.
   1. A presentation or speech is always made more interesting with the use of flip charts, posters, or film.

SOLUTION

A. Recall (33 points each)
   1. b 2. a

B. Inference (34 points)
   1. False

SELF-TEST 28
Chapter 13

A. Recall (25 points each). For each multiple-choice question, select the most accurate answer.

1. If you want to feature the sweep and flow of data, you should use a:
   a. Pictograph
   b. Bar chart
   c. Arithmetic scale
   d. Ratio scale
   e. Line chart
2. Which one of these statements is true?
   a. Charts are more accurate than tables.
   b. Governmental agencies supply more analytical tables than repository tables.
   c. Rows are horizontal arrangements of data.
   d. When a table will not fit on the page on which it is introduced, leave the rest of that page blank and start at the top of the next page.
   e. A footnote refers to all items in the body of a table.
3. Which one of these statements is true?
   a. Given this series of data for the Y-axis, 18; 7; 200; 8,983; 46; 299, a chart would require a break in the axis.
   b. The Y-axis plots for a frequency polygon appear at the lower limits of the classes.
   c. The frequency polygon is a bar chart.
   d. The Y-axis of the arithmetic graph must begin with zero.
   e. A major advantage of the overhead projector is that the speaker may face the audience while using it.

B. Inference (25 points). Indicate whether this statement is true or false.

1. Nonpersonal nonverbal communication is less important to business than is personal nonverbal communication.

SOLUTION

A. Recall (25 points each)

1. e
2. c
3. e

B. Inference (25 points)

1. False

STUDENT'S OBJECTIVES:

1 To extend and reinforce the suggestions for good written communication to oral communication

2 To apply communication principles to the interpersonal level, including conversations and dialogues, interviews, and small-group exchanges

3 To apply communication principles to the mediated level, including the telephone, private intercommunication system, two-way radio, closed circuit television, and dictating equipment

14

SENDING THROUGH ORAL CHANNELS

4 To apply communication principles to the person-to-group level, including informative, persuasive, ritual-function, and entertaining speeches

5 To apply communication principles to the mass level, including radio, television, and film

GUIDELINES FOR EFFECTIVE SPEAKING

- ☐ *Define purposes, participants, and environment for speaking and listening*
- ☐ *Identify speaking channel*
- ☐ *Control interference with speaking and listening*
- ☐ *Select, form, and transmit message*
- ☐ *Use feedback from and to listener*
- ☐ *Evaluate at each stage and at end of transaction*

Because both the written and oral communication channels involve words, many of the suggestions in the preceding chapters on writing also apply to speaking. Extend and reinforce those suggestions while reviewing the different kinds of speaking at the interpersonal, mediated, person-to-group, and mass levels of communication.

SPEAKING AT THE INTERPERSONAL LEVEL

The interpersonal channels include (1) conversations and dialogues, (2) interviews, and (3) small groups.

Conversations and Dialogues

A great deal of communication occurs through conversations. The relatively unstructured, informal, and nonpurposive on-the-job conversation may deal with such topics as making an appointment, basic exchanges about the health and well-being of family members, the latest company gossip, and current national and international news. People cannot completely separate their personal lives from their working lives. To the extent that simple conversation helps them maintain good human relations and reduce their personal problems, it improves their performance. A *dialogue* (a conversation with a purpose) takes place in a relatively structured setting. It has distinct, significant, and usually preannounced decision-making purposes. Two or three people in a business setting can open a dialogue with such purposes as deciding on the details of a contract bid, dividing the work on a project, discussing an annual performance review, and deciding whether to hire or to dismiss someone.

As a participant in a simple conversation or dialogue, bring all of the effective communication guidelines to bear. Take advantage of the immediacy of the feedback by raising questions to test and clarify your perceptions. Provide good feedback. Listen actively, and observe nonverbal cues keenly.

Interviews

As a special type of dialogue, the interview involves such preset goals as:

- Evaluating for promotion
- Appraising an applicant for a job

- Disseminating information to the media
- Counseling for careers, personal problems, etc.

Types

The interview involves at least some structure. Types of interviews include the directive, nondirective, stress, and depth.

Directive The directive interview puts the interviewer in relative command of the transaction. He or she sets the meeting time, determines the objectives, decides how to proceed, asks the questions, and controls the entire process. The interviewee plays the role prescribed by the interviewer. However, the interviewee still must contribute to the success of the interview.

Nondirective The nondirective interview puts both parties into shared roles. Together they set the meeting time, determine the objectives, decide how to proceed, and take turns in leading the transaction.

Stress The stress interview, a special type of directive interview, determines how well the interviewee can handle emotion-laden and leading questions. An example of the type of question is, "When was the last time you stole anything from the company for which you were working?" The stress interview requires a highly qualified interviewer.

Depth As the name implies, the depth interview involves an assertive, directive probe into a topic. It also requires a skilled interviewer who can ask an open question, let the interviewee respond in free fashion, ask specific questions about the points introduced by the interviewee, and continue until the interviewee gets to the bottom of the issues. The approach applies particularly well to motivational research.

Roles

The roles of interviewer, interviewee, and shared-responsibility interviewer/interviewee have important characteristics and responsibilities.

Interviewer As the interviewer, prepare for the interview by defining purposes, participants, channel, interference, messages, feedback, and evaluation. Make the interviewee comfortable. Discuss purposes. Find a natural, common ground to open the discussion.

Use a prestructured list of questions (a patterned interview) or an unpatterned approach to the questioning. Encode questions to meet the educational level of the interviewee. Also avoid emotional symbols—unless conducting a stress interview. Use closed or open questions, all of them brief and clear. If taking notes, avoid making a flourish of it. Proceed discreetly, and do not try to write down every word.

Ask permission before using a tape recorder. Know how to use the equipment and have it in working order before meeting with the interviewee.

To interview an authority on some subject, send a list of questions ahead of time. Avoid varying too much from the original list, particularly to introduce a controversial or demanding topic.

Interviewee As an interviewee, prepare for the transaction just as fully as does the interviewer. Define your purposes and try to define the interviewer's. Learn about the interviewer.

Picture the interview. Think not only about the physical conditions, but about what the interviewer will ask and how you will answer. Practice answers aloud. However, maintain a natural and adaptable speaking style.

Prepare the questions *you* would like to ask the interviewer. Memorize them to avoid the negative appearance created by having to read them. Anticipate the kinds of interference that may occur, and plan how to overcome them. Dress appropriately. Arrive on time. Leave the control to the interviewer. However, contribute to making the interview a success.

Interviewer/interviewee The nondirective interview imposes joint responsibilities. To make such a joint venture successful, in addition to applying the preceding suggestions, exercise turn-taking fairly. Do not dominate. On the other hand, do not allow the other participant to dominate either. Case Study 3 illustrates the application of the communication guidelines to an interview.

Case Study 3: Appraisal and Promotion Interview

You work as a collection correspondent for a large firm. You have been in the position for nearly three years. Your job involves telephoning people to ask them to send payments.

The manager of the collection department has scheduled your annual performance-appraisal interview for next week. You already have completed the self-appraisal form and have met with the collection supervisor about it. You believe the interview went well.

The position of collection supervisor will open within the next few months. You plan to apply for it and thus want the appraisal interview with the manager to go particularly well.

You apply the guidelines:

1. You establish purposes.
   - **a.** To receive a higher composite appraisal rating than last year.
   - **b.** To receive the highest step raise possible.
   - **c.** To have the manager record your desire to become a supervisor and eventually to go into management.
   - **d.** To learn exactly how to activate your application for the supervisory position.
2. You identify the manager's purposes.
   - **a.** To evaluate your performance correctly.
   - **b.** To recommend the highest step raise only to the highest performer.

c. To identify a person who is qualified and motivated to move into supervision.

3. You define yourself in this context.
   a. Strengths.
      (1) Age.
      (2) Performance record.
      (3) Communication ability.
      (4) Relations with manager, supervisor, and all but one other correspondent in the area.
      (5) Motivation.
      (6) Attendance record.
      (7) Health.
   b. Weaknesses.
      (1) Sometimes overbearing and zealous in arguing beliefs.
      (2) Occasional temper flare-up.
      (3) One correspondent with obviously negative feelings.
      (4) Lack of experience as a supervisor.
4. You define the manager in this context.
   a. Strengths.
      (1) Skillful interviewer; allows time for input from interviewee.
      (2) Interested in finding the best people for jobs.
      (3) Professional attitude.
      (4) Not hesitant to recommend pay increases when deserved.
   b. Weaknesses.
      (1) Sometimes difficult to "read" for clues to feelings about employees.
      (2) Wary of taking the risk of promoting an untested employee.
5. You analyze the interview channel for its weaknesses and strengths.
6. You anticipate interference with the message and your purposes, and plan how to overcome it.
7. You plan and practice how you will answer anticipated questions and what you want to volunteer.
   a. You decide that the manager probably will ask some probing questions related to your professed interest in a promotion. You think about how you will answer in a manner that will be self-enhancing instead of self-effacing or bulldozing. Some of the questions and types of proposed answers are:
      (1) "How do you expect to overcome your lack of experience?" You decide to suggest that (a) you continually think, read, and take courses on supervision, (b) you know that the firm's training program provides excellent instruction, and (c) you have had organizational experiences that show your supervisory ability.
      (2) "How do you propose to overcome conflicts such as the one you already have with the correspondent in your area?" You decide to say that you will attempt to identify the source of the conflict, approach it directly, and work positively to overcome it.
      (3) "I've noticed that you lose your temper—even with a customer—once in a while. What do you propose to do to overcome that

problem?" You decide not to deny that the problem exists, but to state that you already have improved significantly (no flare-up at work in at least two months). You will also state that you are confident that you can control it, because you have identified practical and healthful alternatives to the outbursts.

8. Before and during the interview, you choose appropriate nonverbal messages.
   a. Appropriate dress and grooming.
   b. Timely arrival at the manager's office.
   c. A firm handshake.
   d. Good posture that shows confidence.
   e. Eye contact and genuinely pleasant, controlled variations that express dynamism, but not nervousness.
   f. Careful observation of nonverbal cues for appropriate turntaking.
   g. Materials in a clean folder and in proper order on your lap or on the desk.
9. During the interview, you select and transmit appropriate verbal messages in response to the manager's messages.
10. You use feedback opportunities fully.
11. You interject self-enhancing questions and comments not introduced by the interviewer.
12. You evaluate.
   a. You evaluate continually during the interview and adjust appropriately.
   b. You conduct a thorough evaluation at the end of the interview.
      (1) Decide whether you need a follow-up on any part of the interview.
      (2) Decide whether you were successful in attaining your objectives.
      (3) Decide where you might have improved your performance.
      (4) Decide what you will do differently in the next interview or dialogue.

Small Group

Small-group communication has characteristics from several levels. However, the face-to-face, immediate-feedback features of small-group transactions align them most closely with the interpersonal level. (Review defining elements, methods, and roles.)

Defining Elements

Defining elements include size, location, time, topic, purpose, formality, designation, and cohesion.

Size forms an important feature of small groups. Conversations, dialogues, and interviews include no more than three people. Small groups include four to ten people, with five to seven people probably representing the ideal size. When a large group wants the advantages of small-group discussion, it breaks into small groups. Each then summarizes its work and reports in person-to-group fashion to the reconvened larger group.

The effective small group meets in a small, comfortable, and attractive room convenient to the participants. A round table contributes to the work. Thus, *location* has an impact on the communication. Set a meeting *time* and honor it. Collectively keep the meeting moving so that the group does not waste time—one of the most serious complaints about group meetings.

Topics for small-group deliberations parallel those for conversations, dialogues, and interviews. The small group just changes the scenario by including more people. The small-group meeting exists for some well-defined *purpose*. The purpose usually relates to problem-solving and decision-making circumstances.

The *formal,* structured meeting may take on some of the characteristics of the person-to-group channel. It usually involves a previously designated chairperson who sets the meeting time, prepares an agenda, appoints a recorder, presides, and may deliver a monologue at the beginning of the meeting. Once the discussion begins, however, even the formal chairperson usually acts only as a facilitator.

The *informal,* unstructured small-group session begins with no previously named chairperson or agenda. Instead, the recorder and leader emerge from the group—by consensus, election, or volunteerism. If the group sets a second meeting, however, the members usually designate someone to coordinate the activities for the next time. That person may have the title of chairperson, chair, coordinator, facilitator, or convener.

Groups and their meetings go by many different *designations*. The designations include task force, committee, team, work group, council, staff meeting, departmental meeting, and production meeting. The *task force* serves well because it brings together a small group of specialists representing all of the major areas involved in addressing the issue. For example, a marketing strategy group could include specialists from marketing, advertising, research, finance, and production.

The good group unifies into a *cohesive* whole. The people work as one in their concentrated efforts toward attaining the established goal. Working in whatever capacity, the members of a group should individually and collectively apply the principles and guidelines for good communication. They should establish not only the collective purpose for the group, but specific purposes for each member.

Methods

Methods for conducting group meetings include problem-solving, educating, brainstorming, and role-playing.

Problem-solving Probably the most common pattern for business groups to follow, the problem-solving method introduces a scientific approach to accomplish the objectives. When a group uses this method, it follows eight steps:

1. *Organize* by deciding on a plan of action. Choose a strong leader. Also choose a recorder if desired. Establish the structure and rules of conduct.

2. *State the problem* precisely. Write it on paper. *State the short-term objectives* for the first meeting. Also *state long-term objectives* if the solution requires a series of meetings.
3. *Analyze the problem* by considering every factor associated with it. Deal with the who, what, when, where, how, and why. Break the problem into its elemental parts. Think of every possible symptom, cause, effect, force, and variable. Study their relationships to the problem.

When the group has identified all possible factors, arrange them in the order of importance to the discussion. The brainstorming process works well for this part of the problem-solving sequence.

4. *Establish criteria* for evaluation. Do so early in the process. This step fits well into the problem-defining, purpose-setting stage. Examples of problem-solving criteria include:

   The solution will yield at least $2,000 more sales than at present.

   The solution will stop the production of excessive numbers of defectives.
5. *Propose possible solutions* to the problem. Assess the effectiveness of each. Again, the brainstorming process can facilitate this step.
6. *Choose the best solution* by applying the criteria to each suggested solution.
7. *Communicate the solution* to the authorizing person, or put it into effect if you have authority to do so.
8. *Evaluate* the problem-solving discussion. Such evaluation often must await some delayed application of the suggested solution. However, the group should establish a follow-up procedure to determine whether the solution met the criteria.

Educating Some small-group meetings occur simply to share information or to educate the members. For such situations, the leader states or reads a new policy statement or similar message (person-to-group activity). Then he or she opens the floor to discussion (interpersonal activity). The leader and the members of the group may raise points for clarification, ask questions, give examples of applications, and tell what the message means to them.

Brainstorming As introduced in the data-gathering section of Chapter 11, brainstorming provides an important group device for generating ideas. As suggested in the coverage of the problem-solving method, it also serves other purposes.

The process of brainstorming involves these steps:

1. Organize. Announce the ground rules and perhaps designate people to act as coordinator and recorder. The coordinator may use the chalkboard as the recorder uses pencil and paper. If everyone knows the rules for brainstorming, the leadership may emerge from the group—and may rotate among several participants during a session. The ground rules include:

   a. The group will not evaluate the contributions or reach a decision until the group has exercised the creative process fully. Some groups have an additional session before evaluating and deciding which ideas to use.
   b. Each group member should feel free and responsible to take an active part.
   c. No member may pressure any other member.
   d. No member may evaluate or criticize the contributions of another.
2. Define the task and establish the objective. The commonly felt need initiates the chain of expressions. For example, suppose a group holds a brainstorming session to identify the possible causes of shipping delays. The problem then becomes: What causes shipping delays? The objectives include naming every possible cause and then, afterwards, evaluating and organizing the suggestions into a list in order of importance as possible causes.
3. State the ideas as quickly as possible and record them on a chalkboard and/or paper. As soon as a member states one idea, another member immediately states another. The free-wheeling associations go forward rapidly. Role-playing the problem sometimes helps stimulate thinking. (The next section reviews role-playing.)
4. Organize the ideas. Reject duplications. Combine similar ideas under a single heading.
5. Arrange the ideas in the order of importance for resolving the original task or issue.
6. Act upon the listing or give the listing to the person authorizing the group to develop it.

Role-playing Small groups sometimes use role-playing. Role-playing provides an exciting way to involve people in active communication transactions and to solve problems in groups. David Potter and Martin P. Andersen state that in role-playing, "people act out problems containing human conflicts and then analyze their actions and reactions with the help of the other role-players and observers."[1] Also according to Potter and Andersen, role-playing usually includes:

1. Selecting a problem that approaches reality as closely as possible—one that is steeped in meaning for the individuals portraying the roles or witnessing the unfolding of the action. Generally, the situation or plot is constructed in barest outline and is simply and clearly stated.
2. Structuring a problem only to the point where the problem is clear and the players have a mental picture of the roles that they are to portray. Usually no lines are written or memorized.
3. Choosing the role-players from within the group.
4. Instructing and, on occasion, "warming up" the players.
5. Instructing the observers.
6. Role-playing the problem situation; cutting or stopping the role-playing when the issues of the problem have been delineated.
7. Analyzing the role-playing in order to explore further the insights revealed and in order to put the behavior modifications suggested into practice.[2]

Roles

Group members take three basic roles: participant, leader, and recorder.

Participant Participants determine the success of the process. Not only do they bring their knowledge, arts, and skills to bear, but they also assume specific roles as they perform in the group. Theoreticians suggest that the behavior of group members may appear in three broad types of roles: task-oriented, process-oriented, and destructive roles.

The *task-oriented roles* concentrate upon the subject matter of the meeting—the job to be done:

- *Seeker of information*—asks for factual data
- *Giver of information*—provides factual data
- *Seeker of opinions*—asks others to express their opinions
- *Giver of opinions*—provides opinions
- *Seeker of ideas*—asks for ideas
- *Giver of ideas*—provides ideas
- *Starter*—starts group activities
- *Coordinator*—clarifies, paraphrases, explains, elaborates, connects, and suggests illustrations for the ideas of the group
- *Expediter*—keeps the group on the subject
- *Analyzer*—applies logic to the subject
- *Summarizer*—periodically summarizes the material to that point

Process-oriented roles concentrate upon the human interactions:

- *Climate maker*—establishes a friendly, supportive atmosphere
- *Harmonizer*—tries to reduce conflict and misunderstanding
- *Gatekeeper*—facilitates interactions by restraining dominant speakers and encouraging hesitant ones
- *Setter of standards*—preserves objectivity, removes emotionalism, listens well, and maintains momentum
- *Leader of games*—interjects humor and other diversions into the work
- *Compromiser*—brings differing viewpoints together
- *Public-relations person*—interacts well with external entities

Destructive roles prove counter-productive:

- *Withdrawer*—retreats from the group activity and acts bored or indifferent
- *Aggressor*—criticizes and blames others
- *Competer*—expresses differing views on every issue—simply for the sake of the attention and the competition
- *Blocker*—uses a wide variety of tactics to block the group from unifying on an issue
- *Limited-idea person*—repeats the same one or two ideas
- *Clown*—disrupts the interactions of the group through clownish activities

- *Monopolizer*—dominates the discussion
- *Side-stepper*—dodges issues by raising unrelated topics, dwelling on minor arguments, and otherwise avoiding responsibility

In conjunction with the roles, some summary suggestions for good participation are:

- Plan for the meeting by applying the guidelines
- Contribute actively to the discussion
- Select and play the appropriate positive roles; eliminate the negative roles
- Cooperate with the leader and other members
- Listen
- Accept new or different ideas
- Do everything possible to make the meeting successful

Leader Just as participants tend to adopt certain roles as they interact with one another, leaders do the same. This section covers three basic types of leadership: authoritarian, democrat, and permissive leader.

The *authoritarian* takes a dictatorial view of the process. The authoritarian distributes a fixed agenda, sets the rules, procedures, tasks, roles, and evaluative criteria and tells people what to do when, where, and how. The authoritarian meeting usually accomplishes more work than either the democratic or permissive meetings do. Therefore, many situations require autocratic leadership. However, when time and other variables allow, avoid the authoritarian approach. It seems to engender discontent, belligerence, dependence, and blind conformity.

The *democrat* takes a shared-participation view of the process. The democrat offers alternatives, but joins with the other group members to set the rules, procedures, tasks, roles, and evaluative criteria. The leader and members together decide which people will do what, when, where, how, and why. Though the democrat may distribute an agenda ahead of time, he or she invites members to contribute items to it and to amend it once the meeting begins. The democratic meeting usually accomplishes less work than the autocratic meeting. However, the democracy tends to yield better creativity, motivation, positiveness, human relations, and cohesiveness than the autocracy does.

The *permissive leader* takes a noninterfering view of the process, serving only to supply information—and then only when asked to do so. The leader does not join with the other group members to set any rules, procedures, tasks, roles, and evaluative criteria. Without the participation of a leader, the members decide which people will do what, when, where, how, and why. The permissive meeting accomplishes the least work of the three types of meetings. In effect, the permissive leader does not lead, and the leaderless group tends to struggle aimlessly. Therefore, use the permissive style only for rare circumstances: (a) when the members of the group function efficiently without any leader, (b) when the situation requires some seemingly directionless exploration, even to find a basis upon which to select a leader, (c) only until the group establishes enough of a structure that an appropriate leader emerges, and (d) when no one can lead.

A composite role for the effective leader includes these activities:

- Create a positive climate for discussion. Tend to both the physical and psychological settings.
- Establish, or lead in establishing, the agenda and the grounds rules.
- Select or coordinate the selection of a recorder.
- Introduce or stimulate the introduction of the members to one another.
- Introduce the subject of the discussion.
- Guide the discussion. Keep the discussion on the subject and keep it moving. Change to brainstorming when the group reaches a stalemate. Introduce role-playing if it will help the discussion.
- Supply appropriate transitions and intermediate summaries.
- Control the meeting. Take charge. Block the destructive members. Observe the rules established for the meeting so long as they contribute to progress. Handle any event that may interfere with the meeting.
- End the discussion efficiently. Conduct voting or consensus-taking. Evaluate the work of the group in line with preestablished criteria. Make a final summary, including the findings of the group, the results of voting, and the evaluation. Conclude with a plan for the next step.

Recorder Someone should record the key points and results of the discussion. The person who makes the record has the title of recorder or secretary. The leader or group may select someone, or someone may volunteer. The person may come from the group or from outside. The good recorder must write quickly and summarize well, because the recorder must think, listen, organize, and write all at the same time. The recorder often prepares reports for dissemination to others and thus needs to write well.

SPEAKING AT THE MEDIATED LEVEL

The most common oral mediated transactions depend on the telephone, the private intercommunication system, the two-way radio, or the closed-circuit television (CCTV) as the mediating instrument. In addition, although dictating messages to a transcriber or a machine does not qualify as a full-fledged one-to-one interaction, it does involve an intermediary. Therefore, dictating appears in this section on the oral mediated level.

Telephone, Intercommunication, Two-Way Radio, and Closed-Circuit Television

Certain techniques improve the use of the telephone, intercommunication system, two-way radio, and closed-circuit television.

Telephone

A telephone conversation involves rapid turn-taking between sender and receiver. Therefore, good listening proves just as important as good speaking.

Sending When placing a telephone call, decide what you want the receiver to do as a result of it. Establish criteria for evaluating how well the receiver meets your objectives.

Learn all you can about the receiver. Decide why the receiver would want to receive the call and provide the desired action. Picture the receiver and the environment. Identify the potential human and external interference, and plan the communication to overcome it. Select the messages carefully. Jot down ideas and make a brief outline from them. Couch messages in language correct for the occasion and the receiver. Leave space in the outline to record information supplied by the receiver. Particularly plan how to indicate the desired action.

To begin transmission, establish a relaxed but alert physical and mental position. Hold the microphone of the telephone handset about one-half inch from your mouth. As soon as anyone answers, identify yourself and ask for the ultimate receiver. When the receiver answers, identify yourself again, exchange pleasantries if appropriate, and move quickly into the topic. Follow the outline, but adapt to changes the receiver introduces.

Use a moderate voice pattern. Adopt a positive and courteous approach. Use all of the devices necessary to introduce appropriate vocal reinforcements such as emphasis, subordination, color, variety, and cordiality. Listen carefully. Block interference. Stimulate and use verbal and nonverbal feedback.

End the conversation appropriately. As the caller, take leave first. Some communicators suggest that "Bye" and "Bye-Bye" do not fit business conversations. However, choose leave-taking words for naturalness and appropriateness. Avoid abruptness, but convey a courteous finality. Evaluate during and after the conversation. Determine whether the receiver's actions meet the original criteria and purposes.

Receiving When answering a business telephone, begin with the firm's name, followed by yours if appropriate. Do not just say, "Hello."

If someone else receives a call and transfers it to you, treat the initial receiver courteously, but switch to the sender immediately. Do not restate the firm's name. If the initial receiver has told you the caller's name, you may answer with something like: "Hello, Mr. Tompkins." However, if you do not know the person well, you may answer with just your name: for example, "Doris Turner."

Use relaxed, moderate, and receptive tones. Avoid the drawn tones that often come from repeating a company name or your name many times a day. Keep the enunciation and attitude fresh.

When transferring calls to others, always explain each step. Do not leave the caller on "hold" too long. Return frequently to explain delays. Offer to have the ultimate receiver return the call if a delay becomes very long. Offer to help the caller yourself.

After identification, begin the conversation with a question to start the transaction. Common phrases include: "May I ask who is calling?" "May I help you?" "How are you?" "What may I do for you?" "How may I help you?" and "How may I be of service?" However, use custom phrases for senders when possible.

Apply the communication guidelines: Define yourself, the caller, purposes, and environments. Use the channel to its fullest; help overcome interference. Let the sender speak fully, but interject appropriate feedback. Use paraphrasing and repetition to assure correct perception. Make responses and actions clear. Use good vocal techniques and courtesy. Write down the things needed for accuracy and storage. Read them back to assure accuracy. Evaluate the ongoing stages of the transaction and adjust to them as necessary.

Allow the caller to close the conversation. Respond in kind to the sender's leave-taking words. Evaluate during and after the closing.

Two-way Radio

The two-way radio requires the same techniques as the telephone. It also requires proper use of a hand microphone. Experiment to learn how far to hold it from your mouth. Also practice using the switch that activates transmission. For AM channels, learn some of the special jargon for the two-way radio. The FM channels use little of it. In both situations, use a natural conversational style even while meeting the customs of other users.

Closed-Circuit Television (CCTV)

The most common use of CCTV involves one-directional transmission of picture and sound to a selected group of people. However, if the system adds the capacity for vocal return by telephone (talkback television) or two-way projection of both visual and vocal messages, it becomes a two-way mediated transaction. With talkback television, the speaker should solicit telephone feedback and respond to it quickly and naturally when it does come. The receiver who uses the telephone for feedback usually just lifts the receiver and talks. Use the telephone; it adds an important dimension to the transaction.

When using a two-way video/audio television channel, look directly at the camera as if looking at the receiver. Speak and move naturally within the allowable space. Take advantage of the full range of nonverbal symbols to improve the interaction.

Techniques for Dictation

Dictating acts as a common link in the chain leading to a written message. Consider roles as both sender and receiver of dictated messages—with emphasis upon the sending act.

Sending

Application of these six communication guidelines adapted for the dictator can improve the transaction:

- Define the intermediate receiver (that is, the word processor); the ultimate receiver; the purposes of *you,* the intermediate receiver, and the ultimate receiver; and the environments for all.
- Understand the characteristics of the channel. When dictating to a live word processor (a transcriber), you have greater opportunity to sense

immediate feedback and make immediate adjustments in the message. When dictating to a machine, you must learn how to use it correctly—how to start, stop, make corrections, and give instructions.

- Understand the interference that can occur between you and the word processor and between you and the ultimate receiver. Try to control both.
- To select and encode the messages, use the principles and procedures described for writing for the specific channel (letter, memorandum, etc.), and for the telephone. Plan ahead. Jot down ideas and organize them into an outline. Think through your message before you begin to speak. Speak clearly. Concentrate on enunciation, pronunciation, a reasonably slow pace, a normal pitch, and sufficient volume. Give clear and complete instructions at the beginning of the session. Supply all necessary data. Make corrections. Eliminate rough drafts. Through the entire sequence, picture the ultimate receiver. When dictating to a live transcriber, speak to her or him as a substitute for the ultimate receiver. When speaking into a microphone or telephone, picture both the transcriber and the ultimate receiver—and adjust to the perceived needs of both.
- With a live word processor, watch for and adjust to immediate feedback. Even solicit it. However, when dictating to a machine, prevent and adjust to delayed feedback. The transcriber has to telephone or ask in person for clarification or correction. Such contacts waste a great deal of time and money.
- Evaluate in terms of the needs of the transcriber, the ultimate receiver, and you.

Receiving

As a transcriber or word processor, take appropriate responsibility for the oral part of the process. When taking notes in the presence of the dictator, keep interruptions to a minimum. Ask for clarification when the natural flow of the composition halts. Listen carefully. Know the language of the firm.

Give subtle nonverbal feedback during the dictation. Make more overt suggestions about the messages if the dictator receives them well. Read segments of your notes to the dictator upon request. Interpret the dictator's nonverbal messages as well as the verbal ones. Adapt to them.

Think of your purposes, those of the dictator, and those of the ultimate receiver. Such thoughts improve decisions during both dictation and transcription.

SPEAKING AT THE PERSON-TO-GROUP LEVEL

The person-to-group speaker takes only a short step from the interpersonal and mediated-level transactions. That step involves dominating the transaction, increasing the length of speaking time, reducing or eliminating turn-taking, speaking to many instead of one, and controlling the process.

Treat a speech (presentation) as any monologue of any length made to any group from any location relative to that group. Therefore, if you fear the concept of "making a speech," just realize that you already have made hundreds of thousands of speeches in your life. You make many of them every time you talk with a group. You have the essential experience. Therefore, to become an effective person-to-group speaker, make some minor adjustments to what you already know how to do.

Classify person-to-group presentations first by content and purpose, then by style of transmission. Then review some suggestions for applying the communication principles and guidelines.

Types of Speeches Classified by Content and Purpose

This book classifies speeches as: (1) informing, (2) persuading, (3) performing ritual functions, and (4) entertaining. Though the titles seem to describe one-directional communication, understand that they intend to describe a spiraling interactive communication.

Informing

Speakers inform when they convey information to groups. They may volunteer the information spontaneously or give it as the result of a request. They may supply it with or without completing extensive research into an assigned or unassigned topic. They may convey it formally or informally for two minutes or two hours. They may combine informative presentations with question-and-answer sessions with larger groups. They may make the presentations, break larger bodies into small groups for discussions, and reconvene the larger groups for summaries.

When speaking to inform, collect and convey accurate information. Begin with something the listeners already know, and build from that point. Select symbols that meet the listeners' abilities. Solicit feedback, and use evaluative techniques that show whether the audience actually comprehends the information.

Persuading

Persuasive messages have as the purpose the receivers' actions or acceptance—for example, vote on a motion, buy a product, accept a suggestion. To persuade, use facts. Use logical, psychological, and personal appeals to wants and needs. Provide clear avenues for acting on the persuasion. Add nonverbal demonstrations to verbal presentations. Show how acting in the suggested manner will benefit the listener or solve some problem.

Techniques for persuasive written messages appear in Chapter 9. Most of the techniques work just as well for spoken messages. The AICA formula proves particularly appropriate: To gain *attention,* use words and nonverbal accompaniment that catch the listener's imagination, but relate to the topic. Use the amusing, the startling, the enveloping, the unusual, the familiar, the suspenseful, the dynamic. Move smoothly and naturally into the topic in such a way that the listener becomes *interested* enough to continue listening. Then develop the persuasive conviction arguments. Supply facts that *convince* the listener. After completing development of the conviction segment, stimulate the listener to take the *action* suggested in the closing statement.

Performing Ritual Functions

Business communicators often speak before groups to perform rites such as introducing a speaker, paying tribute to retiring employees, giving a welcome speech, and giving an invocation or benediction.

The rituals just described have traditional formats. However, still try to make them fresh. Think of the specific person about whom you speak. Think about your relationship with that person. Think about the audience. Find some original, creative way to tie the three together.

Match the presentation to the occasion. Avoid giddy, gushing, and overstated speeches. Instead, create a tone of sincerity and warmth. Offer honest praise. Concentrate on the positive accomplishments of the honored person. However, you may want to acknowledge some small human foibles in a positive or humorous way.

Keep ceremonial presentations brief. However, make them dynamic. Apply the techniques for colorful, attention-getting messages. Be sure to present accurate facts. Pronounce the name of the honored person correctly. Explain not only the accomplishments of the person, but the characteristics of the award or honor being bestowed.

When introducing a speaker, present a brief sketch of the speaker and her or his background. However, also use the message to gain the attention of the audience and to merge the introduction into the speaker's topic.

When giving invocations or benedictions, respect the makeup of your audience. Such respect means to use words neutral in terms of religious preference and gender of the deity. You may even suggest that those present meditate silently in their own way for a few moments.

Entertaining

Sometimes an entire speech has a core purpose of entertaining the listeners. At other times, entertaining messages serve as means for gaining attention or breaking tension within a speech for another purpose. Both require a special style.

The word *entertainment* includes much more than humor. An entertaining piece also may arouse curiosity, calm, excite, create a pleasant state of mind, or hold attention. Business speakers usually use humor, personal anecdotes, human experiences or foibles, suspense stories, unusual twists to ordinary happenings, and vivid descriptions. Above all, they create mental pictures that will hold audiences.

Drollery, witty sayings, jokes, puns, satire, irony, sarcasm, and ridicule fall into the realm of humor. However, as a business speaker, avoid the last two categories. Sarcasm and ridicule often cause the audience embarrassment, discomfort, and offense. Also avoid humor that disparages individuals or classes of people on the basis of nationality, race, ethnicity, sex, age, mental or educational level, geographic location, handicaps, or other stereotypes. Avoid "sick" jokes—or anything in bad taste. Avoid the hackneyed, mechanical, "stock" joke. Also avoid telling a joke because you think all speakers should tell jokes—at least at the beginning of every speech. Unless you can find a joke that naturally fits your subject, and unless you can tell it well, use some other entertaining or attention-getting device. Otherwise, you will appear clumsy and artificial.

Apply the principles and guidelines for developing entertaining messages just as carefully as for developing any other type. Carefully define the audience and your own capabilities. Set objectives to reflect whether you want to receive only a sense of pleasant acceptance, flickers of smiles, polite laughter, or loud guffaws. Human-based interference seriously affects entertainment—particularly humorous entertainment. Obtaining a laugh from a resistant audience can prove quite difficult.

Select, encode, and deliver entertaining messages to recognize the features of the audience. Use the indirect developmental style most of the time. Use verbal elements and nonverbal devices (good timing, in particular) to create the greatest impact in the transmission. For an entertaining opening to a speech with some other major purpose, keep the opening brief and focused and relevant to the theme.

Use feedback from the audience wisely. If the material does not work, shift it. Skip some planned material if the audience does not respond favorably to earlier material. When an audience warms well enough, you may create new entertaining messages on the spot. Evaluate entertaining presentations as you do any others.

Types of Speeches Classified by Style of Transmission

Styles of transmission of person-to-group presentations fall into five major categories: (1) written, (2) memorized, (3) extemporaneous, (4) impromptu, and (5) round-table.

Written

A speech transmitted from a written manuscript does not actually constitute speaking; it constitutes reading. Therefore, avoid it. Use it when necessary to convey highly technical or formal information, for direct quotations from the works of others, and when providing a copy of the presentation for publication or release to the media.

The oral presentation of a manuscript seriously limits your ability to (1) exhibit a natural style, (2) maintain eye contact, (3) observe and evaluate feedback, and (4) adjust the messages. Therefore, never use the written style just out of fear of facing an audience, of forgetting the material, or of encoding messages improperly. Overcome that fear through practice and experience.

If the formality or complexity of an occasion demands the use of the manuscript, observe these important procedures:

- Apply all the communication guidelines presented in Chapter 2.
- Write a draft of the speech according to sound writing principles.
- Revise by reading the written speech aloud sentence by sentence and

making adjustments necessary to convert a readable piece into a speakable piece.

- Type the revised manuscript in double- or triple-spaced, wide-margined form on only one side of the paper, possibly all in capital letters.
- Practice reading aloud several times before a videotape camera, friends, or a mirror to improve delivery, eye contact, etc.
- Mark the points of some of your important pauses, phrases, emphases, and other nonverbal cues directly on the manuscript. Practice several more times.
- Apply all of the suggestions for good verbal and nonverbal presentations.

Memorized

The memorized speech may lead to the poorest delivery of all. Speakers must concentrate so completely upon recalling memorized material that they do not make contact or observe, evaluate, and adjust to feedback. Additional flaws exist in the memorized approach: (1) the difficulty of memorizing more than a few paragraphs, (2) the possibility of forgetting material during the speech, and (3) the difficulty of presenting a memorized speech in a nonmechanical manner.

Extemporaneous

Choose the extemporaneous style over all of the others. It has the advantages of preparation, naturalness, flexibility, spontaneity, and full interaction with the audience. To develop an extemporaneous speech:

- Apply all of the guidelines.
- Develop the speech by first writing and revising an outline. Write only a few key sentences—and perhaps the opening and the closing.
- Place the outline or key words and phrases, possibly all in capital letters, on only one side of note cards. Leave plenty of space around and between lines.
- Using the note cards only when necessary, practice speaking aloud several times before a videotape camera, friends, or a mirror to improve delivery, sentence construction, eye contact, etc.
- Avoid practicing to the point that you memorize a fixed pattern of words. Practice only until you know that you will speak in a coherent but spontaneous manner.
- Apply all of the suggestions for good verbal and nonverbal presentations.

Impromptu

The impromptu speech occurs with little or no time for preparation. The reduced chances for analyzing the audience, organizing, and encoding require a fast-thinking speaker. When delivering an impromptu speech, use these suggestions:

- At even a hint that you may have to speak, begin to apply the guidelines, even while walking or turning to face the audience.
- Move the planning directly to the specific topic, objectives, and key points. Write them on paper if you have the seconds necessary to do so.
- When first facing the audience, take a few seconds to form the first words silently before speaking them.
- Watch for feedback to know when to repeat or clarify.
- Speak briefly, and conclude firmly.
- If appropriate, ask if the group has questions.

Round-table

Although the round-table discussion overlaps with the other four forms, it warrants special treatment. Other names for, and variations of, the round-table discussion include the forum, panel, symposium, group discussion, lecture-discussion, film-discussion, debate, public dialogue, and public interview. These characteristics and rules apply to many of the types:

- The participants sit or stand facing the audience, sometimes in a semicircle so that they face each other.
- A neutral moderator coordinates and controls the activities of the presentation.
- Time limits control the stages of the presentation.
- Each participant prepares at least a brief statement for delivery at the beginning of the presentation. The delivery may involve written, memorized, or extemporaneous techniques.
- Each participant responds in an impromptu manner to the other participants' statements, to questions directed by the moderator, and/or to questions written or spoken by members of the audience.
- Each participant makes a final statement.

The round-table presentation has the advantage of offering a variety of personalities and viewpoints to the audience. Thus, it may hold attention better than a single speaker. However, the speakers rarely have enough time to develop their ideas fully. Audiences often feel cheated.

To be a good member of a round-table group, combine the arts and skills applicable to extemporaneous, impromptu, and small-group speaking. Also apply the listening and other techniques appropriate to small-group transactions. In addition, learn to interact with the other participants in the forum while also interacting with the larger audience.

Additional Suggestions for Making Good Speeches

Techniques for effective speech-making appear throughout this section. However, these additional suggestions will also contribute to good speeches:

- Speak from a position that faces the largest possible number of people in the audience.

- Sweep the entire audience with your eyes. Make an extra effort to include the people who sit at the extreme right and left ends of wide rows near you. The natural tendency is to make contact with a triangular or wedge-shaped group, with the narrowest point closest to you.
- Avoid locking eyes with individual members of the audience. Brush past their eyes, or look a little above them, and move on.
- Avoid turning for security to the most supportive of the nonverbal senders. Continue to include everyone in your sweeps. If, in a question-and-answer period, someone asks a direct question, fix most of the response on that person. However, occasionally shift your attention to the others in the transaction.
- Relax. Know your material.
- Try stepping away from the speaker's stand.
- Use natural motions and gestures. Avoid tentative, off-rhythm, mechanical gestures.
- Stand or sit relatively erect, but occupy enough space to display appropriate confidence. Avoid shifting and shuffling on the feet and propping a foot on the base of the speaker's stand. Avoid plunging hands in and out of pockets. Avoid rustling papers. Avoid twiddling with hair, ears, or anything else; avoid rocking or swaying; control any other distracting motion.
- Let your face come alive with pleasant, facile expressions, but avoid a false, Cheshire-cat smile.
- Speak loudly enough to reach the persons sitting in the back row. To check, just ask those at the back of the room whether they can hear you.
- When you must use a microphone, try to experiment with it prior to the speech. If you cannot, watch others ahead of you to learn proper distance for clarity of voice, how to change its position, how to put it around your neck, and other features. When you must use a stationary microphone, you will have to give up some movement away from the speaker's stand. Otherwise, your voice may fade in and out and bother an audience. Practice.
- Make sure audiovisual equipment works. Have someone else operate it as you talk unless you can maintain contact as you operate it. Whether you or someone else operates it, practice ahead of time.
- While referring to audiovisual aids, keep eye contact with the audience. Do not speak while facing a chalkboard, screen, poster, flip chart, etc. With such visual aids, face the audience as you speak, turning between sentences just long enough to write or point to an item with a long pointer.
- When using the overhead projector, face the audience while you point to the transparency on the projector. Do not turn around to point to the screen. The opaque projector also has a pointer that allows the speaker to remain in contact with the audience.
- Choose the correct style of transmission to fit the occasion, the content and purposes of the speech, and your abilities. You certainly would not choose the written speech for a greeting to a group of

teenagers gathered for a pep rally. On the other hand, you would not choose the impromptu speech for presenting a research paper to a group of peers at a convention.

- Observe time limits set by the occasion.

SPEAKING AT THE MASS LEVEL

The major oral channels at the mass level include radio, television, and films. Business communicators sometimes speak on radio or television, but not often on movie film. Many books and entire courses of study deal with the development of professional radio, television, and film skills. Therefore, the minimal set of suggestions made in this book are for the person who rarely uses mass channels.

Television and Film

A business communicator on television—taped or live—or on film usually appears in one of four modes: the interview, the informative statement, the round-table discussion, or the speech. The basic characteristics, arts, and skills for the four modes extend to their application to the mass media. However, some special suggestions may help make the application smooth:

- If a photographer tapes or films an appearance before a live audience, pretend he or she is not even there. Do not look at the camera or acknowledge the photographer's presence in any way.
- If you make a statement or speech specifically for mass transmission, treat the camera as the audience. Maintain eye contact with it. Restrict nonverbal messages to camera range. Speak extemporaneously with notes.
- When appearing as a panel member or interviewee, ignore the camera. Talk to the moderator, another panel member, or the interviewer in a natural manner. If the camera operator shifts to pick up a direct shot of your face, still do not look at the camera. Try not to use note cards—and certainly not full-sized pages. Speak extemporaneously from a memorized outline or use impromptu skills well.
- Because you usually have much less time for a mass-media appearance than for a standard one, establish the key points you want to make. If the appearance involves an interview on a "talk show" or some other program, suggest, learn, or anticipate the questions, and practice the answers.
- Dress professionally. Arrive at the suggested time. If appropriate, thank the interviewer, moderator, or director for the opportunity to appear—both on and off the air. Let the professionals control the appearance. They likely will talk with you briefly just before moving before the cameras. Relax. Treat the transaction as naturally as possible.
- Apply the principles and guidelines. The audience includes a large number of people representing a wide variety of demographic factors.

Therefore, keep language at the lower range of educational ability. Avoid anything shocking or sarcastic. You usually receive no feedback from the larger audience; thus, trust your own abilities to assess their reactions.

Radio

When you speak by radio, you engage in a mediated experience similar to that of being before television or movie cameras, but without the visual components. Therefore, place all of the weight of the presentation upon spoken words and nonverbal vocal qualities.

Interact with someone in the studio or on the other side of the microphone. The key to a good radio presentation lies in your ability to picture an audience and to speak naturally as if in their presence. Approach and complete the interview, panel, statement, or speech in a prepared and confident manner. (521 words)

Take and score Self-Test 29 over speaking at the mass level on page 416.

This review of the oral channels completes Part C—sending. Part D includes two chapters that integrate sending and receiving as you present messages necessary for finding employment and developing a career. Chapter 15 gives suggestions for career planning, the resumé, and the application letter.

SUMMARY

Many of the suggestions made for writing also apply to speaking. Therefore, this chapter extends and reinforces those suggestions while reviewing speaking at the interpersonal, mediated, person-to-group, and mass levels of communication.

Interpersonal channels include conversations and dialogues, interviews, and small groups. Conversations involve unstructured, informal, and slightly purposive communication transactions. They may not relate directly to business, but nonetheless contribute to smooth business functioning. Dialogues introduce purpose in relatively structured and formal transactions. The interview is a special type of dialogue. It involves purposes such as appraising an applicant for a job or disseminating information to the media.

In the directive interview, the interviewer commands the transaction. In the nondirective interview, both parties give direction to the interview. The stress interviewer uses emotion-laden questions to determine how well the interviewee handles stress. The depth interview involves a directive probe into the topic. As the interviewer, try to make the interviewee comfortable, state your purposes, and ask what the interviewee would like to accomplish. As an interviewee, prepare for the meeting just as fully as the interviewer does.

Small groups include four to ten people, with location, time, topic, purpose, formality, designation, and cohesion having an impact on the transaction. Methods for conducting group meetings include problem-solving, educating, brainstorming, and role-playing.

Three basic roles define group members: participant, leader, and recorder. Participants take three basic types of roles: task-oriented roles, process-oriented roles, and destructive roles. Three roles define the leader: authoritarian, democratic, and permissive. The recorder must write quickly, summarize well, and think, listen, organize, and write all at the same time.

The mediated level of speaking often involves the use of the telephone, private intercommunication system, two-way radio, closed-circuit television, or dictating equipment. The major difference between the interpersonal and mediated levels arises from the loss of important nonverbal feedback.

The person-to-group level deals with four types of purposes: to inform, to persuade, to perform ritual functions, and to entertain. An informing speech conveys information. A persuasive speech develops a message with the purpose of having the receiver engage in the desired action. Speaking to perform ritual functions occurs in conjunction with such things as introducing a speaker or giving an invocation. Speaking to entertain may occur as the central purpose or for gaining attention or breaking tension during a speech for another purpose.

Person-to-group presentations fall into five categories defined by styles of transmission: (1) written, (2) memorized, (3) extemporaneous, (4) impromptu, and (5) round-table.

Try to avoid making a speech straight from a written manuscript. You will not speak, you will read. When you cannot avoid speaking from a manuscript, try to make the presentation seem extemporaneous. The memorized speech may lead to the poorest delivery of all. Because of complete concentration on the memorized material, you may not have the added capacity to make eye contact and to observe, evaluate, and adjust to feedback. Choose the extemporaneous style over the others. It has the advantages of preparation, naturalness, flexibility, spontaneity, and full interaction with the audience. It uses skeletal notes and outlines. The impromptu speech allows little or no time for preparation. Therefore, it requires the application of the communication guidelines even as you speak. Variations of the round-table speech include the forum, panel, symposium, group discussion, lecture-discussion, and debate. They have some common characteristics, and each has its own defined characteristics and rules.

These suggestions will help you make good speeches:

- Place yourself in a position that faces the largest possible number of people in the audience.
- Sweep the entire audience as you make eye contact.
- Avoid locking eyes with individual members of the audience.
- Relax; know your material.
- Observe the audience carefully.
- Use appropriate nonverbal accompaniments.
- If you use audiovisual equipment, use it well.
- Choose the correct style of transmission to fit the occasion, the content and purposes of the speech, and your own abilities.

- Observe time limits set by the occasion.
- Maintain proper vocal qualities.

When you speak at the mass level, apply the special communication arts and skills associated with that level. The major oral mass channels include radio, television, and film.

EXERCISES

1. *[Your professor will time the written part of this exercise.]* Prepare a three- or four-minute speech on vocal segregates. In the speech, define vocal segregates, give some examples, and explain why they are not necessary. Put the main points of your speech on cards. Practice the speech in front of a mirror. Now meet with your group. You and every other group member stand and give the speech. Evaluate each of the speeches. Have one of your group members give her or his speech to the rest of the class. (The section on vocal segregates is on page 94.)
2. Meet with your group. Choose four people to read this short play.

   Dale: I don't understand why we have to meet now. I have a lot of work to do.
   Chris: Well, we have to decide whether or not to bid on the Warner contract this week, you know.
   Lane: We never get anywhere in these meetings.
   Lou: If we'd just . . . .
   (Dale interrupts.)
   Dale: We don't get any help from management.
   Lane: Yeah. Did you hear that they fired old Rankin? They're trying to get rid of all the good people.
   Chris: You're right. Lorner will be the next one to get canned.
   Lou: Probably. Listen, we'd better get back to the contract.
   Lane: Sure, Lou. But I don't think we have enough information to make a decision yet.
   Lou: Oldfield gave us this assignment six weeks ago!
   Dale: I'll bet he's the one who fired Rankin.
   (Lou sighs.)

   THE END

   Discuss these questions as a group:
   a. What went wrong with Dale, Chris, Lane, and Lou's meeting?
   b. What could they have done to make the meeting more productive?
   c. How would you respond to Dale's "We don't get any help from management" statement?
   d. Is Lane's "lack of information" a valid excuse for not discussing the contract?
   e. Have you ever participated in a similar discussion? What, if anything, did you do to try to make it more productive?
   f. Was Dale, Chris, Lane, and Lou's meeting to have been a meeting to solve a problem, educate, or brainstorm?
3. Decide what role each of these people is taking.
   a. Ruth suggests a name for the potato chips your company is introducing.

b. Ray politely asks the other group members to refrain from talking so that Nora can speak.
c. Al says that Mona does not know what she is talking about.
d. Liz always says "I believe that this is right" instead of "You are wrong" when expressing an opinion.
e. Leonard says "Hey, this isn't *that* important" when Sheila and Stan begin a verbal battle over an issue.
f. Leona suggests a script for the meeting.
g. James says that he cannot work around women because he likes to look at them; thus, he's distracted by them.
h. Joanne says that labor unions are the problem, regardless of the issue.
i. Harvey has an opinion on every subject. Some don't make much sense.
j. Lisa listens intently to what other group members say and offers suggestions when people differ on an issue.
k. Ron is an engineer. He provides technical information during meetings.
l. Cathy makes lots of jokes. That's about all she does.

4. Many communication and management specialists believe that authoritarian leadership is not appropriate in *any* business situation. Support or refute.
5. Exchange phone numbers with another class member. Call her or him and then have your partner call you to explain the important elements of making an entertaining speech or a speech punctuated with humorous anecdotes. When you initiate the call, evaluate yourself as a sender and your classmate as a receiver. Your classmate should also evaluate you as a sender and herself or himself as a receiver. Both of you should answer these questions:
   a. Did the sender know precisely why he or she was making the call?
   b. Did the sender make clear at the outset why he or she was calling and tell you his or her name?
   c. Did the sender speak clearly and at an appropriate volume?
   d. Was the sender's message well organized and concise?
   e. Did the sender solicit your comments during the call?
   f. Did you feel that the call was satisfactory in general? Why?
   g. What could have been done to make the call more productive?
6. Write one- or two-paragraph examples of each of the types of speeches (informing, persuading, performing ritual functions, and entertaining).
7. Meet with your group. Choose one group member to serve as the recorder. For a few minutes, discuss ways to best conduct problem-solving meetings. Now ask the recorder to read what he or she has written. Is the record of the meeting correct and complete? Choose another recorder and continue the discussion. Have the new recorder read her or his notes. Repeat the process until everyone in the group has served as the recorder.
8. Meet with your group. Your task is to hold a brainstorming session so that you can begin to write an informative, entertaining speech on the subject of different approaches to leadership. (Do not limit yourself to the three basic approaches listed in the book.) Pretend that one of you will give the speech at a meeting of the local Rotary Club. Do not write the speech. Just have a no-holds-barred idea session. Commit all of your ideas to paper, and have one group member read your ideas to the class.
9. Develop a five-minute extemporaneous speech on a business or economic topic of your choice. Make the speech to inform, persuade, or entertain. Deliver the speech to the entire class or to your group—as your professor prescribes. Each member of the audience will complete an anonymous evaluation form in summary

of your performance. You will get to see the completed forms. In addition, the group will discuss your performance with you.

10. Your professor will read a brief sketch of a case to the entire class. S/he will then ask for volunteers for, or make assignments of, the described roles to several in the group. The role-players will play the scene. Following the scene, the group at large will evaluate the solution of the case and the contributiveness or destructiveness of each of the roles.

11. Meet in groups of three. Take the roles of interviewer, interviewee, and observer. For just a few minutes simulate an interview between a supervisor and an employee about an alleged misuse of the expense-account privilege by the employee as the observer looks on. After the simulation, have the observer offer constructive criticism about the performances of both parties—paying attention to both the verbal and nonverbal aspects of the transaction. Change roles and repeat the process. Repeat one more time so that all three play all three roles. Convene the entire class and have one member of each three-member group summarize the findings of that group.

12. Your professor will assign a topic and lay down ground rules for a panel discussion to be conducted during a class meeting. Each member will prepare to be a member of the panel. On the day of the panel discussion, the professor will use a random method to select five members to serve on the panel, with the remainder of the class acting as audience/evaluators. Following the panel presentation the panel will interact with the audience in a question-and-answer period. Following the Q-and-A session, the entire class will engage in written and oral evaluations of the process.

13. Meet with your group. Role-play some randomly chosen leader and participant roles. To accomplish the randomization, first write the names of the types of leaders (authoritarian, democrat, and permissive leader) on three slips of paper, fold them, and place them in a container. Draw one and without looking at it, lay it aside. Then write the names of the 11 task-oriented participant roles on slips of paper and place them in a container. Draw a number of slips equal to about one-third of the size of your group. Lay the slip(s) with the one for leadership style. Repeat the process for the 7 process-oriented roles and then with the 8 destructive roles. (Draw only enough additional slips to bring the total of the selected slips to equal the number in your group and to contain at least one destructive role.) Then draw from the selected slips so that each member has one. Do not tell each other which role you drew. Take a few minutes to review the descriptions of your roles and to plan how you will play them. Reconvene. Have each person play her or his role during a five- to ten-minute simulation of a meeting to deal with this case:

    Absenteeism, tardiness, and lengthy coffee breaks and lunch hours have all increased among the workers this quarter. Your purpose is to find a way to overcome the problem without losing the goodwill and productiveness of the workers.

    At the end of the simulation, try to identify which role each person played. (Each participant will either confirm the group's decision or name the role if not identified properly.) Evaluate the success of the meeting according to the contribution of (a) leadership style and (b) mixture of task-oriented, process-oriented, and destructive roles involved. If time allows, eliminate the roles used for the first simulation and repeat the process using the remaining roles.

14. Use your dictionary and thesaurus to create meanings for these words. Use the words when you think, write, and speak so that you feel comfortable using them.

- a. Aural
- b. Bent (as noun)
- c. Cohesive
- d. Consensus
- e. Eclectic
- f. Enliven
- g. Foible
- h. Intermediary
- i. Monologue
- j. Precede
- k. Principal
- l. Principle
- m. Purposive
- n. Spontaneity
- o. Stalemate
- p. Symbiotic

15. Take and score Self-Test 30 over Chapter 14.

SELF-TEST 29
Excerpt about Speaking at the Mass Level

A. Recall (33 points each). For each multiple-choice question, select the most accurate answer:
   1. If you make a statement or speech specifically for television, you should:
      a. Try not to look into the camera
      b. Read straight from your manuscript
      c. Treat the camera as your audience and maintain eye contact with it
      d. Always speak without notes
      e. Dress in bright colors and patterns
   2. The key to a good radio or television appearance is to:
      a. Picture your audience and speak naturally as if you were in their presence
      b. Avoid sounding the least bit frightened
      c. Have complete control over the technical side of the program
      d. Refrain from practicing beforehand so that your answers will be honest
      e. Avoid all controversial subjects

B. Inference (34 points). Indicate whether this statement is true or false.
   1. When you appear on a television or radio program, you would do well to concentrate more on what you are saying than on trying to look and sound like a professional television or radio personality.

SOLUTION

A. Recall (33 points each)
   1. c   2. a

B. Inference (34 points)
   1. True

SELF-TEST 30
Chapter 14

A. Recall (25 points each). For each multiple-choice question, select the most accurate answer.

1. Which of these is *not* a true statement?
   a. You spend a great deal of your business life engaged in informal conversation.
   b. The stress interview is used to determine how well a person can handle emotion-laden and leading questions.
   c. As an interviewer, you should tell the interviewee what your purposes are for the interview.
   d. If you do not know much about the person who will interview you, you can do little to prepare for the interview.
   e. The nondirective interview requires joint responsibilities for both parties.
2. In a brainstorming meeting you want to avoid:
   a. Stating and recording the ideas as quickly as possible
   b. Allowing each group member to take an active part in the meeting
   c. Evaluating and criticizing the contributions of another person
   d. Offering too many ideas
   e. Such methods as role-playing
3. When you speak to persuade, you do *not:*
   a. Use logical, psychological, and personal appeals to wants and needs
   b. Provide clear avenues for acting upon the persuasion
   c. Show how acting as you suggest will benefit the actor or solve some problem
   d. Usually use the indirect method of development
   e. Try to stimulate the listener to take an action that you suggest in your closing statements

B. Inference (25 points). Indicate whether this statement is true or false.

1. A meeting cannot be successful without a leader.

SOLUTION

A. Recall (25 points each)

1. d
2. c
3. d

B. Inference (25 points)

1. False

ENDNOTES

1. David Potter and Martin P. Andersen, *Discussion in Small Groups: A Guide to Effective Practice,* 3d ed. (Belmont, Calif.: Wadsworth Publishing Company, Inc., 1976), 143.
2. Potter and Andersen, *Discussion in Small Groups.*

D

SEEKING EMPLOYMENT

STUDENT'S OBJECTIVES:

1 To apply the guidelines and principles for effective sending and receiving to messages of employment

2 To learn to plan for a career

3 To learn to plan a campaign for a job

15

EMPLOYMENT: Career Planning, Résumé, Application Letter

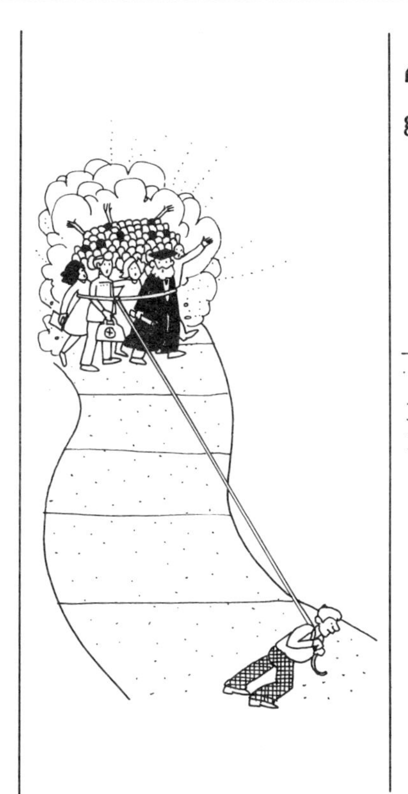

4 To learn to develop a good résumé

5 To learn to develop a good letter of application

GUIDELINES FOR POSITION-SEARCH COMMUNICATION

The generic guidelines provide the foundation for playing all communication roles in the position-search process:

- ☐ *Define purposes, participants, and environment*
- ☐ *Identify the channel*
- ☐ *Control interference*
- ☐ *Select, encode, decode, transmit, and receive messages*
- ☐ *Use feedback*
- ☐ *Evaluate at each stage and at end of transaction*

The campaign for employment calls on the full range of communication abilities. It involves written, oral, and nonverbal messages. It requires both sending and receiving. It includes some routine activity and a great deal of creative and persuasive activity. It requires formality and informality. It depends on the skills of both a collector and a supplier of information. Above all, a campaign for employment requires skillful application of the communication principles and guidelines. This chapter reviews career planning, the résumé, and the application letter. Chapter 16 completes the coverage of employment communication.

PLANNING FOR A CAREER AND A JOB

To review some of the basic principles and techniques associated with career planning, you should begin with setting goals and conducting self-evaluations. Reviewing these principles will help create the kinds of communication transactions that will yield desired results in long-term career development.

Planning for a Career

Seven stages can help you plan for a career:

1. Assess your current status
   a. Present employment
   b. Education and training
   c. Experience
   d. Intelligence and knowledge
   e. Attitudes, beliefs, values, interests, and aptitudes
2. Establish what you would like your career status to be:
   a. Twenty years from now
   b. Ten years from now

   c. Five years from now
   d. Three years from now
   e. One year from now
3. Identify barriers to the attainment of the levels listed in No. 2
   a. Internal
   b. External
4. Determine what you need to do to reach each level specified in No. 2
   a. Education and training
   b. Experience
   c. Strengths
   d. Weaknesses
   e. Barriers
5. Establish a precise plan and a time schedule for accomplishing the stages listed in No. 4
6. Activate the plan
7. Review and revise the plan periodically

Tests

The completion of the assessment and goal-setting stages just described in the outline can take a great deal of time. The assessment may involve taking some evaluative tests at a counseling or testing center. Such tests may measure intelligence, achievement, values, aptitude, personality, and interest.

Publications

To learn about available careers, employers, and positions, conduct a search of the literature on jobs and careers. Such a search might involve the publications about specific jobs or organizations, including annual reports and stock market reports. It also might involve general sources about careers, including some of the following published sources:

General Sources

Business Periodicals Index
Career Planning
Guide to American Directories
Occupational Literature
Occupational Outlook Handbook
Reality and Career Planning: A Guide for Personal Growth
World Trade Directory Reports
World Wide Chamber of Commerce Directory

Specific Sources

Annual Guide to Business Opportunities
Career: The Annual Guide to Business Opportunities
Career Information Service
College Placement Annual
College Placement Directory
Careers Research Monographs

Dictionary of Occupational Titles
Dun & Bradstreet
Journal of College Placement
Moody's Industrial Manual
Moody's Manuals of Investment
Poor's Register of Directors and Executives; United States and Canada
Public Affairs Information Service
Standard and Poor's Manuals
Thomas' Register of American Manufacturers

Interviews and Counseling

In addition to searching the literature, talk with people who presently occupy positions in the career paths of your interest. You also may want to participate in some career counseling—either on an individual basis or as part of a group.

Timing

To set the timing for your goals, try to combine realism and optimism. Above all, understand the need to retain some flexibility in the plan. To do so, establish a schedule for reassessing the plan periodically. Also recognize that many jobs become obsolete as conditions change.

Education, Training, Experience, and Strengths

To gain the education, training, experience, and strengths necessary to research goals, identify appropriate people and situations. Libraries, counseling centers, and other sources provide information on how to proceed in such a search. For a campaign to receive scholarships and grants, engage many of the same techniques used to find jobs. To obtain the appropriate experience, identify and obtain the kinds of positions that yield it. At each stage of application for a position or promotion, review your overall career goals. Then establish specific plans and objectives to fit the larger goals.

Barriers

Identify and attack barriers early, set strategies for overcoming them, and employ the strategies with perseverance and a positive attitude. Above all, do not let the existence of barriers and chance prevent the development of your plans. Many people move through an all-too-short life being nudged here and there by forces they do not even try to control.

Internal Most barriers to success lie within a person's mental, emotional, and physical being. Obstacles to career growth include the following:

- Hesitation to take risks because of the fear of failure
- Lack of the mental ability needed for a given discipline
- Lack of the will to work hard
- Value system that runs counter to the operational reality of a chosen field

- Lack of the physical size and strength necessary to do the desired work
- Lack of interest
- Allowing the opinions and attitudes of others to have undue influence

Sources that help to overcome internal barriers include:

- Obtaining traditional education and training
- Counseling with experts
- Working with groups to practice such things as interpersonal relations and receiving constructive criticism
- Joining organizations or taking courses that give experience in speaking before groups
- Participating in assertive training

External Some barriers to employment do exist outside of a person:

- High unemployment rates
- Family responsibilities
- Military service requirements
- Personal biases or grudges held by people in positions of power
- Attitudes of others about race, ethnic origin, sex, physical being, religion, or age
- Years of service and accompanying benefits at one firm or in one field that prevent a desired shift
- Legal or policy requirements for physical and mental abilities for certain kinds of work

To overcome or adapt to such barriers, use the same devices as for internal ones. (818 words)

Take and score Self-Test 31 over planning for a career on pages 448–49.

Planning a Job Campaign

After setting general career goals and plans, you can develop plans for a specific job campaign. Establish objectives that reflect the appropriate stage of your career plan. A job campaign usually involves a series of objectives and associated criteria. The final objective of a campaign may call for a given firm to hire you at a given salary by a given date under a given set of conditions. However, seven other objectives build toward that one:

1. To learn everything possible about the firm and the people within it
2. To develop and test a résumé and letter of application specific to the firm
3. To send the letter and résumé to reach the appropriate officer at a time beneficial to the campaign
4. To receive a notice that the personnel officer wants an interview
5. To perform so well in the interview that the firm calls you back for the second interview

6. To perform so well in that interview that you receive the offer of the position at the desired salary by the desired time with the desired conditions
7. To encode a message of acceptance that convinces the firm of its wise choice

Applicants rarely deal with just one firm at a time. When a job campaign does involve several firms, you must expand the objectives to include appropriate priorities and actions. Establish the objectives to include alternatives reflecting how such actions relate to one another and to the preferences.

Focus objectives carefully at each stage of your job campaign, even as the stages fit into a greater whole. Also maintain a flexibility that will take advantage of positive events and overcome negative ones. Without the flexibility, vision may fix so rigidly to one narrow course that you miss an opportunity for even greater success than that originally sought.

WRITTEN MESSAGES AND ACCOMPANYING NONVERBAL MESSAGES

Career and position-search plans often require written messages. Of course, nonverbal messages always accompany the verbal ones. Always typewrite résumés, letters, and most other employment messages. When possible, even use the typewriter to complete application blanks. When an application form requires handwriting or when not using a typewriter, write legibly and neatly. Some applicants have résumés professionally printed. However, readers sometimes gain the impression that such applicants broadcast résumés indiscriminately.

Also attend to the nonverbal aspects of written messages. Such aspects include format, color, weight of paper, texture of paper, size and style of type, underlining, use of upper-case and lower-case letters, neatness, and placement of parts of the page.

The résumé and the letter of application represent two major types of written and nonverbal messages in a job campaign.

Résumé

The *résumé* (personal data sheet, data sheet, vita) is the backbone of the communication process for gaining a desired position. It contains the key information about the applicant's qualifications for employment.

Develop the résumé before developing any of the other messages. Use it to accompany application letters. Give it to employment agencies or bureaus. Have it put in placement-office files. Make your résumé informational, yet inherently persuasive. Like the research proposal, the résumé accomplishes most of its persuasion through the quality of the contents and their presentation, rather than through overt techniques. Arrange the contents of the résumé in an order that emphasizes the desired features. Basically, then, begin and end with your strongest points, and place the others between. However, custom sometimes runs counter to the rules of emphasis, particularly in the placement of the names of references at the end of the résumé. Maintain parallel structure in all parts and subparts.

Develop your résumé as part of your self-assessment, goal-setting, and subsequent stages of the career-planning process. You may need to develop several forms to feature the different elements of your background to fit a variety of positions. A specific search often calls for a custom-made résumé. As time passes, revise your basic résumé to account for the changes in your history.

Though typically rather formal, the résumé sometimes expresses some creativity and flair, particularly for a position in the creative realms. However, avoid using abbreviations, contractions, and other such informalities.

The well-written résumé may include a persuasively arranged summary of such components as:

Heading
Objectives
Education and training
Experiences
Research and publications
Activities and accomplishments
Memberships
Honors and awards
Personal information
Hobbies and interests
Desired action
References

Figures 15–1, 15–2, 15–3, and 15–4 provide examples of résumés. The résumé in Figure 15–1 shows a traditional format and language style. Figure 15–2 illustrates some variation in a still-traditional style. Figures 15–3 and 15–4 introduce some flair even as they retain the traditional components.

Heading

The heading of the résumé serves as an introduction as well as a title. It should include your name, the type of work or position you want, and perhaps some identifying word such as "qualifications," "credentials," "assets," or "strengths." Some applicants still include "résumé," "personal data sheet," "data sheet," or "vita" in the heading. However, many authorities recommend omitting them, suggesting that this position of prominence can be better used. After all, we do not put "Report" at the top of a report or "Letter" at the top of a letter.

Objectives

A brief statement of objectives often follows the heading. Use the statement to continue the persuasion begun with the heading. Use this emphatic position to illustrate enthusiasm for the position or type of work cited in the heading.

MILTON A. ROSEN

Candidate for Bachelor of Science Degree in Management
University of Dillon, Dillon, Utah

OBJECTIVE: A challenging position of responsibility as a personnel director, personnel specialist, or organization development specialist in private industry anywhere in the United States

PERSONAL INFORMATION

Permanent Address: 3641 Alvin Elber Drive
Salt Lake City, Utah 33113

School Address: 400 Skinner Street, Apartment 14B
Dillon, Utah 33129

Telephone: (555) 322-8963 (School)
(555) 331-3110 (Home)

Date and Place of Birth: September 25, 1959, Boise, Idaho

Marital Status: Single

Health: Excellent

EDUCATION:

Bachelor of Science in Management, University of Dillon, Dillon, Utah—May, 1981 (expected month of graduation)

Organization Development Certificate, Wyler Institute of Management, Dillon, Utah—August, 1980 (completed 320-hour summer program in organization development)

UNDERGRADUATE CONCENTRATION (in semester hours):

Management—22 hours; Marketing—12 hours; Accounting—6 hours; and Finance—6 hours

FIGURE 15-1 Traditional résumé for soon-to-graduate student.

Education and Training

Recite education and training early in the résumé. Place it first if it forms the most important of your qualifications. List the latest educational or training level first and work chronologically backward from there. Account for any significant gaps between major educational training events. Include your degree or diploma, major field, institution, and date of attainment for each level.

MILTON A. ROSEN 2

WORK EXPERIENCE:

Tutor (part-time), University of Dillon Study Center—1978-present (tutor undergraduates in both management and marketing subjects)

Typist (full-time), University of Dillon Library—summer of 1977 (typed overdue notices and order forms)

UNIVERSITY ACTIVITIES:

President, Kramer Dormitory—1977-1978

Member, Management Club—1978-1981

Editor, Business School Weekly—1980-1981

UNIVERSITY AWARDS AND HONORS:

Dean's Honor Roll—1979-1981

Chamber of Commerce Scholarship—1980-1981

PROFESSIONAL ORGANIZATIONS:

Member, Management Society of Utah—1980-present

Member, Dillon Business Association—1980-present

REFERENCES (permission obtained from all references):

Dr. Alice Symington, Professor of Management,
School of Business, University of Dillon, Dillon, Utah 33129;
phone—(555) 322-8666

Mr. Edward Winters, Assistant Professor of Marketing,
School of Business, University of Dillon, Dillon, Utah 33129;
phone—(555) 322-8667

Dr. Deborah Wechsler, Director, Study Center,
University of Dillon, Dillon, Utah 33129;
phone—(555) 322-8680

Mr. Delbert Irving, Supervisor, Library Business Office,
University of Dillon, Dillon, Utah 33129;
phone—(555) 322-8770

FIGURE 15-1 (Continued).

Courses and grades You may list and group courses you have had that relate to the position or field you want to enter. Put them in descending order of importance. Use titles that explain the content. If you include individual grades, use letters or some generally accepted system. You may show grade-point averages for total programs, your major, or a block of courses. However, if you do, state the numerical base for the average (for example, 4.0 = A).

JANET E. SMITH

2332 Pine Road 555-721-6231 (home)
Anthony, Idaho 44662 555-721-4992 (message)

Objectives

A challenging position, with opportunities for promotion, in financial planning, financial management, or investment counseling.

Education

Master of Business Administration degree in Finance, Anthony University (3.42 grade point average, based on 4-point scale)	1980
Bachelor of Science degree in Finance, Anthony University, Anthony, Idaho (academic scholarship student)	1979
Associate of Science degree in Business Administration, Linwood Community College, Linwood, Idaho	1977

Experience

Investment Assistant, DiRenzio and Barber, Inc., Anthony, Idaho (full-time)	Summers of 1978 and 1979

Assisted two investment counselors in preparing investment folders on major Idaho corporations. Also worked as an investment counselor on several occasions.

Carpenter, Leland and Daughters Construction Company, Anthony, Idaho (full-time)	Summers of 1976 and 1977

Built kitchen and bathroom cabinets in new homes and new office buildings.

FIGURE 15-2 Traditional résumé for recent graduate.

Related experiences Include citations of related educational and training experiences. Usually such experiences either did not result from traditional or formal settings or did not result in a diploma or degree. Examples of such experiences include participation in seminars, workshops, practicums, study groups, retreats, and audited courses offered by local libraries, military personnel, traveling consultants, in-service-training personnel of a firm, or educational institutions. They may cover general topics like leadership, supervisory

Activities

Panelist, Women in Management Workshop, Anthony University	1978
Vice President, Anthony University Finance Club	1978-1979

Memberships

Member, Finance Association of America	1978-present
Member, Anthony Downtown Business Club	1979-present

Honors and Awards

Outstanding Business Student Award, Linwood Community College	1977
Elizabeth Blanchard Scholarship, Anthony University	1977-1978
Susan Stanton Finance Award, Anthony University	1978

Personal Information

Married, two children, excellent health

Hobbies and Interests

Cross-country skiing, furniture building, and reading

References

References provided upon request

FIGURE 15-2 (Continued).

and managerial functions, assertiveness, self-awareness, human relations, or communication (oral and written). They may also cover topics related to a career field (C.P.A. review, law review, insurance workshops, banking seminars, etc.). When you do include a list of learning experiences, indicate the who, what, when, and where of each activity. If it resulted in some sort of recognized documentation of participation (a certificate, for example), report it. Also indicate the number of hours actually spent in the classroom. Include

MARIA E. MARTINEZ 2

Experience (continued)

Organization Development Planner — Darmer Real Estate
January 1, 1976-February 20, 1978 — Danville, West Virginia

As the only planner in the three-person organization development department, I developed and implemented the two organization development programs that were in themselves responsible for a 16 percent reduction in the turnover rate among all Darmer personnel. I also conducted a number of group dynamics and team building workshops for both the managers and salespersons.

Education

I earned the Master of Business Administration degree in June, 1980, from the Boston Business Institute. I completed 60 semester hours in graduate courses at the institute, and I earned a 3.9 out of 4.0 grade point average.

I was graduated from the University of Danville, Danville, West Virginia, with a Bachelor of Business Administration degree in December, 1975. I completed 124 semester hours of coursework, and I earned a 3.6 out of 4.0 grade point average.

Publications

Organization Development: Developing Socio-Technical Systems. Boston: Business Books Press, 1979.

"Training the Professional Systems Manager," Training Digest 12 (October 1978): 112-119.

Professional Affiliations

Member, Training Society of Boston, 1979-present
Member, Association of Organizational Developers, 1976-present

Personal

I am married, and I am willing to relocate.

References

I will furnish references upon request.

FIGURE 15-3 Résumé for person with professional experience.

4321 Vine Street
Boston, Massachusetts 99496

555-666-1319 (home)
555-666-3422 (message)

Qualifications of

MARIA E. MARTINEZ

for a career in training and development

Employment Goal

I seek an extremely challenging position as the training and development director for a major United States corporation.

Summary of Qualifications

Training and Development

- 2 years of experience as the training and development manager for Adams and Ross, Inc., Boston
- 12 semester hours in graduate training and development courses (earned a perfect—4.0—grade point average in these courses)
- 9 semester hours in undergraduate training and development courses (perfect—4.0—grade point average)
- 2 years of experience in teaching undergraduate training and development courses

Organization Development

- 2 years of experience as an organization development planner for Darmer Real Estate, Danville, West Virginia
- 12 semester hours in graduate courses in organization development (perfect—4.0—grade point average)
- 3 years of experience in conducting organization development workshops and seminars for professional groups

General Business

- 60 semester hours of graduate work in business (earned a 3.9 out of 4.0 grade point average)
- 45 semester hours of undergraduate work in business (earned a 3.75 out of 4.0 grade point average)
- 1 year of experience in teaching undergraduate accounting courses

Experience

Manager, Training and Development
March 1, 1978-April 15, 1980

Adams and Ross, Inc.
Systems Management Group
Boston, Massachusetts

I began the first training and development programs at Adams and Ross. When I left, 75 percent (380) of the company's professional and managerial employees were voluntarily participating in the 15 training and development sequences that I developed. As the first manager of training and development, I hired and supervised a staff of 10 training and development associates and 8 clerical workers.

FIGURE 15–3 (Continued).

13 Walker Avenue
Argyle, Maine 22914
(555) 231-9964

LEE WU'S

qualifications for the position of

SALESPERSON

OBJECTIVE	To secure a challenging position as a salesperson for a major, growing pharmaceutical company
EDUCATION AND TRAINING	Bachelor of Arts degree in business, with a major in selling, from the University of Argyle, Argyle, Maine, 1981 Twelve semester hours of selling and marketing courses at the Claire Moran Sales Institute, Argyle, Maine, 1980-1981
SELLING AND MARKETING COURSES AND GRADES	Selling Basic Personal Selling—A Advanced Personal Selling—A Salespersonship—A Selling Problems—A Managing Sales Districts—A Marketing Basic Marketing Management—A Managing the Marketing Function—B Consumer Behavior—A Marketing Reseach—A

FIGURE 15-4 Résumé for salesperson.

LEE WU'S PAGE 2

SELLING EXPERIENCE	Full-time chemical salesperson for the Argyle Chemical Company, summers of 1977-1980. Responsible for entire Vermont sales district. Always exceeded monthly sales quotas. Part-time clothing salesperson at the Argyle Department Store, school years of 1977-1981. Responsible for boys' department. Exceeded sales quotas most every month.
UNIVERSITY ACTIVITIES	President, Salespersons' Club, 1980-1981 Member, Argyle Business Students' Club, 1980-1981 Coordinator, Salespersonship Workshop, 1979
PROFESSIONAL ACTIVITIES	Member, Salespersons of America, 1979-present Member, Argyle Selling Association, 1980-present
PERSONAL	Age 21, single, perfect health
REFERENCES (by permission)	Ann Sleth, Ph.D., Professor of Marketing University of Argyle Argyle, Maine 22914 Richard Mackin, Ed.D., Professor of Salespersonship University of Argyle Argyle, Maine 22914 Ms. Carol Dimitri, Marketing Director Argyle Chemical Company 6231 North Wayne Road Argyle, Maine 22914 Mr. Warren Ochoco, Manager Argyle Department Store 18 North Broadway Street Argyle, Maine 22914

FIGURE 15-4 (Continued).

only significant activities that contribute to indirect persuasion. Do not fill valuable space with a citation of events that will not persuade the reader of your abilities for the specified career or position.

Certification Consider certain kinds of certification either as education and training or as a distinct category. Such certification involves not only extensive education, but also significant testing by an agency independent of educational institutions. Examples include testing for the designations of Certified Public Accountant, Chartered Life Underwriter, Certified Professional Secretary, and admission to the bar. The appropriate acronym for such certification may appear after your name at the top of the page—either in place of, or in addition to, featuring it in a listing. Thus, a name might appear as "Y. R. Self, CFA."

Experience

Include any experiences you have had that will contribute to success in the career you seek. Such experiences usually relate to paid civilian work. However, they also may relate to the military, sometimes to significant volunteer work with a not-for-profit organization, or sometimes even to positions of responsibility in major professional organizations.

List everything since graduation from high school or college—depending upon the status of your career—but distinguish between full- and part-time work. Cite experiences in logical groupings—and generally in reverse chronological order within the groupings. Thus, the latest position in a particular grouping will appear at the top of the list. Give dates, names of organizations, job titles, and a summary of responsibilities. Highlight the work that shows the most valuable and related experiences.

When including experiences like internships, consulting, and self-employment, treat them in a separate section or combine all such types under the heading "Experience."

Research Projects and Publications

A summary of research projects and publications that relates to the desired work can show the quality of the applicant's background. The section on research and publication provides evidence of additional effort that some employers respect. Applicants for positions in universities often include such a section, as do applicants for certain kinds of positions in business.

For a listing of research and publications longer than a half page, one approach calls for including a section in the body of the résumé that features a few of the major works, but refers the reader to a complete listing attached as an appendix to the résumé. Another approach calls for a heading indicating that the section lists selected research and publications, with reference to the number of those not cited. Figure 15-3 illustrates organization of a part on publications.

Activities and Accomplishments

Some major activities and accomplishments require a separate category:

- Speeches or panels
- Workshops and seminars for organizations, civic groups, or programs at public schools and colleges
- Volunteer counseling for people in the community
- Supervision of business-school interns who worked for your firm for a period of time
- Tutoring
- Service in a major capacity for some professional organizations—officer of a local, regional, or national unit
- Work without pay in a businesslike position for a not-for-profit organization (sometimes listed as part of experience)
- Extensive travel or residence in a foreign country in which a firm has holdings
- Speaking the language of a foreign country in which a firm has holdings
- Nonremunerated consulting work that provided valuable related experience (sometimes listed as part of experience)

In a section on activities and accomplishments, include only those relevant to your objectives and significant enough to add support to the persuasive thrust. Unless you have just completed high school, do not include high-school activities unless they show substantial maturity, responsibility, or relevancy to the position. Do not list such activities as cheerleading, social fraternities and sororities, pep clubs, sports, choirs, and other musical groups unless they relate directly to your objectives or exemplify significant leadership abilities.

Once you complete a post-secondary degree, drop all high school activities from your résumé. Until you establish some experience after completion of a degree, you may include some collegiate activities. However, again, do not include activities unless they exhibit leadership or relate closely to your career field. Certainly do not include the kinds of activities listed in the preceding paragraph. Include a separate section on activities only when pertinent activities do not fit naturally into the other sections. Do not feel that you have to include one. (Figures 15–1, 15–2, and 15–4 contain sections on activities.)

Memberships

Some of the types of activities and accomplishments suggested for the previous section relate to memberships in professional, honorary, and civic organizations. Therefore, a single section may show a combination of activities and affiliations. Whether combined or separate, however, a listing of pertinent organizational memberships and participation belongs in many résumés. Put in the list only those organizations that represent current educational and career status. Include only the names of those organizations in which you currently and actively take part. Thus, include active honorary organizations, but leave the inactive ones for the subsequent section on honors.

Honors and Awards

When *significant* honors and awards relate to your career plan, report them in your résumé. They need not form a separate section. (However, Figure 15–2 includes honors and awards under a distinct heading.)

High school If you have not been out of high school long, you may include significant honors from your high school career. Appropriate honors include such earned recognitions as *Who's Who,* honor societies, valedictorian, salutatorian, and scholarships awarded upon graduation. Appropriate honors do *not* include such designations as kingships, queenships, beauty-pageant titles, sweethearts, class favorites, or "most-popular" designations. Sometimes honors such as being named "most likely to succeed," "outstanding business student," or "outstanding athlete" may qualify as preparation. However, many readers consider them unrelated to the serious pursuance of a career.

College Once you receive a degree from a college or university, drop the high school honors, and add those gained during the collegiate years. Include in the post-secondary listing such honors as Phi Beta Kappa, Rhodes Scholar, Mortar Board, *Who's Who,* scholarships, valedictorian, salutatorian, class marshall, *summa cum laude, magna cum laude, cum laude,* and awards for outstanding scholarship in special fields of study. Omit the same kinds of designations cited for omission from the high school listing.

Post-college As soon as you have built some career experience, drop all of the collegiate honors and awards except those that carry a lifetime meaning. (For example, retain a designation like Phi Beta Kappa.) Replace collegiate honors and awards with professional ones: outstanding man/woman of the year; leading a city, region, or the nation in annual sales; or some other kind of recognized achievement. Consider carefully whether to include some of the "who's who" publications. Many of them have reached the point that almost anyone's name appears if he or she completes a form and buys a copy of the publication. Some personnel officers have begun to dismiss them as meaningless affectations by those who do list them.

Personal Information

The traditional résumé (Figure 15–2) includes a section on personal information, usually placed at the beginning. However, many people now omit the section entirely. Others who do include such a section include minimal information and place the section after more important components.

If you do include a personal information section, decide carefully what you want to include in it. Recent laws and rulings have greatly reduced the amount of personal information that you must provide. In the same vein, you no longer have to include the photograph so common to the résumé of a few years ago. Many employment decision-makers prefer not to know any personal information for fear of accusations of discrimination or reverse discrimination.

A middle-ground approach calls for including address(es), telephone number(s), and times when you can be reached at each, while omitting the photograph and any personal characteristics believed negative to chances of fair treatment. However, you may want to include additional information that will not lead to prejudice against you or that will not make the reader uncomfortable. For example, giving family status (married or single, children or no children, etc.) sometimes has no impact upon the reader except to suggest something about you as a human being. Similarly, the inclusion of such physical characteristics as height, weight, and general health may help create a nonprejudiced personal sketch.

If you do decide to include a photograph, do not fix it permanently to the page. The reviewers may want to remove it. The inclusion of a statement of interests and hobbies can replace some of the questionable personal items. Figures 15–1 through 15–4 illustrate some different treatments of the personal sections of résumés.

Hobbies and Interests

Sometimes a résumé includes a part that lists hobbies and interests. However, with the movement away from revealing much personal information, this section may gradually become the major portion of the personal section. It may no longer exist as a distinct one. Briefly naming and describing some personal hobbies, pleasures, and interests often provides relief from the heaviness of the other information in a résumé. In any case, such a listing does not take much space and usually introduces no risk. Observe how the writer treats the sections on hobbies and interests in Figure 15–2.

Desired Action

Résumés sometimes must stand alone, for example in placement or employment office folders. Therefore, some writers elect to include closing persuasive calls to action. When including such a call, keep it brief. Make it fit the format and style of the preceding sections. Also create a heading for the action section that parallels the previous structure. Introduce overt persuasion into a résumé cautiously. Most decision makers probably still expect the traditional factual style. They might tend to reject anything that departs too much from that expectation. In fact, many people believe that directly persuasive statements have absolutely no place in résumés.

References

References usually occupy the final position in a résumé. They do so out of custom, not out of any realistic consideration for emphasizing the most important component. When listing the names, titles, addresses, and telephone numbers of references, obtain their permission prior to submitting the résumé. Indicate on the résumé that you did obtain the permissions. Carefully choose the people whom you include as references. Try to select people with knowledge representing the range of various facets of your career and professional talents and experiences. Because you usually will list no more than five or six, do not include character references unless specifically requested to do so.

Writers often omit a list of references in the résumé. However, they usually do include the heading and simply note that the applicant will provide references upon request. Figures 15-2 and 15-3 include such notations.

Application Letter

A letter of application usually accompanies a résumé. Figures 15-5 through 15-8 present a variety of styles for letters of application. Whatever the style, though, the letter of application must be a strong effort to persuade the reader to action.

Format and Style

Use the basic letter format for the message of application. Always adapt the style to fit your analysis of the receiver and her or his environment. For example, for an unsolicited message, you may have to add some flair to gain the desired attention. On the other hand, you may need to retain a moderate approach so that you will not risk alienating the receiver because of an unusual style. The decision depends upon a careful analysis of the circumstances and the probable nature of the receiver.

Even when adding persuasive touches of color and informality to application messages, preserve most of the amenities. Typewrite the letter using correct basic format and mechanics. Use good-quality paper. Include your return address properly positioned. Include the inside address. Include or omit the salutation depending upon the choice of style. Use subject and attention lines if appropriate. Except for the simplified style, include an appropriate complimentary close. Use the signature block to establish your name and desired courtesy title. Use the enclosure notation to acknowledge the résumé and any other enclosure. Always refer to the résumé in the body of the letter as well. Address the envelope correctly, and fold and insert the letter and other materials properly. For a bulky mailing, use an envelope large enough to hold the materials without having to fold them.

Whenever possible, write each letter of application uniquely and personally to the appropriate person(s) at the firm for which you want to work. If you simply cannot obtain that information, include in the inside address and salutation a traditional title. One such title is "Personnel Director." Figure 15-8 illustrates this approach. If you decide to omit the unknown name, title, and thus the salutation, you may replace the salutation with the kinds of attention-getting phrases and statements used for any persuasive letter (for example, in Figure 15-8).

Use the basic AICA plan of development. Apply the principles for gaining attention: stimulating interest, developing conviction, and calling for action. Apply all of the other suggestions relating to such features as emphasis, vocabulary, active voice, transition, and coherence. Even retain the "you"

400 Skinner Street, Apt. 148
Dillon, Utah 33129
April 15, 1981

Ms. Lee Wong, Human Relations Manager
Mariel Lumber Company
15 Mariel Way
Frilen, Washington 99432

Dear Ms. Wong:

I have taken more courses in organization development than have most of my contemporaries. As an entry-level specialist in your organization development program, I could put my excellent training and extensive knowledge to work for you and for Mariel Lumber Company.

The 320-hour program that I completed at the prestigious Wyler Institute of Management afforded me the opportunity to complete the exploration of organization development that I had begun as a management major at the University of Dillon. My training would allow me to make meaningful contributions to your organization development program, the program I read about in the March issue of Human Resources Monthly. Your program is the most current and ambitious program that I have ever seen.

I am confident that I could perform in a variety of roles in your program because of my unique training as an organization development specialist, because of my two years of experience as a management tutor, and because of my solid general training in business and the arts and sciences at the University of Dillon.

Because I know my unique training would be an asset to your top-notch program, I am eager to become a part of your organization development team, I will be available for work on May 15, a week after I complete my Bachelor of Arts degree in business at the University of Dillon.

By referring to the enclosed résumé and contacting the people I list as references, you will be able to acquire an overall picture of my specialized qualifications.

Please call me or write me soon because I am eager to have a personal interview with you. I will be able to come to Frilen at your convenience.

Sincerely,

Milton A. Rosen

Milton A. Rosen

Enclosure

FIGURE 15–5 Application letter accompanying Milton A. Rosen's résumé.

2332 Pine Road
Anthony, Idaho 44662
June 1, 1980

Mr. Eric Hendricksen, Personnel Director
Shapiro, Hart & Wenner, Inc.
Willtoe, Nevada 33963

Dear Mr. Hendricksen:

As the daughter of two farmers, I learned the meaning of hard work at an early age. The lessons I learned on the farm have been invaluable, and I have devoted all of my energy to every job, project, or school course that I have ever undertaken.

Your advertisement in the May 29 edition of the Daily Nevadan asked for an energetic, hard-working person. Your advertisement also asked that the job applicant be a competent investment counselor.

My two degrees in finance and my experience as an investment assistant make me a competent investment counselor. My years on the farm and the fact that I paid my own way through rigorous, expensive undergraduate and graduate finance programs make me a hard working, competent investment counselor. As you will notice on the enclosed résumé, my work at DiRenzio and Barber, Inc., involved both investment planning and investment folder preparation.

I want to use my farm-hand energy and common sense, my excellent training in finance, and my considerable intelligence to give your Shapiro, Hart & Wenner clients sound investment advice. I can begin work for you immediately.

May I please hear from you soon concerning a personal interview? You can contact me at my home address, at 555-721-6231, or at 555-721-4992.

Sincerely,

Janet E. Smith

Janet E. Smith

Enclosure: Résumé

FIGURE 15-6 Application letter accompanying Janet E. Smith's résumé.

4231 Vine Street
Boston, Massachusetts 99496
August 3, 1980

Ms. Linda Kelsoe, Industrial Relations Manager
Quarel Foods, Inc.
13904 Industrial Triangle Drive
Boston, Massachusetts 09498

Dear Ms. Kelsoe:

My background makes me confident that I can creatively perform as the training and development manager for Quarel Foods, Inc.

As my resume indicates, I have four years of full-time experience in training and development and organization development. Perhaps my most notable accomplishment in the training field was the extremely successful training and development program that I developed and implemented at Adams and Ross, Inc., a systems management group. By the time that I left Adams and Ross, 75 percent of the managerial and professional employees were voluntarily participating in my program's 15 training sequences.

While earning the B.B.A. and M.B.A. degrees in management, I took 33 semester hours of training and development and organization development courses, and I earned a perfect—4.0—grade point average in those courses. The Boston Business Institute, the institution from which I earned my M.B.A. degree, is well known for its excellent training and development courses.

Because I am familiar with your Quarel Foods, Inc., operation, I know your industrial relations department is most impressive. I would very much like to be a part of the food manufacturing industry and of your fine department as the manager of training and development at Quarel Foods. Your interest in team building is an interest that I share, and the team-building workshops that I conducted at Darmer Real Estate were both successful and enjoyable.

Please call me at 666-1319 so that I can answer any of your questions. Sometime during the next two weeks I would like to meet with you at your convenience. I am eager to discuss my many training and development ideas with you.

Sincerely,

Maria E. Martinez

Maria E. Martinez

Enclosure

FIGURE 15–7 Application letter accompanying Maria E. Martinez's résumé.

13 Walker Avenue
Argyle, Maine 22914
August 15, 1981

Personnel Director
Waygo Pharmaceuticals, Inc.
333 East Main Street
Silverton, New Hampshire 33692

YOUR COMPANY COULD PUT AN ENERGETIC,
SUCCESSFUL SALESPERSON LIKE ME
TO WORK IMMEDIATELY.
AND YOU'D GET FANTASTIC RESULTS!

HERE'S WHY:

1. For the four summers that I managed the entire Vermont sales district for the Argyle Chemical Company, I exceeded my sales quota every month.

2. While working my way through the University of Argyle, I was a top part-time salesperson for the Argyle Department Store.

3. My major at the University of Argyle was selling, and I earned my Bachelor of Arts degree in business. Twenty-seven quarter term hours in selling and marketing made up a significant portion of my coursework.

As my résumé notes, a challenging position as a salesperson for a major, growing pharmaceutical company like yours is my objective. Remember, both my selling experience and business education would allow you to put me to work immediately. You could have me exceeding sales quotas for you every month of the year.

Selling is the thing I do best. Please call me at (555) 232-1194 so that I can begin work for you immediately.

Sincerely,

Lee Wu

Lee Wu

Enclosure

FIGURE 15–8 Application letter accompanying Lee Wu's résumé.

attitude. Appeal to the reader's needs. Try to convince the reader that hiring you will benefit her or him. Even with the "you" attitude, you will have to use the first-person pronouns. However, try not to overuse them, and space them well through the message.

Whatever the circumstances of the transaction, apply the guidelines and principles particularly carefully. Never will you encounter a situation that requires you to sell anything more important; you essentially sell yourself.

Techniques for Successful Application Letters

David Gootnick lists 13 techniques for developing successful messages of application:

1. Be positive and confident, but not presumptuous or arrogant.
2. Talk of key credentials to fulfill the job requirements.
3. Show interest in working for the company.
4. Show knowledge of the company.
5. Show knowledge of the job requirements.
6. Prove that your capabilities and experience fulfill key requirements.
7. Be forthright in seeking the interview, but still respectful.
8. Compliment the firm's work or reputation but avoid obvious or insincere flattery.
9. Refer to the résumé for evidence of your qualifications.
10. Avoid any negative remarks about yourself, others, and the company.
11. Use the letter opening to excite the reader about you and to let the reader know what you want, namely the job. You capture attention and build interest by mentioning such things as:
    a. the job-ad source
    b. a person well known to the reader
    c. a person of fame
    d. a comment that assures reader agreement
    e. a significant accomplishment of the firm
    f. an accomplishment of the reader
    g. an award or honor of the reader
    h. a significant change in the field
    i. an important and felt need of the firm
    j. a personal qualification currently in need by the firm
12. Use the letter middle to create desire. Prove, in this part, that you have what it takes to excel in the job. Whet the reader's interest by highlighting key capabilities and by using the enclosed résumé as a reservoir of key accomplishments to prove your strengths. If you have prepared a nutshell summary in the résumé, be certain that this part of the letter is phrased or slanted somewhat differently.
13. Use the letter ending to request the interview and stimulate action.[1]

Even as you try to include all of these elements, however, try to limit your letters to one page. Carefully develop the theme and the key points, and tie them together in a warm, but concise package.

Analyze Figures 15-5 through 15-8 to determine how well you think they meet the criteria. Would the recipients read the résumés? Would they invite the writers for interviews? Would they acknowledge receipt of the material even if an opening does not exist? Would they hand the letters to others for consideration? Would they simply file them?

As you review the figures, also notice how the general-search letter (Figure 15-8) lacks some of the precision and zest possible in the specific letters (Figures 15-5, 15-6, and 15-7). Similarly, notice how the writer responding to an advertisement (Figure 15-6) cannot include the focus on a specific theme that a writer with more detailed information about the firm can. The contrast between that letter and Figures 15-5 and 15-7 illustrates the difference.

To develop a successful letter of application, retain a basic honesty in a message that reflects a sound application of the principles and guidelines for good communication. Let your personal style emerge even as you meet the requirements that custom and good form impose.

The final chapter in this book—Chapter 16—concludes the discussion of employment messages. It does so by covering some additional written messages, interviews, appearance, and careers in communication.

SUMMARY

The campaign for employment involves sending and receiving written, oral, and nonverbal messages. Thus, the guidelines for effective communication and the principles for reading, listening, observing, writing, speaking, and sending nonverbal messages all apply.

Planning for a career requires several steps: (1) Assess your current status. (2) Establish goals for career status at selected points in time in the future. (3) Identify barriers to the attainment of your career-status goals. (4) Determine what you need to do to reach the specified career-status goals. (5) Establish a precise plan and time schedule. (6) Activate the plan. (7) Review and revise the plan periodically.

To aid in career planning, you may want to take tests, consult publications, and interview knowledgeable people. Use both optimism and realism in setting time schedules, and identify and set strategies to overcome internal and external barriers. After setting career goals and plans, set them for a specific job campaign. The goals and plans relate to learning about the firm, developing and testing a résumé and letter of application, interviewing, and receiving the job offer.

Many written messages characterize a job search. The résumé and letter of application represent two of the major types. The résumé—also called a personal data sheet, data sheet, or vita—contains information about you and your qualifications for employment. Arrange the contents of the résumé in an order that emphasizes the features pertinent to the job you want. The résumé may include as many as 12 parts: (1) heading, (2) objectives, (3) education and training, (4) experience, (5) research and publications, (6) activities and accomplishments, (7) memberships, (8) honors and awards, (9) personal information, (10) hobbies and interests, (11) desired action, and (12) references.

The letter of application presents a relatively formal but persuasive message. Adapt the format and style to fit your personality and the circumstances of the application. Apply the writing principles and communication guidelines fully and carefully. Some of the techniques for a successful letter of application include: (1) Set a positive and confident tone. (2) Talk of key credentials. (3) Show interest and knowledge. (4) Refer to the résumé. (5) Avoid negative remarks. (6) Use the opening and closing positions for gaining attention and soliciting action. (7) Try to contain the letter on one page.

EXERCISES

1. You stand a good chance of getting hired at Aldridge, Inc., if you can get an interview with Alice Rogers, a very powerful Aldridge vice president. The normal procedure is to send an application to the personnel department, but you know that few people make it past the personnel department. Write a letter directly to Rogers. Try to persuade her to grant you an interview. Remember that Rogers will not be following the normal employment procedure if she decides to interview you.
2. *[Your instructor will time this exercise.]* You just learned that a position opened up at the firm for which you want to work. The opening is for an entry-level marketing associate who will develop marketing plans for small toys. The toys will be sold only in the local area. You have already prepared a résumé that emphasizes your abilities as a marketer. Now write a one-page letter of application that you will send with your marketing résumé. Address the letter to:

   Mr. Arnold Benner, Personnel Director
   Dorn Marketing Group
   2233 Fisher Lane
   Savelle, Mississippi 26919

3. Prepare your own résumé. Do not tailor it to any specific position, but do emphasize your best qualities in a traditional form. Try to include all of the résumé components listed on page 427 except for the section on desired action.
4. Convert your conventionally designed résumé (Exercise No. 3) into a résumé with creativity and flair. Include a section on desired action. Meet with your group to discuss and evaluate both forms of résumés. Decide whether you think prospective employers generally would react more favorably toward the conventional or creative résumé in each case—and why. Choose a member to report the group's decision and reasons to the class.
5. You plan to apply for a position as an accountant at a local accounting firm. You have been told that you are to send only your résumé; the firm wants no letters of application. You decide that because your résumé must stand alone, you should include a section that makes explicit the action that you desire. Write the desired-action paragraph.
6. With your group, use the brainstorming technique to identify the interpersonal

strengths and weaknesses of each member of the group. Allow each person to participate in her or his own analysis. After the brainstorming, allow each member to discuss her or his list—questioning the validity of it if desired. Summarize any strengths or weaknesses common to the members of the group. Choose one member to report the findings to the class.

7. Select a career field which you would like to enter upon graduation. Check the literature to learn all you can about it. Write a two-page paper reporting your findings.
8. Identify and analyze an actual firm in the career field selected in Exercise No. 7. Write a letter of application for a desired position within that firm.
9. Complete for yourself the first five stages of career planning (see pages 422–23).
10. Develop a schedule of how and when you will activate, review, evaluate, and possibly revise the career plan you developed in Exercise No. 9. Make the plan a practical one that you actually will use.
11. Visit the testing/counseling center on your campus. Learn what services, tests, etc., are available to help in your personal career planning. Write a one- or two-page paper summarizing your findings and indicating which of the services and tests you plan to use. Include an actual time schedule for that use.
12. Meet with your group. Develop an interview guide for interviews with businesspeople to learn what they consider to be the major mistakes made by applicants for positions with their firms. Have each member select a businessperson who has contact with applicants, schedule and complete the interview, and report the findings in a one- or two-page paper. Reconvene the group to summarize the papers. Select a group member to report the summary to the class.
13. Interview representatives of a private employment agency and a government employment office. Develop an interview guide before doing so. Write a report comparing the findings of the two interviews.
14. Use your dictionary and thesaurus to create meanings for these words. Use the words when you think, write, and speak so that you feel comfortable using them.
    - a. Cardinal
    - b. Characterize
    - c. Coherent
    - d. Defuse
    - e. Evolve
    - f. Exemplify
    - g. Innocuous
    - h. Orientation
    - i. Peer
    - j. Perceive
    - k. Protocol
    - l. Remuneration
    - m. Scenario
    - n. Unorthodox
15. Take and score Self-Test 32 over Chapter 15.

SELF-TEST 31
Excerpt about Planning for a Career

A. Recall (33 points each). For each multiple-choice question, select the most accurate answer.

1. The first step in planning your career is to:
    - a. Find several references
    - b. Prepare your résumé, letters of application, and placement files
    - c. Identify all the jobs available in your city
    - d. Assess your current status in employment, education and training, experience, intelligence and knowledge, and attitudes and interests
    - e. Visit an employment agency

2. Which of these is a career barrier over which you have some control?
   a. You do not have the education necessary for the jobs that you want.
   b. Unemployment in your field is high.
   c. You simply cannot find a job that will pay enough to allow you to get the education that you need.
   d. General unemployment is high.
   e. You are the "wrong" sex or race, have the "wrong" ethnic background, belong to the "wrong" church, or have some physical limitations.

B. Inference (34 points). Indicate whether this statement is true or false.
   1. When you engage in careful career planning, you exercise more control over your life.

SOLUTION

A. Recall (33 points each)
   1. d 2. a

B. Inference (34 points)
   1. True

SELF-TEST 32
Chapter 15

A. Recall (25 points each). For each multiple-choice question, select the most accurate answer.
   1. Which of these is probably the best channel to use for your initial job contact?
      a. Telephone
      b. Letter
      c. Face-to-face interview
      d. Telegram
      e. a and b
   2. Which of these entries does *not* belong on a résumé that you will use to secure a position as a financial analyst?
      a. Member, Finance Club
      b. M.B.A. in Accounting, University of Arizona
      c. Baton Twirler, Del Ray High School
      d. B.A. in journalism, University of Kansas
      e. Salesperson, Alling Pharmaceutical Company
   3. Which one of these statements is true?
      a. The guidelines for position-search communication are significantly different from those for other types of communication.
      b. The résumé usually is overtly persuasive.
      c. Letters of application generally allow for more creativity and persuasion than do résumés.
      d. Nonverbal messages have no impact on the written parts of the employment process.
      e. The most important information in a résumé or letter of application should be placed in the middle (body) of the message.

B. Inference (25 points). For the multiple-choice question, select the most accurate answer.

1. Which one of these statements is *false*?
   - **a.** Exercise modesty about listing post-college honors and awards in a résumé.
   - **b.** No universal suggestions exist for the content of the personal information section of the résumé.
   - **c.** A résumé may take on some of the features usually reserved for the letter of application.
   - **d.** The inclusion of a list of references in a résumé is declining.
   - **e.** The closing part of a letter of application may be used to stimulate the reader to contact you about an interview.

SOLUTION

A. Recall (25 points each)

1. b **3.** c

2. c

B. Inference (25 points)

1. a

ENDNOTES

1. David Gootnick, *Getting a Better Job* (New York: McGraw-Hill Book Company, 1978), 85.

STUDENT'S OBJECTIVES:

1 To continue to apply the guidelines and principles of effective communication to employment messages

2 To learn to write a follow-up letter to reinforce interest and ability for a job

3 To learn to develop messages that respond to an offer of a job: a letter of acceptance, a letter of rejection, and a letter of delay

4 To learn to write a letter of thanks for an interview

16

EMPLOYMENT: Other Written Messages, Interviews, Appearance, Business Commmunication Careers

5 To learn to complete application blanks

6 To learn strategies for placement- and employment-office files, particularly as they concern confidentiality

7 To learn to give a good interview

8 To learn the proper dress and appearance for an interview

9 To review some careers in the field of business communication and reinforce the importance of communication to all careers in business

Chapter 16 completes the coverage of employment messages. The first section deals with additional written messages (building on the foundation of Chapter 15). Subsequent sections cover interviews, appearance and dress, communication and careers, and business as a communication-centered operation.

ADDITIONAL WRITTEN MESSAGES

The résumé and the letter of application represent the two major written messages of an employment-seeking campaign. However, several other written messages often enter into that process. Such messages include letters of follow-up, acceptance, rejection, delay, and thanks; application blanks; and other messages.

Letter of Follow-up

Sometimes during the application process, you may need to create new messages as follow-ups to others, such as following up an application or contact from a prospective employer.

Initial Application

Sometimes an initial application message elicits no response, or at best a routine one. (This situation arises more often for unsolicited applications than for solicited applications.) In routine-response or nonresponse circumstances, a follow-up letter often proves useful. It can initiate or intensify interest in your application.

Make the follow-up message brief and persuasive. While reinforcing some of the key points included in the original message, use attention and action techniques to stimulate the reader to review the original. Perhaps send two or three such letters, or even move to the more effective telephone channel. However, after a few unsuccessful follow-up contacts, dismiss that company and move on to another strategy. Figure 16–1 illustrates a follow-up letter written after the application letter received no response.

Initial Contact from Prospective Employer

Another stage of the application process, after a successful contact with a potential employer, may also call for a follow-up letter. In one case, a nonroutine letter or telephone call by the prospective employer may follow your initial application. In another case, it may follow your initial interview. In both cases, either you or the prospective employer may decide that you need to supply additional information or develop an idea introduced in the first transaction. The follow-up letter in Figure 16–2 shows how messages at this stage may continue to build the persuasion toward action.

13 Walker Avenue
Argyle, Maine 22914
August 30, 1981

Personnel Director
Waygo Pharmaceuticals, Inc.
333 East Main Street
Silverton, New Hampshire 33692

YOU HIRE SUCCESS IF
YOU HIRE ME!

Perhaps you haven't had time to respond to my first letter? As I wrote in that letter, I am an experienced, educated, and extremely successful salesperson who would like to sell for you at Waygo.

My bachelor's degree is in business—with a major in selling. More important, I have four years of solid experience as a quota-bursting salesperson. My resume tells my success story well, so I enclosed another one for your convenience.

Though I am eager to work for you, I have a number of offers to consider. You could give me a chance to accept yours. I could come for an interview almost any time next week.

Please call me at (555) 232-1194. You'll get an energetic, successful salesperson on the line.

Hire immediate success.

Sincerely,

Lee Wu

Lee Wu

Enclosure

FIGURE 16-1 Lee Wu's follow-up letter.

Letter of Acceptance

A prompt response should follow the potential employer's offer of a position. The response might take the form of an *acceptance* message. Write it to convey satisfaction at receiving the offer, to indicate your intent to accept it, and to reinforce confidence in your ability to do the job.

Because the letter of acceptance basically carries good news, use the direct style of writing. Keep the message direct and brief. Figure 16-3 provides

13 Walker Avenue
Argyle, Maine 22914
September 7, 1981

Ms. Wenoma Drum, Sales Manager
Waygo Pharmaceuticals, Inc.
333 East Main Street
Silverton, New Hampshire 33692

Dear Ms. Drum:

Thank you so much for taking some time out of your busy Thursday to discuss selling opportunities at Waygo with me. The advice you gave me was most informative.

The prospect of selling for Waygo Pharmaceuticals, Inc., still interests me very much. I am confident that I could bring success to one of the three entry-level sales positions we discussed.

As I pointed out, I know how to sell, and I enjoy selling immensely. Your Waygo sales quotas would be barriers that I could cross in no time; at Argyle Chemical I never let a sales quota go unsurmounted. Also, my bachelor's degree in business—with a major in selling—gave me a solid educational background from which I can continually create both new selling approaches and innovative distribution techniques.

Now that I've had a chance to discuss the Waygo operations with you, Ms. Drum, I am absolutely convinced that I want to work for you as a Waygo salesperson.

Again, I so appreciate the time you spent with me.

Sincerely,

Lee Wu

Lee Wu

FIGURE 16–2 Lee Wu's post-interview follow-up letter.

an example of a letter of acceptance. Examine it to determine whether it carries out the suggestions.

Letter of Rejection

The letter of rejection delivers bad news, because it usually rejects an actively sought position. Because of the negative response, select the indirect developmental method for the letter of rejection. Build to the rejection by citing the

13 Walker Avenue
Argyle, Maine 22914
September 25, 1981

Ms. Wenoma Drum, Sales Manager
Waygo Pharmaceuticals, Inc.
333 East Main Street
Silverton, New Hampshire 33692

Dear Ms. Drum:

I most definitely accept your offer to join Waygo as an entry-level salesperson in the Vermont sales district. My familiarity with Vermont will allow me to seek out new customers as well as provide excellent service to your established clients.

The $14,500 annual salary and the sales commission schedule are most satisfactory. Your $500 salary advance will make it much easier for me to move to Silverton before Monday, October 15, the day that you want me to report to work. I will come to your office at 9 A.M. on that Monday, as you asked.

Thank you for making me a part of your Waygo sales team. You will get excellent work from me every day that I sell for you.

I look forward to meeting with you on October 15.

Sincerely,

Lee Wu

Lee Wu

FIGURE 16-3 Lee Wu's letter of acceptance.

reasons for it. Retain courtesy and the "you" attitude throughout. Figure 16-4 illustrates a letter of rejection. It uses the positive sandwich to carry the bad news.

Letter of Delay

A letter of delay asks for a postponement on the decision of whether to accept a job offer. The need to delay may arise when an offer comes from a firm before completion of other interviews. The need also may arise because the offer comes from a lower-priority firm, although it could serve if a preferred offer does not materialize. Requests to delay a decision about an offer also may arise from personal reasons or external circumstances.

13 Walker Avenue
Argyle, Maine 22914
September 25, 1981

Ms. Wenoma Drum, Sales Manager
Waygo Pharmaceuticals, Inc.
333 East Main Street
Silverton, New Hampshire 33692

Dear Ms. Drum:

Thank you for your generous job offer. I realize that the Vermont sales district is a plum, and I think that your sales department is one of the best that I have seen.

The Morey Drug Company just offered me the job of heading its entire Pacific sales district. I would supervise the district's thirty salespersons, and I would also travel extensively. Because the sales manager acts as a salesperson, manager, and world traveler all at once, I have decided to join the Morey Drug Company staff.

Again, thank you for taking the time to discuss your company with me. And more important, thank you for the appealing job offer.

I am sure that this will be a record-breaking sales year for you, and I hope that I'll be fortunate enough to meet you again someday.

Sincerely,

Lee Wu

Lee Wu

FIGURE 16–4 Lee Wu's letter of rejection.

The letter of delay is a combination of bad-news and persuasive messages. Thus, use the positive sandwich to accompany the indirect development style. Logically support the request for action—the receiver's agreement to the delay. Figure 16–5 shows an example of a request for postponement of the decision in response to an offer of a position. Does it meet the requirements for such a letter?

Letter of Thanks

Sometimes an employment-seeking campaign calls for thank-you messages. For example, a thank-you message may acknowledge an interview with an

2332 Pine Road
Anthony, Idaho 44662
June 10, 1980

Mr. Alvin Swagner, Personnel Manager
Scanlon Investment Services, Inc.
326 West Ninth Avenue
Dariel, Tennessee 72221

Dear Mr. Swagner:

Your offer to have me join Scanlon Investment Services, Inc., as a financial analyst is most appealing. The job sounds both interesting and challenging.

I have not yet completed interviews with three other investment firms; my last interview will take place early next week. Because I want to base my career decisions on as much information as possible, I would like to respond to your offer by phone next Friday, June 24, after my last interview. If June 24 is not satisfactory, please call or write me so that we can discuss a more convenient time for you.

I was very impressed with both Scanlon Investment Services and the city of Dariel when I visited you last week. As a financial analyst in your international division, I know that I could make sound contributions to your fine company.

Sincerely,

Janet E. Smith

Janet E. Smith

FIGURE 16–5 Janet E. Smith's letter of delay.

important prospect. It will show thoughtfulness, fix your application in the mind of the interviewer, and reinforce the persuasion. Follow the traditional rules for writing a routine thank-you message. However, insert just enough information to support your original application purpose. Figure 16–6 is an example of a thank-you message appropriate to an employment-seeking campaign. Examine it for style and content.

Application Blank

Your ability to complete an application blank properly will have a great deal to do with the success of your application. The attainment of many entry-level jobs depends entirely upon proper completion of an application form.

2332 Pine Road
Anthony, Idaho 44662
June 21, 1980

Ms. Mary Shapiro, Partner
Shapiro, Hart & Wenner, Inc.
Willtoe, Nevada 33963

Dear Ms. Shapiro:

Thank you so much for taking the time to discuss the bright future of your investment firm with me. Your five-year plan takes into account every conceivable economic change.

I am even more interested in working as an investment counselor for Shapiro, Hart & Wenner, Inc., now that I have talked with you, Ms. Shapiro. The company is in very good hands.

Again, thank you for the fine interview. Please let me know if you have any questions.

Sincerely,

Janet E. Smith

Janet E. Smith

FIGURE 16-6 Janet E. Smith's thank-you letter.

These suggestions aid in completing application forms:

1. Keep your résumé up to date, and carry a copy of it (or a skeleton outline of the key points of it) with you any time you may have to complete an application form.
2. Read the instructions on the form carefully before beginning to complete it. Follow them precisely.
3. If the instructions specify printing or handwriting responses, do as required. Otherwise, use the style that creates the better nonverbal impression.
4. Complete every blank on the form—even if you have to insert entries like "None," "Not applicable," "0," or "—."
5. Complete the form correctly and neatly. Carry a small dictionary with you if you need it to spell words correctly.
6. For open-end questions, organize your thoughts carefully and write a

draft of the answer on a piece of scratch paper before transferring it to the form.

7. Answer questions honestly, but in a manner that will emphasize strengths, not weaknesses.
8. As suggested for the résumé, consider carefully whether to include or omit answers to questions that you may not legally have to answer.
9. If the form includes a question about what salary you expect to receive, write an actual figure or range of figures if you have made such a decision, or write something like:
   a. The typical salary paid for the position to someone of my ability
   b. To be discussed during interview
   c. Negotiable
   d. Open for discussion
10. Upon completion, review the entries for completeness and accuracy.

The completion of an application form has as its major purpose obtaining a desired position. However, it may also become a permanent part of your personnel file. Figure 16-7 provides an example of a completed application form. Check it for all ten suggestions for good completion.

Other Messages

Additional written messages in an employment-seeking campaign take a routine or special form. Examples include (1) tests and (2) placement- and employment-office files.

Tests

Many firms require applicants to complete employment tests. Anticipate and review the kinds of questions that may appear on such tests. Obtain sample tests and take them. As in completing any form, read test instructions and follow them carefully. Try to relax. Take account of the time factor involved. Answer open-end questions particularly carefully; they show not only knowledge, but also your ability to write.

Placement and Employment Office Files

A campus placement office or an employment agency can sometimes aid your search for a position. Both types of service usually require the same kinds of messages that one prepares for an independent job search.

Carefully make the decision about whether to mark recommendation forms "confidential" or "nonconfidential." If marked confidential, the persons writing the recommendation may feel freer to communicate frankly. Readers also may feel that the information holds more meaning than nonconfidential recommendations. If you mark the forms nonconfidential, you do have the right to review them. Thus, you can make sure that no one has included false information—or information that may interfere with your opportunities to obtain jobs. Most directors of placement offices recommend marking the forms "confidential." However, you do have the choice.

SHAPIRO, HART & WENNER, INC., Willtoe, Nevada 33963

General Information

Date June 6, 1980 Job wanted Investment Counselor Salary wanted $18,000/year

Full name Janet Ellen Smith

Address 2332 Pine Road, Anthony, Idaho 44662

Message phone (555) 721-4992 Home phone (555) 721-6231

Social Security number 448-000-000

Of what country are you a citizen? U.S.A.

Equal Opportunity Information

You are not obligated to complete this section. Your decision will not affect your chances for a job.

Sex Female Age 31 Race Black Are you handicapped? No

Legal Information

Have you ever been convicted of a felony? No

Have you ever had your driver's license suspended? No

If you answered "yes" to one or both of the above, explain the circumstances here: Not applicable

Educational Information

Name the high schools, colleges, and other training institutions that you attended. Include the school's address, the degree you received, and the dates that you attended.

1. Linwood High School, Linwood, Idaho 44621
   High school diploma.
   From September, 1972, through May, 1975.
2. Linwood Community College, Linwood, Idaho 44621
   Associate of Science degree in Business Administration.
   From September, 1975, through May, 1977
3. Anthony University, Anthony, Idaho 44662
   Bachelor of Science degree in Finance.
   From September, 1977, through May, 1979.
4. Anthony University, Anthony, Idaho 44662
   Master of Business Administration in Finance.
   From June, 1979, through May, 1980.

FIGURE 16-7 Janet E. Smith's completed application blank.

Employment Information

List your current or last positon first.

Firm's name DiRenzio and Barber, Inc.

Supervisor's name Kathryn Barber

Address 98 East Fourth Street, Anthony, Idaho 44662

Phone (555) 721-4999 Starting salary $650/month Ending salary $710/month

Period worked June 5, 1978 & June 5, 1979 to Sept. 5, 1978 Sept. 5, 1979 Part-time ______ Full-time X

Title Investment Assistant

Duties Prepared investment folders and counseled clients

Reason for leaving Went back to school

Firm's name Leland and Daughters Construction Company

Supervisor's name Carolyn Leland

Address 46 Dayfield Plaza, Anthony, Idaho 44662

Phone (555) 721-4332 Starting salary $4/hour Ending salary $6/hour

Period worked June 1, 1976 & June 1, 1977 to Sept. 1, 1976 Sept. 5, 1977 Part-time ______ Full-time X

Title Carpenter

Duties Built kitchen and bathroom cabinets in new homes and office buildings.

Reason for leaving Went back to school

References

Give the names, addresses, occupations, and phone numbers of three references. Do not name the supervisors you listed in the employment section.

1. Sidney Lewis, Ed.D., 32 Farley Hall, Anthony University
   Anthony, Idaho 44662—professor. Phone: (555) 721-1343
2. Denise Flanagan, 462 Albert Place
   Anthony, Idaho 44662—investment counselor. Phone: (555) 721-3368
3. Wallace Erickson, 16 Avell Road
   Linwood, Idaho 44621—banker. Phone: (555) 821-9175

The information I have given is to the best of my knowledge correct and complete.

Janet E. Smith 7/5/1981

Signature Date

FIGURE 16–7 (Continued).

INTERVIEWS

The search for a position involves many oral transactions, such as telephone conversations, face-to-face conversations, introductions to potential co-workers, and interviews. The interview, however, forms the hub of the oral application process.

The first interview usually occurs with a professional interviewer from a personnel office. The second interview usually occurs with one or more of the superiors who must approve offers and hirings. Although the interview takes place in a rather formal, subdued setting, it takes the form of a verbal and nonverbal sales presentation. To a great extent, that setting falls under the control of the interviewer.

Techniques

Chapter 14 contains general descriptions and suggestions for interviews. However, these suggestions illustrate some special techniques for a successful employment interview:

1. If possible, make an anonymous and unobtrusive visit to the interview site a day or so before the interview. Observe both the people and the environment.
2. Arrive for an interview about ten minutes ahead of time—well-rested and calm, but alert.
3. Announce your presence and the time of your appointment to the person in the outer office.
4. Remove your coat and leave it in the outer office.
5. Follow the lead of the interviewer, of course, but generally shake hands with her or him. Make the handshake firm.
6. Enter the office with confidence.
7. Remain standing until the interviewer invites you to be seated.
8. Establish the proper posture, and command the desired amount of territory as you sit. Minimal occupation of space communicates passivity and weakness, but maximum occupation of space communicates a power status that may threaten the interviewer.
9. Do not have gum, candy, mint, cough drop, cigarette, cigar, or pipe in your mouth in either the outer or inner office.
10. Avoid the negative messages associated with fidgeting with hair, clothing, jewelry, handbag, briefcase, papers, or something on the interviewer's desk.
11. Use facial expression properly. Too much smiling transmits weakness and servility, but too little smiling may threaten the interviewer.
12. Use your voice as an instrument for establishing the desired level of confidence and enthusiasm.
13. Make good eye contact with the interviewer. If you continually look away, the interviewer may attribute unwarranted negative traits to you.
14. Carry only small briefcases, handbags, and folders. Place all loose articles in them before entering the interviewer's office. Place the items in your

lap or on the floor rather than on the interviewer's desk. Do keep a pen or pencil and a note pad within easy reach.

15. If the interviewer has not seen your résumé ahead of time, give her or him time to read it as you sit quietly and organize your thoughts.
16. Let the interviewer take the lead in the interview, but contribute your part by answering questions with more than a mere "yes" or "no."
17. If you take notes, do so quickly and quietly. Do not be disturbed if the interviewer also takes notes.
18. Do not use profanity even if the interviewer does.
19. Do not tell jokes, but do exchange pleasantries when the interviewer establishes that pattern.
20. Always use "Mr.," "Ms.," or other preferred title, never the first name of the interviewer.
21. Avoid the servile attitude exhibited by overuse of "ma'am" or "sir."
22. If the interviewer receives a telephone call during the interview, just remain seated and quietly look through some of your material. Try not to listen; at least give the impression that you are not listening.
23. If the interviewer receives a caller while you are in the office, remain seated and facing the original direction. However, if the interviewer introduces you to the caller, rise, shake hands, and interact appropriately.
24. Avoid a show of anger toward the interviewer—even for an improper line of questioning. Use a controlled, reasoned approach if you must stop such a line of questioning.
25. Never look at your watch during an interview. The interviewer will end the interview when he or she wants to do so. However, carefully observe nonverbal cues that may signal the end of the interview.
26. Never part with a question like "Do I get the job?" Instead say, "I am very interested in the position; when do you think I might hear from you about your decision?" or "When might I call?"
27. As you leave, express appreciation for the interview.
28. Immediately after the interview, record any notes you want to make. Also analyze and evaluate your performance. Decide what you might do to improve the next interview.

Style

Style (charisma) alone probably does not often lead an interviewer to hire an incompetent candidate. However, style often does lead the decision-maker to choose a slightly less qualified person over a more highly qualified one. Such a choice may occur at the subconscious level—and may occur more often than interviewers realize or will admit. Particularly at the managerial level, interviewers tend to choose someone with the right "chemistry."

If you think your personal style may harm your chances, analyze and try to improve it.

Content

These suggestions may help you effectively communicate during an interview:

1. Review your analysis of the firm and the particular job just before the interview.
2. Review your self-analysis and résumé just before the interview.
3. Anticipate the kinds of questions the interviewer might ask. Rehearse responses to them.
4. Make a list of the information you want to give—even if the interviewer does not ask for it. Rehearse how you might insert it by making a smooth transition from specific answers to the volunteered information.
5. Develop and memorize the questions you want to ask; rehearse them. Generally, do not talk about salary or fringe benefits until the interviewer introduces the topics—usually in a post-offer interview.
6. Answer and introduce questions in clear, concise, and specific terms. However, avoid being curt.
7. Tell the interviewer the truth, but couch negative messages in positive-sandwich terms—without being defensive or self-deprecating.
8. Maintain a natural, conversational style, but avoid using slang and jargon.
9. State your qualifications in straightforward language, but avoid leaving the impression that you are bragging.
10. Avoid undue criticism of your present employer. The interviewer may wonder whether you tend to criticize everyone.
11. Observe and listen carefully to the content of the messages the interviewer sends. Adjust your messages accordingly.
12. Feature your strengths, and subordinate your weaknesses.
13. Speak in grammatically correct and complete sentences. Avoid run-on sentences that do not allow the interviewer to interject comments.
14. Understand and adapt to the circumstances that define your relative chances of selection. If you have a strong bargaining position, interview differently than if you have a weak one.
15. Learn and apply the techniques of negotiation on employment issues such as salary and location. Understand that everyone must win something for negotiation to succeed.
16. As soon as the interview nears its end (usually after about thirty minutes), emphatically transmit the information that you want to introduce. Finish strong.

Types of Questions

Interview questions take many forms. This section summarizes some ways to deal with them.

General Questions

1. *Tell me about yourself.* Take this opportunity to present the rehearsed persuasive exposition of your key qualities and your interest in and understanding of the firm.
2. *What kind of work do you want to do?* Stress capabilities and determination related to the work for which you apply. Also indicate your ambition to advance beyond the level of the particular job.

3. *What are your weaknesses (faults)?* Indicate that you know that everyone has flaws in innate ability, personality, education, experience, or other factors that go into defining a good employee. Stress that you have analyzed both your strengths and weaknesses and have found that your strengths far outweigh your weaknesses. State that you have already conquered some of the weaknesses and have a strategy for overcoming the remainder. Possibly cite one or two minor weaknesses along with evidence of strategy to overcome them. End on a positive note—solutions and strengths rather than problems and weaknesses.
4. *Why have you chosen this career (position, company, etc.)?* Use this question to express knowledge about the topic. In addition, use it to emphasize the strength of your interest in it. Incorporate your central persuasive thrust into it.
5. *What makes you think you are qualified for this position?* Convert this question from one that could make you defensive into one that lets you feature your qualifications. Stress the education, training, experience, and personal abilities that specifically fit you to the position.
6. *What do you do in your leisure time?* Answer honestly about some of your less serious activities. Interviewers are interested in your ability to relax—to lead a balanced life. However, if you spend some of your leisure time in the pursuit of additional education, training, or experience, report that too.
7. *Why are you leaving your present job?* Stress the reasons that place you in the best light. Do not criticize your employer, no matter how justified the criticism.
8. *What salary do you expect?* During a first interview, try to dodge this question. Suggest that you would prefer to await a job offer, but that you know that the salary should fit your ability to contribute to the firm's goals. If the interviewer in a first interview presses you, or if you receive an offer, then meet the salary question directly. Negotiate from a realistic assessment of your bargaining position. Try to get the interviewer to state the first figure. Then, if you have a strong position, you may ask for more—but still probably within the range you have learned most people at this position receive. If you have a poor bargaining position, you may have to accept the offer—or only slightly higher than it. You may even have to accept a salary at the low end of the usual range.
9. *Tell me about your family.* Describe your home life briefly. Do not show photographs. Avoid directing too much attention away from the purpose of the meeting—your qualifications for the work for which you apply. Show a realistic concern for family responsibilities, but leave the clear impression that they will not interfere with your duties. If you prefer not to discuss marital status, children, living arrangements, or other areas, phrase your declining statement carefully. Though you have a legal right not to discuss these matters, you may lose ground with the interviewer by not responding.
10. *Do you smoke? drink? use drugs?* Avoid an emotional reaction if the interviewer asks this question. You may choose to answer. If you smoke, say so. If you consume alcoholic beverages, indicate that you do so in

moderation and for social reasons. When speaking of the other drugs, tread lightly. For example, even if you believe that marijuana should be legalized, the interview does not provide a forum in which to express such views. Basically, answer truthfully, but also protect yourself from adverse reactions if you have tried drugs. You could state that you consider such information private. Add that if you do use any of the substances, their use in no way impairs your ability to perform the job. Make such statements forthrightly, and without a show of irritation.

11. *Though we cannot require it, would you agree to take a polygraph test?* If you agree, you may be giving up some of your rights. If you disagree, you may irritate the questioner—and even arouse suspicions. If you disagree, explain that you have nothing to hide, but that your principles do not permit you to submit to the test.
12. *Have you ever stolen anything from a store or from a former employer (padded an expense account)?* The question on drugs and this question on stealing often occur in conjunction with polygraph tests or stress interviews. You may decide that you do not want to work for a firm badly enough to answer such probing, personal, possibly self-incriminating questions. However, do not answer in an irritated fashion or leave in a huff. Instead give the kind of answer that shows strength combined with control.

    One strong response uses words like: "Though I have nothing to hide, I do not choose to answer this sort of question. I believe my record of education and experience establish my competency to perform the work for which I am applying." Such an answer may please the interviewer because it shows evidence of maturity. As another way to handle such a stressful question, answer candidly. Show no surprise and use words such as these: "Oh, I took some candy a couple of times as a child and have taken a few pencils and paper clips from the office where I worked, a generally accepted practice there. However, I more than replaced the value of any office supplies I ever took. I worked overtime many times for no pay. I occasionally used my own car to run errands for the firm without being reimbursed. If a firm has a strict rule against using its supplies for an occasional personal purpose, I can certainly abide by such a rule."
13. *What salary do you expect to receive in three years? five years? ten years?* Answer to show knowledge of your chosen career field and the salaries paid in it. Also answer to show confidence in your ability, but not to show outright conceit by stating an unrealistically high figure. Use ranges or approximations. Try to cite an actual published source of the information reported.
14. *What kinds of working conditions do you like best?* Stress the satisfaction you feel when you do your job well and when you meet challenges. Also stress the importance of contributing to the solution of problems and working with talented and cooperative people. Establish a clear picture of yourself as self-motivated. Omit or subordinate any mention of such insecure feelings as the need for "appreciation" or "good treatment." Avoid any emphasis on salary and benefits at this point. Emphasize the

environment only as it contributes to your doing your job—not for your personal benefit.

15. *Name your strengths.* List in a forthright manner the education, experience, and personal characteristics that portray you as one capable of occupying the prospective position. In addition, feature the strengths that show that you can grow beyond that position rapidly.
16. *Why should XYZ Corporation hire you?* Reinforce your understanding of the firm, of your qualities, and of how the two match. Impress the interviewer with your realistic confidence and adaptability.
17. *Aren't you overqualified for this job?* If you do have excess qualifications, yet need the job, indicate how your additional qualifications will help you perform the work in superior fashion. Through such an approach, persuade the interviewer that your additional qualifications do not constitute overqualification in the traditional sense. Assure the interviewer that you have the ability to function productively at many levels without being bored, condescending, or dissatisfied.

Stereotyped Questions

An interviewer may ask anyone the preceding types of questions. However, some questions show evidence of stereotypes and the biases associated with them. The stereotypes run the gamut—race, ethnic origin, sex, marital status, age, religion, cultural heritage, and handicaps, for example. This section covers examples of questions that relate to only one of the major classes—sex.

Women Stereotyped questions that might be asked of a woman are:

- I observe that you prefer the courtesy title "Ms." You're not one of those "women's libbers," are you?
- Who will take care of your children?
- What will you do when your children are sick?
- Don't you think a mother's place is in the home?
- What if we hire you, and then in a year or so your husband is transferred?
- I see you're not married. Do you live with a man?
- Do you ever plan to get married?
- Are you a divorcée?
- Do you plan to have children? What birth-control method do you use?
- This job requires a great deal of travel. Do you think women should travel with men?
- You have listed volunteer work on your résumé. Do you actually think that volunteer work will help you in the real business world?
- Is your work attendance record better than most women's?
- Can you control your emotions?
- Do you type? (To an applicant for a nontyping position)
- Most people don't like to work for women. Why do you think you're the exception?
- You're an attractive woman. Do you think your looks will be a distraction to the men in the office?

- Do you really think you will be able to be a boss and get along with the men you supervise?
- At meetings with the other supervisors (all male), will you be willing to serve coffee and take notes?
- What do you think about all this flurry about alleged sexual harrassment on the job? You don't really mind a little kidding and fun between the sexes, do you?
- You seem to be rather aggressive. Do you think aggressiveness is attractive in a woman?
- Do you think you can do this job and retain your femininity?
- What does your husband think about your wanting to work? Would the pressure of your work be a strain on your marriage?
- Does your husband let you work overtime (travel, attend company functions alone, etc.)?
- I see you were graduated from college in 19XX, worked only two years, and have been out of the job market for 20 years. How can you claim you are qualified to apply for a supervisory position?
- Have you ever filed a claim against a company on the basis of sexual discrimination or sexual harrassment?
- The women we hire usually start in secretarial positions. You would be willing to start there, wouldn't you?
- Do you think that affirmative action requirements are fair to firms?

Many of these questions will not take a direct form; many have illegal implications. However, a woman should prepare to answer them directly or to insert the "answers" to them in an indirect way while building persuasion.

Develop responses that:

- Enhance your image as one capable of doing the job
- Do not betray other women
- Do not show aggressiveness, servility, or passivity
- Separate your private life from your company life
- Indicate assertion, strength, courage, and capability—and the compatibility of femininity with such abilities
- Do not show a negative, reactionary defensiveness to the questions
- Briefly explain any refusal to answer certain questions

Men The presence of men in the higher ranks of business remains the norm. Therefore, the list unique to men has fewer questions than the list unique to women:

- I see you're not married. You probably know that we like our executives to have wives who can do some of the entertaining for the corporation—and to accompany their husbands to important functions. How do you propose to overcome this problem?
- I see you're married and have children. We have found that our single executives have more freedom to transfer and to travel than married

ones do. Will family responsibilities cut down on your flexibility? (This one is similar to some of the questions for women.)

- Have you met your military obligations? (This question comes and goes with the draft. At the time of the publication of this book, the question has always applied to men. However, it may eventually apply to women as well.)

Answer these questions just as women answer those aimed stereotypically at them. Answer in a self-enhancing manner. Be straightforward and composed. Try not to react defensively or in a negatively reactionary way. If you choose not to respond, briefly explain why.

(2110 words)

Take and score Self-Test 33 over types of interview questions on page 481.

APPEARANCE AND DRESS

Dress and appearance create only a part of the nonverbal messages transmitted during an interview. Chapter 5 covers dress and appearance in general terms. However, this section includes some specific suggestions for dress and appearance for the interview.

General Suggestions

Some suggestions for good appearance apply to men and women alike. The overriding one requires following the standard rules for good grooming and cleanliness.

An anonymous visit to the site of an interview ahead of time allows for the observation of the appropriate manner of dress. However, an applicant cannot always dress as casually as can those already working in an office. As an alternative to an anonymous visit to the site, check similar offices or read into the literature about the dress appropriate to the position. If doubts remain, lean toward conservatism.

Some other general suggestions include:

- Wear fingernails at a short to medium length. Have them clean and well manicured.
- Choose a haircut and style that fits the standard for the work. Have it cut a week or so before the interview.
- Have freshly cleaned and pressed clothing—including overcoats and raincoats.
- Use a minimum amount of shaving lotion, cologne, or perfume.
- Choose clothing appropriate for the season. However, do not choose unusually lightweight or lightly colored clothing even in the summer.
- Choose styles that enhance your personal characteristics.
- Choose clothing that fits comfortably.
- Avoid wearing obviously brand-new, untested clothing.

- Just before going into the outer office of the interviewer, check your clothing and grooming—preferably where no one can see you.
- Once in the office, forget your clothing and appearance. Do not shift and adjust clothing, check hair, or do any of the myriad of other things that indicate preoccupation and nervousness.
- Wear a minimum of jewelry. Make it tasteful. Wear a watch.

Special Suggestions for Men

Though overlapping with the general suggestions, these suggestions apply specifically to men:

- If you have facial hair, have it cut in an acceptable style. Have it well trimmed and groomed.
- Wear a traditional two- or three-piece business suit in a dark, solid color in a hard-finished fabric. Do not wear a leisure suit.
- Choose a conservative shirt, tie, socks, belt, and shoes to coordinate properly with the color and style of the suit.
- Even if you wear a necklace during your leisure hours, leave it off for the interview.
- Choose shoes in a calf leather, dark color, and traditional style. Keep them shined and in good repair.
- Carry an unworn billfold or wallet in a traditional style. Remove all unnecessary bulk from it.
- Have a cleanly laundered handkerchief in a pocket.
- Remove all unnecessary keys, change, and other items from your pockets.
- If you wear a hat, be sure that it is well cleaned and blocked. Leave it in the outer office with your coat.

Special Suggestions for Women

These special suggestions apply to women:

- Wear a two-piece, below-the-knee, skirted business suit or a simple, tailored dress in a dark, solid color and a hard-finished fabric. Do not wear a vest, pants, or pants suit, sheer fabrics, flimsy fabrics, tight-fitting jacket or skirt, low-cut dress, short or unusually long skirt, or any high-fashion clothing.
- Choose a conservative, medium- to high-cut blouse coordinated properly with the suit. Do not choose a low-cut, sheer, or clinging blouse or sweater.
- Choose medium-colored, sheer stockings. Do not wear opaque or high-fashion stockings.
- Wear closed-toed, closed-heeled, low- to medium-heeled pumps in a dark-color kid or suede leather coordinated with your suit. Do not choose high heels, sandals, open toes, open heels, boots, white or other light colors, or patent leather.

- Wear little or no jewelry. Do not wear large-looped or dangling earrings.
- Have a full-length winter coat or raincoat longer than your skirt.
- Choose a hair style that will convey moderation and confidence. Avoid high-fashion or out-of-date styles—particularly the highly sprayed, backcombed, beehive styles.
- Use conservative makeup.
- If you use nail polish, choose a medium color.
- If you do not carry a briefcase, carry a small, dark-color, leather handbag that coordinates with your suit and shoes. Carry nothing in it that you do not absolutely need. Close it before entering the office.
- Never use compact or lipstick in either the outer or inner office.
- Choose accessories such as scarves, belts, gloves, and hats to show moderate taste and an understanding of acceptability for that office. Put any removable items such as gloves in your coat pocket or purse before being called into the interviewer's office.

COMMUNICATION AND CAREERS

"Communication . . . is the growth area of the next decade—bringing with it tremendous career possibilities."[1] So writes Sandra E. O'Connell, who cites four reasons for such a claim: (1) technical advances and the accompanying information explosion, (2) interdependence and the resultant need for integration of activities through communication, (3) legislation leading to requirements for more—and better—communication, and (4) the growth in employee communication.[2]

Walter F. Giersbach echoes O'Connell's claim:

> The field of business communications has come into its own. Gone are the days when a multi-million dollar corporation relied on an under-budgeted, unattractive "house organ" and called it communications . . . .
>
> The growth in internal and external business communications means that you need not leave the field to continue climbing the career ladder.[3]

Though small firms often have one or two professional communicators, the best opportunities lie with large corporations or in independent consulting. The positions available to the career communicator include:

Vice president for communication (responsible for all company publications, advertising and promotion, and employee training in communication)
Director or manager of
 Employee relations
 Customer or consumer relations
 Public relations
 Corporate relations

Government relations
Administrative/office services
Communication
Credit and collections
Word processing

Administrative assistant or other staff position, such as
Interviewer
Editor
Writer
Counselor
Photographer
Designer
Audiovisual specialist
Trainer
Self-employed consultant
College teacher

Preparation for a business communication career should include work in written and oral communication, business, and human behavior. O'Connell suggests that "written communications—publications and management newsletters—are the foundation of corporate communication."[4] However, she also found in a survey that

> business was conducted primarily by oral communication. Print was used for documentation, followup, and with large audiences. Clearly, the key to business transactions is in oral communication, face-to-face and over the phone. This results, of course, in a need for training: presentation skills, interviewing, negotiation, performance review discussions, and participation in meetings.[5]

O'Connell summarizes the abilities needed by the communication professional in this paragraph:

> 1) be knowledgeable in a broad range of communication processes; 2) be well grounded in theory—the whys and complexities of the communication process; 3) possess the ability to bridge the gap between theory and application and move between these two worlds; and 4) have some understanding of the business environment.[6]

O'Connell suggests that a career communicator needs to obtain education and experience related to the four areas just reported, get an entry level job, and set career goals.

As a final admonition, she writes that not many organizations send recruiters to campuses to find communication professionals. Instead, people interested in the area will need to take responsibility for their own careers, seek out potential employers, and take the initiative in selling their own abilities.[7]

BUSINESS AS A COMMUNICATION-CENTERED OPERATION

In surveys, respondents have consistently ranked communication as the most important or among the most important of the business arts and skills. In addition, they have tended to assign more importance to oral communication than to written communication.

The Importance of Communication Compared to Other Business Skills

In 1971, James C. Bennett sent questionnaires to top executives in the 58 California-based corporations listed among *Fortune* magazine's 500 largest U.S. industrial corporations. With a 60 percent return, Bennett reported:

> Every one of the respondents felt that effective business communication skills had played a part in their advancement to a top executive position in their company. Sixty-six percent of the respondents indicated that "effective communication skills" had played a "major part" in their advancement while only 34 percent indicated "some part" in their advancement.[8]

John M. Penrose conducted a survey of businesspeople in Austin, Texas, in 1976. The 157 respondents rated 11 business-related abilities from "1" (Very Valuable) to "7" (Not Valuable). These mean responses for the abilities appear in ranked order: public relations (1.84), marketing (1.92), accounting (1.96), finance (2.25), business speaking (2.32), business writing (2.34), mathematics (2.35), office administration (2.39), business law (3.03), statistics (3.46), computer methods (4.01), and government (4.06).[9] Thus, the research places public relations and marketing (both communication-related fields), business speaking, and business writing in the top half of the array.

In affirmation of the importance of communication to management, Henry Mintzberg writes:

> We need to pay particular attention in our management development programs to the development of verbal [oral] skills. In fact, we should develop methods to train management students in the use of all the managerial media. The telephone, the scheduled and unscheduled meetings, the tour, and the mail are the manager's prime tools. We should train the student systematically in their use.[10]

The Relative Importance of Various Communication Skills

The preceding excerpt from Mintzberg's book revives interest in the relative importance of types of channels. Mintzberg emphasizes the oral channels as the primary vehicles for managerial communication, even as he acknowledges the necessity for the written channels. He bases his argument on a review of the literature and his own research involving observation of managers at work:

> The manager uses five basic media: the mail (documented communication), the telephone (purely verbal), the unscheduled meeting (informal face-to-face), the scheduled meeting (formal face-to-face), and the tour (visual). . . . Documented communication requires the use of a formal subset of the language, and involves long feedback delays. All verbal [oral] media can transmit, in addition to the messages contained in the words used, messages sent by voice inflection and by delays in reaction. In addition, face-to-face media carry information transmitted by facial expression and by gesture.
>
> . . . managers demonstrate very strong attraction to the verbal [oral] media. Virtually every empirical study of managerial time allocation draws attention to the great proportion of time spent in verbal [oral] communication. . . . My own findings bear this out. . . . verbal [oral] interaction accounted for 78 percent of the . . . managers' time and 67 percent of their activities.[11]

Notice how Mintzberg's findings confirm the proportions of time spent in the various sending and receiving activities reported in Chapter 5 (45 percent—listening; 30 percent—speaking; 16 percent—reading; and 9 percent—writing). Together they show that the components associated with oral communication occupy more time than the written ones.

In a survey of businesspeople in 1974, J. Donald Weinrauch and John R. Swanda found slightly different proportions, but similar results:

> Generally, listening consumes from one-fourth to one-third of a practitioner's time spent in communication.
>
> . . . Speaking was found generally to be the second significant form of communication by business personnel. It consumed about one-fifth to one-fourth of the business practitioner's time. Writing was the least relevant form. It was utilized between one-eighth and one-sixth of the time spent in communication. An interesting sidelight to this study is that the respondents were engaged about 20 percent of the time in indirect communication activities [planning messages and the mental activity associated with preparing messages].[12]

In research conducted among businesspeople, Homer Cox found similar proportions. He reported estimates of the percentages of job time spent on activities in an average month: "Listening, 29 percent; speaking, 26 percent; writing, 25 percent; reading, 20 percent."[13]

Jon M. Huegli and Harvey D. Tschirgi conducted research in 1974 to determine communication skills needed by entry-level business employees. Of 13 skills listed, the first four ranks represented oral skills, the next five, writing skills, and the final four, oral skills. Converted to combined percentages of frequency of use, 64 percent involved oral communication and 36 percent involved written.[14]

During 1974–1976, a committee of the American Business Communication Association (ABCA) conducted a survey to determine evaluations of the basic collegiate business communication course. The committee sent questionnaires to 151 graduating students in 1974; 85 responded. Of the 85 receiving the follow-up questionnaire in 1975, 49 responded. Of the 49 receiving the follow-up questionnaire in 1976, 36 responded.

In summary of the consistent findings for the three years, the study reports:

1. The course time spent on letter writing and long-report writing should be *decreased.*
2. The time spent on memoranda, speaking, interpersonal and small-group communication, interviewing, listening, nonverbal communication, barriers to communication, and psychology of communication should be *increased.*
3. The time spent on short report writing, dictating, job applications, communication theory and semantics, and other topics should be *maintained.*
4. The course time spent on lectures should be *decreased.*
5. The time spent on group activities should be *increased.*
6. The largest proportions of communication time on the job are spent in nonwriting activities.[15]

With minor exceptions, two important communication facets—the intrapersonal and the nonverbal—have received little, if any, attention in the reported research. The indirect communication activities cited by Weinrauch and Swanda hint at the intrapersonal. However, they represent only the intrapersonal associated with the multi-human levels of communication.

The ABCA survey indicates the need to increase the coverage of nonverbal communication in the collegiate business communication course. The researchers probably intended to imply that the proportion of time spent on each of the stated skills includes the nonverbal, but that implication proves difficult to draw.

The purpose for delineating some of the research about the relative importance of the communication arts and skills lies in the need for a balanced view. For example, some people equate business communication with writing—particularly letter writing and report writing.

Although writing remains an indispensable tool in the communication kit, wise communicators must add listening, speaking, reading, and their nonverbal accompaniments to that kit. In addition, theory should join practice in order that each may grow.

Everyone employed in business communicates. Thus, whether planning to function in business as a communication specialist or in some other capacity, you should strive to develop the full spectrum of arts, sciences, and skills that define the communication process. Whatever your specialty, you can serve your career and your life no better than to meet the requirements of the ultimate binder of business and living—communication.

SUMMARY

Chapter 16 completes the coverage of employment messages by dealing with additional written messages, interviews, appearance and dress, communication and careers, and business as a communication-centered operation.

A follow-up letter reminds a prospective employer of your keen interest in a job. The follow-up letter should reinforce some of the key points made in the résumé and the letter of application. The follow-up letter may also reinforce important statements made during an interview.

Following the offer of a job, write a letter of acceptance, a letter of rejection, or a letter of delay. In the letter of acceptance, convey your satisfaction at receiving the offer. Also write that you intend to accept the job and have confidence that you can do the work well. As a bad-news message, the letter of rejection calls for the indirect developmental method. Just build to the rejection by listing the reasons for it first. End with a buffer statement. A letter of delay asks for additional time in which to make a decision about whether to accept or reject an offered position. You may need the time to complete other interviews or to resolve personal or external factors. A letter of thanks—particularly for an interview—provides the opportunity to maintain the momentum of the job search.

Carry your résumé with you during a job search to aid in completing application blanks. Assure neatness, accuracy, and persuasion when completing the blanks. Some prospective employers look at nothing else.

Tests and placement- and employment-office files often enter into a position search. Decide carefully whether you want confidential or nonconfidential files.

Before an interview, learn as much as possible about the firm and the people who will interview you. Apply self-enhancing techniques as you prepare for and participate in interviews. Develop the content of the interview to improve your chances for success. Anticipate and practice answering the general and special questions the interviewer may ask, particularly the difficult ones. Establish appearance and dress appropriate to the occasion of the interview. Lean toward conservatism.

Careers in business communication may well form the growth field of the eighties. Positions available in the communication field include vice president, director, manager, administrative assistant, self-employed consultant, college teacher, and others. Whatever your career field, it likely will require communication arts and skills. Your communication abilities must cover sending and receiving written, oral, and nonverbal messages.

EXERCISES

1. You applied for the position of personnel manager at the local telephone company. It represents the job that you really want. A bank to which you applied has offered you the position of assistant personnel manager. You would like to wait for a response from the telephone company before committing yourself to the bank. Write a letter of delay to the bank president. Make up the necessary names, addresses, and other information.
2. [*Your professor will time this exercise.]* Karen Creek just interviewed you for the position of insurance salesperson at Creek & Fuller Insurance, Inc. Creek, a co-owner of the firm, took you to lunch. She also gave you a great deal of information about the insurance industry. Write a thank-you letter to her. Use your imagination to create addresses and to add information.
3. You sent a letter of application and your résumé to an insurance company over a month ago. The company, which had been advertising for salespeople, has not responded to your letter. Write a follow-up letter that briefly emphasizes your general competence, your selling abilities, and your interest in working for the company. Create the company name, address, and other needed information.
4. Alice Snedley, the owner of the small hardware store that you want to manage, will interview you next week. You have taken great pains to learn about the store, Snedley Hardware, and Snedley herself. Here is what you have discovered:
   a. Snedley's mother built the store 50 years ago. The mother died, and Snedley has been managing the store herself for the last 35 years.
   b. Snedley employs five salespeople, all of whom have been working at the store for at least 10 years. None of the employees has a college degree. Nor does Snedley.
   c. Snedley is now 65 years old. She is hiring a manager so that she can go into semiretirement.
   d. Snedley, a Democrat, opposes labor unions, supports both minority rights and women's rights, and dislikes what she terms "giddy, giggly people."
   e. Snedley once said that she finds aggressive, creative people very interesting.
   f. Snedley has always worked over 15 hours a day, Monday through Saturday.
   g. Snedley Hardware has not been in the black since the new suburban shopping center was built two years ago.

   Make a list of the questions that you believe Ms. Snedley might pose during the interview. Develop answers for all of the questions. Which of the questions do you consider difficult?
5. Apparently Snedley (Exercise No. 4) was impressed with you because she just called you and wants to hire you. First write a letter of acceptance. Now assume that you do *not* want the job, and write a letter of rejection. You do not want the job because you have been offered a better-paying job at the hardware store in the new suburban shopping center.
6. Meet with your group. Have one group member play the role of an interviewer, and have another group member act as the job applicant. Have them conduct a short interview while the other group members evaluate the interviewer's and applicant's performances. Have the interviewer ask at least one difficult or stressful question in the process of the interview. Continue the interviews until everyone in your group has played both roles. Discuss both performances immediately after each interview.
7. Obtain and complete an application blank for a firm. Analyze the form and your ability to answer the questions in a self-enhancing manner.

8. Meet with your group. Design a simple survey. Design the instrument to determine whether the firms to which you will submit it have any career positions in the field of business communication. Pool the designs of all the groups. Divide the work among the class members. Compile the results. Have each member of the class write a brief report of the research.
9. Based upon the literature and/or observation, write a brief paper about the mode of dress and appearance appropriate for the position you want to hold.
10. Meet with your group. Briefly discuss any or all of these topics. After the discussion, a spokesperson for each group will report to the class.
    a. The issue of open files and whether to mark recommendation forms confidential or nonconfidential
    b. Hints about taking employment tests
    c. Handling interview questions about drugs, theft, and other difficult subjects
    d. Responding to a leading question; e.g., "You don't like . . . , do you?"
    e. Developing a good personal style
11. Visit your campus placement office to learn its procedures for aiding people in obtaining jobs. Also obtain copies of any forms used as part of those procedures. Evaluate both the procedures and the forms and write a one-page paper summarizing the evaluation. Meet with your group to discuss and summarize the independent evaluations of the group members. Designate one person to present the group's summary to the class. After the presentations from all of the groups, the class may want to establish a team to develop a set of written and oral recommendations to be presented to the placement office. If you are nearing graduation, you may want to complete your placement-office file at this time.
12. You were interviewed last week by Elton Ables of the X. Acting Corp. in your city for a position as a personnel officer. You received a call today from one of Ables's assistants indicating that Ables would like to have a written statement about the salary you would expect to receive if you join the firm. He needs the statement within two days. The assistant did not say that Ables wants to see you again at this point. Write the statement, supplying any additional information you may need. Indicate how you would transmit the statement to arrive within the specified two days.
13. Recall (without looking, if you can) the six guidelines for effective communication. Write a two- or three-page paper explaining how you would apply each of the guidelines to the transactions associated with your career planning and search for employment.
14. You are scheduled to be interviewed by Donna Lofgren, president of the small accounting firm for which you wish to work. The Lofgren firm is the only accounting firm in town, and you know that competition is stiff for jobs there. Describe how you will apply the six communication guidelines for next week's interview. Summarize the application in a one- or two-page paper.
15. Use your dictionary and thesaurus to create meanings for these words. Use the words when you think, write, and speak so that you feel comfortable using them.

    a. Aggressive
    b. Aptitude
    c. Assertive
    d. Belligerent
    e. Entity
    f. Facile
    g. Impasse
    h. Militate
    i. Obsolete
    j. Preoccupation
    k. Raucous
    l. Self-deprecating
    m. Self-incriminating
    n. Servility
    o. Strategy
    p. Succinct

16. Take and score Self-Test 34 over Chapter 16.

SELF-TEST 33
Excerpt about Types of Interview Questions

A. Recall (25 points each). For each multiple-choice question, select the most accurate answer.

1. Which one of these questions involves a stereotyped approach to interviewing?
   - **a.** What are your weaknesses?
   - **b.** Tell me about your family.
   - **c.** Will you be able to travel?
   - **d.** Are you married?
   - **e.** Has your husband given you permission to work?
2. Which one of these statements is true?
   - **a.** When asked about the salary you expect to receive, always state some figure.
   - **b.** When asked about personal matters, tell the interviewer, "It's none of your business."
   - **c.** If you choose not to answer certain questions, briefly and assertively explain why.
   - **d.** Never refuse to answer a question.
   - **e.** Avoid reciting your qualities, honors, or awards; the interviewer will think you are conceited.
3. Which one of these approaches is correct?
   - **a.** By using a positive answer, try to turn a negative question to your favor.
   - **b.** When asked why you are leaving your present employer, be sure to describe the employer's flaws to the interviewer.
   - **c.** Use a question about leisure time to report only serious activities.
   - **d.** Always agree to take a polygraph test; otherwise the interviewer will think you have something to hide.
   - **e.** When asked about the kind of working conditions you like, be sure to emphasize salary and benefits.

B. Inference (25 points). For the multiple-choice question, select the most accurate answer.

1. You are interviewing for the position of loan officer at a bank. The interviewer asks you what you think of the military draft. Which answer would most likely allow you to be true to your beliefs and avoid a disagreement at the same time?
   - **a.** I think all able-bodied people should be drafted.
   - **b.** I am opposed to the draft, aren't you?
   - **c.** *I* certainly don't want to go to war, but I do think the draft is a good thing.
   - **d.** What does your question have to do with this job?
   - **e.** I've heard a number of interesting discussions on both sides of the question. The draft is certainly a complex issue.

SOLUTION

A. Recall (25 points each)

1. e **3.** a

2. c

B. Inference (25 points)

1. e

SELF-TEST 34
Chapter 16

A. Recall (20 points each). For each multiple-choice question, select the most accurate answer.

1. A letter of follow-up:
   a. May have the purpose of initiating or intensifying interest in a previously submitted application
   b. Should be long and comprehensive
   c. Must not be repeated
   d. Should not include additional information
   e. Must not include any persuasion

2. When an employer uses the mail to offer you a position with a firm,
   a. Always wait several days before responding
   b. Write a response of acceptance in the indirect style
   c. Write a response of rejection in the direct style
   d. Include no reasons in a response asking for more time to make a decision
   e. Treat a letter asking for a delay as a combination of persuasive and bad-news messages

3. Before and during an interview, you should *not:*
   a. Ask such questions as: "Are you going to give me this job?" or "Will you give me a decent salary?"
   b. Arrive for the interview ten minutes ahead of time
   c. Remain standing until the interviewer invites you to be seated
   d. Make good eye contact with the interviewer
   e. Let the interviewer take the lead

4. Which one of these statements is true?
   a. You need not complete every blank on a questionnaire.
   b. Always mark recommendation forms "confidential."
   c. Show photographs of your family at the first interview to indicate allegiance to your family.
   d. High-fashion clothing impresses the interviewer because it shows that you are up to date.
   e. Whether in a business communication career or another career in business, written, oral, and nonverbal communication arts and skills are critically important.

B. Inference (20 points). For the multiple-choice question, select the most accurate answer.

1. Which one of these statements is *false?*
   a. Even though careers in business communication are expanding, a business-communication major would be wise to prepare in a second field.
   b. Most interviewers are unaware of the impact that interviewees' personal styles have on them.
   c. The first impression created by dress and appearance may override many other of the interviewee's characteristics.
   d. An interviewee is hypocritical if he or she does not deliberately state views on controversial issues.

e. Business-communication students tend to believe that the proportion of class time devoted to group activities, speaking, and discussion should be increased.

SOLUTION

A. Recall (20 points each)
1. a **3.** a
2. e **4.** e

B. Inference (20 points)
1. d

ENDNOTES

1. Sandra E. O'Connell, "Communication: Growth Field of the Seventies," *Journal of Business Communication* 15 (Spring 1978):37.
2. O'Connell, "Communication: Growth Field," 37–39.
3. Walter F. Giersbach, *Sell Yourself as a Pro. Communicator* (New York: New York Business Communicators, 1979), 12.
4. O'Connell, "Communication: Growth Field," 41.
5. O'Connell, "Communication: Growth Field," 41.
6. O'Connell, "Communication: Growth Field," 44.
7. O'Connell, "Communication: Growth Field," 44–45.
8. James C. Bennett, "The Communication Needs of Business Executives," *Journal of Business Communication* 9 (Spring 1971):8.
9. John M. Penrose, "A Survey of the Perceived Importance of Business Communication and Other Business-Related Abilities," *Journal of Business Communication* 13 (Winter 1976):21.
10. Henry Mintzberg, *The Nature of Managerial Work* (New York: Harper & Row Publishers, Inc., 1973), 190–91.
11. Mintzberg, *Managerial Work,* 38.
12. J. Donald Weinrauch and John R. Swanda, Jr., "Examining the Significance of Listening: An Exploratory Study of Contemporary Management," *Journal of Business Communication* 13 (Fall 1975):31.
13. Homer Cox, "The Voices of Experience: The Business Communication Alumnus [*sic*] Reports," *Journal of Business Communication* 13 (Summer 1976):37.
14. Jon M. Huegli and Harvey D. Tschirgi, "An Investigation of Communication Skills Application and Effectiveness at the Entry Job Level," *Journal of Business Communication* 12 (Fall 1974):25.
15. American Business Communication Association *Ad Hoc* Committee, Bobbye Sorrels Persing, Chairperson, "The 1976 ABCA Followup Evaluation of the Course Content, Classroom Procedures, and Quality of the Basic Course in College and University Business Communication," *ABCA Bulletin* 40 (March 1977):18–24.

APPENDIX A

READING RECORDS

RECORD OF READING EFFICIENCY
CAREFUL READING

Date	Material Read (Page No., Self-Test No., or Other ID)	No. of Words	No. of Seconds	Words per Minute (w.p.m.) $\frac{\text{No. of Words} \times 60}{\text{No. of Seconds}}$	Comprehension Test Score (c.t.s.)	Reading Efficiency Score (r.e.s.) w.p.m. × c.t.s.

RECORD OF SPEED
CAREFUL READING

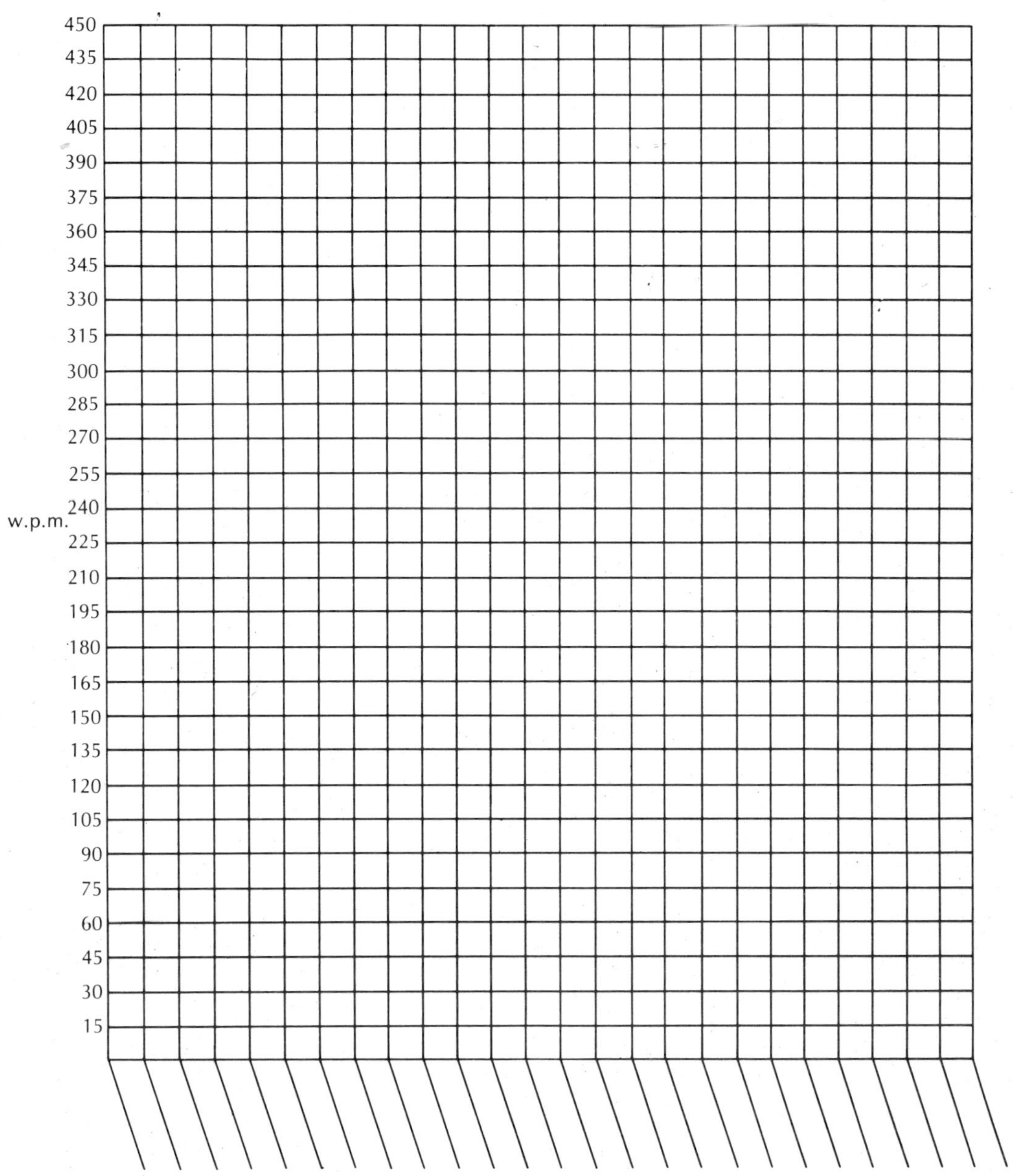

RECORD OF READING EFFICIENCY SCORE

CAREFUL READING

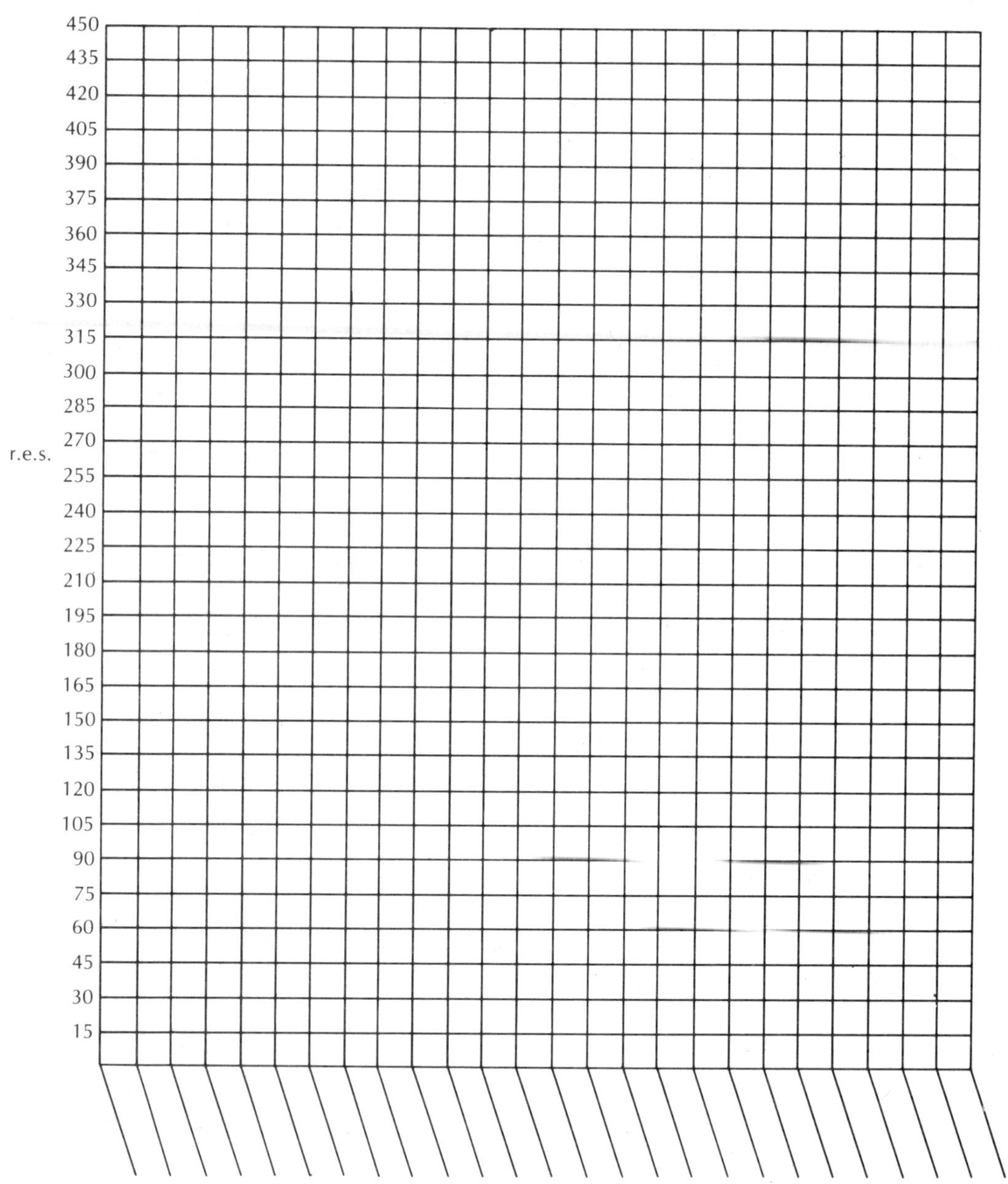

RECORD OF READING EFFICIENCY
RAPID READING

Date	Material Read (Page No., Self-Test No., or Other ID)	No. of Words	No. of Seconds	Words per Minute (w.p.m.) $\frac{\text{No. of Words} \times 60}{\text{No. of Seconds}}$	Comprehension Test Score (c.t.s.)	Reading Efficiency Score (r.e.s.) w.p.m. × c.t.s.

RECORD OF SPEED
RAPID READING

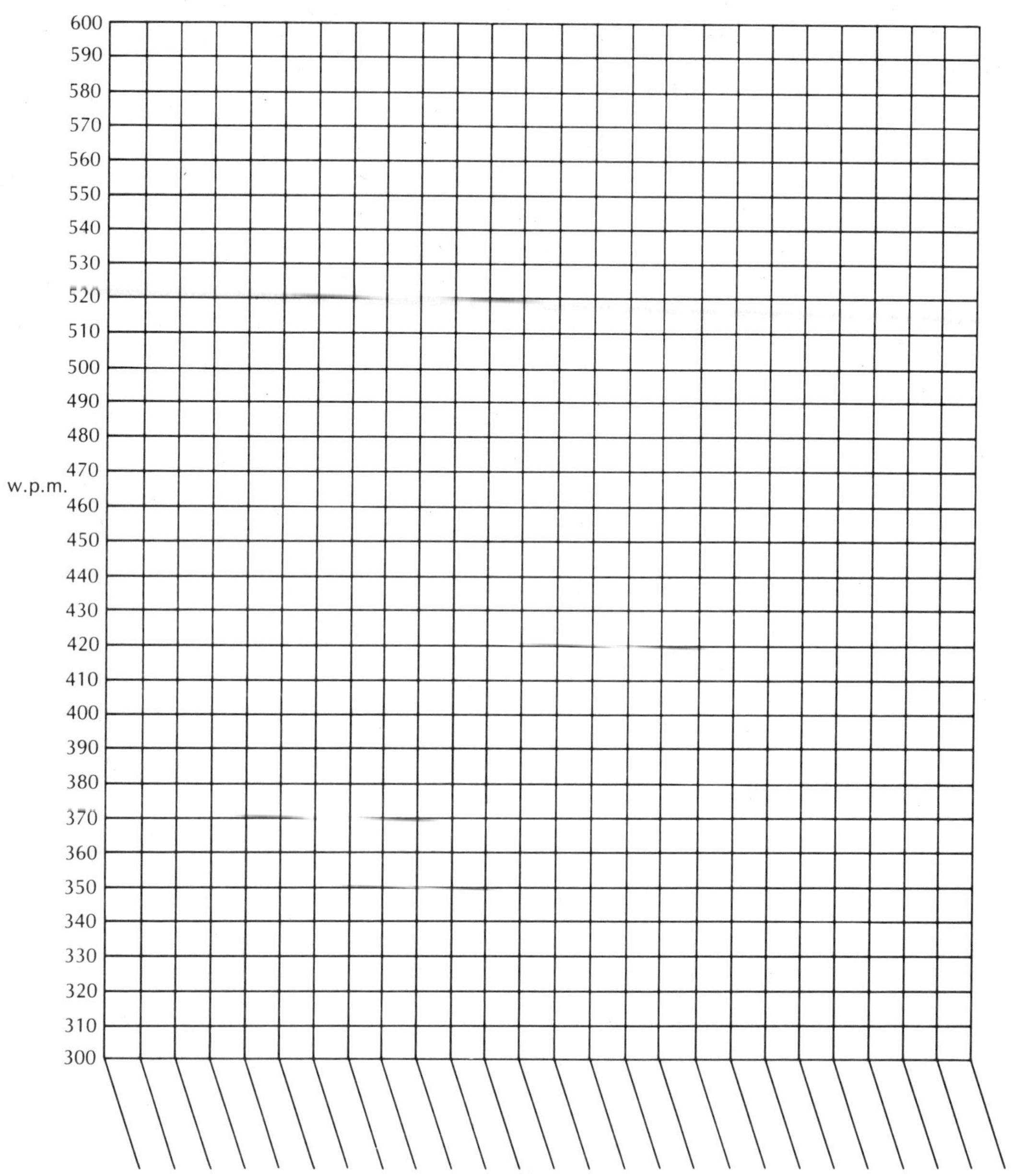

RECORD OF READING EFFICIENCY SCORE

RAPID READING

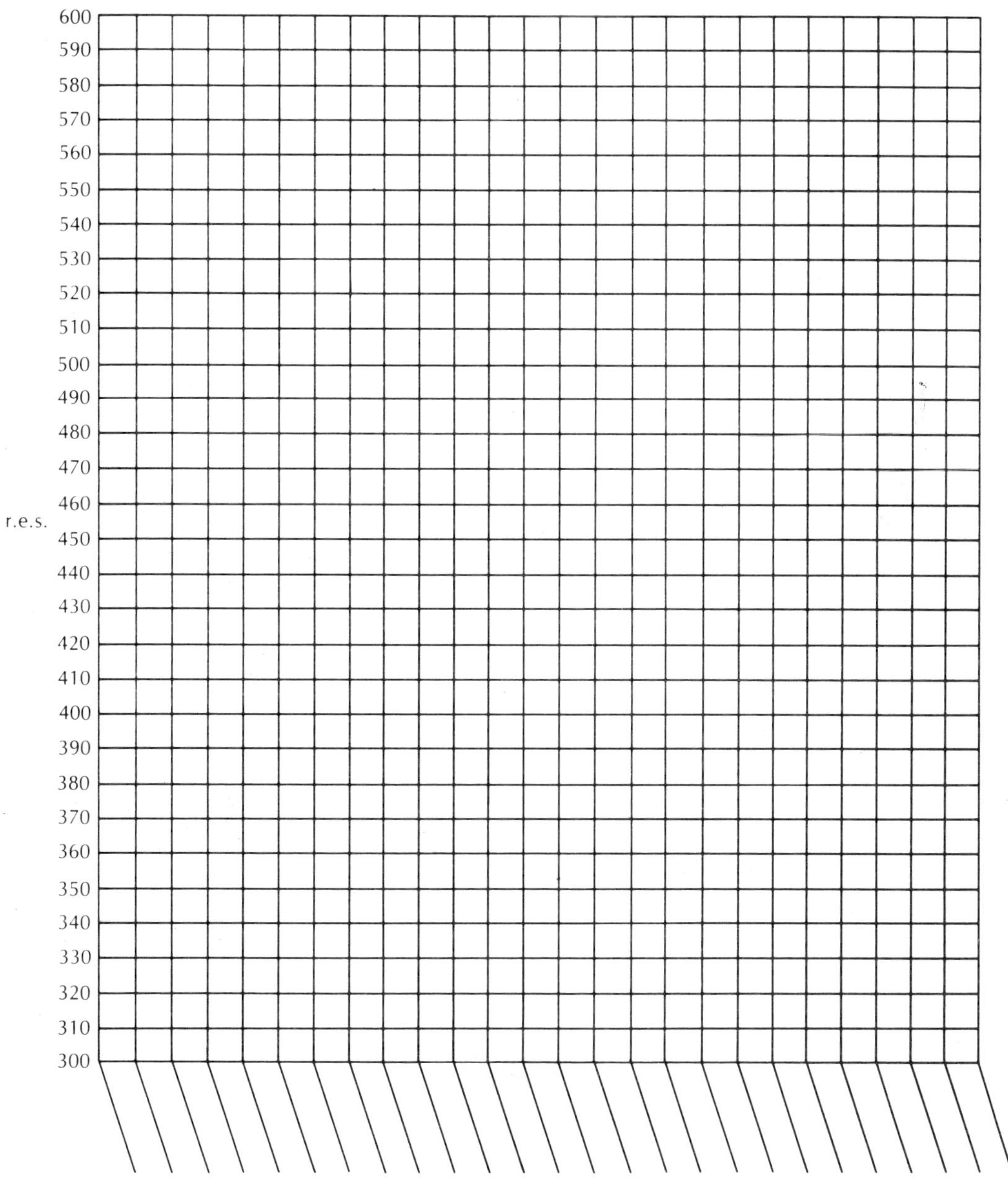

Date

RECORD OF READING EFFICIENCY
SKIMMING

Date	Material Read (Page No., Self-Test No., or Other ID)	No. of Words	No. of Seconds	Words per Minute (w.p.m.) $\frac{\text{No. of Words} \times 60}{\text{No. of Seconds}}$	Comprehension Test Score (c.t.s.)	Reading Efficiency Score (r.e.s.) w.p.m. × c.t.s.

RECORD OF SPEED

SKIMMING

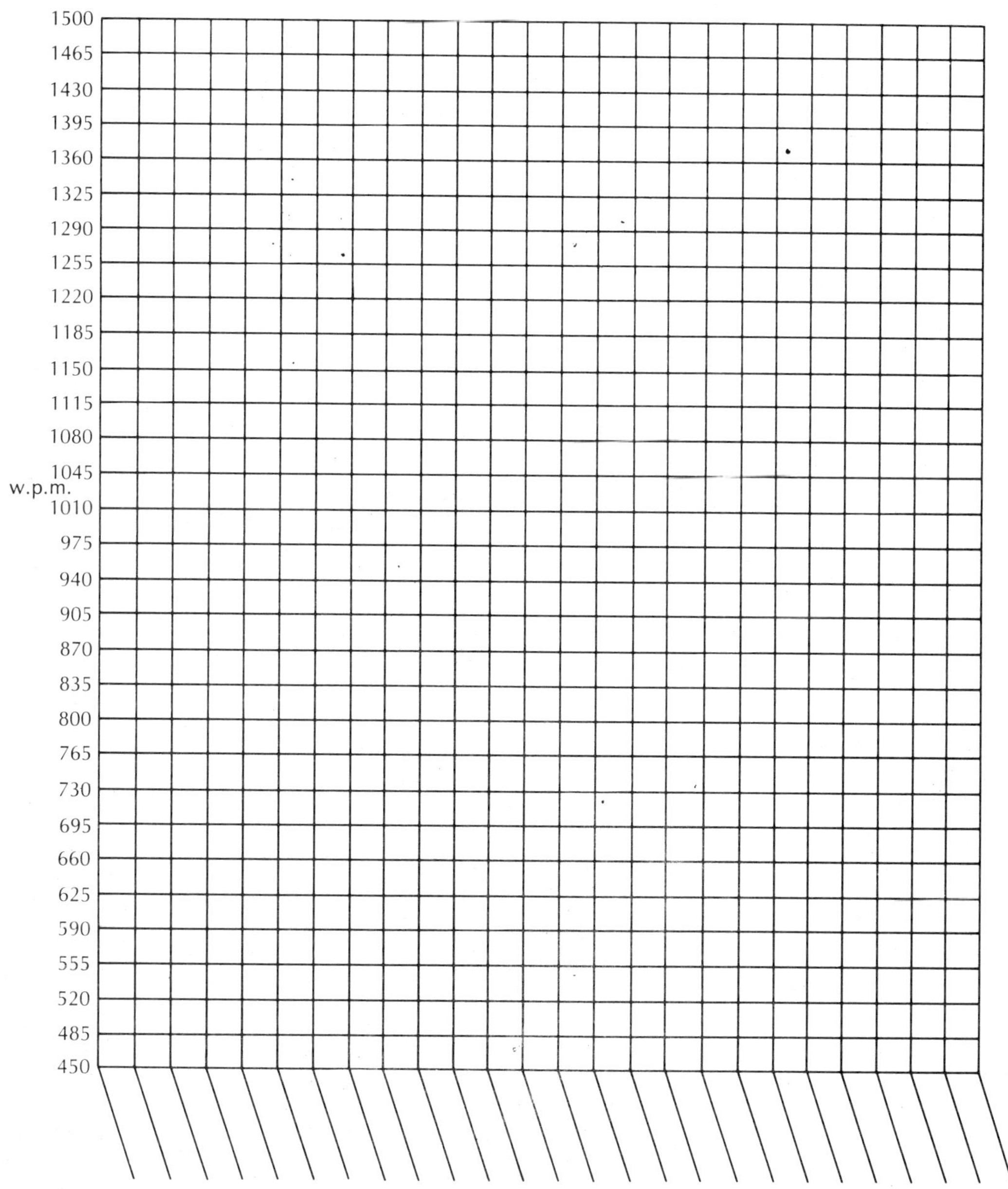

RECORD OF READING EFFICIENCY SCORE

SKIMMING

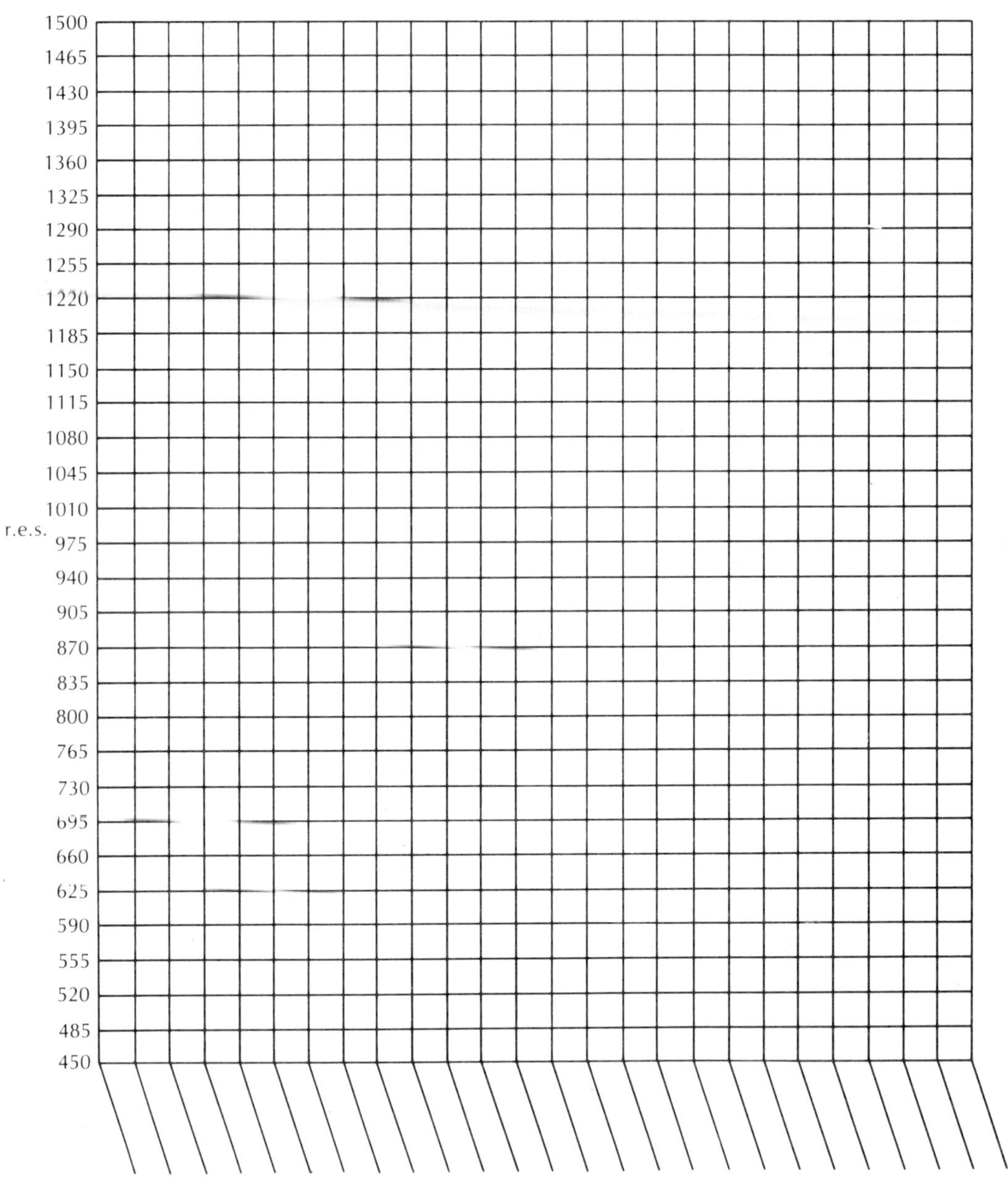

RECORD OF READING EFFICIENCY
SCANNING

Date	Material Read (Page No., Self-Test No., or Other ID)	No. of Words	No. of Seconds	Words per Minute (w.p.m.) $\frac{\text{No. of Words} \times 60}{\text{No. of Seconds}}$	Comprehension Test Score (c.t.s.)	Reading Efficiency Score (r.e.s.) w.p.m. × c.t.s.

RECORD OF SPEED
SCANNING

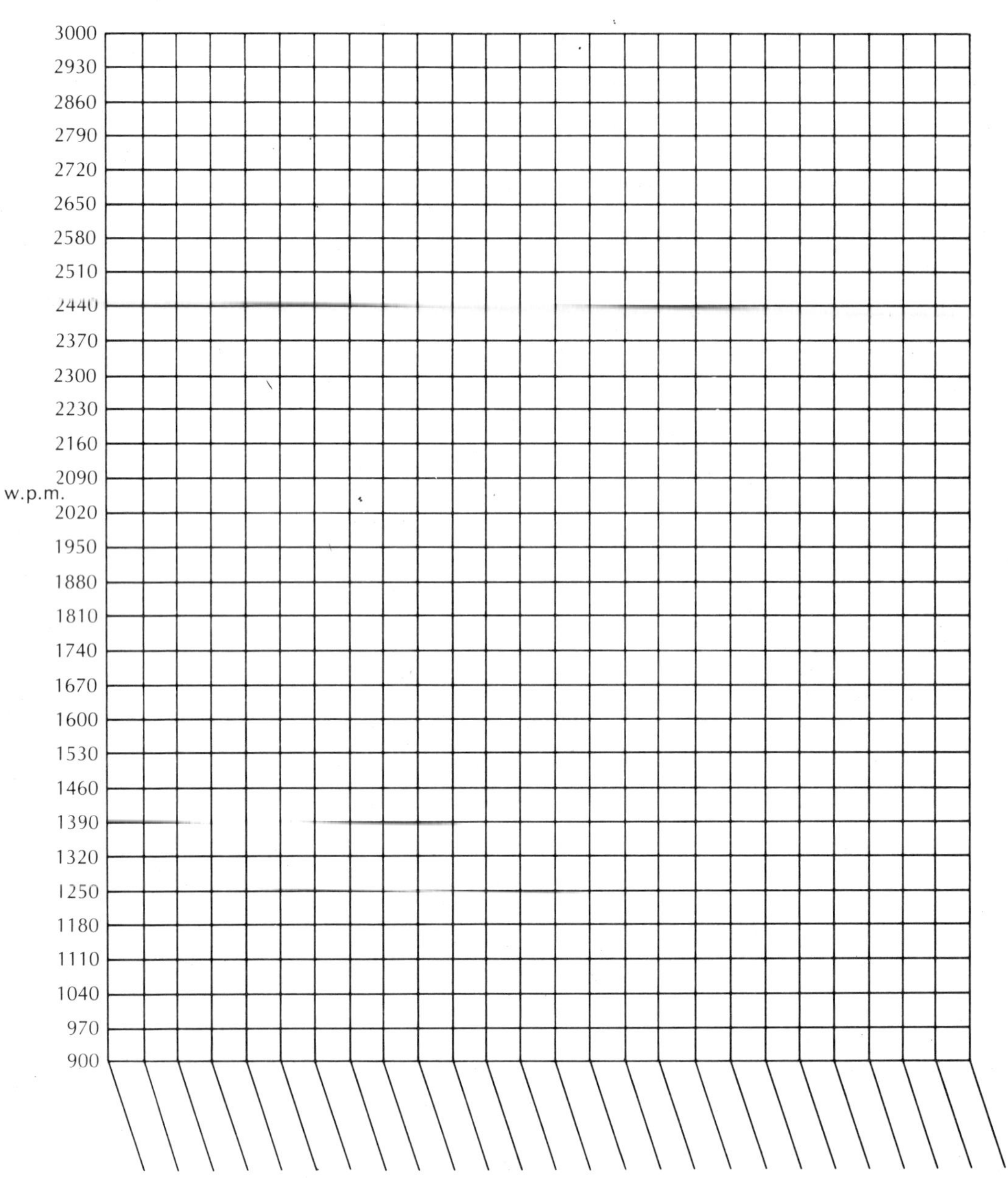

RECORD OF READING EFFICIENCY SCORE

SCANNING

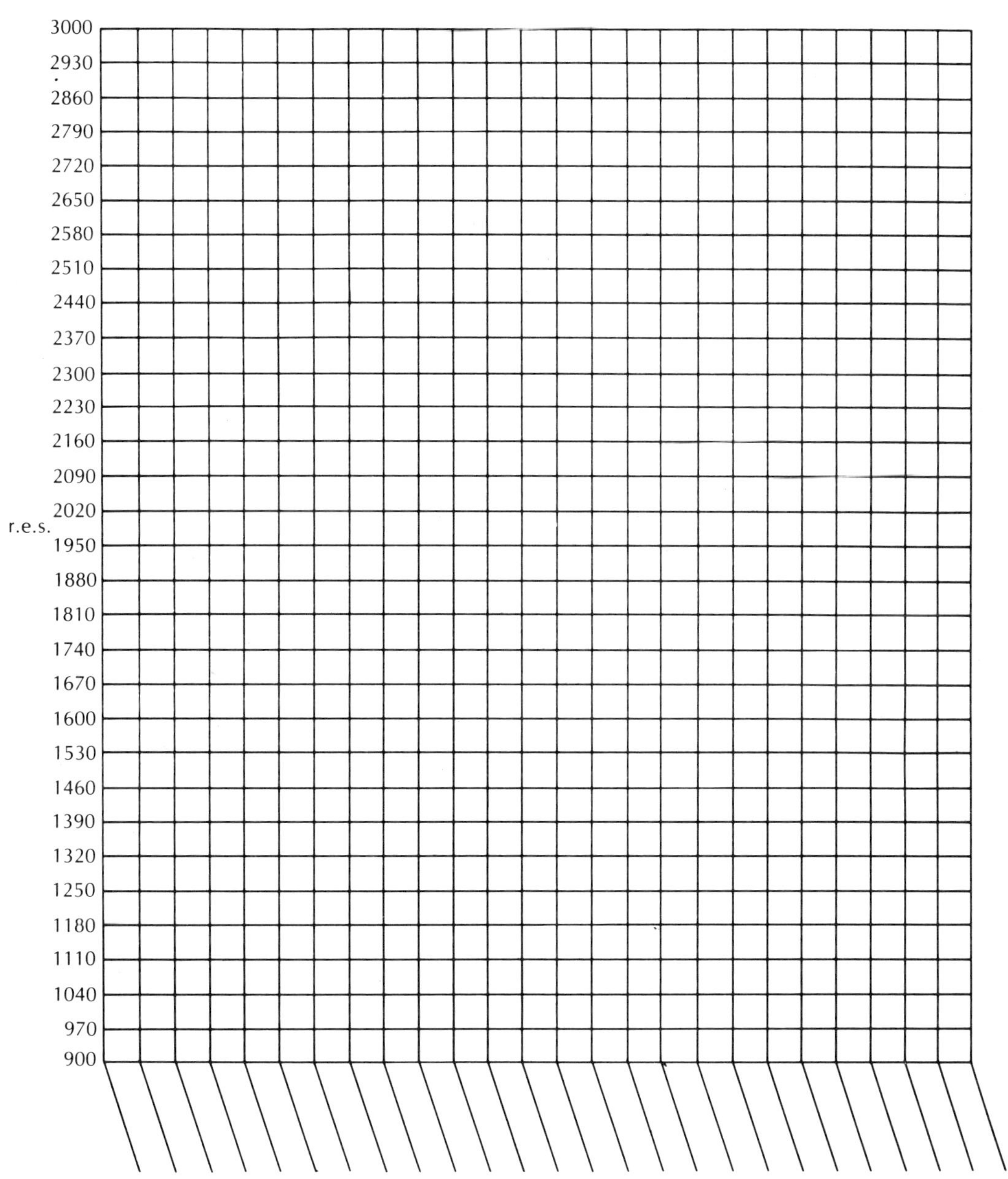

APPENDIX B

ENGLISH REVIEW

GRAMMAR

When people make grammatical errors in their writing, speaking, and thinking, they usually make one or more of the mistakes described in this section. Study the examples that illustrate each of the grammatical rules so that you can avoid making these errors.

1. **MISTAKE:** *The subject and the verb in a sentence or clause do not agree.* In other words, the subject is singular and the verb is plural, or the subject is plural and the verb is singular.
   SOLUTION: When the subject is plural, its associated verb should be plural. When the subject is singular, its associated verb should be singular. The subject and verb must agree regardless of the number of words separating them.
   HINT: When several words separate the subject and the verb, mentally remove them so that they do not confuse your thinking. For example, if a sentence such as "The person for the Higgs and Suggs accounts is Daren" is confusing, just think of the sentence as "The person is Daren" for a moment. Clearly both the subject and the verb are singular in this instance, though "accounts" is plural. Again, just put mental parentheses around the words that separate the subject and its associated verb.

INCORRECT	CORRECT
The manager (of the shoe and hosiery departments) are absent.	The manager (of the shoe and hosiery departments) is absent.
They was at the meeting.	They were at the meeting.
The number (of times the books is used) are inconsequential.	The number (of times the books are used) is inconsequential.

INCORRECT	CORRECT
Neither (Frank nor Alice) were asked back for another interview.	Neither (Frank nor Alice) was asked back for another interview.
If either (Rachel or Lane) go, I will write the report.	If either (Rachel or Lane) goes, I will write the report.
If either Ms. Baum or the Fabers joins us, we will have to order more coffee.	If either Ms. Baum or the Fabers join us, we will have to order more coffee.

(Note: Here the subject closest to the verb determines whether the verb is singular or plural. "Fabers" is plural, so the verb "join" is plural.)

2. **MISTAKE:** *"Each," "everyone," "everybody," "anyone," and "anybody" are used as if they were plural.*
   SOLUTION: "Each," "everyone," "everybody," "anyone," and "anybody" are singular. Use them as such.

INCORRECT	CORRECT
Everybody and their parents will attend.	Everybody and her or his parents will attend.
Each of the accountants are working on the audit.	Each of the accountants is working on the audit.
We want everyone to have their chance.	We want everyone to have her or his chance.
Each of the department heads will contribute their time, and all of the employees are planning to donate old clothes.	Each of the department heads will contribute her or his time, and all of the employees are planning to donate old clothes.

3. **MISTAKE:** *"Us" is used in the subjective case and "we" is used in the objective case.*
   SOLUTION: Always use "we" as part of the subject and "us" as part of the direct or indirect receiver of the subject's action.
   HINT: When trying to decide whether to use "us" or "we," think of the sentence without the word or words following "us" or "we." For example, say the sentence in the first example without the word "employees." "Us want a better grievance system" sounds odd, but "We want a better grievance system" sounds, and is, correct.

INCORRECT	CORRECT
Us employees want a better grievance system.	We employees want a better grievance system.
The manager gave the new guidelines to we salespeople.	The manager gave the new guidelines to us salespeople.
The report that us board members want should be ready tomorrow.	The report that we board members want should be ready tomorrow.

4. **MISTAKE:** *"I" is used in the objective case and "me" is used in the subjective case.*

SOLUTION: Use "I" as the subject and "me" as the direct or indirect receiver of the subject's action.

INCORRECT	CORRECT
Fred gave the presentation to Laura and I.	Fred gave the presentation to Laura and me.
Him and me share an office.	He and I share an office.
It is me.	It is I.
The party was given for Adam and I.	The party was given for Adam and me.

5. **MISTAKE:** *"Who" is used as an object and "whom" is used as a subject.*
SOLUTION: Use "who" in the subjective case and "whom" in the objective case.
HINT: Substitute "he," "she," or "we" for "who," and substitute "her," "him," or "us" for "whom" when you are confused.

INCORRECT	CORRECT
Rhoda Sills, whom works for us, will make the trip.	Rhoda Sills, who works for us, will make the trip.
You will be giving the raise to who?	You will be giving the raise to whom?
Who are you talking about?	Whom are you talking about?

(Note: Here you can restate the sentence as "You are talking about her?", which sounds, and is, correct.)

INCORRECT	CORRECT
Whomever wrote this knows her or his subject.	Whoever wrote this knows her or his subject.

PUNCTUATION

Because numerous punctuation rules exist, the treatment of the rules in this appendix is by no means exhaustive. However, some of the important rules do appear here.

1. **THE PERIOD, THE EXCLAMATION POINT, AND THE QUESTION MARK:** *The period, exclamation point, and question mark are used to end sentences.* A sentence, of course, is a complete thought which includes at least a subject and a verb, such as: "Mr. Skibbs is the manager." A sentence can also be a command, such as "Sit", where the subject, you, is understood. *A period is used to end most sentences. An exclamation point is used to end a command or a sentence expressing great excitement, grief, or something of extraordinary significance. A question mark ends sentences that are questions.*

INCORRECT	CORRECT
If I could write well. I would write more.	If I could write well, I would write more.

Please send me a sample copy of *City Executive!*	Please send me a sample copy of *City Executive.*
Congratulations, Forrest. *(You want to express excitement.)*	Congratulations, Forrest!
I plan to look for a job after I go to Europe I want to teach business writing my strengths are in punctuation and spelling.	I plan to look for a job after I go to Europe. I want to teach business writing. My strengths are in punctuation and spelling.
Do you know which desk is hers.	Do you know which desk is hers?

2. **THE COMMA:** *Commas are used within sentences to cause the reader to pause, and then continue reading.* Commas make sentences more readable. When you are trying to decide whether to use a comma, say the sentence out loud. Often you will need to put commas in the places where you paused when speaking the sentence. Commas serve a number of functions, most of which are described in this section.

   a. *Commas set off introductory and parenthetical words, and commas signal a direct reference to the reader.*

INCORRECT	CORRECT
Curiously Jane and Felix refused to finish the project.	Curiously, Jane and Felix refused to finish the project.
Even so I will talk to Ms. Rames.	Even so, I will talk to Ms. Rames.
Given that the reorganization plan should be written by a third party.	Given that, the reorganization plan should be written by a third party.
The Simmons Plan I believe is due on Wednesday.	The Simmons Plan, I believe, is due on Wednesday.
The candidate I chose however speaks very well.	The candidate I chose, however, speaks very well.
I am pleased to inform you Ms. Blue Sky that you will receive your certificate at the employees' luncheon.	I am pleased to inform you, Ms. Blue Sky, that you will receive your certificate at the employees' luncheon.

   b. *Commas set off introductory clauses and phrases.*

INCORRECT	CORRECT
If I choose a company outside of Omaha it must be located in the San Francisco area.	If I choose a company outside of Omaha, it must be located in the San Francisco area.
The company I choose, must be located in the San Francisco area.	The company I choose must be located in the San Francisco area.
When Mr. Li makes a speech most people listen.	When Mr. Li makes a speech, most people listen.

Because the offices are too crowded now the Roy Company will move to a new building.	Because the offices are too crowded now, the Roy Company will move to a new building.

c. *Commas connect two complete sentences joined by a conjunction.*

INCORRECT	CORRECT
I fully intend to complete the appendixes on time and I plan to begin preparing the index next week.	I fully intend to complete the appendixes on time, and I plan to begin preparing the index next week.
I do hope that you are pleased with your first Bilmark Briefcase and I do want you to visit our store soon so that you can receive your free gift.	I do hope that you are pleased with your first Bilmark Briefcase, and I do want you to visit our store soon so that you can receive your free gift.
Ms. Dorn did quite well in her interview and Ms. Ross was impressed by Mr. Schapp's credentials.	Ms. Dorn did quite well in her interview, and Ms. Ross was impressed by Mr. Schapp's credentials.

d. *Commas set off nonrestrictive clauses.* Nonrestrictive clauses give additional information, but do not provide information essential to the sentence.

INCORRECT	CORRECT
Sharon who is a C.P.A. is the head of the Accounting Department.	Sharon, who is a C.P.A., is the head of the Accounting Department.
The five-year plan I wrote is sixty pages long which is twice the length of the plan Wellings wrote in 1979.	The five-year plan I wrote is sixty pages long, which is twice the length of the plan Wellings wrote in 1979.
The Lansing office which is located in Farmer Michigan had an extremely high turnover rate last year.	The Lansing office, which is located in Farmer, Michigan, had an extremely high turnover rate last year.

e. *Commas set off longer introductory prepositional phrases.*

INCORRECT	CORRECT
To everyone but Sam Alice was the best marketing manager in the history of the firm.	To everyone but Sam, Alice was the best marketing manager in the history of the firm.
For reasons only he knew the new orders were canceled.	For reasons only he knew, the new orders were canceled.
In response to Faye's letter Tom withdrew his proposal.	In response to Faye's letter, Tom withdrew his proposal.

f. *Commas set off words or phrases in a series.*

INCORRECT	CORRECT
Dan ordered paper clips pencils and rubber bands.	Dan ordered paper clips, pencils, and rubber bands.

I reviewed the report attended a meeting wrote a memorandum and discussed a problem with Mona.	I reviewed the report, attended a meeting, wrote a memorandum, and discussed a problem with Mona.
Check the progress report for errors type the report and then give the report to me.	Check the progress report for errors, type the report, and then give the report to me.

g. *Commas set off two or more words that modify a noun.*

INCORRECT	CORRECT
An intelligent articulate financial analyst is easy to find in this town.	An intelligent, articulate financial analyst is easy to find in this town.
No company should be without a reliable inexpensive phone system.	No company should be without a reliable, inexpensive phone system.
The first, preliminary report was both informative and interesting.	The first preliminary report was both informative and interesting.

h. *Commas set off words that emphasize differences.*

INCORRECT	CORRECT
The person for the job should have experience in the private not public sector.	The person for the job should have experience in the private, not public, sector.
We assumed that Pam not David would do the honors.	We assumed that Pam, not David, would do the honors.

i. *Commas set off clauses beginning with "but," "yet," "or," "nor," and "for."*

INCORRECT	CORRECT
I answered the phone but the caller said nothing.	I answered the phone, but the caller said nothing.
She received excellent performance ratings yet was never considered for promotion.	She received excellent performance ratings, yet was never considered for promotion.
The supervisors did not cross the picket lines nor did the janitors clerks or mechanics.	The supervisors did not cross the picket lines, nor did the janitors, clerks, or mechanics.

j. *Commas set off academic degrees, titles, parts of personal names, cities, states, countries, dates, and "Inc." and "Ltd."*

INCORRECT	CORRECT
Arnold Schwartz Jr. Ed.D. will give the major address at the production managers' conference in Kansas City	Arnold Schwartz, Jr., Ed.D., will give the major address at the production managers' conference in Kansas

INCORRECT	CORRECT
Missouri on Monday February 6, 198X.	City, Missouri, on Monday, February 6, 198X.
Stella Vale Vice President is married to an artist.	Stella Vale, Vice President, is married to an artist.
Conway Inc. is a wholly-owned subsidiary of Lentek Ltd. of London England.	Conway, Inc., is a wholly-owned subsidiary of Lentek, Ltd., of London, England.

k. Commas set off direct quotations.

INCORRECT	CORRECT
John asked me "Who are you to disagree?"	John asked me, "Who are you to disagree?"
What she said was "All of the employees in my department have equal rights and responsibilities."	What she said was, "All of the employees in my department have equal rights and responsibilities."

3. **THE COLON:** *The colon marks the beginning of a series of words. The colon also introduces descriptions, long quotations, and lists.*

INCORRECT

Joan Elliott, an expert on motivation and work behavior, said

> No employee should have to view herself or himself as a nobody. The manager should tell the employee that she or he is an important part of the organization and then behave in a manner that supports, not contradicts, the employee's feeling of importance.

Six people are being considered for the job Joe, Louise, Fred, Martha, Henry, and Rita.

Please answer these questions
1. What is your name?
2. What is your job title?
3. What is your home address?
4. What is your home telephone number?
5. What amount do you wish to donate?

CORRECT

Joan Elliott, an expert on motivation and work behavior, said:

> No employee should have to view herself or himself as a nobody. The manager should tell the employee that she or he is an important part of the organization and then behave in a manner that supports, not contradicts, the employee's feeling of importance.

Six people are being considered for the job: Joe, Louise, Fred, Martha, Henry, and Rita.

Please answer these questions:
1. What is your name?
2. What is your job title?
3. What is your home address?
4. What is your home telephone number?
5. What amount do you wish to donate?

4. **THE SEMICOLON:** *The semicolon serves to cause a more definite pause than the comma.* The most important uses of the semicolon are described in this section.

   a. *Semicolons connect two complete sentences.* Here, the sentences must be related, and no conjunction is used to separate them.

INCORRECT	CORRECT
I was the first person to voice an opinion James was the first person to take offense.	I was the first person to voice an opinion; James was the first person to take offense.
Dave has worked for the firm for six years his work record is exemplary.	Dave has worked for the firm for six years; his work record is exemplary.

b. *Semicolons connect two main clauses, the second of which begins with a conjunctive adverb.*

INCORRECT	CORRECT
Good health contributes to good learning however, not every healthy person is a quick learner.	Good health contributes to good learning; however, not every healthy person is a quick learner.
You have sold more merchandise than any other salesperson, consequently you have been named Shoe City Salesperson of the year.	You have sold more merchandise than any other salesperson; consequently, you have been named Shoe City Salesperson of the Year.

c. *Semicolons separate long or complex items or phrases in a series, including phrases or clauses that contain commas.*

INCORRECT	CORRECT
These people participated in the workshop: Susan Morris, marketing, Randy Fein, accounting, Lisa Foo, typing pool, and Walter Nern, editorial services.	These people participated in the workshop: Susan Morris, marketing; Randy Fein, accounting; Lisa Foo, typing pool; and Walter Nern, editorial services.
Marilyn DiRicci volunteered to write the training plan, including the training schedule, to talk to Joe Byrne about the marketing, accounting, and payroll problems, to call Anna Friend, and to conduct the next meeting.	Marilyn DiRicci volunteered to write the training plan, including the training schedule; to talk to Joe Byrne about the marketing, accounting, and payroll problems; to call Anna Friend; and to conduct the next meeting.

5. **THE DASH:** *Dashes mark a major shift in the structure of a sentence, enclose some words of significance, or set off explanatory words that contain commas.*

INCORRECT	CORRECT
Albert takes the time to talk to his employees and believe me they are pleased with the attention.	Albert takes the time to talk to his employees—and, believe me, they are pleased with the attention.
The District Five states Kansas, Nebraska, Missouri, and Arkansas were slow to adopt our new dog food, Doggie Palace.	The District Five states—Kansas, Nebraska, Missouri, and Arkansas—were slow to adopt our new dog food, Doggie Palace.

6. **QUOTATION MARKS:** *Quotation marks are placed before and after the unaltered words of a speaker or writer. Quotation marks also enclose titles of newspaper or magazine articles, reports, songs, short poems, and other short pieces of writing.* Remember that commas and periods go inside the quotation marks, and colons and semicolons are placed outside the quotation marks. If a quotation is a question or an exclamation, the question or exclamation point should be placed inside the quotation marks. If the entire sentence is a question or an exclamation, the question mark or exclamation point should be placed outside the quotation marks. *Also, quotation marks can be used to enclose slang or unusual words, words used sarcastically, and words used to mean something other than their dictionary meaning. Finally, words that you are describing should be enclosed in quotation marks.*

INCORRECT	CORRECT
Ms. Wane said, Every human being has a right to food and shelter.	Ms. Wane said, "Every human being has a right to food and shelter."
How to Organize Your Day, an article in *Business First,* was quite helpful.	"How to Organize Your Day," an article in *Business First,* was quite helpful.
Mr. French thinks that cool has something to do with temperature.	Mr. French thinks that "cool" has something to do with temperature.
I, you, he, she, it, we, and they are pronouns in the subjective case.	"I," "you," "he," "she," "it," "we," and "they" are pronouns in the subjective case.

7. **THE HYPHEN:** *Hyphens connect words that modify the same noun, connect compound words, and divide words too long to fit at the end of a line.*

INCORRECT	CORRECT
The half written paper was of no use to me.	The half-written paper was of no use to me.
The instructions were self explanatory.	The instructions were self-explanatory.

8. **PARENTHESES:** *Parentheses suggest that the words they enclose are not critical to the sentence.* The words in parentheses are usually explanatory words, "aside" words that do not flow well in the sentence. Avoid overusing parenthetical structures.

INCORRECT	CORRECT
The current interest rate, too high, I think, is the topic of my finance paper.	The current interest rate (too high, I think) is the topic of my finance paper.
I wrote, remember how poorly I wrote in high school, a report that will be read before the commission.	I wrote (remember how poorly I wrote in high school?) a report that will be read before the commission.

9. **ITALICS AND UNDERLINES:** Italics are used in printed material for words that are underlined in typewritten material. *Italics and underlines are used to emphasize words, signal foreign words that are not generally used, and set off titles of books, pamphlets, magazines, newspapers, plays, operas, movies, and long poems.*

INCORRECT	CORRECT
I "do not" want my name to be used.	I do *not* want my name to be used.
Elaine considers herself a member of the bourgeoisie.	Elaine considers herself a member of the *bourgeoisie.*
The article in "Newsweek" was reprinted in "Professional Secretary."	The article in *Newsweek* was reprinted in *Professional Secretary.*

10. **THE APOSTROPHE:** *The apostrophe is used to make words possessive, to form contractions, and to make some abbreviations, letters, and words plural.*

a. *Apostrophes make nouns and indefinite pronouns possessive.* In most cases, you make a singular noun or pronoun possessive by adding an apostrophe followed by an "s." An apostrophe is placed after the "s" in plural nouns and indefinite pronouns.

INCORRECT	CORRECT
The managers office is imposing. *(Note: Only one manager occupies the office.)*	The manager's office is imposing.
The manager's offices are located on the fifth floor. *(Note: Several managers occupy the offices.)*	The managers' offices are located on the fifth floor.
The manager's will meet in my office.	The managers will meet in my office.

(Note: If a word is plural but not possessive, no apostrophe is needed. In this example, the managers do not own or possess anything, so "managers" is not possessive.)

INCORRECT	CORRECT
Davids home is in the suburbs.	David's home is in the suburbs.
She has six months experience in computer programming.	She has six months' experience in computer programming.
She has six months' of experience in computer programming.	She has six months of experience in computer programming.
The Liss son is one of the applicants.	The Liss's son is one of the applicants.

Carol and Johns paper is excellent.	Carol and John's paper is excellent.

(Note: Here both Carol and John wrote the paper.)

Robert and Nancys papers are late.	Robert's and Nancy's papers are late.

(Note: Here Robert and Nancy wrote separate papers.)

The door handle was broken.	The door's handle was broken.
They had a years worth of food.	They had a year's worth of food.

b. *Put apostrophes in the place of missing letters in contractions.*

INCORRECT	**CORRECT**
I have'nt finished the report.	I haven't finished the report.

(Note: Here the apostrophe goes between the "n" and the "t" in place of the missing "o.")

Its enough to be here.	It's enough to be here.
Is'nt the chart ready?	Isn't the chart ready?
Wer'e on our way.	We're on our way.

(Note: Here the apostrophe goes between the "c" and the "r" in place of the missing "a.")

c. *Apostrophes make plural both abbreviations and letters.*

INCORRECT	**CORRECT**
Lonnie made two Aes and three Bes.	Lonnie made two A's and three B's. OR Lonnie made two As and three Bs.
Always put "ss" after the apostrophe in singular nouns and pronouns that are possessive.	Always put "s's" after the apostrophe in singular nouns and pronouns that are possessive.
The accountants had three Ph.D.s among them.	The accountants had three Ph.D.'s among them.

d. *Apostrophes can be used to make numbers, years, and symbols plural. Also, words that are referred to in a sentence can be made plural with an apostrophe and an "s."*

INCORRECT	**CORRECT**
Things were calm in the 1970es.	Things were calm in the 1970's.
Six "7es" appeared in the sentence.	Six 7's appeared in the sentence.
Do not overuse "howevers" and "therefores."	Do not overuse "however's" and "therefore's."
Put "%s" after the numbers in the third column.	Put "%'s" after the numbers in the third column.

SPELLING AND PRONUNCIATION

The best way to learn to spell and pronounce words correctly is to practice the troublesome words until you have them committed to memory. When the least bit unsure about how to spell or pronounce a word, check a dictionary. Recall, however, that the order of pronunciations in a dictionary does not indicate the order of correctness or preference.

This section lists words that are often misspelled and mispronounced.

WORDS THAT ARE OFTEN MISSPELLED AND MISPRONOUNCED
(Second column alphabetized correctly)

INCORRECT	CORRECT
abscent	absent
accomodate	accommodate
accounant	accountant
acknowledgement	acknowledgment
accross	across
ajust	adjust
administrate	administer
advise (for advice)	advice
adviseable	advisable
advice (for advise)	advise
alright	all right
all most	almost
anlysis	analysis
analyse	analyze
anxous	anxious
arguement	argument
asteriks	asterisk
athalete	athlete
athaletics	athletics
(Note: "Athlete" has only two syllables; "athletics" has only three.)	
attendence	attendance
atitude	attitude
attornies	attorneys
auxilary	auxiliary
batchler	bachelor
babtise	baptize
bargan	bargain
begining	beginning
believeable	believable
beleiving	believing
benefical	beneficial
bookeeper	bookkeeper
bullitin	bulletin

WORDS THAT ARE OFTEN MISSPELLED AND MISPRONOUNCED
(Second column alphabetized correctly)

burocracy	bureaucracy
busyer	busier
bussiness	business
calender	calendar
campane	campaign
catagory	category
changable	changeable
chargable	chargeable
colesterol	cholesterol
chose (for choose)	choose
choose (for chose)	chose
commited	committed
commitee	committee
companys	companies
compatant	competent
concieve	conceive
congradulate	congratulate
consientous	conscientious
concious	conscious
controled	controlled
convience	convenience
corelate	correlate
correspondant	correspondent
couragous	courageous
curteus	courteous
criteria (for criterion)	criterion
curiousity	curiosity
data (for datum)	datum
deficent	deficient
dependant	dependent
discribe	describe
desireable	desirable
desert (for dessert)	dessert
developement	development
discrete (for discreet)	discreet
discrepency	discrepancy
eficent	efficient
elgible	eligible
embarass	embarrass
inclose	enclose
envirorment	environment
equiped	equipped
excape	escape
expecially	especially

WORDS THAT ARE OFTEN MISSPELLED AND MISPRONOUNCED
(Second column alphabetized correctly)

INCORRECT	CORRECT
excede	exceed
excelent	excellent
excitment	excitement
exersize	exercise
exausted	exhausted
existance	existence
extention	extension
familar	familiar
famos	famous
feasability	feasibility
feasable	feasible
Febuary	February
financialy	financially
finnish	finish
forcable	forcible
formost	foremost
forseen	foreseen
gambel	gamble
goverment	government
grammer	grammar
grievence	grievance
garuntee	guarantee
gilt (for guilt)	guilt
habet	habit
handleing	handling
happyness	happiness
harras	harass
half to	have to
heighth	height
hygene	hygiene
illigitimate	illegitimate
inaguration	inauguration
incidently	incidentally
indispensible	indispensable
insistance	insistence
inteligent	intelligent
interferred	interfered
introduceing	introducing
irrevelant	irrelevant
jelousy	jealousy
jewls	jewels
journies	journeys
legable	legible
liesure	leisure

WORDS THAT ARE OFTEN MISSPELLED AND MISPRONOUNCED
(Second column alphabetized correctly)

INCORRECT	CORRECT
liason	liaison
lisence	license
maintainence	maintenance
managment	management
medium (for median)	median
median (for medium)	medium
momento	memento
memorandem	memorandum
merchent	merchant
miscelanious	miscellaneous
mispelled	misspelled
morale (for moral)	moral
moral (for morale)	morale
naturel	natural
neccessary	necessary
negetive	negative
negociate	negotiate
niether	neither
nuetral	neutral
nineth	ninth
noticable	noticeable
nucular	nuclear
numberous	numerous
obveous	obvious
ocassion	occasion
ocurred or occured	occurred
ocurrence	occurrence
origenal	original
oweing	owing
pamplet	pamphlet
paralell	parallel
preform (for perform)	perform
permanant	permanent
personnell	personnel
prespiration	perspiration
preceed	precede
preceeding	preceding
presise	precise
prefered	preferred
prevelent	prevalent
priveledge	privilege
proceedure	procedure
procede	proceed
proposel	proposal

WORDS THAT ARE OFTEN MISSPELLED AND MISPRONOUNCED
(Second column alphabetized correctly)

INCORRECT	CORRECT
psycology	psychology
quanity	quantity
questionaire	questionnaire
rasberry	raspberry
realator	realtor
realaty	realty
recieve	receive
reccommend	recommend
referrence	reference
refered	referred
reguard	regard
revelant	relevant
rediculous	ridiculous
runaway (for runway)	runway
sells (for sales)	sales
scrutany	scrutiny
seperate	separate
sherbert	sherbet
silance	silence
simalar	similar
solvant	solvent
spaded	spayed
stastistics	statistics
suficient	sufficient
summery	summary
supercede	supersede
tacktics	tactics
tenative	tentative
tho	though
thoughtfull	thoughtful
thru	through
tonite	tonight
tradgedy	tragedy
transfered	transferred
transfering	transferring
truely	truly
unlikly	unlikely
useage	usage
wif	with
witholding	withholding
writting	writing

WORD USAGE

People sometimes use words incorrectly or confuse them with words that have similar spellings. Some of the words that give people trouble appear in this section.

1. **ACCEPT AND EXCEPT:** When you *accept* something, you receive it. When you *except* something, you leave it out—you exclude it. Remember, when you accept, you receive; when you make an exception, you exclude something.

INCORRECT	CORRECT
I excepted the job because I have wanted to be an executive secretary all of my life.	I accepted the job because I have wanted to be an executive secretary all of my life.
Everyone accept Johnny has a degree in business.	Everyone except Johnny has a degree in business.
All of the computers excepted the data accept the computer programmed in BASIC.	All of the computers accepted the data except the computer programmed in BASIC

2. **ADAPT, ADEPT, AND ADOPT:** When you *adapt* something, you make an adjustment so that it will work or fit. When you are *adept* at something, you are very good at it. Finally, when you *adopt* something, you take it and use it as your own.

INCORRECT	CORRECT
Recent graduates often find that it takes several weeks to adopt themselves to a full-time job.	Recent graduates often find that it takes several weeks to adapt themselves to a full-time job.
Rose was adapt at both writing and speaking.	Rose was adept at both writing and speaking.
The committee adepted the guidelines listed in Fran's proposal.	The committee adopted the guidelines listed in Fran's proposal.

3. **ADVERSE AND AVERSE:** Something is *adverse* when it is quite hostile or unfavorable. You are *averse* to something when you are opposed to it or are reluctant to face it.

INCORRECT	CORRECT
The averse publicity forced the company to withdraw its Sugar Fun Cereal from the market.	The adverse publicity forced the company to withdraw its Sugar Fun Cereal from the market.
A person is said to be risk-adverse when he or she carefully avoids risks.	A person is said to be risk-averse when he or she carefully avoids risks.
I am adverse to aversity.	I am averse to adversity.

4. **AFFECT AND EFFECT:** When you *affect* something, you bring about a change in it. When you *effect* something, you make it happen. Also, an *effect* is a result.

INCORRECT	CORRECT
The recent staff changes will effect morale.	The recent staff changes will affect morale.
If a person is to affect changes in this organization, he or she must be willing to take some risks.	If a person is to effect changes in this organization, he or she must be willing to take some risks.
What affect will the move have on the regional vice presidents?	What effect will the move have on the regional vice presidents?

5. **ALL READY, ALREADY, ALL TOGETHER, AND ALTOGETHER:** When something is *all ready,* it is prepared or completely done. When something is *already* done, it was done previously. Things that are *all together* are things that are together in one group. When you are *altogether* something, you are entirely something.

INCORRECT	CORRECT
She was all ready late.	She was already late.
The packages were already for shipping.	The packages were all ready for shipping.
They were altogether in the conference room.	They were all together in the conference room.
He was not all together wrong in his assessment of the situation.	He was not altogether wrong in his assessment of the situation.

6. **APPRAISE AND APPRISE:** When you *appraise* something, you evaluate it or estimate its worth. When you *apprise* someone of something, you inform her or him.

INCORRECT	CORRECT
The insurance company sent a woman to the garage to apprise the value of the damaged car.	The insurance company sent a woman to the garage to appraise the value of the damaged car.
Six people were chosen to appraise the affected employees of the reasons for the changes in the salary structure.	Six people were chosen to apprise the affected employees of the reasons for the changes in the salary structure.

7. **ANXIOUS AND EAGER:** When you are *anxious,* you are worried about something that may happen. When you are *eager,* you look forward to something or want something to happen.

INCORRECT	CORRECT
I am eager about the probable cut in my pay.	I am anxious about the probable cut in my pay.

I am anxious to meet all of you.	I am eager to meet all of you.

8. **CAPITAL AND CAPITOL:** A *capital* is a city, and the *capitol* is the main government building in the capital. *Capital* is also money or property.

INCORRECT	CORRECT
We went to Oklahoma's capitol, Oklahoma City, to take a tour of the capital.	We went to Oklahoma's capital, Oklahoma City, to take a tour of the capitol.
We do not have enough capitol to incorporate.	We do not have enough capital to incorporate.

9. **CITE, SIGHT, AND SITE:** You *cite* a person when you quote her or him or when you commend her or him for good service. You *sight* a person when you locate her or him with your eyes. A *site* is the place where something was, is, or will be located.

INCORRECT	CORRECT
The attorney sited *Marks* v. *Lainer.*	The attorney cited *Marks* v. *Lainer.*
We last cited Don and Meyer in the park.	We last sighted Don and Meyer in the park.
We need to find a suitable sight for the new insurance office.	We need to find a suitable site for the new insurance office.

10. **COMPLEMENT, COMPLIMENT AND COMPLIMENTARY:** Something *complements* something else when it completes it or perfects it. Someone *compliments* someone else when he or she gives praise or expresses admiration. Something is *complimentary* when it is given at no charge as a courtesy.

INCORRECT	CORRECT
The chair compliments the desk.	The chair complements the desk.
She rarely gives complements.	She rarely gives compliments.
A complementary drink is given to every passenger.	A complimentary drink is given to every passenger.

11. **CONFIDANT AND CONFIDENT:** Your *confidant* is a trusted friend. You are *confident* when you are relatively sure about someone or something.

INCORRECT	CORRECT
Sally is my confident; I tell her everything.	Sally is my confidant; I tell her everything.
I am confidant that I will be promoted to group leader.	I am confident that I will be promoted to group leader.

12. **CONSCIENCE AND CONSCIOUS:** Your *conscience* is what distinguishes between right and wrong. You are *conscious* when you are aware of something about yourself or about your environment.

INCORRECT	CORRECT
My conscious was bothering me because I had neglected my family.	My conscience was bothering me because I had neglected my family.
I was conscience of your problem, but not of Milt's.	I was conscious of your problem, but not of Milt's.

13. **CONTINUAL AND CONTINUOUS:** Something that happens *continually* happens often. Something that takes place *continuously* takes place without interruption.

INCORRECT	CORRECT
Harry continuously stayed after closing time.	Harry continually stayed after closing time.
The continual buzz of the clock distracts me.	The continuous buzz of the clock distracts me.

14. **COUNCIL, COUNSEL, COUNCILOR, AND COUNSELOR:** A *council* is a group of people. You *counsel* someone when you discuss something with her or him. You are a *councilor* when you are a member of a council. You are a *counselor* when you act as an adviser.

INCORRECT	CORRECT
I am a member of the city counsel.	I am a member of the city council.
I council my clients to invest in money market certificates.	I counsel my clients to invest in money market certificates.
I was a city counselor for sixteen years.	I was a city councilor for sixteen years.
I am a career councilor at Synne High School.	I am a career counselor at Synne High School.

15. **CREDIBLE AND CREDITABLE:** You are *credible* when you are perceived to be honest and knowledgeable. When you do good work, your work is *creditable*.

INCORRECT	CORRECT
I would not quote him because most people do not consider him a creditable source.	I would not quote him because most people do not consider him a credible source.
The work you did on the sales campaign is credible.	The work you did on the sales campaign is creditable.

16. **DISINTERESTED AND UNINTERESTED:** When you are *disinterested,* you are unbiased or impartial. When you are *uninterested,* you are simply not interested in the subject.

INCORRECT	CORRECT
Most circuit court judges are said to be uninterested because they are impartial.	Most circuit court judges are said to be disinterested because they are impartial.
Claudine seemed disinterested in my book about Australian wheat.	Claudine seemed uninterested in my book about Australian wheat.

17. **EVERY ONE, EVERYONE, ANY ONE, AND ANYONE:** *Of* usually follows the words *every one* and *any one. Everyone* means everybody and *anyone* means anybody.

INCORRECT	CORRECT
Everyone of you is responsible.	Every one of you is responsible.
I want every one to have a chance to speak.	I want everyone to have a chance to speak.
Anyone of you could be the next chairperson.	Any one of you could be the next chairperson.
Any one caught divulging company secrets will be suspended.	Anyone caught divulging company secrets will be suspended.

18. **FARTHER AND FURTHER:** *Farther* is a greater distance in space that can be measured in such units as inches or miles. *Further* usually refers to a distance in space or time that cannot be measured in standard units or refers to a greater degree for a qualitative factor. *Further* also refers to advancing something.

INCORRECT	CORRECT
My new car can go further on a gallon of gasoline than my old car.	My new car can go farther on a gallon of gasoline than my old car.
The farther I get into this project, the more I like it.	The further I get into this project, the more I like it.
The completion of my degree will farther my career.	The completion of my degree will further my career.

19. **FOREWORD AND FORWARD:** A *foreword* is a preface or introduction. You move toward the front when you move *forward.* Also, if you are aggressive, you might be considered *forward.*

INCORRECT	CORRECT
The forward of the book was too long.	The foreword of the book was too long.
I sometimes wonder why he is not moving foreword in his career.	I sometimes wonder why he is not moving forward in his career.

20. **FORMALLY AND FORMERLY:** You do something in a formal way when you do something *formally.* You were something or did something *formerly* when you were something or did something previously.

INCORRECT	CORRECT
Carnes will formerly hand over the reigns of power at the banquet.	Carnes will formally hand over the reigns of power at the banquet.
Louise Frankel, formally of Biggs and Weinberg, will direct all research projects.	Louise Frankel, formerly of Biggs and Weinberg, will direct all research projects.

21. **ITS AND IT'S:** *Its* is used as a possessive pronoun. *It's* is used as the contraction of *it is* or *it has.*

INCORRECT	CORRECT
The agency applied for it's license after the deadline.	The agency applied for its license after the deadline.
Its unfortunate that the company will not allow it's employees to have flexible work hours.	It's unfortunate that the company will not allow its employees to have flexible work hours.

22. **LAY AND LIE:** You place something on a surface when you *lay* it down. You yourself rest or recline on a surface when you *lie* down. Objects *lie* after they have been placed on a surface. The past tense of *lie,* however, is *lay.*

INCORRECT	CORRECT
Please lie down your papers so that you can write on the board.	Please lay down your papers so that you can write on the board.
The books just laid there unused for a week.	The books just lay there unused for a week.

23. **LEAD AND LED:** You *lead* if you are directing, guiding, or conducting something or someone now or in the future. You *led* if you directed, guided, or conducted something or someone in the past. *Lead* is also a metallic substance.

INCORRECT	CORRECT
I lead a fund drive last summer.	I led a fund drive last summer.
The type bars are made of led.	The type bars are made of lead.

24. **LOOSE AND LOSE:** Something is *loose* when it is not tight. When you *lose* something, you are unable to find it or you do not win it.

INCORRECT	CORRECT
The drawer handle is lose.	The drawer handle is loose.
If we loose the contract, we will be in financial trouble.	If we lose the contract, we will be in financial trouble.

25. **PASSED AND PAST:** *Passed* is the past tense of *pass. Past* is an adjective that refers to something that has gone by or something that is no longer current.

INCORRECT	CORRECT
We past the school on the way to work.	We passed the school on the way to work.
The bill is passed due.	The bill is past due.
What happened in the passed is of no concern to me.	What happened in the past is of no concern to me.

26. **PERSECUTE AND PROSECUTE:** You *persecute* someone when you purposely harm her or him. You *prosecute* someone when you bring a legal action against her or him.

INCORRECT	CORRECT
We aren't giving you suggestions for the purpose of prosecuting you.	We aren't giving you suggestions for the purpose of persecuting you.
Do you intend to persecute the person who altered your firm's books?	Do you intend to prosecute the person who altered your firm's books?

27. **PERSONAL AND PERSONNEL:** Something that is *personal* is something that is yours. The employees of an organization are its *personnel.*

INCORRECT	CORRECT
I try to keep my personnel life separate from my life at work.	I try to keep my personal life separate from my life at work.
We offer an excellent package of benefits to our personal.	We offer an excellent package of benefits to our personnel.

28. **PERSPECTIVE AND PROSPECTIVE:** Your *perspective* is your point of view. *Perspective* also refers to the relationship of the parts to each other and to the whole. A *prospective* something is an expected something.

INCORRECT	CORRECT
Your prospective on the matter seems to differ from mine.	Your perspective on the matter seems to differ from mine.
The perspective client wants us to give her a presentation.	The prospective client wants us to give her a presentation.

29. **PRACTICAL AND PRACTICABLE:** Something that is *practical* is something that is useful or something that is acquired through action, not through theory. Something that is *practicable* is something that is capable of being put into use. Though *practical* can refer to both things and people, *practicable* refers to only things.

INCORRECT	CORRECT
Because he wears clothes that are both stylish and functional, I consider him to be practicable.	Because he wears clothes that are both stylish and functional, I consider him to be practical.

The plan for modifying the computer network is most likely practical.	The plan for modifying the computer network is most likely practicable.

30. **PRECEDE AND PROCEED:** When something *precedes* something, it comes before that something. You *proceed* when you continue.

INCORRECT	CORRECT
The foreword proceeds the chapters in the book.	The foreword precedes the chapters in the book.
I told Ms. Wong to precede with her work on the financial reporting requirements.	I told Ms. Wong to proceed with her work on the financial reporting requirements.

31. **PRINCIPAL AND PRINCIPLE:** A *principal* something is the most important something. A person who is a *principal* is the head of a school or is an important person in some organization or activity. *Principal* can also refer to the amount of a loan before interest. A *principle* is a law, rule, assumption, or fundamental truth. *Principle* is used only as a noun.

INCORRECT	CORRECT
The principle of Waller High School is Sharon Kline.	The principal of Waller High School is Sharon Kline.
The principle reason I chose to become an accountant is that I have always liked to work with numbers.	The principal reason I chose to become an accountant is that I have always liked to work with numbers.
Most of the money we pay each month goes to pay off the interest, not the principle, of our loan.	Most of the money we pay each month goes to pay off the interest, not the principal, of our loan.
The examination covered basic accounting principals.	The examination covered basic accounting principles.

32. **SALES AND SELLS:** *Sales* is a noun. You hold a sale. You make a sale. Your sales for the year are high. *Sells* is a verb. A person sells something.

INCORRECT	CORRECT
Jane, who sales vitamins to health food stores, made more sells in December than the other four sellspeople combined.	Jane, who sells vitamins to health food stores, made more sales in December than the other four salespeople combined.

33. **SOME TIME AND SOMETIME:** When you refer to a period of time, you use *some time*. When you refer to an occasion, you use *sometime*.

INCORRECT	CORRECT
I will need sometime to drive to my appointment in Jersey City.	I will need some time to drive to my appointment in Jersey City.
I will call you some time.	I will call you sometime.

34. **STATIONARY AND STATIONERY:** You do not move when you are *stationary*. You write letters on *stationery*.

INCORRECT	CORRECT
I exercise on the stationery bicycle in the family room.	I exercise on the stationary bicycle in the family room.
When I write letters to prospective employers, I use my best stationary.	When I write letters to prospective employers, I use my best stationery.

35. **TACK AND TACT:** When you use a certain plan of action, you take a certain *tack*. When you know how to act in a socially appropriate manner, you are said to have *tact*.

INCORRECT	CORRECT
The correct tact is not always obvious.	The correct tack is not always obvious.
A public relations person should have tack.	A public relations person should have tact.

36. **THEIR, THERE, AND THEY'RE:** Their is a possessive form of *they*. *There* refers to a place. *They're* is the contraction of *they are*.

INCORRECT	CORRECT
There office is located on the seventh floor.	Their office is located on the seventh floor.
There office is located over their.	Their office is located over there.
Their due here in an hour.	They're due here in an hour.

38. **TRACK AND TRACT:** A *track* is some sort of mark or path. A *tract* is either a piece of land or a propaganda paper.

INCORRECT	CORRECT
The visitors left muddy tracts in my office.	The visitors left muddy tracks in my office.
The right-wing political party's track was written by a college professor.	The right-wing political party's tract was written by a college professor.

39. **USE AND UTILIZE:** Though both *use* and *utilize* mean practically the same thing, *utilize* sounds stilted and is usually not necessary. *Utilize* should be used only when referring to something rather technical or formal, such as "The Facilities Utilization Plan," where *utilization* means the profitable and efficient use of the facilities. *Utilized* is used too frequently.

INCORRECT	CORRECT
When I write, I utilize my pen or pencil.	When I write, I use my pen or pencil.
Turn off the typewriter after you utilize it.	Turn off the typewriter after you use it.

40. **WHO'S AND WHOSE:** *Who's* is a contraction of *who is. Whose* is the possessive form of *who* and *which.*

INCORRECT	CORRECT
Whose going to lunch with her?	Who's going to lunch with her?
Mr. Farias, who's daughter is an electrical engineer, plans to go back to college to finish his degree in business.	Mr. Farias, whose daughter is an electrical engineer, plans to go back to college to finish his degree in business.

41. **YOUR AND YOU'RE:** *Your* is the possessive form of *you. You're* is the contraction of *you are.*

INCORRCT	CORRECT
You're department is more productive than mine.	Your department is more productive than mine.
Your one of the finest employees I have had the good fortune to know.	You're one of the finest employees I have had the good fortune to know.

SENTENCE STRUCTURE

Eight major types of errors in sentence construction receive treatment in this section. Examples illustrate incorrect and correct sentence construction. English grammar and style books supply additional suggestions for controlling sentence structure.

1. **MISTAKE:** *Commas are put in places where they do not belong.* The result is a sentence that does not flow well.
   SOLUTION: Review the section on commas in the Punctuation section of this appendix. Note just when and where commas *are* used. Remember that a sentence *without* the necessary commas usually reads better than a sentence *with* unnecessary commas.
   HINT: As suggested in that section of the appendix, read your sentence out loud. If you do not pause, the sentence probably does not need a comma. If you do pause somewhere in the sentence, you probably need a comma there.

INCORRECT	CORRECT
Mr. Wince is, a valuable employee.	Mr. Wince is a valuable employee.
She would like to apply, for a promotion.	She would like to apply for a promotion.
Danny, Christine, and Mary won, scholarships.	Danny, Christine, and Mary won scholarships.

2. **MISTAKE:** *Commas are placed between two complete, distinct sentences.* This mistake is often called a *comma splice.*

SOLUTION: Commas link two sentences only if they are related, if they are relatively simple, and if the comma precedes a conjunction such as *and* or *but.* Remember that most complete sentences are *not* linked by commas or semicolons.
HINT: If you wish to put a comma between two complete sentences, put *and, but, or, nor, for,* or *yet* after the comma. If you are at all confused, however, just end each sentence with a period.

INCORRECT	CORRECT
Carol uses the communication guidelines whenever she writes, speaks, or communicates nonverbally, Arnold uses the guidelines too.	Carol uses the communication guidelines whenever she writes, speaks, or communicates nonverbally. Arnold uses the guidelines too. OR Carol uses the communication guidelines whenever she writes, speaks, or communicates nonverbally; Arnold uses the guidelines too.
She wants to work for an investment firm, I want to be a real estate broker.	She wants to work for an investment firm, and I want to be a real estate broker.
When he studies, he tries to find a quiet room, he also likes to take frequent exercise breaks.	When he studies, he tries to find a quiet room. He also likes to take frequent exercise breaks.
Sheila is doing well, she just got a job at the marketing firm.	Sheila is doing well. She just got a job at a marketing firm. OR Sheila is doing well because she just got a job at a marketing firm.
George seems quite capable, however his performance is inconsistent.	George seems quite capable; however, his performance is inconsistent.

3. **MISTAKE:** *Incomplete thoughts are used as sentences.* In other words, the sentences do not contain both a subject and a verb. Incomplete sentences are often called *sentence fragments.* Sentence fragments are used sometimes as attention getters; however, they are not usually employed in formal writing.
SOLUTION: Check your writing to make sure that all of your sentences are complete thoughts. Complete thoughts include both a subject and a verb.

INCORRECT	CORRECT
Of course. You are going to get a raise!	Of course you are going to get a raise!

For the reasons I cited in my letter. I plan to pursue a career in teaching.	For the reasons I cited in my letter, I plan to pursue a career in teaching.
What do you plan to do? With that book?	What do you plan to do with that book?
She will join the staff in February. Which is two months after Herman is scheduled to leave.	She will join the staff in February, which is two months after Herman is scheduled to leave.
When you are not sure about the spelling of a word. Look it up in the dictionary.	When you are not sure about the spelling of a word, look it up in the dictionary.

4. **MISTAKE:** *Two or more sentences that should be separated by a punctuation mark are not separated at all.* These sentences are referred to as *run-on sentences.*
   SOLUTION: Two or more complete thoughts must be separated by a period, a question mark, an exclamation point, a semicolon, or a comma followed by a conjunction, whichever is appropriate.
   HINT: Read the sentences out loud. You likely will need to end a sentence where you pause *longer* than briefly. Commas or semicolons are usually needed at the places where you pause *only* briefly.

INCORRECT	CORRECT
Karen is the very antithesis of an authoritarian manager she studied under Katherine Ingalls, Ph.D., the author of *Employees Deserve Respect.*	Karen is the very antithesis of an authoritarian manager. She studied under Katherine Ingalls, Ph.D., the author of *Employees Deserve Respect.*
When he receives an assignment he quickly writes down everything that he knows about the subject he then goes back to organize the material.	When he receives an assignment, he quickly writes down everything that he knows about the subject. He then goes back to organize the material.
She wrote the report Don typed the bibliography I designed the cover.	She wrote the report, Don typed the bibliography, and I designed the cover.
We hope that you will order the desk, an order form is enclosed.	We hope that you will order the desk. An order form is enclosed.

5. **MISTAKE:** *Words that are intended to modify certain other words are put in the wrong place in the sentence.* As a result, the wrong words are modified.
   SOLUTION: Always place the modifying words directly before or directly after the words they are intended to modify.
   HINT: Think about the sentences you write or speak. Do they say what you intended them to say?

INCORRECT	CORRECT
The man prepared the minutes with a degree in secretarial science.	The man with a degree in secretarial science prepared the minutes. OR The man who has a degree in secretarial science prepared the minutes.
She bought a hamburger at the cafeteria with cheese, lettuce, tomatoes, and mayonnaise on it.	She bought a hamburger with cheese, lettuce, tomatoes, and mayonnaise on it at the cafeteria.
He received a letter from a financial analyst with résumé attached.	He received a letter with a résumé attached from a financial analyst.
The person will write the newsletter who wins the writing competition.	The person who wins the writing competition will write the newsletter.

6. **MISTAKE:** *A modifying phrase or a modifying word does not modify anything in the sentence.* This modifier is called a *dangling modifier* because it relates to nothing in the sentence.
   SOLUTION: Put words of modification in the *same* sentence as the words they modify.

INCORRECT	CORRECT
Without any warning, who will attend the staff meeting?	If given no warning, will anyone attend the staff meeting?
Having no knowledge of the problem, the door was shut in my face.	Because he had no knowledge of my problem, he shut the door in my face.
Without any brakes, I took it to the garage.	Because my car had no brakes, I took it to the garage.
Born to a wealthy family, the university was the most expensive in the area.	Born to a wealthy family, she was able to attend the most expensive university in the area.

7. **MISTAKE:** *The sentence contains nonparallel phrases or mixed phrases.*
   SOLUTION: Always make sure that your sentences do not arbitrarily mix active voice and passive voice, infinitives and gerunds, and infinitive phrases and relative clauses. You want the phrases and clauses in a sentence to be similar, or parallel, in construction.

INCORRECT	CORRECT
He likes writing, to read, and cross-country ski trips.	He likes writing, reading, and cross-country skiing.
She decided to buy a machine that can collate and to print on both sides of the paper.	She decided to buy a machine that collates the pages and that prints on both sides of the paper.

Obviously, the report was written by Sara and Dan typed it.	Obviously, Sara wrote the report and Dan typed it.
Not only is the vice president involved, but the president did it too.	Not only is the vice president involved, but the president is involved as well.

8. **MISTAKE:** *A verb, preposition, conjunction, or noun is omitted in the second and subsequent phrases or clauses in a sentence.* Such an omission is not necessarily a grammatical error.
   SOLUTION: In order to make the meaning of a sentence more clear, include the appropriate verb, preposition, conjunction, or noun in all parts of the sentence.

SOMETIMES UNCLEAR	CORRECT
She was hired as a management analyst, and he as a financial assistant.	She was hired as a management analyst, and he was hired as a financial assistant.
They are and always will be hard workers.	They are hard workers and always will be hard workers.
The first report will be typed by Frances, and the second by Albert.	The first report will be typed by Frances, and the second report will be typed by Albert.

OTHER MECHANICS

In this section, some of the mechanics of writing and speaking that were not covered elsewhere are described. The topics include numbers, possessives, syllabication, capitalization, abbreviations, contractions, footnotes, and the bibliography.

1. **NUMBERS:** Style manuals contain many rules for writing numbers. Consider 12 of them here.

   a. *Always spell out numbers that begin a sentence.*

INCORRECT	CORRECT
60 pages were missing.	Sixty pages were missing.

   b. One set of rules has you *spell out numbers one through ten* when no larger numbers are part of the same sentence. *If larger numbers appear in the sentence, however, use figures for all the numbers.*

INCORRECT	CORRECT
I want 3 copies of *Small Business Week* and 9 copies of *Maryland Executive.*	I want three copies of *Small Business Week* and nine copies of *Maryland Executive.*

He ordered six company bowling shirts, nine trophies, and 105 programs for the bowling awards banquet.	He ordered 6 company bowling shirts, 9 trophies, and 105 programs for the bowling awards banquet.

c. *When two numbers come together in a sentence, write out the smaller number.*

INCORRECT	CORRECT
She requested 2 48-inch typing tables.	She requested two 48-inch typing tables.
They forgot to deliver the twelve 3-pound postage scales.	They forgot to deliver the 12 three-pound postage scales.

d. *Spell out one- or two-word approximate numbers.*

INCORRECT	CORRECT
He invited about 60 people to the reception.	He invited about sixty people to the reception.
Approximately six hundred and fifty people attended the strike rally.	Approximately 650 people attended the strike rally.

e. *A person's age, when given in years, is spelled out.* If the person's exact age (years, months, and days) is given, use figures without commas separating them.

INCORRECT	CORRECT
The chairwoman will be 54 years old on Friday.	The chairwoman will be fifty-four years old on Friday.
John's daughter, Emily, is one year, two months, and eleven days old.	John's daughter, Emily, is 1 year 2 months and 11 days old.

f. *Figures precede "A.M." and "P.M." Words precede "o'clock."*

INCORRECT	CORRECT
The meeting is scheduled to begin at eight A.M.	The meeting is scheduled to begin at 8 A.M.
She never leaves before 6 o'clock.	She never leaves before six o'clock.

g. *Always use figures when referring to distances, cents, dollars, percents, page numbers, weights, and heights. When a dollar amount is even, use no zeros or decimal points. Commas separate millions, thousands, and hundreds in the same figure.*

INCORRECT	CORRECT
He will be reimbursed for eight miles of travel.	He will be reimbursed for 8 miles of travel.
Just pay the driver eighty cents.	Just pay the driver 80 cents.

We presented him with $25.00.	We presented him with $25.
The sales volume for September, 1983, was $1416982.24.	The sales volume for September, 1983, was $1,416,982.24.
Meetings take up at least ten percent of my time.	Meetings take up at least 10 percent of my time.
Please begin on page three.	Please begin on page 3.
The carton weighs two pounds.	The carton weighs 2 pounds.
A police officer must be at least five feet three inches tall.	A police officer must be at least 5 feet 3 inches tall.

h. *When no other numbers appear in a sentence, spell out fractions. When a whole number and a fraction are part of the same number, write them as figures.*

INCORRECT	CORRECT
He wrote ¼ of the memorandum.	He wrote one-fourth of the memorandum.
Multiply the number by one and one-fourth.	Multiply the number by 1¼. OR Multiply the number by 1.25.

i. *When the month precedes the day, do not add a "th," "d," "nd," "rd," or "st" to the number of the day. However, when the day precedes the month, use words or figures with "th," "d," "nd," "rd," or "st,"* whichever one is appropriate. *Remember always to write out the month in a sentence.*

INCORRECT	CORRECT
The conference begins on September 25th.	The conference begins on September 25.
The 23 of October is the date of the school party.	The 23rd of October is the date of the school party.
She will meet us in the lobby on Dec. sixth at 3 o'clock.	She will meet us in the lobby on December 6 at three o'clock.

j. *Use figures for house numbers 11 through infinity. Street numbers one through ten usually are written out.* Use figures for all other street numbers.

INCORRECT	CORRECT
She will be at 1 Delano Street.	She will be at One Delano Street.
Please send the brochure to Sixteen Rodriguez Avenue.	Please send the brochure to 16 Rodriguez Avenue.
Andrew lives on 8th Street.	Andrew lives on Eighth Street.

Joyce once lived on Sixty-fourth Avenue.	Joyce once lived on 64th Avenue.

k. When numbering a list, use figures.

INCORRECT	CORRECT
Please answer these questions:	Please answer these questions:
One. Are you satisfied with your job?	1. Are you satisfied with your job?
Two. What are your career plans?	2. What are your career plans?
Three. Do you plan to go back to school?	3. Do you plan to go back to school?

l. When completing forms, use numbers.

INCORRECT

CATALOGUE NUMBER	NAME	QUANTITY
Six	pencils	eight sets
Seven	rubber bands	four boxes

CORRECT

CATALOGUE NUMBER	NAME	QUANTITY
6	pencils	8 sets
7	rubber bands	4 boxes

2. **POSSESSIVES:** A possessive noun or pronoun is someone or something that owns or possesses someone or something else in the sentence. *You usually make a singular noun or pronoun possessive by adding an apostrophe and an "s." You usually make a plural noun or pronoun possessive by adding an apostrophe after the "s."* Take care to not confuse possessives with plurals. Plural words that are not possessive do not need an apostrophe.

   a. Apostrophes make singular nouns and indefinite nouns possessive. *An apostrophe and an "s" follow singular possessive words.*

INCORRECT	CORRECT
Joans husband is a salesperson.	Joan's husband is a salesperson.
Alberts children live in Bristow.	Albert's children live in Bristow.
The boss work philosophy differed from mine.	The boss's work philosophy differed from mine.

   b. An apostrophe followed by an "s" makes plural nouns that do not end in an "s" possessive.

INCORRECT	CORRECT
The childrens' goals were numerous.	The children's goals were numerous.
The peoples' requests are written here.	The people's requests are written here.

c. *Place an apostrophe after the "s" in other plural nouns in order to make them possessive.*

INCORRECT	CORRECT
We value our employees suggestions.	We value our employees' suggestions.
Our clients questions were easy to answer.	Our clients' questions were easy to answer.
My daughters-in-laws careers are as important as my son-in-laws career.	My daughters-in-law's careers are as important as my son-in-law's career.
The suburban branches roles vary.	The suburban branches' roles vary.
He had six years experience in the U.S. Navy.	He had six years' experience in the U.S. Navy.
My book's were stacked in the bookcase's.	My books were stacked in the bookcases.

d. *An apostrophe and an "s" make an abbreviation possessive.*

INCORRECT	CORRECT
An M.B.A.s first job is usually a good one.	An M.B.A.'s first job is usually a good one.
The C.P.A.s convention is held in Houston once a year.	The C.P.A.'s convention is held in Houston once a year.

3. **SYLLABICATION:** Several rules govern how words are divided in written communication. Some rules and examples that illustrate the rules appear in this section.

   a. *A word should be divided between syllables.* A dictionary shows where the syllables begin and end.

INCORRECT	CORRECT
He had no knowled- ge of the problem.	He had no knowl- edge of the problem.

   b. *Do not divide a one-syllable word.*

INCORRECT	CORRECT
She was a sta- unch supporter.	She was a staunch supporter.

The figures were bas- ed on data from 1968.	The figures were based on data from 1968.

c. *Do not divide words that contain fewer than five letters.*

INCORRECT	CORRECT
He was ver- y capable.	He was very capable.
He makes ov- er $39,000 a year.	He makes over $39,000 a year.

d. *Divide hyphenated words at the hyphens.*

INCORRECT	CORRECT
He is self-ef- facing.	He is self- effacing.

e. *Do not divide numbers, names, contractions, or abbreviations.*

INCORRECT	CORRECT
The plan is for 19- 90 and after.	The plan is for 1990 and after.
Her name is Dor- othy Jensen.	Her name is Dorothy Jensen.
He said that he wo- n't worry.	He said that he won't worry.
He will earn an M.- B.A. in finance.	He will earn an M.B.A. in finance.

f. *Do not separate one- or two-letter prefixes, suffixes, or syllables from the rest of the word.*

INCORRECT	CORRECT
He is an ex- pert in his field.	He is an expert in his field.
She has never been a complain- er.	She has never been a complainer.

g. *Do not divide words between double vowels, except when one of the vowels is part of another syllable.*

INCORRECT	CORRECT
He wants to be a bookke- eper.	He wants to be a book- keeper.
There is no agre- eing with Marvin.	There is no agree- ing with Marvin.

Reading, skii- ng, and running are my hobbies.	Reading, ski- ing, and running are my hobbies.

h. Words can be divided between their double consonants.

INCORRECT	CORRECT
I was a boo- kkeeper.	I was a book- keeper.
They were committ- ing errors.	They were commit- ting errors.

i. Divide a word that contains a one-letter syllable after the one-letter syllable.

INCORRECT	CORRECT
I would elim- inate the chart.	I would elimi- nate the chart.
Running is exhil- arating.	Running is exhila- rating.

j. Do not divide the word at the end of the list line on a typewritten page. Also, do not divide the last word in a paragraph.

k. Do not divide words in two consecutive lines, if possible. Divide no more than three words on a page.

l. Do not divide a word in a place that confuses the reader.

INCORRECT	CORRECT
She is com- passionate.	She is compassionate.
The young soldier re- signed in May.	The young soldier re-signed in May.

4. **CAPITALIZATION:** Selected rules for capitalizing words constitute this section.

a. Capitalize a person's title when it directly precedes her or his name. Do not capitalize the title when it follows the person's name.

INCORRECT	CORRECT
vice president Sue Anders	Vice President Sue Anders
aunt Kathleen	Aunt Kathleen
Ron Rames, President, will speak to his company's employees.	Ron Rames, president, will speak to his company's employees.

b. A title used in place of a name is not capitalized. The President of the United States is always capitalized even when it is used alone.

INCORRECT	CORRECT
My Aunt wrote to me.	My aunt wrote to me.
The Vice President wrote the letter.	The vice president wrote the letter.
Our nation's president will give a speech.	Our nation's President will give a speech.

c. *Always capitalize a person's title when it is part of an address or signature block.*

INCORRECT	CORRECT
Ms. Alice Foine, president Lexington Manufacturing, Inc. 666 Olive Avenue Sother, Nevada 11111	Ms. Alice Foine, President Lexington Manufacturing, Inc. 666 Olive Avenue Sother, Nevada 11111

d. *Capitalize the complete names of organizations.* Do not capitalize such words as *company, university,* or *firm* when used instead of the full name of the organization. Also, do not capitalize *federal, government, navy, army,* or *air force,* when used alone.

INCORRECT	CORRECT
Bysar products, inc., is located in Waynesberg.	Bysar Products, Inc., is located in Waynesberg.
The Company makes bathroom fixtures.	The company makes bathroom fixtures.
The Federal Government and Navy offices are located in Washington.	The federal government and navy offices are located in Washington.

e. *When you are writing about your own company's departments, it is correct to capitalize them.* Do not capitalize the names of other company's departments, though.

INCORRECT	CORRECT
Our finance department is made up of six analysts.	Our Finance Department is made up of six analysts.
I hope to work in an Organization Development Department.	I hope to work in an organization development department.

f. *Capitalize the official names of courses, but not general areas of study.*

INCORRECT	CORRECT
She is taking calculus II.	She is taking Calculus II.
He wants to take a Shorthand course.	He wants to take a shorthand course.

g. Capitalize all of the words in the titles of publications except for the articles, prepositions, and coordinate conjunctions. Always capitalize the first and final words in a title, however.

INCORRECT	CORRECT
"What are your Goals in Life?", an article in this month's *Wealth For The Masses,* is worth reading.	"What Are Your Goals in Life?", an article in this month's *Wealth for the Masses,* is worth reading.

h. Days of the week, months, holidays, and very special events or periods in history should be capitalized.

INCORRECT	CORRECT
She is a world war II veteran.	She is a World War II veteran.
Please read a book on the industrial revolution.	Please read a book on the Industrial Revolution.

i. Capitalize the official names of places. Do not capitalize general references to places.

INCORRECT	CORRECT
They live on rockhound street.	They live on Rockhound Street.
We visited the Mountains in Idaho this weekend.	We visited the mountains in Idaho this weekend.

j. Capitalize regions of the country. Do not capitalize directions when they modify other words.

INCORRECT	CORRECT
She was born in the south.	She was born in the South.
She lives South of here.	She lives south of here.
They went to Northwestern Wyoming.	They went to northwestern Wyoming.

k. Capitalize the adjectival forms of countries and other proper names.

INCORRECT	CORRECT
I bought a chinese vase.	I bought a Chinese vase.
Their jewish heritage is very important to them.	Their Jewish heritage is very important to them.

l. Capitalize most nouns that precede numbers.

INCORRECT	CORRECT
The data are part of table 6.	The data are part of Table 6.
The meeting will be held in room 14C.	The meeting will be held in Room 14C.

5. **ABBREVIATIONS:** *Avoid using many abbreviations in formal writing.* The rules in this section illustrate the most common uses of abbreviations.

   a. These abbreviations appear in *both formal and informal writing.*

SINGULAR	PLURAL
A.D.	———
B.A.	B.A.s or B.A.'s
B.C.	———
B.S.	B.S.s or B.S.'s
CPA; C.P.A.	CPAs or CPA's; C.P.A.s or C.P.A.'s
Dr.	Drs.
M.B.A.	M.B.A.s or M.B.A.'s
M.D.	M.D.s or M.D.'s
Mr.	Messrs.
Mrs.	Mesdames
Ms.	Mses.
U.S.	———

   b. These abbreviations are used in *informal writing.*

SINGULAR	PLURAL
apt.	apts.
B.t.u.	B.t.u.'s
c.o.d.	c.o.d.'s
dept.	depts.
f.o.b.	f.o.b.'s
ft. (foot)	ft. (feet)
g (gram)	g (grams)
gal.	gals.
hwy.	hwys.
in. (inch)	in. (inches)
Inc.	———
L (liter)	L (liters)
lb.	lbs.
Ltd.	———
mgr.	mgrs.
mo.	mos.
oz. (ounce)	oz. (ounces)
p. (page)	pp. (pages)
qt.	qts.
yd.	yds.
yr.	yrs.

   c. *Spell out addresses in most formal writing. The two-letter state abbreviation can be used in an address, however.*

INCORRECT	CORRECT
Ms. Meredith Wiley 16 N. 6th St. Tulsa, Okla. 73000	Ms. Meredith Wiley 16 North Sixth Street Tulsa, OK 73000

6. **CONTRACTIONS:** *A contraction is one word that represents a longer word or two words.* A contraction always contains an apostrophe. The apostrophe usually replaces one or several of the missing letters. The missing letters are often vowels. The apostrophe never goes between the original two words, but does replace a letter or letters in the second word. Study the incorrect and correct versions of the list of contractions so that you do not make the common error of putting the apostrophe in the wrong place. Remember that contractions do not belong in formal writing.

COMPLETE WORDS	CONTRACTIONS INCORRECT	CORRECT
are not	are'nt	aren't
cannot	ca'nt	can't
have not	have'nt	haven't
he will	h'ell	he'll
I am	Im	I'm
is not	is'nt	isn't
it is	its	it's
she will	sh'ell	she'll
there is	theres	there's
they are	the'yre	they're
they will	the'yll	they'll
we are	w'ere	we're
we will	w'ell	we'll
were not	were'nt	weren't
will not	wo'nt	won't
you are	yo'ure	you're

7. **FOOTNOTES:** *When you write another person's written or spoken words, you have the responsibility to identify the person you have cited.* You need not identify the person, however, if what he or she said is common knowledge. (If you write that Washington, D.C., is the nation's capital, you need not cite a source for that information.) When you do use someone's work, though, consult a style manual for information on how to identify the cited material. These are examples of footnotes that you may find helpful:

   a. *You cite from a book with one author.*

      [6]Ann Grico, *Statistics for Business and for Life* (New York: Oro Press, 198X), 81–82.

   b. *You cite from a book with two authors.*

[1]Edna G. Grown and Robert Frank, *Business Writing for Children* (London: Smythe and Waco Publishing Co., 1976), 251.

c. *You cite from a book with three authors.*

[5]Albert Fox, Marsha Wiler, and Nancy Toledo, *Always Writing* (Kansas City, Mo.: PRA Co., 1976), 11.

d. *You cite from a book with more than three authors.*

[3]Simon Wales et al., *Accounting in America* (San Francisco: Wechsler Press, 198X), 314.

e. *You cite from a book with no author.*

[9]*Business, Money, and Ethics* (Eugene, Oreg.: Davlyn Press, 198X), 92.

f. *You cite from a book with an editor acting as the author.*

[2]Susan Woodell, ed., *Women in Business and Industry* (Corning, Tex.: Corning University Press, 1968), 460–61.

g. *You cite from a report with one, two, or three authors.*

[3]Elizabeth Hart, Mark Tunis, and Irene Perez, *Report on Foreign Exchange Rates* (Portland, Oreg.: Floridian Investments, Inc., 1978), 8.

h. *You cite from an article in a journal.*

[4]Wayne Limone, "Writing Without Fear," *Journal of American Communication* 61 (August 198X): 47.

i. *You cite from an article in a magazine.*

[9]Lucille Phillips, "Organizations Cannot Survive the Decade," *Business Digest,* September 198X, 137.

j. *You cite from a newspaper article.*

[4]"Allensnapco Raises Prices," *McKenzie Times,* 16 February 198X, sec. B., B17.

8. **THE BIBLIOGRAPHY:** The bibliography lists all of the sources of material cited, consulted, or recommended. Place the bibliography at the end of the paper. Again, consult a style manual for a detailed treatment of the preparation of bibliographies. The footnotes used as examples in the preceding section of this appendix are in bibliographical form in this section. Note that the author's names are reversed and that the form of the entry differs from that of the footnote.

a. *Your bibliography includes a book with one author.*

Grico, Ann. *Statistics for Business and for Life.* New York: Oro Press, 198X.

b. *Your bibliography includes a book with two authors.*

Grown, Edna G., and Frank, Robert. *Business Writing for Children.* London: Smythe and Waco Publishing Co., 1976.

c. *Your bibliography includes a book with three authors.*

Fox, Albert; Wiler, Marsha; and Toledo, Nancy. *Always Writing.* Kansas City, Mo.: PRA Co., 1976.

d. *Your bibliography includes a book with more than three authors.*

Wales, Simon; Deutsch, R. F.; Michaelson, Denise P.; and Wendstrom, Gloria S. C. *Accounting in America.* San Francisco: Wechsler Press, 198X.

e. *Your bibliography includes a book with no author.*

Business, Money, and Ethics. Eugene, Oreg.: Davlyn Press, 198X.

f. *Your bibliography includes a book with an editor acting as the author.*

Woodell, Susan, ed. *Women in Business and Industry.* Corning, Tex.: Corning University Press, 1968.

g. *Your bibliography includes a report with one, two, or three authors.*

Hart, Elizabeth; Tunis, Mark; and Perez, Irene. *Report on Foreign Exchange Rates.* Portland, Oreg.: Floridian Investments, Inc., 1978.

h. *Your bibliography includes an article from a journal.*

Limone, Wayne. "Writing Without Fear." *Journal of American Communication* 61 (August 198X): 44–50.

i. *Your bibliography includes an article from a magazine.*

Phillips, Lucille. "Organizations Cannot Survive the Decade." *Business Digest,* September 198X, 135–41.

j. *Your bibliography includes a newspaper article.*

"Allensnapco Raises Prices." *McKenzie Times,* 16 February 198X, sec. B, B17.

APPENDIX C

NONSEXIST COMMUNICATION

Discriminatory communication practices exist for many human factors; for example, race, ethnicity, nationality, age, handicap, religion, and sex. All such practices require correction. However, sexism has the most pervasive impact. It threads its way through every level of communication, and, until recently, it has had the perpetuating stamp of approval of all who teach and use the sexist communication system. However, most communicators no longer teach or use sexist communication patterns. The growth in awareness, the sense of justice, the desire to apply the most current communication practices, the recognition that most audiences expect nonsexism, and the intent to avoid the possible legal ramifications of sexism have led to that change.

Sexist communication occurs when the structure reflects female and male stereotypes, with the male treated as the norm and the female treated as the "other." Thus, to remove sexism, simply remove all sex-role stereotypes and all usage that assumes maleness until proven otherwise.

The Nonsexist Communicator provides a complete development of the nonsexist communication patterns available.[1] However, this appendix presents some guidelines to help you bring a commitment to nonsexist communication into practice.

PRONOUNS

Use neutral references instead of male pronouns for reference to a person, animal, or thing that could be either male or female. Use neutral references instead of female and male pronouns in reference to stereotyped roles.

SEXIST	NONSEXIST
Have each participant bring his own sack lunch and his own equipment.	Have each participant bring a sack lunch and equipment.
Feed your cat the food he loves—Catsies.	Feed your cat the food it loves—Catsies.
Jack loves his new car. She submits to his every command.	Jack loves his new car. It follows his every command.
Every lawyer should give his secretary her own office.	All lawyers should give their secretaries their own offices.
A good supervisor creates a supportive climate for his workers.	A good supervisor creates a supportive climate for her or his workers.

WORD ENDINGS

Revise words that include such sexist endings as *-man, -ette, -ix,* and *-ess.*

SEXIST	NONSEXIST
Chairman	Chairperson, chair
Mailman	Mail carrier
Usherette	Usher
Aviatrix	Aviator
Stewardess	Flight attendant

MALE WORDS USED TO INCLUDE BOTH FEMALES AND MALES

Change to neutral form any words that treat the female as a subspecies of the male.

SEXIST	NONSEXIST
Mankind	Humankind
Brotherhood of man	Humanity, association of humans
Scholastic fraternity	Scholastic organization

ADJECTIVES

Remove sex-marking adjectives and reverse sex-marking adjectives.

SEXIST	NONSEXIST
Woman driver	Driver
Female attorney	Attorney
Male nurse	Nurse

COURTESY TITLES

Use courtesy titles that do not show marital status for both males and females.

SEXIST	NONSEXIST
Miss	Ms.
Mrs.	Ms.
	Mr.

SALUTATIONS AND SIGNATURE BLOCKS

Use salutations and signature blocks that remove sexism. Retain sexist courtesy titles only for receivers who indicate they want you to use them. A nonsexist signature block should not contain a courtesy title. However, a woman who leaves off "(Ms.)" in the signature block may receive letters addressed to "Mr." or "Miss" until all writers adopt nonsexism.

SEXIST	NONSEXIST
Tabular Displays, Inc.	Tabular Displays, Inc.
....	....
Gentlemen:	Ladies and Gentlemen:
Director, Personnel Department	Director, Personnel Department
....	....
Dear Sir:	Dear Director:
Response to a person who signed name "Reba Courtney"	
Miss Reba Courtney	Ms. Reba Courtney
....	....
Dear Miss Courtney:	Dear Ms. Courtney:
Sincerely yours,	Sincerely yours,
(Mrs.) Joan Farrell	Joan Farrell OR (Ms.) Joan Farrell

NONPARALLEL REFERENCES AND ORDER

Use equal and parallel references to females and males. For fair order in paired references to males and females, include the female in first position half the time or use alphabetical order.

SEXIST	NONSEXIST
Men and ladies	Men and women OR Gentlemen and ladies
Jones [for Mel Jones] and Mary [for Mary Smith]	Jones and Smith OR Mel and Mary
Girls and men (all 18 or older)	Girls and boys OR Women and men
Man and wife	Husband and wife

Everybody should take his or her turn (all the time)	Everybody should take her or his turn (half the time, or all the time if using alphabetical order for all female/male pairs)
Woman and man (all the time)	Woman and man (half the time, unless using alphabetical order for all female/male pairs)

STEREOTYPES

Remove all stereotypes from oral, written, and nonverbal messages.

SEXIST	NONSEXIST
Portraying women only as homemakers and mothers, secretaries, nurses, etc.	Seriously portraying women part of the time as attorneys, managers, physicians, builders, welders, etc.
Portraying women as giddy dumbbells, sex objects, and servants	Portraying women as capable humans who both love and are loved and who both serve and are served
Portraying men only as workers outside the home in male-stereotyped positions	Seriously portraying men part of the time as homemakers and fathers, secretaries, nurses, etc.
Portraying men as macho womanizers and insensitive dictators	Portraying men as capable humans who both love and are loved and who both serve and are served

RELIGIOUS AND MONARCHIAL REFERENCES

Revise or omit sexist religious and monarchial references.

SEXIST	NONSEXIST
Lord God	God
God . . . His	God . . . the . . . .
She sat there like a little princess.	She sat there quietly. OR She asked some good questions.
The good leader must be king of the hill.	The good leader must take command.

SECONDARY INFORMATION

When citing from secondary sources, remove sexism by using summaries and paraphrases instead of direct quotations, by using *sic,* and by using ellipses to show omissions and brackets for insertions. Only the first procedure works well for oral transactions.

SEXIST	NONSEXIST
Murphy writes, "Man must take responsibility for his environment."	Murphy writes that humans must take responsibility for their environment.
Ellis suggests, "Only the right kind of manpower can solve this problem."	Ellis suggests, "Only the right kind of manpower [sic] can solve this problem." OR Ellis suggests, "Only the right kind of . . . [employees] can solve this problem."

ENDNOTES

1. Bobbye D. Sorrels, *The Nonsexist Communicator* (Englewood Cliffs, N.J.: Prentice-Hall, Inc., 1983).

APPENDIX D

LETTER-WRITING MECHANICS

Letters apply general principles of writing to a specific process. This appendix covers some of the mechanics of writing letters, with particular emphasis on formats and components of letters.

FORMATS OF LETTERS

A company almost always specifies its format for letters. This section reviews four of the major styles and the parts composing them: block, modified block with blocked paragraphs, modified block with indented paragraphs, and simplified. In addition, the format of the continuation page has special characteristics.

Block

In the block style, every part of the letter begins at the left margin. Figure D–1 shows that format—as well as displaying many of the traditional letter components of letters. The components themselves receive treatment in a subsequent section.

Modified Block with Blocked Paragraphs

Figure D–2 illustrates that with the exception of the date line and signature block, every line of the modified-block, blocked-paragraph letter begins at the left margin. The components for the modified-block form remain the same as for the traditional block format.

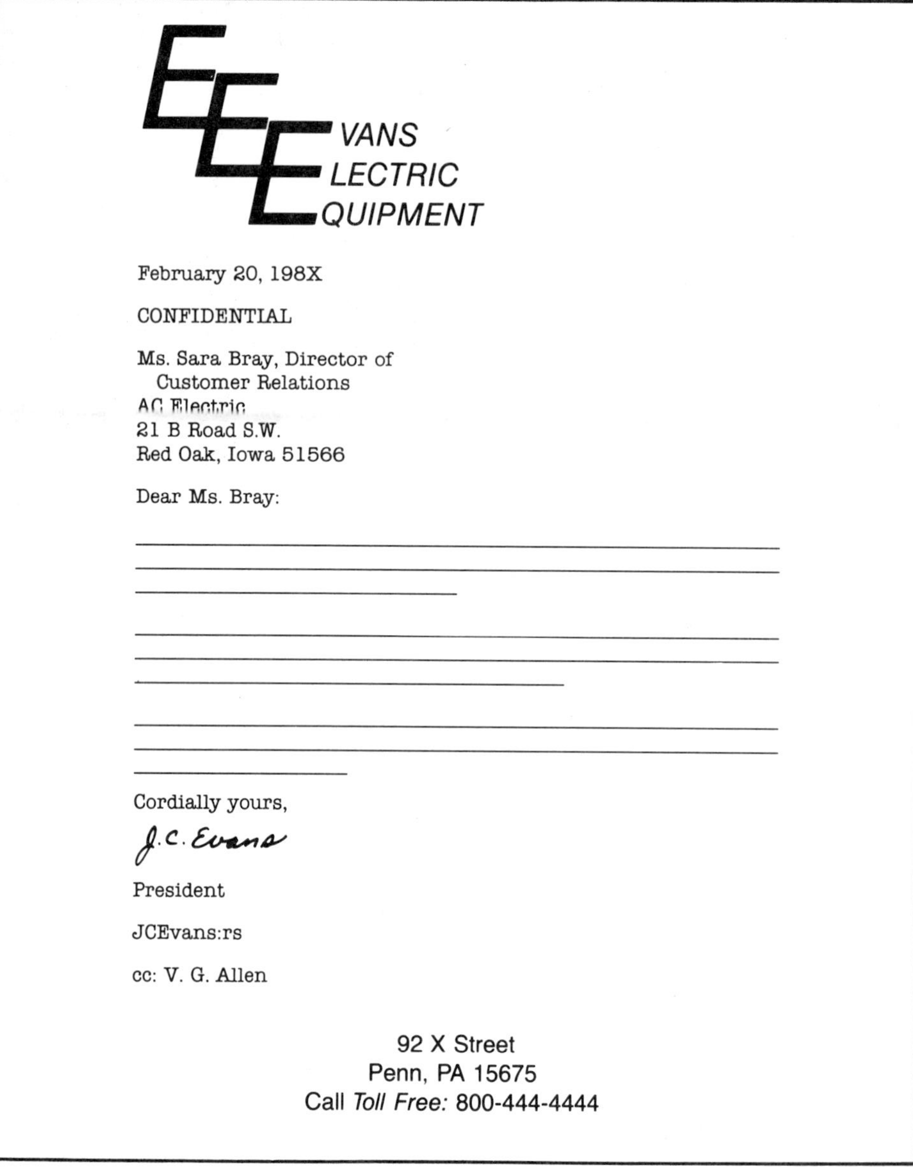

February 20, 198X

CONFIDENTIAL

Ms. Sara Bray, Director of
Customer Relations
AC Electric
21 B Road S.W.
Red Oak, Iowa 51566

Dear Ms. Bray:

Cordially yours,

J. C. Evans

President

JCEvans:rs

cc: V. G. Allen

92 X Street
Penn, PA 15675
Call *Toll Free:* 800-444-4444

FIGURE D–1 Block; mixed punctuation; classification notation; copy notation.

Modified Block with Indented Paragraphs

The modified-block, indented-paragraph format simply indents the paragraphs of the basic modified-block plan. Figure D–3 shows the style.

Simplified

The simplified format follows the block setup for the letter. In addition, it eliminates the salutation and the complimentary close, while including a subject line as a standard part. Thus, the simplified form discards some of the

SEEKERS, INC.

7834 Firefighter's Lane/Shiloh, Virginia 22549
(666) 666-6666

Board of Directors

A. A. Ashe
President
Ashe Corp.

B. B. Barnes
President
Barnes Company

C. C. Carney
Vice President
Oak Tree, Inc.

D. D. Dalley
Director
Public Relations
Freebie Co.

E. E. Ellis
General Manager
Cellar Corp.

F. F. Frates
President
Future Shock

19 April 198X

Onlycoping, Inc.
One 58 Street
Niantic, IL 62551

Attention: Claims Agent

Ladies and Gentlemen

CLAIM—INVOICE NO. 79243

Sincerely yours

SEEKERS, INC.

J. J. Jeffers

Ms. J. J. Jeffers
Assistant

rp

bc: A. A. Alton

We search the globe for rare and exotic gifts

FIGURE D-2 Modified block with blocked paragraphs; open punctuation; attention line; subject line; typewritten company name; blind copy notation (appears only on copy); postscript.

HAPPEE CORPORATION
222 High Street
Guthrie, Oklahoma 73044
(405) 111-1111

Office of the Manager   20 January 198X

Sales Manager
Oano, Inc.
Hilo, HI 96720

Dear Sales Manager:

Sincerely,

Alice Jenkins, Manager
Production and Distribution

AJ/dlp

Enclosures: Sales brochure
Order form

copies: Sharon Carr
David Furr
Carl Hull

FIGURE D–3 Modified block with indented paragraphs; mixed punctuation; enclosure notation; copy notation.

older letter components, and becomes the most nontraditional of the formats considered. Figure D–4 illustrates the simplified form.

Continuation

When a letter does not fit on one page, use a continuation page. Do not use letterhead stationery for that page. Instead, use plain paper of the same quality

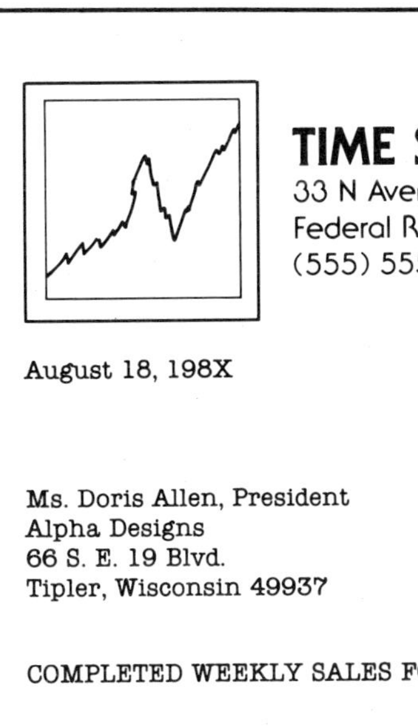

TIME SERIES ANALYSIS
33 N Avenue
Federal Reserve, Georgia 30303
(555) 555-5555

August 18, 198X

Ms. Doris Allen, President
Alpha Designs
66 S. E. 19 Blvd.
Tipler, Wisconsin 49937

COMPLETED WEEKLY SALES FORECASTS FOR 198X

Dale Sellers

DALE SELLERS, CHIEF CONSULTANT

cp

Enclosure: Forecast Report

FIGURE D–4 Simplified; enclosure notation.

as the letterhead, and typewrite the heading. Use the same margin settings as those for the first page. Place the first line of the heading about one inch from the top of the page. Leave two blank lines after the heading.

The heading includes the name of the receiver, the date, and the page number. A continuation page must contain at least one paragraph of the body of the letter—followed by the closing parts. Figure D–5 illustrates two acceptable continuation-page formats.

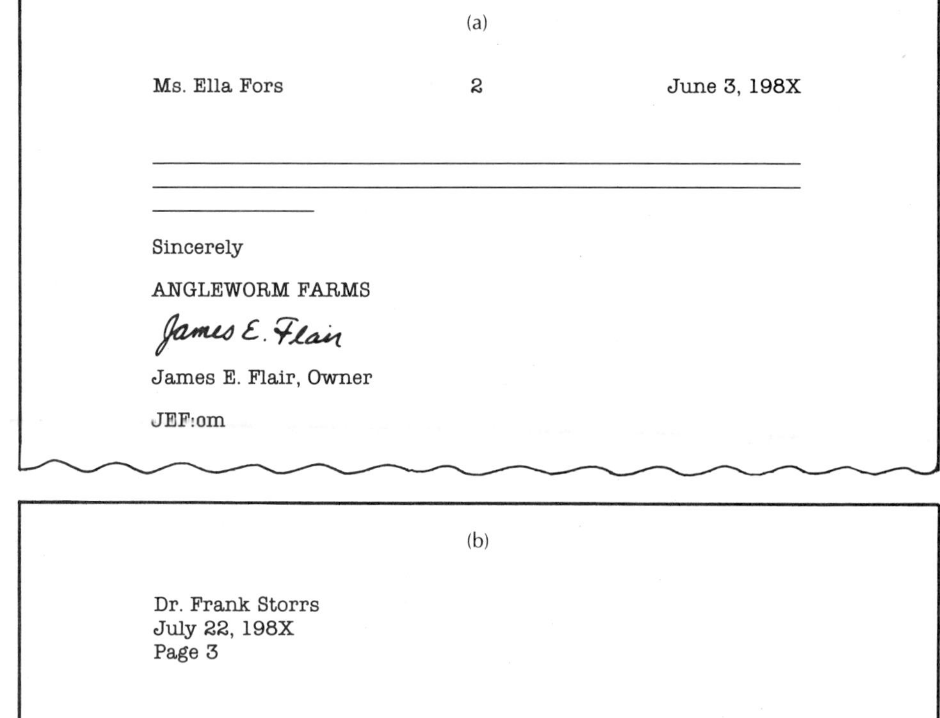
(a)

Ms. Ella Fors 2 June 3, 198X

Sincerely

ANGLEWORM FARMS

James E. Flair

James E. Flair, Owner

JEF:om

(b)

Dr. Frank Storrs
July 22, 198X
Page 3

Respectfully yours,

Jerry Marn

Jerry Marn
Sales Representative

cd

FIGURE D-5 Continuation pages.

COMPONENTS OF LETTERS

A letter can include as many as 15 components: (1) stationery and letterhead/return address, (2) date line, (3) special designations, (4) inside address, (5) attention line, (6) salutation, (7) subject line, (8) body, (9) complimentary close, (10) company name, (11) signature block, (12) reference initials, (13) enclosure notation, (14) copy notation, and (15) postscript.

The stationery and letterhead, date line, inside address, salutation, body, complimentary close, signature block, and reference initials form the standard parts of the business letter. Use the remaining seven parts as needed or desired. Of course, the simplified format omits the salutation and complimentary close and adds the subject line as a fixed part.

Stationery and Letterhead/Return Address

Stationery and the letterhead/return address contribute significantly to a message. The wording and design of the letterhead/return address contribute both verbally and nonverbally. The stationery contributes nonverbally.

Design

Companies usually engage specialists to design letterheads and envelopes. (Many of the figures in Chapters 7–9 illustrate letterheads.) The good letterhead should include at least the firm name, telephone number, and address. It may include a short explanation of what the firm does in a simple, straightforward design. Additional information often creates a jumbled, distracting appearance that defeats the letterhead's communicative purpose—that of pleasant identification. For example, Figure D–2 shows printed stationery that may contain too much information.

Letterhead designers use color, embossing, standard or unusual styles of type, and a variety of sizes and arrangements of type. Through them, they try to make the letterhead communicate the desired image.

When using paper without a printed letterhead, include a return address. Place it at the top in a position that fits the format chosen. Include only the mailing address, not your name. In the block and simplified formats, the return address begins at the left margin. In the modified-block formats, the return address either begins at horizontal center or ends at the right margin. For all formats, the return address starts about one and three-fourths inches from the top of the page. Figure D–6 illustrates the proper placement of return addresses on plain paper.

Stationery

The quality, weight, texture, fabric content, size, and color of paper also have an important impact on the communication. For letterheads, envelopes, and plain sheets, use a quality bond. Most offices use a 20-pound watermarked paper with some fabric content. Some use 16-pound paper without the watermark or fabric content.

Always insert the paper so that the typewriting appears on the *felt side*. For watermarked paper, the felt side allows the watermark to appear in the correct reading position. For paper without a watermark, the wrapper usually includes a notation identifying the felt side. Without such information, identify the felt side by using a magnifying glass to select the side with the smooth, felt-like appearance. The other side—the screen or wire side—has a rough, granular appearance.

The most common size for letterhead stationery measures 8½ inches wide by 11 inches long, with the letterhead placed across the top of the width

(a)
Block and Simplified

1111 18th Street
Souder, MO 65751
March 15, 198X

Dr. Jan Cory
14 Dover Street, N.W.
Woodstock, VA 22664
Dear Dr. Cory:

(b)
Modified Block

1111 18th Street
Souder, MO 65751
March 15, 198X

Dear Jan,

FIGURE D–6 Typewritten return address for (a) block and simplified formats in a formal letter and (b) modified-block formats in a personal letter; mixed punctuation.

of the page. However, companies sometimes make the page 11 inches wide by 8½ inches long, with the letterhead at the top of the width (Figure D–7). Occasionally, the letterhead appears at the bottom of the sheet.

Other sizes for stationery include the 7½- by 10½-inch, 7½- by 11-inch, and 5½- by 8½-inch sheets. Information usually appears at the top, but may appear at the bottom of such sheets.

Most designers use white stationery. However, some designers use color, particularly if the products or services of the firm warrant the added nonverbal flair.

Avoid the erasable papers. Generally, they smudge and smear easily and have a slick finish that makes marking on them difficult.

Always use the same quality and weight of paper for second and successive pages of a letter as used for the first page. Never use a letterhead as a second sheet.

Lightweight paper works well for carbon copies. Some offices use onionskin for file copies.

For carbon copies for distribution to receivers, make the print sharp and dark. Make corrections on the carbon copies as well as on the original copies.

Management
Consulting

THE SERIOUS CORPORATION

785 Nirvana Drive / Panacea, Florida 32346 (333) 333-3333

June 3, 198X

My dear Mr. Collins:

Yours very respectfully,

Sharon Phelps

Sharon Phelps
Consultant

Mr. Ernest Collins
Executive Secretary
Evermore, Inc.
88 Frontier Place
Oxford, Indiana 47971

sp:cm

FIGURE D–7 Official letter format; closed punctuation; letterhead placed on 11-inch width of paper.

Provide ribbons, inks, type bars, and other such materials and equipment that make clean, sharp impressions. Carbon ribbons generally do a better job than reusable ribbons. Unless cleaned regularly, the type bars will imprint filled-in letters and numbers.

Date Line

All four basic letter designs include the date line as part of the format. Place it at least two lines below the letterhead. Start it at the left margin in the block and simplified styles (Figures D–1 and D–4). For the modified-block styles, start the date line at horizontal center, or end it at the right margin (Figures D–2 and D–3).

Business firms often adjust or revise these customary placements to enhance visual appearance. For example, notice how the date line complements "Office of the Manager" in Figure D–3. Observe in Figure D–2 how moving both the date line and the signature block to end with the right margin would improve artistic perspective.

Place the date line for a plain-paper return address one line below the city and state. Examples in Figure D–6 show the arrangement.

Business organizations still seem to prefer the standard style for dates: May 14, 198X. However, some offices use the military format: 14 May 198X (Figure D–2). Never use the "5/14/8X" style in business letters. Spell out the month, omit such endings as "-nd" for the day, and include all digits in the designation of the year.

Special Designations

Place special designations two or three lines above the first line of the inside address. Capitalize or underline the letters to set the designation apart from the address itself: Priority Mail, AIR MAIL, SPECIAL DELIVERY, Confidential, PERSONAL, Hold for Arrival. Figure D–1 illustrates the placement.

Inside Address

The inside address includes the name and address of the person and/or organization to receive the letter.

Standard Formats

For the standard formats, the inside address appears at the left margin several lines below the date line or two or three lines below a special designation when the letter includes one. Figures D–1, D–2, D–3, D–4, and D–5**a** include examples.

Nonstandard Formats

For two nonstandard forms—the formal official letter style and the informal personal business letter—the inside address goes at the left margin two or three lines *below* the last line of the signature block. Figure D–7 illustrates the setup for the official letter, and Figure D–8 illustrates it for the personal

STRUGGLING
GROCERY
WHOLESALERS
740 Freedom Boulevard Woodville, Alabama 35776

July 22, 198X

Dear Terry,

Cordially,

Jim

James L. Friar

Ms. Terry McLendon
14 Oak Circle, Apt. 132
Pine Bluffs, WY 82082

FIGURE D–8 Personal business letter; mixed punctuation.

business letter. Both official and personal business-letter formats usually take the modified-block format with indented paragraphs. A personal letter on plain paper may or may not include an inside address. Figure D–6**a** includes it; Figure D–6**b** does not.

Order of Elements

Generally, put the elements of an address in order logically from the last destination on the top line through the first destination on the bottom line. To remember the order, just picture postal workers following steps from the bottom line up to the top line. Some writers now use variations of this order.

Courtesy Titles

When a person's name appears as the first line of the address, begin that line with an appropriate title. Some of the most common ones include:

Mr.	President
Ms.	Professor
Miss	Senator
Mrs.	Representative
Dr.	The Reverend
Dean	The Honorable

Notice both the abbreviated and the spelled-out titles. They show conventional usage.

Position Title

A position title often follows the name of the addressed person. Depending on its length, the title may appear on the line with the person's name, placed on a separate line, or divided between two lines. Figures D-1, D-4, and D-7 illustrate the technique.

For a person of unknown name, you may address the letter to the appropriate title. Figure D-3 shows this approach.

Organization Name

An organization name usually follows the name of the person or a position title—or can stand alone as the first line of the address. Write the name of the organization exactly as firm representatives write it. If the company name includes such abbreviations and symbols as &, *Inc.*, *Co.*, and *Corp.*, copy them exactly. Likewise, spell *Company* in full if the company does.

Street Address

A street address normally comes after the name of the person or organization. For the street number, use figures and omit the number endings such as *-st*. Spell out a one-word number for clarity, however (Figure D-2). If a designation such as *N.W.* belongs after a street number, either separate it from the street number or name by a comma (Figures D-1 and D-6) or omit the comma. If a street address represents an apartment house, include the apartment number (Figure D-8).

Acceptable abbreviations include *Apt.* for Apartment, *Blvd.* for Boulevard, *S.W.* for Southwest, and state abbreviations such as *TX* for Texas and *IL* for Illinois. However, the cluttered look created by the excessive use of abbreviations offends some people. Thus, a middle-ground approach might include state abbreviations and abbreviations for nontitle words of two or more syllables, but spelled-out other words. A list of the two-letter state abbreviations appears in Figure D-9.

Each address must include the appropriate zip code. It follows the state name—always on the same line and one or two spaces after it. Though the

Alabama	AL
Alaska	AK
Arizona	AZ
Arkansas	AR
California	CA
Canal Zone	CZ
Colorado	CO
Connecticut	CT
Delaware	DE
District of Columbia	DC
Florida	FL
Georgia	GA
Guam	GU
Hawaii	HI
Idaho	ID
Illinois	IL
Indiana	IN
Iowa	IA
Kansas	KS
Kentucky	KY
Louisiana	LA
Maine	ME
Maryland	MD
Massachusetts	MA
Michigan	MI
Minnesota	MN
Mississippi	MS
Missouri	MO
Montana	MT
Nebraska	NE
Nevada	NV
New Hampshire	NH
New Jersey	NJ
New Mexico	NM
New York	NY
North Carolina	NC
North Dakota	ND
Ohio	OH
Oklahoma	OK
Oregon	OR
Pennsylvania	PA
Puerto Rico	PR
Rhode Island	RI
South Carolina	SC
South Dakota	SD
Tennessee	TN
Texas	TX
Utah	UT
Vermont	VT
Virginia	VA
Virgin Islands	VI
Washington	WA
West Virginia	WV
Wisconsin	WI
Wyoming	WY

FIGURE D–9 Two-letter abbreviations for states.

examples in this book illustrate the five-digit zip codes, the United States Postal Service introduced nine-digit codes on a limited and voluntary basis in 1981.

Attention Line

The attention line does not form a part of the inside address. However, it does represent a destination and does come immediately after the inside address.

The attention line indicates that a letter addressed to an organization should go to the person or position title designation in the attention line. Though declining in usage, the attention line still remains a proper part of the letter.

Position an attention line two lines below the inside address and two lines above the salutation. Start it at the left margin, or indent it with indented paragraphs, or center it. Underscore it if desired. Figure D–7 includes an attention line.

Salutation

A salutation usually follows the inside address (or attention line, if included). It begins at the left margin, two lines below the last line of the address. As established, the simplified letter form omits the salutation.

The salutation greets the receiver. For a person or a title, it usually takes the "Dear . . ." form. Use a colon or comma (mixed-punctuation style) or no punctuation at all (open-punctuation style). For mixed punctuation use the colon for all business letters except the personal business letter, in which you may use the comma (Figure D–8). Use the comma for mixed punctuation in the salutation of a personal letter or plain paper (Figure D–6).

Designated Person

Figures D–1, D–3, D–6, D–7, and D–8 include salutations directed to designated people or titles. Observe the use of the first name of the addressee for the informal, personal style (Figures D–6 and D–8). Observe also that moderately formal salutations include "Dear" followed by the correct courtesy title and the surname (Figure D–1) or by a position title (Figure D–3). Figure D–7 shows a formal salutation: "My dear" followed by a title and surname. Avoid the stilted salutations: "Dear Sir," "Dear Madam," "My dear Sir," and "My dear Madam."

Company

A letter to a company, with or without an attention line, has traditionally included "Gentlemen" as the salutation. However, because of the sexism of the word, use "Ladies and Gentlemen"—a familiar form of address already customary in oral communication. (See Figure D–2). *Never* use "Dear Sirs," "Dear Mesdames," or "Dear Ladies and Gentlemen."

Appendix C includes other suggestions for correcting the discriminatory language of the old forms.

Formality

This list of salutations illustrates formality—in descending order:

Sir/Madam
My dear Sir/My dear Madam
Dear Sir/Dear Madam
Gentlemen (for a firm comprised only of men)/Mesdames or Ladies
(for a firm comprised only of women)
Ladies and Gentlemen (for a firm comprised of men and women,
or of unknown composition)
My dear Mr. Jones/My dear Ms. Jones
Dear Mr. Jones/Dear Ms. Jones
Dear Director
Would you like to be part of an important survey?
My dear Mary/My dear Fred

Dear Mary/Dear Fred
Mary/Fred
Hello
Hello, Mary/Hello, Fred
Hi, how are you?

When an informal phrase such as "Would you like to be part of an important survey?" takes the place of a salutation, it combines elements of the salutation and the subject line. The phrase acts as a greeting, but also often introduces the topic of the letter.

Subject Line

The subject line provides a preview of what the letter covers. The simplified format requires a subject line. Other formats may include it.

For a letter with both a subject line and a salutation, place the subject line two lines below the salutation at the left margin, or two lines above the salutation at the left margin, or centered on the salutation line. Typewrite it with solid capitals, with key-word capitals, and/or with underlines.

The subject line in the simplified format goes three lines below the last line of the inside address and three lines above the first line of the body of the letter. It begins at the left margin, typewritten in solid capitals. Figures D–2 and D–4 include subject lines. Neither includes the words "Subject," "About," "In re," or "Re." Such words still appear occasionally, but most writers omit them.

Body

The encoded message forms the body of the letter. Therefore, apply the writing guidelines discussed in Chapter 6 to its composition.

The chosen letter format dictates whether to indent the paragraphs. The first line of the body begins two lines below the salutation or subject line for all but the simplified style. For the simplified style it begins three lines below the subject line.

With the exception of certain novelty letters, all business letters require single spacing, with double spacing between paragraphs.

Carefully choose the margin settings and vertical placement of the body and other parts to create an attractive, picture-framed layout. Decisions depend primarily on the length of the letter, but also on the letterhead design. Control vertical placement through variation in the number of spaces between date line and the first line of the inside address. Control horizontal placement through the margin settings.

Complimentary Close

The complimentary close forms the leave-taking phrase that parallels the greeting phrase in the salutation. Therefore, its formality should correspond with that set by the salutation. This list of complimentary closes shows the order from most formal to least formal:

Very respectfully yours
Yours very respectfully
Respectfully submitted
Respectfully yours
Respectfully

Very truly yours
Yours very truly
Yours truly

Very sincerely yours
Yours very sincerely
Yours sincerely
Sincerely yours
Sincerely

Yours cordially
Cordially yours
Cordially

Yours faithfully
Faithfully yours
Faithfully

Yours for good television viewing
Best wishes
Good luck
See you at market
Till the convention
Goodbye
Your friend

Use the less conventional complimentary closes only for informal or personal business letters—and for personal letters as well. However, avoid the contrived or "cute." Also consider the receiver's tastes.

Place the complimentary close two lines below the last line of the body. Start it at the left margin or at the center of the page, depending upon the style of the chosen format. Capitalize only the first word. Follow the complimentary close with a comma (mixed punctuation) or include no punctuation mark (open punctuation). Match the punctuation style of the salutation.

Except for Figure D–4, all the samples shown so far include complimentary closes. Figure D–4 shows the simplified format; by definition, that format does not include a complimentary close.

Company Name

Some organizations include the typewritten name of the company after the complimentary close—particularly in a two-page letter. The original purpose for including the company name with the signature was to assign legal responsibility to the company for the employee's message. However, court decisions have now established that responsibility even when the typewritten company name does not appear.

When included, the company name appears in solid capitals two lines below the complimentary close. Figures D–2 and D–5a show the placement.

Signature Block

The signature block consists of the signature and typewritten name of the signer and/or the signer's position title. Penwrite your signature personally. If circumstances ever dictate that another must sign for you, that person should place her or his initials after the signature (Figure D–3).

For the traditional style, place your signature in the space between the complimentary close and the typewritten name or title, or between the company name and the typewritten name or title. For the simplified style, sign between the last line of the body and the typewritten name (Figure D–4).

Depending on the level of formality of the letter, your signature may differ from your typewritten name. For example, for a letter to a receiver you know well, you may sign only your first name even though your full name appears in the typewritten line (Figure D–8).

The typewritten name and position title of the encoder belong four lines below the complimentary close or company name in the traditional letter. Typically, five or more blank lines fall between the last line in the body and the typewritten name in the simplified letter (Figure D–4).

A woman needs to decide how to sign and typewrite her name. The contemporary style calls for the omission of the courtesy title just as for men (Figure D–3). However, as a woman, if you use initials or have a name common to both men and woman (for example, Gale, Dale, Chris, Jan, Marion, Dana, Leslie, Lynn, Jerry, Terry), you may want to include "Ms." with your name on the typewritten name line (Figure D–2). Otherwise, you might receive mail addressed as "Mr." on return correspondence. Consider the dilemma of Doris Allen as she prepares to respond to the letter from Dale Sellers (Figure D–4). She will not know whether to use "Mr." or "Ms." However, because of historical assumptions, she may choose "Mr."

A custom still observed by some people calls for women to include "Miss" or "Mrs." on the typewritten name line. Therefore, you will still receive letters following that custom. When responding to such a woman, respect her wishes by using the implicitly requested marital-status courtesy title in your return letter.

If you are a man, you should not include "Mr." on the typewritten name line. However, as conventions change, you may want to begin doing so if you have a sex-neutral name (Gale, Dale, etc.).

Reference Initials

Most business letters include reference initials. They appear at the left margin two lines below the last line of the signature block. Usually, the letter includes only the stenographer's initials (Figures D–2, D–4, and D–5**b**). However, the dictator's initials can precede the stenographer's initials (Figures D–3 and D–5**a**).

In addition, if the writer's typewritten name does not appear in the signature block, her or his name should appear with the stenographer's initials. Figure D–1 illustrates that setup.

Enclosure Notation

If you insert anything other than a letter into the envelope, show an enclosure notation on the letter. The enclosure notation begins at the left margin two lines below the reference initials. It includes the word or abbreviation *Enclosure(s), Encl(s).,* or *enc(s).,* followed by a colon and either the number of enclosures or a list of the enclosure items. Figure D–3 includes an enclosure notation.

Copy Notation

The copy notation lets the receiver know who, other than the addressee, receives a copy of the letter. The notation cc stands for *carbon copy(ies),* but appears even for copies made by other processes (Figure D–1). The word *copy(ies)* or the phrase *copy(ies) to* may supplant *cc* (Figure D–3). Some writers now use the notation *xc* for *xerox copy*.

The notation *bc* stands for *blind copy* and appears only on the copy, not on the original letter. Use it when you do not want the receiver to know that you have sent a copy to someone else. Figure D–2 includes a blind copy notation as it would appear only on the copy. The original would simply show a blank space for that line. The copy notation begins at the left margin. It falls two lines below the enclosure notation, or two lines below the reference initials if no enclosure notation appears.

Postscript

The postscript—typewritten or handwritten, preferably without "P.S."—forms the last part of a letter. It falls at least two lines below the preceding letter component. It should contain no more than a few sentences. Depending on the format, indent it or start it at the left margin.

Avoid using the postscript—particularly if it includes an obvious afterthought. Preplan letters so that you do not need a postscript. If your plan suggests that a postscript can reinforce some point already made in the body, though, go ahead and use it. Figure D–2 shows a postscript following a blind copy notation.

ENVELOPES

The type of paper, weight, and color in envelopes should match those of the letterhead stationery. Type sharp, clean impressions on them, using good equipment.

The imprinted return address on an envelope usually appears in the upper left-hand corner of the front of the envelope. Occasionally, it appears on the flap of the back. The design should match that of the letterhead reasonably well, but should include little more than the firm name and address. Excessive use of drawings and slogans detracts from the desired impression.

For plain envelopes, type the return address in the upper left-hand corner. Unlike the typewritten return address on a letter, the return address on an envelope does include the sender's name (Figure D–10**b**). Begin the return address on the second or third line from the top edge and in the third or fourth space from the left edge.

Most businesses use the No. 10 envelope (9½ by 4⅛ inches). However, writers use the smaller No. 6¾ envelope (6½ × 3⅝ inches) quite frequently. Unusual kinds of mailings may require different sizes and shapes. However, make sure the dimensions of such envelopes meet postal requirements.

With the exception of the placement of the attention lines and special designations, addresses on envelopes should parallel inside addresses. For best use of electronic mail sorters, however, the United States Postal Service offers these guidelines:

1. Block and single space all lines of the address.
2. Put the city, state, and zip code on the bottom line, with the street address on the line just above it.
3. Include the number of an apartment, room, suite, or other unit immediately after the street address on the same line—never above, below, or in front of the street address.
4. Place the address well within a scanning field that meets these specifications:
    a. A margin of at least 1 inch on the left
    b. A margin of at least ⅝ inch on the bottom
    c. No print to the right of or below the address[1]

To place the address horizontally within the electronic scanning area, start the address several spaces to the left of the center of the envelope and end it to leave a margin of at least 1¼ inches. To place the address vertically within the scanning area, start it about 2½ inches from the top of a No. 10 envelope and about 2 inches from the top of No. 6¾ envelope. Such placement not only meets postal requirements, but also creates a visually attractive balance.

Though not required for electronic scanning, these additional features for addresses receive recommendation from the Postal Department:

1. Two-letter abbreviations for states
2. All capital letters for all words in the address
3. The omission of punctuation[2]

Figure D–10 shows several acceptable styles for envelope addresses, including these features:

1. Envelope **b** shows the receiver's name and address in capital letters.
2. Envelope **c** includes an attention line. The attention line also may appear on the third line below the last line of the return address.
3. Envelopes **b** and **d** show special notations properly placed at the left.
4. Envelopes **a, c,** and **d** have imprinted return addresses.
5. The imprinted company name and address on envelope **d** leaves space for insertion of a person's name.
6. Envelope **b** has a typewritten return address. Observe that the typewritten return address includes the writer's name as well as the address.

Figure D–11 illustrates how to fold and insert 8½- by 11-inch pages into a No. 10 envelope, and 5½- by 8½-inch pages into a No. 6¾ envelope. Figure D–12 shows the same procedures for inserting 8½- by 11-inch pages into a No. 6¾ envelope. To use a window envelope, type the receiver's name and address in the appropriate position on the letter. Then fold the letter accordian-style so that the address shows through the window. Stationery suppliers and office manuals usually provide instructions for placement and folding.

Transmit a letter so that it does not fall prey to the external interference identified at the planning stages. Consider timing, distance, security, cost, and

(a)

Action
Advertisers
30 N.E. Front Bay
Dexter, ME 04930

Mr. Blair Coates, Chairperson
United Fund Drive
77 55 Street
Craftsbury Common, VT 05827

(b)

Joan Bard
One Trail's End
Vildo, TN 38072

SPECIAL DELIVERY

MS. CLAIRE DALE
SALES AGENT
FORESEE DISTRIBUTORS
44 WEST 42 STREET
NEW YORK NY 10036

FIGURE D–10 Envelope formats.

CENTURY CO.
78 Madison Street, S.E.
Medanales, NM 87548

(c)

Truetolife Paintings
Attention Ms. S. T. Stipes
404 Cliff Road
Effie, MN 56639

-Albert Foote, Manager
TRADEWINDS SOUTH
202 TREE LANE
SEABREEZE, FL 32020

(d)

Hold for Arrival

Professor Lynn Shore
Hallsofivy University
Essex, MA 02112

FIGURE D–10 (Continued).

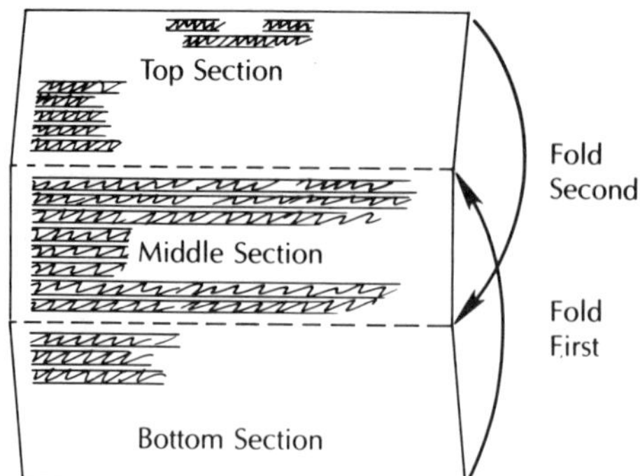

Step 1. Fold bottom section (one-twelfth inch less than one-third of the page) up over middle section. Fold top section down so that it overlaps the bottom and middle sections by one-fourth inch. (Try to make creases straight.)

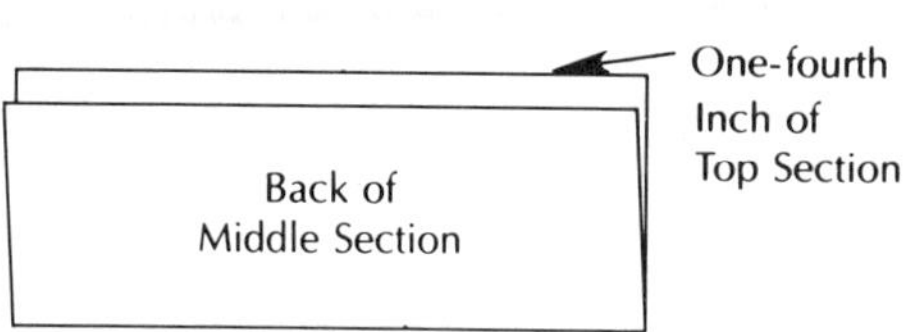

Step 2. Turn the letter so that its top section is farthest from you. The one-fourth-inch section of the top of the page should be visible.

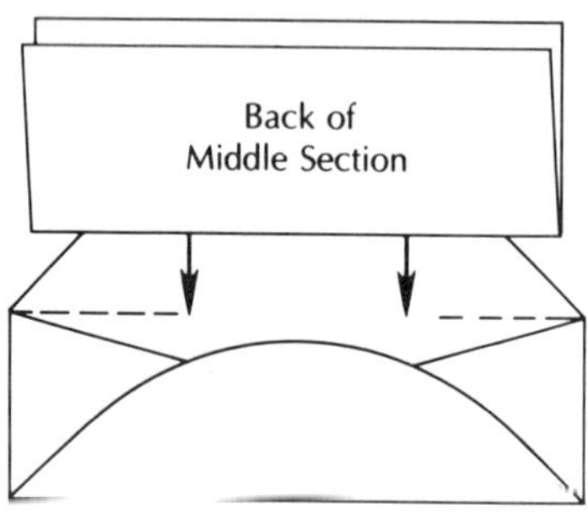

Step 3. Insert the letter as indicated.

FIGURE D–11 Procedure for folding and inserting 8½- by 11-inch pages into a No. 10 envelope, and 5½- by 8½-inch pages into a No. 6¾ envelope.

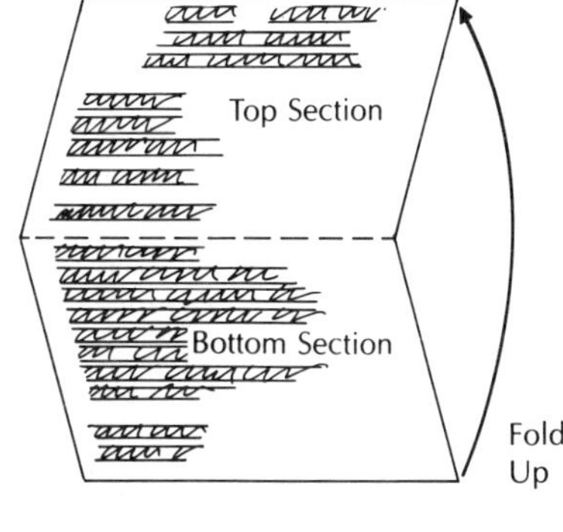

Step 1. Fold bottom section over top section so that the bottom edge is about one-fourth inch from the top edge after folding. (Try to make straight creases.) Leave letter in place.

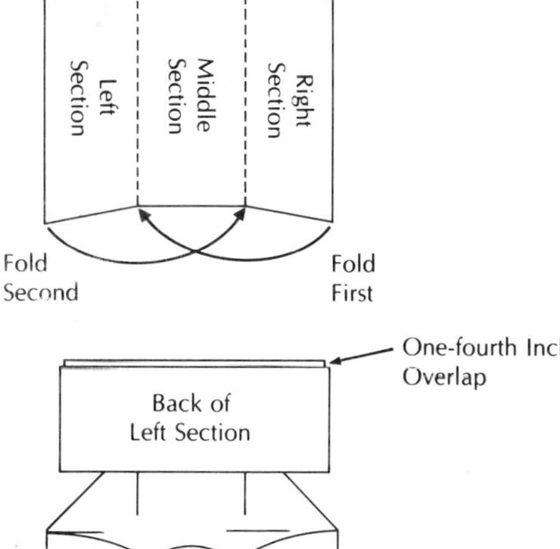

Step 2. Fold right section (one-twelfth inch less than one-third of the width) over middle section. Now fold the left section over the other two sections so that the left section overlaps the other two sections by one-fourth inch.

One-fourth Inch
Overlap

Back of
Left Section

Step 3. Turn your letter so that the back of the left section is nearest you and the one-fourth-inch overlap faces you at the top. Now insert the letter into a small envelope as indicated.

FIGURE D–12 Procedure for folding and inserting 8½- by 11-inch pages into a No. 6¾ envelope.

1. **Express Mail.** Articles received by 5:00 P.M. delivered by 3:00 P.M. the next day. For any mailable article up to 70 lbs. High rates.
2. **First Class.** Letters, post cards, presort rates, business reply mail. Two- to three-day service for higher rates.
3. **Second Class.** Newspapers and periodicals with second-class mail privileges.
4. **Third Class.** Circulars, books, catalogs, and other printed matter; merchandise, etc. weighing less than 16 ounces. Low rates. Bulk rate available.
5. **Priority Mail** (heavy pieces). Equivalent of first class service for pieces weighing over 12 ounces up to 70 lbs.
6. **Fourth Class** (Parcel Post). Parcels weighing up to 70 lbs. Slower service and lower rates than priority mail and express mail.
7. **Special Handling.** Careful handling. For third and fourth class only. Additional fee
8. **Special Delivery.** Personal delivery by letter carrier. Cannot be left in mail box. For all classes. Additional fee.
9. **COD** (Cash on Delivery). Receiver pays for goods and COD fee upon receipt.
10. **Certified Mail.** Provides proof of mailing and delivery. For first class only. Additional fee.
11. **Return Receipt.** Shows to whom and when delivered. For insured certified and registered mail. Additional fee.
12. **Insurance.** For coverage against loss or damage. Additional fee according to liability up to $400.
13. **Registry.** For maximum protection and security. For first class only. Additional fee according to value.

FIGURE D–13 Selected services of the United States Postal Service.

the legal aspects of the situation. On the basis of the analysis, choose a messenger service, a mail service, an electronic mail service, or a courier service.

If you choose the conventional mail, know the range of choices available to you. The United States Postal Service offers many different services. A summary of them appears in Figure D–13.

ENDNOTES

1. U.S. Postal Service, *Mailroom Addressing for Automation,* Customer Services Dept. Notice 23-C (October 1977).
2. U.S. Postal Service, *Mailroom Addressing.*

SOURCES

Articles

ABCA Bulletin 38 (December 1975). (Contains 14 articles on communication for employment.)

Almaney, Adnan. "The Effect of Message Treatment on Feedback in Business Communication." *Journal of Business Communication* 9 (Spring 1972):19–23.

American Business Communication Association *Ad Hoc* Committee, Bobbye Sorrels Persing, Chairperson. "The 1976 ABCA Followup Evaluation of the Course Content, Classroom Procedures, and Quality of the Basic Course in College and University Business Communication." *ABCA Bulletin* 40 (March 1977):18–24.

Bennett, James C. "The Communication Needs of Business Executives." *Journal of Business Communication* 8 (Spring 1971):5–11.

Cox, Homer. "The Voices of Experience: The Business Communication Alumnus [*sic*] Reports." *Journal of Business Communication* 13 (Summer 1976):35–46.

Ekman, Paul, and Friesen, Wallace V. "The Repertoire of Nonverbal Behavior: Categories, Origins, Usage, and Coding." *Semiotica* 1 (1969):49–93.

Fisher, Jeffrey D.; Rytting, Marvin; and Heslin, Richard. "Hands Touching Hands: Affective and Evaluative Effects on Interpersonal Touch." *Sociometry* 39 (1976):416–21.

Flesch, Rudolf. "A New Readability Yardstick." *Journal of Applied Psychology* 32 (June 1948):221–33.

Holland, Winford E.; Stead, Bette Ann; and Leibrock, Robert C. "Information Channel/Source Selection as a Correlate of Technical Uncertainty in a Research and Development Organization." *IEEE Transactions on Engineering Management* EM-23 (November 1976):163–67.

Huegli, Jon M., and Tschirgi, Harvey D. "An Investigation of Communication Skills Application and Effectiveness at the Entry Job Level." *Journal of Business Communication* 12 (Fall 1974):24–29.

Johnson, H. G.; Ekman, Paul; and Friesen, Wallace V. "Communicative Body Movements: American Emblems," *Semiotica* 15 (1975):335–53.

O'Connell, Sandra E. "Communication: Growth Field of the Seventies." *Journal of Business Communication* 15 (Spring 1978):37–46.

Pauly, John. "The Case for a New Model of Business Communication." *Journal of Business Communication* 14 (Summer 1977):11–23.

Penrose, John M. "A Survey of the Perceived Importance of Business Communication and Other Business-Related Abilities." *Journal of Business Communication* 13 (Winter 1976):17–24.

Persing, Bobbye Sorrels. "Search and Re-search for Solutions to Communication Problems." *Journal of Business Communication* 16 (Winter 1979):13–25.

———. "Sticks and Stones *and* Words: Women in the Language." *Journal of Business Communication* 14 (Winter 1977):11–19.

Rogers, Carl R., and Roethlisberger, F. J. "Barriers and Gateways to Communication." *Harvard Business Review* 30 (July–August 1952):46ff.

Trager, G. L. "Paralanguage: A First Approximation." *Linguistics* 13 (1958):1–12.

Weinrauch, J. Donald, and Swanda, John R., Jr. "Examining the Significance of Listening: An Exploratory Study of Contemporary Management." *Journal of Business Communication* 13 (Fall 1975):31.

"Who Is the Real Family?" *Ms.,* August 1978, 43.

Books

Agee, Warren K.; Ault, Phillip H.; and Emery, Edwin. *Introduction to Mass Communications.* 5th ed. New York: Harper & Row, 1976.

American Business Communication Association Research Committee, C. Glen Pearce, Chairperson. *Guidelines for Research in Business Communication.* Urbana, Ill.: American Business Communication Association, 1977.

Andersen, Kenneth E. *Introduction to Communication Theory and Practice.* Menlo Park, Calif.: Cummings, 1977.

Berlo, David K. *The Process of Communication: An Introduction to Theory and Practice.* New York: Holt, Rinehart and Winston, 1960.

Berne, Eric. *Games People Play.* New York: Random House, Grove Press, 1964.

Blake, Reed H., and Haroldsen, Edwin O. "Humanistic Studies in the Communication Arts." In *A Taxonomy of Concepts in Communication,* edited by George N. Gordon. New York: Communication Arts Books, Hastings House, 1975.

Blumer, Hubert. "Symbolic Interaction: An Approach to Human Communication." In *Approaches to Human Communication,* edited by Richard W. Budd and Brent D. Ruben, 401–19. Rochelle Park, N.J.: Spartan Books, Hayden, 1972.

Bonner, William H. *Better Business Writing.* Homewood, Ill.: Richard D. Irwin, 1974.

Bonner, William H., and Voyles, Jean. *Communicating in Business: Key to Success.* Houston: Dame Publications, 1980.

Bowman, Joel P., and Branchaw, Bernadine. *Successful Communication in Business.* New York: Harper & Row, 1980.

Branchaw, Bernadine P. *English Made Easy.* New York: Gregg Division/McGraw Hill, 1979.

Brendel, Leroy A.; Donnelly, Frank P.; and Peterson, John C. *Communication Word Power: Vocabulary and Spelling Mastery.* New York: Gregg Division/McGraw-Hill, 1968.

Brennan, John. *The Conscious Communicator: Making Communication Work in the Work Place.* Reading, Mass.: Addison-Wesley, 1974.

Brooks, William D. *Speech Communication.* 4th ed. Dubuque, Iowa: Wm. C. Brown, 1981.

Brown, Leland. *Communicating Facts and Ideas in Business.* 2d ed. Englewood Cliffs, N.J.: Prentice-Hall, 1970.

Brusaw, Charles T.; Alred, Gerald J., and Oliu, Walter E. *The Business Writer's Handbook.* New York: St. Martin's Press, 1976.

Butera, Mary C.; Krause, Ruthetta; and Sabin, William A. *College English: Grammar and Style.* New York: Gregg Division/McGraw-Hill, 1967.

Campbell, James H., and Hepler, Hal W. *Dimensions in Communications: Readings.* 2d ed. Belmont, Calif.: Wadsworth, 1970.

Clover, Vernon T., and Balsley, Howard L. *Business Research Methods.* 2d ed. Grid Series in Management. Columbus, Ohio: Grid, 1978.

Cornwell, Robert C., and Manship, Darwin W. *Applied Business Communication.* Dubuque, Iowa: Wm. C. Brown, 1978.

Damerst, William A. *Resourceful Business Communication.* Harcourt, Brace and World, 1966.

Dance, Frank E. X. "Toward a Theory of Human Communication." In *Human Communication Theory: Original Essays,* edited by Frank E. X. Dance, 288–309. New York: Holt, Rinehart and Winston, 1967.

Dance, Frank E. X., and Larson, Carl E. *Speech Communication: Concepts and Behavior.* New York: Holt, Rinehart and Winston, 1972.

Dartnell's Glossary of Word Processing Terms. Chicago: Dartnell, 1975.

Dawe, Jessamon, and Lord, William Jackson, Jr. *Functional Business Communication.* 2d ed. Englewood Cliffs, N.J.: Prentice-Hall, 1974.

Ekman, Paul, and Friesen, Wallace V. *Unmasking the Face.* Englewood Cliffs, N.J.: Prentice-Hall, 1975.

Fabun, Don. *Communications: The Transfer of Meaning.* Beverly Hills, Calif.: Glencoe Press, 1968.

Fast, Julius. *The Body Language of Sex, Power, and Aggression.* New York: M. Evans, 1977.

Felber, Stanley B., and Koch, Arthur. *What Did You Say?* 2d ed. Englewood Cliffs, N.J.: Prentice-Hall, 1978.

Flesch, Rudolf. *The Art of Readable Writing.* 25th anniv. ed. New York: Harper & Row, 1974.

Freeman, Michael J. *Writing Résumés, Locating Jobs, and Handling Job Interviews.* Homewood, Ill.: Richard D. Irwin, 1976.

Giersbach, Walter F. *Sell Yourself as a Pro. Communicator.* New York: New York Business Communicators, 1979.

Gootnick, David E. *Even You Can Give a Talk.* East Elmhurst, N.Y.: Communication Dynamics Press, 1975.

_______. *Getting a Better Job.* New York: McGraw-Hill, 1978.

Gunning, Robert. *More Effective Writing in Business and Industry.* Boston: Industrial Education Institute, 1963.

_______. *The Technique of Clear Writing.* rev. ed. New York: McGraw-Hill, 1968.

Hall, Edward T. *The Silent Language.* Garden City, N.Y.: Anchor Press/Doubleday, Anchor Books, 1959.

Haney, William V. *Communications and Interpersonal Relations.* 4th ed. Homewood, Ill.: Richard D. Irwin, 1979.

Harris, Thomas A. *I'm OK—You're OK.* New York: Harper & Row, Avon Books, 1969.

Hatch, Richard. *Communicating in Business.* Chicago: Science Research Associates, 1977.

Hayakawa, S. T., in consultation with Arthur Asa Berger and Arthur Chandler. *Language in Thought and Action.* 4th ed. New York: Harcourt Brace Jovanovich, 1978.

Henley, Nancy M. *Body Politics: Power, Sex, and Nonverbal Communication.* Englewood Cliffs, N.J.: Prentice-Hall, 1977.

Henley, Nancy, and Thorne, Barrie, comps. *She Said/He Said: An Annotated Bibliography of Sex Differences in Language, Speech, and Nonverbal Communication.* Pittsburgh, Pa.: Know, Inc., 1975.

Himstreet, William C., and Baty, Wayne Murlin. *Business Communications.* 6th ed. Belmont, Calif.: Wadsworth, 1981.

Howard, C. Jeriel; Tracz, Richard Francis; and Thomas, Coramae. *Contact: A Textbook in Applied Communications.* 3d ed. Englewood Cliffs, N.J.: Prentice-Hall, 1979.

Huseman, Richard; Lahiff, James; and Hatfield, John. *Business Communication: Strategies and Skills.* New York: Dryden Press, 1980.

———. *Interpersonal Communication in Organizations.* Boston: Holbrook, 1976.

International Association of Business Communicators. *Without Bias: A Guidebook for Nondiscriminatory Communication.* Edited by Judy E. Pickens, Patricia Walsh Rao, and Linda Cook Roberts. San Francisco, Calif.: International Association of Business Communicators, 1977.

Jacobus, Lee A. *Improving College Reading.* 3d ed. New York: Harcourt Brace Jovanovich, 1978.

Janis, J. Harold. *Writing and Communicating in Business.* 3d ed. New York: Macmillan, 1978.

Klare, George R. *A Manual for Readable Writing.* Glen Burnie, Md.: REM Company, 1975.

Knapp, Mark L. *Nonverbal Communication in Human Interaction.* 2d ed. New York: Holt, Rinehart and Winston, 1978.

Korzbski, Alfred. *Science and Sanity: An Introduction to Non-Aristotelian Systems and General Semantics.* Lancaster, Pa.: Science Press, 1933.

Larson, Charles U. *Communication: Everyday Encounters.* Belmont, Calif.: Wadsworth, 1976.

———. *Persuasion: Reception and Responsibility.* 2d ed. Belmont, Calif.: Wadsworth, 1979.

Leedy, Paul D. *Practical Research.* 2d ed. New York: Macmillan, 1980.

Leonard, Donald J. *Shurter's Communication in Business.* New York: McGraw-Hill, 1979.

Lesikar, Raymond V. *Basic Business Communications.* Homewood, Ill.: Richard D. Irwin, 1979.

———. *Business Communication: Theory and Application.* 4th ed. Homewood, Ill.: Richard D. Irwin, 1980.

———. *Report Writing for Business.* 6th ed. Homewood, Ill.: Richard D. Irwin, 1980.

Level, Dale A., Jr., and Galle, William P., Jr. *Business Communications: Theory and Practice.* Dallas: Business Publications, 1980.

Lewis, Phillip V., and Williams, John. *Readings in Organizational Communication.* Grid Series in Management. Columbus, Ohio: Grid, 1980.

Lipman, Michel, and Joyner, Russell. *How to Write Clearly.* San Francisco: International Society for General Semantics, 1979.

McCabe, Helen M., and Popham, Estelle L. *Word Processing: A Systems Approach to the Office.* New York: Harcourt Brace Jovanovich, 1977.

McGough, Elizabeth. *Your Silent Language.* New York: William Morrow, 1974.

McIntosh, Donal W. *Techniques of Business Communication.* 2d ed. Boston: Holbrook Press, 1977.

Mangieri, John N., and Baldwin, R. Scott. *Effective Reading Techniques: Business and Personal Applications.* New York: Harper & Row, Canfield Press, 1978.

Maslow, Abraham H. *Motivation and Personality.* 2d ed. New York: Harper & Row, 1970.

Mehrabian, Albert. *Silent Messages.* Belmont, Calif.: Wadsworth, 1971.

Menning, J. H.; Wilkinson, C. W.; and Clarke, Peter B. *Communicating Through Letters and Reports.* 6th ed. Homewood, Ill.: Richard D. Irwin, 1976.

Michulka, Jean H. *Let's Talk Business.* Cincinnati, Ohio: South-Western, 1978.

Miller, Casey, and Swift, Kate. *Words and Women.* Garden City, N.Y.: Doubleday, Anchor Press, 1976.

Mintzberg, Henry. *The Nature of Managerial Work.* New York: Harper & Row, 1973.

Montagu, Ashley, and Matson, Floyd. *The Human Connection.* New York: McGraw-Hill, 1979.

Murphy, Herta A., and Peck, Charles E. *Effective Business Communications.* 3d ed. New York: McGraw-Hill, 1980.

National Lexicographic Board. *The New American Roget's College Thesaurus in Dictionary Form.* New York: World, 1962.

Pearsall, Thomas E., and Cunningham, Donald H. *How to Write for the World of Work.* New York: Holt, Rinehart and Winston, 1978.

Persing, Bobbye Sorrels. *The Nonsexist Communicator.* East Elmhurst, N.Y.: Communication Dynamics Press, 1978.

———. *Business Communication Dynamics.* Columbus, Ohio: Charles E. Merrill, 1981.

Poe, Roy W., and Fruehling, Rosemary T. *Business Communication: A Problem-Solving Approach.* 2d ed. New York: Gregg Division/McGraw-Hill, 1978.

Potter, David, and Andersen, Martin P. *Discussion in Small Groups: A Guide to Effective Practice.* 3d ed. Belmont, Calif.: Wadsworth, 1976.

Robert, General Henry M. *Robert's Rules Newly Revised.* Edited by Sarah Corbin Robert. Glenview, Ill.: Scott, Foresman, 1981.

Ruesch, J., and Kees, W. *Nonverbal Communication: Notes on the Visual Perception of Human Relations.* Los Angeles, Calif.: University of California Press, 1956.

Scheaffer, Richard L.; Mendenhall, William; and Ott, Lyman. *Elementary Survey Sampling.* 2d ed. North Scituate, Mass.: Duxbury Press, 1979.

Schneider, Arnóld E.; Donaghy, William C.; and Newman, Pamela Jane. *Organizational Communication.* New York: McGraw-Hill, 1975.

Shannon, Claude E., and Weaver, Warren. *The Mathematical Theory of Communication.* Urbana, Ill.: The University of Illinois Press, 1964.

Sheridan, Donald H. *Basic Communication Skills.* Columbus, Ohio: Charles E. Merrill, 1971.

Sigband, Norman B. *Communication for Management and Business.* 2d ed. Glenview, Ill.: Scott, Foresman, 1976.

Sigband, Norman B., and Bateman, David N. *Communicating in Business.* Glenview, Ill.: Scott, Foresman, 1981.

Simon, Julian L. *Basic Research Methods in Social Science: The Art of Empirical Investigation.* New York: Random House, 1969.

Sorrels, Bobbye D. *The Nonsexist Communicator.* Englewood Cliffs, N.J.: Prentice-Hall, 1983.

Stewart, Daniel K. *The Psychology of Communication.* New York: Funk & Wagnalls, 1968.

Stewart, Marie M.; Lanham, Frank W.; Zimmer, Kenneth; Clark, Lyn; and Stead, Bette Ann. *Business English and Communication.* 5th ed. New York: Gregg Division/McGraw-Hill, 1978.

Swindle, Robert E. *The Business Communicator.* Englewood Cliffs, N.J.: Prentice-Hall, 1980.

Thayer, Lee. *Communication and Communication Systems.* Homewood, Ill.: Richard D. Irwin, 1969.

Treece, Malra. *Communication for Business and the Professions.* Boston: Allyn and Bacon, 1978.

———. *Successful Business Writing.* Boston: Allyn and Bacon, 1980.

Turabian, Kate L. *A Manual for Writers of Term Papers, Theses, and Dissertations.* 4th ed. Chicago: The University of Chicago Press, Phoenix Books, 1973.

University of Chicago Press. *A Manual of Style.* 12th ed., rev. Chicago: The University of Chicago Press, 1969.

Vardaman, George T., and Vardaman, Patricia Black. *Communication in Modern Organizations.* New York: John Wiley & Sons, 1973.
Verderber, Kathleen S., and Verderber, Rudolph F. *Inter-Act: Using Interpersonal Communication Skills.* 2d ed. Belmont, Calif.: Wadsworth, 1980.
Verderber, Rudolph F. *Communicate!* Belmont, Calif.: Wadsworth, 1975.
Weitz, Shirley, ed. *Nonverbal Communication: Readings with Commentary.* 2d ed. New York: Oxford University Press, 1979.
Wells, Walter. *Communications in Business.* 3d ed. Belmont, Calif.: Wadsworth, 1981.
Whalen, Doris H. *Handbook for Business Writers.* New York: Harcourt Brace Jovanovich, 1978.
Wittenberg, Mary Alice, and Voiles, Price R. *Modern Business English: A Text-Workbook for Colleges.* 6th ed. New York: Gregg Division/McGraw-Hill, 1979.
Wolf, Morris Phillip; Keyser, Dale R.; and Aurner, Robert R. *Effective Communication in Business.* 7th ed. Cincinnati, Ohio: South-Western, 1979.
Wolf, Morris Phillip, and Stead, Bette Ann. *Easy Grammar: A Programmed Review.* Dubuque, Iowa: Kendall/Hunt, 1970.
Zall, Paul M., and Franco, Leonard N. *Practical Writing in Business and Industry.* North Scituate, Mass.: Duxbury Press, 1978.
Zelko, Harold P., and Dance, Frank E. X. *Business and Professional Speech Communication.* 2d ed. New York: Holt, Rinehart and Winston, 1978.

Other

Conference Board. *Federal Budget.* Economic Road Maps, nos. 1860–1861. New York: The Conference Board, August 1979.
———. *Long Term U.S. Energy Trends.* Economic Road Maps, nos. 1866–1867. New York: The Conference Board, November 1979.
———. *Older Workers.* Economic Road Maps, no. 1835. New York: The Conference Board, July 1978.
———. *The Two-Way Squeeze, 1980.* Economic Road Maps, nos. 1876–1877. New York: The Conference Board, April 1980.
———. *Worldwide Foreign Investment in Manufacturing.* Economic Road Maps, nos. 1862–1863. New York: The Conference Board, September 1979.
Guidelines for Creating Positive Sexual and Racial Images in Educational Materials. New York: McGraw-Hill, 1972.
Massey, Morris E. "What You Are, Is Where You Were When." Videotape. Boulder, Colo.: University of Colorado, 1978.
Monthly Energy Review (May 1980):13.
Monthly Labor Review 103 (May 1980):6.
Oklahoma. *Oklahoma Labor Market.* March 1980, 1, 26.
Rainey, Bill G. *Writing Business Proposals: A Teaching Unit.* Ada, Okla.: East Central State College, 1971.
U.S. Department of Labor, Bureau of Labor Statistics. *How the Government Measures Unemployment.* BLS Rept. 505. Washington, D.C.: Government Printing Office, 1977.
U.S. Department of Labor, Bureau of Labor Statistics, Region 6. *Consumer Prices: April 1980.* Dallas: Region 6.

U.S. Department of Labor, Manpower [*sic*] Administration. *Job Title Revisions to Eliminate Sex- and Age-Referent Language from the Dictionary of Occupational Titles, Third Edition*. Washington, D.C.: Government Printing Office, 1975.

U.S. Postal Service. *Domestic Postage Rates, Fees, and Information*. Notice 59 (June 1979).

U.S. Postal Service. *Mailroom Addressing for Automation*. Customer Services Dept. Notice 23–C (October 1977).

INDEX

H

I

J

K

L

M